GOD EVERY DAY
365
life application devotions

Mike Lutz

Foreword by Crystal Lewis

Revised & Expanded

BRIDGE LOGOS

Alachua, Florida 32615

"In this devotional, Mike does an excellent job of taking a verse from Scripture and giving practical application for daily living to the reader. It's thoroughly biblical, personal, and practical. I enjoyed it, and I'm sure you will, too."
—Brian Brodersen, *Senior Pastor, Calvary Chapel Costa Mesa*

"The Spirit of God will allow you to have a new perspective every day as you stop for a few moments to enjoy the riches of these devotionals. Mike has done it right, taking us through the Bible in our daily devotion for the year and allowing us to meditate on a precept of Scripture each day as we make the decision to include the miracle-working God in our lives."
—Gerry Brown, *Pastor and founder of U-Turn for Christ*

"With a fresh perspective and a heart for God's Word, Mike's take on the common yearly devotional brings a wow to your daily quiet times. His devotional gives you 365 days of challenging reading to take you through the Bible in a year. For those who struggle with daily quiet times, each day gives you poignant ideas and vivid word images that help bring the Bible to an easy, everyday level of understanding. From Genesis to Revelation, some days brought laughter, and some brought quiet introspection, but each day left me contemplating throughout my day. A must-read for anyone looking for a daily devotional."
—Lenya Heitzig, *Author and women's ministry speaker*

"I love that the pages are not just filled with inspirational ideas and motivational meditations . . . although those abound! Rather, at the core of this book is a desire to draw us deeper into Scripture and truth."
—Crystal Lewis, *Grammy-nominated Christian recording artist*

"When I wake up in the morning, I love to start my day with time in the Bible. In addition to reading the Scriptures, I enjoy reading a daily devotional. Mike Lutz does a great job with his one-year devotional, taking you through the Word of God. He highlights great passages with practical insights that stay with you throughout the day."
—John Randall, *Senior Pastor, Calvary Chapel San Juan Capistrano*

"Mike Lutz is a man who deeply loves the Bible and people. His new devotional book takes people through the Bible in a year while emphasizing and applying the key passages of Scripture. It is a great way to go through the Bible in just a few minutes a day. It is unlike any other devotional book I have seen."
—Dave Rolph, *Senior Pastor, Calvary Chapel Pacific Hills*

"Say good-bye to quick-fix Scriptures and artificial anecdotes with your morning coffee. Mike's thoughtful, substantive lessons from the daily text provides all-day caffeine for the soul."
—Tim West, *English Pastor, Chinese Baptist Church of Greater Hartford*

My utmost desire is
that this book's primary triumph
is the supreme exaltation of God!

May Christ be magnified,
and God's people be edified
as they read and apply the principles of this book to their lives.

To God be the glory.

Acknowledgments

FIRST AND FOREMOST, I would like to thank my wife, Colette, for standing beside me throughout the writing of this book. You have been an inspiration to me and have motivated me to pursue excellence in everything that I do.

Thanks to Tracilee for your encouragement and willingness to read through my rough draft and provide me with your always-valuable and thought-provoking comments and suggestions.

Thanks to Karla for understanding my vision for this book and working tirelessly to edit it in such a way that brought style and grace to the finished work.

Thanks to Crystal for your enthusiastic support of this book and the abundant blessing that your inspiring and heartfelt words added to this project.

Foreword

WHEN I WAS A LITTLE GIRL, I knew I would find my father in "his chair" every morning. When I woke for school, I could guarantee that he would be planted in that same spot each day, Bible in hand, without a doubt. His discipline and diligence in seeking the Lord through His Word and prayer was consistent and inspiring. As a child, I was not aware of the struggle and stress that accompany life in ministry. However, today I understand and realize that his perseverance makes perfect sense.

The Bible is a sword, a weapon against Enemy of our souls, and unless we are intimately acquainted with it, having honed our skills and become well-equipped, we run the risk of being ineffective and unproductive (see 2 Peter 1:4–8). My dad knew the value, the eternal significance, of spending time digging in to God's Word.

I am forever grateful for the example he set, and continues to set, for me. How could either of us have known that a life in ministry would be my calling as well? I have now learned firsthand, from both mistakes and successes, how invaluable the Bible is not only to my life and work, but also to my heart every day.

Music, too, has played an immeasurable part in my life. Obviously, as I have grown up not only in the music industry, but in church as well, Christian music has shaped my days. My mother was a faithful teacher of Scripture through song. Many of the songs that come to my mind during quiet times as I seek the Lord are simply verses put to music that were taught to me as a child. Continuing that tradition in my own home, with my own children, brings me great joy.

Had my parents neglected to diligently seek after God through the regular reading of the Word, many of the lessons I learned would be obsolete. The foundation on which my spiritual life has been built holds fast because of their faithfulness and God's grace, all of which grew out of a deep love for and trust in the Word.

God Every Day provides the tools we need to build blocks of understanding, knowledge, and wisdom (see Proverbs 3:13–23). Digging into this book unearths the treasure that is the truth, making massive cornerstones to add to our foundations of faith. I love that the pages are not just filled with inspirational ideas and motivational meditations . . . although those abound! Rather, at the core is a desire to draw us deeper into Scripture and truth, an invitation to grow in those character-building beliefs that shape our hearts and minds, and encouragement to acquire the principles that help us become adept at wielding the Word.

Crystal Lewis
Christian recording artist

Bridge-Logos
Alachua, FL 32615 USA

God Every Day: 365 Life Application Devotions
by Mike Lutz

Edited by Karla Pedrow

Library of Congress Catalog Card Number: 2014944644
International Standard Book Number 978-1-61036-127-9

COS 06-19-15

Contents

January

"God created man in His own image; in the image of God He created him; male and female He created them. Then God blessed them." (Genesis 1:27–28)

JANUARY

1

New Beginnings

A NEW YEAR often means considering the good and the bad from the previous year and looking forward with expectancy and hope to a bright future in the year to come. Since the beginning of time, no one in all of existence could have had a brighter future than God's first human representatives, created in His divine image: Adam and Eve. What a beginning!

After all, this was the first day of the first year of human existence. The day had to be bright and sunny in that garden of perfection. As the sun reflected a beautiful array of colors all around the garden and the fresh fragrance of a new creation, like that fresh scent after a rain, filled the air, all of creation must have been singing in perfect harmony with mankind and God. A perfect oneness existed that day as the pleasures of a pure paradise and the fullness of such majestic splendor lay ahead of God's human representatives. Mankind, at that moment, was full of heavenly potential and unlimited possibilities.

At the beginning of a New Year, like at the beginning of Creation, every child of God is full of heavenly potential and unlimited possibilities.

Notice that before God gave His mission to mankind, He first gave mankind a special blessing (Imagine how beautiful that first blessing upon mankind must have been!). The blessing was personal, filled with the utmost love, care, and compassion. God blessed His crowning achievement before mankind embarked on the greatest journey in the entire universe: life. God was the initiator of this blessing upon mankind and therefore displays to us that God's nature and His desire is to bless humanity. God is the same yesterday, today, and forever, so His nature and desire to bless humanity is the same today just as was His nature and desire were that incredible first day in the Garden of Eden.

God wants to bless you this year, and you should see the gift of a new year as the gift of a new beginning from Him. Entering a new year is like standing in the garden, looking at a new creation that lay ahead. Today is a beautiful day and a new chance to worship God as never before; a chance to see Him in a bright new light; a chance to see the wonder and majesty of our Creator through fresh eyes; a chance to serve Him as never before; and a chance to worship Him with garden simplicity this next year. What better way to start off your new year than to begin as creation began, with a blessing from our Creator! He knows us because He made us; therefore He is uniquely qualified to bestow a blessing of immeasurable depth upon His people.

Before taking another step into the future of this year, stop and ask God to bless the days ahead with all the hope and promise and potential that awaited Adam and Eve, and pray that you may walk in a way that reflects the image of our Creator.

The book of the genealogy of Jesus Christ. (Matthew 1:1)

Roots That Run Deep

JANUARY

2

WHEN was the last time you opened your Bible, only to discover that your daily reading began something like this: "Hezron begot Ram, and Ram begot Amminadab; Amminadab begot Nahshon, . . ." and so on and so on? Then after a few minutes of struggling to pronounce names like Abiud (that is uh-BI-ud in case you were wondering), you began asking yourself, "What is the point? Do I really need to know all these names? Does it matter to me who begot whom?"

Biblical genealogies are much more than tongue-twisting exercises in pronunciation. They serve a purpose, and here in Matthew's Gospel, we have the most significant, most important, and most beautiful genealogy of all time recorded: the genealogy of our precious Messiah and King, Jesus Christ.

If you were a Jew during the time of Christ, being able to prove your ancestry was not only important, but under certain circumstances, was also essential. If you wanted to transfer land, you needed to know where the roots of your family tree extended. If you wanted to serve in the temple, you had to be able to prove your priestly pedigree, and if you wanted to be king, you would have to prove your royal birthright—and your evidence would have to be indisputable.

The genealogy of Jesus Christ is imperative, and, moreover, the entire New Testament depends on the validity of this lineage. If Jesus is Messiah and King, then His royal heredity must be confirmed.

The genealogy of Jesus is significant for a few more reasons. One, by mentioning Abraham, we are introduced to the fact that Jesus will be the fulfillment of the promise given to Abraham in Genesis 12: "All peoples on earth will be blessed through you" (verse 3 NIV). Two, Jesus' genealogy shows that God was preparing and paving the way from the beginning of human history for Christ's entrance into the world. Three, through the genealogy of Jesus Christ, we see the grace of God being displayed.

Some have even called this the Genealogy of Grace because through Christ we see a historical account of God's grace throughout history. This is a Genealogy of Grace because we see, grafted into the family tree of God, four wild branches, four outcast women in an otherwise male record: a harlot, a prostitute, a Gentile, and an adulteress—all four weak things used by God to show His amazing grace. As 1 Corinthians 1:27 reminds us, "But God has chosen the foolish things of the world to put to shame the wise, and God has chosen the weak things of the world to put to shame the things which are mighty". By including these four women, weak and foolish in the eyes of the world, in the royal lineage of Christ, God shows us that He has always desired to seek and save that which was lost.

This kingly genealogy gives hope to all sinners. Because of His great grace, He has so constructed his family that anyone can be grafted into the royal line of our most holy and precious God and King. May you never see this genealogy as just another list of names again, but may you view the sovereignty and grace of God through this list, and may that cause you to glorify the King of kings.

> Then the Lord God called to Adam and said to him,
> "Where are you?" (Genesis 3:9)

Seek, Do Not Hide

JANUARY
3

HIDE AND SEEK. Just the thought of this popular kid's game brings back a flood of childhood memories. I can remember a few favorite hiding spots: behind bushes, up a tree, under a porch, or underneath some leaves. I would think, "No one will find me in here!" I also remember the fear I felt when I had not found that perfect hiding place and heard the words, "Ready or not, here I come!"

Imagine trying to hide from God. Sound ridiculous? It should. Psalm 33:13 tells us, "The LORD looks from heaven; He sees all the sons of men." So, what in the world was Adam thinking by trying to hide from God? Did he actually think hiding was possible? And because God sees everything, why did He bother asking "Where are you?"

Adam's response to his sin was to hide.

Have you ever done anything so embarrassing that you wished you could just crawl under a rock and hide? Have you ever sinned and felt that the last place you wanted to be was close to God, because you were ashamed? Well, as sin entered the world for the first time in the Garden of Eden, hiding was Adam's reaction. Disobedience led to fear, fear led to shame, and shame led to hiding from God. That is what sin does; sin leads to separation. Sin causes a break in our fellowship with our Creator, which is why sin is so dangerous and damaging. Sin pushes us away from the One we need to be drawing ever closer to.

God's response to Adam's sin was to seek. From that came the simple question: *Where are you?* God does not ask because He does not know the answer. God knows all (see 1 John 3:20). The question God asked Adam was designed to expose Adam's sin. I find the questions God asks to be very interesting, not simply because God always knows the answers; the questions are interesting because God uses questions for our benefit. God's questions are often used to bring about sin-realization leading to repentance, ultimately bringing restoration to humanity's relationship with God.

Adam's sin brought consequences and when we sin, we face consequences , but God always wants to bring restoration through confession and repentance. God asked Adam where he was in order to draw him out from hiding and to bring Him back into fellowship. God's heart in the question was not to bring condemnation, but to bring restoration.

Hiding from God is not a game. When we make mistakes, when we wander away from God, when we sin, or when we feel guilt and shame, we feel a desire to go and hide from God. Yet that feeling should serve as a reminder to us that something is wrong with our relationship with Him. Instead of hiding from God, we should run to Him and, in those moments, seek Him.

Do not allow your feelings to drive you away from God. Fight that urge, and immediately return to His presence, confessing your sin to Him. Then, you can walk once again in close fellowship with your Creator who loves you.

Then Jesus was led up by the Spirit into the wilderness to be tempted by the devil. (Matthew 4:1)

JANUARY
4

Tried and True

JUST after coming up from the waters of baptism, Jesus was taken into the wilderness of temptation. Moments before, Jesus heard the voice of His heavenly Father speaking a blessing upon Him. Then Jesus heard the hiss of the snake, whispering words of enticement. After fasting for forty days in preparation for the start of His public ministry, Jesus would face the Father of Lies. The meeting had to happen; this was a showdown that was planned and predestined somewhere in the history of time. Jesus needed to be tempted.

Why? Why would Christ, our Lord, our Savior, need to be tempted? The reason is that if Jesus is to be our King, He must first demonstrate to us His power over the ruler of this world. If Jesus is to be our Savior, He must at all points prove His purity through sinlessness.

The Spirit led Jesus to the place of temptation, but He was not the source of temptation. God was not surprised. God was not ambushed. This meeting was expected, necessary, and allowed. The nature of the word *tempted* helps us gain further insight into the necessity of this encounter. *Tempted* is often used in both Hebrew and Greek to mean "to test or to prove." We could say that these tests were allowed to prove the purity of the One being tested. Through this process, Jesus could be proven as an acceptable sacrifice for the sins of mankind: "Therefore, in all things He had to be made like His brethren, that He might be a merciful and faithful High Priest in things pertaining to God, to make propitiation for the sins of the people" (Hebrews 2:17).

You can be sure that Satan held nothing back, because a victory here for Satan would reverse the redemptive plans of God and keep Satan from the Great Abyss. So only Satan's best weapons would do. Three proven, persuasive, and highly effective strategies that had been used in times past would also be used here: the lust of the flesh, the lust of the eyes, and the pride of life. With rapid-fire succession the Enemy of God would attack, tempting Jesus to serve self, to test God, and to worship the created rather than the Creator.

Some have said that before a king can rule others, he must first prove he can rule himself. Before Jesus could ask His disciples, past and present, to obey, He first had to be obedient to the will of the Father. Jesus responded to each temptation with a decisive and precise use of the Word of God, which is the key to our own victory when we are tempted.

If we want to be victorious over temptation, if we want to have the same victory over the Enemy that Jesus had, then we must also know the Word, we must use the Word, and we must obey the Word. And we must remember that Jesus also allowed the Enemy to try and test Him, because through His victory He can help us in times of testing. As Hebrews 2:18 reminds us, "Since he himself has gone through suffering and testing, he is able to help us when we are being tested" (NLT).

Do you find yourself struggling with temptation today? There is hope! Jesus' victory can be our victory because Jesus has given us all the resources we need to resist any and all temptation. Take hold of the Word of God, rely on the power of the Holy Spirit of God, and follow the example of Jesus.

And Enoch walked with God. (Genesis 5:24)

A Walk to Remember

AT CERTAIN TIMES IN LIFE you may feel as though you are a walking billboard for Murphy's Law, that says, "Anything that can go wrong will go wrong." Maybe you have had one of those days, weeks, or even years where everything just seems to be going wrong. Even your closest relationships seem to be difficult. No matter what you say, words are misunderstood, feelings get hurt, an awkward tension develops, and before you know, you feel as though you are trapped in a silent movie because no one is talking.

How can you break the cycle? Can there ever be peace again? The answer may sound overly simplistic, but the results can be surprisingly positive. Take a walk! (I told you the answer was simple.) Taking that first step is always the hardest. Begin by determining to make the time, and then just go for a walk together. Whether this applies to one of your earthly relationships that can use some quality time of togetherness or whether the even more important relationship with your heavenly Father could use a boost, purpose to take the time and go for a walk. A walk often strikes up thoughts of peacefulness and tranquility. A walk is a time to unwind and reflect. And when someone joins you on your walk, an added facet of fellowship enhances the walk. Something amazing happens on walks: during this time of limited distractions and few interruptions, we are able to focus all of our attention on the relationship and simply pour out what is on our hearts and minds to the one who is listening.

The Bible mentions a man who walked with God. His name was Enoch, and he is one of those enigmas of the Bible, where not much is said about him or the mystery surrounding his heavenly abduction. What we do know is that Enoch walked with God. As hard as that may be to imagine, those walks must have been unforgettable times of cherished fellowship for Enoch—times that would have strengthened his faith, times when he would have learned about the nature and character of God, and times when he would have gleaned counsel, instruction, and guidance from intimate moments of fellowship. Can we walk with God like Enoch?

A few things need to be present first. For example, we cannot walk with God without faith. Second Corinthians 5:7 tells us that "we walk by faith," and we read in Hebrews 11:6 that "without faith it is impossible to please Him." Also, in order to walk with God there must be mutual agreement, as the prophet Amos reminds us: "Can two walk together, unless they are agreed?" (3:3). We must agree to let God lead us. The first thing Jesus asked His disciples to do was to follow Him. By faith we believe, by faith we agree, by faith we follow, and by faith we walk.

Times may be tough, relationships may be strained, and circumstances may be difficult. You may not understand why you are where you are in life, but by faith choose to walk with God. While you are on the path, He will show you so much as you pour out your heart to Him in faith, believing that He can direct your steps. You will certainly have a walk to remember.

"Blessed are you when they revile and persecute you, and say all kinds of evil against you falsely for My sake." (Matthew 5:11)

JANUARY

6

Rejoicing in Reviling

A.W. TOZER once said that to be right with God has often meant to be in trouble with men. Being a Christian in today's world is not easy. For that matter, living the Christian life in this world that is not friendly toward Christ or those who follow Christ has never been easy. The resulting persecution against Christians should be no surprise, especially in light of the fact that Jesus said this was the way life would be.

Jesus included a teaching about persecution in a portion of the Bible commonly called The Beatitudes, which can be found at the beginning of His greatest sermon, the Sermon on the Mount. Jesus began by giving several simple statements of profound significance that hold the keys to God's abundant blessing in the life of every Christian. In these "blessed are" statements, Jesus offered characteristics that are to be found in every Christian's life, thereby bringing blessing.

Blessed, which is commonly translated "happy," certainly includes happiness, but includes much more than just happiness alone. Happiness is situational and often limited to circumstances, making happiness short-lived and temporary. *Blessing*, on the other hand, goes beyond happiness and transcends a person's circumstances in the purest sense. Blessing comes from a closer union with God, a contentedness with God that surpasses any current life circumstance. The Beatitudes teach us that the blessings of God are not found in this world and, therefore, are permanent.

Of all the beatitudes, this last one seems to be the most at odds with human logic. How can blessing come from persecution? How can good come from hatred? To understand the dynamics of this irony, we must first consider why criticism comes upon the Christian. Living righteously will lead to reviling; living like Christ will result in Christlike treatment. When we live a right life, which, simply stated, is living according to God's Word, our actions will conflict with those who have decided not to live according to God's Word. This disparity in lifestyles causes those who walk in darkness to resent those who walk in the light. The blessing comes because we are found worthy to share in the sufferings of Christ. Peter and the apostles responded with this when they were mistreated in Jerusalem: "So they departed from the presence of the council, rejoicing that they were counted worthy to suffer shame for His name" (Acts 5:41).

Can people see Christ in you? If they can, then expect to encounter persecution, because the closer you walk with Christ and the more you look and act like Him, the more you will suffer for Christ's name. Not all Christians are currently experiencing persecution, and not all Christians experience the same type of persecution. But no Christians will be exempt from some persecution if they live as Christ called them to live.

When you are persecuted, rejoice in your reviling and find the blessing in living like Christ, even when others are rejecting you for it.

> And they said, "Come, let us build ourselves a city, and a tower whose top is in the heavens; let us make a name for ourselves, lest we be scattered abroad over the face of the whole earth." (Genesis 11:4)

**JANUARY
7**

Fame and Failure

IN EVERY COMMUNITY AND EVERY CULTURE, from politics to performing arts, on the Broadway stage or in the boardroom, from London to Los Angeles, are ordinary people who want to be famous. Some are looking for their moment in the sun or their two seconds of fame, or perhaps some want a lifetime of notoriety.

As Alan Richardson wrote, "The hatred of anonymity drives men to heroic feats of valour or long hours of drudgery; or it urges them to spectacular acts of shame or of unscrupulous self-preferment. In its worst forms it tempts men to give the honour and glory to themselves which properly belong to the name of God."[1]

The fame craze has gone global, and no place is this more evident than on the reality shows that saturate the television line-up. Shows like *America's Got Talent, America's Next Top Model, The Next Food Network Star, Survivor, Project Runway,* and, of course, the reigning champion, *American Idol.* But before you think mankind's pursuit of fame is a new phenomenon, you should know that this has been around for thousands of years. One tragic example goes back to one of the earliest civilizations located in the region of Babylon in a city called Babel.

After the great flood, , people began to settle in the plain of Shinar or Babylon under the leadership of the mighty Nimrod. Once there, they began to build a city and a tower in the hope that these would make them famous. The people of Babel wanted to make a name for themselves, and they wanted the world to sit up and take notice of who they were and what they could accomplish. While being famous is not a sin, the pursuit of fame at all costs is, and what happens next in their story explains why.

The relentless pursuit of fame led the people of Babel to disobey and rebel against God. God had told the people to spread out after the flood, but they decided to come together and settle instead. God was to be exalted, but they chose to exalt themselves. They were told to be God-centered, but they chose instead to be self-centered. The saddest consequence is that the people of Babel got their wish; they did become famous, but for all the wrong reasons. Now they are forever immortalized in the pages of Scripture for their rebellion against God. They are now infamous, serving as an example also that not all fame is good fame!

We should seek to make God famous, to use our talents and gifts to exalt the One true God who is the only one worthy of all praise, honor, glory, and the only one who deserves to be famous. By seeking to make God famous, you will gain in return something far greater than anything this world has to offer through the pursuit of fame. A better choice is to follow the advice of James: "Humble yourselves in the sight of the Lord, and He will lift you up" (4:10). Rather than trying to exalt yourself, only to be humbled by the hand of God, why not seek to live in humility and let God make much of you?

"But I say to you that whoever looks at a woman to lust for her has already committed adultery with her in his heart."
(Matthew 5:28)

JANUARY

8

The Eye of the Beholder

JESUS, in what is referred to as the Sermon on the Mount, spends much of His time speaking about the issues of Christian conduct. In this great and wide-ranging sermon, Jesus gave more than just a list of dos and do nots; He gave everyone, young and old, male and female, insight into God's heart on the everyday issues of life.

One such issue is sexual purity. In today's society, sexual purity sounds like an oxymoron because everywhere we turn, the media and advertisers use sex to sell everything. A casual and carefree attitude about sex pervades our culture's values, in an "anything goes" kind of approach (and, quite frankly, anything often does go in our society today). But a people giving in to a pleasure-seeking, self-indulgent way of life is nothing new; human struggles with sexual desires throughout history led Jesus to take a radical stand against sexual sin by redefining when sexual activity becomes a sin.

What Jesus explains in Matthew 5:28 goes beyond just adultery; He draws our attention to the origin of sin. We know that we sin, when we commit a sinful action. What Jesus clarifies is that sin is committed *before* the action (in this case, adultery) is actually committed. Here, Jesus teaches that lust—and in His previous example, anger—are both considered sin because sin begins in the heart and is committed in our thoughts long before becoming an action. In other words, from God's viewpoint, the thought of sin equals the action of sin.

The importance of this explanation is essential for us to understand—as Jesus knew, of course—because this insight gives us the ability to appropriately deal with sin by identifying its origin. Jesus goes on to give us the remedy: Sin must be dealt with in its earliest stage, and must be dealt with absolutely and aggressively. The shocking illustration used by Jesus drives this point home. Jesus tells us to pluck out our eye or chop off our hand if these things cause us to sin. Jesus is speaking metaphorically here, and by looking at this metaphor, we see the answer to the struggle against sin. Jesus chooses the eye and the hand as examples of how we are led into sin.

The eye and the hand also provide the way for us to avoid sin. If we look at those things that honor and please God (see Philippians 4:7–8), we promote right thinking. For as we think, so we also do. Or, as Ralph Waldo Emerson said, "Sow a thought, and you reap an action." This leads us to the hand. If our aim is to put our hand to the works of righteousness, then our hand will promote right living. Right thoughts lead to right actions, and all thought begins with whatever the beholder chooses for his eyes to see.

Now the Lord had said to Abram: "Get out of your country, from your family and from your father's house, to a land that I will show you." (Genesis 12:1)

Not Seeing, Yet Believing

EVERY DAY we exercise faith of some kind. When I sit down in a chair, I have faith that the chair will hold my weight and not collapse. When I eat in a restaurant, I have faith that my food is safe to consume. When I set my alarm at night, I have faith that the alarm will wake me up in the morning.

Not surprisingly, the Bible has much to say about faith. For example, we are saved by faith (Ephesians 2:8–9), we stand by faith (2 Corinthians 1:24), we edify by faith (1 Timothy 1:4), we receive righteousness by faith (Romans 4:13), and we are justified by faith (Romans 5:1). Because faith is so important in our relationship with God, seeking to better understand faith is imperative.

The Bible says in Hebrews 11:1, "Now faith is the substance of things hoped for, the evidence of things not seen." I like to explain this scripture this way: Faith is not seeing, yet believing. Often the genuineness of someone's faith is most clearly revealed when that person is not afraid to move forward as God leads, even though the details of how God is going to provide the means to get to the desired destination is yet unseen.

This was the case with Abram, who was called to leave everything behind and go out, not knowing where God was leading. God told Abram to leave everything he knew: his family, his friends, and his community. God was asking Abram to leave all that was comfortable, all that was familiar, and all that brought him security.

On the surface for God to ask Abram to walk away from everything may seem strange, maybe even a little cruel. But God was seeking to lead Abram to a new physical land as well as new land in the spiritual sense; his spiritual destination was a place where Abram would find his security in God and not in the people, places, or things of this world.

God may not call you to leave everyone and everything you know and step out in the same way that He called Abram to step out, but God does want the same thing from you as He did from Abram: faith. He wants you to have a faith that says, "Lord, wherever You lead, I will go." He wants you to have faith that can say, "This seems impossible but I trust nothing is impossible for God." God desires that your faith has a trust that can be expressed like this: "Though I may not see how I am going to get to where God is calling me, I still will believe in the One who is calling me."

Allow God to take you places and show you things that you would have never thought possible, and, in so doing, experience the blessing of living by faith.

"Therefore I say to you, do not worry about your life, what you will eat or what you will drink; nor about your body, what you will put on. Is not life more than food and the body more than clothing?" (Matthew 6:25)

No Worries

AMONG THE MANY EXPRESSIONS people use in everyday conversation, none has risen to the height of the Australian saying, "No worries." This expression has become so popular in Australia that people have considered to be the nation's national motto. The sentiment is often used to communicate *"don't worry about that"* and has become a positive, uplifting social exchange that denotes a carefree attitude. However, "no worries" is far more than just an optimistic expression from Australia; the saying is actually one of the teachings of Jesus.

Jesus teaches that worry is sinful and that worry and faith cannot coexist in the Christian life. Therefore, if you are worrying, you are not walking by faith, and if you are walking by faith, then you are not caught in the trap of worry. Worry exchanges the potential of today for the possibility of problems tomorrow. Worry fails to trust in the promises of God and focuses on self rather than on the Savior. Worry chooses to see the impossibilities of mankind and forgets to believe in the God of possibilities.

The word *worry* literally means "to strangle." This definition paints a vivid picture of what worry does in the life of any believer who allows worry to wrap its hands around the neck of their faith and squeeze. Worry is a killer. Jesus illustrates this in Matthew 13:22: "The seed that fell among the thorns represents those who hear God's Word, but all too quickly the message is crowded out by the worries of this life and the lure of wealth, so no fruit is produced" (NLT). Worry chokes out the Word of God and leads to unfruitfulness in the life of a Christian.

So what are Christians to do? How are we to rid ourselves of worrying about our next paycheck, our next meal, or the clothes we need? Jesus gives us a few recommendations that are sure to drive worry away, if we adhere steadfastly to them.

First, He directs our attention to His past and present faithfulness. As we look to Creation, we are sure to see all the marvelous ways He has provided for the creatures of the earth. God has been faithful to provide food and shelter for even the smallest sparrow, and He will do the same for you and me.

Next, we are to seek the righteousness of Jesus above all other things. We do this in part by aiming to keep our eyes fixed on Him, by observing the character and nature of Jesus, and by looking at what He did and how He lived.

Finally, we take Jesus as the example and the Bible as our guide, and use them both as a filter for our lives by pouring our decisions, cares, and concerns through this heavenly filter, allowing them to catch and purify our lives.

As we seek Jesus and seek to imitate His life as the Spirit works in and through us, we will set ourselves up for living a life in which we can honestly say, "No worries!"

> *Then she called the name of the Lord who spoke to her,*
> *You-Are-the-God-Who-Sees.* (Genesis 16:13)

El Roi

HAGAR was an Egyptian slave girl, a servant, of Sarai, the wife of Abram who was unable to have children of her own. As a servant, Hagar held no position of authority; she was not a person of influence. She was poor and about to be pregnant. Sarai therefore decided to use Hagar as a surrogate so she could give Abram a child. As if life was not already hard enough for this slave girl, the resulting success of the surrogacy added jealousy and cruel mistreatment from Sarai to the list of her sorrows. Feeling used and abused, Hagar ran away. But what happened next is both wonderful and astonishing.

The Angel of the LORD, who is commonly identified as the Lord Jesus Christ, appears to Hagar. God finds Hagar at what might be considered the lowest point in her life. Here God reveals himself to her and lets her know that He has heard her cries of sadness and understands her hardships. He tells her to name her son Ishmael, which means "God hears." What a wonderful picture of God's love and grace to this runaway slave girl! He not only appears to Hagar, but also blesses this poor Gentile girl.

God hears the cry of the afflicted, He sees their needs, and because He cares, He offers help to the afflicted when they cry out to Him.

Hagar responded by calling God, *El Roi*, The-God-Who-Sees. She calls God this because she came to realize that even when she felt abandoned and alone, God was there. He saw her, He knew her troubles, and He would not forsake her or her unborn child.

Just as God saw Hagar and her child and had a plan for their future, God is able to see us personally, constantly, and completely, and He is able to meet our needs in the same way. God sees us personally in that He knows who we are and what we are experiencing, and He is not distant or detached from our lives. He sees us constantly because never a moment goes by when God does not know where we are, what we are doing, and what are experiencing. Lastly, He sees us completely, not only where we are and what we are doing, but also who we are. He knows our every thought and our every desire, He knows us in our innermost being, and He knows the beginning and the end of all things. In essence, He knows us inside and out, more completely than we even know ourselves.

Have you ever been unfairly mistreated? Have you ever suffered from illness or injury, brokenheartedness, or frustration? Maybe you are depressed or discouraged. Maybe you are suffering from loneliness or disappointment, or life simply has gone in a direction you never expected. Perhaps you have thought to yourself, *There is no one who knows what I am going through! There is no one who cares about me!* Well, you are re wrong. The all-knowing, all-powerful, ever-present God of the universe knows everything about you. He cares for you, and He is working in and through the circumstances of your life to accomplish His perfect will.

Never forget that *El Roi*, The-God-Who-Sees, is watching out for you and is watching over you. If you doubt that, just call out to The-God-Who-Sees. Do not be surprised if He allows you to see Him in a very practical way.

"Do not judge, or you too will be judged." (Matthew 7:1 NIV)

Snap Judgments

WE can be so quick to point the finger at others but slow to consider our own weaknesses. If the truth be told, we are all a little (or maybe even a lot) guilty of taking a magnifying glass to other people's lives while turning a blind eye to our own. Perhaps, because we are all sinners ourselves, we are so good at sniffing out the sin in other people's lives. We judge others by one standard and ourselves by another. We bad-mouth others for certain actions or attitudes while brushing off the same actions or attitudes when they surface in our own lives. What was Jesus calling for when He said, "Do not judge"? Did He want us to close our eyes to error and evil? Should we never address wrong behavior in another person because, after all, none of us are perfect?

No, Jesus was not forbidding the Christian from judging others entirely, but He was giving the boundaries by which we can judge others properly. The type of judging Jesus was denouncing is judgment that tries to evaluate the motives of another person when, quite simply, no one knows or understands why people do what they do. We are limited in our understanding because all we see are the outward actions of others, but God is able to discern the inner intentions of a person's heart. Therefore, He alone is able to rightly judge a person's motivations.

Jesus also spoke out against judgment that seeks to condemn another person. As Chuck Swindoll has pointed out:

> How often we have jumped to wrong conclusions, made judgmental statements, only to find out later how off-base we were. . . . What keeps us from being qualified to judge? We do not know all the facts. We are unable to read motives. We find it impossible to be totally objective. We lack "the big picture." We live with blind spots. We are prejudiced and have blurred perspective.[2]

God does not forbid our judging of wrong and evil actions, but says instead, rather than looking at others condemningly, we should look at others restoratively. Jesus is not calling us to blindly accept wrong or evil but, when appropriate, to benevolently confront those wrongs with grace, leaving the final judgment in the hands of God.

Our main priority should always be "How am I living?" not "How are you living?" We cannot properly help others deal with sin in their lives if we have not properly dealt with sin in our own lives. The sin we are quick to judge in someone else may be the very sin we struggle with ourselves. This is why the sin is so easy for us to identify, because we are well acquainted with the same struggle. Before we judge others, we must judge ourselves. Jesus said, "First remove the plank from your own eye, and then you will see clearly to remove the speck from your brother's eye" (Matthew 7:5). After we have judged ourselves and have removed those things that blur our vision, then we can see clearly to properly judge, or make an accurate evaluation, of someone else, with the purpose of restoring them (see Galatians 6:1).

Avoid making snap judgments of others by prayerfully looking at your own life first and making the changes you need to make. Then you will be in a better position to lend a hand to someone else who is struggling with an issue.

> *But Lot's wife looked back and turned into a pillar of salt.*
> (Genesis 19:26 MSG)

No Turning Back

IF SOMEONE SAID TO YOU, "Do not look now," what is the first thing you would want to do? Of course you would want to look! Well, this was the warning given to Lot and his family as they were being rescued from the Lord's judgment that was about to be poured out on Sodom and Gomorrah. As to be expected, someone could not resist the urge to look back, and that person was none other than Lot's wife. What would be the punishment for sneaking a peak? Well, God instantly turned Lot's wife into a pillar of salt. Whoa! Why such a severe punishment for what may seem like a minor infraction? And why should we pay special attention to this punishment?

In Genesis 19, we learn about Sodom and Gomorrah, a pair of immoral cities that were scheduled to be destroyed because of their unrestrained wickedness. A man named Lot, his two daughters, and his wife were the only ones on God's short list to be spared. Two angels were assigned to escort the family to safety, and the angels gave clear instructions to Lot and his family that they would have to hurry if they wanted to escape alive. After some hesitation and a little forceful persuasion, Lot and his family cleared the city limits, where the angels then instructed them to, "Flee for your lives! Don't look back, and don't stop . . . or you will be swept away!" (Genesis 19:17 NIV) Here, the story takes an unexpected twist. Whether in a moment of weakness, worldliness, or wistfulness, Lot's wife took one last, fleeting look back toward her home. We do not know whether she was considering returning to her sinful past or missing what she was leaving behind, but what we do know is that she looked when she was explicitly told not to. Why was looking back such a horrible sin, causing the judgment of God to fall on her? First, her action was outright disobedience to God, and well, that is never a good choice. God warned of severe consequences for disobedience, and yet Lot's wife still chose to disobey Him. Second, her action was an abuse of God's grace she was just freely given; God graciously saved her and her family from destruction. Yet instead of being appreciative, she was filled with ingratitude.

If you have trusted in Christ, God has delivered you from destruction! He has called you to flee from your old life, to look forward rather than back, to keep moving forward and do not stop or consequences will await you. We are not to love anything more than God, for when we do, we are tempted to look back toward those things for fulfillment, instead of looking to God for fulfillment. Whatever direction a person is looking is the direction he or she will walk. As a result, you are either walking toward God, or you are walking toward something other than God. This is why Jesus said, "No one, having put his hand to the plow, and looking back, is fit for the kingdom of God" (Luke 9:62).

Would you have trouble walking away from anything in your life if God were to call you to something new? Do you believe that whatever and wherever God is calling you is better than what you are leaving behind? Are you willing to move forward with God, no turning back?

And do not fear those who kill the body but cannot kill the soul. But rather fear Him who is able to destroy both soul and body in hell." (Matthew 10:28)

JANUARY

14

Fearless Faith

JOHN HUS, a 14th century Christian and philosopher believed that the Bible was the flawless and final authority in all matters. He was burned at the stake for this belief at the young age of about thirty-five. Before he was burned, he was given a final opportunity to renounce his faith and be spared from the flames, but he refused. As the fire began to blaze and the heat began to burn, instead of forsaking his faith, Hus boldly cried out from the flames, "What I taught with my lips I now seal with my blood."[3]

The pages of Christian history are filled with many such men and women who possessed such a fearless faith in Christ that, when torture or death drew near, they remained steadfast and proved themselves to be faithful until the end. The unfortunate fact is this type of fate is not just historical truth, but also a present reality for so many in the world, and is a future certainty during the Tribulation. Modern-day martyrdom is worldwide and widespread, and sadly, to say is not going to change anytime soon.

More Christians, by many estimates, have been martyred for their faith in the twentieth century than in all previous centuries combined. From the church's first martyr, Stephen, through today, countless men and women have been tortured and brutally murdered simply for believing in Jesus Christ. What are we, humanity, to do in the face of such a possibility?

Jesus warns us three times in the verses surrounding Matthew 10:28, "Do not fear." Well, this certainly sounds easier said than done, especially when we are faced with the prospect of rejection, persecution, or even execution. But Jesus is not leaving us with just three commands not to fear; He quickly counters our fears with three reasons not to fear. Whether we face the possibility of death or simply the rejection of friends or family because of our faith, we need to remember what Jesus says to us in light of what may lie ahead.

One, we should not fear mankind, "for there is nothing covered that will not be revealed" (verse 26). In other words, Jesus was saying that truth will eventually be triumphant, wickedness will be uncovered, evil that was done in darkness will be brought to light, and God will judge evil.

Two, we should not fear mankind, but "fear Him who is able to destroy both soul and body in hell" (verse 28). This body is a temporary dwelling place, which means anything a human can do to a body is also only temporary. The soul, however, lasts forever, so what God can do to your soul is eternal. Our fear, which includes reverence, should be toward God.

Third, we should not fear mankind because nothing that happens to us that

God does not first know about and also ordain (see verse 29). He is sovereign over all, and everything happens for a reason: His reason.

When our eyes are firmly fixed on God, we will have a fearless faith that will shine forth like the sun because we have the Son. Any opposition comes that our way is only for a moment in light of the blessed eternity that lies ahead.

God visited Sarah exactly as he said he would; God did to Sarah what he promised. (Genesis 21:1 MSG)

Promises, Promises

PROMISE! We have all made promises to other people, and we have all had promises made to us. We have also all suffered the disappointment that comes when a promise made to us is broken. Keeping a promise is a reflection of our character. That is why we teach our children, "Do not make a promise you cannot keep." A broken promise can sow seeds of doubt in a person's heart, damaging relationships and leading to a loss of faith that a person will fulfill their promises and do what they say they will do.

Sarah was the beautiful, loyal, and strong wife of the patriarch Abraham, but she had one struggle: she was barren. In that culture, at that time, not only was being barren personally heartbreaking for a woman,, but also often brought about cultural criticism as well. As time passed, the prospect of pregnancy faded for Sarah, and the age of childbearing became nothing more than a distant memory. God chose this time to make her a promise so extraordinary that would have been ludicrous coming from anyone else, In fact, God so caught Sarah off guard that she initially allowed doubt to diminish her faith in His Word. The promise was that Sarah would bear a son. When Sarah heard the promise of God, her heart did not leap for joy; rather, she laughed. In fact, if her laugh itself could have been translated, the translation might have been heard as, "You must be kidding me! I am eighty-nine years old, and my husband is ninety-nine years old! There is *no way* we are having a child this late in our lives!"

How did God respond to this laugh of disbelief? He did so with a loving rebuke and a reaffirmation of His promise. He said, "Is anything too hard for the LORD? At the appointed time I will return to you, according to the time of life, and Sarah shall have a son" (Genesis 18:14). God had to remind Sarah that His promises are accomplished by His power. The promise that God made to Sarah was not dependent on her, nor did her momentary doubt revoke God's promise to her. A promise is only as good as the one making the promise, and the promises of God are based on His faithfulness and rooted in His nature and His character. This is why chapter 21 opens with the proclamation that God did for Sarah as He said because He promised He would.

When you read about the promises of God, do you believe He can and will do all that He has said? Do not let doubt creep into your heart, diminish your faith, and rob you of the blessings God has in store. If you are tempted to doubt the promises of God, remember, nothing is too difficult for God. When God makes a promise, He will deliver on that promise. For Him to do anything else would be contrary to His nature and character. God never makes a promise He cannot keep. The birth of Abraham and Sarah's son, Isaac, is one perfect proof that God is the Promise Keeper.

Find reassurance in the countless promises that God has given to us in His Word.

"Then many false prophets will rise up and deceive many."
(Matthew 24:11)

JANUARY

Warning: False Prophets Ahead

16

A PROPHET is someone who is chosen by God to speak for God. In the Old Testament, the role of the prophet was taken very seriously and came with very strict consequences for anyone proven to be a fraud. The punishment for being a false prophet was death, which would certainly make someone think twice before teaching lies or making false predictions.

The problem with false prophets is nothing new, but the Bible teaches that, as time draws closer to the second coming of Christ, their numbers will increase by epic proportions. This drastic increase is undoubtedly the Devil's final and desperate attempt to deceive the world, which ultimately culminates in the False Prophet's leading people to worship the Antichrist (see Revelation 16, 19, 20).

So how do you protect yourself against the deceitfulness of false prophets, false religions, and anything that might lead you astray from the one true God? Our first warning is given to us in 1 John 4, where we are encouraged to test the spirits. We are not to believe someone just because he opens his mouth and makes a claim, holds some title or position, or can perform signs, because even Satan can perform false signs and false wonders. The true test centers on what they believe about Jesus Christ; of first importance here is how a person views the Incarnation whereby Jesus, as God, came to mankind in the flesh of man. Jesus was fully God, and He also was fully man. How someone handles the divinity of Christ is a surefire test for determining the nature of a prophet. Any compromise that lessens Jesus as fully God is to be fully rejected.

Next, in John's Gospel, chapter 1, we have another non-negotiable in proper discernment of truth. John teaches us that Jesus Christ and the Word of God are one and the same. In fact, Jesus is the Word made into flesh. So, when considering the incarnation of Jesus, not only must we not separate the deity of Jesus from the Incarnation, but we also cannot allow the separation of the Word of God from the Son of God. This means that when we seek to discern what is truth and what is false teaching, we need to consider what is being said about the Word of God as well as the relationship of the Scriptures to Jesus.

We are warned many times in the Scriptures to be watchful for the Enemy, and to be on our guard. We must be alert and prepared. We must stand firm and never compromise on who Jesus is, because if we give the Enemy a foothold against the truth of who Jesus is, we are sure to be led astray into false teaching.

Do not wait until you are faced with false teaching to turn to the Word of God, because you may lose your ability to detect the lie. Stay in the truth every day, and false teachers will not be able to mislead and deceive you.

*Then Jacob was left alone; and a Man wrestled
with him until the breaking of day.*
(Genesis 32:24)

Wrestling with God

JACOB'S NAME MEANS "HEEL CATCHER," which proved to be a very appropriate name for this Jewish patriarch. Most of Jacob's life was spent trying to get what he wanted by using his own strength, always grabbing and scheming just to get ahead. He believed in God but was not fully surrendered to Him. He duped his brother, deceived his father, and defrauded his father-in-law, and all this was done in an attempt to bring blessings into his own life. Jacob, like many of us, needed to learn that blessings come at the hand of God and not by the hand of mankind.

Jacob would learn this one night while he was all alone in the wilderness and suddenly met with God in the most unusual of ways. Arms became interlocked, heads bowed down, and shoulder pressed against shoulder, as each used his weight and leverage to try and overpower the other. God was wrestling with mankind! We must realize that God was the initiator of this unusual encounter. He came to Jacob, and He was the one who reached out and wrapped him in a heavenly headlock.

Jacob was not so much wrestling with God as he was simply refusing to yield to God. Keep in mind that the point of any wrestling match is to bring your opponent to the place of total submission. This was something Jacob still needed to learn. Hour after hour, the two remained intertwined until God decided enough was enough, and the time had come to drive the lesson home. So, God touched Jacobs's hip and permanently dislocated the joint. Now, that had to hurt! God one, Jacob zero.

The result was that Jacob could no longer wrestle. All he could do at that point was to hold on for dear life. As Jacob clung to God, he sought God's grace and blessing in that moment. God, in His grace, saw a change in Jacob's heart and gave him a new name: Israel. His new name means "governed by God." With a new name came a new way of life for this former heel catcher. No longer was he seeking to live life his way by grabbing and scheming for blessings. He saw that the only way to true blessing was received by submitting to and clinging to God. Jacob was physically weakened from His encounter with God, but spiritually he was made stronger.

Have you ever wrestled with God? Have you ever fought to have things your own way, only to have God dislocate your plans? As we wrestle against the hand of God, we always will be on the losing end of that struggle. Only when we realize how weak we really are do we truly win. Only when we submit to and surrender to God can the true blessing of a newfound intimacy with Him be experienced.

Save yourself from walking with a limp because you wrestled with God for your own way! Surrender your will to His today.

And about the ninth hour Jesus cried out with a loud voice, saying, "Eli, Eli, lama sabachthani?" that is, "My God, My God, why have You forsaken Me?" (Matthew 27:46)

JANUARY

18

The Darkest Day

SUDDENLY a divine darkness moved in and surrounded the earth. When Jesus came into the world, a light shone in the sky to mark his birth. But on this day, darkness covered the earth as the world prepared for His death. As Jesus hung on the cross, the sun was reaching the highest position in the sky while the Son of God was experiencing His lowest point on earth.

Nothing like this had ever happened before, and nothing comparable would ever happen again. This day was the appointed day, and this hour was the appointed hour for the Son of God to take the sins of the world upon His shoulders. During the divine darkness, which lasted for three hours, Jesus, who never sinned, would *become* sin for us. Jesus, who was perfect in righteousness, would exchange that righteousness for sin so that all who would believe might exchange their sinfulness for His righteousness. God's great and glorious plan to redeem mankind and provide the way to everlasting life was revealed in this horrific act.

But this plan of grace, prepared from before the foundations of the earth were set, came with a painful price; more painful than the physical suffering inflicted on the flesh of Jesus would be the moment of supreme spiritual pain. The beating, the torn back, and the bloodied brow would not compare to the pain Jesus experienced when He was temporarily estranged from God the Father. Never a time existed in all of eternity past that Jesus did not enjoy oneness with the Father. The closest and most intimate of relationships was about to experience the pain of separation.

From the greatest agony ever experienced, Jesus cried out, "My God, My God, why have You forsaken Me?" This was the only time that Jesus called God anything but Father because this was the only time the Father turned His back on the Son. Jesus never lost His divinity and never ceased being a part of the Trinity, but for a short time, He lost intimacy with the Father.

Great is the mystery of our salvation, yet let us never forget or minimize its cost or trivialize the severity of sin. Jesus was abandoned so that we might be accepted; He was forsaken so that we might be forgiven. What was the darkest day for the Son of God is also the gateway to marvelous light for all who trust in Christ. We are now called to testify to the fact that Jesus is the Light of the World as He paid for the darkness of mankind's sins on the cross and died that dark day in history so that we might live. We no longer need to walk in darkness if we accept His sacrifice on our behalf. We can walk in the light of His glory and grace.

Jesus gives us all the invitation to trust in Him and receive His sacrifice. Have you accepted His gift of grace? If you have, then is your life a testimony to what Jesus has done for you?

*Now Joseph had a dream, and he told it to his brothers;
and they hated him even more.* (Genesis 37:5)

Brotherly Hate

THE story of Joseph is a beautiful portrayal of the providence of God. His was largely a story of the foreknowledge of God that unfolds through the divine, behind-the-scenes choreography of God through the life of Joseph. Much of God's mighty maneuvering was accomplished through the ordinary, everyday events of Joseph's life, even though God's plan was anything but ordinary.

Joseph's family had a fair amount of dysfunction, and Joseph bore the brunt of much of his family's mistreatment. Joseph, the second youngest son of twelve, was his father's favored son and was given the place of preference that was normally reserved for the oldest. Reuben, being the firstborn son of Jacob and the rightful heir and benefactor of his father's benevolence, would not receive this birthright, however. Because he had an incestuous relationship with his father's concubine, he thereby forfeited his father's favor and lost his household rank. This action now freed Jacob to choose someone to replace Reuben. For Jacob the choice was a no-brainer. Hands down, his choice would be Joseph. This decision was made official when Jacob adorned Joseph with a royal robe, signifying his newfound position in the family hierarchy.

A thread of brotherly hatred already ran against Joseph among his siblings, but this repositioning in the family added fuel to their already smoldering disgust. The straw that would break the camel's back of family tension would be the dreams given to Joseph by God.

Now, Joseph was far from perfect, but the dreams that God gave him were a glimpse into God's perfect purposes for him. Joseph's dreams were a clear foreshadowing of Joseph's future position of prominence over his family. No one knew the details of God's plan, but the result was unmistakable to all, as evidenced by his brother's remark, "Shall you indeed reign over us?" (Genesis 37:8). This was more than the brothers were willing to bear. Already skating on thin ice, Joseph was living with his family on borrowed time. The brothers made their plans to rid themselves of their younger brother.

The dreams of Joseph set in motion a series of divine events that, when seen from the outside, look hard, harsh, and unhelpful in accomplishing anything good and godly. But when you have a sovereign God in control of everything, even when others intend things for evil, God can turn them into blessing and use them to further accomplish His perfect plans.

No matter how hated we might be, no matter how hurt we may feel from the actions of others, and no matter how hopeless our situation may be, if we remain faithful to God in the same way we see Joseph remaining faithful to God despite the many years of hardships, we can rest assured that He will remain faithful to accomplish His perfect, providential purposes in our lives as well. As God did for Joseph, He can do for all who remain faithful to Him.

"Go therefore and make disciples of all the nations, baptizing them in the name of the Father and of the Son and of the Holy Spirit, teaching them to observe all things that I have commanded you; and lo, I am with you always, even to the end of the age." Amen. (Matthew 28:19–20)

JANUARY
20

Get Going

FEW COMMANDS have haunted the church more than the final words of Jesus to His disciples. These words have been called the Christian Magna Carta and are considered to be the marching orders for the church. Jesus clearly and concisely communicated His charge to the church in these final verses.

The command is simple: make disciples. The process begins by going, which means that we head out and take the good news of the Gospel of Christ to people where they live, work, and play. The goal never has been for us to say, "Come to us and hear the good news," but, instead, we are to say, "Let us rise up and go out to the people with the good news." Some will go to foreign lands and others will stay close to home, but either way, the command to make disciples implies that as Christians, we are already going. Whether or not you have consciously purposed to "go out," know this: you already have. You are always out walking, talking, working, and living as an example of a disciple of Jesus Christ, wherever you are. The question is not so much whether you are going, but what you are doing while you are already out.

Baptism is the next part of the process of making disciples and is a mark that signifies the new life that a believer has found in Christ. Baptism is our identification with Christ, His death, His burial, and His resurrection, and represents a conscious decision that can only be made by an individual for himself or herself. No outward act involving water has any significance unless the one getting baptized makes the choice. The mere act does not indicate a genuine decision to follow Christ, and is not a means for attaining salvation; instead, baptism is to *follow* salvation. Baptism is a representation of our communion with and commitment to Christ and all those who follow Christ. Making disciples involves inviting others to publicly proclaim their identification with Christ through baptism.

All of this is vital, but a failure to teach all that Jesus commanded will only leave disciples weak and immature in their faith. Far too often today, preachers focus solely on feel-good messages, prosperity preaching, and entertaining rather than teaching. This type of message results in a failure to communicate the sinfulness of mankind and the holiness of God, thereby fails to convict people of their need to be saved and sanctified. We all must be teachers of the whole counsel of God, from Genesis to Revelation and everything in between. We must be dedicated students of the Bible so that we can teach others effectively and completely.

This command has so haunted the church throughout the centuries because every generation, every church, and every believer bears the responsibility of discipleship. The command is not exclusively for missionaries, pastors, or evangelists; all who believe are so commanded. Millions of people are traveling on the wide road that leads to destruction. As the church of Jesus Christ, we must get going and make disciples of every tribe, tongue, and nation.

Let us not make the Great Commission, given to us by God, become the Great Omission of the church today.

So he looked this way and that way, and when he saw no one, he killed the Egyptian and hid him in the sand.
(Exodus 2:12)

JANUARY

21

The Wrong Way

ONCE, while I was, driving in a foreign country, I came across a series of signs that, although not written in English, made exactly clear what they were saying by their bright red letters. The signs were warning drivers that this way was the wrong way! Just ahead, I could see the street that I needed to get to, just a block away. If I missed that street, I knew I would be in trouble because I had no idea how I would get back to where I needed to go.

I was faced with a choice: Do I knowingly go the wrong way, or do I turn around and go the right way and be delayed indefinitely? With limited information, I chose to go the wrong way. Apart from a few evil eyes and horns honking, I made the journey successfully, no worse for the wear. I was willing to take a shortcut to get to where I needed to go. But one thing is for sure: no shortcuts exist to accomplishing God's will.

Moses had not received God's Law yet, so you could say that he was operating with limited information. But, honestly, he did not need the Law to know that all the signs ahead of him were saying, "Wrong way!" Moses chose to go the wrong way when he took matters into his own hands and killed the Egyptian taskmaster. Moses thought he could accomplish God's will in his time and in his own way. All the education of Egypt and privileges of living in the palace of Pharaoh would not properly prepare Moses for doing things God's way. This is most clearly seen when Moses looked to the right and looked to the left to see if anyone was watching. But he failed to look in the one direction where he needed to look the most: *up.* Moses looked this way and that way, but he did not look God's way.

Before we are too hard on Moses, let us keep in mind that he did have noble intentions. He saw injustice and could not just stand there silently and allow justice to fail. He knew the Hebrew people were under harsh treatment, and he wanted to help them get out from under their oppression. But his good intentions do not negate his wrong direction and wrong action. So, God sent Moses to the desert so he could learn to wait on Him and learn to do things His way. Moses needed time to unlearn the worldly methods he was taught under the king of Egypt so he could be ready to learn from God the right way to accomplish His will.

The next time you think that you are ready to do something for God, take the time to look up. Wait for God's direction to ensure that you do not go the wrong way when doing His will. Look to God and His Word to make sure the street you are about to go down is the right one, and that you are going in the right direction.

Now there was a man in their synagogue with an unclean spirit. And he cried out, saying, "Let us alone! What have we to do with You, Jesus of Nazareth? Did You come to destroy us? I know who You are—the Holy One of God!"
(Mark 1:23–24)

JANUARY

22

Confessions of a Demoniac

*A*MAZING, mysterious, miraculous, and even *bizarre* . . . these are just a few words that describe what took place while Jesus was teaching in the synagogue one Sabbath morning. The Bible occasionally gives us a glimpse into the workings of angels and demons, and undoubtedly those encounters can often leave us mystified and bewildered. But we can learn a great deal from the confessions of the demon-possessed man.

What exactly is a demon? Demons are fallen angels who once enjoyed the beauty of heaven, only to be cast out because they chose to follow Satan and rebel against God (see Revelation 12:7–9). Demons also have the power to occupy the bodies of the unsaved and use them for evil.

Even though demons may be able to hassle and cause trouble for a believer, they can never inhabit the person who has made Jesus the Lord of his or her life. As one author wrote, "Demons cannot live in Christian hearts, but they perch on Christian shoulders and whisper in Christian ears."

Additionally, demons know their time is short, and a day will arrive when they will be bound and thrown into the great abyss (see Luke 8:31). With that understanding, demons are also fully aware of who Jesus is. Notice the two main aspects of this demon's confession with regard to who Jesus is:

"What have we to do with You, Jesus of Nazareth?" This is a confession that acknowledges the humanity of Christ, and demonstrates a belief in the Incarnation, when God became man.

"I know who You are—the Holy One of God!" This is a confession that acknowledges the deity of Christ and voices a belief that Jesus is God. But a mere acknowledgment of these facts of who Jesus is does not lead to an eternity in heaven. Acceptance of Jesus as Lord over our lives is required, and this is something the demons refused to do.

Jesus was no stranger to demons; He faced them many times throughout His earthly ministry, and in every instance, His authority over them was complete and absolute. Jesus' supremacy over all earthly and demonic powers demonstrates that a person can never come to a saving knowledge of Jesus Christ too late. Although the demons have made their choice and are doomed to spend eternity in hell, such a fate does not need to be the end of anyone who still has breath in his or her lungs.

No evil exists from which God cannot rescue someone, even if that evil is in the form of a person being overcome by a demon. Jesus is greater and more powerful than any evil force, including demons, and His desire is to set the captives free. So if you find yourself enslaved to evil, turn to the only One who has the power to set you free: Jesus of Nazareth, the Holy One of God.

> But Moses said to God, "Who am I that I should go to Pharaoh, and that I should bring the children of Israel out of Egypt?" (Exodus 3:11)

What is Your Excuse?

THE GERMAN POET Christian Hebbel once said, "Whoever wants to be a judge of human nature should study people's excuses." Whether it is "I forgot," "I'm too busy," "I had car trouble," "There was traffic," or the all-time favorite excuse of students, "The dog ate my homework," we have all heard them and maybe even used them ourselves at one time or another. People fundamentally use excuses to justify their own actions or avoid getting involved in something they would prefer to stay out of.

Have you ever made an excuse to God? Have you ever sought to justify your actions before God or attempted to offer an excuse to avoid involvement in some opportunity that He was making available to you?

For Moses, forty years had passed since he attempted God's will. At that time, Moses was presumptuous, impulsive, and prideful, but now, after forty years in the backside of the desert, he had become reluctant, cautious, and humble. Only then did Moses have an encounter with God at the burning bush, and he was overwhelmed by what God asked him to do.

Moses' reaction to this phenomenal opportunity that God placed before him was to make an excuse: "Who am I?" Perhaps Moses was thinking he was too old, or perhaps his past failures haunted him, or perhaps he had fear of being rejected. I suspect that all of the above, and more, that led Moses to offer God a series of excuses.

God took the time to reassure Moses that He would be with Him, that He would guide Him, and that He would give Him the words to speak and the miracles to perform. In short, God was telling Moses, "I will take care of everything." All Moses had to do was trust God.

We need to keep in mind here that Moses' reluctance to do God's will was not a rejection of God's will, but the starting point for Moses. He had to learn and understand that if he was going to do God's will, then he would have to do things God's way. Through Moses' reluctance he recognized his weaknesses, was able to admit his failures, could see his inadequacies, and was able to understand his need for God's help. God used Moses' excuse to reveal to him that who Moses was did not matter; what mattered was who *God* is! Eventually Moses let go of his fears and weaknesses and allowed God to use him.

Recognize your weaknesses, because the reality is, we all have weaknesses and limitations. But we cannot allow them to keep us from what God wants to do in and through our lives. If we allow our excuses to get in the way of following God, then we are demonstrating a lack of faith in God's ability to accomplish His plans and purposes through us. Everyone has shortcomings; no one can do everything. And the sooner we recognize our weaknesses, the sooner God can work by His strength through us.

Do not let reluctance turn to rejection. Do not let inadequacy lead into inactivity. God gives us what we need, in His perfect time, in order to accomplish what He wills. What excuse is holding you back from obeying God and serving Him with all your heart? Do not let excuses keep you from experiencing the blessings that God wants to give you.

"Go home to your own people. Tell them your story—what the Master did, how he had mercy on you." (Mark 5:19 MSG)

JANUARY

24

What is Your Story?

GOD has given us all a story that speaks of how God came into our lives, how He changed our lives, and how He is currently working in our lives. Your story is a powerful bridge that gives you easy access into the lives of the people that God has placed in your world. While sharing the gospel can be an intimidating task at times, sharing your story is a natural and stress-free way to talk about God with anyone, anytime.

In the gospel of Mark, chapter 5, we learn of one man's startling story. One day, Jesus and His disciples sailed into a region called the Gadarenes, where they would meet one wild and crazy guy—a guy whose story was about to change forever because God would radically transform his life. Up until this point, this man's story was dark and dismal. He was forced to live in a cemetery just outside of town because he was untamable, uncontrollable, and terrorized by an unclean spirit. His life was filled with such shame and despair that he would often resort to cutting himself in a twisted effort to feel anything. In pain, he was often heard in the nearby towns as his tormented soul caused him to cry out like a coyote, night after night.

But everything changed the moment he met Jesus. His demons were cast out, his sanity returned, and his soul, which had been supernaturally hijacked, was finally free. Full of amazement and appreciation for all that Jesus had just done, this man wanted to leave his home and travel with Jesus, but Jesus told him to stay and tell his story to anyone who would listen.

God wants to use your story, too. He wants to use your experiences, what you have seen God do, how God has spoken into your life, and the ways in which He has changed your life so that other people will begin to see that God is real, that miracles happen, that prayer works, and that their lives can be transformed too. Sharing your story can inspire others to seek God, to turn from their sins, and to give their lives over to God.

Your story is unique to you and powerful as is, so do not try to embellish or exaggerate your story in an attempt to sound more dramatic. God wants to use you just the way you are and your story just the way it is, because the story really is not about you anyway; the story is all about God and what God has done and is doing in your life. Take the time to think about your story and be ready when Jesus gives you an opportunity to share your story with someone.

But Moses protested again, "What if they won't believe me or listen to me? What if they say, 'The LORD never appeared to you'?"
(Exodus 4:1 NLT)

JANUARY
25

Faith, Not Fear

HAVE you ever been afraid of what people might think of you? Maybe you felt this way during that awkward, overly self-conscious period in junior high school, where popularity and acceptance from peers meant everything. Or perhaps you had to give a speech in front of a group of people and could feel all the eyes in the room were on you. Possibly, you felt this way at that first job interview, or maybe when you were trying to make a good impression on your future spouse. Whether you share one of these experiences or have one of your own, we all have been concerned at one time or another about what others may think about us.

As Christians, we, too, can be assaulted with the fear of how others will perceive us, but these fears are not justified in God's social economy. If we fall prey to the god of perception, image, and acceptance, we will only handicap ourselves as we seek to serve God.

Moses was certainly afraid of how he would be perceived by his fellow comrades, and he wondered if they would even receive him and God's message of deliverance. Moses' fearfulness nearly prevented him from entering into the joy of the Lord's service and all the blessings that come with being used by God. God had a Promised Land flowing with milk and honey awaiting Moses and the children of Israel, but Moses seemed content to stay in the desert.

We can do the same. We can limit the fullness of God's blessing in our lives when we allow ourselves to be swayed by fear. Many people are crippled by fear. Unfortunately, allowing fear to keep you frozen only leads to your hurting yourself. Yet 2 Timothy 1:7 tells us,

"For God has not given us a spirit of fear, but of power and of love and of a sound mind."

Do not miss out on God's best, and do not forfeit what God has for you simply because of the fear of failure. We can get so comfortable and set in our ways that we are unwilling to change. We can be unyielding to change, even when we know that change is for the best. What we need is more faith and less fear. As 1 John 5:4 tells us, "For whatever is born of God overcomes the world. And this is the victory that has overcome the world—our faith." By faith, we can overcome any fear.

Do not miss out on the abundant life that God has planned for you by allowing fear to keep you from serving and following God's plan for your life.

Immediately He made His disciples get into the boat and go before Him to the other side. (Mark 6:45)

The Perfect Storm

AFTER JESUS FED THE FIVE THOUSAND, the crowd grew eager to make Jesus king (see John 6:15). Why not? After all, He did just single-handedly eliminate the hunger problem for over five thousand people that day. This act alone certainly had to go a long way in making him the people's choice for king. But this was not God's plan. Jesus, sensing that a social storm was brewing, decided to withdraw and send the twelve disciples across the sea in a boat while He went to spend the night in prayer.

As Jesus was on the mountain overlooking the sea, He knew the disciples were headed for a storm. This was a storm that would not only test the disciples physically, but would also challenge them spiritually. The disciples went from a nice dinner by the lake to danger on the stormy sea; they went from blessing to testing. Yet as the storm rolled in, Jesus never lost sight of His friends. As He watched them, He saw these experienced fishermen working and straining hard not to lose control. How many times do we look just like those disciples that day on the sea, struggling not to lose control?

The storms of life will come to us all. For some, maybe the heartache and sorrow of broken relationships will be our storm. Others will experience the stress and worry of a financial crisis, and yet for others, the pain and suffering of health problems or the grief surrounding the death of a loved one.

The disciples were never out of the sight of their Master, and we are never out of the sight of our loving Savior. Jesus not only sees the storms of life approaching, but He may be the very one who puts us in the boat and sends us into the wind and rain to test our faith. So, naturally, we may wonder, How will we weather the storm? Will we continue to trust and stay afloat as the waves crash against the boat, or will we allow fear to sink us?

As the familiar saying goes, the night is always darkest just before the dawn. At this dark hour, Jesus decided to come out to His weather-beaten disciples. The disciples who had just witnessed Jesus as the Great Provider now lacked the faith to believe that He also could be their Great Protector.

Jesus met their fears head-on as He walked on the water in the midst of the storm, demonstrating His complete control over all that was causing them to fear at that moment. When He reached them He said, "Be of good cheer! It is I; do not be afraid" (Mark 6:50). Jesus addressed their fear by dealing with their lack of faith (which is the cause of fear in the first place) and directed them to focus on Him.

We would do well to remember that "faith is the substance of things hoped for, the evidence of things not seen" (Hebrews 11:1). Just because the disciples could not see Jesus did not mean that He was not there, or that He forgot them, or that He could not rescue them. But the disciples' fear had blinded them when their faith should have given them the spiritual eyes to see that God was there for them, even in the storm.

Do not let the fear of life's storms blind you from seeing the reality of the fact that Jesus is with you, even in the midst of those storms.

> *Then the whole congregation of the children of Israel
> complained against Moses and Aaron in the wilderness.*
> (Exodus 16:2)

JANUARY
27

The Complaint Department

AFTER THE ISRAELITES were delivered out of Egypt by the mighty hand of God, they entered into a time of wandering in the wilderness; here they were tried and tested, and God provided for His people and sought to purify His people. This also was a time filled with the grumblings of discontented people.

Only a month had passed since God parted the Red Sea and miraculously led the Israelites across dry ground to freedom, but all of these grand acts became a distant memory for them. As their stomachs began to grumble, their mouths began to murmur. The Israelites were witnesses as God plagued the Egyptians and protected His people. They watched as God drowned the Egyptian army while they were delivered on dry ground, and they tasted His goodness as He made the bitter waters at Marah sweet to drink. But even after all, that God had done for them, they still complained. How could they do that? Wait...before you answer the question; remember that we are just as guilty when we complain.

Complaining is being forgetful. The Israelites were complaining in part because they had selective memories. They chose to forget all the great and mighty things the Lord had done for them, and instead focused on their current problem while forgetting the Great Problem Solver.

Complaining is blinding. The Israelites had allowed their complaining to blind them to the promises of God. In other words, they failed to see the big picture. God promised to bring them to a land flowing with milk and honey (see Exodus 3:8), and He did not bring them out of Egypt just so they could starve to death.

Complaining shows a lack of faith. Someone with a lack of faith is impatient with the timing of God, doubts the providence of His provision, questions the power of His protection, and lacks a personal proximity to His presence. All of this leads to fearfulness, which chokes out the flow of faith in our lives.

God is gracious through all we face, even when we complain. God, in His grace, chose not to deal harshly with the Israelites and their sin of complaining. Rather, God saw an opportunity to teach His people a lesson in trusting, and also display His glory to His people so their faith might be strengthened (see Exodus 16:7, 12).

We can always find something to complain about. But remember, complaining shows discontentedness with the plans and purposes of God.

So instead of saying, "Woe is me," seek to worship the King. Instead of finding fault, focus on the promises that God has given to us in His Word. The sooner we learn not to complain, the better off we will be because not complaining shows that our faith is stronger than our circumstances.

Heaven does not have a complaint department. Do not allow complaining to blind you to the blessings you have in Christ.

"But who do you say that I am?" (Mark 8:29)

Is That Your Final Answer?

IF YOU WERE TO ASK PEOPLE THE QUESTION, *Who do you think Jesus was?* You would get a variety of answers. Some would say that Jesus was a prophet, while others would consider Him a good moral teacher, and while some may classify Him as a rabbi, a sage, or a charismatic leader.

As Jesus walked north of Galilee on His way to Caesarea Philippi one afternoon with His disciples, He asked them, "Who do men say that I am?"

People's opinions of Jesus in that day were as varied as people's opinions are today. The word on the streets of Israel back then was that some people thought Jesus was John the Baptist, others thought He was Elijah, while others believed that He was a prophet. People were certainly impressed with Jesus, but most people did not see Him for who He really was. Not much has changed in two thousand years. Jesus' question was not designed to boost His ego or to check his approval rating. Rather, He was preparing to see whether His disciples were going to share in the popular opinion of the day or whether they could see Him for who He really was.

After hearing what the word on the street was, Jesus turned the tables on His disciples and asked them the same piercing question: "But who do *you* say I am?" (emphasis added). The question is not subjective in nature, but rather, objective. The question is not relative, but absolute in nature because only one answer is correct. Peter supplied us with that answer when he responded, "You are the Christ" (Mark 8:29).

This was a divinely inspired confession from the human lips of Peter that also included the acknowledgment that Jesus was the Son of God (see Matthew 16:16–17). Peter's confession was an acknowledgment of the divinity of Jesus as God's Son and recognition of His position and title as the Promised Messiah (see Daniel 9:25).

The popular opinion of the day does not matter regarding the person of Jesus. What matters is, *who do you say that Jesus is?* One day we will all stand before God, and the way we answered this question while we were here on earth will determine whether or not we inherit eternal life. To see Jesus as anything less than the Christ, the Son of God is to not see Jesus for who He really is. This is not a multiple-choice question; this is a true-or-false question. Either He is the Son of God or He is not. Either He is the Christ or He is not. As the Bible tells us, "Whoever believes that Jesus is the Christ is born of God" (1 John 5:1).

Make sure that you take the time to search out the truth about Jesus. You owe yourself a thorough investigation into His life, His ministry, and His teachings before you give your final answer as to who you say that He is!

""You shall have no other gods before Me." (Exodus 20:3)

Priority Is Job One

*T*HE TEN COMMANDMENTS. Perhaps the words conjure up the image of Charlton Heston's Moses, with white hair and a sunburned face, wearing a red robe and holding two stone tablets as he stood on top of Mount Sinai. Or perhaps all that comes to mind is a bunch of rules and regulations that you consider to be old and outdated.

How should people in today's culture see the Ten Commandments that were given nearly 3,500 years ago? First, the Commandments are absolutely indispensable and altogether applicable. Second, they are far from irrelevant for us today. The Commandments are the most concise summation of how we are to relate to God and how we are to relate to one another. Nothing could be more important for us to understand.

In the first four commandments, God addresses how we are to relate to God. In other words, God addresses the issue of our worship, what is acceptable and unacceptable for our worship of God, and what our relationship toward God should look like.

The commandments then shift away from our vertical (or upward) relationship involving man and God to the horizontal (or parallel) plane, explaining what God's expectations are concerning our relationship one with another: mankind's relationship to mankind.

All of the Ten Commandments are important and worthy of study, but if we fail to worship God properly, then the rest of the Ten Commandments are essentially worthless. God begins these important instructions with our relationship with Him, first and foremost. Take, for example, oxygen. If we are unable to breathe, nothing else matters until we take care of what is impairing our ability to breathe oxygen. Is eating important? Yes. Do we need to drink water? Of course. However, breathing is our first priority. Why? Well, we can go weeks without eating and can go days without water, but we can only go minutes without oxygen. The same is true spiritually. The commandment not to murder or steal is important? Certainly. But if something else is coming before our worship of God, then we must make corrections as our first priority.

The Israelites were surrounded by nations that worshiped other gods. God needed to make the point unmistakably clear that He was not first among *many* gods. Rather, He was the *only* God, and apart from Him, no other God existed. Since only one God exists, to worship anything other than Him is to worship created things rather than the Creator.

The same temptation exists today. People can place their worship of other *things* before their worship of God, and in so doing, create other gods. These gods may not be made of wood and stone like in ancient days, but whatever you spend your time pursuing, whether money or appearances, appetites or things, you have made the objects of your pursuits into gods because you have placed your quest of objects before your pursuit of God.

There is only one true God. Everything else is a fake. Make your worship of the one true God priority number one.

This kind can come out by nothing but prayer and fasting."
(Mark 9:29)

Power Outage

MAYBE YOU HAVE EXPERIENCED a power outage that lasts for several days due to downed power lines or because of some natural disaster that struck. No electricity means no refrigerator or freezer, no lights, no heat, and worse than that (for some people), no television! As inconvenient as a power outage can be, with a little planning and preparation, you can be ready for one, if and when an outage occurs.

Have you ever suffered from a spiritual power outage? Nobody wants to fail, fall short, or frustrate the work of God in his or her life. Unfortunately, most of us can say that we have done just that at one point or another in our lives. If we were to look closely at the reason we fell short, we would discover a lack of power was at fault. In Mark, chapter 9, we read that the disciples also fell short and frustrated the Lord due to their own spiritual power outages.

Back in chapter 3, Jesus had given the disciples the authority to heal the sick and to cast out demons, but when faced with a particular demon-possessed boy, something went terribly wrong for the disciples. They ran out of power. Perhaps the miraculous had become mundane for them, or perhaps pride crept in, and they were relying on their own power to do the work of God. Maybe they were feeling sorry for themselves because they were left to do the work while Peter, James, and John were given a special glimpse of the glory of Christ on a nearby mountain.

Jesus gave the disciples the authority to accomplish great things for God, but in order for them to exercise that authority, they needed to stay connected to the endless supply of power that only comes from God.

Jesus went on to explain to the disciples why they were unable to cast out this demon. Their failure was not because God's power was insufficient or the demon was too strong; rather, they had allowed themselves to become complacent in their relationship with God. Laziness led to powerlessness in their lives. We are powerless, just as the disciples were powerless that day, to accomplish the work of God if we unplug ourselves from the only source of spiritual power.

The power to exercise our faith comes from tapping into the power generator, which is God. Prayer and fasting play an important role in keeping the power flowing from God into our lives. Constant communion with God is essential in accomplishing the work of God, and prayer is a crucial part of that shared relationship with God. Fasting represents a life that is totally surrendered and submitted to God. These last two aspects of our relationship with Him can act like the positive and negative charges needed to produce the necessary power in our lives and prepare us for anything that comes our way.

If you feel like your spiritual batteries are running low, or if you are experiencing a total spiritual power outage, then cast out anything that has come between you and God and reconnect to the only spiritual power source: God. Living a power-filled life that brings glory and honor to God means that you must live a disciplined life that includes both prayer and fasting.

"You shall not covet. . . ." (Exodus 20:17 NIV)

I Want What You Have

HAVE YOU EVER looked at your situation in life and thought to yourself, "If I just had what they had, my life would be great"? Looking at someone else's life, their job, their success, their ministry, their car, their home, their family, their kids, or even their spouse and thinking that the key to your happiness is found in what someone else has is a real temptation. God calls this covetousness, and the problem is big enough to have made God's Top Ten list. But why is coveting so dangerous?

When God was giving the Ten Commandments to Moses, last on the list, but certainly not least, came "You shall not covet." Covetousness as a sin often goes unrecognized, yet is frequently committed. So, what does God mean by "to covet"? To covet is simply to want what belongs to someone else. We covet when we set our hearts on something that is not ours and should never be ours. As Philip Ryken and R. Kent Hughes have said, "We often want the wrong thing, in the wrong way, at the wrong time, and for the wrong reason, and this is what the tenth commandment rules out."[4]

Coveting is what causes that feeling of disappointment to creep in whenever someone else gets what we want. We covet when a friend goes on the vacation of our dreams, when a coworker gets the promotion we have been chasing, or when a neighbor gets the car that we have been longing to own. The apostle James said the reason we fight and complain is because we want what we do not have and are jealous of what others have, so we scheme to try to get what belongs to someone else (see James 4:1–2 NLT).

To want bigger and better things is not wrong. To want to succeed is not wrong. To admire someone or something is not wrong. But to feel discontentment with our current life situation and therefore turn to what our neighbors have and want what is theirs *is* wrong. Are you looking at someone or something and are thinking that you would do anything to have what they have? Stop before covetousness causes mayhem in your heart and distress in your life.

Human nature has not changed much since the time that the Law was given to Moses. Covetousness is still a big problem because to covet leaves God out. Looking for things to satisfy when God is the only source of genuine satisfaction is a problem. Stuff never satisfies; only God can satisfy. To avoid coveting, begin thanking God for what you do have. As you realize and recount the numerous blessings that God has already given you, you will not be tempted to want what someone else has.

February

Jesus entered the temple courts and began driving out those who were buying and selling there. He overturned the tables of the money changers and the benches of those selling doves. (Mark 11:15 NIV)

Turning the Tables

MOTHER THERESA holding a machine gun? Billy Graham wearing combat fatigues and brandishing a machete? Do these images seem a little strange to you? That is because what we know about these individuals is juxtaposed to the image.

Many people think of Jesus as "gentle Jesus, meek and mild" and not angry Jesus, firm and forceful. That is why, when gentle Jesus went into the temple with a whip and kicked over tables, the scene is juxtaposed to how we picture the Lamb of God. What made Jesus react so strongly?

Imagine for a moment that you are driving to church for Sunday service. A sense of anticipation is about you as you are eager to worship God, share in communion, and give your tithe and offering to God. But when you get to church, the parking lot is full. Okay, no problem, you eventually find a place to park on the street and walk the extra five minutes. All the while, you are thinking, *Is something going on this weekend that I forgot about?*

As you approach the front of the church, you notice there is a long line to get in, and a series of tables set up, almost like checkpoints, where people are required to stop. As the line slowly moves you closer, you discover a new church currency, mandatory for all tithes and offerings, has been established. At the first table, you discover that you need to change your money into this new church currency, and the exchange rate is twenty dollars for ten dollars' worth of new church bucks. Feeling a little cheated, you move on to the next table, where you find out the worship lyrics no longer will be displayed on the big screen at the front of the sanctuary, and the church is requiring everyone to buy their own personal hymnal at a cost of $19.95 each. Finally, just up ahead, you notice a sign on the last table in today's chaos says, "Communion cups, $7.00; grape juice, $4.00; wafers, $3.00." At this point, you become so frustrated and discouraged that you no longer want to go to church because you feel that you are being taken advantage of.

The above scenario is a modern version of what Jesus saw in the temple court. Jesus saw that the temple, the place of worship, had lost its way. The temple was to be a "house of prayer" where worshipers could have an encounter with their God and Father. But church was no longer about God; church had become nothing more than a business.

God gets angry when we allow anything to interfere with our worship of Him. As believers, we are temples of the Holy Spirit. How much of your temple is dedicated to prayer and genuine worship, and how much is dedicated to worldly, nonspiritual things? Jesus' explosion in the temple demonstrates his passionate jealousy. God is eagerly longing for our heartfelt devotion and genuine worship.

Then everyone came whose heart was stirred, and everyone whose spirit was willing, and they brought the LORD'S offering for the work of the tabernacle of meeting.
(Exodus 35:21)

FEBRUARY

2

To Give or Not to Give

GIVING has become a delicate subject in many churches today. Some churches have gone overboard, teaching that giving to God will make all your financial dreams come true, while others have erred on the side of never speaking about the subject of giving at all. Both approaches are extreme, and both approaches are wrong. A biblical balance concerning the subject of giving to God does exist, and we can observe this balance is in the book of Exodus.

In Exodus 25:1–2, God told Moses to speak to the Israelites, asking all who were willing to give an offering toward the tabernacle-building project. God knew that the people needed to be made aware of the opportunity in order for them to participate in the work of God. Moses faithfully communicated this to the people, and their response was so overwhelming that Moses had to stop the people from making any further contributions (see Exodus 36:6–7).

God did not tell Moses to command the people to give or to manipulate them or play with their emotions to get something from them. Rather, God was searching for those whose hearts were stirred and whose spirits were willing.

God does not need our gifts to accomplish His purposes; He is all-sufficient and all-powerful. But He does graciously give us the privilege to partner with Him. One way we can do this is by giving to the work of the ministry.

When we give to God, we reflect the love of God. The Bible tells us, "For God so loved the world that He gave His only begotten Son" (John 3:16). His love for us was His motivation for giving us His only Son. Our only motivation for giving back to God should be our love for Him.

The children of Israel gave diversely to God; some gave gold and others gave goat hair, and some, who were unable to give assets, gave their abilities. From woodworkers to jewelry cutters, all gave freely and willingly to God. You may be able to only give two pennies to God, but quantity is not in the standard by which God determines the value of the gift. Rather, He looks at the willingness and the motivation with which you give the gift.

The subject of giving should not be avoided, nor should the topic be overemphasized. Part of giving involves our being made aware of opportunities as they arise, then prayerfully considering the how, when, and where of our giving that will most glorify Him. God then invites us into partnership and gives us the privilege to participate in His heavenly mission.

We are never to give to God out of compulsion. We should not give to God because we feel guilty or so that others will see us give. We give willingly and freely because of our love for Him and our desire to see His will done on earth as it is in heaven.

And being in Bethany at the house of Simon the leper, as He sat at the table, a woman came having an alabaster flask of very costly oil of spikenard. Then she broke the flask and poured it on His head. (Mark 14:3)

The Fragrance of Worship

TIME WAS SHORT. His crucifixion was rapidly approaching. The burden of bearing the sins of mankind profoundly weighed on the mind of Jesus. Death was only days away. This heavy burden led the Savior to seek solace at one of His favorite safe havens, Bethany. This small, quiet town was less than a thirty-minute walk from the hustle and bustle of Jerusalem and would often provide Jesus with the much-needed rest He sought during His public ministry.

On one such occasion, as the Savior was enjoying dinner with close friends, the sweetest of scents would soon fill the air. The lovely scent was not the aroma of freshly baked bread, nor the bouquet of herb-roasted vegetables or even the smell of stew simmering. No, the fragrance that would fill this feast would be the fragrance of worship.

Eager to express the inexpressible gratitude he had for the healing he received at the hands of Jesus, Simon threw a feast for Jesus, His disciples, and a few close friends. Here, during this intimate gathering, the most unexpected and extraordinary of things would take place. A woman would forever be immortalized in the Bible for her extravagant offering to the Lord, as she poured out a bottle of expensive perfume over the head of Jesus. In the Gospel of John, chapter 11, we find out who this mystery woman was. She was none other than Mary, the sister of Martha and Lazarus.

Mary is only mentioned a few times in the Bible, but each time we encounter her, we see her at the feet of Jesus, listening intently to His every word. On this occasion, at the home of Simon, Mary expressed her deepest devotion to Jesus by anointing Him for His impending burial. Her offering was no small gift; the monetary value of the perfume would have been the equivalent of a year's wages. But to her, the gift represented only a fraction of her affection and dedication to her Lord.

As this fragrant worship continued, Mary fell to her knees and took her hair, which was considered the glory of a woman (1 Corinthians 11:15), and wiped the feet of her Lord and Master. In the sweetest and simplest of ways, she expressed her humility, submission, and devotion to the only one worthy of glory, the King of glory (see Psalm 24:8).

Mary's actions brought rebuke by those who failed to see the significance of her worship. This was not the first time she experienced the nearsightedness of others. Both here and in Luke 10:38-41, she is criticized for worshiping Jesus, and in both instances, Jesus came to her defense and called her service "good."

Mary's offering of perfume was good, not simply because she gave her best to the Lord but because she gave her all to the Lord. Motivated by her love for the Lord, she was obedient to respond to the prompting of the Holy Spirit and gave sacrificially to God. Her offering, originating out of the mercies of God that she had experienced (see Romans 12:1–2), led her to sacrifice and surrender her

35

life to the Savior. For these reasons, her gift will forever be remembered as the sweet fragrance of worship.

What can you do today that demonstrates your love for God?

"If his offering is a burnt sacrifice of the herd, let him offer a male without blemish; he shall offer it of his own free will at the door of the tabernacle of meeting before the LORD."
(Leviticus 1:3)

FEBRUARY
4

Up in Smoke

THE BURNT OFFERING was a bloody, brutal, yet beautiful event through which sinful man was to relate to a holy God. The burnt offering signified a relationship that was marked by total commitment and complete consecration to God. The entire animal was sacrificed and placed on the altar to be burned, representing how a true worshiper of God should live a sacrificial life, thoroughly surrendered to and totally set apart for God.

In the opening chapters of the book of Leviticus, we are introduced to five offerings: the burnt offering, the grain offering, the peace offering, the sin offering, and the trespass offering. These offerings speak of the commitment, cleansing, and communion that were necessary for a right relationship to exist between created mankind and the Creator God.

The burnt offering may seem very bizarre to a modern person in a contemporary culture where many faint at the sight of blood. To the ancient Jew, however, the offering was an important and central part of life, which involved the worshiper of God bringing his sacrificial animal to the entrance of the holy dwelling place of God, the tabernacle, where he would go no further because he was not a priest. He would present his sacrifice to the priest and, standing near the altar, would place his hand on the head of the sacrifice. Then, with one quick slice across the throat, he would kill the animal. As the animal's blood gushed out, the priest would catch the flow of blood in a basin to throw against the altar. The worshiper then cut up the sacrifice and the priests would arrange the pieces on the burning altar. Soon, a thick smoke would rise up to the heavens, and the bloody sacrifice was complete.

The burnt offering allowed worshipers to express their faith and devotion to God through sacrifice. This offering allowed commitment, cleansing, and communion between mankind and God.

The beauty of this sacrifice far surpassed its brutality. Beauty can be found in the fact that God has made provision for all who are willing to come and offer themselves to Him. Even though we are sinners and God hates sin, He has provided a way, through the sacrificial system, to bring Himself and humanity back together.

A far more surpassing beauty is found in the provision for all who are willing to come to Christ, the ultimate burnt offering sacrifice. Jesus beautifully embodied the burnt offering as He willingly laid himself on the altar of the cross, pure and undefiled. He accepted and atoned for sin through the brutal shedding of His blood, and through His offering and sacrifice, He has made all who believe in Him to be a sweet-smelling aroma to God. Christ became our burnt offering so that we might be His living sacrifices.

God requires willing, voluntary, and complete surrender of our lives to Him as we hold nothing back and lay our all on the altar, seeking to be a sweet-smelling aroma to Him.

> *John answered, saying to all, "I indeed baptize you with water; but One mightier than I is coming, whose sandal strap I am not worthy to loose. He will baptize you with the Holy Spirit and fire." (Luke 3:16)*

A Witness in the Wilderness

JOHN THE BAPTIST was a mysterious and often misunderstood man of God. When your diet consists of grasshoppers and honey, when your clothing is made from camel's hair, and when, during your preaching, you call your listeners a bunch of vipers, the odds are very good that you will be frequently misunderstood and labeled a little eccentric, to say the least. Jesus would further add to the intrigue that surrounded this prophet by declaring him to be the greatest man born of a woman (see Matthew 11:11).

Unique and uniquely privileged, John was the first prophet to break the four hundred-year silence between God and His people, bringing to a close the time gap between the Old and New Testaments. John's mission was to prepare the way for the Messiah, and his message was one of repentance.

The people in John's day were disinterested and unenthusiastic about the things of God. The priests were corrupt and unethical, and a general spiritual hypocrisy was prevalent among the scribes and Pharisees. This led John the Baptist to speak out about the coming judgment of God on those who refused to repent, that is, to turn away from their sin and go in the opposite direction. Conversely, for those who would choose repentance, God would offer His grace and salvation to all who were willing to receive them.

As his name indicates, John the Baptist was concerned about baptism. Baptism was nothing new in Judaism because Gentile converts were commonly baptized into their new Jewish faith. What was different about what John was doing was that he was baptizing those who were already Jews. John's baptism was a baptism of preparation, a baptism that looked forward to the coming Messiah, a baptism that signified, much like today, identification with Jesus. Christian baptism today looks *back* to the finished work of the Messiah; for the Jews listening to John, their baptism looked *forward* to the work of the Messiah.

Part of John's preparation also included announcing that the Messiah would baptize with the Holy Spirit and with fire. The Holy Spirit baptized the believers at Pentecost (see Acts 2:4), and today when a person trusts in Jesus Christ as their Lord and Savior, the Holy Spirit baptizes him or her into God's family as the Holy Spirit indwells a believer. For the person who does not trust in Christ, the baptism of fire speaks of future judgment.

John, though a little mysterious and unconventional, is an example of faithfulness to the work of God. He was committed to elevating people's awareness of Jesus Christ, while at the same time, deflecting attention and his own self-promotion. For all the unknowns that still surround this prophet, one thing is abundantly clear: this man, his mission, and his message can be best summed up by his own words about his relationship to Jesus: "He must increase, but I must decrease" (John 3:30).

Any individual, ministry, or church that aims to magnify Jesus and deflect self-promotion and glory seeking, while being more concerned about boldly proclaiming the message of Jesus Christ, has learned well from this mysterious witness from the wilderness.

"For I am the LORD your God. You shall therefore consecrate yourselves, and you shall be holy; for I am holy." (Leviticus 11:44)

FEBRUARY 6

Hitting Holiness Head-On

HOW WOULD YOU ANSWER this question: If you were to describe yourself in one word, what word would you choose?

In 1989, one book hit store shelves that was destined to become a bestseller. Geared toward giving people the tools they need to enjoy powerful and effective living, the book was saturated with advice on leadership, life management, and relationships. The whole premise of the book was centered on the inside-out concept that old behavior is learned, not instinctive. Therefore, old habits can be discarded and replaced by new, effective habits.

That book, written by Stephen R. Covey, was called *The Seven Habits of Highly Effective People.* According to Covey, if you exhibit in your daily life the seven habits outlined in his book, you could rightly describe yourself in one word: *effective.*

Many words can be found in the Scriptures that we would like to say describe ourselves. But here are just seven words that should describe God's people: *honest, patient, kind, giving, loving, selfless,* and *humble.* But what about *holy*? Perhaps our reluctance to describe ourselves with such a word as *holy* is based on some common misconceptions of its meaning. The word *holy* does not mean super religious, or perfect, and neither does it mean better than someone else. Holy simply means to be separate or set apart.

When the Bible calls God holy, this primarily means that God is transcendentally separate. He is so far above and beyond who we are that He would be totally unfamiliar to us if not for the fact that He has revealed himself to us through His Word and through Jesus Christ. To be holy is to be "other" or to be different in a special way.

Since the beginning, back in the Garden of Eden, humanity was created to reflect the image of God (see Genesis 1:26). Part of how we reflect His image is through holiness. We are called to live lives that are separate, set apart, consecrated, and dedicated to God, lives that magnify and glorify God, and lives that are obedient to His Word. Living a life of holiness, a life dedicated to obeying God's Word, definitely means you are living separately from the world around you. You will be living a life in the world, but a life that is also very different from that of others in the world.

In the book of Leviticus God goes to great lengths to describe many different aspects of holy living and how His people are to remain pure, clean, and righteous in an unclean and unrighteous world. Throughout His Word, God continues to encourage His people to pursue purity, to seek to live set apart unto God, and to be committed to consecration—all of which will lead a person to holy living.

Now, before you think, *I cannot live a holy life!* remember that God does not call His people to anything He has not enabled them to accomplish. God has given us His Word on holiness. When you show evidence of a life lived in a way that is set apart for Him, where His character and nature can be seen in you and in your daily life, then you could rightly describe yourself in one word: *holy.*

"Love your enemies, do good to those who hate you, bless those who curse you, and pray for those who spitefully use you." (Luke 6:27–28)

FEBRUARY 7

Love-Hate

WHEN SOMEONE DISLIKES US, says evil things about us, is cruel to us, or takes advantage of us, hatred can easily sneak in and consume our emotions. Hatred has been the cause of many of the problems in the world, both past and present, but hatred never has done anything to solve these problems. Instead, hatred only serves to fuel the flames of animosity.

On the other hand, love is different. We find loving to be very easy towards those who are kind or supportive to us, or those who demonstrate concern for our well being. This is why, when we read Jesus' command to "love your enemies, do good to those who hate you," our knee-jerk reaction is to resist, stiffen up, and think, *That is easy for you to say, Jesus* Hating those who hate us and loving those who love us is much easier, but Jesus calls us to rise up to the standards of heaven, not live down to the prevailing principles of this world. Responding with an eye for an eye against those who hate and harm us does nothing more than to leave us in a blind world, holding on to hate, which is a great hindrance to the work of God.

Every Christian must learn to make the godly replacement of hate with love. This exchange of divine proportions begins with the realization that we are unable to accomplish this exchange apart from the power of God. We must also recognize that this love does not originate from our emotions or from anything within ourselves; rather, this love is a conscious act of surrendering our will to God. In other words, to love this way is a choice that we make to respond to the commands of God.

Jesus went on to explain what these "love choices" look like in everyday life. A love choice is reflected in a lifestyle of goodness, a life that chooses to do good, even toward those who hate us. Choosing to seek to encourage and speak well of those who curse and speak evil of us is another love choice. Another example is choosing to lift up our enemies before God in prayer, or choosing to turn our cheek to personal offense. Love choices give what is needed to those who need a helping hand, while at the same time does not seek to be repaid, even if cheated. Jesus equates these love actions with the Golden Rule: treat others how you want to be treated.

Christ demonstrated the very love choices that He calls us to live out. Jesus did good to those who hated Him, as in the case of Malchus, the servant of the High Priest who came to the Garden of Gethsemane to arrest and imprison Jesus. Yet, Jesus chose to heal this man's severed ear. Jesus turned the other cheek when the priests struck Him across the face, He prayed on the cross for those who were nailing Him to it, and He offered salvation to the thief being crucified next to Him, even though he initially hurled insults at Jesus. Ultimately, Jesus demonstrated all of these love actions through His willingness to go to the cross and pay the penalty for sin on behalf of a world that has repeatedly shown hatred toward Him.

How quick we can be to quarrel. How fast we are to engage in a fight. How ready we are to revile another. Instead, let us live up to the standard that Jesus calls us to live by. Let us choose not just to demonstrate love, but to live a life of love, and not live down to the baseness of hate.

"On the fourteenth day of the first month at twilight is the LORD'S Passover." (Leviticus 23:5)

FEBRUARY

8

Food for Thought

ONE OF THE GREATEST DAYS in the history of Israel was the day God delivered them from the bondage of Egypt. Part of this miraculous event included an awesome display of destruction and protection known as the Passover. During the Passover, God killed all the firstborn males in the land of Egypt who were not protected by the blood of the Passover lamb. God's instructions to the Israelites were simple: sacrifice a lamb and place his blood on the doorposts of your home on the fourteenth day of the first month, and all firstborns would be spared.

The feast of Passover was instituted to commemorate and celebrate the mighty powers of God, displayed in His deliverance of His people out of Egypt. The feast and the food are full of significance and symbolism, intended to remind God's people of what God had done for them. The unleavened bread shows the haste in which the people left the land of Egypt. The bitter herbs reflect the bitterness of their slavery. The saltwater represents the tears that were shed during the years of bondage. The savory chutney, which has a mortar-like texture, is reminiscent of the brick making and hard labor in Egypt. The red wine embodies joy, and, most importantly, the roasted lamb, sacrificed before the meal, illustrates redemption.

The apostle Paul said in 1 Corinthians 5:7 that Jesus Christ is our Passover Lamb. On the night that Jesus was to be betrayed, He took His disciples aside to celebrate the Passover feast together. During the celebration of the Passover with His disciples, Jesus became the fulfillment of the Passover feast and ushered in a new feast, the Lord's Supper. He said, "For this is My blood of the new covenant, which is shed for many for the remission of sins" (Matthew 26:28).

Just as the blood of a lamb was placed on the doorposts to save God's people, Jesus, as the Lamb of God, shed His blood on a wooden cross to save all who would believe in Him. God's wrath was poured out on Jesus, delivering us from judgment and setting us free as He leads us through this life to the Promised Land of our inheritance that is, awaiting us in heaven. The blood of Christ has therefore protected us, and we are passed over by God's judgment, being protected, delivered, and set free because of the blood of the Lamb.

The Christians' Passover feast today is represented through the taking of communion. Time is set aside when we celebrate, commemorate, and remember the work of God's deliverance in our lives. He has freed us from the bondage of sin and allowed himself to be the Lamb that was sacrificed to save us from the judgment of God. The bread of Communion represents the body of Christ, which was broken for us. The wine (or grape juice) represents His blood, which was shed for the forgiveness of our sins. God has used food as part of the process to make us think and recall the goodness of God.

May we never forget.

And He said, "To you it has been given to know the mysteries of the kingdom of God, but to the rest it is given in parables." (Luke 8:10)

FEBRUARY
9

Unlocking the Mystery of Parables

HIS POPULARITY WAS GROWING, word was spreading, and people were coming out in large numbers to see the Great Miracle Worker, Jesus of Nazareth. With these large crowds, questions began to arise: *Who came to see Jesus because they really wanted to hear what He had to say? Who came out to see a show? Who came out because they wanted to try and get something for free?* Jesus had a solution, a way that would feed those who were hungry for the truth while at the same time drive away all the lookie-loos who were there for selfish reasons. His solution was to speak in parables.

A parable is a story in which something familiar is used to explain something unfamiliar. Parables use common, everyday examples to communicate a heavenly or spiritual truth. In the New Testament, a "mystery" is a spiritual truth understood only by divine revelation. Many have said that a biblical mystery could be called a "sacred secret," known only to those on the inside, those who were seeking to learn from the Lord and obey Him.

The parable of the sower in Luke 8 serves as a warning for some of us and as an encouragement for others. Jesus draws on the common agricultural image of a farmer planting seeds in the ground to communicate His spiritual truth. Jesus explains that the seed is the Word of God and that whenever the Word of God is preached, that word goes out in the same way that seed goes out in a field. The soil represents how the heart of mankind receives the seed, or the Word of God. Some hear the Word and, due to a hard heart, the seed is quickly stolen by birds. A second type hears the Word and, due to a shallow heart, the Word springs up fast but has no roots to sustain life. Next is the seed that lands among the weeds, which is a heart that has allowed cares and pleasures to choke out

41

any chance of producing fruit. Finally, the last seed lands in the good soil, which is a heart that receives the Word and produces fruit of different quantities.

Jesus explained that this parable is a pattern for all parables, and that by unlocking the secret mystery here, we are able to see the meaning behind every parable, which is to *reveal* truth to those who are seeking truth and to *conceal* truth from those who are self-seeking.

The Word of God never changes. The parable and the accompanying meaning do not change. The only thing different is the attitude of the hearer and the condition of his or her heart, because the condition of the heart is the key to unlocking the parables.

What type of listener are you? Do you approach listening to God's Word casually? Do the cares of the world and other pursuits distract you from making a personal application of the Word to your life? Or, are you the type of listener who is seeking in order to receive and produce a good crop?

Cultivate a heart of receptivity and let the Word of God grow, bringing forth fresh life, which will yield an abundant harvest of blessing in your life.

"The LORD bless you and keep you." (Numbers 6:24)

God Bless You

FEBRUARY 10

IS THERE REALLY ANYONE who *does not* want God to bless his or her life? I seriously doubt it! But does being blessed mean having a big house, a new car in the driveway, low cholesterol, a high-paying job, a happy family that includes a husband, a wife, straight-A children, and a dog named Spot?

Blessings in the Bible come in many different shapes and sizes and, without a doubt, everything in the above list can be considered a blessing. But biblical blessing is more than getting what you want; this type of blessing means getting what God wants. What, then, does God's blessing look like?

To begin with, the word for *blessed* is often translated "happy," and in reality, an element of happiness is associated with being blessed. However, happiness is temporary and subject to change. Therefore, happiness can come and go like the wind, where blessedness carries a sense of permanence and a joy that is unchanging. When Jesus said in Matthew 5, "Blessed are those who mourn . . ." (verse 4), *happy* just does not seem to completely capture all that Jesus was communicating. You see, you can be experiencing some very difficult circumstances in life that do not make you particularly happy, but you can still be blessed in the midst of them.

This may cause you to ask, "How is that possible? How can I mourn yet be blessed, or how can I experience any of the vast number of difficult circumstances in life yet still be blessed?" The answer to all these questions is found in the source of blessing.

In Numbers 6:23–27, we find the Aaronic Blessing (*not* the Ironic Blessing). Here, God gave instructions for the priests, who at that time were Aaron and his sons, on how to bless the people. A priest had two main responsibilities: one, to stand before God as humanity's representative; and two, to stand before the people as God's representative. As God's representative to the people, the priest was given the responsibility and privilege of pronouncing a blessing on the people. Even though the priests were the instruments used by God to proclaim the blessing of God, that the source of the blessing is God is unmistakable.

The Lord is the one who blesses (verse 24), who keeps (verse 24), who makes His face to shine upon us (verse 25), who is gracious (verse 25), the Lord lifts up His countenance (verse 26), and gives peace (verse 26). And, just to avoid any confusion, the passage ends with "and I will bless them." God is the source of all blessing.

In much the same way in the Beatitudes (see Matthew 5), where Jesus lists a series of blessings, a blessing can be found in each example that comes from God. The blessing may be comfort, mercy, adoption into God's family, and so forth, but the point is, all the blessings come from God.

True blessings can only come from God; someone cannot give you one, and you cannot bless yourself. Blessings are a gift from God. And here is the key: Blessings are gifts *of* God. Every genuine blessing from God is the gift *of* God. God gives us some aspect of himself, His mercy, His grace, His provision, His peace, and so on.

Seek more than happiness in life. Look to God for more of Him, and you will be blessed.

Then He said to them all, "If anyone desires to come after Me, let him deny himself, and take up his cross daily, and follow Me." (Luke 9:23)

FEBRUARY
11

Cross Walk

WHEN YOU CONFESS JESUS CHRIST, not only are you accepting His sacrificial death on the cross, but you are also accepting your own cross to bear. Jesus demands daily self-denial from His disciples; He commands constant commitment from every Christian. He allows no exceptions, no exemptions, and no excuses. Sound difficult? Well, that is because it is! The road that Jesus walked was a difficult one, and He tells all who desire to follow Him that the road ahead of them also will be a difficult road to walk.

Jesus' cross walk was more than the two thousand feet He walked from the Praetorium to the hillside of Golgotha the day He was crucified. Every day of His earthly life, Jesus walked in the shadow of His cross. He lived each and every day in faithful obedience to all that His heavenly Father commanded Him, which meant knowing hunger, thirst, and temptation. His burden meant being despised, rejected, misunderstood, and mistreated. For every true disciple living in the shadow of the cross of Christ, life also will include times of hunger, thirst, and temptation, times of being despised, rejected, misunderstood, and mistreated.

The Christian life is more than a code of conduct; to be a Christian is identification with Christ. Doing so includes carrying your cross and sharing in the sufferings of Christ as you live a life of sacrifice, submission, and suffering, just as the Savior did. Carrying your cross begins by saying yes to Jesus and no to self. Carrying your cross means saying yes to His lordship over your life and no to self-lordship. Carrying your cross is a daily discipline that must be a daily priority.

Saying no to self and to self-lordship does not mean that you are doomed to live a boring life that is empty of enjoyment and lacking in occasional luxuries, but does mean saying no to *anything* and *everything* that comes between you and your relationship with Jesus Christ.

Be aware, however, that carrying your cross is more than dealing with the regular challenges and difficulties that happen in life. For example, having to deal with heavy traffic every day is not an instance of carrying your cross. Also, carrying your cross is not found in dealing with the sicknesses and diseases that may come to pass in life. Carrying your cross can only come as a result of following Jesus. You bear your cross when you are despised for living like Jesus, for having a life that looks like Jesus' life, and for loving others the way Jesus loved others. When you face difficulties because you are caught cross walking, *then* you are bearing your cross.

Seek to find your identity in Christ and not in self. Look to glorify God and not to seek your own personal interest. Work to advance His kingdom and not expand your own. Then you will begin to know how you feel when you pick up your cross and walk as Jesus did.

So Moses made a bronze serpent, and put it on a pole; and so it was, if a serpent had bitten anyone, when he looked at the bronze serpent, he lived. (Numbers 21:9)

FEBRUARY
12

Just What the Doctor Ordered

GOD'S PEOPLE are not born perfect; no one is. We are all "in process," which means many failures as well as successes will go into shaping us.

During the forty years that the children of Israel wandered in the desert, we witness two generations of God's people and how life in the wilderness affected their relationship with God. The first generation was made up of those who experienced the exodus out of Egypt, while the second generation consisted of those who were born during the desert years. All in the first generation were sentenced to die in the wilderness and prevented from entering the Promised Land as punishment for their repeated unbelief and disobedience to the commands of God. The time soon came for the next generation to show what they had learned from their parents' successes and failures.

Numbers 21 opens with a great success. The second generation is faced with an attack by the enemy, which leads them to turn to God for His help. God heard their prayer and gave them victory over their enemies. Yet, as quickly as they had turned toward God in prayer, they turned against God, suspicious about His sovereignty, doubting His provision, and questioning His love. Why the sudden discontent so soon after God's blessing? The short answer is *sin.* The slightly longer answer is they became discouraged because they were on the brink of the Promised Land when they were forced to take an unexpected detour, which meant they would have to do some backtracking before they could move forward. This led them to complain against God.

What was God's response to their deliberate sin? Judgment and grace. In judgment, God sent a plague of poisonous snakes into the camp of the Israelites to bite them with deadly venom, "for the wages of sin is death" (Romans 6:23). Because of sin, the judgment of death entered the world and remains today; because of sin, all have been bitten by the snake's deadly venom.

God had every right to let His judgment stand against that rebellious generation and leave them all to die in the wilderness, just as the previous generation was sentenced. In the same way, every person who has ever lived is deserving of death because we have all sinned and deserve His judgment. Enter the grace of God, in which God provided a remedy for all those who were doomed to die. God commanded Moses to make a bronze snake and hang it from a pole, and all who would look at it would be healed. No magic existed in the bronze serpent; and the healing did not come from the people's power to look. The people's salvation from death came through their faith in God to heal them. Their faith was in the power of God to take away the punishment for their sin, and looking upon the hanging serpent was only the expression of their faith.

Simple faith was all mankind had to have, yet some looked at God's remedy and doubted and laughed in disbelief, thinking, *It cannot be that simple! What I really need is some antivenin medicine!* Those who saw their sinfulness and responded to the grace of God by faith were saved.

In the same way, God has graciously provided the remedy for the deadly snakebite of sin from which all men suffer. In order to be healed, will you, by faith, look at the cross where Jesus hung?

The younger son gathered all . . . , journeyed to a far country, and there wasted his possessions with prodigal living. (Luke 15:13)

Finding Your Way Home

FEBRUARY 13

LOSING YOUR WAY in this world is easy. One step in the wrong direction can lead you down a dead-end road. Everywhere you turn, neon signs and flashing lights entice you to buy whatever is being sold. The personal philosophy adopted by many has become, "Life would be great if I could just do whatever I want, whenever I want, with whomever I want." So off they go.

Jesus told the story of one son who decided to take his inheritance early and head out on life's open highway where he could be his own boss, answer to no one but himself, and live footloose and fancy-free. So off he went.

In the beginning, all seemed to be going great. The money was flowing, so that meant the very best of everything, starting with some new clothes, a nice apartment, and parties every night with gourmet food and free drinks for all his friends. His living was lavish, but life seemed to be getting a little darker every day. What was supposed to be fulfilling and freeing only brought emptiness and bondage. Hard times came, as they often do, and this young man was not ready because he had wasted his wealth. Out of money, he discovered that his "friends" were nowhere to be found, and the once king of the hill found himself as a servant of slop, where his only friends were eating better than he was. How did this happen to him? How does anyone wind up living in life's pigpen?

This process begins by being focused on self. Pursuing selfish desires instead of being committed to God begins the downward spiral that leads to serving the swine instead of serving the sovereign King. We all must come to the point where we see our own poverty of spirit. We must experience our own personal hunger for the things of God before we can ever hope to get out of life's pigpens.

This realization led the prodigal son to come to his senses or, as Jesus said, "He came to himself" (Luke 15:17). We are never living as God intended when our *sole* purpose is not living for our *soul's* purpose. When we live for ourselves while we should be living for God, our only hope of finding our way home is to come to our senses. This realization sparked within the prodigal son a deep desire to return to his father because he came to see that only in his father's house could he experience true freedom. Upon his son's return home, the father, who had been watching and waiting all this time for his son's return, was filled with great joy and celebrated with a feast.

The way home to our heavenly Father begins with the realization that this life is not about doing whatever we want, whenever we want, with whomever we want. We must see that we are headed for something worse than a pigpen unless we come to our senses and see our own sinfulness and rebellion against our heavenly Father. When we repent and return to our Father, we find that He has been watching and waiting for us, and his heart is filled with great joy when we return home: "Likewise, I say to you, there is joy in the presence of the angels of God over one sinner who repents" (verse 10).

It's never too late to leave the pigpen and return home.

"Therefore know that the Lord your God, He is God, the faithful God who keeps covenant and mercy for a thousand generations with those who love Him and keep His commandments." (Deuteronomy 7:9)

FEBRUARY
14

The Gem of Faithfulness

THE FAITHFULNESS OF GOD is like a diamond, where the pages of the Scriptures are facets that brilliantly and brightly capture and reflect the beauty of this truth. But a diamond is more than just a beautiful gem; this stone is also one of the strongest materials in the world. Its very name means "unbreakable." So too, the faithfulness of God is not only a beautiful truth, but is also one of the strongest truths in the entire universe, and truly unbreakable.

The faithfulness of God is more than a characteristic describing the personality of God; faithfulness is an essential element found at the core of His being. Faithfulness means that God never fails, never falters, never forgets, never forfeits, and never speaks falsehood. Every declaration He makes is true, every promise will come to pass, and every covenant will be kept.

God is faithful to forgive (see 1 John 1:9), for without this facet of His faithfulness, we would be eternally lost. He is faithful to help in times of temptation (see 1 Corinthians 10:13), for without this facet we would be utterly helpless. He is faithful to protect us from evil (see 2 Thessalonians 3:3), for without this facet we would be completely defenseless. Even if we are faithless, God always remains faithful because He cannot go against His own nature (see 2 Timothy 2:13). Without this facet, everything would be totally hopeless. God's faithfulness is so important to Him that He has chosen to define himself in terms of His faithfulness: "Know that the LORD your God, He is God, the faithful God" (Deuteronomy 7:9).

The faithfulness of God is the basis for our security and an endless source of our encouragement. His faithfulness is a rock in our foundations and an anchor for our souls. Just as the faithfulness of God comes from the core of His being, so, too, the core of every believer's faith in God must include the comprehension of and confidence in God's faithfulness. God is who He says He is, and God does what He says He will do. This is an absolute that cannot be denied, disproven, or disputed. For all who believe and keep God's commands, the blessing of His faithfulness is extended in mercy and covenantal blessing.

The faithfulness of God has no spot or blemish, but is perfect and pure. Like a diamond formed in high-pressure and high-heat environments, so too is life for the believer, often filled with high-pressure and high-heat situations, used to make us who we are: precious gems in which God's faithfulness can shine forth most brilliantly.

"Father Abraham, have mercy on me, and send Lazarus that he may dip the tip of his finger in water and cool my tongue; for I am tormented in this flame." (Luke 16:24)

FEBRUARY
15

Dead Man Talking

DEATH IS NOT THE END. This life is not all there is. We have been created as eternal beings, and this physical world that we reside in is only the beginning of our endless existence. After death, in this existence, we will not be given a second chance to get things right. We will not be doomed to walk this earth as some sort of phantom beings, and we do not return as reincarnated life forms. Death takes place when the soul leaves the physical body, at which point the soul is either headed for heaven or bound for hell.

C. S. Lewis once said, "Indeed the safest road to hell is the gradual one—the gentle slope, soft underfoot, without sudden turnings, without milestones, without signposts."[5] Hell is not a subject that often comes up in casual conversation, even among churchgoers. Hell is not a subject that finds its way into many pulpits today either. Yet, despite its lack of public popularity, hell is a very real place and was repeatedly spoken of by Jesus. For this reason, the subject of hell is worthy of our attention. One such occasion in which Jesus spoke about hell was in the illustration of Lazarus and the rich man.

Two individuals comprise this story. The first was a rich man who lived well, but cared little for his fellow man, and even less for the things of God. The second was a homeless beggar who was poor materially, but rich spiritually toward God.

Death came for them both, as death does for all, and yet again, these men found themselves at opposite ends of the spectrum. The rich man found himself in hell, while Lazarus experienced paradise. The rich man was tormented, while Lazarus was comforted. The torment experienced by the rich man was related not only to the burning flames all around him, but also to a greater torment that he seemed to experience, a torment of awareness. The awareness was twofold: first, he was aware of the eternal consequences resulting from his rejection of God during his lifetime, and second, he was aware that others whom he loved were destined for his fate.

The ending is a sad one for the rich man, but his does not need to be anyone else's ending. This fate that can be corrected, but only while a person is alive on this earth, not after he or she leaves this life. In death, no divine do-overs are given, and a great divide which cannot be bridged eternally separates those who rejected God. The divide has only been bridged in the realm of the living, by the cross of Jesus Christ, and can only be crossed by faith. Faith serves as the feet of the soul and propels someone into paradise.

This man's riches did not send him to hell any more than the poverty of the beggar sent him to paradise. True riches are not found in silver and gold, but in a right relationship with God, and true poverty is a soul that considers God, but not until too late.

The direction of your eternal destiny is determined in the here and now; heed the warning from this dead man talking.

And the Angel of the LORD said to him, "Why have you struck your donkey these three times? Behold, I have come out to stand against you, because your way is perverse before Me." (Numbers 22:32)

FEBRUARY
16

Dumber than a Donkey

TALKING DONKEYS AND ANGELS, kings and clairvoyants, bribery and greed, blessings and curses—now those have the makings of a good story! But this is no fairy tale, and is not mere folklore. The following story, although unusual, comes straight from the Word of God.

This biblical story begins with Balak, the king of Moab, observing the Israelites, his newest neighbors. Balak became filled with fear because the Israelite community was large and had many conquests in the surrounding region, so Balak decided to hire someone to curse Israel, today's equivalent to calling 1-800-Rent-a-Prophet. One prophet named Balaam had just the reputation Balak sought. Balaam was certainly a puzzling figure, a sort of cross between a shady fortune-teller and a genuine prophet of God. What is even more intriguing is that God used him despite his less-than-stellar credentials.

Next, Balak sent a few of his higher-ups to go and make Balaam an offer for his unique services. Balaam heard them out and decided to take the matter before God. God's answer to Balaam was plain and simple: no. No cursing could be done upon those whom God had chosen to bless. So Balaam, with a hint of reluctance, sent the messengers and money back to the king. But Balak refused to take no for an answer. This time he sweetened the pot by sending more prestigious messengers, a blank check for Balaam to fill in any amount, and, to top it off, the promise of notoriety.

This is so often the strategy of Satan. If at first he does not succeed, he tries, and tries again. In the sequence of this second offer, we see more of this part-time prophet's true heart. Balaam wanted to go. He wanted to accept all offered to him, so he went to God again, hoping that God might change His mind, even though He had already given Balaam an unmistakable no.

How guilty we can be of committing this same offense with God! When His Word has been clearly no, we often return to Him later in prayer, hoping that maybe we were mistaken or maybe we misheard Him or maybe there was a chance that He would change His mind.

God granted Balaam permission to go, but only with a yes designed to test his obedience, which was clearly lacking. Balaam set out, but along the way, he was stopped by his donkey, which saw an angel of the Lord blocking the way and refused to move. So, Balaam struck the donkey, and the donkey, in turn, struck up a conversation with Balaam. God opened the eyes of Balaam to see the angel before him, and the angel declared, "Your way is perverse" (Numbers 22:32).

Balaam's heart was not submitted to God. He may have been going through the motions on the outside, but God looks at the heart, and here He saw the corrupt heart of Balaam.

We must do what is right because it is right before God, and we must do so for the right reasons: glorifying God. Otherwise, what we do will be rejected by Him.

Do not go the way of Balaam (even if the idea of hearing a talking donkey sounds cool). If God were to open the mouth of a donkey for you to hear, I doubt good news would be the result.

In the beginning was the Word, and the Word was with God, and the Word was God. (John 1:1)

First Impressions

PERHAPS YOU HAVE HEARD the truism, "You never get a second chance to make a first impression." An opinion only takes a moment to formulate, as does an immediate evaluation when you first meet someone. Therefore, how you present yourself goes a long way in shaping the type of impression you will make. The Apostle John recognized that he had the great privilege, as well as the awesome responsibility, of introducing people to Jesus Christ. How he presented Jesus would go a long way in shaping the type of impression Jesus would make on someone. Along with this privilege and responsibility came the overwhelming challenge of capturing the complexity of Christ, the height of His holiness, and the depth of His divinity.

Just like a flash of lightning that instantly lights up the dark sky, or a sudden quake that shakes the earth to its core, John lights up a dark world and shakes the mind of humanity with the profound truth that Jesus is the Word of God.

Words reveal much about who we are. We are even told in the Bible that the words we speak come out of our innermost being (see Luke 6:45). Therefore, our words are a reflection of who we really are. Jesus, as God's Word, reveals to us much of who God is, because Jesus is a reflection of God's innermost being. No one would know who God is, His nature, His character, or even how humans were to relate to God unless God told us, and the way God chose to communicate His truths to humanity was through His Word.

This extraordinary relationship linking Jesus and the Word of God is further described by the apostle as he explains to us that Jesus as the Word of God means that Jesus *is* God and that Jesus has always been *with* God, signifying both His deity and His distinctiveness as part of the Holy Trinity of God. John goes on in verse 3 to describe Jesus as the creative Word of God, meaning that Jesus is not a created being, but Jesus created all things. A final dimension of this glorious truth that John gives us here is that Jesus is the incarnate Word of God (see John 1:14). If you are confused, perhaps this will help: Jesus is God in human form, and the Bible is God in written form.

Where the other three Gospels present us mainly with the *events* of Jesus' life, John presents us with both the *meaning* of His life and those events, and how we are to respond to His life with faith that leads to eternal life. No doubt, that is why John's gospel is considered the best place for both new believers and those who have never opened a Bible before to start reading. In the reading of John, so many Christians receive their first impression of God, their first look at His Word, and their first exposure to Jesus.

I cannot think of a better introduction to God than through the Gospel of John.

"Be sure your sin will find you out." (Numbers 32:23)

You Can Run, but You Cannot Hide

FEBRUARY
18

SIN is like a boomerang that eventually returns to the one who threw it. The Bible is filled with many examples of people who thought they could throw sin aside with hopes that sin would never come back to haunt them. Adam and Eve thought they could hide in the Garden of Eden (see Genesis 3:8), Cain thought he could bury his sin in the ground (see Genesis 4:10), Achan thought he could hide his sin under his tent (see Joshua 7:21), and Ananias and Sapphira thought they could hide their sin with a lie (see Acts 5:1–10). Yet, in every case, God exposed their sin.

Moses said, "Be sure your sin will find you out," and he made that statement to the tribes of Reuben, Gad, and half the tribe of Manasseh. Moses spoke from experience; he, too, had earned himself a rightful place on the list of men and women in the Bible who thought they could hide their sin. Remember, Moses killed an Egyptian taskmaster and then, in an attempt to hide what he had done, buried the Egyptian in the sand, only to wake up the next morning to find out that his sin had been discovered.

So, Moses knew what he was talking about when speaking of the truth of this principle regarding sin, and he warned these Israelite tribes to make good on their promise to support Israel when they went to battle. You see, Reuben, Gad, and half the tribe of Manasseh wanted to live on the outskirts of God's Promised Land. They wanted to live in the land east of the Jordan River, while the rest of the Israelites were going to live in the land west of the Jordan River. God allowed them to make this choice, but Moses warned that they had better make good on their promise when the time came to support the other tribes. If they did not, their sin would have consequences.

Do not be fooled. Sins have a way of coming out. Sin can affect your health. The sin of gluttony can cause obesity and many other adverse health conditions. A life of alcoholism, which involves the sin of drunkenness, can cause liver damage. Just to be clear, not all health problems are directly related to sin; but we cannot ignore the fact that some sins can affect our health.

Sin also can affect our conscience, which is the ability to understand our moral responsibility. Living a lie or suppressing the truth, which is the sin of both hypocrisy and lying, can severely damage our ability to judge right and wrong. As 1 Timothy 4:2 points out, those who depart from the faith in the last days will "[speak] lies in hypocrisy, having their own conscience seared with a hot iron."

Apart from the worldly consequences of our sin, our sin ultimately will find us out before God. One day, everyone will stand before God at His judgment seat and give an account (see Romans 14:10; 2 Corinthians 5:10). You can run from your sins, but you cannot hide your sins from God. The good news is you can run to Jesus Christ, who willingly took our sins and bore the consequences of them on the cross.

God no longer will count your sin against you if you have put your faith in Christ. Although earthly consequences of your sin may still occur, the boomerang effects of sin will not follow you into heaven.

And Nathanael said to him, "Can anything good come out of Nazareth?" Philip said to him, "Come and see."
(John 1:46)

Leading Someone to Christ

MANY PEOPLE overcomplicate what is required in bringing someone to Christ. We often feel that before we can even raise the subject of believing in Jesus Christ with someone else, we must first be super theologians who are ready to leap tall arguments in a single bound, faster than a speeding atheist and more powerful than a false religion. Sadly, because most of us think we do not have what it takes to tackle the tough questions from our challengers, we can avoid sharing Christ altogether.

First, make no mistake; the work of salvation is not mankind's work. Rather, salvation is a work of God. God does not need mankind to accomplish His plan of salvation, yet He has chosen to allow mankind to participate in this great and glorious work. Salvation is always a divine work of God. Grace, mercy, and forgiveness of sins are all divine actions accomplished by God and connected to salvation, but salvation does require mankind's response of faith. The two sides are intertwined in such a way that the mind of humans cannot distinguish where

God's sovereign work ends and mankind's faith begins.

But the truth that salvation is the work of God does not change the fact that mankind plays a part in bringing others to Christ. We must recognize that we are not responsible for the conversion of a person's soul toward God, but we do have the responsibility to introduce people to Christ and let God take the reins from there.

Christ's story began with apostles, and as we look at how several of them came to follow Christ, we can see that these men came to Him in different ways. Andrew and John responded to the preaching of John the Baptist, Simon Peter was brought to Jesus by the witness of his brother Andrew, Philip was given a personal invitation from Jesus himself, and Nathaniel was encouraged by a friend to go see for himself who this Jesus was. In this, we can see that God used various methods to introduce people to Jesus Christ, and He still uses that same diversity. Equally as important and obvious as God's diversity in drawing people to Christ, however, is the wonderful simplicity involved in sharing Christ with others.

Philip painted a beautiful picture of how simple personal evangelism often can be, if one is willing to be used. Philip began his journey with a personal encounter with Jesus Christ, an encounter rooted in the Word of God. Philip explained to Nathaniel that he had found the Christ (see John 1:45), which means the Anointed One of God, the very one that Moses and the prophets said would one day come. Philip's faith in Jesus came "by hearing, and hearing by the word of God" (Romans 10:17). Next, Philip was willing to share Christ with someone else. He did not have all the answers, but he was willing to invite a friend to meet Jesus, who did.

You should know your Bible and to be able to defend it. Every believer should be able to clearly explain the gospel to someone else. Understanding Christology, soteriology, eschatology, and other biblical doctrines is great, but you do not have to have all the answers when you are leading someone to Christ.

Sometimes all God is looking for is someone who is willing to say, "Come and see." *Come and see this Jesus that I have found. He changed my life, and He can change yours.*

"And these words which I command you today shall be in your heart. You shall teach them diligently to your children, and shall talk of them when you sit in your house, when you walk by the way, when you lie down, and when you rise up." (Deuteronomy 6:6–7)

FEBRUARY 20

How to Raise Godly Children

EVERY PARENT wants what is best for his or her children, but parenting is a challenge. Newborns do not come with instruction manuals, and teenagers do not come with tracking devices. But despite the numerous challenges parents face in today's world, raising godly children is still possible today.

Did you know that God's wisdom is timeless? This means the advice we find in the Bible is timeless as well. God gave Moses advice for parents nearly 3,500 years ago, and that advice was sound instruction that is just as relevant and true today as the day the instruction was given.

The first thing to know is that to raise up your children in the way they should go, you as a parent must have gone there first. God begins by reminding parents that they must first have the Word of God firmly planted in their own hearts before they can hope to plant the Word in the hearts of their children. Nothing could be more basic and more true. You cannot teach someone something if you have not first learned what you are teaching. God wants parents to be able to say to their children, "Follow my example." Therefore, God reminds parents that faith in the home begins with their faith in God.

You cannot make children believe what you believe, but you can be faithful to teach them what you believe. God reminds parents that the Word of God, which is to be planted in their own hearts, must be taught diligently to their children. Diligence is a key factor in teaching faith to children, according to God, and therefore should be understood clearly. To teach diligently means to teach carefully, thoroughly, persistently, and perseveringly. Also, the teaching must be done lovingly, thoughtfully, tenderly, and unselfishly.

God even goes a step further by giving us a practical picture of what this looks like in a parent's everyday life. God declares that you, as a parent, are to be speaking about His Word and teaching His Word to your children while you are sitting around the house. This means doing so while you are watching TV together, playing games, eating meals together, and working around the house. Next, you are to take that teaching out with you as the family is out and about, walking to school, driving to soccer practice, and shopping in the grocery store, whenever and wherever you go together. Finally, when you tuck your kids in at night and when you wake them up in the morning for breakfast, you are to teach them God's Word. More importantly, live God's Word, and your life will reinforce what you are teaching your children.

God wants parents to see life as an endless opportunity to share the truth of His Word and be a living example of how to relate his Word to their lives. Be a living demonstration of God's Word to your children. Do this when you feel like doing it and when you do not, live this way of life out when someone cuts you off on the freeway and when someone blesses you with a gift. Speak and teach the truth all the time and in every situation.

If you are faithful to follow God's advice for parenting, then there is no reason the promise of Proverbs 22:6 should not rest on your children: "Train up a child in the way he should go, And when he is old he will not depart from it."

This beginning of signs Jesus did in Cana of Galilee, and manifested His glory; and His disciples believed in Him.
(John 2:11)

FEBRUARY
21

A Big Fat Jewish Wedding

WEDDINGS are special events that capture the imagination of many girls from a very young age. They dream of their big day and everything associated, long before the wedding day ever arrives. Countless pictures of wedding dresses may have been collected from magazines, long hours have maybe been spent searching for the perfect match with the wedding colors and bridesmaid's dresses, the food and flowers have been carefully considered, and the father of the bride has spent many years counting the cost of his daughter's big day. Now imagine for a moment what your reaction might be if, during your meticulously planned event, you ran out of food for your very special guests. How would you feel?

Jesus and His disciples were invited to a big Jewish wedding in Cana of Galilee where, nearly halfway through the celebration, the unthinkable happened: the wine ran out. On the surface this may seem like nothing more than an annoyance, but this was a social and cultural no-no that not only would have involved public embarrassment, but also could have resulted in the family being ostracized and, in some cases, even fined.

Jesus performed His first miracle during this wedding celebration: He turned water into wine. This certainly was an interesting choice for Jesus to perform His first miracle, but we must see this miracle as more than just a practical solution to an embarrassing social pickle. The act of turning water to wine is full of both spiritual significance and prophetic imagery.

John calls this a "beginning of signs" (John 2:11). Usually, signs are intended to get our attention and to point us to something else. Jesus' intention was not to point people to the wine or even the miracle, but to point people to Him. We must remember that as Jesus continued throughout His public ministry, He would perform many signs and wonders, seeking to use them all as an opportunity to reveal who He really was so that people might believe in Him.

In addition to the spiritual significance of belief in Jesus through the manifestation of His glory through signs, a lack of belief is represented in the empty water pots. These stone pots were commonly used for religious purification, and by Jesus' using these pots to perform His miracle, He was bearing witness to the fact that the old religious rituals were finished, and God's people were now entering into a new way of relating to God, no longer approaching Him through ritual, but through intimate relationship.

Wine is often a symbol for joy in the Bible. Arthur W. Pink, a biblical expositor, wrote, "Judaism still existed as a religious system [there were purifications], but it ministered no comfort to the heart. It had degenerated into a cold, mechanical routine, utterly destitute of joy in God. Israel had lost the joy of their espousals."[6] Jesus came to change that by offering a new type of relationship with God, illustrated by the new wine. Jesus came to replace the emptiness of ritual with the fullness of relationship, and He came to replace empty religion with the fullness of himself.

Now every Christian can dream of the "big day" when we will celebrate the wonderful wedding feast with our bridegroom, Jesus.[7]

"There shall not be found among you anyone who makes his son or his daughter pass through the fire, or one who practices witchcraft, or a soothsayer, or one who interprets omens, or a sorcerer, or one who conjures spells, or a medium, or a spiritist, or one who calls up the dead."
(Deuteronomy 18:10–11)

FEBRUARY
22

Double, Double, Toil and Trouble

IN RECENT HISTORY, fascination with anything having to do with the occult has been renewed, including all forms of sorcery, witchcraft, magic, Wicca, Satanism, divination, and necromancy. People are seeking out mediums, fortune-tellers, and psychics. They are dabbling with Ouija boards, holding séances, and turning to the stars for guidance. This fascination even has reached into the entertainment world, creating a mass appeal among young people by portraying the occult as innocuous and amusing.

In ancient history, the fascination with the mysterious practices of the mystical, transcendental world compelled God to speak out. The Israelites were God's chosen people, and He always had been there for them, leading them, providing for them, and protecting them. God spoke to His people through His prophets and gave His people all the instruction they needed for living a life that would both honor God and bless them personally. But no matter where God's people lived geographically, neighbors were always close by, practicing the Dark Arts. The Egyptians worshiped the sun, practiced magic, and cast spells. The Canaanites worshiped Moloch and participated in demonic child sacrifices. Even the church in the New Testament had to deal with magic and sorcery (see Acts 8:9–25; 13:4–12; 19:13–20), all of which sought to oppose the work of God and His people.

The Bible strongly warns God's people to have nothing to do with any of these activities. God calls these practices and all who participate in them an abomination (see Deuteronomy 18:12).

If you are wondering why God is so unyielding and unwavering about things of the occult, he does so because everything involved in the occult comes from Satan. The magic arts are rebellious and unrepentant, like Satan; the edicts are unholy and untrue, like Satan; the practices are deceptive and deceitful, like Satan; and practicing this type of activity will leave people lost and permanently separated from God, like Satan. Satan has placed himself in direct opposition to God and everything that is true. As a result, the occult and its practices elevate the demonic and minimize the heavenly. The occult always takes and yet never gives, serves as a surrogate for truth, offering only a lie in return, and says to eat fruit from the very Tree of the Knowledge of Good and Evil from which God has said to abstain.

God wants to bless His people. So be wise about the occult and simply stay away. Do not dabble in its practices, do not play around with its spells and trickery, and certainly do not be fooled into thinking that anything about the occult is harmless fun. You have no need to seek hidden knowledge when God has given us His revelation of truth through His Word and in the person of Jesus

Christ. Jesus Christ is God's fullest revelation of truth. All the knowledge and power we need is found in Him and in His Word, and nowhere else.

For God so loved the world that He gave His only begotten Son, that whoever believes in Him should not perish but have everlasting life. (John 3:16)

FEBRUARY
23

The Difference a Verse Can Make

A CLICHÉ is an expression so overused that the original intent is lost. A few examples are "knock on wood," "play it by ear," "one in a million," and "let sleeping dogs lie."

One of the most well-known and beloved verses in the Bible is in jeopardy of becoming so overused that this important scripture becomes nothing more, to some, than a mere Christian cliché. John 3:16 can be seen on cardboard signs at baseball games, painted on the stomachs of overweight football fans, and often tattooed on people's bodies as a mere fashion accessory. Many people consider this verse to be the single most powerful sentence ever written, but sadly, the significance behind the verse is often overlooked, and even considered outdated.

Even though some may treat this verse casually, its importance never should be overlooked. How people view this verse not only will shape the way they look at life, but will also will determine where they spend eternity.

No other single verse in all the Scriptures so overwhelmingly presents us with the love of God. In one verse, we are given a glimpse into the magnitude of God's love, the scope of God's love, the expression of God's love, the quality of God's love, and the purpose of God's love.

Consider for a moment this amazing love.

Consider how God *so* loved. Could a greater understatement exist, characterizing the magnitude of God's love, yet so completely summarizing the limitless height and immeasurable depth of the greatest love expressed to mankind?

God so loved *the world*. Every language group, every country, every community, and every individual is welcomed into a relationship with God because of the scope of His love.

God so loved the world that He *gave*. Selflessly, God provided and sacrificially He made available the ultimate expression of His love through giving freely and without compulsion.

God so loved the world that He gave *His only begotten Son*. Within the heavenly storehouses could not be found a single item more dear and more highly valued than that of God's only Son, for in such a gift, God gave His best because He gave of himself.

God so loved the world that He gave His only begotten Son, that whoever believes in Him should not perish but have *everlasting life*. Motivated by love, God purposed to provide a way for mankind to be saved from the penalty of sin and guaranteed everlasting life.

Within twenty-five words, one verse—a verse which has been called the

Gospel in Miniature, and far from trivial—is a truth so great that it divides the eternal destinies of men.

Which side of this verse are you on? Do you treat this important verse as nothing more than a cliché? Or when you consider the verse, do you see an awe-inspiring, life-altering, destiny-dividing expression of God's great love and grace? Trust in this verse, and watch and see the difference that trust can make in your life.

"As an eagle stirs up its nest, Hovers over its young, Spreading out its wings, taking them up, Carrying them on its wings." (Deuteronomy 32:11)

FEBRUARY
24

Learning to Fly

TO AN EAGLET, nothing could be more terrifying than learning to fly. Why leave the comfort of a warm nest with ample provision and protection? Eventually the day comes, however, when the parents stir up the nest. The first thing the parents do is to remove the soft fur and down feathers that have been carefully placed in between the jagged sticks that make up the nest—fur and feathers which, up to this point, have acted much like the eaglet's personal security blanket. Next comes a loving nudge or the flapping of wings to encourage the young one to get up and get out of the nest. Standing hundreds of feet up, looking down at an intimidating valley floor below, the eaglet prepares to spread its wings and fly.

Moses had led the children of Israel for forty years, and the time came for him to leave the children of Israel. Moses would not be permitted to enter the land God had promised to the Israelites because he had misrepresented God to the people (see Numbers 20:1–13). As Moses and the Israelites stood on the border of the Promised Land, looking down at the intimidating valley floor below and all that was about to be theirs, they needed a nudge. So Moses began to recount to them their history, a history that was filled with the provision and protection of God, a history that at times even included God acting much like an eagle acts toward her young when she stirs up the nest.

One of the best ways to prepare for the future is to consider the past. Moses knew that the children of Israel had some fears about entering the Promised Land, and even though blessings were ahead, times also awaited when the Israelites would feel as though God were stirring the nest.

The stirrings of life can appear to be a great disturbance or interruption. Sometimes, a stirring may even seem destructive and dangerous. But we must recognize that God is not trying to hurt His children. Rather, He is preparing them to fly.

We can become complacent, lazy, and waste away as we sit wrapped in the warmth of our nests, never venturing out. So, God comes along to stir up our lives and nudge us up and out of our comfort zones where we must spread our wings and fly. If we are not accustomed to flying, then we must start with short flights, ever increasing our strength and ability to fly further and soar higher.

To a Christian, nothing can be more terrifying than stepping out of a comfort zone and flying by faith. But if we sit in the security of our nests too long, the day will come when God must stir things up, not because He wants to make our lives miserable, but because He has given us wings. Why sit when you can soar?

An eagle is never quite as beautiful as when seen soaring high above this world, and Christians are never quite as beautiful as when they allow the wind of God's Spirit to carry them higher and higher. When God stirs things up in your life, when He begins to nudge you on into new areas, seek how you can allow the wind of His Spirit to take you higher and fly farther than ever before.

"But the hour is coming, and now is, when the true worshipers will worship the Father in spirit and truth; for the Father is seeking such to worship Him." (John 4:23)

FEBRUARY
25

Authentic Worship

SOME BELIEVE that "Christian worship is the most momentous, the most urgent, the most glorious action that can take place in human life."[8] However, many Christians consider worship today to be a style, a sound, a vibe, or an atmosphere. Worship has become an experience, not a way of life, as worship was intended to be. Perhaps that is why A.W. Tozer said, "Worship is the missing jewel in modern evangelicalism."

God has created us to be authentic worshipers, not irregular or indiscriminate worshipers, and not careless or carefree worshipers. We have been created to worship God completely, wholeheartedly, and endlessly, and our worship is to involve both spirit and truth.

Because worship is intended to be such an essential part of the Christian's life, Jesus, naturally, outlined what is needed to ensure that our worship is authentic. Jesus confronted the subject in a conversation that took place in the most unlikely of locations. He did not discuss authenticity of worship in a synagogue, where you might expect a conversation about worship to take place. No, this conversation took place in the detested city of Samaria. The conversation took place between Jesus and one of the most unlikely of people, not with a rabbi or priest whom you might expect Jesus to speak to concerning this subject. This conversation was with an ostracized woman of questionable moral character. Lastly, this conversation resulted in the most unlikely of conclusions. The conversation did not lead to a new-and-improved intellectual understanding regarding the subject of worship; instead, the spoken words explained the complete and total life-changing experience of how to become an authentic worshiper.

In dealing with the subject of authentic worship, Jesus had to cut through a common misconception of the day, which was the emphasis on the external aspects of worship. This focus on aspects of worship still exists among us today. This "worship" believes that where you worship is more important than how you worship, places the spotlight on the superficial instead of allowing the substance to light the way, and focuses on form over function. Jesus says, in essence, that God is not looking for external worshipers. God seeks those whose worship flows out of worshiping hearts.

The defining characteristic of authentic worship, according to Jesus, is worshipping in spirit and truth. Worshiping in spirit is worshiping God from the spiritual core of one's being, while seeking the most intimate fellowship and communion with God. God is spirit, and for authentic worship to take place, we must worship God from our spirit. The invisible and immortal part of mankind must meet the invisible and immortal God. Authentic worship must equally be rooted in the truth of God's Word. As we read the Bible, as we meditate on its truths, as we pray over scriptures, as we live according to the Word, we are worshiping in truth. In other words, worshiping in truth is our response to the truth.

Worship is less about seeking what we get from worship, less about methods and styles, and less about an experience. Authentic worship is more about a lifestyle and more about what we give to God. Authentic, worship must be perfectly balanced in spirit and truth, because this is the type of worship God seeks from us.

"This Book of the Law shall not depart from your mouth, but you shall meditate in it day and night, that you may observe to do according to all that is written in it. For then you will make your way prosperous, and then you will have good success." (Joshua 1:8)

FEBRUARY
26

The Secret to Success

HOW DO YOU MEASURE SUCCESS? All too often, success is wrapped up in the accumulation of things. Many people think that success is achieving prominence, becoming rich, having a great marriage, raising good kids, climbing the corporate ladder, or having lots of friends. Although nothing is wrong with any of these things, God measures success very differently.

Joshua took over leading the Israelites after the death of Moses, and he had some pretty big sandals to fill. Moses was the picture of godly leadership, a humble servant who was filled with compassion, obedient, and not faultless, but faithful. Moses was the man God chose to deliver the Israelites out of slavery, to communicate the Law of God to the people of God, to perform miracles, and to lead the people during the wilderness years. Joshua was understandably a little nervous about his new position and concerned with how the people would react to the new leadership. God understood Joshua's hesitancy, and not only gave him the necessary encouragement to rise above his fears, but also gave him what he needed to know in order to be successful in all that he endeavored to do for God.

In Joshua 1:8, God gave the new leader three secrets to living a successful life, and each one is rooted in a right relationship with God's Word.

First, God instructed Joshua that His Word "shall not depart from [his] mouth." God's

Word was to be such a major part of Joshua's life that the words of scripture would naturally and perpetually spill over into his regular day-to-day speech. Every follower of God should be talking about the Word of God constantly and continually, not out of obligation but because the Word is such a part of life that speaking the Word aloud has become the normal overflow of having God's Word written on his or her heart.

Second, meditation on God's Word is essential for success. The biblical practice of meditation is not some transcendental or mystical experience that involves repetitive chanting. Rather, meditation is the deliberate and thoughtful consideration of the principles found in God's Word, and practical application of the principles to our own lives. For Christians, meditation means to seek to understand the Word of God personally and apply the meaning practically.

The final secret to godly success is the most important: obedience to the Word of God. Joshua's success was directly tied to his obedience to God's Word, and our success will be as well. We cannot pick and choose from the Scriptures those commands we will obey and will not obey, and we cannot give God partial obedience. We must be totally and completely obedient to all that He commands.

Who you are or what you are going through in life does not matter; you can be truly successful at whatever you do if you pay attention, pick up, and put into practice what God proclaimed to Joshua. Rise above what society deems as success and realize that the secret to success comes from a life devoted to the Word of God.

"I am the bread of life." (John 6:48)

The Jesus Diet

FEBRUARY
27

JESUS HAD JUST FED FIVE THOUSAND PEOPLE with five loaves of bread and two small fish. This day was the day after this miraculous all-you-can-eat buffet, and the whole region buzzed with excitement. The word was spreading, the crowd was growing, and Jesus was preparing to speak. As everyone converged upon the small sea town of Capernaum, Jesus seized the opportunity to speak about what really mattered in life. He would give a sermon that day that not only was custom-made for His audience, but also would be timeless enough to speak to every subsequent generation. And the turning point of His message would be the statement, "I am the bread of life. Whoever comes to me will never go hungry, and whoever believes in me will never be thirsty" (John 6:35 NIV). Jesus knew this would get everyone's attention. After all, He had just filled their stomachs, and now He wanted to fill their souls.

Mankind is born with a natural hunger for God, and nothing else will satisfy that hunger. Only Jesus Christ is able to provide the bread of life that fulfills the inmost hunger and deepest cravings within the heart and soul of humanity. Jesus challenged the crowd that day to look past the carnal and think for a moment about the eternal. Jesus knew that the crowd really was only there because they were looking for another free meal. Most of the people there that day were concerned only all about what Jesus could do for them. So, Jesus changed the menu and said that this life is more than food, more than physical passions, and more than the pursuit of the short-term pleasures of this world. In other words, "Stop wasting so much time thinking about all the things that won't last, that won't make you happy, and that will never satisfy your soul, and start thinking about what really matters and what really satisfies: the Bread of Life" (which is Jesus).

After Jesus finished this sermon, most of the people turned and walked away from Him, never to follow again. These fickle, fair-weather followers left Jesus after they got what they wanted from Him. John's Gospel provides this detail: "Then Jesus gave the Twelve their chance: 'Do you also want to leave?' " (John 6:67 MSG). This presses us to ask ourselves the same thing. Are we seeking God so that He may fill our stomachs, pay our bills, and give us new clothes to wear? The Bible is clear that Jesus is the Bread of Life. *He* is God's provision for our deepest spiritual needs. He alone satisfies. He alone meets our needs. He alone gives life.

Jesus is essential to our spiritual diet. By faith, we feed on Christ as He saves us and gives us eternal life, becoming to us an inexhaustible feast for our souls that will satisfy us in this life and last forever.

Israel crossed over on dry ground, until all the people had crossed completely over the Jordan. (Joshua 3:17)

Getting Your Feet Wet

FEBRUARY 28

Every obstacle in life is an opportunity to obey God, every complication is a chance to be conformed into the image of Christ, and every trial gives us the choice of whether we will trust in the timing of God or not.

After wandering in the desert for what seemed like an eternity, Joshua and the children of Israel were on the verge of entering the blessing of God's Promised Land. God made a promise to Abraham nearly six hundred years earlier concerning the land that was now before his descendants (see Genesis 15). As Joshua and the children of Israel stood on the edge of receiving God's promise, they had one more barrier to cross: the Jordan River.

During most of the year, the Jordan would not have been much of a barrier to cross at all, but during the spring, when the Israelites were there, the river had swelled to a mile wide. Not only that, a strong current was flowing, making crossing the river nearly impossible.

God had led the Israelites to this place, to this point in time, knowing they would face this obstacle. This encounter is very similar to the way God led the Israelites to the edge of the Red Sea before parting the waters of their deliverance. But this time, God would choose to do things differently. This time God would require His people to get their feet wet before He would make a way across the Jordan.

Before moving forward, the people would have to sanctify themselves to prepare their hearts to receive the blessing of God. Sanctifying ourselves can simply be seen as cleansing ourselves; sanctification begins by examining our hearts and putting away those things that are contrary to the Word of God.

Next, the Ark of the Covenant, which represented the presence of God, was to go before the people. In order to follow God, we must allow Him to go first. He must precede His people in everything they do and everywhere they go.

Finally, the people had to take a step of faith and make their way into the water. The priests were told they had to step out into the Jordan before God would remove the obstacle of the remaining water. This process would require one step at a time, one foot in front of the other, until God made the water disappear and allowed the children of Israel to walk across on dry ground.

What is your Jordan River? Has God been preparing you to cross over and receive the blessing of His promises, yet there is one more hurdle of obedience before you? Whatever the Jordan River is in your life, view that river as an opportunity to obey God. The obstacle is a chance to be conformed into the image of Christ, and having the obstacle there gives you the choice of whether you will trust in the timing of God or not.

Leave the desert, make your way down to the banks of the river, and sanctify yourself. Allow God to go before you as you step out, willing to get your feet wet as you trust and watch God dry up the waters of your Jordan River and lead you to the land of promise.

March

Now Martha said to Jesus, "Lord, if You had been here, my brother would not have died." (John 11:21)

Where Is God When You Need Him?

YOUR PAIN has a purpose with God. Your problems are possibilities for God to be glorified. No one lives a pain-free life, and no one's life is free from the occasional problem, whether big or small. When we realize how big our God is, then we will see how small our problems really are.

Mary and Martha, two close friends of Jesus, had what we would call a big problem. Their brother, Lazarus, was sick with a critical illness, and the sisters sent word to Jesus to come quickly. They must have assumed that Jesus would drop everything and rush to where they lived in Bethany. After all, Jesus loved Lazarus (see John 11:3, 5).

But Jesus did not come right away. In fact, He waited two more days before He left for Bethany. Why would He wait? For that matter, if Jesus loved Lazarus so much, why did He allow him to get sick in the first place? Furthermore, why did Jesus not just heal Lazarus from a distance, as He did the nobleman's son (see John 4:43–54)?

Meanwhile, back in Bethany, Mary and Martha no doubt were expecting Jesus' imminent arrival. Minutes turned into hours, and hours turned into days as they waited eagerly, expectantly looking out their window and wondering when exactly would be the moment Jesus would make His appearance. To the sisters' dismay, Lazarus died and was buried before Jesus even arrived. With his death, the sisters' hope died as well. One more day went by, then a second, then a third, and finally a fourth day passed before Jesus showed up. But, to the girls, his arrival had come too late. What could He do now? Mary and Martha, in their disappointment and despair, both said to Jesus—with a hint of rebuke in their voices—"If You had been here, my brother would not have died."

Are we not guilty of the same sarcastic skepticism when we say to God, with a hint of rebuke, *Where were You? Why did You allow this to happen? If You would have been here, none of this would have happened.*

What Mary and Martha missed is that while they wanted Jesus to heal their brother, but Jesus wanted to do something far greater than what they expected; He wanted to raise Lazarus from the dead.

Sometimes when we pray and God does not come through, at least not the way we expect. And when the answers do not come, we often wonder, *Where is God in my pain? Why won't He help me with this problem?* We can be so focused on a particular solution that we miss God's greater good. The day that Lazarus was raised from the dead, many believed in Jesus and the faith of Mary, Martha, and the disciples was strengthened.

Whatever you are going through, remember, your pain has a purpose with God. Your problems are possibilities for God to be glorified. And who knows? Maybe, like Lazarus, Jesus wants to do something far greater than you can begin to imagine.

"Only Rahab the prostitute and all who are with her in her house shall be spared, because she hid the spies we sent."
(Joshua 6:17 NIV)

MARCH

2

From Harlot to Heroine

IN THE DARK SHADOWS of an ancient city lived a heroic prostitute. . .
Stop! Wait. What did you say?
You read that right: a heroic prostitute in the Bible. Rahab made her living by selling herself to strangers, yet the Bible praises her as a woman of faith. She would not let her bad reputation keep her from the good that God wanted to do in her life. Rahab would rise above her reputation and trust in God, and she eventually would be placed in the lineage of the Messiah. So how does a woman like this go from a harlot to a heroine of the faith?

Rahab lived in the city of Jericho, in a house that was built into the outer partition of the fortified wall that surrounded and protected the people living within the city's borders. Word was spreading about God's wandering people of Israel, new to the area and in the process of conquering the land. When news came to Jericho that the Israelites were coming to Jericho next, the people readied themselves to do battle. While the city was preparing to fight, Rahab was preparing to worship. She was the only one in Jericho who decided to fear and obey Israel's God.

So it seemed only natural that when Joshua sent two secret agents to scout out Jericho to determine how the city could be captured, Rahab was the one who turned her roof into a hiding place for these fugitives. When the king of Jericho heard that spies from Israel had entered his city, he immediately sent soldiers to search out Rahab's house. But Rahab trusted God, acted in faith, and risked her own safety to hide the wanted men from the king. As a result, her life was spared.

Rahab was a remarkable woman for a number of reasons. First, she is the only other woman beside Sarah mentioned in the Bible's Hall of Faith, found in Hebrews 11 (see verse 31). Second, she is one of two women mentioned in the lineage of Jesus (see Matthew 1:5). Third, she is the mother of Boaz, the kinsman redeemer whose life was like a picture of Christ. And finally, the Apostle James used her as an example of how faith and works should go together in the life of a believer (James 2:25).

Rahab lived by faith and not by sight. She believed and was spared, and that changed her life forever. She did not continue living as a harlot, but chose instead to live among the people of God. Rahab's faith changed a harlot into a heroine.

If you have a past that you are not proud of, or if you have done things that you wish you could forget, all is not lost! No sin, no matter how shocking or scandalous, exists that God cannot forgive. No one is out of God's reach or beyond God's grace. If God can turn a harlot into a heroine, then He can transform your life, too. But you must begin with faith. Start by first placing your faith in God, and then live your life by faith for God.

As you let God work in your life, do not be surprised if He also uses your life as an example of faith for others to follow.

"If I then, your Lord and Teacher, have washed your feet, you also ought to wash one another's feet." (John 13:14)

MARCH

3

Watch and Learn

SOMETIMES THE MOST EFFECTIVE WAY to communicate a concept or to teach a theory is through demonstration. A watch-and-learn approach many times communicates more to the intended audience than the spoken word alone is able to express. If a picture were worth a thousand words, then this portrait of Jesus would fill an entire library.

The day arrived when Jesus was to be betrayed. A flood of emotions were rushing upon Him like a tidal wave and a flurry of thoughts assaulted His mind from every direction as the crucifixion rapidly approached. In these final hours leading up to the greatest sacrifice in history, Jesus did not choose to distance himself from His disciples. Rather, He saw an opportunity to teach His disciples an unforgettable lesson.

As the disciples gathered that night in what could be considered an ancient apartment known as the Upper Room, Jesus stooped down, grabbed a bowl of water and a towel, and took on the role of a household servant by washing the feet of His disciples. Jesus even washed the feet of the man whom Jesus knew would soon betray Him. No doubt, you could have heard a pin drop in that room as the Master humbled himself as a servant in the presence of these men.

After Jesus washed their feet, He asked them if they understood what He had just done for them. He went on to explain that what they had seen and experienced was an example of what a humble servant looked like; Jesus demonstrated that no person is to consider his or her self so highly that they cannot lower themselves in service to others. His example taught that if God was willing to humble himself and serve others, then all who follow Him must be willing to humble themselves in the same way.

To know how to be a humble servant is one thing; actually being a humble servant is altogether different. This is why Jesus told His disciples to go and do likewise, and here, the blessing that Jesus promised enters. Jesus was not making foot washing another sacred practice like Communion; instead, Jesus was teaching the principle of humble servanthood, which may take the form of washing someone's feet, or picking up trash that does not belong to us. Servanthood may be found in volunteering to clean bathrooms, or visiting the sick. Whatever the action, Jesus finished His lesson by saying that if we practice a life of a humble servant, then we will be blessed.

In washing his disciples' feet, Jesus not only painted a beautiful picture of humble service, but also showed that no one is above this type of servanthood. In fact, His entire life teaches us, by example, what humility wrapped in servitude looks like. His life was the ultimate classroom, and His actions communicated as much, if not more, than all of His sermons.

Look to Jesus, and watch and learn from the Master. Then go, and do likewise.

"Neither will I be with you anymore, unless you destroy the accursed from among you." (Joshua 7:12)

MARCH

4

Secret Sins

THE DIFFERENCE between spiritual success and failure is often a thin line called sin. Success can quickly turn to defeat when we allow sin to gain a foothold in our lives. No one can bear witness to this fact more than Joshua. The Israelites just had one of their greatest victories in the new land as they defeated the walled city of Jericho. This victory came as the result of strict obedience to their God-given battle plan. The celebration, however, would be short-lived, as the Israelites were soon to suffer an embarrassing defeat at Ai, a much smaller city with a much smaller army. What should have been an easy victory became a humiliating failure. What made the difference?

Joshua went to God in prayer and asked Him why they had suffered such a crushing defeat. God's response was, "Israel has sinned" (Joshua 7:11). During the battle of Jericho, God commanded the entire city be destroyed; all the gold, silver, bronze, and iron objects were to go into the temple's treasury, while everything else was to be burned. No personal plundering was allowed. Initially, all signs seemed to show that everyone had listened and obeyed, until time came to fight again. Then, the Israelites became painfully aware that something was terribly wrong. Sin was in the camp. Someone had violated the command of God, and everyone was suffering the consequences. Eventually the culprit, a man named Achan, confessed and admitted that he had stolen items that rightfully belonged to God. Achan thought he could get away with sin by hiding the sin from everyone else, but the truth is no sins are secret sins because God sees and knows all.

Achan's problem started before he actually stole what did not belong to him. His problem began with his dissatisfaction with the provision of God, which in turn laid the groundwork for his disobedience. In 1 Timothy 6:6 (NIV), we are told, "godliness with contentment is great gain." In Achan's discontent, he wanted that which did not belong to him. Soon his desire took over, and he acted on impulse. To make matters worse, in a vain attempt to hide his sin, Achan buried what he had stolen, thinking no one ever would find out. The Bible tells us that a day will come when all of our sins will be exposed, and everything will be laid uncovered before God. In Achan's case, the day for his sin to be uncovered came swiftly, and his punishment was severe.

Never underestimate the pain and damage that can come to you and others by trying to hide your sin. God wants us to walk in victory and not defeat, but victory can only come through a steadfast obedience to His Word. If we want to walk in the land of promised blessing and see God knock down the walls of the enemy like He did at Jericho, we must deal with our sin when we fall short rather than hiding. Confess your sin instead, because even if you can successfully hide your sin from others, you cannot hide it from God.

As long as you let sin have the victory in your life, you will live in spiritual defeat. Take the victory for yourself instead, and confess.

"No branch can bear fruit by itself; it must remain in the vine. Neither can you bear fruit unless you remain in me."
(John 15:4 NIV)

MARCH
5

Life in the Vine

HOW PRODUCTIVE you are in the Christian life does not depend on your strengths or your skills; productivity is totally dependent on how connected your life is to God. Like the branch of a grapevine should produce grapes, a Christian should produce the fruit of Christlikeness. However, only a branch that is connected to the vine can bear fruit. God wants you to live a fruitful and productive life, so if you find seeing the spiritual fruit in your life to be a difficult task, then perhaps a lesson from the grapevine will help.

Jesus and the disciples were walking through the city, making their way out to the Garden of Gethsemane after eating their final meal together, when Jesus painted a vivid picture of how to live a fruitful Christian life. Perhaps as Jesus and the disciples passed by the temple the golden vine that was part of the decoration on the temple door shimmered in the moonlight and caught the eye of the Master. Or maybe, as Jesus strolled past the city gates, He observed a dead branch still clinging to a barren grapevine, so He snapped the dead off and twisted the twig in His hands as He walked and talked. Whatever inspired Jesus to use this imagery, the lesson we should take away is unmistakable: Jesus is the vine and we are the branches. As such, He is the source of our lives, He is the nutriment of our fruitfulness, and He is the giver of our increase. As we abide in Jesus, we allow Him to develop in us all we need to live a fruitful life.

Life in the Vine means that we must stay connected to Jesus in order to receive the life-giving nourishment that allows us to grow and be fruitful. Just as a branch can produce nothing apart from the vine, a Christian can produce nothing apart from Christ.

The best way to abide in the Vine, or to abide in Christ, is by staying connected to His Word. We must allow the Bible to fill our minds, direct our steps, and transform our hearts. We must obey what the Bible declares so that nothing restricts the flow of fruitfulness. The Word of God and the Spirit of God produce the fruit of God.

By living in the Vine, we will produce fruit naturally because fruit is produced by abiding, not striving. Fruitfulness is not based on outward success. The bigger the vine does not necessarily mean the better the fruit. As we abide in the Vine, the fruit that God is working to produce is the fruit of the Spirit, which is "love, joy, peace, longsuffering, kindness, goodness, faithfulness, gentleness, self-control" (Galatians 5:22–23). As part of our lives in the Vine, God the Father, the caretaker and cultivator of the vine, occasionally will cut and clip our spiritual branches so that fruitfulness will increase in the life of believers. God's process of pruning is never intended to hurt or destroy; the purpose is always productivity.

If you want to live a more fruitful and productive life, then stay connected to the Vine. When a Christian abides in Christ, God is glorified, fruit is produced, and abundant life is experienced. Fruitfulness comes into your life as the result of your connection to the Vine.

Then the men of Israel took some of their provisions; but they did not ask counsel of the LORD. (Joshua 9:14)

MARCH

6

Avoiding Spiritual Blind Spots

WHAT YOU SEE is not always what you get. Have you ever purchased something on a whim, only to realize that what you received was not all it was cracked up to be? What is worse is making an investment in something or someone, only to find out that you were cheated. Joshua and the Israelites were tricked into thinking that what they saw exactly was what they were getting. They trusted in their intellects, they relied on their senses, and they acted without seeking God. The result was a bad decision, as usual.

The Gibeonites heard that the Israelites had destroyed Jericho and Ai, and they were afraid they would be next on the conquered list. So the Gibeonites came up with a devious plan to deceive the Israelites in order to ensure survival. The Gibeonites arrived at the camp of the Israelites pretending to have journeyed from a faraway country, when they were actually next-door neighbors. To add believability to their story, the Gibeonites dressed in worn-out clothes, brought with them some moldy bread, and carried old luggage. The Gibeonites must have been good actors because Joshua and his leaders were taken in by their story and agreed to enter into a peace treaty with them.

Imagine the Israelites' surprise when then they found out they had just been cheated. For some reason, Joshua and the leadership team either did not feel the need to consult God, or the thought just never entered their minds. Either way, this omission was bad news. God's wisdom was available to them, but they never sought that wisdom. They had not because they asked not.

The Bible tells us that if we lack wisdom, all we have to do is ask God, and He will give this wisdom to us (see James 1:5). Some decisions in life can be made with our own senses and intellect. For example, if the weather is wet and rainy, prayer is not necessary to decide whether to take an umbrella when we leave home. If the meat you have in the refrigerator has changed color and now smells funny, your senses tell you not to eat the spoiled meat. In these instances, your senses are right. But the danger is in thinking that spiritual decisions can be made this way.

We have been created as spiritual beings, and a spiritual dimension is integral to the way we are to live our lives. In the spiritual dimension, the child of God should never seek to make a decision apart from prayerfully petitioning God. To faithfully follow God, serve Him, and honor Him in and through our lives, the children of God should not rely on their senses, their understanding, or their intellect. Rather, we should seek the divine wisdom of God, patiently wait for His direction and do not act hastily.

To live a life full of faith, we cannot walk by sight or any of our other senses. The only way to avoid spiritual blind spots in our lives is by seeking God's wisdom and waiting on His Holy Spirit and the Word of God to give us direction for our decisions.

"I do not pray for these alone, but also for those who will believe in Me through their word; that they all may be one."
(John 17:20–21)

MARCH

7

When God Prays for You

NINETEENTH-CENTURY Scottish pastor Robert Murray M'Cheyne wrote, "If I could hear Christ praying for me in the next room, I would not fear a million of enemies. Yet distance makes no difference. He is praying for me."[9] Did you know that Jesus prays for you and for me? How amazing and wonderful to know that God prays for us! Hebrews 7:25 tells us that Jesus is constantly praying to God the Father on behalf of all those who believe in Him. If you could hear what Christ was praying for you, how would that change the way you lived today?

The Bible gives us the ability to listen in on one of Jesus' prayers for all future believers. Do you know what Jesus asks the Father for? He asks God the Father for a divine oneness among all who believe in Him. As Christ was preparing to go to the Cross, He had a tremendous burden on His heart that His people would be marked by unity. Unity does not mean uniformity; Jesus was not asking that we all should be the same. He was not saying that we all look the same, listen to the same music, like the same things, or even "do church" the same. Unity and diversity are not mutually exclusive.

The oneness that Jesus was asking for is both incredible and incomprehensible because this is a oneness displayed in the unity between God, the Father, and God, the Son. Jesus prayed, "You, Father, are in Me, and I in You; that they also may be one in Us" (John 17:21).

Unity is all about relationship: Jesus' relationship to the Father and the Father's relationship to Jesus. The unity of the church is equally about relationship; our relationship to Jesus affects our relationships with one another. The closer we are to Christ, the stronger the unity we can have with one another.

Also, our relationship to the truth is vitally important in terms of unity. Simply stated, no unity can exist apart from truth. The truth of God's Word must be at the center of all our unifying efforts. We cannot forsake the truth in the name of unity.

Finally, the unity of believers in Christ has a direct impact on the relationship we have to the world around us, and perhaps this was the main reason for Jesus' prayer request. When society looks at the church and sees disunity, division, backbiting, and bitterness, these failures of relationship only serve to drive them away. Why would anyone want to have any part of that? If disunity drives people away from Christ, then unity must draw people to Christ. Genuine unity is supernatural and should lead people to the only explanation for such a supernatural phenomenon, which is Jesus Christ in us.

How will you respond, having heard a prayer of Jesus for you? Unity is not automatic or easy. I suppose that is why Jesus prayed believers to develop unity. True oneness begins with one person at a time making a commitment to be an answer to this prayer of Jesus. Let unity begin with you as you seek to be an instrument of unity among believers.

When Joshua had grown old, the LORD said to him, "You are now very old, and there are still very large areas of land to be taken over." (Joshua 13:1 NIV)

MARCH

8

You are Never Too Old to Serve!

WHAT ARE YOUR THOUGHTS about getting old? If you are not already there, before you realize, you, too, will be driving ten miles below the posted speed limit, eating dinner at 4:30 PM, and telling kids to get off your lawn. Growing old also includes retirement from the workforce and those long-awaited golden years after a life of hard work. But before you plan on moving to some deserted island to sit on the beach and sip umbrella drinks, know that God never intended for us to retire from spiritual activity. God has a purpose for His people in every stage of their lives.

Joshua was an old man who faithfully served God throughout his life, and as he was approaching one hundred years of age, God had another job for him to do because there was still kingdom work to be done. As the children of Israel took possession of the Promised Land, the property needed to be divided and distributed among the tribes of Israel. Long gone were the days of Commander Joshua leading the troops into battle; God had a more fitting job for this aging servant.

Joshua was not the only senior citizen to serve God faithfully and heroically. Moses began his ministry at the age of eighty, Caleb was still climbing mountains for the Lord at eighty-five, Abraham was promised a son when he was ninety-nine, and of course there were Daniel, Zacharias, Simeon, and others whom God used powerfully in their golden years.

Do you feel that your age has affected your ability to serve God? Do you worry about your usefulness as you get older? Know this: you are never too old to serve God. If you are getting up there in years and think you do not have anything more to contribute to the work of God, you are mistaken. You may not be able to do all the things that you used to do, but for the people of God who remain in touch with God, their lives will remain involved in the work of God. Age does not matter as much as having a willingness to serve. God still has a plan for your life as a senior citizen, and Psalm 92:14 reminds us, "They shall still bear fruit in old age."

Senior citizens have many ways to continue serving God in the golden years. For example, mentoring is always needed in the church today, where the older men encourage and exhort the younger men, and the older women instruct and inspire the younger women (see Titus 2). The Bible also pays tribute to "a widow of about eighty-four years, who did not depart from the temple, but served God with fastings and prayers night and day" (Luke 2:37). Calls can always be made, cards can be sent, and visits are especially meaningful when they come from seasoned saints who have already experienced the highs and lows of life.

As long as God has you here, He still has a worthwhile ministry for you to accomplish. So, keep on serving the Lord! Retirement years can be among the most fruitful of your life if you search for ways to serve God.

"What is truth?" (John 18:38)

Truth or Consequences

MARCH
9

THE TRUTH has become one of the world's most endangered species. Truth has been manipulated and mistreated, despised and distorted. However, one thing is for certain: no matter how people may treat truth, they will never succeed in its destruction. The Bible tells us that a day will come when people will completely turn away from the truth and will choose instead to believe in myths. When people come face-to-face with truth, they have only three ways to respond: they may choose to totally reject the truth, be indifferent toward the truth, or accept the truth.

"What is truth?" Pontius Pilate asked Jesus this famous question when the religious leaders brought Him in to stand trial. Pilate's question was not unique; he was not the first person to raise the question, and he will not be the last. For centuries, mankind has been looking for the answer to that question. The only difference is when Pilate asked the question, he was standing face-to-face with the very answer he sought. Jesus was sent on a mission by God to answer this question. He declared, "For this cause I was born, and for this cause I have come into the world, that I should bear witness to the truth" (John 18:37). Jesus spent His life bearing witness to the truth about God, sin, heaven and hell, love, life and death. His entire life was a testament to the truth about all that mankind ever needs to know.

In seeking to find the definition of truth, we need only to look at two of the greatest summation statements about truth ever made.

In the first statement, Jesus was speaking to His disciples when He declared, "I am the way, the truth, and the life" (John 14:6). Jesus was born to bear witness to the truth, which He did by the words that He spoke, by the miracles He performed, and by the perfect life He lived. Therefore, when you seek to be built up in truth, just look to Jesus, read the Gospels, and get a fresh perspective on the truth as you reflect on His life and ministry.

In the second statement, Jesus was praying to God the Father for His disciples when He proclaimed, "Your word is truth" (John 17:17). No greater source of absolute truth than the Word of God exists. The Word of God bears witness to the truth through inerrancy, prophetic accuracy, moral significance, and through the lives changed by and through the Word.

When you come face-to-face with the truth of Jesus Christ and the Bible, how do you respond? Do you sarcastically sneer at the truth like Pontius Pilate?

Or, do you receive Christ's testimony about truth? One day we all will stand face-to-face with Jesus. How you respond to His declarations of what the truth really is will determine your eternal destiny.

Do not choose to be indifferent like Pontius Pilate. Accept and obey the truth given to us by God in Christ, or be ready to accept the consequences for rejecting that truth.

"Choose for yourselves this day whom you will serve . . . as for me and my house, we will serve the LORD."
(Joshua 24:15)

MARCH
10

Home Improvement

WHAT MAKES A GODLY HOME? These days you can tune in and watch a multitude of television shows that focus on home improvement. Entire channels are dedicated to helping you cultivate a better home and garden. You can watch shows that motivate you to do the home improvement yourself or programs that showcase the work of interior designers. We cannot forget the ever-popular extreme makeover type of show that completely transforms an ordinary house into a personal castle. Given our obvious obsession with home improvement, the question remains: do any of these "improvements" really improve your home?

The time had come for Joshua to give his farewell speech to the people, but before he gave them a personal challenge to improve their homes, he recounted the blessings of God. Joshua began by reminding the people of God's great promise to Abraham to give his descendants a land of their own. Joshua described how God had provided for His people, protected His people, and fought on behalf of His people as He brought them into the Promised Land. As if to add an exclamation point to his speech, Joshua delivered his message to the people at Shechem, the very place God spoke to Abraham about the Promised Land (see Genesis 12:6–7).

Joshua knew that God had been good to His people, and he was afraid they might begin to take God for granted, turn away from Him, and begin to worship other gods. Joshua sought to communicate in such a way that the people would consider the greatness of God and willingly choose to serve Him. As their leader, Joshua was not calling the people to do anything he was not also willing to do himself. Joshua's bold proclamation that he and his house would be dedicated to following and serving God still reverberates today with the same power and conviction as the day Joshua declared those words.

Joshua spoke to the people about a choice that was not to be a one-time event. Instead, he spoke of a lifelong commitment, lived out in the day-to-day choices that are made while following and serving God, just as Joshua exemplified to the people.

Today every home is faced with the same choice of whether or not to follow God and serve Him throughout day-to-day life. Joshua understood that the only way to have a godly nation would be to begin by having godly homes. Although nothing is wrong with spending time and money on home renovation (and a finely decorated house certainly is nice to have), in the end, none of this kind of home improvement can compare to having a godly home.

The type of home improvement Joshua would challenge us to make would not take the do-it-yourself approach to renovation; Joshua would urge us closer to the extreme makeover style in which we allow God to completely and radically change our house from the inside out, into a godly home. After all, a godly home is not determined by décor but by devotion to God.

And He, bearing His cross, went out to a place called the Place of a Skull, which is called in Hebrew, Golgotha, where they crucified Him. (John 19:17–18)

The Beauty of Skull Mountain

THE CRUCIFIXION OF JESUS CHRIST is both gruesome and full of grace. At the cross, we see mankind at his cruelest and God at His most compassionate. Before Jesus hung on the cross, the crowd yelled, "Crucify Him!" Yet while Jesus hung there, beaten and bloodied, He would pray, "Father, forgive them . . ." As the nails were being driven into the hands of the Savior, Satan thought he was successful in stopping God's plan of salvation. Yet, when the stone was rolled away from Jesus' tomb, the victory was found in the empty tomb of a risen Redeemer. The most striking contrast found at the cross is His death actually became new life in Him.

When we look to the events that led up to and included Jesus' dying on the cross, the beauty in what God was accomplishing through something so grotesque may have been difficult to see. Perhaps the first step in the right direction for understanding this method of redemption is to understand that sin is, in fact, grotesque; sin is also gruesome, distressing, and detestable to God. God is holy and pure, and therefore He cannot have anything to do with sin, nor can He be anywhere near sin. Naturally, therefore, the Christian should have nothing to do with sin nor be anywhere near sin. Sin represents everything that goes against God's will, His nature, and His Word.

When Adam sinned in the Garden of Eden, all mankind became permanently and fatally flawed because of sin's insidious consequences. Sin is now a disease that courses through the veins of every human being and is incurable, inoperable, and impossible to treat, apart from God. As part of God's judgment against sin, death was the prescribed penalty. As part of God's mercy toward mankind, a substitution sacrifice would be allowed. God's hatred for sin and His love for mankind compelled Him to offer the only acceptable sacrifice: His Son, Jesus Christ. Now, instead of having to die *for* our sins, we must die *to* our sins.

The compassionate cure for our disease came through the crucifixion of Christ on a cross in a place called Skull Mountain. The physical pain involved in the event, as great and agonizing as one could imagine, would be only a fraction of the pain suffered by Christ; the greatest pain would come from bearing the full weight of mankind's sin upon Himself. But here, at the location of such an ugly event, also lies beauty; Skull Mountain, is also the place where we see the willing self-sacrifice of a loving Savior.

Every Christian needs to look upon Skull Mountain and see sin the same way that God does, as grotesque, gruesome, distressing, and detestable. Our sin put Jesus on that cross. He became repulsive, taking on our sin so that we could become redeemed, taking on His righteousness.

As we look to the cross and see the sacrifice of our Savior, we should be motivated to follow Him with the same dedication that led Him to the Place of a Skull: "Greater love has no one than this, than to lay down one's life for his friends" (John 15:13). Only a love so beautiful could make someone willingly accept such an ugly death.

And it came to pass, when the judge was dead, that they reverted and behaved more corruptly than their fathers, by following other gods, to serve them and bow down to them. (Judges 2:19)

MARCH
12

Breaking the Cycle of Sin

BAD HABITS are hard to break. Whether your habit is nail biting, knuckle cracking, fidgeting, or procrastinating, putting an end to these types of habits can be hard work. Sinful habits are even harder to break. Just ask the Israelites.

After the death of Joshua, the Israelites entered into a cycle of sin that lasted for more than four hundred years. The Book of Judges takes us through a period of disobedience and judgment for the nation of Israel that could have been avoided if only they had been willing to break free from their sin cycle. The cycle of sin starts with one small step in the wrong direction and leads to habitual sin where personal devotion to God is slowly eroded, eventually leaving us tolerant of sin, comfortable with disobedience, and friendly with selfishness.

The Israelites' cycle of sin came in four stages: sin, slavery, supplication, and salvation.

Stage 1: Entering into sin. The Israelites turned away from God to worship idols. This worship came about through forsaking God's Word, which led to forsaking God himself. No one is immune. If we are not careful and watchful, we, too, can start down this road by allowing something other than God to capture our attention, and before we even become aware, we are living for something other than God.

Stage 2: The bondage of slavery. Because of their sin, God allowed the Israelites to become enslaved to surrounding nations. God refused them victory over their enemies because with their worship of other gods, they were making God their enemy. By choosing disobedience, they reaped defeat. Ironically, obedience to the one and only God would have led to victory.

Stage 3: The shout of supplication. Because of the chastening of the Lord, the people cried out to God. Sadly, for some today, many do not call out for God's help until they experience the darkness of their bad choices and begin to cry out for the light of God to show them the way.

Stage 4: God's gracious salvation. God heard their prayers and, in His mercy and grace, delivered the people by raising up a judge to defeat their enemies and set His people free. Sadly, after their deliverance, the Israelites failed to learn from their affliction. They grew comfortable and complacent and eventually began the cycle of sin all over again.

If we fail to overcome sin, sin will overcome us. So how can we reverse the cycle of sin?

- **Stage 1: Turn back to God.** Place Him in the center of your life, seeking to please Him and not self.
- **Stage 2: Obey His Word.** Continual and faithful obedience to the Word of God is what will keep you from forsaking God and seeking sin.
- **Stage 3: Pray.** Pray, pray, and yes, pray some more! Ask God daily for His help and strength to resist sin and follow Him.
- **Stage 4: Listen and remain yielded to the Holy Spirit's guidance.** God has given every Christian a Helper, the Holy Spirit. Walk in the freedom that He provides.

If we repeat this cycle of holy living, then the cycle of sin will have no power over us.

"Unless I see in His hands the print of the nails, and put my finger into the print of the nails, and put my hand into His side, I will not believe." (John 20:25)

MARCH
13

The Skeptic's Guide to God

AUTHORS Norman Geisler and Ronald M. Brooks pointed out that "before we can share the Gospel, we sometimes have to smooth the road, remove the obstacles, and answer the questions that are keeping that person from accepting the Lord."[10] Doubt is often viewed as a bad word in Christianity, but doubt is not the opposite of faith; doubt can actually be an essential stepping-stone for developing a person's faith in Jesus Christ.

No greater personification of doubting in the Bible exists than that of the Apostle Thomas. He got his reputation for doubting from missing an important meeting with the other apostles after the resurrection of Jesus. This is a good place to interject that we should seek not to miss gathering together with God's people at church (see Hebrews 10:25). Who knows what blessings we will miss? We do not know why Thomas missed gathering with the others that day. Maybe he had a legitimate reason. But what we do know is that he missed out on the tremendous blessing of having an experience with the risen Lord.

When the other apostles came to Thomas and gave him the astounding news of what had happened, he refused to believe, saying, "Unless I see . . . , I will not believe." But before we come down too hard on Thomas, we must remember that, at first, none of the other apostles believed that Jesus had risen from the dead either. Not until the Lord revealed himself to them behind closed doors did they believe. Thomas, though often harshly criticized for his doubt, was actually looking for a way to solidify his faith, not reject his belief.

When Jesus appeared to the apostles the following week, Thomas was with them this time. In this encounter, Jesus lovingly helped Thomas to see clearly, drawing Thomas's attention to His nail-scarred hands and His spear-pierced side.

This caused Thomas to make the most profound confession of faith a person can make about Jesus: "My Lord and my God!" (John 20:28).

No matter what the other apostles said to Thomas prior to this encounter with Jesus, they were unable to change his mind in the end. We, too, are unable to change someone's mind about God; only the work of God and His Holy Spirit can completely and totally bring about the spiritual sight that removes doubt. God may choose to use us in the process, but the results are in His hands, not ours. Our job is much the same as that of John the Baptist: to prepare the way for Jesus. The way we do this is, again, to "smooth the road, remove the obstacles, and answer the questions that are keeping that person from accepting the Lord."[11] We can help prepare the way for Jesus to deal with people who initially doubt.

Doubt that drives a person deeper into discovery of the truth about Jesus is an honest doubt that can produce a strong faith. Honest doubt should not be avoided or condemned, but instead, looked upon as an opportunity to make Jesus known.

Remember, when you are dealing with people's doubts, deal with them lovingly as Jesus did with Thomas. Remain fully aware that the final result is not found in your ability to persuade, but in whether they will see Jesus and believe.

"Look, I shall put a fleece of wool on the threshing floor; if there is dew on the fleece only, and it is dry on all the ground, then I shall know that You will save Israel by my hand, as You have said." (Judges 6:37)

MARCH
14

A New Fleece on Life

KNOWING GOD'S WILL can sometimes feel like attempting to assemble a thousand-piece jigsaw puzzle, blindfolded. How can you know what God's will is for you in your daily life? When you are facing tough decisions, how can you know which decision best honors God? Or, when you come to a fork in the road, how can you know which direction guarantees that you are walking in obedience to His will? These are the types of questions that a man named Gideon wrestled with in his efforts to know God's will.

His story begins during a time when a nearby enemy, known as the Midianites, was terrorizing the Israelites. The Midianite method of intimidation involved allowing the Israelites to spend the year tending to their crops and raising their livestock. Then, just as harvest time was approaching, the Midianites would swoop in, clean out their crops, and loot their livestock, leaving the Israelites impoverished and disheartened. After a few years of this type of treatment, the Israelites cried out to God, and He responded. God came to an ordinary man named Gideon and declared to him that he was being chosen to deliver the people from the cruel hand of the Midianites.

Now, instead of responding confidently to God's call, His commissioning, and the promise of His presence, Gideon demonstrated a lack of faith. Once God reveals His will to us, our responsibility is to simply obey. This may sound like an oversimplification of the truth about His will, but still remains true. Gideon, however, like so many of us, heard the Word of God and decided that he needed more, so he asked for a sign from God as confirmation. He did this by putting out a fleece before the Lord. A fleece involves asking God to do something out of the ordinary or asking Him to meet some arbitrary condition we have set to receive direction from Him. Although Gideon already had received a direct revelation from God—God's will was understood from God's word to Gideon—God nonetheless graciously accommodated Gideon's request, not just once, but twice.

Does this mean we should use the fleece method to determine God's will in specific situations? The answer is simple: no! Using a fleece as some sort of spiritual compass is not a biblical approach to discovering God's will. God had already spoken to Gideon, and God has already spoken to us. The place to turn when you are seeking direction and when you need help making the right decision is none other the Bible.

Nothing is wrong with asking God to direct your steps, and nothing is wrong with wanting to be certain of God's will for your life. But the answers you look for will not come from testing God; they will come from trusting God. Answers will not be found by fleecing God but by seeking God through His Word.

If you are trying to know God's will, then seek God, do not fleece Him. Open His Word and let Him direct your steps.

So when they had eaten breakfast, Jesus said to Simon Peter, "Simon, son of Jonah, do you love Me more than these?" He said to Him, "Yes, Lord; You know that I love You." He said to him, "Feed My lambs." (John 21:15)

MARCH 15

Failure Is Not the End

WHEN YOU HEAR the name Thomas Edison, you probably think of a great inventor who revolutionized the world with his innovations. However, what most people do not realize is that during his work on the light bulb, Thomas Edison tried more than six thousand different fibers, only three of which worked. Giving up would have been easy for him after 5,999 tries, but each failure brought him that much closer to fulfilling his dream. The pioneering car maker Henry Ford once said, "Failure is only the opportunity to begin again more intelligently."

Have you ever felt as though you have failed God and therefore, He would never want to use you again? If you have failed, I have good news: failure is a starting point for God to refashion your heart. The Bible is filled with great men and women of God who, at one time in their lives, messed up on a grand scale with God. Yet God restored them, and eventually, they went on to be used by Him in mighty ways for His glory. One such person was the Apostle Peter, a spiritual giant,leader of the early church, and powerful preacher. But he also failed the Lord on more than one occasion. Despite his failures, restoration came to Peter one day over breakfast.

Peter had denied the Lord three times on the night before Jesus' crucifixion, and he was crushed by his failure. Even though he would rejoice in a few days over the resurrection of Jesus, he still was utterly discouraged because of his failure. Based on what he did next, he seemed to question his future usefulness to God. Peter was told by Jesus to wait, but Peter decided instead to go fishing. As H. A. Ironside has said:

"It is so much easier to go fishing than to give yourself to prayer! You know how that is. When the Spirit of God would call you to a season of waiting on the Lord, it is so much easier to get up and do something. We would rather do almost anything than wait quietly on God. That is the flesh."[12]

Jesus met up with Peter and the other disciples who joined him that day and made breakfast for them by the sea. Over this intimate time of fellowship, Jesus restored Peter. The road to personal restoration with God can only be found through intimate fellowship with God. Jesus restored Peter by dealing with the main issue: Peter's love for Jesus. Three times Jesus called Peter to affirm his love for Him (one for each of Peter's denials, no doubt), and three times, Peter publicly proclaimed his love for Jesus. After Jesus reaffirmed Peter's affections, He gave Peter his assignment: *Go and be a shepherd to My people.*

If you have failed the Lord and feel that you can no longer be effective for Him, know this: you can be restored to ministry, but this restoration begins by reaffirming your love for Jesus. Jesus is love, and if you are to serve Him faithfully, you must be steadfast in your love for Him, rekindling the flames of an intimate relationship with the Savior.

One of the greatest expressions of love for the Savior is through our service to Him. As you seek to be restored, you must be willing to wait, because restoration and re-commissioning can only come at the hand of the Lord, and will happen only according to His divine timetable. Then, as your love is refreshed, be ready to be re-commissioned for service.

And she said, "The Philistines are upon you, Samson!" So he awoke from his sleep, and said, "I will go out as before, at other times, and shake myself free!" But he did not know that the LORD had departed from him. (Judges 16:20)

MARCH 16

How the Mighty Have Fallen!

H ELLO. My name is Samson. My name means "little sun." I can tell from the looks on some of your faces that you recognize my name. I'm not surprised. After all, when I lived here on earth I was anything but "little." I was a larger-than-life legend. I was not a "little sun," I was an enormous sun. I had a bright and glorious future. I was the most famous man in the world. Everyone knew the name of Samson. And they spoke it with respect. They had to. I was the strongest man who ever lived. If I was on earth today, you'd not only admit me into your Olympics, but you'd have to set up a special category for me. Because I'm the strongest man of all time.[13]

The life of Samson has become a dramatic story, depicting squandered potential and a tragedy that portrays the cost of compromise. The story is a valuable tool that offers us several lessons to be learned. Samson's life began like only one other person's in the Old Testament, in that his birth was foretold by an angel. He began life consecrated to God as a Nazarite, which meant that he was entirely set apart to God. Symbolic of his consecration, he drank no wine and allowed his hair to grow, untouched by a razor. By the age of twenty, he was the leader of the Israelites. And as already mentioned, he was blessed with superhuman strength, tearing a lion in two with his bare hands and pulling huge wooden gates off their iron hinges that were anchored to a city wall. No questioning that Samson was an extraordinary man.

Sadly, even though Samson had such promise and potential, this powerhouse of a man had a powerful weakness that would eventually be his downfall. Easily overcome by temptation, Samson's unbridled lust continued to lead him astray. Repeatedly choosing to allow the same sin to dominate his life choices, he eventually anesthetized his spiritual senses.

What caused this consecrated man to cave? The slow decline of compromise was the culprit. Repeated compromise led him straight into a trap, where the enemies of God exploited Samson's weakness and were then able to defeat him. Samson had become so numb to spiritual truth that he was totally unaware that the Spirit of God had left him. The cost of compromise for Samson was his sight, his freedom, and his life. Samson's many compromises damaged his relationship with his family, and His compromise caused others to blaspheme the name of God. Samson's grand finale was as heartbreaking as his life. His final show of strength in destroying the Philistines may have signified a spiritual renewal because his strength always had been a symbol of God's presence in his life, but also cost him his life.

Christians are to be consecrated to God, set apart to serve God with the spiritual gifts God has given us. Our ability to be effective for God is related to our consecration to God. Our strength comes only as a result of God's presence in our lives. Compromise is a surefire way to allow weakness to overpower strength and to make ourselves vulnerable to temptation. Simply put, compromise kills consecration and has severe consequences in our lives.

Do not allow compromise to gain a foothold. Seek the grace of God to give you the strength of God to remain consecrated to God.

"But you shall receive power when the Holy Spirit has come upon you." (Acts 1:8)

MARCH
17

Power Up!

WHAT DO ONE-HUNDRED-MEGATON BOMBS, gravity, the Colorado River, tornadoes, and rhinoceros beetles have in common? They are all extremely powerful forces. Now, you may be thinking, *A rhinoceros beetle? What is a rhinoceros beetle?* Well, this little beetle, with a head shaped like a rhino, is proportionally the strongest animal on the planet, with the ability to lift objects up to 850 times its body weight. Here is an example of this power, just to give you some perspective: If you weighed 150 pounds, you would have to lift over 127,000 pounds to be as strong as this little beetle. (A friendly reminder: do not try this at home!) Even with the variety of power we see displayed on earth, nothing compares to the power of the Holy Spirit.

The time had come for Jesus to leave this earth and return to heaven. Forty days had elapsed since His resurrection, and He had spent this time teaching and preparing His disciples for their gospel mission. You can imagine their anxiety, their fear, and their general feeling of powerlessness as they considered life without Him.

Perhaps you, too, have felt powerless to live the life that God wants you to live and do the work God has called you to do. You may have feelings of inadequacy, anxiety, and a general powerlessness to accomplish what God has set before you.

The disciples had been with Jesus for three-and-a-half years, and now they would be on their own, or so they thought. Jesus told the disciples they were to wait in Jerusalem a few more days so they might receive the Promise of the Father, the Holy Spirit. This Promise would deliver to the disciples all the power they needed to do all the ministry God would give them. Prior to the Holy Spirit's coming upon and empowering the disciples, they simply did not have the power they needed to get the job done. In the spiritual work of ministry, the work is accomplished not by man's strength or ability. Rather, it is the work done only by God's Spirit.

If you are a Christian and feel as though you lack power, the good news is that all believers in Jesus Christ already have within themselves the most powerful resource in the entire universe: God's Holy Spirit. All we need to do is tap into that power source. The power that raised Jesus from the dead is the same power available to you and me today: "But if the Spirit of Him who raised Jesus from the dead dwells in you, He who raised Christ from the dead will also give life to your mortal bodies through His Spirit who dwells in you" (Romans 8:11).

In order to experience the power of the Spirit of God working in your life and through your life, you must be surrendered to the Holy Spirit. Every believer has access to God's Spirit and the power of His Spirit, but living yielded to the Spirit is a must if you want to experience the release of that power in your life.

The Bible exhorts us to be filled with the Spirit, to walk in the Spirit, not to smother or quench the Spirit, and to make sure that we do not grieve the Spirit. All these aspects are involved in being yielded to the Spirit. Follow these principles, and you will be powered up to accomplish the glorious plans that God has prepared for you to do.

In those days there was no king in Israel; everyone did what was right in his own eyes. (Judges 21:25)

It is Not All Relative

MARCH
18

MANY PEOPLE TODAY make their choices and live their lives according to personal philosophies that frequently can be boiled down in one of the following ways: *If it makes you happy, then it cannot be that bad; If it feels good, do it;* or *Life is short, so grab all the enjoyment you can.* Looking around the world today, everyone seemingly wants what he or she wants right away, like, right now! Sincerity has replaced moral absolutism, and no responsibility to a higher authority remains because most people view themselves as the final authority. The end result of this type of self-first outlook on life will be much the same as the fate of the children of Israel at the end of the Book of Judges.

The Book of Judges concludes with the sad declaration: "Everyone did what was right in his own eyes." The saddest portion of this statement was that "everyone" was a description of those who should have known better: God's people. If any group of people should have known the devastation that can come from holding on to a self-centered, God-rejecting approach to life, the Israelites should have known. As a nation without a king, they also rejected the one-and-only King of kings and decided to live according to their own individual standards, declaring themselves wise in their own eyes. They let their own hearts govern their lives rather than allowing God to govern them.

Making choices and decisions in life based solely on our personal preferences and emotions can be so easy, never giving a second thought to considering what God has to say about the situations we face. In a society with an absence of a governing authority, evil will prevail. The same is true individually. In the absence of a governing authority in our lives, evil to will prevail. Above all, spiritually if we do not stand for God and let Him govern our lives, we will fall for every lie whose core is the notion that we can do as we please. This choice rejects God's rule as King over our lives. Living as though no absolutes, no boundaries, and no consequences exist, when, in fact, absolutes, boundaries, and eternal consequences are a certainty for the choices we make today.

The Bible stands in direct opposition to the way of relativism; the truths within boldly oppose subjectivism and shamelessly assert the existence of absolute truth. The Bible upholds the idea that universal moral principles have been established by God to govern individual behavior, as well as the behavior of society as a whole.

The Bible continually reveals to us, time and time again, that if we choose to abandon God's moral governance, whether individually or as a society, then we are headed for ruin. In the end, what is right in our own eyes does not matter; all that matters is what is right according to God's Word.

And they continued steadfastly in the apostles' doctrine and fellowship, in the breaking of bread, and in prayers.
(Acts 2:42)

MARCH 19

The Church Checklist

FOR MANY, the word *church* conjures up images of wooden benches, stained-glass windows, large, elaborate buildings, organ music, and potlucks. Added to that is everyone's individual opinion of what "church" should be and should not be.

Given the diversity of denominations, countless number of congregations, and vast assortment of worship styles to choose from, choosing the right church can seem as overwhelming as viewing the entire breakfast cereal aisle of your local grocery store. However, finding the right church does not have to feel like aimlessly shopping in a spiritual supermarket if you have a good checklist. We were given a checklist when church was born two millennia ago.

Nearly two thousand years ago, a sudden and sizable baby boom occurred as three thousand people were born into the family of faith. In one single day, as God created church the number of believers increased from 120 to 3,120. The apostles were faced with an instant church, and to ensure that the first church was a place where spiritual maturity and growth was fostered, they dedicated themselves to four fundamentals that are still needed in the church today.

Priority must be given to the teaching of the Word of God. Acts 2:42 tells us, "They continued steadfastly *in the apostles' doctrine*" (emphasis added). The Apostles were a teaching church with learning people. A Spirit-filled church must promote solid biblical teaching, because only through the Word of God are we able to come closest to the heart and mind of God.

Next, the church must have *fellowship*. Fellowship, of course, begins with our fellowship with God and then extends to include God's people. Fellowship, in essence, is a partnership or sharing together in the life of the local church. Fellowship is choosing community over isolation, connectedness over separation, and involvement over detachment.

Another fundamental of the church is dedication to continue *the breaking of bread.* Our commitment to communion is not optional, as Jesus instructed us to "do this in remembrance of [Him]" (Luke 22:19). Commitment to communion is a means of keeping the work of Christ on the cross always before us, and the act helps us to remain Christ-centered.

Last, but certainly not least among the fundamentals, is continuing *in prayers.* Persistent prayer is one of the most neglected—yet most essential aspects of church life. Prayer shows the supremacy of God and is a sign of our dependence on God. A church persistent in prayer will undoubtedly be a church that sees the power of God at work.

G. K. Chesterton once said, "We don't want a church that will move with the world. We want a church that will move the world." The early church was a church that moved the world and was described in Acts 17 as "these who have turned the world upside down."

Personal preferences in the search for a good church should influence your decision of where to attend church, as long as the essentials above are also present. So, whether you like contemporary or traditional services, large churches, or small churches, make sure that wherever you go, you can check off the fundamentals from your list and be ready for your church to move the world.

"Do not call me Naomi; call me Mara, for the Almighty has dealt very bitterly with me." (Ruth 1:20)

Angry at God

WHEN WE HAVE BEEN HURT or offended by someone, those feelings can quickly take root in our hearts and become resentment and bitterness, if we are not careful. Bitterness turns that which was sweet into something sour; bitterness turns the fragrant into something foul, and the healthy into something harmful. Bitterness is a thief that seeks to sneak in under the cover of darkness and steal joy, rob relationships, and plunder faith. Bitterness turns our gaze away from the goodness of God and sets its sights on the sting of disappointment.

Naomi and her family, which included her husband and two sons at the time, left Bethlehem because a famine came upon the land. They decided to live in the region of Moab, just on the other side of the Jordan River. During that time, Naomi's sons married two local girls, one named Orpah, and the other, Ruth. Life in Moab soon took a nasty turn for Naomi when her husband and two sons died. Being freed from her family ties, Orpah left Naomi and returned to her family, while Ruth decided to stay with her mother-in-law. The two women returned to Bethlehem ten years after Naomi and her family had initially left.

But Naomi's experiences in Moab had changed her. She no longer was the same sweet woman she had been when she left. She no longer wanted to be known as Naomi, which means "pleasant" or "sweet." Rather, she wanted to be called Mara, which means "bitter."

We cannot control what happens to us in life, but we can control how we respond to what happens to us. In a similar series of tragedies, Job was able to say in the midst of his suffering and loss, "The LORD gave, and the LORD has taken away; Blessed be the name of the LORD" (Job 1:21). Joseph also was able to see that even though he had been a slave and a prisoner, God meant his suffering all for good (see Genesis 50:20). On the other hand, Naomi, though she did not abandon God, allowed bitterness to creep into her heart. She became angry with God for her experiences. She accused God of dealing bitterly with her, and in so doing, she turned her gaze away from the goodness of God and focused on the sting of disappointment.

Naomi did not forget God, but she did forget that God still has a good plan and a purpose for His children, even in the hardships, difficulties, and losses that we encounter in this life. Was her pain real? Yes. Was she wrong to feel that hurt and pain? Not at all! But her bitterness was blinding her to the goodness of God that was still at work around her. Her bitterness made her say that she had returned empty when, in fact, she was not empty-handed; Ruth had come with her. Naomi's bitterness could only allow her to see the negative things in life.

Through hardships we are to draw closer to God, not drift farther away. Trials are not intended to be a spiritual curse, but a gateway to blessing. When we stop believing in the goodness of God, when we no longer believe that He has our best interests in mind, or when we allow ourselves to think and live this way, life will turn bitter and so will we.

If you feel gripped by bitterness or are angry with God for the difficulties you are going through, remember that God has not forsaken you; He has a good plan and purpose for everything you face. Keep looking to Him and start to reverse the spread of the acidic taste of bitterness. Instead, start tasting the sweet blessings you have in Christ.

Now when they saw the boldness of Peter and John, and perceived that they were uneducated and untrained men, they marveled. And they realized that they had been with Jesus. (Acts 4:13)

MARCH
21

A Master's Degree

BENJAMIN FRANKLIN once said, "an investment in knowledge pays the best interest." In a recent ranking, *U.S. News & World Report* included such universities as Princeton, Harvard, and Stanford among the "best values" in the country. Undeniably, education is one of the best investments a person can make, but a good education is more to than attending an Ivy League school or graduating at the top of your class. A higher education exists that has more value and is a much better investment.

Two unschooled fishermen stood before the most esteemed religious leaders of their day. Two regular guys confronted rabbis who had received extensive education and had dedicated their lives to the study and observance of their religious law. These were the same leaders whom Jesus himself stood before a few weeks earlier when they were condemning Him to death. These two fishermen, Peter and John, were ignorant in the ways of rabbinic wisdom, yet they boldly declared to these men the way of salvation. They proclaimed to the high priest and others who were there that day that salvation is found in no other name except the name of Jesus (see Acts 4:12). Peter and John declared the truth before these men confidently and unashamedly, and in so doing, they astonished these pious leaders and led them to realize that these men had spent time with Jesus.

Ten minutes with Jesus is worth more than an ocean of theology. Time with Jesus gives a person more than head knowledge; time with Jesus delivers a living knowledge, a transforming education, and a true, comprehensive world-view. The apostles had spent three years with Jesus. They watched His every move, they hung on His every word, they marveled at His every miracle, they scrutinized His social conduct, and they shared in His private life. Now that is an education! As an added bonus, this education does not cost $35,000 a year, and does not require you take an entrance exam. The only requirement: time with Jesus.

Every person is afforded the same opportunity to spend time with Jesus and learn through the study of His Word. In the Word, we are able to watch His every move, hang on His every word, marvel at His every miracle, scrutinize His social conduct, and share in His private life. Now that is an education! we can receive no higher education than that which comes by allowing the Holy Spirit of God to teach us all things about Jesus, which we find in the Word of God.

Make an investment in something that pays eternal dividends, and get a degree from *the* Master by spending time with Jesus.

> *So she fell on her face, bowed down to the ground, and said to him, "Why have I found favor in your eyes, that you should take notice of me?"* (Ruth 2:10)

MARCH
22

Gleaning in Fields of Grace

THE NATURE AND CHARACTER OF GOD is to exhibit unmerited kindness toward mankind. God generously and lavishly gives us good that we do not deserve and have not earned. This is the essence of grace, something that reverberates throughout the pages of the Scriptures.

Some mistakenly believe that God is portrayed in the Old Testament as a God of wrath and that not until we turn to the New Testament do we see God as a God of grace. But God's grace is not hidden in the Old Testament. On the contrary, countless pictures of His spectacular and amazing grace are found in this book. In the Book of Ruth, we come face to face with such a demonstration of God's grace, and the timeless significance of this story still impacts us today.

As an impoverished woman, widow, and stranger in a new land, Ruth was stuck at the bottom of the social ladder. However, with human choice and the divine providence of God, Ruth would stumble upon God's grace. Ruth went out looking for a field to gather the grain left behind by the harvesters, which was a basic welfare program established by God, allowing those in need to work for their food. Ruth, however, was not from Bethlehem, and as a newcomer in town, she was shocked at the kindness she received at the hand of Boaz, the owner of the field where she was gathering. Not only was she allowed to gather grain, but she also was invited to have lunch with Boaz and the harvesters. After lunch, Boaz gave instructions to the workmen to watch over her and help her with her gathering. Boaz went above and beyond what was required in providing for this poor widow Ruth. In her amazement she asked, "Why have I found favor in your eyes, that you should take notice of me?"

The answer is simple: because of grace. The grace of God led her to that field on that day, the grace of God that made Boaz "happen" to see, God's grace gave her favor with Boaz, and God's grace was displayed through the heart of Boaz, enabling Ruth to return home that day having received an overflow of both grain and grace.

The grace that Ruth received not only made an impact on her, but also affected Naomi. God's amazing grace began to take away the bitterness that had taken root in Naomi's heart, and her bitterness was changing into an overwhelming sense of God's blessing. What a difference grace can make! Even in the ordinary routine of our everyday circumstances, the grace of God can break through and change everything.

As we seek to gather in the fields of God's grace, we can see in Ruth an example for us all when receiving His grace. She recognized her unworthiness, which prompted her to gratefully and humbly receive the grace shown to her. Truly seeing all that God has done for us should force us to look upon His grace toward us with gratitude and humility and say, like Ruth, "Why have I found favor in your eyes, that you should take notice of me?"

God's grace should produce thankfulness in our hearts that is expressed in our lives as we seek to live in a way that imparts grace to those around us. May we show grace like Boaz showed to others, and may we receive grace like Ruth.

"But we will give ourselves continually to prayer and to the ministry of the word." (Acts 6:4)

A Pitfall for Pastors

MARCH
23

TO FILL THE JOB description of today's pastor sounds like a job for Superman. A pastor is expected to make house calls as willingly as yesterday's country doctor, to shake hands and smile like a politician on the campaign trail, to entertain like a stand-up comedian, to teach the Scriptures like a theology professor, and to counsel like a psychologist with the wisdom of Solomon. He should run the church like a top-level business executive, handle finances like a career accountant, and deal with the public like an expert diplomat at the United Nations. No wonder so many pastors are confused about just what is expected of them and how they will ever manage to live up to all those expectations.[14]

The apostles were being blessed with wonderful church growth. God was adding those who were being saved to the church daily, but with this rapid church growth came a few problems. The early church had a food program to help the widows in the congregation, but as the church grew, the food program grew as well. The result was the apostles were in jeopardy of spending too much time serving food themselves and not enough time praying and ministering the Word of God. Delegation became necessary. The apostles could not do everything themselves, nor were they supposed to try to do everything themselves. The solution was to appoint some qualified men who could step up and serve this growing need in the church.

The apostles were not too good to serve food to those in need, but more important was that they serve the Word of God. If the apostles would have tried to do everything themselves, they would have discouraged others who may have wanted to serve, and they would have neglected their responsibility to pray, prepare, and preach the Word.

Some pastors today are too busy for their own good and the good of their congregations. They are trying to do too much, and the result is they are not spending enough time praying and preparing so they may preach the Word effectively and with the full anointing of the Holy Spirit. None of this means that the pastor is to neglect his congregation, but he is to find a balance, always keeping the majority of his time for his primary responsibility, which is praying, teaching, preaching, and studying the Word of God.

Many churches would be healthier if this were the focus of their pastor, and many pastors would be happier if they functioned as they were called to function. Everyone has a spiritual gift given to them by God, a job, if you will, and the majority of the time we spend serving in the church should involve that which we have been called and gifted to do in the church.

Be a blessing to your church leadership by fulfilling your calling and coming alongside them so they can fulfill their responsibilities. Your pastor is not Superman, and he should not have to do ministry all alone.

"And now, my daughter, do not fear. I will do for you all that you request, for all the people of my town know that you are a virtuous woman." (Ruth 3:11)

MARCH
24

A Virtuous Woman in a Modern World

SOCIETY'S PICTURE of the modern woman has changed significantly from the quintessential Suzy Homemaker of the 1950s to the career woman of today. Today's woman is still expected to cook, clean, and keep a neat home, raise well-adjusted children, and be a supportive wife. But now added to those expectations for today's woman are the ability to balance a successful career and be assertive and goal-driven, all the while remaining feminine. With all the demands placed on today's woman, the question is, can she be both a modern woman *and* a virtuous woman?

In a day and age when everyone was doing what was right in their own eyes, a woman stood who set her sights on doing what was right in God's eyes. When society was given over to selfish pursuits, wild living, and moral compromise, a woman who was devoted to moral excellence and the pursuit of God could still be found. Ruth's godly life was the talk of the town, and when her name was mentioned in the markets, when the local women gathered at the well, when people saw her coming, everyone said the same thing: Ruth is a woman of virtue.

What distinguished her as a virtuous woman? She was devoted and loyal to her family, she delighted in her work, she was diligent in all she did, she was dedicated to godly speech, she showed a dependence on God, she dressed with modesty, she kept her relationships with men proper, and she was a blessing to others. Ruth was not a perfect woman, but she was a purposed woman. Ruth rose above the societal norm of her age, and she did not allow the mentality of "every one is doing it" to sway her from living God's way. She did not withdraw from her culture, but chose to be an example of a woman of virtue *in* her culture.

So, what is a modern girl to do? Today some women are doctors, lawyers, or CEOs, some serve in the military, some stay at home, some work in an office, some are married, some are single, some have children, and others do not. Despite the many differences, they all have one thing in common: no matter who they are or what they do, all of them can be women of virtue. The progress of a society should not determine the priorities of its people.

Perhaps you have heard the expression, *It is not what you say but how you say it.* Well, we could say that *It is not so much what you do, but for whom you do it.* Are you devoted and loyal to your family? Do you delight in your work (whatever your work is)? Are you diligent in all your efforts? Are you dedicated to godly speech? Do you show a dependence on God? Do you dress with modesty? Are you above reproach with men? And finally, do you seek to be a blessing to others?

If you are seeking to put God first in your life and to pursue His purposes no matter what you do, then you will be a priceless woman of virtue.

"Saul, Saul, why are you persecuting Me?" (Acts 9:4)

Can God Really Use Me?

MARCH

25

THROUGHOUT HISTORY, the world has seen its share of evil people who have been responsible for horrible crimes against humanity such as oppression, persecution, murder, and enslavement. Names like Adolph Hitler, Joseph Stalin, and Mao Tse-Tung brought fear to millions of people during their time in power, and these names still bring chills to those who read of the notorious leaders' atrocities. In the early years of the church, a similar name struck fear in the hearts of Christians. His name was Saul of Tarsus.

Have you ever wondered, *Can God really use me?* Maybe you have done things of which you are ashamed, or acted in a way that has hurt your reputation. You may be feeling inadequate and incapable of rising above your mistakes and your past and have convinced yourself there is no way you could serve God. If so, good news! You will be encouraged as you see how God turned a persecutor of Christians into a killer Christian.

Saul of Tarsus made tracking down and persecuting the early church of Jesus Christ his mission in life. He was present during the murder of the church's first martyr, Stephen (see Acts 7:58). A relentless bloodhound with an uncanny ability to hunt Christians down, Saul was treacherous, rebellious, callous, and cold-hearted. But one day, everything changed for this former Wyatt Earp of religious apprehension. Eventually, he would go on to become a bold and courageous witness for Jesus Christ and one of the greatest preachers of the Word of God.

Saul was on his way from Jerusalem to Damascus, where he was hoping to arrest and bring back in chains as many Christians as possible to stand trial for preaching that Jesus was God. As Saul approached the city of Damascus, Jesus knocked him off his horse and asked, "Saul, Saul, why are you persecuting Me?" (Acts 9:4). The subsequent conversation with Jesus eventually would lead to the conversion of Saul, the persecutor of the church, changing him into Paul, an apostle of the church. Paul's conversion was definitely amazing and dramatic, but every conversion is a miracle of God, and no one becomes a Christian apart from a very real and personal encounter with Jesus Christ.

Any service to God must begin with a total surrender of one's life to God. Our service begins with our salvation, and our personal encounter with Jesus must include, but not be limited to, an acknowledgment that Jesus died for our sins, that God raised Him from the dead, and that if we believe in Jesus as Lord, we can be saved. This salvation encounter acts like a divine eraser that effectively wipes away our sins and gives us a fresh start, a new life in Christ. Because of this new life, we have a new lease on life that allows us to get out from under our past mistakes, sins, and failures and serve the Lord, free from condemnation and full of joy.

Never give up on yourself or someone else. Do not write someone off as a lost cause or consider yourself as being too far gone to be saved and used by God. God can use you, He wants to use you, and He has work prepared for you to do, if you allow Him to take control of your life.

If a former bounty hunter of Christians can become one of the greatest leaders in the church, then God can use you if you allow Him to take the reins.

"Speak, your servant is listening." (1 Samuel 3:10 NTL)

Stop, Look, and Listen

FRANKLIN ROOSEVELT, who often endured long receiving lines at the White House, complained that no one really paid any attention to what was said. One day, he decided to try an experiment during a reception. As each person came down the receiving line and shook his hand, he murmured, "I murdered my grandmother this morning."

The guests responded with phrases like, "Marvelous! Keep up the good work. We are proud of you. God bless you, sir."

Not until he was greeting the ambassador from Bolivia at the end of the line were Roosevelt's words were actually heard. Not quite knowing what to say, the ambassador leaned over and whispered, "I'm sure she had it coming."

Are you a good listener? Better yet, are you a good listener, hearing God speak to you?

Samuel had grown up in the tabernacle, the dwelling place of God among His people. He had been serving in the tabernacle from a very young age, but he did not yet have a personal relationship with God, until one night when he was just twelve years old and God called out to him. Initially mistaking the voice of God for that of Eli the priest, who was also Samuel's guardian, Samuel eventually responded to God's voice with a ready ear and an attentive heart. During this encounter with God, Samuel began his lifelong journey as a follower, a servant, and a prophet of God as he responded to God's call.

God wants a relationship with every person, and subsequently, as He did with Samuel, God calls out to each person in a distinct and personal way. Yet, despite the methodology by which God gets our attention, hearing God speak begins with responding to His call to salvation. If you have not yet entered into a personal relationship with God, then the first thing to do is to *stop, look* to the Bible, which is the way God speaks to us today, and *listen* to what the Bible has to say about Jesus.

The Word of God may come differently to each of us. For example, some may hear a sermon and respond to God's call. Others may respond to God's voice through a conversation with a friend or by reading a book. No matter how we hear Him speaking to us for the first time, if God truly is speaking, then He always will be directing us to belief in Jesus, "for God so loved the world that He gave His only begotten Son, that whoever believes in Him should not perish but have everlasting life" (John 3:16).

Once you respond to God's call into a personal relationship with Him, you can be certain that your communication with God has just begun. God desires to speak to you, and He desires us to speak to Him. Developing a ready ear and an attentive heart to ensure that you hear from God means that you continue to look to His Word, listen to His Spirit as He speaks to your heart ("a still small voice" as 1 Kings 19:12 says), receive godly counsel like Samuel did from Eli, and wait on God's timing for Him to bring His Word to pass.

If you are ready for God to speak to you, then begin by saying, "Speak, your servant is listening."

Then immediately an angel of the Lord struck him, because he did not give glory to God. And he was eaten by worms and died. (Acts 12:23)

MARCH
27

The Diet of Worms

PRIDE COMES BEFORE A FALL or, in at least one case, before being eaten by worms. This may even sound like the makings of a bad science fiction movie with a title like *Attack of the Killer Worms* or *War of the Worms*, where fifty-foot worms are terrorizing cities and forcing people to join renegade worm resistance movements to preserve the human race. But I assure you that what we have in Acts 12 is not science fiction, but a very real and very graphic warning concerning how we handle the glory that belongs to God.

King Herod Agrippa I is the king mentioned in this chapter, and he is the fourth Herod in a string of five family Herods that ruled in Israel from 34 BC to AD 100. While in the coastal region of Caesarea, King Agrippa determined to make a speech to the people, and with great pomp and circumstance, he arrayed himself in his royal garments and gave what must have been a rousing speech because the people all cried out, "The voice of a god and not of a man!" Hearing the great praise from the people, Herod made a fatal mistake and failed to give the glory to God. The result was a gruesome warning to all who would consider making the same mistake.

Not everyone who fails to give God the glory will be eaten by worms, but occasionally God will use drastic actions to make a drastic point so we will never forget what He is trying to teach us. In Isaiah 48:11, God makes clear that He will not share His glory or allow someone else to claim what belongs to Him. Also, in Revelation 4:11, we find these exemplary words of praise: "You are worthy, O Lord, To receive glory and honor and power; For You created all things, and by Your will they exist and were created." This is not some self-centered demand of an egotistical Creator; rather, this is the appropriate response of people who recognize the all-powerful hand and the all-loving nature of God from whom all things flow.

Consider for a moment the reaction we have when we behold beauty. Often, a welling up of praise and admiration within our being arises that cannot be contained. Take the brilliant colors of a sunset, or witnessing the miracle of a child being born. The amazement, wonder, and joy cause an involuntary response of praise for the beauty before our eyes. In the same way, when we begin to recognize that everything comes from God, that He is the giver of all life, beauty, and ability, then we should feel a similar, involuntary response to give God the praise, honor, and glory. Doing so is merely the natural response of praising the one who is worthy of praise.

When others seek to praise you for something you have done, remember that God deserves the glory for the great things He has done through you. Seek to make much of God and little of yourself, and you will be on your way to living a life that glorifies God and not one that may become the diet of worms.

"For the Lord does not see as man sees; for man looks at the outward appearance, but the Lord looks at the heart." (1 Samuel 16:7)

MARCH 28

What God Is Looking For

A MAN needs only to be tall, dark, and handsome to often win the affection and confidence of others. People's perceptions many times go no deeper than the skin. The opinion commonly formed is that a beautiful exterior in some way represents an equally beautiful interior. God, however, is looking for something deeper, and we need His help to do the same.

Israel wanted a king to rule over them so they would look like the other nations. God gave them Saul, who is described in the following way: "There was not a more handsome person than he among the children of Israel. From his shoulders upward he was taller than any of the people" (1 Samuel 9:2). The people were immediately drawn to him and rejoiced greatly over their new king, but this feeling would be short-lived. Perhaps because of his good looks and stature, Saul thought he was the best thing before sliced bread and therefore better than everybody else. But what we do know is that Saul started off okay but did not finish well, and because of his rebellious heart, God eventually rejected him, ripped the kingdom out of his hands, and gave this reward instead to a man after God's own heart.

Who would be God's chosen replacement? And how would God make His selection? Samuel the prophet was instructed to go to the house of Jesse to find the next king. The father of eight sons, Jesse paraded seven of his boys before Samuel to choose from, but shockingly everyone was passed over by the prophet. Only one more was left to be considered. Although he was not thought worthy of this informal Mr. Israel Pageant, he would be the one chosen to wear the crown. In David, the youngest and the least of the brothers, God saw something that was lacking in the others, despite their outward qualifications. God saw in David a heart devoted to Him, "for the eyes of the LORD run to and fro throughout the whole earth, to show Himself strong on behalf of those whose heart is loyal to Him" (2 Chronicles 16:9).

Danger lies in making choices based on appearances. The Bible tells us that charm is deceitful and beauty is passing (see Proverbs 31:30). But how many times are choices made solely on those types of qualities? Attractiveness is not to be looked down on, but also is not something to be highly exalted, either. Superficial choices go beyond choosing the most attractive person for the job. We can also make a choice based on other obvious talents. Perhaps someone is a great speaker, but not every great presenter is called to be a pastor. Or someone may have a high IQ, but not every genius should be an elder in a church. Any number of other talents may be obvious in people, but God is more interested in a person's character, not their capabilities. Many who are very talented trust in their talents to succeed, when God is seeking those who will rely on Him.

We should strive to be people who are cultivating a beautiful heart for God, people who base our opinions of others on character. And when we are put into a position where we are looking to hire someone, place them in ministry, make them a leader, marry them, or put trust in them of any kind, we must look at others as God would look at them. We must go beyond the charisma or wow appeal and make decisions based on godly character, demonstrated by an indwelling and inner working of God in their lives.

They received the word with all readiness, and searched the Scriptures daily to find out whether these things were so. (Acts 17:11)

MARCH
29

The Truth Test

DO YOU BELIEVE everything you hear or read? Many "Christian" doctrines out there are anything but Christian. Some pastors preach unbiblical principles and books that propagate feel-good philosophies at the expense of truth, and many people fall prey to these false teachings. How can you be sure whether what you are hearing or reading is genuine Christian truth or nothing more than a phony philosophy?

As the Apostle Paul made his way through the European continent on his second missionary journey, one noteworthy stop was in the town of Berea, which is located in northern Greece. Here, Paul encountered a group of people hungry for truth and eager to investigate what they heard. The great Apostle Paul, who wrote nearly two-thirds of the New Testament, was not offended by the Bereans' desire to check out his preaching. He was not worried they might conclude that he was a fake, and he did not care if they compared his words to the Word of God. In fact, Paul said this was a very noble characteristic for God's people. This desire to corroborate preaching with the Word of God is not only a noble characteristic, but also a *necessary* characteristic, necessary to ensure good spiritual health and well being.

Paul believed that a Christian should not believe something just because someone spoke it, taught it, or wrote about it, but that all Christians have a responsibility to open up the Scriptures and check things out for themselves. We must learn to be testers of the truth and not hearers only. Doers of the Word must be knowers of the Word. Believers must know what they believe and not simply adopt someone else's ideology. Above all, we must be willing to investigate what we hear and read, or else we can be led astray.

So how can we be like a Berean in our approach to the things we hear and read? Here are a few tips.

When you hear someone quote from the Scriptures, make sure you compare the Scriptures with the Scriptures. The Bible is the best commentary on the Bible, so make sure you can find the principle elsewhere in the Bible. Do not allow yourself or others to isolate a verse and build an entire doctrine or belief around one idea. Removing a text from its surrounding context can lead to a distorted and inaccurate interpretation of the biblical meaning.

Next, be willing to allow the Bible to shape your ideas, theology, and beliefs. When what you believe is different from what the Bible teaches, then be willing to lay down what you have come to believe and take up what God has said concerning the matter. A final test to help protect yourself and others from heresy, false teaching, and Christian over-spiritualization is to hold what you hear up to a threefold test: One, did Jesus teach it? Two, did the apostles address it? And three, did the early church practice it?

Do not be afraid to apply the truth test to everything you hear and read, and if what you learn stands up to the truth test, then receive that information with gladness.

Then David said to the Philistine, "You come to me with a sword, with a spear, and with a javelin. But I come to you in the name of the Lord of hosts, the God of the armies of Israel, whom you have defied." (1 Samuel 17:45)

MARCH
30

Vanquishing the Voldemorts

MANY FEAR-PROVOKING VILLAINS are found in movies and literature, whether the daunting Darth Vader, the herculean Terminator, the just plain creepy Hannibal Lecter, or the wicked Voldemort. These characters often embody our worst fears. But where villains lurk, often unlikely heroes, underdogs, and individuals also are found, who, against all odds, are able to overcome their fears and gain the victory. Something within us wants to root for the "little guy," enjoying watching the long shot come from behind to win the game. We love to see ordinary people overcome extraordinary odds.

Despite the feel-good factor we receive from reading these stories or watching them on the big screen, they offer us no actual help. However, one larger-than-life story has all the makings of a Hollywood blockbuster, yet is grounded in truth, and therefore, offers real help and real hope for when we are facing real giants in life.

When was the last time you came face-to-face with a nine-foot-six-inch-tall warrior? Probably never! How many of us have come face-to-face with a giant problem? Probably all of us. If you have ever said to yourself, *How am I going to get through this?* or *What am I going to do?* then you have come face-to-face with a giant of a problem.

Most people have heard the story of David and Goliath and how this "little guy" defeated a real giant, a soldier nearly twice his size, and he did so with a rock and a sling. What we can often overlook is that David's victory was not because he was a good shot or because he was very courageous, but because of his confidence. His confidence was not in himself, mind you, but in God. David knew God, and he knew that God could defeat the giant that was in front of him. Everyone else only saw the giant, and he was definitely an intimidating giant, but

David saw things differently. David saw a God who was bigger than any giant. David's faith allowed him to see the problem from God's perspective.

The battle was not finished simply because David believed that God would give him the victory. David also needed to act! Genuine faith requires action, and David picked up a few rocks and made his way toward the giant. A sling in the hand of a faithful man is mightier than a sword in the hand of a giant. Working together with David's faith was a pure motive. David's desire was for God to receive all the glory. From beginning to end, David wanted God's name to be exalted and not his own.

You can vanquish any villain and defeat any enemy that stands in opposition to God by trusting that God is bigger than any giant you face. What giant are you facing? Sin, setbacks, or selfishness? Fear, finances, or failure? Discouragement, depression, or disappointments? Faith sees that God is bigger than any giant. Faith sees what God can do. Faith seeks to give God the glory and stands on the promises of God, then steps out, knowing the victory is God's.

With a faith like David's, you can slay any giant as you see your situation from God's perspective. Nothing is too big for God to handle.

Then Paul stood in the midst of the Areopagus and said, "Men of Athens, I perceive that in all things you are very religious." (Acts 17:22)

MARCH 31

Reaching People with the Gospel

ORDINARY PEOPLE like you and me can change the world one person at a time, but we must be willing to invest the time and effort to build a bridge to the lives of those we seek to reach with the gospel.

As Christians, we have the greatest news in the entire world—scratch that—the entire universe. We know forgiveness of sins comes through Jesus Christ, and through that forgiveness, we can have a relationship with God and spend eternity in His presence. Really, news does not get any better than that. But if we fail to make a connection with the people we are speaking to, they may never receive what we have to share. I will preface all this with the fact that ultimately, whether a person will respond to the invitation to trust in Jesus Christ for their eternal salvation is all the work of the Holy Spirit. However, we have a responsibility to do all we can to present the truth clearly, in a way to which they can relate, and in a way in which they will see the need to respond. The Apostle Paul gives us a textbook example of how to relate to those we are speaking to.

Apostle Paul came to Athens about four hundred years after their Golden Era, a classical period that saw great economic and cultural growth. Athens was still a cultural center in the world during Paul's day, and many still gathered there to discuss philosophy. One day, Paul went to the center of the city and decided to join in their philosophical discussions and share about Jesus. Paul gave an incredible sermon as he used logic, philosophy, and religion to get their attention and build a bridge to his listeners that day. He used that connection to move into a discussion about the one true God.

Sometimes when we share, many will respond, sometimes only a few will respond, and at other times no one will respond. But no matter the outcome, our responsibility remains to step up and make the effort to reach people with the gospel. Whether you are speaking to a large group of people or sharing one-on-one with someone, connecting with your listener(s) is essential. Look for obvious commonalities. Maybe the surrounding location is common, a person's vocation is similar, or perhaps you share the motivation for being where you both are on that day. If you are speaking to a group, know your audience. How you speak to a group of senior citizens will be vastly different from how you speak to an auditorium filled with high school seniors. Speaking to a coworker will be different than speaking to your neighbor, and so on. But in each and every case, start with what you have in common, thereby preparing the way for them to be more receptive to what you have to share about God.

Pray for opportunities, be prepared to share when those opportunities come, be an example, and build bridges. This was so often the method of Jesus as He shared the truth in practical ways, building bridges to those He encountered on the way.

Be flexible, be available, and be bold.

April

Then Jonathan said to David, "Go in peace, since we have both sworn in the name of the Lord, saying, 'May the Lord be between you and me, and between your descendants and my descendants, forever.'" (1 Samuel 20:42)

APRIL

1

Best Friends Forever

A FRIEND has been defined as someone who walks in when the rest of the world walks out. This is especially true when you are looking for friends to help you move (I mean really, the only fun thing about moving is popping bubble wrap!). But if you have one special friend, a best friend, a friend who remains close your entire life, then consider yourself blessed.

David had such a friend in Jonathan, King Saul's son, a friend who was there for him when everyone else was walking out on him. In their friendship with each other, we can learn a few lessons about how to have lasting friendships.

David was God's chosen man to replace Saul as King, and Saul was becoming more and more aware that he was reigning on borrowed time. His jealousy was getting the better of him, and instead of repenting before God for his sinfulness and rejoicing in a right relationship with Him, Saul sought to add to his sins by repeatedly trying to kill David. Here, among the hatred and rage of Saul, we see a beautiful picture of unconditional love in the friendship between Jonathan and David. If ever David needed a friend, he needed one during this troublesome time in his life.

Jonathan was the king's son and the rightful heir to the throne, yet Jonathan knew that God had chosen David to become the next king of Israel. We see that, instead of jealousy on Jonathan's part, he was committed to God's plan for David and sought David's best, even if that meant he would take second place. One of the hardest things to do is to rejoice in other people's successes, especially if you are not experiencing similar success. But a true friend is able to genuinely share in the joys of his or her friends, making sure the friendship is free from envy, jealousy, competition, and covetousness. Jonathan also purposed to protect David when he was being unjustly persecuted, even when such a stand placed him in the line of fire, literally. Saul threw a spear at his own son because Jonathan was looking out for David's best interest. Jonathan's friendship with David was sincere, selfless, and sacrificial. One of the greatest demonstrations of Jonathan's friendship was when he went to David and "strengthened his hand in God" (1 Samuel 23:16). Godly encouragement is one of the greatest gifts you can give to a friend.

Having a close friend who will faithfully stand with you in good times and in bad is a true gift. Being a true friend to someone means that you are there when they need you, no questions, and no judgments, just there. Maybe you have a friend like Jonathan. If so, you are blessed.

But maybe you do not have such a friend. Perhaps the place to start is not by seeking a best friend, but by seeing how you can be a friend like Jonathan to others. Be kind, be there, be honest, be genuine, be an encouragement, be loyal, be forgiving, be selfless, and be available, and you will find yourself being someone's Jonathan. And do not be surprised if you become best friends forever.

In a window sat a certain young man named Eutychus, who was sinking into a deep sleep. He was overcome by sleep; and as Paul continued speaking, he fell down from the third story and was taken up dead. (Acts 20:9)

APRIL

2

How to Be a Good Listener

MANY HOLD THE BELIEF that "the mind can only absorb what the seat can endure." We have all seen those people in church (or perhaps we have been one of them, even) whose eyes are getting heavier and heavier, whose bodies are starting to slump forward, and before long, they are out: sound asleep in church. Once they fall asleep, maybe you keep watching them, as I do, to see if they will do the head-bob or maybe even snort themselves awake. Then comes my favorite: the full-body sleep-jerk.

If we were honest with ourselves, we all would admit that we have struggled at one time or another to stay awake in church, sometimes through no fault of our own. Maybe we were sick, on medication, overworked, up all night with a newborn, or simply unable to get a good night's sleep. But how would you like your name to be in the Bible for falling asleep in church? Eutychus will be forever immortalized as the guy who fell asleep while listening to the Apostle Paul in church.

As the first-century believers began meeting on Sundays, the first day of the week, we have a glimpse into what church looked like for these Christians. One of the most important aspects of their gatherings was the teaching of God's Word. On this particular evening, Paul had been teaching for several hours and showed no signs of slowing down, which leads me to a quick aside. The early Christians' hunger for teaching should certainly make us reevaluate our ability and willingness to sit and listen to a forty-five-minute sermon without looking at our watches. Nonetheless, for Eutychus, as the hour was nearing midnight, the room was stuffy and filled with people, and the flickering candlelight was just enough to cause him to doze off. Unfortunately for him, this little catnap would kill him as he fell from a third-story window. Thankfully, that is not the end of his story. The group rushed out to find his lifeless body, but Paul came over, and by the power of God, he brought Eutychus back to life. I would bet that Eutychus never fell asleep in church again!

Now, you may have never closed your eyes and drifted off into the land of sugarplum fairies and gingerbread houses during a church service, but are you really listening in church? Lack of attention can certainly lead you to drift off, even if you do not drift off to sleep. You may be sitting there physically, but are you there spiritually? When you go to church, you want to make sure that you are listening with the intent to grow spiritually and not thinking about what is for lunch or stressing out about all the things you need to get done before the weekend is over. How you listen to the Word of God is a reflection of your view of God.

Help yourself be a good listener by bringing your Bible and following along during the sermon. Take notes, as this is good for future reference and will help keep you focused. Give visual encouragement to your speaker by making eye contact and nodding in agreement. Remove distractions like your cell phone or iPad, and above all, remember God wants to speak to you.

No matter who is delivering the sermon, ultimately God is trying to speak to you through the teaching of His Word. And *He* definitely deserves *all* your attention.

Now David was greatly distressed. . . . But David strengthened himself in the Lord his God. (1 Samuel 30:6)

APRIL

3

Going from Bad to Worse

WHEN LIFE GIVES YOU LEMONS, are you the type to try and make lemonade? The down side to that is that sometimes while you are trying to make lemonade, things do not always go as planned, like when the lemon squirts in your eyes and then drips onto the only finger that has a paper cut. What about when the storm clouds are threatening? Do you look for the silver lining, only to get struck by lightning? Sometimes looking on the bright side is not so easy. Sometimes things go from bad to worse, and finding the silver lining is like finding a needle in a haystack by stepping on the sharp end. What should you do when things go from bad to worse in your life?

David found himself in a real mess. While he and his men were away from home, their enemies, the Amalekites, raided Ziklag, the town where David and his men were living. The Amalekites burned the town to the ground and took the women and children captive. When the men returned, they were beside themselves with grief, having lost everything. They cried until they were completely emptied of tears. David, who shared in their loss and pain, had an added hurt to deal with as his men turned on him, blaming him for this tragedy. In their grief, they spoke of stoning David. Overwhelmed by trouble, emotionally bankrupt, physically exhausted, depressed, stressed, and fearing for his life, David saw things go from bad to worse.

When things go from bad to worse in our lives, we can either allow despair to overcome us, or we can determine to overcome obstacles God's way. Notice what David did: he strengthened himself in the Lord (see 1 Samuel 30:6). Practically, this means to start by taking your eyes off your trouble and putting them on God. Now you may think, *I cannot actually see God, so how do I "put my eyes on God"?* Putting your eyes on God means looking to the only place where you can see God, which is the Bible. As the psalmist wrote, "My soul melts from heaviness; Strengthen me according to Your word" (Psalm 119:28).

David continued to strengthen himself in the Lord by talking with Him. Our relationship with the Lord is a two-way street. He speaks to us through the Bible, and we speak to Him through prayer. Prayer is essential if we want to climb out of those periods of despair. Prayer involves praising God for who He is, thanking

God for all He has done and has yet to do, and confessing our sins to Him. Prayer also involves accepting His forgiveness, and asking God for those things that are in accordance with His will, and resting in *His* will to be done and not *our* will. Prayer involves waiting as well. God rarely answers prayers immediately, so be patient and learn to wait. "Wait on the LORD; Be of good courage, And He shall strengthen your heart" (Psalm 27:14).

David next responded to what God told him to do. Through David's obedience to the Word of God, he put distance between himself and his despair. The fastest way to weakness in the Lord is through disobedience. Conversely, as you are obedient to God's Word, you will build up your strength in the Lord.

Sometimes in life, things go from bad to worse. Do not wait for someone to come along to help you out of your situation, because you may be waiting a long time. Turn to the Lord, strengthen yourself in Him, and walk through the valley of despair to His fields of strength.

For the wrath of God is revealed from heaven against all ungodliness and unrighteousness of men, who suppress the truth in unrighteousness. (Romans 1:18)

APRIL

4

Warning: The Wrath of God Ahead!

SOME THINGS just make us feel warm and fuzzy inside, like sitting by a fire in the middle of winter with a cup of hot chocolate, playing with puppies, or hearing a child say "mommy" or "daddy" for the first time.

The wrath of God does not usually fall into the category of things that give us the warm fuzzies. The whole subject of God's wrath is usually avoided by most and certainly is not a subject that will help you to win friends and influence people. But to fully understand the grace of God, we must endeavor to understand the wrath of God. To know how good salvation is, we must know how bad our sin is in the eyes of God.

First, we must understand that the wrath of God is *not* like human anger. Mankind's anger is most often sinful, although not sinning when angry is possible (This is usually the exception, not the rule). Our anger is often irrational, unreasonable, and rooted in selfishness. The wrath of God is nothing like that. God does not have uncontrollable outbursts, His wrath is not emotionally based, and not vindictive. Rather, God's wrath is an execution of judgment against ungodliness, and a total intolerance of iniquity. God is holy, and therefore, He must reject everything that is unholy. Because God is good, He must reject that which is evil.

Next, God made His wrath obvious to mankind from the beginning, starting when His wrath brought death into the world as a punishment for Adam's sin in the Garden of Eden. Also, God's wrath is seen through the great flood that came upon the earth, and we can see His wrath in the destruction of Sodom and Gomorrah. Also, in many other places throughout the Bible, God has shown His wrath against ungodliness.

God has continually shown humanity the seriousness of sin by carrying out His wrath, and mankind's response generally has been to reject God's warnings.

Nowhere is this more evident than through the greatest outpouring of wrath, which was also the greatest demonstration of love: Jesus dying on the Cross for our sins. He took the full force of God's punishment, a punishment that we all deserved. Mankind's predictable response has been mostly denial, suppression, and rejection of the truth. One reason humanity chooses to deny and suppress the truth of God's wrath is to avoid the fact that God judges ungodliness and sin. We reject the truth that mankind is held responsible for his or her actions, and that sinful actions have consequences.

Although understanding the wrath of God may not normally give you the warm fuzzies, but the result of his wrath should, if seen this way: through the wrath poured out on Jesus, all who believe in Him can be spared from God's wrath. Our understanding of God's wrath should cause us to have the same hatred for sin and motivate us to live a life of obedience to God. Our understanding of the nature of God's wrath also will give us a burden and a desire to share how others can experience the grace of God and be forever spared from facing His wrath. Do not forsake understanding the issue of God's wrath, because a shallow view of God will lead to shallow Christianity.

The deeper we are willing to dive into the truths found in His Word, the closer we will walk with Him.

So they set the ark of God on a new cart. (2 Samuel 6:3)

Do the Ends Justify the Means?

APRIL

5

IF YOU COULD SAVE THE WORLD by killing one person, would you? Would you lie to spare someone's feelings? What about a little white lie to get a job or holding back important information in order to close a deal? In other words, is doing something unethical, illegal, or immoral ever acceptable, even if you do so for a "good" outcome? If you answer yes to these questions, then you must consider where you draw the line. If you are making your decision from an ethical standpoint, you may weigh the "good" end against the "bad" means, and if the good end is greater than the bad action, then you might say that yes, the ends justify the means.

What about when you are carrying out the will of God? Does God care how you get the job done or just that you do the job to completion? King David found out firsthand about God's opinion on the subject of *how* we do and *what* we do for God.

David was now the king over all Israel, and as he began ruling from Jerusalem, he had a desire to bring the sacred Ark of the Covenant back to the Holy City. David decided that for such a special project, he would bring out the big guns, pull out all the stops, and spare no expense. He gathered thirty thousand of the best men of Israel for an unforgettable parade, he placed the Ark on a brand-new cart, he had Uzzah (whose name means strong) drive the cart, and he had Ahio (whose name means brotherly) go out in front of the cart to prepare the way.

What a scene unfolded: a sea of people following this shiny new cart being driven by a muscleman, with the welcoming guy out front, shaking hands and working the crowd. All the while, the royal marching band was playing music. Now that is a parade! But this display has one big problem. God had given specific instructions back in the Book of Numbers on how to transport the Ark (see Numbers 7:1–10), and this was not the way. But did that really matter to God? I mean, David was doing a "good" deed by bringing the Ark back to Jerusalem after all. Did the specifics of the Ark's transfer really matter? Let us continue.

Suddenly everything changed. As the caravan was moving the Ark, the cart hit a bump and Uzzah reached back to grab hold of the Ark to prevent damage from falling. But Mr. Muscles was instantly struck dead by God for violating the Law concerning the Ark (see Numbers 4:15). David immediately stopped the parade, went back to Jerusalem, and searched God's Word to find out what went wrong and to see what God said about *how* to move the Ark, something he should have done from the beginning. Apparently, logistics on how David accomplished God's will did matter to God after all.

The first step in accomplishing God's will is to find out whether God has said something in the Bible about what we are planning to do. If God gives us clear instructions, then our answer is simple. Follow what the Bible says, and if there is an absence of direction from the Bible, then carry out the task in a way that best honors God and does not violate other biblical truths.

When making a decision about whether or not the ends justify the means, we must first realize that this is not an ethical question; this is a biblical question. Therefore, look to the Bible to discover how to do God's will God's way, because God cares about how we do what we do.

For he is not a Jew who is one outwardly, nor is circumcision that which is outward in the flesh; but he is a Jew who is one inwardly; and circumcision is that of the heart, in the Spirit, not in the letter; whose praise is not from men but from God. (Romans 2:28–29)

APRIL 6

Losing Your Religion

THE NINETEENTH-CENTURY Danish theologian Soren Kierkegaard said there were two kinds of religion: Religion A and Religion B. Religion A, he said, is faith in the name of religion only. Those in this group will act as though they are religious, but they will reject the power that could make them godly. They will be involved in attending church without genuine faith in the living God. Religion B, on the other hand, is a life-transforming, destiny-changing experience. Religion B followers have a definite commitment to the crucified and risen Savior, which establishes an ongoing personal relationship between a forgiven sinner and a gracious God.[15]

So, what does *God* have to say about religion? Is God looking for more "religious" people? Is being "religious" and not getting into heaven possible?

In Paul's day, the most religious people were the Jews. They had been blessed by God in many ways. They were the chosen people through whom the Messiah would come, and they had been given the Word of God. The name

"Jew" meant "God be praised." The Jews had been protected by God, provided for by God, delivered by God, and directed by God. The Jews were dedicated to living a very religious life and therefore believed everything was okay in their relationship with God. But the Apostle Paul challenged their view of religion and showed them that religious activity does not mean a right relationship with God.

Paul confronted the religious person who thought that ritual brought redemption. He challenged the one dedicated to works but devoid of worship, and he rebuked those who performed sacraments yet failed to live surrendered to the Word of God. Paul, like Jesus, was saying, "Your heritage doesn't save you, sacraments don't save you, service doesn't save you, knowledge doesn't save you, and for the Jew, not even circumcision saves you." These are all outward acts, and although they are not wrong, they are not what bring salvation. In other words, being religious does not mean that you will go to heaven.

The principle is the same today. Whatever you call yourself—Baptist, Methodist, Presbyterian, Catholic, or non-denominational—does not matter. Whether you grew up in a Christian home, were baptized, took communion, went to confirmation, or were christened as a baby, does not matter. Religious activity, and even religious profession without transformation, is empty religion. We must be careful not to fall into the trap of thinking, *Because I go to church, I am okay,* or *Because I have done this religious service or that ritual, I am going to heaven.* Salvation is by faith in Jesus Christ alone and not because we act religious. We must not think that godly rituals without a personal relationship with God in Christ will do us any good.

Do not simply go through the religious motions. Lose your religion and gain a relationship with Jesus that changes you from the inside out, because you never will be changed from outside in.

"I've sinned against God." (2 Samuel 12:13 MSG)

Coming to Your Senses

APRIL 7

HAVE YET TO SEE a song called "Repentance" make the top of the Billboard charts. As a matter of fact, you will not even hear too many songs about repentance sung in church, and unfortunately, you will not hear too many sermons preached on the subject of repentance, either. The whole subject of repentance simply makes people fidget in their seats and causes them to avoid making eye contact with the pastor who delivers such a message. None of which has been helped by the movies, which portray sweaty preachers pounding pulpits and shouting, "Repent or perish!" This behavior does not exactly engender someone to the subject of repentance. Add to this our natural tendency to resist repentance, trying to sweep the subject under the proverbial carpet in an attempt to move on with life, hoping that we never have to deal with the issue again.

Even King David, the man after God's own heart, tried to avoid the subject of repentance at one point in his life. If I were to ask you to complete the phrase "David and . . ." you might finish with *Goliath,* or you might choose *Bathsheba.*

If David's greatest victory was when he killed Goliath, then David's greatest failure was his sin with Bathsheba, which nearly killed him. Of course, David's adultery with Bathsheba was not the end of his sin cycle; David resorted to deception and even murder in an attempt to cover up his sinful actions. David then spent a year in denial as his heart grew callous and his conscience became seared, while his unrepentant sin began to ruin his life.

The inevitable course of unrepentant sin is to harden the heart and numb the mind of all who refuse to repent swiftly and completely. Sooner or later, God will work to disrupt His complacent child. God will use a variety of circumstances to unsettle the complacency that is taking root in the heart, and He will use those circumstances to bring conviction of sin, which will lead the child of God to repentance.

For David, God sent Nathan the prophet to disrupt his complacent heart, confront him, and allow the Spirit of God to convict him of his guilt. When David finally saw the darkness that had grown in his own heart, he was quick to turn from the darkness, which is the very essence of repentance: turning and going in the opposite direction, away from sin. Out of David's repentant heart came the greatest song of repentance, Psalm 51. In this Psalm, we hear the cry of a repentant heart that says, "I have sinned," "I have done evil in your sight," "cleanse me," "create in me a clean heart," and "restore to me the joy of my salvation."

Although few songs have been written on the subject of repentance, David's song gives us a good picture of genuine repentance. Repentance is not just a mere change of your *mind* about sin; it is a change in your *heart* about sin. That change will demonstrate itself in changed behavior as conviction about sin leads to confession of sin before God and results in walking away from sin.

The next time you sin and fall short of God's standards, be quick to come to your senses and repent.

For all have sinned and fall short of the glory of God.
(Romans 3:23)

APRIL 8

Houston, We Have a Problem!

YOU HAVE A PROBLEM! A *big* problem! You are not alone, though. I have the same problem, and for that matter, every other human being shares this problem. The problem is sin. Sin means to miss the mark, to stumble, to wander from the path of God's righteousness, to do wrong, or to violate God's law. Sin is any thought, word, or action that falls short of God's standard of living. As sin entered the world through Adam, so we enter this world as sinners by nature because of our identification with Adam's original sin. But we are also sinners by choice because of our own actions.

Because of sin, a great divide exists between God and mankind. Our problem is made worse by the fact that God only will accept total righteousness from mankind, yet because of sin, humanity is totally unrighteous. God is also just, and because of His just nature, He cannot excuse sin. He cannot look the other way or simply pretend that everything is okay. Without the right solution, we have no chance to get to heaven. (I told you we have a *big* problem!)

So how do we fix such a *big* problem? We cannot. God does. In the book of Romans, the Apostle Paul builds his case and demonstrates that no one can measure up to God's standard. No one is good enough. No one is religious enough. No one seeks God. Therefore, no one can have a right relationship with God on his or her own. That is the bad news. Now, the good news.

Humanity's problem is sin, and God's solution is grace. There is no more magnificent word than *grace*, and grace shines brightest against the backdrop of mankind's sinfulness. Grace means unmerited favor or kindness shown to one who is totally undeserving of such kindness. God's greatest demonstration of grace comes to mankind in the form of the forgiveness of sin through faith in Jesus Christ.

Paul declares that by God's grace through faith in Jesus, we can be justified. The simplest way to think about the process of justification is to look at the word this way: when a person is justified by faith in Jesus, he or she can say, "It is *just-as-if-I'd* never sinned." Justified! The reason God sees us as justified is because Jesus never sinned. He was holy and divine, and when we place our trust in Him for our salvation, God makes a divine transfer and now sees us through the sinlessness of Christ. Just as sin identifies us with Adam, faith identifies us with the righteousness of Jesus.

Sin is a *big* problem, and there is nothing you can do on your own to fix it, period. No amount of good works will reverse the judgment against sin, and no amount of religion will set you free from sin's penalty. But God, who is full of grace, has solved humanity's biggest problem:

> God sacrificed Jesus on the altar of the world to clear that world of sin. Having faith in him sets us in the clear. God decided on this course of action in full view of the public—to set the world in the clear with himself through the sacrifice of Jesus, finally taking care of the sins he had so patiently endured. (Romans 3:25 MSG)

Problem solved!

"The Lord is my rock, my fortress and my deliverer." (2 Samuel 22:2 NIV)

A Rock Song

APRIL
9

WE ARE WEAKER than we are willing to admit, and God is stronger than we are able to comprehend! We are easily moved, yet God is immovable. We are unsteady, yet God is unshakable. Do you currently feel as though your life is on shaky ground? Do you feel like your strength is nearly gone and you are on the brink of giving up? Then today is a perfect day to remember that God is your rock, your refuge, and your strength.

Music often grabs our attention, captures our emotions, and inspires our imaginations, and in the Bible, no one enjoyed music more than King David. Music was the instrument of expression for this man after God's own heart. He wrote countless songs that trumpeted the heights of his love for God, and he also sang psalms that sounded the depths of his soul's despair. His words resonate deeply with us today because an emotional and spiritual harmony is shared through our mutual struggles, fears, and joys.

Here in 2 Samuel 22 (and in Psalm 18), David wrote a "rock" song of thanksgiving that summed up his life and relationship with God. David praised God for who He is. David recognized and lifted his voice to God his rock, his fortress, and his deliverer. David was well acquainted with anxiety and often found himself on shaky ground, but God had been a stronghold for David, and when David cried out to God in his times of distress, God delivered him. After David was delivered from the hand of Saul and all the enemies of Israel, he sang this song of praise to God for His deliverance.

God was a refuge for David, and He is a refuge for His people today. He is a shelter, a stronghold, and a safe place to run to for all who trust in Him. He is a firm foundation upon which we can stand and upon whom we can build our lives. As much as we need to recognize these truths, we must also go beyond the mere realization that God is all these things and more to His people. We must also personalize these truths. Ask yourself this: Is God *my* rock? Is God *my* fortress? Is God *my* deliverer?

The best way to move from the realization that these things are true to the personalization that they are true for *you*, is to consider the words of Jesus: "Anyone who listens to my teaching and follows it is wise, like a person who builds a house on solid rock" (Matthew 7:24 NLT). When your life is built on Jesus, you can trust Him to be a rock in shaky times, a fortress in hard times, and a deliverer in fearful times. Build your life on the solid rock of Jesus, because there is no rock like our rock, and there is no God like our God!

We have peace with God through our Lord Jesus Christ.
(Romans 5:1)

APRIL
10

War and Peace

ON MARCH 10, 1974, Second Lieutenant Hiroo Onoda finally surrendered, not from the Vietnam War, but from World War II. He had been left on a Philippine island in December, 1944, with the command to "carry on the mission, even if Japan surrenders." And that is exactly what he did. All efforts to convince him to surrender failed. He ignored messages from loudspeakers announcing Japan's surrender and that Japan was now an ally of the United States. Leaflets begging him to surrender were dropped, but he refused to believe that the war was over. He lived off the land and raided the fields and gardens of local citizens, and he was responsible for killing some thirty individuals during his almost thirty-year personal war. Thirteen thousand men and almost $500,000 were used to try and locate the army officer and convince him to surrender. Finally, in 1974, Onoda handed over his sword; his war was over.

What a tragedy to spend so many years fighting in a war that had long since been over. The Apostle Paul writes much on the subject of peace throughout the New Testament, but here we discover that the war with God is over and peace with God begins. Our souls were created *by* God and exist *for* God, and therefore, our souls are never at peace until they rest *in* God. The only way to have rest in God is through the peace that God offers, and that comes by faith in Jesus Christ. Jesus Christ is the peace treaty between God and humanity, and the terms are complete faith and total surrender to the lordship of Jesus Christ.

What a tragedy to choose to fight with God when He has made a way for peace! Yet still, some refuse to believe that peace has been made between God and mankind. James reminds us, "Whoever therefore wants to be a friend of the world makes himself an enemy of God" (4:4). We have been at war with God because of our sin, but day and night God seeks to convince us that the war is over for all who will believe in Jesus by faith. Because of the grace of God, we are now able to experience peace with God. This is no small matter that Paul is addressing because without peace with God, there is no way to please God. Without peace *with* God, there is no enjoying the peace *of* God. We will consider the peace of God in the future, but for now, the peace of God is the ability to go through the cares and concerns we face in this life with the calm assurance of His presence and power.

Through peace *with* God, we gain access *to* God. Prior to this, His presence was limited and temporary, but now, through peace with God, His presence is perpetual and permanent among His people by His Spirit. Through peace with God, we have the glorious hope of heaven and a promised inheritance that awaits us. Through peace with God, we allow God to work in us to conform our character into the holy character of Christ.

Apart from peace with God, we cannot enjoy these and many other spiritual blessings that God offers us. God is desperately calling out to all to lay down their arms, to surrender their swords, and to enjoy the peace that He offers. Apart from Christ, no end to the war between God and mankind is in sight. But by God's grace, we can move from combat to comfort, from battle to blessing, and from war to peace. If we will surrender our will to His and believe, then our war is over.

God said, "Ask! What shall I give you?" (1 Kings 3:5)

Got Wisdom?

APRIL
11

IF GOD CAME TO YOU and said that He would grant you one wish, what would you ask for? Would you ask for all the wealth in the world? Would you want to be the most powerful or the most famous person in the world? Maybe you would ask for a long life, or maybe you would try and beat the system by asking for more wishes. But seriously, if you could have anything in the world, what would you want? With an open-ended offer like that, many of us would be quick to consider wishes like health, happiness, money, or influence. But what about asking for wisdom? Now be honest. Did that thought even cross your mind? Well, the wish for wisdom certainly did come to the mind of King Solomon.

Solomon was new to the throne, a young man around the age of nineteen. The boy king took over as king of Israel after his father, David. As you can imagine, expectations were high for the new king, and Solomon was feeling a little overwhelmed, underqualified, and inexperienced for the work of

God. Such a feeling is certainly understandable! Perhaps God has given you a job, position, or responsibility that you feel overwhelmed, underqualified, and inexperienced to carry out. Notice what happened next. After Solomon worshiped the Lord, God came to him and basically said, "Make a wish." Solomon, recognizing the awesomeness of serving God and the immense responsibility of leading God's people, asked for the only thing that could offer him any real help in his situation and the only thing that is of value: wisdom from God.

Now, "wisdom is the power to see and the inclination to choose the best and highest goal, together with the surest means of attaining it."[16] There is a difference between knowledge and wisdom. Knowledge is information; wisdom is application. Knowledge is theoretical; wisdom is practical. Wisdom is using knowledge to do the right thing at the right time, and applying truth to everyday life. Solomon asked for wisdom, and God gave him wisdom.

Before you say, "Lucky Solomon! But that will never happen to me, so what is the point?" consider this. God is not a genie in a bottle who is just waiting to grant wishes to people. God will probably not appear to you and say, "Make a wish." But God does offer wisdom to those who wish for it.

How can we get godly wisdom? First, if we want to get wisdom, we must ask God. In other words, we must spend time praying for wisdom: "If any of you lacks wisdom, let him ask of God, who gives to all liberally and without reproach, and it will be given to him" (James 1:5). Charles Spurgeon said:

> There is no "if" in the matter, for I am sure I lack it [wisdom]. What do I know? How can I guide my own way? How can I direct others? Lord, I am a mass of folly, and wisdom I have none.
>
> Thou sayest, "Let him ask of God." Lord, I now ask. Here at Thy footstool I ask to be furnished with heavenly wisdom for this day's perplexities, ay, and for this day's simplicities; for I know I may do very stupid things, even in plain matters. . . .
>
> I thank Thee that all I have to do is to ask.[17]

Second, we must have a desire to acquire godly wisdom for the glory of God. God cares about our motives, and if we come to Him with impure or selfish motives, then we should not expect to get what we asked for.

Finally, we must spend time reading the Bible. The Bible is the greatest source of godly wisdom available. The more time you spend in reading the Bible, the wiser you will be.

Since we have died to sin, how can we continue to live in it?
(Romans 6:2 NLT)

Decisions, Decisions

APRIL
12

ON AVERAGE we make 35,000 decisions a day, decisions that can include whether to wake up or hit the snooze button, whether today is going to be a regular or decaf day, whether to exercise or not, and whether to update our Facebook status or actually disconnect from all social media for five minutes. Then those bigger decisions loom, such as whom to marry, what college to go to, and what job to take. At times, your very life may hang in the balance of your decision, and the choice you make could be the difference between life and death.

Of course, no greater decision exists than whether you will choose to trust in Jesus Christ for your eternal salvation. But before you think this is where your spiritual decisions end, here is one more thing to consider. The Apostle Paul makes clear that the daily decisions we make will determine the type of Christians we will be.

Some of the Christians in first-century Rome were trampling on God's grace. They were assuming that the more a person sinned, the more grace that person could enjoy because God was so gracious to forgive all their sins. This is an incorrect way of thinking and might be voiced today in this way: "Well, I am saved, so I can do whatever I want because God will forgive me," "I am going to heaven, so it does not matter how I live on earth," and even "Live it up today and let God forgive me tomorrow."

The response to such manipulative Christian thinking is that although God is abundant in grace and willing to forgive any and all sins, this is not permission to choose to continue sinning. The forgiveness of God is not a blank check that gives us permission to abuse the grace of God. Once we become Christians, we do not become sinless, but we should be choosing to sin less. As Christians, we are no longer to be controlled by sin, and we are no longer to habitually practice sin. God's grace does not free a person *to* sin, but God's grace should free a person *from* sin.

If you make the choice to follow Christ, then you must have a life that consistently chooses not to sin. What about Christians who continue to routinely practice sin? They are not hard to find. All we have to do is look, and we will see people who say they believe in Christ, yet make no change in their lives, and show no sign that sin is shrinking in their lives. The answer is, they are not Christians. You cannot choose Christ and continue to choose sin. Sin must be decreasing in your life, and Christlikeness must be increasing.

If any doubt remains in your mind as to what the right decision is, then let me appeal to your rationale for a moment. Usually, when a decision needs to be made, we consider the pros and cons, and this is exactly what Paul does in Romans chapter 6. He says that choosing sin will lead to enslavement (verses 16–17), lead to lawlessness (verse 19), cause shame (verse 21), and end in death (verse 23). On the other hand, choosing *not to* live in sin leads to righteousness (verse 16), freedom (verse 18), holiness (verse 19), and eternal life (verse 22). Given this information, the decision does not seem like much of a choice if you ask me.

Do not choose to live in habitual sin any longer. Break free and make the smart decision today to stop sinning and walk in the freedom and fullness of God grace.

For it was so, when Solomon was old, that his wives turned his heart after other gods; and his heart was not loyal to the Lord his God. (1 Kings 11:4)

APRIL

13

The Destructive Power of Ungodly Influences

WHO DO YOU SPEND TIME WITH? What do you like to do in your spare time? Who has had the greatest impact on your life? Who do you go to when you need advice? What do all these questions have in common? The answer is influence. A simple definition of influence is the power to affect. Whether you are consciously aware of this or not, the people you surround yourself with, the activities that you are interested in, and what you watch and listen to all have an influence on you. Influence can be either positive or negative. Unfortunately for King Solomon, he found out the hard way the damage that can be caused by allowing the wrong things to have an influence in your life.

Watching an athlete fall in the Olympics, get injured in the first quarter of the Super Bowl, or have to sit on the bench during the World Series is so heartbreaking; we think of such an occurrence as such a waste of ability and potential. When we look at Solomon, we feel the same kind of heartbreak. Solomon had all the ingredients necessary for a long and successful reign as king, but in the end, he traded in the wisdom of God for the foolishness of the world. What a waste of ability and potential! Solomon's failure and fall can be attributed to the negative influence he allowed his wives to have on him. First of all, God warned Solomon as a king not to multiply his wives, yet Solomon did anyway. The result was Solomon was poisoned by his passions. His lust for women opened the door for their idolatrous worship to take root in his heart. No doubt the turning of Solomon's heart away from God was a slow and steady change, which made the transition all the more dangerous. This kind of change can go unnoticed in our lives if we do not take precautions to prevent such a disastrous end.

First Corinthians 15:33 says, "Do not be deceived: 'Evil company corrupts good habits.' " We could simplify this way: "Evil corrupts good" or "The ungodly corrupt the godly."

Let us get personal and practical for a moment. If you are spending more time with non-Christians than Christians, if you are devoting more time to certain activities, interests, hobbies, movies, or music than to godly pursuits, then be warned: you are in danger of having your heart turned away from God. Do not mistake this principle. This does not mean that you cannot have non-Christian friends. You should! We are called to be salt and light in this world, and that can only happen as you spend time in the world with people who basically live for this world.

Of course, we can still enjoy sports or other spiritually neutral interests from time to time, but these things are not to be our priority. This means that if you are spending more time with those activities than with God, then something needs to change.

Also, a brief word about marriage: take a lesson from Solomon and marry someone who worships God. You put yourself in a compromising position when you allow the person closest to you, the person who has the most influence on you, to be someone who does not share your core beliefs.

Who we spend our time with and what we spend our time doing will determine the direction our lives will go. Stay focused on God and allow Him to have the most influence on your life.

Therefore, there is now no condemnation for those who are in Christ Jesus. (Romans 8:1 NIV)

The Mountaintop View

APRIL 14

HIKING UP A MOUNTAIN takes determination as you fight the steep inclines, struggle to keep your footing, and battle the various weather conditions, but there comes that moment when all the hard work pays off and you are standing on the summit. The very first thing that grabs your attention is the amazing view! From your new vantage point, you can see miles and miles in either direction as you scan the horizon.

What if we had a spiritual vantage point that would allow us to see the plans and purposes of God for miles and miles in either direction? Romans 8 gives us a glimpse of that mountaintop view.

You would be hard-pressed to find another chapter in the entire Bible that leads you from the depths of the flesh to the summit of the Spirit, from the basin of bondage to heights of freedom, from the valley of death to the peak of eternal life. As Charles G. Trumbull said:

> Beginning with "no condemnation," ending with "no separation," and in between, "no defeat." This wondrous chapter sets forth the gospel and plan of salvation;. . . the hopelessness of the natural man and the righteousness of the born again; the indwelling of Christ and the Holy Spirit; the resurrection of the body and blessed hope of Christ's return; the working together of all things for our good; every tense of the Christian life, past, present, and future; and the glorious climactic song of triumph, no separation in time or eternity, "from the love of God which is in Jesus Christ our Lord."[18]

Standing on the mountaintop, you can see in the distance the Roman Road that brought you to the peak—a road that brought you through the wrath of God (Romans 1:18), the depravity of man (Romans 1:24–32), the weakness of works (Romans 2), the righteousness of God (Romans 4), justification by faith (Romans 5:1), the gift of grace (Romans 5:15), the process of sanctification (Romans 6), the struggle with sin (Romans 7), and freedom in Christ (Romans 8).

With a bold declarative statement, chapter 8 begins, "There is . . . now no condemnation for those who are in Christ Jesus." We have been freed from the penalty of sin, from the bondage of sin, and from the oppression of the flesh. And because of what Jesus Christ has done for us, we are able to stand on the mountaintop. We must remember that verse 1 does not say there are "no mistakes," "no failures," or even "no sins" for those who are in Christ; rather, the verse says there is no condemnation! Do not mistake no condemnation for no discipline, no correction, no rebuke, or even no suffering. No condemnation means positionally, before God, we have been set free in Christ, free to become all that God wants us to be, free to achieve all that God wants us to achieve, and free to enjoy all that God wants us to enjoy.

The view from the mountaintop shows us that the Christian is completely victorious. We are free from judgment because Christ died for us, we are free from defeat because Christ lives in us, and we are free from discouragement because Christ is coming for us. So the next time you are walking through the valley, remember your mountaintop view.

> And behold, the Lord passed by, and a great and strong wind tore into the mountains and broke the rocks in pieces before the Lord, but the Lord was not in the wind; and after the wind an earthquake, but the Lord was not in the earthquake; and after the earthquake a fire, but the Lord was not in the fire; and after the fire a still small voice. (1 Kings 19:11–12)

APRIL
15

God's Way or the Highway

WHAT A TREMENDOUS HIGH POINT for the prophet Elijah! He had just seen a wonderful and glorious display of God's power on Mount Carmel as the false gods of Baal were utterly defeated and the pagan priests who promoted idolatrous worship were killed. No doubt Elijah must have been thinking that this was only the beginning of some big changes and that the evil King and Queen of Israel, Ahab and Jezebel, would repent of their wickedness, leading to a great revival in all the land. But no such happy ending was in store for Elijah, and when the opposite became apparent to him and the queen put him at the top of Israel's most wanted list, Elijah decided the best thing to do was to run for the hills.

When Elijah saw that God was not going to work the way he wanted Him to, Elijah became discouraged and fearful. Elijah thought that God should do things his way. After all, he believed this was a great opportunity for God after such a dynamic display of absolute authority. God should have definitely capitalized on this, Elijah thought, kept the momentum going, and continued to work in big ways. Have you ever thought God should do things a certain way, only to watch Him work in a different way altogether? When God did not work the way you thought He should, did you respond like Elijah and allow yourself to become discouraged and fearful?

Elijah's place, is not to dictate to God the means and the methods by which He should work, nor is such dictation our place. While Elijah was having a pity party for himself, God reached out to the prophet and brought a strong wind, an earthquake, and a fire before Elijah, but God was not to be found in them. Instead, God chose to speak to Elijah by way of a still, small voice. God demonstrated to Elijah through the wind, earthquake, and fire that no lack of power or resources were at His disposal and He will use the big guns at times in order to accomplish His plans, as Elijah recently saw on Mt. Carmel. But this was not one of those times. This was a time for God to use stillness and quiet to speak His word into the heart of His chosen prophet.

Elijah needed to realize that God's ways were not his ways. At the root of Elijah's discouragement and fear were his misconceptions about the ways in which God works. God may use the big guns—the dramatic use of miracles, signs, or wonders—to get people's attention. But the lasting change that God seeks really occurs as the Word of God is received in the stillness and quiet of one's heart.

God will accomplish all that He has planned. We do not need to worry about that. And we have no responsibility to counsel God on how He ought to accomplish His plans. Our responsibility is to trust and obey. Keep yourself in the place where you are able to hear the still, small voice of God speaking to your heart through His Word, and remain yielded to God in such a way that your main desire is to see God accomplish His will, His way.

And we know that all things work together for good to those who love God, to those who are the called according to His purpose. (Romans 8:28)

APRIL
16

The Greatest Good

THE PROMISES OF GOD are either wishful thinking or wonderful truths. If they are wishful thinking, then they are nothing more than optimistic clichés like "Look on the bright side," "Things could be worse," "Keep your chin up," and "Every cloud has a silver lining." All of these clichés offer little hope, even less comfort, and no confidence in times of trouble. On the other hand, the wonderful promises of God, which are true, not only offer these helps, but also security and stability, even in our worst times. How good are you at receiving promises of God?

Paul gives us a bold, radical, and life changing promise of God that is definitely more than a mere optimistic cliché.. He tells us that *all* things work together for good! You may be thinking, *ALL things? Really, Paul, are you serious?* You may be willing to acknowledge that certainly *some* things are working for good, you may even agree that some difficult situations can prove to have valuable lessons and therefore accomplish some good, but *all* things?

Do all things work together for good then when a baby dies? What about when a loved one is diagnosed with a terminal illness? Are all things still working together for good? What about when we lose our job, or when a marriage falls apart, or we lose our home? How are all things working together for good then?

For Paul, he had not an ounce of doubt in this truth because he said, "We *know* that all things work together for good . . ." (emphasis added). The reason for Paul's certainty was rooted in the Resurrection of Jesus Christ. God fulfilled some of the greatest promises through the Resurrection, including proof that God is able and will deliver on His promises, and proof that God honors His word. The resurrection is proof that God is all powerful, and proof that gives us the certainty to *know* that when God makes a promise, He will keep that promise, and this promise will be accomplished.

This does not mean that everything in life will work out the way we hoped, or that only good things will happen to us, or that all things are good. Paul is not saying that death, suffering, disease, and tragedy are good things. The death of a child is not a good thing. The end of a marriage is not a good thing. God never looks at bad and calls bad good, but when God looks at bad, He sees how He can use that for good in our lives. He sees how He can accomplish a greater purpose than anything we ever expected could come out of such difficulty.

One condition to God's promise to make good out of bad exists: this promise is reserved only for the Christian. As Paul tells us, this is for *those who love God . . . those who are the called according to His purpose.* We must therefore be careful how we apply and share this verse with others, because its application is limited to those who have put their faith in Christ, those to whom God promises that whatever they face in this life, He will use for good.

God can do much good in our lives through the circumstances we face, but one ongoing good that God does is to conform us into the image of Jesus (see Romans 8:29). I do not know what you are facing today or what issue is weighing heavily on your heart. But *know* this: God is at work, and there is nothing He cannot use to conform you into the image of Christ, which is God's greatest good for your life.

"Why don't we add on a small room upstairs and furnish it with a bed and desk, chair and lamp, so that when he comes by he can stay with us?" (2 Kings 4:10 MSG)

APRIL
17

Some Good Old-Fashioned Hospitality

SOMETHING WARM and welcoming comes with being invited to someone's house to share a home-cooked meal. We have all been in a house where, as soon as you step over the welcome mat and walk through the doorway, you immediately feel at home. You have the freedom to kick off your shoes and put your feet up. You are shown around and are invited to enjoy everything as your very own. You experience no guilt, no mention of cost, and no worry about drinking the last soda or grabbing the last dinner roll because second helpings are not only welcomed, but they are also encouraged. A simple and sincere concern for your comfort is apparent as you are instructed to relax and enjoy the blessing of genuine hospitality. As wonderful as this is, the Bible challenges the Christian to take hospitality a step further.

Elijah the prophet's ministry had come to a close, and his successor, *Elisha,* was on the scene. Elisha was what you might call a prophet to the people, as his ministry was done modestly and mostly among the ordinary people of Israel. One such person who was blessed *by* Elisha and a blessing *to* Elisha was the Shunammite woman. She was a woman of great character who was given to hospitality. As she observed the prophet traveling through her town, she graciously began to open her home to this servant of God and welcomed him into her home to rest, relax, and enjoy a refreshing meal whenever he was in town or just passing through.

If that is all she did, that would have been a great demonstration of hospitality, but this woman and her husband took hospitality one step further as they built a bed and breakfast onto their home where the prophet could stay whenever he was traveling. In those days, no Motel 6 was around to leave the light on for you while you were away from home, but a call was out for the Jews to be hospitable not only to their own people, but also to strangers who might be in need of some traveling kindness (see Leviticus 19:34).

This is the essence of true hospitality that the Christian is to extend to others. This hospitality goes above and beyond, extended not just to those we are close to, because that is normally what people already do. No, the Christian is to go beyond the norm and extend hospitality on a much broader scale. Like the Shunammite woman, we may seek to bless those who minister the gospel or missionaries who are home from the front lines of service. Perhaps this means opening your home to host a Bible study or small group. For some, maybe this means the prayerful consideration of making provision for someone in need to stay with you while they get back on their feet, or even being a foster parent. Hospitality, however, does not need to be as large as what was done by the Shunammite woman. We do not all have the ability or the resources to convert a portion of our home into a motel room for ministers, but we can all find ways to bless others with the gift of hospitality.

Hospitality is a sign of maturity in the believer (see 1 Timothy 3:2), but the practice of being hospitable is the responsibility of every believer. While some may certainly have a knack for or the gift of hospitality, we are all called to practice being hospitable, so start by looking around you for ways you could bless someone with some good old-fashioned hospitality.

> Does this mean, then, that God is so fed up with Israel that he'll have nothing more to do with them?
> (Romans 11:1 MSG)

APRIL

18

Israel, Israel, Israel

HAVE YOU EVER WONDERED what happened to the special relationship between God and the nation of Israel? Are the Jews still God's "chosen people"? Are the promises that God made to Abraham, Moses, David, and other Old Testament Hebrews still in effect? Or did God reject Israel when the nation rejected His Son, Jesus?[19]

Israel's special place in the Bible is unmistakable. God's relationship with Israel goes back a few thousand years, beginning with a man called Abraham, also known as the father of the nation (see Genesis 12:1). God entered into a covenant relationship with Abraham (see Genesis 15:18), promising to bless his descendants and make them a great nation (see Genesis 12:1–3). This is where Israel formally became God's "chosen people." God's covenantal relationship was confirmed by the people at Mount Sinai when they promised to do all that the Lord commanded (see Exodus 24:3). Unfortunately, God's people would break their promise with God eventually and even go so far as to reject the Son of God. But God never broke His promise to Israel; He always does what He says He will do. Therefore, He never has and never will break His promise to Israel or to us.

The apostle Paul confirms the fact that "God has not cast away His people" (Romans 11:2) and He still has a great purpose for them in His future plans. At times, seeing what God is doing may be hard, or we may find understanding His ways to be difficult, but we can be assured that "He who has begun a good work in [us] will complete it" (Philippians 1:6). That is His promise to us, and God is and always will be faithful to His Word.

Do you ever wonder what your future with God looks like? Do you ever worry that the situation you are going through, the struggles you are wrestling with, or the pressures you are experiencing are an indication that God is not working things out for a good purpose in your life? If so, this section of Romans is designed especially for you, as Paul used Israel's past, present, and future as an illustration that God is faithful, even when His people are not. No matter your situation, no matter your struggles, God is faithful—even when we are not.

We can take God at His word—we can trust His promises. He will be faithful to do all that He has said He will do, and if you are wondering how you can know that for sure, then look at God's relationship with the nation of Israel.

"If the prophet had told you to do something great, would you not have done it? How much more then, when he says to you, 'Wash, and be clean'?" (2 Kings 5:13)

APRIL
19

Receiving God's Remedy

YOU HAVE HEARD THEM ALL BEFORE: "Nothing in life is free"; "Nothing worth having comes easy"; and "You get what you pay for." These expressions remind us that hard work and persistence are essential to make a difference, to succeed, or to get where we are going in life. The statements express that we are often skeptical of receiving anything that we do not have to pay for or did not earn. When something is free, we are tempted to think, *What is wrong with it?* Unfortunately, we can be guilty of carrying these ideas over into our understanding of salvation, which means that we may hopelessly be trying to purchase or work hard for that which is freely offered to us by God.

Naaman was a man who carried over his strong work ethic and skepticism of freebies into his understanding of how God works. He was a man of great power and influence, and he was popular and highly respected. As the commander of the Syrian army, he would have had to work hard to rise through the ranks and into his highly respected and powerful position. Naaman also was considered a mighty man of valor, and the Lord used him to bring great victory to Syria. But Naaman had one fatal flaw: he had leprosy, which was a dreaded and incurable disease that would spread quickly throughout a person's body. And because of the devastating effects of leprosy and its incurable nature, the disease is often considered to be a picture in the Bible of the devastating effects of sin.

Despite all the power and influence that Naaman had, he remained powerless to cure himself. When sin is involved, we are all like Naaman:

powerless to cure ourselves of this deadly disease. Having tried everything he could think of to make himself whole again, neither Naaman nor anyone else could do anything to reverse the effects of his leprosy.

Here, the grace of God was extended to Naaman through the prophet Elisha, as Elisha called for Naaman to come to him. Naaman proudly arrived with a large entourage and was fully prepared to pay a great price for a personal miracle at the hands of this man of God. But to Naaman's surprise and dismay, Elisha simply conveyed a message for Naaman to go to the Jordan River and wash in the waters seven times. With his pride wounded, Naaman refused. His self-importance expected some elaborate work to be done to bring about his healing. His pride thought this was too easy, as if to say, "If this is going to work, surely it cannot be free."

Naaman eventually was healed as he let go of his pride, humbled himself, and by faith trusted in God's remedy. In the same way, we, too, can be saved from the disease of sin that plagues our spiritual bodies. If we let go of our pride, humble ourselves, confess our sins to God, and place our trust in Jesus' sacrifice on the cross, then we will be healed. When we come to God, we must be willing to abandon self-importance and realize that we cannot work harder to gain the grace of God. We must recognize that the forgiveness of sin is not for sale, but the free gift of God. All we must do is be willing to receive God's remedy.

And do not be conformed to this world, but be transformed by the renewing of your mind, that you may prove what is that good and acceptable and perfect will of God. (Romans 12:2)

APRIL
20

Mind Matters

MORE AND MORE PEOPLE TODAY are taking the time to read food labels. While we are grocery shopping, we pick up cereal boxes, snack foods, and canned goods, looking at the labels for answers. What are the ingredients? How many calories? How many grams of fat? How much sugar? How many carbs, and how much protein? We take great care in watching what we put into our bodies, but are we taking the same kind of care to watch what we put into our minds? Are we asking ourselves, *What is in this movie we are about to spend two hours watching?*; *Is this television show appropriate?*; or *Are the ideas in this book that I am about to read immoral or destructive?*

Paul understood that belief determines behavior, convictions determine conduct, and attitude determines action, which means that how we think is not only important, but also indispensable. Paul challenged all Christians to take control of their minds and to stop letting the world influence the way they think and the way they act. The J. B. Phillips translation of this passage is worth inserting here: "Don't let the world around you squeeze you into its own mould, but let God re-mould your minds from within, so that you may prove in practice that the plan of God for you is good, meets all his demands, and moves toward the goal of true maturity."

How should Christians think, then? To begin with, as Christians, we are not to allow the culture to determine our conduct, or let the world shape our worldview. The values, principles, beliefs, and morals that Christians are to hold are not to be found in the newspapers, politics, or the media of the day; they are found in God and God alone.

The Bible tells us that we are to have the mind of Christ, which is the same as saying we are to have a godly mind. A godly mind lets God shape opinions, perspectives, philosophies, and morality. Instead of having a worldly worldview, we should approach life from a Godview, which means we look at life from God's view, found in the Bible. When we are confused about an issue, or seek clarity on a subject, when we need direction, when we seek to understand the meaning and purpose to what we are experiencing in life, we are to look to what God has to say about our situation.

Renewing our minds is more than just reading the Bible, however. True renewal involves meditating on what you have read, which simply means that we must spend time going over what we read, thinking about the meaning, and considering how this scripture applies to our lives personally. Also, memorizing passages from the Bible will help make what we read become a part of who we are. Just as the food we eat shapes our physical body, what we feed our minds will shape our spiritual body.

A type of radical, life-transforming change should be evident in the life of a Christian, beginning in every believer's mind , when God's Holy Spirit, and Word are regularly nurtured within the heart, shaping our thoughts, totally converting the innate worldliness of our minds into a glorious, heavenly, consecrated mind like Christ. Believers undergo a metamorphosis of divine proportions evident in day-to-day lives as we take on a biblical Godview. Out of this process, we will be changed into new creations that understand and live the will of God.

Josiah also got rid of the mediums and psychics, the household gods, the idols, and every other kind of detestable practice, both in Jerusalem and throughout the land of Judah. (2 Kings 23:24 NLT)

APRIL 21

Spring Cleaning

WHEN YOU LOOK OUTSIDE and see the sun shining, the birds singing, and the flowers blooming, only to look inside and see a garage full of garbage, the closets piled high with odds and ends, and a refrigerator that no longer contains edible food but has been transformed into a science experiment, you know time for some spring cleaning has arrived. Spring cleaning is that time of year when you give your house a complete top-to-bottom cleansing and that time when you get rid of all the unwanted, outdated, and useless piles of junk.

But what may be easy to see in your house may not be so easy to see in your spiritual life. Has the time come for some spring cleaning in your life?

The nation of Israel was long overdue for some spiritual spring cleaning. They had allowed the garbage of idolatry to pile up, accumulated the odd practitioners of sorcery and witchcraft, developed a foul smell in the land because of incense being burned to pagan gods, and priests had perverted the house of God by storing up unholy images. King Josiah had the courage to do what needed to be done and began by taking out and burning the irreligious trash. But he did not stop there. He also kicked to the curb anyone who did not share his burden for the Lord, and he uprooted any practices that had sprouted up like weeds among God's people.

What do you see when you look inside yourself at your spiritual condition? Have you allowed the spiritual cobwebs to accumulate? Has the idolatry of worshiping things over God piled up? Are the closets of your mind filled with the odds and ends of trivial information, which have therefore pushed the things of God into a small shoebox in the corner that you never open because you have forgotten the box exists? When devotion to other things has taken your attention away from God, when work is more important than worshiping God, and when you have lost sight of the sacred because of the stuff in your life, then the time has come to clean house.

Josiah gives us a great example of what is necessary if we want to get our house in order. First, he was convicted by the Word of God. You never will want to make the necessary changes in your life if you first do not spend time reading the Bible. Out of the time you spend reading the Bible, God will reveal the junk and the clutter that you have allowed to pile up. Out of this renewed awareness from the Word of God will come a conviction brought on by the Spirit of God, which will lead to a commitment to obey God, just as Josiah experienced when he made a commitment to follow God and adhere to His Word (see 2 Kings 23:3).

Next, Josiah acted. All the conviction, commitment, and planning will amount to nothing if you do not follow through with your actions.

Do not allow worthless junk to take the place of worship. Do not let cobwebs form over your spiritual gifts. If you find things starting to pile up that keep you from serving and worshiping God, then take the time to do some spiritual spring cleaning and keep yourself uncluttered in your walk with the Lord.

Let every soul be subject to the governing authorities. For there is no authority except from God, and the authorities that exist are appointed by God. (Romans 13:1)

APRIL
22

In God We Trust

*P*OLITICS AND *RELIGION*. If you say these two words together, you are likely to get many different and often passionate reactions from people. Some believe that the two topics should never meet, and social etiquette says to never discuss religion and politics in polite company. Despite opposition to the idea, the two are related. One philosopher said, "Those who say religion has nothing to do with politics do not know what religion is." So, what does God say about politics and religion? How is the Christian to interact with the government and authority? And what are we to do if the government we live under is evil?

God has established three institutions: the family, which began with Adam and Eve; the state, as God gave Noah some post-flood regulations for civil authority; and the church at Pentecost. Now, during the time that Paul was writing his epistle to the Romans, the political climate was tense, filled with persecution, corruption, injustice, and instability. Yet despite the oppressive and abusive rulers in government that were beginning to construct anti-Christian policies, Paul still wrote, "Let every soul be subject to the governing authorities." The reason for such broad submission is because God has ordained and approved government. Think about this: If God is behind all the authority on earth, when we disobey authority, we dishonor God. God has created government primarily to prevent chaos and restrain evil.

Accepting the fact that God is behind government when the government is good is easy, because God is good. But is He behind the governments that are evil as well? The answer is still yes. This does not in any way mean that God is evil or condones evil rulers, but the Bible makes clear that God can turn evil, even evil governments, into good. God worked through evil rulers like Pharaoh, Nebuchadnezzar, Pilate and others to accomplish good purposes. Just because bad men may be in government does not mean that all government is bad.

Now, Paul skips over one difficult problem with government that we should briefly mention, and that is, what happens when the government orders you to do something that goes against your biblical responsibilities as a Christian? For example, what if the government passed a law forbidding the preaching or sharing of the gospel? Then, Acts 5:29 reminds us, "We must obey God rather than any human authority" (NLT). God is the highest authority, and His Law overrules any law that comes from mankind. If I have to disobey the word of mankind so that I can obey the Word of God, then I need to be willing to accept punishment as a result of my disobedience, and I am still required to act with integrity. Daniel, Paul, Silas, Peter, and John all had to disobey mankind's authority in order to obey God's higher authority. They suffered the consequences for disobeying the government, but they still disobeyed in a way that honored God.

We submit to authority knowing that God has allowed that person to be in that position for a purpose and that God's will is being accomplished through that person, even if we do not see how or understand why. God says, "By me kings reign" (Proverbs 8:15). He takes responsibility for the raising up of a ruler and the pulling down of another.

Respect authority because in God we trust, not mankind.

And Jabez called on the God of Israel saying, "Oh, that You would bless me indeed, and enlarge my territory, that Your hand would be with me, and that You would keep me from evil, that I may not cause pain!" So, God granted him what he requested. (1 Chronicles 4:10)

APRIL
23

The Jabez Prayer

SOMETIMES WE CAN BE GUILTY of opening our Bibles in search of some sort of God-formula, like *x* plus *y* equals success, or *a* times *b* equals happiness, or *c* minus *d* equals holiness. The Bible is undoubtedly full of commands, covenants, promises, and principles that bring blessing in our lives, but caution must be taken when presenting the promises of God as nothing more than a mere formula in which all that is required is that we insert the appropriate action into a God formula and then wait for Him to provide the expected results.

When considering this simple yet insightful prayer of Jabez, we must not see a mere formula in which we insert our names and wait for God to provide us with the same results that He provided to Jabez. We know very little about this man that God highlighted from among the long list of names in 1 Chronicles, but the little we do know is certainly noteworthy and helpful.

A brief look at the prayer of Jabez gives us some understanding as to the type of man that he was. Jabez prayed for four things: (1) God's blessing, (2) God's provision, (3) God's presence, and (4) God's protection.

Jabez began his passionate plea by humbly seeking the blessing of God, which included God's favor but went much deeper than any general kindness sought after by God toward Jabez. His blessing went on to include a deepening of his relationship with God. Jabez sought a blessing that would bring him nearer to God and increase his knowledge of God in a more personal way.

As Jabez sought God's provision by enlarging his territory, some degree of physical provision may have been included in what he was seeking, but the greater emphasis would no doubt be a desire for greater spiritual opportunity. We might ask this today in the following manner: "Lord, open the doors" or "Grant me more opportunities to glorify you."

Realizing he could do nothing apart from God, Jabez asked for God's presence to be with him, guiding and directing his every step. Finally, Jabez had some understanding of sin and the damage caused by sin, so he asked for God's protection, just as Jesus taught the disciples to pray, "Do not lead us into temptation, But deliver us from the evil one" (Matthew 6:13). Jabez knew that only God had the power to keep him from sin and help him live a God-honoring life.

Verse 9 of 1 Chronicles 4 tells us that "Jabez was more honorable than his brothers." Jabez was upright, moral in character, God-honoring, and God-fearing in his personal perspective. This proved to be the source and supply of his prayer and where the true "secret" of his success lay, and sheds light onto why God chose to answer his prayer.

Although nothing is wrong with wholeheartedly praying this prayer of Jabez, the key to unlocking a Jabez-like blessing in your life is not through paying careful attention in copying or mimicking his prayer. Rather, such blessing is found by living a God-centered life that includes passionate, humble, and heartfelt prayer, focused on honoring and fearing God.

God answered Jabez's prayer not because the prayer was what God was looking for, but because Jabez was the type of man whom God was looking for.

Welcome with open arms fellow believers who don't see things the way you do. And don't jump all over them every time they do or say something you don't agree with—even when it seems that they are strong on opinions but weak in the faith department. Remember, they have their own history to deal with. Treat them gently. (Romans 14:1 MSG)

APRIL
24

United We Stand or Divided We Fall

ARE YOU RELIEVED that Christians never disagree? That we see eye-to-eye on every issue? And we do not let petty differences divide us? *R-i-i-i-g-h-t!* (Insert sarcasm here!) The truth is, the church has always struggled to keep unity. In Corinth there were cliques, in Galatia there was bad-mouthing, and in Philippi there was arguing. Even Paul and Barnabas had their differences. Many issues face us today that Christians have differing opinions on, like: Should baptism be a full-body dunk, or is sprinkling with water okay? Should single Christians date? Is drinking wine or beer okay? How often should a church take communion? Is the use of birth control wrong? Is smoking a sin? Can you leave a church just because you do not like the music? Are overeating, playing cards, dancing, wearing makeup, or going to the beach all sins? These may seem trivial to you, but throughout church history, some of these very issues have divided churches. So, what should we do when we disagree?

The Bible is black-and-white on many issues, such as do not steal, do not lie, do not commit adultery, help the poor, and love one another. The Bible is equally black-and-white on doctrinal issues like the divine nature of Jesus, His payment for sin on the cross, salvation by grace, and the authority and inerrancy of the Bible. These are nonnegotiable issues or the absolutes of our faith. In Romans 14, Paul helps us understand what to do when we do not see eye-to-eye on issues that fall into the gray zone. Gray zone issues are not black or white and are where we have been given no clear instruction or command in the Bible.

For the Christians in Rome, their issues were: Should a person eat meat sacrificed to an idol? Was one day holier than another day? Despite their differences, Paul said they should strive for unity. Not every issue is essential for us to agree on. Paul said some things are disputable, so when considering something that the Bible does not make a big deal about, why should we argue? Instead, seek unity and let Jesus be the judge, because He is the one we will stand before to give an account for what we say, do, and believe. At the moment when you stand before God, whether or not you watched *Dancing with the Stars* or ate meat or only vegetables will not make a difference. What will matter is why you made the choices that you made.

Now, what is the best way to make sense of the gray zone issues? Let us look to Romans 14. First, figure out what your opinions are (verse 5). Then, ask yourself, "Does this honor the Lord?" (verse 8). Next, determine any lasting or eternal value in those actions or beliefs (verse 10). Also, make sure this does not cause another Christian to stumble in his or her walk with Christ (verse 13). And lastly, decide if this is an accurate expression of your faith (verse 23).

God is not trying to create uniformity, but He is seeking a community committed to unity. Theologian Rupertus Meldenius wrote, "In essentials, unity; in nonessentials, liberty; in all things, love." Let your love for Christ and your love for one another be greater than your opinions on disputable matters.

Now these are the men whom David appointed over the service of song in the house of the LORD, after the ark came to rest. They were ministering with music before the dwelling place of the tabernacle of meeting. (1 Chronicles 6:31-32)

The Ministry of Music

WHETHER YOU PREFER "Amazing Grace" or "How Great Is Our God," whether you like drums or no drums, guitar or no guitar, a big choir or a small band, traditional hymns or contemporary praise songs, everyone has particular likes and dislikes when it comes to worship music in church.

Music is powerful, and has the ability to express our deepest thoughts, feelings, and emotions in a way that stirs our hearts and draws us closer to God. When spiritual truth is put to music, the combination can bring us to a place of complete brokenness and total surrender to God because of the unique way song can engage our thoughts, emotions, and spirit all at once.

David knew better than anyone how worship music can impact the spirit. He wrote countless praise and worship songs, some of which we still have record of in the book of Psalms. With such a powerful medium as music, the question we should ask is, how should music be used in church?

David saw the need for music and song to be included in tabernacle worship, so he appointed men whose sole responsibility was to minister in the tabernacle with music. Today we would call such people worship leaders. Churches today have entire ministries, teams, choirs, and musicians all dedicated to minister through music when the congregation gathers together.

Music in church services today plays an important role and needs to be seen as more than the warm-up act for the message or as an extra cushion that allows for latecomers to find a seat. Equally important is the fact that church music is not designed to be entertainment, and the people on stage are not there to put on a show or to draw attention to themselves. Instead, music and song in church should be used to glorify God and draw His people into His presence.

Just imagine what David's response would have been if the men he had appointed to lead worship in the tabernacle were showing off, putting on a concert, or using worship to whip people up into some sort of spiritual frenzy. David did not appoint worship ministers in order to fill the tabernacle with people. He wanted to fill the tabernacle with the praise of God's people instead.

When we approach music and song in church, we need to begin by checking our attitudes at the door. Do not enter the sanctuary with a critical spirit toward the music. Rather, find a way to focus your mind on the object of your singing, which is God. He is the One we are singing for and the One we are singing to. David approached worshiping through music and song as an integral part of his relationship with God, and when we give worshiping through song a proper place, the music can be a wonderful aspect of our life of worship as well.

Take advantage of the time your church spends worshiping God through music, and let the words of the songs become the prayers of your heart and expressions of your love as you sing praise to God.

Now I myself am confident concerning you, my brethren, that you also are full of goodness, filled with all knowledge, able also to admonish one another. (Romans 15:14)

APRIL

26

A Good Church

CHURCH IS NOT SUPPOSED TO BE A LOCATION, but a lifestyle. Every church is different and has its own vibe, personality, and culture. Some churches have that cutting-edge vibe that affects the way they approach ministry, how they use media, and the styles of worship they enjoy. Other churches have a more casual personality that defines the way they operate, and still other churches have a more traditional culture that has shaped their style.

No matter where your church falls on the ethos scale, and regardless of the collective style of ministry, what would your church look like if you took away those things that often define its culture? No more amazing building? Remove the awe-inspiring music? Do away with the awesome children's ministry? Do not get the wrong idea; these are all wonderful things that are valuable and necessary in the modern church. But they are not what make a healthy church.

When you strip away the outer niceties from what we commonly consider "church," what you are left with is the real makeup of a church. Paul was pleased with the church in Rome, and Paul was not the type of person to casually throw around compliments. If something was wrong, he would not hesitate speak out. He did so with the church in Corinth, when he rebuked them for having divisions (1 Corinthians 1:10), or as he reprimanded the church in Galatia, telling them they had been bewitched (Galatians 3:1). In the letter to the Hebrews, the churchgoers were called out for being immature (Hebrews 5:12–13). But to the church in Rome, Paul handed out an extraordinary compliment as he listed three qualities that made them praiseworthy, three qualities that every church, regardless of vibe, personality, and culture should be known for.

First on the list: goodness. Goodness speaks of moral excellence and involves generosity, thoughtfulness, and charity. Goodness is moral Christian character lived out in everyday life, character that is concerned with the welfare of others and has blameless motivations. Goodness is a fruit of the Spirit (Galatians 5:22) and therefore is on God's list of distinct attributes that are to be evidenced in the life of every believer.

Second on the list: knowledge. Knowledge is the ability to discern what is right and what is wrong and to act accordingly. Knowledge is rooted in our knowing Jesus Christ, "as His divine power has given to us all things that pertain to life and godliness, through the knowledge of Him who called us by glory" (2 Peter 1:3).

Third on the list: admonishing one another. This is the ability to biblically encourage, advise, and teach one another in the issues of the faith. Admonition is not the sole responsibility of elders and pastors; every believer bears this responsibility.

As one commentator pointed out, the church in Rome "morally, was 'full of goodness,' intellectually they were 'complete in knowledge,' and functionally they were 'competent to instruct one another.' "[20] Going to a church that has the right vibe, personality, and culture for you is important, but even more important is that goodness, knowledge, and admonishing one another is part of that vibe, personality, and culture as well.

Talk of all His wondrous works! (1 Chronicles 16:9)

God Talk

IN OUR MODERN WORLD, countless devices abound through which we can communicate with one another. We have a variety of smartphones, computers, and tablets that allow us to blog, tweet, e-mail, text, instant message, update social media, and spend face time. If all this fails, we can turn to the good old-fashioned way of communicating. We can write a letter, send a card, or pick up a pay phone (and yes, they do still exist). With more outlets available today to reach more people with our thoughts and views on life, how much time is spent actually talking about the wondrous works of God?

King David talked often about God and sought to praise God for all His wondrous works. He sang songs, he wrote poems, and he publicly declared the greatness of God and used every means available to him to speak of the God of wonders. When we have experienced the goodness and greatness of God in our lives, we will want to find as many ways to talk about God with as many people as possible, whenever possible.

F. B. Meyer said that as Christians, "We talk about sermons, details of worship and church organization, or the latest phase of Scripture criticism; we discuss men, methods, and churches; but our talk in the home, and in the gatherings of Christians for social purposes, is too seldom about the wonderful works of God. Better to speak less, and to talk more of Him."

We may find working the wonders of God into everyday conversation difficult, but that is only because we have created difficulty for God in the work of His wonders in our hearts. We have allowed our lives and our hearts to be filled with so much that is not God that not speaking much of God is only natural. We have fallen out of the practice of praising Him because we have fallen out of the practice of being captivated by Him.

The simple truth is that no matter how much we talk about God, we can all talk about Him more. If God is the most important part of our life, as He should be, then we should not have to "work" God into our conversations. Our speech should be saturated and overflowing with the wonders of God because He is a God of countless wonders. Anyone can regain a sense of the majesty of God in his or her life, which will naturally result in transforming so many empty words into words that honor and exalt God.

We must begin by remembering the wonderful works God. We remember His works as we look throughout the Bible and see the Creator and Sustainer of life, the Provider and Protector of His people, the Savior and Sanctifier of the faithful. As we remember who God is, what He has done, what He is doing today, and what He has yet to do in the future, we will be moved to give thanks and to glorify His name. Our hearts will be filled with joy, expectation, and anticipation, and out of our hearts our mouths will speak.

We have the tendency to only talk about what is in our hearts. Therefore, if we are having a difficult time talking about God, we need to get more of God in our hearts. Take the time to focus on all God has done in your life and all He has done for His people, and you will not be able to stop all the God talk that pours from your lips.

For the message of the cross is foolishness to those who are perishing, but to us who are being saved it is the power of God. (1 Corinthians 1:18)

APRIL
28

Cross Thoughts

THERE ARE TWO WAYS to look at the cross of Christ: either you see the action upon the cross as the greatest miracle ever exhibited by God toward mankind, or you consider the act to be the most absurd claim ever made by mankind about God. The cross of Christ is both repelling and appealing, horrific and holy, ridiculous and reasonable, outrageous and outstanding, and is both foolishness and wisdom. As Oswald Chambers said, "All heaven is interested in the cross of Christ, all hell terribly afraid of it, while men are the only beings who more or less ignore its meaning."[21] Why does the cross of Christ cause some to fall to their knees in worship and others to walk away, shaking their heads in defiant disbelief?

The answer is found within the message of the cross. In order for us to understand that message, we must first understand what the cross was all about. Crucifixion was a horrific form of capital punishment used by several ancient nations, including the Romans, whereby the convicted criminal would be nailed to a cross to die a slow, agonizing death by asphyxiation. Crucifixion was incredibly painful, tremendously humiliating, and consequently was reserved for only the worst criminals. The thought of God using the cross as the instrument of glory through which He would accomplish His greatest work seemed counterintuitive for most and remains that way even today.

The message of the cross is, at its very core, God's remedy for humanity's terminal disease of sin. The cross was God's plan from before the creation of the world. The cross would be the divine tool through which Jesus, His holy Son, would sacrifice his life in a glorious and victorious demonstration of God's love and power. God knew he would make a bold invitation that anyone who believes in Jesus Christ and what He accomplished through His death on the cross would be given eternal life. Despite God's clear message of love and mercy, some find the story too simple, too foolish, or too humbling to accept.

The Jews were offended at the message of the cross because they wanted a conquering king, not a suffering Savior. The Greeks were offended at the message of the cross because the plan was not polished with rational philosophical sophistication. Others, however, saw in the message of the cross of Christ the perfect display of God's love and power, a faultless example of His forgiveness, and a genuine display of God's genius.

Why the message of the cross of Christ has offended people's sensibilities throughout history is simple; behind every objection to the message and meaning of the cross is the sin of pride. Always and forever, pride calls the message of the cross foolish. Pride believes that mankind's way must be the right way, that human reasoning must be higher than God's reasons, that human intellect must be greater than the infinite mind of an all-knowing God. But the message of the cross is central to Christianity, and a dividing line between foolishness and faith.

In this message, we must never compromise, water down, or eliminate from what we believe, what we stand for, and what we proclaim. Better to be a fool in the eyes of mankind and be found wise in the eyes of God than be considered wise to mankind and found a fool to God.

"If My people who are called by My name will humble themselves, and pray and seek My face, and turn from their wicked ways, then I will hear from heaven, and will forgive their sin and heal their land." (2 Chronicles 7:14)

APRIL
29

The Difficulty of Humility

PERHAPS THE THREE GREATEST VIRTUES of Christianity are humility, humility, and humility. Humility is a great Christian quality, but is often greatly misunderstood, being hard to define and even harder to cultivate. Humility is countercultural, at the core of a cross-centered life, and not something we often pray for with urgency, but something we all desperately need.

Solomon had just completed building the temple in Jerusalem. As part of the temple dedication, people gathered there as Solomon praised God for His faithfulness and declared to the people that people could come there and meet with God through prayer. After an enormous sacrifice and spectacular display of God's power and glory, the Lord appeared to Solomon and gave him a promise in 2 Chronicles 7:14. At the center of the promise is humility.

Humility simply means to be brought low or to have a sense of lowliness, not thinking too highly of yourself, but not putting yourself down. Where pride exalts self, humility exalts Christ; where pride is full of self, humility is emptied of self. So, how can we humble ourselves while living in such a proud world?

Humility begins by being His. God said, "If *My people* who are called by My name will humble themselves . . ." (emphasis added). Humility admits, "I don't have all the answers," "I can't do it all on my own," and, more times than we admit, humility also says, "I need help." Apart from God, you cannot achieve true humility because humility is directly tied to a right relationship with God. As you willingly submit yourself under the authority of Jesus Christ, you can begin to let go of pride and embrace genuine humility.

God also said,that his people should *"pray."* Prayer is recognition that we need God's help to live as He calls us to live. Prayer shows utter dependence on God and is, therefore, an expression of humility.

If you want to get serious about humility, get serious about seeking God. Notice that He said, should pray and *"seek My face"* (emphasis added). Serious seeking involves a second aspect of prayer, which is a desire to know God more deeply. This depth comes as we dive into the Bible with expectancy, knowing that every moment we spend looking at His Word, we are looking directly at the face of God.

One more aspect of this verse must be addressed: God's people must "*turn from their wicked ways*" (emphasis added). Humility is not afraid to say "I messed up," or "I made a mistake," "I have sinned." When you refuse to acknowledge your sin and seek God's forgiveness, you are exhibiting pride, the opposite of everything that humility stands for.

F. B. Meyer once said, "I used to think that God's gifts were on shelves one above the other; and that the taller we grew in Christian character the easier we should reach them. I now find that God's gifts are on shelves one beneath the other; and that it is not a question of growing taller but of stooping lower; and that we have to go down, always down, to get His best gifts."[22]

The fire will test the quality of each person's work. (1 Corinthians 3:13 NIV)

When the Smoke Clears

APRIL
30

WHY DO WE DO WHAT WE DO? As Christians we show up for church services week after week, attend Bible classes, volunteer to usher, help prepare meals for others, participate in work days, counsel couples, teach Sunday school, sing in the choir, give money, and do many other things in the church. But why? Are our Christian activities done out of a sense of duty or devotion? Do we serve so that we might get something in return, or is the purpose of our serving to give something? And at the end of the day, does why we are doing what we are doing even matter if what we are doing is good?

A fine line separates doing acts of service and being a servant. As Christians, we are called to be servants, which naturally will result in acts of service, but acts of service are not always the result of someone being a servant. Often, the difference is found in the reason we do what we do. One day, all Christians will stand before God, where their lives will be examined and their works will be tested. What will God look for as He examines our lives and tests our works? God is most interested in the quality of our work. You see, God is not only interested in *what* we do, but *why* we do what we do. Whether in doing service at church or in attendance at church services and events, what God is looking for are people with the right motivation for doing what they do and the right application for doing what they do. In other words, God wants His people to do the right things, for the right reasons, and in the right way.

Let us consider why we *should not* do what we do! We should not look at our service to God as a means of earning favor with God or earning favor with other people. We should not serve to increase our overall approval rating with God or others. If we are approaching our service or our attendance at church with a perspective that says, "What can I get from this?" then we need to pay close attention to the warning found in 1 Corinthians 3:13, where we are warned that if we do what we do for the wrong reasons and in the wrong way, then our works will not amount to much. Just as wood, hay, and stubble will not make it through fire, neither will our service or our actions pass through the testing by fire. Is our salvation secure in the fire of testing? Yes, but our rewards are not.

Why *should* we do what we do? We should serve God and attend church for two simple reasons. First, our motivation should be rooted in our love for God. We want to serve others because we love God. Second, we should serve others and attend church as an act of worship. We love God, therefore we want to worship God, and by worshiping God, we are ascribing worth (or value) to God as we give Him our adoration and attention, our time and our service, all for His glory.

We want to make sure that we are doing the right things for the right reasons, because only then can we be certain that when our life and works are tested by fire and the smoke has cleared, what remains has been purified and not destroyed.

May

For the eyes of the Lord run to and fro throughout the whole earth, to show Himself strong on behalf of those whose heart is loyal to Him. (2 Chronicles 16:9)

MAY

1

The Loyalty Factor

T HE GREAT EVANGELIST D. L. MOODY once said, "The world has yet to see what God can do with a man fully consecrated to Him. By God's help, I aim to be that man." Many people want to be used by God, to serve Him with enthusiasm, and to see God do great things in and through their lives, thereby having a lasting impact for the kingdom of God. But God wants to see something even more important in us before He shows himself strong in our lives, and that something is loyalty.

King Asa of Judah was a good king who made a bad decision. His decision sparked a series of compromises in his life that would eventually test his loyalty toward God. During a civil war between Judah and Israel, King Asa decided to go against wise counsel, which led him to rob the temple treasury to purchase a peace treaty with the neighboring enemy of Syria. King Asa, in this time of testing, turned away from trusting in the promises of God and chose to forget the past protection and provision that God had always provided. To help himself gain a military advantage over Israel, he traded in his loyalty to God for a temporary truce.

When Asa was rebuked by the prophet Hanani, the king did not repent of his disloyalty and distrust toward God. Subsequently, he became afflicted with an illness, yet still he stubbornly refused to return to trusting God. From King Asa, we learn that a good beginning does not guarantee a good ending. Loyalty will stand the test of time, remains faithful in difficulty, and continues to trust, even in the darkest hour.

King Asa's mistake began when he no longer trusted God to take care of him when things got tough. God is looking for men and women who will remain loyal to Him, faithful as they remember that God is always faithful, and patient in the tough times of testing. God is not waiting on us to accomplish His plans and purposes. The plans of God do not depend on humanity, but God has given us the privilege of being used for heavenly purposes. And as we remain loyal to God, we will see His power and strength displayed.

What happens if we, like King Asa, fail to follow through, fail to remain faithful, and fail to stay loyal to God's Word and to God's promises to us? Do we thwart God's plans? Is God incapable of accomplishing a particular action? Not at all. God is and will always be God. God is and will always be able to accomplish His purposes. The only real question is whether we will be a part of God's plans or not.

We lose out most when we choose to distrust God. We lose out on the blessings of fellowship with God, we forfeit the opportunity to be a part of God's purposes, and fail to see God's power displayed in our lives. King Asa traded in the promises of God for a temporary solution that eventually opened the door for more trouble in his life and for the nation of Israel.

Seek to remain consecrated to God and loyal to His purposes, even when times get tough and you are tempted to trade in your trust for provisional peace. Relying on God and remaining loyal to Him always will guarantee the best outcome, both today and tomorrow.

> *Then you must throw this man out and hand him over to Satan so that his sinful nature will be destroyed and he himself will be saved on the day the Lord returns.* (1 Corinthians 5:5 NLT)

MAY
2

Immorality in the Church

WHO AM I TO POINT THE FINGER? Who am I to judge? Who am I to cast the first stone? When getting involved in confronting the sins of other people, these questions are often the reasons we shy away from getting involved. A social phenomenon has been repeatedly observed in people called the bystander effect. The basic idea is that the greater the number of people present, the less likely someone is to step in to help when observing a person in distress. People think someone else will respond, and therefore they do not need to do anything. But what usually happens is that nothing is done and no one responds. Unfortunately, the church can also suffer from a similar type of bystander effect when observing another believer caught in the distress of sin. This leaves many to shy away from getting involved, thinking they are not obligated to get involved or believing that someone else will step in.

The Corinthian church had a big problem. A member of the congregation was involved in sexual immorality, having a sexual relationship with his stepmom and everyone in the church (and outside the church) knew about the affair, but no one was willing to get involved. Corinth was the party capital of the world back then, and people did as they pleased. This forced the Corinthian church to help with people escape the party lifestyle and get on the road to holy living. With this man, however no one was willing to do the hard work of confrontation.

Sin can never be cured by ignoring its existence or pretending that everything is okay. When a church fails to act against unrepentant sin, whether from the leadership of the church or a member of the congregation, the results can be devastating to the entire body. Paul challenged the church at Corinth to discontinue turning a blind eye to this shocking sin, and to step up and do the hard, but loving, work of confronting this brother in Christ.

When confronting another Christian, we must follow the steps outlined in Matthew 18 and first approach the person privately. Lovingly, take him or her aside and speak the truth, emphasizing the person's need to repent. Our next approach is to return with two or three people and employ the same loving approach. If the sinner still refuses to repent, the final step is to remove that person from the church. The Corinthian church was at the final stage with this man but had been unwilling to go any further. Paul told them to turn the man over to Satan.

That sounds harsh, right? What does "to turn someone over to Satan" mean? In this case, the offending person is expelled from the church, thereby removing him or her from any support, fellowship, and protection provided by the church. The hope is the wrongdoer will grow so weary of living in sin and want to return to life in the body of Christ. Does this really work? For this man, yes. In Paul's second letter, he told the Corinthian church to receive the genuinely repentant person back into fellowship.

Church discipline is never easy or comfortable, but is nonetheless important. God can use discipline to bring conviction and restoration to a wayward believer. The goal of any and all church discipline is restoration, not condemnation, by having the courage to be more than a bystander and help those in caught in the distress of sin.

Then the people of the land tried to discourage the people of Judah. (Ezra 4:4)

Turning Point

MAY 3

LET'S FACE IT, we have all been hit with discouragement at one time or another in our lives. Maybe you have been unemployed for an extended period of time, or chronic health problems have kept you down, or maybe you have suffered repeated rejection or failure. Many situations can leave you feeling discouraged and questioning whether things will ever turn around. Although situations may vary from person to person, the causes and cure often share similarities.

In the year 538 BC, several thousand Jews had returned to Jerusalem, having spent time in what is known as the Babylonian captivity. Their mission was to rebuild the temple of God under the guidance of Zerubbabel, but just as the temple foundation was set in place and work seemed to be moving forward, the enemy attacked the people and work came to a screeching halt. For the next sixteen years, no work would be done on the temple. What kind of weapon could stop so many people for so long? Was this some sort of ancient biological or chemical weapon? On the contrary! The weapon of choice is one of the most effective weapons still in use today by the Enemy of God against the people of God: the weapon of discouragement.

What causes people to give in to the crippling effects of discouragement? One of the first things that will allow discouragement to creep in is fatigue. When physically or emotionally overloaded and overworked, your defenses are weakened and discouragement has an opportunity to gain a foothold. Fatigue often leads to frustration, which further feeds discouragement. Frustration mounts as unfinished projects, begun with optimism, now look insurmountable, and you become overwhelmed. Frustration often turns to fear, allowing discouragement to spread. Fearful questions assault your mind like, *What if I fail?* or *What will others think of me?* Your fears, whether, real or imagined, can discourage you into a total state of paralysis.

The Enemy of God used a progression like this to discourage the hearts and minds of the Jews who were trying to serve God by rebuilding the temple.

He led them from fatigue to frustration, and from fear to failure. If we are not careful, the weapon of discouragement can crush our confidence and set back our service as well.

So, how can we turn discouragement around and regain our resolve? Resting and refueling are important; we cannot neglect our bodies physically and expect to be at our best. However, we must also refresh ourselves spiritually. Ezra 5:1 tells how the Jews overcame discouragement by rededicating themselves to the Word of God. If you disconnect from God's Word, discontent is sure to set in! His Word is an inexhaustible source of wisdom and encouragement, available for anyone who will invest the time. Refreshing yourself in the Word will help remind you of who God is, and that He is bigger than any fear or frustration.

Next, return to the work that God has called you to as soon as possible. Idle hands are the Devil's tools and only breeds more idleness, so just get started wherever you are and allow the Lord to lead you onward and upward in your service to Him. Look past your current situation and look to God, seek Him in His Word, and serve Him faithfully and fearlessly. Make this your turning point away from discouragement.

But I say to the unmarried and to the widows: It is good for them if they remain even as I am. (1 Corinthians 7:8)

MAY 4

Being Single in a Married World

BEING SINGLE does not mean that you pass your time sitting in an empty apartment, watching TV while eating frozen dinners in a room filled with cats. However, if you are single, you may feel pressure from family as they relentlessly ask you, "When are you going to settle down and get married?" Or, friends may constantly try to set you up with Mr. Right or Miss Perfect, but do not feel less than "normal" because you are single. As a matter of fact, your singleness may even be a gift given to you by God and something to be cherished and not embarrassed about (see 1 Corinthians 7:7).

Marriage may be God's plan for most people, but not for everyone. If you are single, God's will for your life may just be that you remain single. You should not feel uncomfortable or insecure for choosing to remain single if that is God's calling for your life. Being single in Christ is not falling short of God's best and, actually may be God's very best for you.

If you have been called to a life of singleness in Christ, God has given you a unique opportunity to serve Him in a way that most cannot. You are not weighed down with the same cares and burdens of married folks, and you have fewer financial, emotional, and physical responsibilities. Single people are free to spend more time developing an intimate relationship with God because fewer pressures and demands assault them. Also, single Christians have freedom to serve the Lord without distraction, allowing them to give Christ their undivided attention and devotion as they serve Him.

However, if you are a single Christian and have *not* been given the gift of singleness, and if you long for the day when you find that special someone, here are a few suggestions on how to wait on God as you wait for Him to provide you with a spouse.

First, learn to be content with your singleness. God has you in your current situation for a season and a reason, so use this time to discover who God wants *you* to be before you worry about who you are to marry. Both the single person and the married person must first find their fulfillment and contentment in Christ.

Second, pursue purity. Sexual temptation exists, but can be resisted. Flee situations that may put you in a compromising position, and do not be pressured into physical intimacy before you are married.

Third, do not seek a relationship with a non-Christian. The Bible is clear that Christians should not marry non-Christians, and that means do not date them either. You are just setting yourself up for heartache if you do.

Finally, pray. Keep your marriage search ever and always in the hands of God. Praying to marry is certainly okay, but allow God to lead you in the process. Do not get ahead of Him.

The Apostle Paul says being single is good, but your singleness does not make you any more or any less spiritual than those who marry. However, have some benefits of being single allow you to serve the Lord in a special way. Whether God has called you to married life or to a life of Christian singleness, you are called to put Jesus Christ first in your life and to serve Him joyfully and faithfully.

For the Lord made them joyful. . . . (Ezra 6:22)

Dedicated to Joy

MAY 5

CHRISTIANS SHOULD BE the most joyful people on the planet. This does not mean that twenty-four hours a day, seven days a week, we are walking around with a song in our hearts and a smile on our faces. Nor does being joyful mean that we do not experience grief, know pain, or suffer setbacks. But being joyful does mean that we should not let circumstances in life steal our joy. The driver that just cut you off on the freeway does not need to send you into an emotional tailspin. The difficult person at work does not need to drain the life out of you. And that unexpected delay is no reason to rant and rave.

Riddled with resistance, stumbled because of setbacks, and nearly overwhelmed by opposition, God's people finally finished rebuilding the temple. The road to completion was long and hard, but with God leading the charge on behalf of His people and for His glory, the temple was completed. Time then came to dedicate the temple to God and celebrate the Passover joyfully. The dedication was a source of joy because the people finished the work that God gave them to do. More than that, however, the dedication filled the people with joy because the temple was a symbol of God's *present* faithfulness.

In addition to the dedication celebration, the people also celebrated the Passover feast, thereby remembering all that God had done for His people in times past. The Passover was a symbol of God's *past* faithfulness to His people.

By reflecting on God's past faithfulness and focusing on His present faithfulness, God's people cannot help but be filled with abundant joy.

What does being filled with abundant joy mean? Joy is a reflection of the presence of God in your life. Joy is not found in circumstances, but in God, because joy is not situational; joy is relational. The amount of joy in your life is directly connected to your proximity to God. The more time you spend with God in His Word and in prayer, and the more often God is on your mind and spoken of by your mouth, the greater joy you will experience in life. Joy is not found in the *what* you do for God, but rather in the *why* you do what you do for God. Joy means that I find total satisfaction in God. I am joyful because I en*joy* Him. He is the Creator and Sustainer of life, and He is the source of all joy.

If you are finding being filled with joy difficult, or if you have been letting the situations of this life steal your joy, then begin by checking your relationship with God. If you have been focused more on your circumstances than on drawing closer to God, then your joy is sure to fade away. Refocus on God. Start by considering the present faithfulness of God in your life, how He is providing and caring for you, and how His Word presently ministers to your Spirit. Then reflect on what God has done for you in times past and how His past faithfulness is an encouragement. As you devote yourself to keeping the faithfulness of God ever present in your mind, the joy of the Lord will be a constant source of strength.

Do you not know that those who run in a race all run, but one receives the prize? Run in such a way that you may obtain it. (1 Corinthians 9:24)

**MAY
6**

Going for the Gold

THE WORLD IS FILLED with die-hard sports fans, rooting and cheering, booing and hissing, as they ride an emotional rollercoaster, rising up with the thrill of victory and plummeting with the agony of defeat. The king of the world in today's sports arena is soccer, with cricket, tennis, volleyball, baseball, golf, and basketball among the other most popular sports in the world. One competition that often turns the entire world into one huge stadium of fanatics for several weeks at a time is the Olympic Games. National pride mixed with emotional intensity provides fans with the perfect sports combination. In every event, only one wins and receives the gold.

How can we live a godly life like an athlete who competes to win? In ancient Greece, the Olympics, held in Athens, and the Isthmian Games, held in Corinth, were the popular sports attractions of the day. The Greeks treated their athletes with much the same fanfare as athletes receive today. In a culture filled with sports fans, Paul had an easy way to illustrate how a Christian should "run," or live life. The difference between the athletic races and the Christian "race" is that every Christian can win. Although we do not compete against other Christians, and we do not compete for our salvation, we are competing against physical and spiritual obstacles that can hinder us from the rewards that God has for us. From Paul, we can learn a few lessons from the wide world of sports.

Paul, like any good coach, zeroed in on two things we all need to practice in order to make sure that we win the prize: discipline and self-control. Discipline is *doing*, where self-control is *denying*. Paul had learned that discipline was just as necessary for the building up of one's faith as is necessary for the building up of an athlete's physical ability. As Christians, we must be disciplined to spend time reading the Bible, praying, spending time in fellowship with other believers, serving, and sharing our faith with those who do not know God (collectively, the *doing*). We must discipline, or build up, our spiritual bodies by conforming our minds, our attitudes, and our desires to those of Jesus Christ (more *doing*). We must also exhibit self-control, like a training athlete, by saying no to self-centered desires that can take our focus off the finish line (the *denying*). We must put aside the pursuit of worldly pleasures and sinful habits, or they will cost us the race (more *denying*).

Self-control is not an act of the will. We do not try harder in order to exhibit more self-control; self-control is a yielding of one's spirit to the Holy Spirit. True self-control is directly related to the extent we let go of control and surrender to God's control over our lives instead.

If you have not been competing to win, then begin your training today. Discipline yourself like a good athlete, doing those things that help bring spiritual growth and equip you to run with endurance. Cast off any sin that weighs you down, slows you down, or wears you down and begin to compete like an Olympian for the everlasting crown of gold that awaits every competitor at the heavenly finish line.

Then I proclaimed a fast there at the river of Ahava, that we might humble ourselves before our God, to seek from Him the right way for us. (Ezra 8:21)

MAY 7

To Fast or Not to Fast?

YOU DO NOT HAVE TO DRIVE FAR these days to find fast food. Golden Arches fill the skylines, huts devoted to pizza line the landscapes, White Castles ruled by Burger Kings reign, and Dairy Queens have babies born with Golden Spoons in their mouths. You can find Church's filled with fried chicken, and take a Subway from Boston Market all the way to the border, where you can hear the Taco Bell ring. With such easy access to an abundance of food options, fasting seems outdated and out of step with the times. So, many Christians are left wondering, *To fast or not to fast?* That is the question at hand.

Ezra was a priest who led a group of a few thousand of his closest friends back to Jerusalem from their time in captivity in Babylon. But during their journey, Ezra put on the brakes and called everyone to participate in a three-day fast. The impromptu fast was to be a time of prayer and waiting on the Lord during their journey. During the three days, the people would ask the Lord for direction, not from a position of pride or arrogance, not demandingly, but in humility, surrendering their will to His.

Some say waiting time is never wasted time, and so often in our lives we can hear the Lord speak the loudest to our hearts only in times when we slow down, sit in silence, turn off the distractions of life, and simply wait.

Fasting is not commanded in the Scriptures, but is clearly implied as something that Christians should practice. When the Lord's disciples were criticized for not fasting, Jesus responded by suggesting that fasting was not appropriate for them while He was still here with them, but the time would come when He would be gone, and would become appropriate (see Luke 5:35). Also, when speaking about fasting, Jesus said, "When you fast, anoint your head and wash your face . . ." (Matthew 6:17). Here Jesus was clearly suggesting that He expected fasting to be regularly practiced, and He gives a few guidelines as well.

What is fasting? Fasting is a spiritual discipline in which one abstains from food for a period of time in order to seek God. Fasting can be as simple as giving up a meal or two in order to spend time in prayer, or can be something that is done for several days or more. During the time that would normally be spent fulfilling the body's physical needs of eating, time is spent meeting spiritual needs. A few reasons for fasting are to focus your attention on the Lord, especially if you are facing a challenge or difficult decision; to seek needed wisdom from God; to submit to the Lord; to fight temptation; or to repent.

God has given us food for enjoyment, nourishment, fellowship, and worship, but we should definitely set aside our physical hunger at times when a stronger spiritual hunger leads us to draw closer to God. Fasting should not be seen as something that only super-committed Christians do, but as something that every committed Christian should do. Never allow a few hunger pangs to quench your appetite for a deeper intimacy with God.

No temptation has overtaken you except such as is common to man; but God is faithful, who will not allow you to be tempted beyond what you are able, but with the temptation will also make the way of escape, that you may be able to bear it. (1 Corinthians 10:13)

MAY 8

Escape from Temptation Island

TEMPTATION RUSHES IN unexpectedly and assaults the mind, quickly diverting all attention away from what one knows is wrong and redirecting every thought toward fulfilling a selfish desire. Masquerading itself as harmless gratification or personal entitlement, temptation distorts your emotions and cravings, tricking you into believing that a particular thought or action you have right to enjoy or a freedom that you should be allowed to exercise. Temptation produces tunnel vision, restricting what the mind's eye can see, and confuses concentration by suspending all rational thought. For the Christian, temptation allows the sensual to supersede the spiritual.

Temptation hits everyone; no one is exempt. Temptation comes daily, as a relentless hunter. Temptation makes promises that cannot be kept: promising sweetness, but only providing bitterness; promising fulfillment, but only providing emptiness; promising satisfaction, and only providing a thirst for more.

Although all of this is true, being tempted is not a sin. Despite its extremely powerful gravitational pull, temptation can be resisted.

Paul realized that temptation is not a game, and therefore should not be taken lightly, especially by those who presume to have the strength in themselves to stand against it. He encouraged the Corinthians to pay attention and learn from the examples of others in the Bible, realizing that the temptations others faced were no different from the temptations the Corinthians faced.

The key to escaping temptation lies in God's faithfulness. His is a faithfulness that will not leave you deserted with no way of escaping. God's faithfulness will not allow temptation to fall upon you like a collapsing building, leaving you trapped beneath the devastation. Through His faithfulness, God promises to preserve His people, to protect them from being overwhelmed, and to always provide an escape, no matter the temptation. Temptation does not inevitably lead to sin. If temptation does lead to sin, the result is no one's fault but our own. We cannot play the blame game with sin and say, "The Devil made me do it." Neither Satan, nor the world can make us sin, and our own flesh cannot force us to sin. We sin because we chose to sin.

Resisting temptation is not easy, and we have all failed at one point or another. But no matter our successes or failures, more temptations will come our way, and we need to be ready. Do not let past failures keep you from present and future victories. Go on the offensive by praying before temptations come. Jesus said, "Watch and pray, lest you enter into temptation" (Matthew 26:41). Be aware that we fall into sin because we allow ourselves to give in to our own selfish desires. Replace your selfish desires with a desire to please and honor Christ with your life, just as Christ made His aim to do all things that pleased the Father. Be consistent in reading your Bible, because as Christ endured temptation by knowing and trusting in God's Word, we can make the right choices in resisting temptation by knowing the truth found in the Bible.

Finally, when temptation comes, the best thing you can do is to just leave! Get out of the situation and setting that is causing the temptation. The next time temptation assaults your senses, look for the spiritual escape route that God provides, and then walk away in victory.

So it was, when I heard these words, that I sat down and wept, and mourned for many days; I was fasting and praying before the God of heaven. (Nehemiah 1:4)

MAY 9

Effective Leadership

EVERY GENERATION has had great leaders, those people who inspire us and bring out the very best in us. We love to read books and watch movies where a strong, decisive individual takes command of a difficult situation, does the right thing, leads people to victory, and saves the day. Historically, men like George Washington have fit that profile, motivating and moving many to rise above their challenges and be part of establishing a new nation. Theatrically, there men like John Wayne stood for rugged individualism and would invariably ride in and save the day. Biblically, men like Nehemiah stand with similar influence and integrity, leading and rallying the people of Jerusalem into a time of revival and rebuilding.

Nehemiah was the cupbearer to King Artaxerxes when news reached him that the temple had been rebuilt in Jerusalem, but the walls that once surrounded the city were still in ruins. The people of Jerusalem were discouraged, disgraced, and defenseless. The news cut Nehemiah to the heart and became a burden that weighed heavily on his soul and moved him with compassion for his fellow countrymen.

So often, any great work of God begins here. As God allows us to be cut to the heart and burdened in our soul for people and we are moved with compassion, God moves us into action. Nehemiah's compassion and burden moved him to take the only action that someone should take before stepping out to serve God: he waited, he fasted, and he prayed. Before he made a plan, he prayed. Before he forged ahead, he fasted. Before walking, he waited.

Every undertaking *for* God must include consecration *to* God. Time must be spent seeking God and waiting upon Him. Simply put, through such times God works in us so that He can work through us. As we pray and wait, we learn that persistence in prayer teaches us perseverance, and perseverance is continuously needed in any work we carry out for God. We need to be prepared in order to be productive.

The lessons in leadership from the Book of Nehemiah are examples for all of us. You may not be called to rebuild a city or lead a spiritual revival, but as Christians, we are all leaders. You may be a husband who is leading his household, a parent who is leading his or her children, a businessperson who is leading at the workplace, or a Sunday school teacher who is leading a classroom of students. Or, you may be the only Christian in your neighborhood or in your family, and therefore your leading is by being an example before others.

Wherever and whomever you may be leading, remember that a good leader is also a good follower. Follow the example of people like Nehemiah, who prepared himself properly for the leadership role that God was preparing for him.

Therefore whoever eats this bread or drinks this cup of the Lord in an unworthy manner will be guilty of the body and blood of the Lord. (1 Corinthians 11:27)

MAY 10

Table Manners

TALKING WITH YOUR MOUTH FULL, reaching over another person to grab a plate, burping, slurping, putting your elbows on the table, and wiping your mouth on your sleeve are all considered to be bad table manners. In today's fast-paced world, everything is becoming more and more about convenience, with casual attitudes and casual attire replacing the former days of formality. Despite cultural trends or social preferences, good manners are always in vogue, and good manners are never more obvious than when they are not being observed. When we come to the Lord's Table to share in the Lord's Supper, as we remember His sacrifice for us, we must make sure that we observe this sacrament with good manners and the right motives.

Paul saw in the Corinthian church something far worse than just bad etiquette. What he saw was an extremely offensive display of selfishness as the church gathered to take Communion. What was originally established to be a celebration, centering on the most selfless act in human history, had now turned into a three-ring circus of complete self-centeredness. That which was intended to promote unity and deepen fellowship only brought division and disgrace. People were getting drunk, gorging themselves, and refusing to share their food with those who were in real need. This was hardly the best way to prepare to participate in one of the most sacred ordinances given to us by Jesus.

Although we may not see people getting drunk in church before taking Communion today, both a right way and a wrong way to approach the Communion table still exists today. How do you prepare yourself to receive Communion?

Communion is an important act of worship in which God's people gather together to remember the sacrificial death of Jesus Christ on the cross. In order to take Communion in the right manner, we need to properly prepare our hearts first. This means we do not simply go through the sacred motions of Communion. We are not to treat the act of Communion like an empty tradition or a rote ritual; this is a holy act of fellowship and worship. No matter how often we choose to partake in Communion, Paul tells us that we must examine ourselves before receiving and ask the Lord to search our hearts for anything that is displeasing to Him.

We must start by examining our personal relationship with Jesus. Communion is all about Jesus, so you must first know Jesus personally; He must be your Lord and Savior. If you know Him, then you must ensure that your relationship with Him is in good standing. You must not take Communion if any sin in your life remains unconfessed, if you are bitter or angry, or if you struggle with recurring sin. Confess and surrender these sins to Jesus before taking Communion. Communion is for the sinner, and we are sinners saved by grace, but we must lay our sins openly before God first through the act of confession so that we do not displease or dishonor Him.

Communion should be approached seriously, with reverence, and with self-examination, but also viewed as a joyous time, which should be filled with thanksgiving as we remember the God's grace, shown to us through the sacrifice of Jesus. The next time you approach the Lord's Table, do so with proper table manners.

Then the king said to me, "What do you request?"
So I prayed to the God of heaven. (Nehemiah 2:4)

Waiting with Purpose

MAY
11

AFTER FINISHING AN APPRENTICESHIP, a newly converted young man named William could not find work for an entire year. This was the most difficult trial of his entire life. He was puzzled because God was not answering his persistent prayer for work. He even had a widowed mother who desperately needed his financial help. But God knew that those twelve months of poverty would later give him the unique ability to identify with the poor. William Booth would go on to create The Salvation Army, which now helps people in need in 124 different countries. Sometimes no matter how much you want something to happen, or what you may try in order to make anything happen, all you can do is wait.. For most of us, waiting is the hardest part. Are you waiting on God right now? Do you know how to wait with purpose?

When Nehemiah received the news that the wall surrounding Jerusalem was lying in ruins, the Lord gave Nehemiah a burden to act. Nehemiah wanted to go to Jerusalem to honor God by being a part of rebuilding the holy city's wall. What happened next for Nehemiah? Nothing! After a week passed? Still nothing! A whole month went by with no word or direction from God. Then two months, then three, and so on. At this point, some questions might naturally come to your mind, like: *God, are you still there? Did I hear you right? Was that message meant for someone else?*

Have you ever thought maybe you heard God wrong? Are you waiting on God for some answers, opportunities, or direction. God often makes us wait before He moves us to action, but:

> "[w]aiting for God is not laziness. Waiting for God is not going to sleep. Waiting for God is not the abandonment of effort. Waiting for God means, first, activity under command; second, readiness for any new command that may come; third, the ability to do nothing until the command is given."[23]

Nehemiah had to wait for God's timing, but he knew how to wait with purpose. He did not know *when* or really even *if* God was going to give him the opportunity to return to Jerusalem to help rebuild, but Nehemiah knew he was going to be ready to go if God gave him the opportunity. Waiting with purpose means doing just what Nehemiah began to do: pray and wait. Nehemiah prayed, trusting and believing God would make a way (see Nehemiah 1:5–11).

Nehemiah also continued to do his job well. His work did not suffer, he was not working with one foot out the door or with his head in the clouds, nor was he waiting for that day when he would be out of there. He was not distracted, and he did not whine or complain as he waited for an opportunity to go to Jerusalem.

Nehemiah had also been planning during his wait, considering in advance what he would need to do the job for God, and he counting the costs. He wanted to be ready if and when opportunity came. A Civil War saying advises, "trust the Lord, but keep your powder dry!" In other words, God is in control, but we should still be prepared. Praying, planning, and waiting on God always precede serving God. The sooner we learn to wait God's way, the sooner we can be used to build God's way.

Now concerning spiritual gifts, brethren, I do not want you to be ignorant. (1 Corinthians 12:1)

Your God-Given Gift

HOW CAN WE LIVE A LIFE THAT MATTERS, moves past the monotonous, makes a lasting difference, and is fruitful, full of joy, and God-honoring? Sound like an impossibility? Well, fear not! The way to find purpose, to get on the fast track to an abundant and active life that honors God is by understanding your place in the body of Christ.

Some Christians think that a Christian bookstore is the only place to find spiritual gifts. To say most Christians have no idea what their spiritual gifts are is an understatement. This means that most are not living up to God's greatest and best for their lives. Adding to this confusion is the misunderstanding between physical *talents* and spiritual *gifts*.

You might say, "Oh, well I love to sing, so singing is my gift" or "I like to work with my hands, so building is my gift."

Simply put, these abilities are talents, not gifts. Although God gives us both talents and gifts, the best way to distinguish between the two is as follows: talents are for earthly or physical benefit or enjoyment, while gifts are given for heavenly or spiritual benefit to bring glory to God. Spiritual gifts build the kingdom of God, benefit the body of Christ, and bring glory to God. Although singing is a talent and not a spiritual gift, the ability to sing *can* be used to complement a spiritual gift, like that of encouragement.

If you want God to use you to make a lasting difference in the lives of others, then the place to start is by knowing your spiritual gifts. Paul lists the spiritual gifts in three places: in 1 Corinthians 12, in Romans 12, and in Ephesians 4. Together, these scriptures list a total of twenty different spiritual gifts. Once you understand what these gifts are and how they operate, then time has come to find yours. Finding your gift is not a matter of picking and choosing, and not a spiritual buffet where you say, "Oh, I like that gift; I think I will take a little teaching with a side of helps and a dash of prophecy." Instead, spiritual gifts are given to each Christian by the Holy Spirit and are given according to God's will, not according to your desire for a particular gift. Most people have more than one gift, no one has all the gifts, and no Christian goes without at least one gift.

So how do you discover your gifts? Start by praying and asking God to reveal your spiritual gift(s) to you. He is not playing hide-and-seek with your gifts; God wants you to know what they are and for you to use them, so ask Him to show you. God will give you a passion for the gifts that He has given you, so as you look over the gifts, pay attention to the ones you are drawn to the most, and start serving. You will most likely encounter a bit of trial and error during the discovery process, so do not get discouraged. Step out and see what God blesses. Take the feedback of a few trusted mentors into consideration as they observe you in action. An outside perspective of a trusted and mature believer can go a long way in narrowing your focus.

Nothing is more exciting and rewarding than using your God-given gifts. God has given us all we need so we can do all that He has prepared for us to do.

Seek to discover your God-given gift, and rise above the humdrum and enjoy a fulfilling and fruitful, God-glorifying life.

Now it happened, when Sanballat, Tobiah, the Arabs, the Ammonites, and the Ashdodites heard that the walls of Jerusalem were being restored and the gaps were beginning to be closed, that they became very angry, and all of them conspired together to come and attack Jerusalem and create confusion. (Nehemiah 4:7–8)

MAY
13

The Law of Opposition

W E ARE ALL FAMILIAR with certain laws of nature. For example, the law of gravity, which is often expressed in the statement, "What goes up must come down." Also, we have Newton's third law of motion, which says that for every action there is an equal and opposite reaction.

Just as physical laws govern the natural world, spiritual laws also govern the spiritual world. One such spiritual law, demonstrated throughout the pages of the Scriptures, is what we shall call the Law of Opposition.

The Law of Opposition says that when the people of God begin to do the work of God, the Enemy of God will try and stop them. For example, Moses was opposed by Pharaoh, David was opposed by Saul, and Jesus came face-to-face with Satan himself. Nehemiah was no exception; he had an opportunity to serve God, and he prayed and waited on God before stepping out in faith. But as soon as he was ready to begin the work, the enemy was right there, trying to stop the work from beginning.

When God opened the door of opportunity, Nehemiah boldly walked through and went to Jerusalem. Upon his arrival, he succeeded in gaining the support of the people whom he needed to help rebuild the city walls, and the work began quickly. What Nehemiah faced next is what every believer will face when stepping out to do the work of God: opposition. Nehemiah's opposition came from both external and internal threats, all attempting to stop the work of God.

Nehemiah responded with both spiritual sense and common sense; he used his Bible and his brain. Instead of firing back when attacked, which is how we often react, Nehemiah talked to God first. We must always remember that we are in a spiritual battle, and we will not win the war if we fight with our flesh. Prayer, the first step, is a very powerful weapon that the Enemy does not want us to use. And quite simply, we should never respond to opposition until we have first spent time in prayer.

After seeking the Lord in prayer, waiting on God for His divine timing, and searching out the Scriptures, Nehemiah then used his common sense. The opposition against the work of God switched from mocking and name calling to intimidation and threats, so Nehemiah responded decisively. Half the people would work on the wall, and half the people would stand guard on the wall with swords. This solution is both practical and spiritual, as the Bible tells us several times to "watch and pray." The people were now ready for God to work in and through them.

Nehemiah both prayed and prepared. He relied on God and stayed ready for the enemy. He prayed for the best and prepared for the worst. Sometimes the answer to prayer is given through the ability God has given you to accomplish the task. Nehemiah kept his eyes on God and his hand to the plow.

When you step out to serve God, be prayed up and prepared, and remain practical when dealing with opposition.

> Though I speak with the tongues of men and of angels, but have not love, I have become sounding brass or a clanging cymbal. (1 Corinthians 13:1)

MAY
14

What's Love Got to Do with It?

WHAT IS THAT ANNOYING SOUND? Is that the sound of someone's nails on a chalkboard? Or the sound of a dentist's drill? Maybe the ear-piercing feedback from a microphone? Or the screech of a train stopping as metal scrapes against metal? No, actually the sound is much worse than any of those: the sound of a Christian who does not have love. Talk is cheap, and "do as I say, not as I do" does not cut muster when living the Christian life. If we want to do God's will in a way that brings the greatest glory to Him, we must do everything with love.

Often called the love chapter, 1 Corinthians 13 gives us an impressive and imposing description of love, a description that proves to be much easier said than done. Despite the difficulty one finds in the application of love, true Christian love must not be confined to our mere admiration of its impressive nature or limited to empty conversations that yield little to no change. The love we are called to exhibit needs to be a comprehensive and complete, all-encompassing, all-consuming expression found in our everyday lives.

Paul strategically placed the subject of Christian love right in the middle of his discussion about spiritual gifts in an attempt to give us the proper perspective of how we are to serve God and exercise our spiritual gifts. Paul is saying, in essence, "It is not *what* spiritual gift you have but *how* you use your spiritual gift that matters." And the *how* is to be with love!

The love spoken of here is not a sensual love, or a brotherly love or a family love, and this love is not based on a feeling or emotion. Rather, this love is the highest form of love a person can have. This giving, generous, and gracious love is sacrificial, selfless, and unconditional, . The love spoken of here is thoughtful, kindhearted, and comprehensive. This love is a choice and a decision; here, love is an action verb, full of life, and a fruit of the Spirit. This love is practical, pragmatic, real-world relevant, everyday applicable, and above all, a Christian's daily obligation. This is a love that finds its fulfillment through living. This love works, serves, and helps, without resentment, flashiness, arrogance, or pride, and expresses itself by being patient and gentle, caring and compassionate, generous, trusting, hopeful, and enduring. This love is not optional or pointless, but is a nonnegotiable that must be the guiding principle in all that we say and do as Christians.

What's love got to do with the Christian life? The answer is everything! What do your works amount to if they are done without love? Nothing! Do not let your life be an irritating sound that drives people away. Instead, let your life be a sweet symphony that finds its expression through a life lived perfectly in tune with the love of God.

So they read distinctly from the book, in the Law of God; and they gave the sense, and helped them to understand the reading. (Nehemiah 8:8)

MAY

15

The Wind of Change

ANY TRUE REVIVAL cannot happen apart from the Spirit of God, working through the Word of God. When the Word of God is given the proper place in the life of a church, the life of a nation, or a person's life, conviction comes by the Holy Spirit, and the wind of spiritual revival begins to blow. Revival can be described as a renewed interest in, or passion for, the things of God. Charles Spurgeon once said during one of his sermons:

> Oh! men and brethren, what would this heart feel if I could but believe that there were some among you who would go home and pray for a revival . . . men whose faith is large enough, and their love fiery enough to lead them from this moment to exercise unceasing intercessions that God would appear among us and do wondrous things here, as in the times of former generations.[24]

In chapters 8 through 10 of Nehemiah, we see the people of God returning to the Word of God and being refreshed by the Spirit of God as a citywide revival breaks out. The Word of God was read and taught and was received willingly by the people, revitalizing their faith in God. As we examine the revival that swept Jerusalem in that day, we notice a few essentials that will cause personal revival to break out in our hearts and corporate revival to sweep through our churches.

The first is *conviction.* The reading and teaching of the Word brought people to a place where godly sorrow had gripped their hearts as they recognized their disobedience toward God and were convicted of their sin against God (see Nehemiah 8:9).

Second, that conviction brought *confession.* The revival sweeping across the city had awakened the hearts of the people to the things of God, and with this new love for the Word came a new hatred for sin, which led the people to humble themselves and confess their sins to God (see Nehemiah 9:2). No spiritual growth or revival can occur until sin is dealt with first. We do not need to dwell on our sin, but we do need to declare our sin to God so that God can forgive us and deal with the sin in our lives.

Lastly, for revival to take root, there must be *commitment.* The people experienced a renewed conviction of sin and repentance, which was followed by an intense desire to continue to live in obedience to God (Nehemiah 10:29). The people realized that their lives needed to match what they believed. Commitment means all or nothing. No such thing as partial commitment to God exists. Some have aptly said that the Christian life is like climbing a greased pole; you are either climbing up or sliding down, with no in-between. If the people of Jerusalem had failed to make a commitment here, everything up to this point would have been just an emotional response and nothing more than lip service. Commitment is where the rubber meets the road. Real commitment means absolute surrender and total submission to God.

Are you are feeling dry and disconnected from God? Are you feeling passionless and purposeless? Dig into the Word of God and allow the wind of revival to bring you to the place of conviction, confession, and commitment before God.

And if Christ is not risen, then our preaching is empty and your faith is also empty. (1 Corinthians 15:14)

This Day in History

MAY 16

WHAT DO YOU THINK is the single most important day in all of human history? Throughout history, the world has seen many important days, so to narrow just one most important is no small task. Some of the days that are certainly worthy of consideration are the day the wheel was invented, the day mankind first entered space, the day the assembly line produced its first product, the day Archduke Ferdinand was assassinated (starting World War I), the day the printing press was invented, or the day the Declaration of Independence was signed. These were all significant, world-changing events that made an impact on millions of people and changed history, but what about the day Jesus Christ rose from the dead?

Paul believed that the single most important event in all of history was the day that Jesus rose from the dead. He went so far as to say that if Jesus did not rise from the dead, then nothing in life really matters or has any real significance. If life is pointless, then do what you want to do, live how you want to live, go for the gusto, eat, drink, and be merry, for tomorrow, you die. If Jesus did not rise from the dead, Paul concluded that life would be meaningless, faith would be useless, and no hope would exist beyond the grave.

On the other hand, if Jesus *did* rise from the dead, then nothing else is more important, and life does have meaning, what you do *is* important, and there is *hope* beyond the grave. Paul declared that the foundation of our faith is built upon the *fact* of the resurrection of Jesus Christ, and from this fact we can boldly stand strong and unshakable in our faith, secure in our salvation, and able to carry out the work of God. As Henry Morris wrote:

> The bodily resurrection of Jesus Christ from the dead is the crowning proof of Christianity. Everything else that was said or done by Christ and the apostles is secondary in importance to the resurrection. If the resurrection did not take place then Christianity is a false religion. If it did take place, then Christ is God and the Christian faith is absolute truth.[25]

The Bible makes much of the Resurrection of Jesus, mentioning the event over three hundred times. This event is highly esteemed and full of significance and power, and a sign for unbelievers (see Matthew 12:38–40). The Resurrection is the answer for the believer's doubt (see Luke 24:38–43), serves as the guarantee that Jesus' teachings are true (see Acts 2:22–24), and is the center of the gospel itself (see Romans 4:24–25; 10:9). The Resurrection is the motivation for evangelism (see Matthew 28:18–20), the source of the believer's daily power (see Philippians 3:10), and the reason for total commitment to Christ (see Romans 7:4). The Resurrection removes the fear of death (see John 11:25), and provides a foretaste of heaven for the believer (see Philippians 3:20–21; 1 Peter 1:3–5).

With all these reasons and many more, the day that Jesus rose from the dead must be the single most important day in all of human history. The Resurrection should be a day that we always remember, and a day that impacts the way we live each and every day.

Thus I cleansed them of everything pagan.
(Nehemiah 13:30)

MAY 17

Beware of Backsliding

NOT SURPRISINGLY, most people like fairy-tale endings. Who does not want life to finish with, "And they lived happily ever after"? The Book of Nehemiah would have finished with one of those happy endings we all love if the book ended after chapter 12. The walls had been rebuilt, conflicts had been resolved, the people were singing "Kumbaya" (or something similar). Before Chapter 13, Jerusalem residents seemed like to have an *It's a Wonderful Life!*- sort of ending.

Unfortunately, chapter 12 is not the end of the story, and a harsh reminder of the cost of compromise and the danger of backsliding follows. Backsliding is refusal to listen to God and often includes returning to one's old, disobedient ways. Compromise, if not dealt with quickly and corrected, can lead to backsliding.

Nehemiah had returned to Babylon, resuming his duties as the king's cupbearer. Meanwhile back in Jerusalem, people were backsliding. The high priest was tolerating sin people chose to pursue financial gain rather than pursuing God, and purity was exchanged for pleasure. The people had become complacent. As one writer said:

> Complacency is a blight that saps energy, dulls attitudes, and causes a drain on the brain. The first symptom is satisfaction with things as they are. The second is rejection of things as they might be. "Good enough" becomes today's watchword and tomorrow's standard. Complacency makes people fear the unknown, mistrust the untried, and abhor the new. Like water, complacent people follow the easiest course—downhill.[26]

When Nehemiah returned to Jerusalem, he determined to set things straight. He first dealt with the traitor in the temple. In Nehemiah's absence, the high priest had allowed an enemy of God to live in the temple, so Nehemiah threw him out (which the high priest should have done long before). Nehemiah did just as Ephesians 4:27 instructs, refusing to "give place to the devil." We must be on guard at all times, or the Enemy will move in and set up residence in our hearts.

Next, Nehemiah ended moneymaking on the Sabbath. People were seeking wealth first, and they lost sight of God and His promises. A Sabbath of rest was made mandatory so the people would always keep a godly perspective. Simply put, the continual practice of worship helps to keep you focused on God, which will help keep you from backsliding.

Finally, our relationships must be pure. The people of Jerusalem became unequally yoked with nonbelievers. Marrying whomever you want to marry, regardless of whether he or she believes as you believe, is one of the fastest ways to damage your commitment with God. This does not mean cannot have friends who do not share our faith in God, but we need to keep a healthy balance, remaining true to our faith. But to keep yourself pure, remember that bad company corrupts good character, and being unequally yoked will always pull you down.

Beware of backsliding, a slow weakening process, which can be very subtle. Protect yourself by remaining unwavering in your commitment to God, steadfast in your perseverance, and determined in your obedience to the Word of God.

Blessed be the God and Father of our Lord Jesus Christ, the Father of mercies and God of all comfort, who comforts us in all our tribulation, that we may be able to comfort those who are in any trouble, with the comfort with which we ourselves are comforted by God. (2 Corinthians 1:3–4)

MAY 18

Comfort from Above

When peace, like a river, attendeth my way,
When sorrows like sea billows roll;
Whatever my lot, Thou has taught me to say,
It is well, it is well, with my soul.

WRITTEN BY CHICAGO LAWYER Horatio Spafford in 1873, these often-sung and much-loved words did not flow from the fountains of blessing. Rather, they rose up like relentless waves pounding the seashore while carrying the most devastating of distresses. Scarlet fever had stolen the life of his four-year-old son, and the great Chicago fires had burned down all his real estate investments. In desperate need of some time away for his family, he planned a trip to England. At the docks in New York, Spafford was called back to Chicago on business, but he sent his wife and four daughters on ahead and promised to meet up with them as soon as possible.

Nine days later, Spafford received a telegram informing him that all four children were killed when their ship to England sank; only his wife survived. Spafford immediately set sail to meet up with his wife and, as the ship he was on passed over the location where his daughters drowned, he penned the great hymn, "It is Well with My Soul," a hymn that has brought comfort to countless people over the years.

The Apostle Paul was no stranger to trouble, trials, tribulation, and anguish. He declared, "Three times I was beaten with rods; once I was stoned; three times I was shipwrecked; a night and a day I have been in the deep, . . . in perils of robbers, . . . in weariness and toil, in sleeplessness often, in hunger and thirst, . . . in cold and nakedness" (2 Corinthians 11:25–27). Out of the depths of his personal suffering to the heights of experiencing God's mercy, Paul was able to declare that even in times of suffering the possibility for blessing is still there, abundant comfort can be found in God, and divine purposes are at work.

How does God comfort us in times of trouble? Comfort begins as we praise God for who He is. As we esteem God for His nature and character, our perspective on our troubles grows dim in the light of our great God. Equally important, as we remember the redemptive work accomplished through Jesus Christ, who gave us eternal life, we see power and love in it all. God, rich in mercy, has promised never to leave us or forsake us, so he gave us The Holy Spirit, sometimes called the Comforter. God comforts us through His presence and His peace.

If we focus our attention on our troubles, they can drown us. As we look to God and consider who He is and what He has done for us, we realize that can He comfort us and also use us to comfort others. God gives us a unique opportunity to use our experiences to help others get through their troubled times. Troubles, as difficult and painful as they may be, are never wasted on the Christian. If you are in trouble, look to Him for comfort. If you have experienced His comfort, then look to Him for an opportunity to share what He has shown you with others who are in need of encouragement.

"Yet who knows whether you have come to the kingdom for such a time as this?" (Esther 4:14)

MAY 19

Once Upon a Time

FROM SLEEPING BEAUTY to Snow White, from Cinderella to Belle, fairy tales with enchanted characters (complete with kingdoms and castles and people who live happily ever after) have long captured the imaginations of more than just children. Stories that begin with, "Long ago in a distant land" or "Once upon a time" prepare the reader for tales of mystery and magic, and adventure and exploration.

Tucked away in the recesses of the Old Testament is an often-overlooked jewel, a true story that reads much like a fairy tale. An orphan girl became a queen and lived in a beautiful palace, where she would eventually save her people from the treacherous hands of an evil nobleman. Her story mixes the foreknowledge of God with the choices of mankind (or in this case, a woman), and illustrates how humanity has been given the privilege to participate in the plans of God. The story's timeless application is relevant for believers of all ages.

Long ago in the land of Susa, a young woman named Esther lost her parents at a very young age. She was taken in as an orphan, and cared for by her uncle Mordecai, who loved her as his own child and taught her about her heritage as a Jew. One day she was selected to participate in a very special beauty pageant for the king of the empire, and when she was presented to the king, he fell in love with her and made her queen. But lurking in the shadows was the evil Haman, a nobleman and trusted adviser to the king. Haman's hatred for Mordecai led him to influence the king to demand the extermination of all the Jews, a decision with which the king agreed, completely unaware that this would lead to the death of his queen.

What was Queen Esther to do? What would you do? She could go to the king and plead her case, but to appear before the king uninvited meant certain death, with only one exception: if the king agreed to pardon the uninvited intruder in his court and extend grace to him or her. Such a plan was risky, with no guarantee of success. But could Esther really afford to do nothing when so much was at stake? Mordecai encouraged Esther, telling her God would accomplish His plans and His purposes with or without her help, but by not choosing to cooperate with God's will for her life, she would be missing out on a great opportunity. After all, God placed her in this predicament, so that she could be used to deliver God's people from the hands of the enemy.

God is in control, and He has placed us all in different lands under different rulers for such a time as this. People are here who need for us to minister to them, lives are in need of our impact, and many people need to be delivered out of the hands of the enemy, and come to trust in the one and only King of kings, Jesus Christ. Nothing is accidental in the life of a believer, even when times are difficult.

God has you right where He wants you. Following God means making hard choices, including the choice to participate with God's plans or not. If you choose not to participate, then God will use someone else in your place. But God wants to use you. He has a plan and a purpose for your life, if you are willing to step up and step out in faith.

Then one day, our King will come, and we will live happily ever after in His heavenly kingdom.

So all of us who have had that veil removed can see and reflect the glory of the Lord. And the Lord—who is the Spirit—makes us more and more like him as we are changed into his glorious image. (2 Corinthians 3:18 NLT)

MAY
20

Mirror, Mirror

HAPPINESS has been described by some as being able to look in the mirror and like what you see. Most of the time, we get up in the morning, look in the mirror, and, after letting out a sigh, we begin to work on the image looking back at us. Men comb their hair, brush their teeth, shave, and get dressed. Women may add primping, curling, moisturizing, and applying makeup to that morning fix-up list. But whether we spend ten minutes or sixty minutes in front of a mirror, we all spend time each and every day working on our appearances, because how we present ourselves is a reflection of who we are. When others look at you, what do they see? What type of image are you projecting to your friends, family, coworkers, and neighbors?

The Apostle Paul thought how a Christian was perceived was important. And although he would have agreed we should take care of ourselves physically, the most important aspect of how we appear to others is less about our hair being picture-perfect or our shoes matching our pants, and more about whether we are reflecting the image of Jesus Christ to the world around us. To help illustrate this, Paul brought in a blast from Israel's past by giving an example from the life of Moses.

During the time when the children of Israel were wandering in the desert, Moses had the exclusive privilege of talking to God face-to-face (see Exodus 33:11). This personal and powerful powwow with the living God had such an effect on Moses that, after leaving the presence of God, his face would shine with an afterglow. The people were both amazed and afraid, so Moses put a veil over his face to hide the glory that resulted from his nearness to God. Moses came to realize, however, that the longer he was away from the presence of God, the more the glow faded.

Now, under the New Covenant, *all* believers are afforded the extraordinary privilege of nearness with the living God. Because of Jesus Christ, we can all look to Christ and behold the glory of God. As we draw close to God, He works in us to transform us into His image so that we can reflect His glory to those around us. Because of the Holy Spirit, we now can have an even closer relationship with God than Moses was able to have because the Holy Spirit lives inside every believer.

The result of this blessed close proximity to God should be a reflection of the living God and a permanent afterglow. Speaking of reflecting Jesus, what do others see when they look at you? We become what we behold; this means if we are spending time looking to Jesus, then we should also be looking like Jesus. In order to look more like Jesus, we need to spend less time looking at ourselves and more time looking at Him. As we fix our eyes on the author and finisher of our faith, we will be a better reflection of our glorious God. The closer you are in proximity to God, the more you will reflect His image. But if you pull away from God, His image in you will begin to fade.

"The Lord gave and the Lord has taken away; may the name of the Lord be praised." (Job 1:21 NIV)

MAY 21

The Choice Is Yours

LIFE IS FULL OF SOME WONDERFUL MOMENTS: falling in love, laughing until your sides hurt, witnessing the birth of a child, spending time with close friends, or watching the sunset, just to name a few. But life has tragedies as well, like the death of a child, the loss of house and home, and economic failure, again, just to name a few. In life's most difficult moments, a person's character is most apparent. When tragedy hits, the choice is yours to either respond in faith and worship God through the pain, or dismiss and denounce God because of the pain.

Job suffered. He lost family and friends, and he lost health and wealth. But he never lost his faith. Job made the choice, in his hour of greatest pain, to say, "The LORD gave and the LORD has taken away; may the name of the LORD be praised" (Job 1:21 NIV). Satan thought for sure that Job could be turned against God and that he would break down under the weight of tragedy and throw away his faith in God. Satan thought no one could possibly choose to worship God after experiencing such terrible tragedy. But through everything, Job refused to blame God. He would not complain, and he would not condemn God's sovereignty. And in so doing, as Chuck Swindoll describes:

> The wicked spirits sat with their mouths wide open as it were, as they watched a man who responded to all of his adversities with adoration; who concluded all of his woes with worship. No blame. No bitterness. No cursing. No clinched fist raised to the heavens screaming, "How dare you do this to me, after I've walked with you all these years!" None of that.[27]

God allowed Job to be reduced to a crust of bread, and even at his lowest point, Job refused to curse God, and instead chose to praise Him. The temptation to kick and scream against the heartbreak that God allows is always there, along with the desire to hold on to what God is taking away. True worship, however, originates in the simple fact that God is worthy of worship, regardless of our circumstances.

Accepting the good things that God gives us is easy. The challenge is to readily receive what tragedy takes away. The challenge is choosing blessing and not bitterness, adoration instead of anger, and worship without whining. We must have a willing attitude and a teachable spirit, always remembering that nothing comes into our lives except what God allows.

Life is full of wonderful moments and terrible tragedies. The real test of our worship is not how loud we sing His praises in times of blessing, but how willing we are to continue singing His praises in our pain. How willing are you? The choice is yours.

For we know that if our earthly house, this tent, is destroyed, we have a building from God, a house not made with hands, eternal in the heavens. (2 Corinthians 5:1)

MAY
22

In the Face of Death

AS AN ENTIRE FAMILY sat together in the doctor's office waiting to hear the update, you could cut the tension with a knife. A few nervous jokes were made to try and lighten the mood before the doctor came in, and the laughter proved helpful, but was only temporary. Several long years of an all-out war with the evil enemy of cancer led up to this day. The combat included countless visits to the doctor, an assortment of intense treatments, repeated scans, and endless medications that led to extreme physical highs and lows. Sitting cramped in the small, sterile exam room, everyone knew the outcome of this visit. The fact that the disease was winning the war against the frail body sitting front and center had become painfully obvious to all.

When the doctor finally said, "There is nothing else we can do, except to make you as comfortable as possible in the time you have left," The moment was almost surreal. Despite the sting of that news, the one who should have been the most disappointed remained a pillar of courage and confidence. How could someone who had been walking in the shadow of death for years, someone who was standing face-to-face with her own mortality, remain calmly confident about the insufficient and unpredictable number of days that lay ahead? And how can we face death with a similar, brave confidence?

The Apostle Paul was no stranger to persecution; he faced death on a daily basis. Knowing that any day could be his last, Paul still had confidence that transcended his circumstances; his confidence was in God and not in circumstances. Paul traded what he did not know about his future for what he did know about God. This gave him the strength to live courageously for Christ, even in the face of death.

Paul tells us that our current body is nothing more than a tent, a temporary dwelling that believers will trade in for a permanent, heavenly home that God is preparing for us: a glorified body, insusceptible to sin, disease, and death. Until that day, God has given all who trust in Christ everything we need for godly living through His Holy Spirit. He is our proof of purchase, our guarantee of a new home in Heaven. Paul declared every believer is guaranteed the hope and confidence that death will lead to an immediate passage into the very presence of Christ. The confidence of our future in heaven with God should be a source of strength and a motivation to live a life that that is well pleasing to God.

For the believer, death is not to be feared, because only through death are we fully released from the restrictions of these bodies into the riches of our heavenly habitations. For believers in Christ, the how and when of our physical death does not limit our ability to live with a courageous faith each and every day, even in the toughest trials, because the light of God's grace will always outshine the darkest of circumstances.

This is how someone can walk through battling cancer with dignity, grace, and confidence. This is how Paul was able to face persecution and eventually execution with boldness. Faith trusts in the promises of God, faith waits patiently for the eternity that lay ahead, and faith knows that all pain is temporary. Faith in the face of death empowers you to live courageously because of your heavenly confidence.

So they sat down with him on the ground seven days and seven nights, and no one spoke a word to him, for they saw that his grief was very great. (Job 2:13)

MAY 23

Helping the Hurting

PEOPLE everywhere are hurting. At any given moment, people are experiencing or recovering from natural disasters such as floods, tornados, hurricanes, earthquakes, fires, or tsunamis. Other tragedies such as shootings, car accidents, plane crashes, bombs, kidnappings, and countless other heartbreaks are happening all around the world. Unexpected tragedies resulting in the loss of property and the loss of life happen every day, leaving people in a state of emotional and spiritual crisis. How can we best help ourselves and others who are in the middle of a crisis?

Job was a man who was blessed by God. He was one of the richest men in the world, blessed with plentiful possessions, a huge house, and a large family that included a wife, seven sons, and three daughters. But Job's greatest asset was not the abundance of his possessions or the size of his portfolio, but his character. Job "was blameless and upright, and one who feared God and shunned evil." (Job 1:1). God even said, "There is none like him on the earth" (Job 1:8).

However, in a sudden and severe series of devastating events, Job would suffer unimaginable loss. Nearby raiders swooped in and slaughtered servants and stole possessions, a fire ignited and quickly consumed even more servants and killed thousands of sheep. Seeing this as an opportunity, other robbers came in and plundered Job's property. In an absolutely crushing blow, a tornado-like wind arose and caused his house to collapse, killing all his children in an instant. If such calamity was not bad enough, Job would then be struck with a painful physical condition that covered his entire body and caused such great agony that he wished he was never born. Job's character was resilient, and spiritually, he demonstrated a remarkably strong faith that allowed him to praise God in the midst of such great sorrow and pain. However, this strength did not remove the fact that Job was still hurting and experiencing a time of crisis.

Job had several "friends" who came to comfort and counsel him during his time of great distress, but overall they were anything but consoling and compassionate. They were accusatory, condemning, and insensitive. His friends were thoughtless, careless, and reckless with their words, and, as the saying goes, "With friends like these, who needs enemies?" Nevertheless, Job's counselors did one thing right. When they first came to see Job, they were in such shock at all the calamities that had befallen Job that all they could do was sit in silence with Job for seven days. The simplicity of their presence and the humility of their silence would prove to be the most sensitive and powerful portion of their ministry to Job.

Most of us will naturally shy away from people in pain. We often do so because we do not know what to say, we do not know how to act, and we do not know the best way to help. Out of this awkwardness, people can say some very thoughtless things to people in pain because they feel they need to say something, as though their words will fix everything. One of the best lessons we can learn from Job's counselors is that often, the first step in counseling people in crisis is to just be there with them, sit with them, cry with them, hold their hand, listen to them, put your arm on their shoulder, and allow the power of your presence to minister to them. Then, when the time is right, you can point them to the strength found in God's presence.

> Now I rejoice, not that you were made sorry, but that your sorrow led to repentance. For you were made sorry in a godly manner. (2 Corinthians 7:9)

MAY
24

A Tale of Two Sorrows

I'M SORRY! These words can be hard to say. For most people, apologies do not come easy. But apologizing with sincerity to someone can go a long way in mending broken fences caused by misspoken words or hurtful actions. However, as good as saying you are sorry is (if you truly are sorry), if your actions do not agree with your apology, two questions remain: Was your apology genuine, and are you really sorry?

The Bible teaches two types of sorrow; one is superficial, and the other, substantial. One is preoccupied with consequences, and the other, motivated by conviction. One is worldly, and the other, godly.

The Apostle Paul, in his first letter to the Corinthians, is stern but loving, uncompromising yet caring, and truthful yet tender. He admonished this struggling church to get right with God and deal with their sins. Paul rebuked the Corinthians for their immorality, carnality, and their self-centeredness, and he told them to stop "playing church" and to start being a church. The letter was difficult for Paul to write, he had to because the church in Corinth needed to be corrected. True love will seek to correct sin, not condone sin. Paul admitted that he was not trying to make them feel bad about their sin, but he did want them to abandon their sin.

With *worldly* sorrow, a person merely feels bad about his or her sin, experiencing regret, guilt, and remorse for something he or she said or did. Motivated by a fear of consequences, he or she seeks to rectify the mistake, which usually involves offering up a white flag with the words *I'm sorry* on it. This is where worldly sorrow usually stops, with no change in behavior. Worldly sorrow is mostly concerned with the effect the wrong will have on the relationship with the individual. *Godly* sorrow, on the other hand, is concerned with the effect the wrong has on the individual's relationship with God.

Worldly sorrow believes the solution is found in saying, "I will try harder next time" or "It will not happen again," which is nothing more than a self-help approach to change. But godly sorrow recognizes that no hope for any lasting change can exist apart from God's help. Worldly sorrow is all talk and no action, while godly sorrow is both talk and action.

How can we ensure that we exhibit godly sorrow after we sin? The answer lies in repentance. Paul said that godly sorrow brings repentance that leads to salvation. As we are convicted about the sin in our lives, we will be moved to make any and all necessary changes to make a clean break from our sin. Godly sorrow will produce a pursuit of purification, a concern for righteousness, and a determination for exoneration, and will respond with separation from sinfulness.

Saying "I'm sorry" to God is good; this is part of confessing our sins to Him. But unless our actions coincide with our apology, our sincerity is questionable. If something is in your life that you need to confess to God, take the sin seriously, confess immediately, and turn from the sin today. Do not just regret your sin; repent from the sin and allow godly sorrow to work in you.

"If a man dies, shall he live again?" (Job 14:14)

The Death Clock

LIFE IS SHORT and then you die. This sounds very pessimistic, but the statement is true nonetheless, and as James 4:14 tells us, "How do you know what your life will be like tomorrow? Your life is like the morning fog—it's here a little while, then it's gone" (NLT). Most people do not like to think of their mortality, and they will often go to great lengths to avoid talking about the subject with others. But in two instances the reality of our mortality rises to the surface and forces us to face the dreaded subject: when we attend the funerals of loved ones and when we are personally suffering from a severe sickness. In these times,, people who previously avoided pondering the subject are often left to wonder, *What will happen to me when I die?*

Job was experiencing both of the above conditions in his life. First, Job had to bury his ten children while still grieving their sudden and unexpected deaths. Second, Job had his own illness to deal with, as his physical suffering brought him near the brink of death. Out of his pain and agony, Job cried out to God, asking if life existed after death. We must remember that Job did not have the same revelation we have today. Although he was a man of faith, he did not have all the answers. Job did not have a Bible that he could open for direction, and he knew nothing of Jesus and His resurrection from the dead. Although Job would later display a strong faith in the living God and demonstrate a confidence that he would one day see God face-to-face (see Job 19:25–26), at this moment, Job was wrestling with the subject of life after death.

During times of grief and pain, hopelessness can cloud your vision and cause you to think that God has forgotten you. Whatever uncertainties Job may have wrestled with regarding life after death, no one needs to wrestle with that kind of uncertainty ever again because Jesus answered the question once and for all by declaring, "I am the resurrection and the life. He who believes in Me, though he may die, he shall live" (John 11:25). These words are not dead, spoken by a dead God. God is not dead. Jesus rose from the dead and conquered the grave, bringing hope and everlasting life to all who believe in Him.

Life is short, and how much you run, walk, bike, swim, or work out does not matter. You can diet, eat right, give up fatty foods, lower your cholesterol, eat more fiber, stop drinking soda, lower your sodium, and take a wide variety of vitamins. These are all good habits for living a healthy life. But in the end, no one can cheat death. No one knows the day or the hour of his or her own death, but one thing we can know for certain. All who have faith in Jesus Christ, all who can say, as Job said, "I know that my Redeemer lives" (Job 19:25), can know that when they die, they will be with God in heaven.

So let each one give as he purposes in his heart, not grudgingly or of necessity; for God loves a cheerful giver. (2 Corinthians 9:7)

The Gift that Keeps on Giving

MAY
26

JESUS CHRIST said more about money than about any other single thing because, when it comes to a man's real nature, money is of first importance. Money is an exact index to a man's true character. All through Scripture, there is an intimate correlation between the development of a man's character and how he handles his money.

—Richard Halverson

How people choose to handle their money is an indication of how their hearts handle God. Where we place our resources is a reflection of our priorities and reveals where we believe contentment is found. How we approach giving to God is more important than what we give to God. What does your giving reveal about your relationship with God?

Paul was surprised by the believers in Macedonia because, although they were poor themselves, they gave generously and abundantly to the needy saints in Jerusalem (see 2 Corinthians 8). They were so eager to give that they actually begged Paul to allow them the opportunity to provide support for their brothers and sisters in Christ. Paul saw this as an opportunity to exhort the Corinthians on the model approach and attitude toward giving, using the Macedonians as an example. Paul told the Corinthians that when Christians give as the Macedonians gave, blessing would result. The givers would be blessed because they were privileged to be used by God, and the people receiving the gift would be blessed because God would meet their needs.

Paul went on to give a few principles that should help shape the way we approach giving to God. First, Paul turned the world's way of thinking about giving upside down, because the world says, "We will have more if we give less." But God says fundamentally, "You will have more if you give more" (see 2 Corinthians 9:6). God's law of *increase* tells us that the more we give to the work of the Lord, the more "fruit" will be transferred to our account.

Next, God's law of *intent* is critical to our giving. Motive gives worth to our giving. No matter how much we give to God, the value of that gift is determined by the motivation for giving. If we are not giving to glorify God, we are giving incorrectly. If we give reluctantly or with a tight fist, God would rather we keep our gift. After all, He does not need our money or gifts to accomplish His plans and purposes because the earth and all its richness are His.

God has said that when we give to Him willingly, generously, thankfully, and joyfully, He will give grace back to us abundantly (see 2 Corinthians 9:8). Paul encourages us to give to the poor, to give to the work of the ministry in our church, and to give to those in the mission field. He said that we should not be motivated by guilt in our giving, but let grace be our guide.

As we have experienced the grace of God in our lives, we should have a desire to give graciously to the work of God so that others may come to know and experience grace as we have. Let God search your heart so that you can properly purpose in your heart what to give, and how to give, so you can give cheerfully. No matter what you give to God, you will surely receive much more than you can ever give.

"Why do the wicked have it so good, live to a ripe old age and get rich?" (Job 21:7 MSG)

Live Long and Prosper

LIFE CAN BE SO UNFAIR SOMETIMES. You may work hard yet still barely make enough money to get by. You may eat right and exercise regularly, only to die young. You may be the best person for the job, but nevertheless watch helplessly as the job goes to someone less qualified. Some people lie, cheat, and steal to get ahead, while others play by the rules, only to spin their wheels and get nowhere fast. So to be honest, life can be unfair. When we see God allowing wicked people to have life so good when upright people have life so bad, we can be left, like Job, asking the haunting question: *Why?*

Job lived near the time of Abraham, making him one of the first people in the Bible to ask, why do the wicked live long and prosper? Job would not be the last person to ask this question. Others, like King David, King Solomon, and the prophet Jeremiah, also wrestled with the success of the wicked while witnessing the suffering of righteous.

Today, people are still puzzled as they notice that wicked people often succeed in the world, while good and godly people are met with misfortune. The prosperity of the wicked has even led some people to consider the apathetic approach of *why bother doing the right thing when those who do the wrong thing still get ahead?* Throughout history, many have "succeeded" while being unscrupulous, irreligious, and downright evil. But this type of success is temporary at best, and even a long life is still fleeting in light of eternity.

Out of the depths of great despair, pain, misery, and loss, Job compared his life to that of other more wicked people, who were not experiencing the same kind of intense loss and suffering. Although Job did question the wealth and success of the wicked, he did not believe long life and material prosperity were the gateways to true blessing. Job looked past the here-and-now good fortune of the wicked and remembered that this life is fleeting. He knew true wealth was measured in the reward of eternity, which comes through a proper relationship with God. One day, the wicked will stand before God and give an account for their wickedness. God may not punish the wicked here and now, but that does not mean that He will not punish them there and then, in the future.

Life can seem so unfair to us because we are prone to focus on our earthly position and possessions rather than our spiritual position and heavenly possessions. We compare our circumstances to the circumstances of others, rather than looking at all we have in Him. The best way to keep your focus off of the success of the wicked, or avoid becoming preoccupied with other inequities of life, is by remembering that God's view of success and prosperity is fundamentally different than the world's. Success is based on *who* owns you, not *what* you own. Either you are ruled by God, or you are ruled by worldliness.

Ultimately, true success is not about how long you lived, how much money you made, or what kind of car you drove down easy street; having lived life in Jesus Christ is all that really matters. Success is not measured by treasure but by trust in God. True prosperity is not found in the abundance of possessions but in an abundant personal relationship with God and His Word. A long life means nothing if you will be spending eternity banished from the presence of God.

"My grace is sufficient for you, for My strength is made perfect in weakness." (2 Corinthians 12:9)

When God Says No

MAY 28

THE SIMPLE TRUTH is that sometimes bad things happen to God's people. God's people get sick, they are involved in car accidents, they lose their jobs, they deal with disabilities, and they suffer pain. God's people experience affliction, persecution, discomfort, misery, heartache, and disease, and they are harassed, oppressed, and suffer tragedy. No guarantee is given in the Bible that those who follow Jesus Christ are immune from pain and suffering. Often, the opposite will be the case for all who follow Christ. We must understand that sometimes, suffering comes because we make bad choices. At other times, God simply allows suffering in our lives to teach us and transform us through the painful lessons of life to live lives that are more holy.

Have you ever prayed to God and asked Him to heal you or a loved one from some sickness, or to deliver you from some affliction, or to spare you from some persecution, only to receive "no" as the answer? What are you to do when God says no to your request? The Apostle Paul, author of thirteen of the New Testament books, was mightily used by God not only through the letters he wrote, but he also spread the gospel and established new churches. He had a bold and fearless faith, but even this giant of the faith received a "no" from God!

Paul enjoyed wonderful revelations from God on more than one occasion, often seeing things the human eye has not seen, hearing things that the ear has not heard, and being left speechless at times because words could not describe what he had experienced. One such occurrence was when the Lord allowed Paul to catch a glorious glimpse of heaven. After seeing such a spectacular vision, God allowed Paul to be afflicted so that he would not become puffed up or exalted beyond measure. God wanted to make sure that Paul's heavenly experience did not go to his head.

The result was that Paul was given a "thorn in the flesh." Although many speculate as to what this "thorn" of Paul's was, no one knows for sure. Regardless, Paul was affected severely enough to ask God three times to remove it, and God's answer was, "My grace is sufficient for you, for My strength is made perfect in weakness" (*No, I will not remove your affliction, Paul*).

The sufficiency of God's grace was enough for Paul, and is to be enough for us. Nothing is wrong with asking God for healing or to eliminate suffering or erase affliction, but sometimes His answer might be no, and that no is for a good reason.

The answer to Paul's prayer was not to be found in the removal of this difficulty from his life, but in what the difficulty was going to produce in him. God used the circumstances of his affliction to produce in Paul a stronger character, that developed a deeper trust in God's sovereignty, which would grow in humility, and a produce character that would see the strength of God displayed through his afflictions. Paul came to see that his affliction was not only drawing him closer to God, but was also being used to keep him from sinning against God.

God's answer of no was not to keep something good away from Paul, but to add something even better to his life, and that something was grace. Oftentimes a no from God is necessary for us to realize that we need to rely on Him more and rely on ourselves less.

Blessed is the man Who walks not in the counsel of the ungodly, Nor stands in the path of sinners, Nor sits in the seat of the scornful. (Psalm 1:1)

MAY
29

The Everyone's Guide to Happiness

ALTHOUGH SOME TRUTHS, like the pursuit of happiness, may stand as self-evident, not everyone enjoys their inalienable, God-given rights. For some, true happiness may seem as elusive as chasing rainbows or as hard to grasp as the wind. True happiness is made available by God for everyone to enjoy, but this happiness does involve a choice. Good or evil, right or wrong, sacred or sacrilege, righteousness or wickedness; you must choose one or the other. No middle ground can be found here; a choice must be made. One road leads to a life of happiness, and the other road dead-ends in despair.

No one should be surprised that God wants to bless His people, and Psalm 1 begins by boldly proclaiming the way of blessing. Although the word *blessed* may sound somewhat sacred, here, blessed simply means, "happy." After all, who does not want happiness in their lives? The good news is a person can have a happy or blessed life, and Psalm 1 gives us the requirements.

Before making that first step out onto the road to happiness, you must watch where you walk. Make sure that you do not choose to walk with those who want nothing to do with God. Do not take advice from those who resist God's Word, and do not receive counsel from those who chose to ignore God's wisdom.

Next, do not stand with those who sin against God. We are all sinners, but once we have been saved by God's grace, we are no longer to live as we once did. We are to separate ourselves from our old way of living and reject those who still choose that lifestyle. This does not mean we no longer associate with those who reject God. In fact, we are commanded to go to them, but we no longer do as they do. Instead, we are to be an example of godliness.

Finally, the road to happiness means avoiding sitting with those who mock or ridicule God. The choices may be small, the progression may be slow, but the momentum is hard to stop, and in the end, you will receive more than unhappiness. Worldly thinking will lead you to take worldly actions, which will lead you to make worldly friendships. James 4:4 reminds us that friendship with the world is hatred with God, and no faster express lane to unhappiness exists than to live a life in opposition to God.

True happiness comes from a life devoted to the Word of God, a life that gives priority to the Word of God, a life that walks in the fullness of God's counsel, a life that stands firm with the faithful, and a life that keeps company with the righteous. The simple truth is that happiness is both earthly and eternal, and arises from living a life of holiness.

Make the choice to walk in the fullness of God's grace by saturating yourself in the Word of God twenty-four hours a day, seven days a week, and you will have a life of happiness and productivity.

But even if we, or an angel from heaven, preach any other gospel to you than what we have preached to you, let him be accursed. (Galatians 1:8)

MAY
30

Demonic Doctrines

"WE BELIEVE IN JESUS, *but. . . ."* This is the cry of the cults, a fabrication of many false religions, and the message promoted by those who are being misled. This is one of the oldest heretical doctrines the church has faced, and continues to be a stumbling block for millions of people today. Any religion or system of beliefs that says you need Jesus *and* something else in order to be saved is preaching a false gospel. The gospel of Jesus Christ is a gospel of grace, which means that we are saved by grace through faith in Jesus . . . *and* nothing else. The gospel of grace is a gospel of *believing*—not one of *doing*—in salvation through Jesus Christ.

The Galatians were in danger of perverting the gospel of grace by making this gift a gospel of *doing*. A group called the Judaizers essentially said, "We believe in Jesus, *but. . . ."* They believed it necessary to add some works to the finished work that Jesus completed on the cross. By doing so, they were turning the gospel of grace into the gospel of Jesus . . . *plus* something else. As the Judaizers' doctrine began to spread, the Galatian churches became confused and were teetering on the verge of leaving the truth of God for this lie.

Paul was quick to react to this demonic doctrine that changed the gospel of grace into a cursed creed. He called the Galatians to absolutely and wholly reject any changing or distorting of the gospel, no matter how small the change or how great the one doing the changing was. Paul went so far as to say that even if an angel were to appear and proclaim the sacrilegious doctrine of Jesus and something else, this must be immediately discarded and denied as truth. Several world religions today claim personal angelic revelation as the source of their belief system, but we must remember that Satan transforms himself into an angel of light (see 2 Corinthians 11:14). We must also remember what Paul says here in Galatians: any doctrine that adds to or takes away from the gospel of grace found in Jesus Christ's sacrifice on the cross is demonic doctrine.

The simple truth of the gospel of grace is that no one can add anything to what God has already done on the cross through the sacrifice of Jesus Christ. God has made the way for forgiveness of sin by faith in Christ alone, and nothing nor anyone can add to that. Only one Gospel is truth. Only one Savior exists. Only one way of salvation is real. The emphasis of the Gospel is not on what we must *do;* we always focus on what Christ *has done* for us.

Salvation is not performance based; salvation is entirely person based, and that person is Jesus Christ. All other religions and belief systems emphasize what mankind must do in order to please God. Rules must be followed and rituals must be performed. Sacraments must be observed and services must be accomplished. For them it is always Jesus plus something.

But Jesus was, is, and always will be sufficient to save us because He was God. Jesus plus nothing equals eternal life.

The heavens declare the glory of God; And the firmament shows His handiwork. (Psalm 19:1)

MAY 31

Stop and Smell the Roses

ON A BEAUTIFUL, sunny Southern California afternoon, a very unexpected event took place. The temperature was perfect, the sky was blue and cloudless, and a light breeze from the ocean was blowing gently up the nearby canyon, making all the leaves on the trees sway back and forth as though dancing to a silent symphony that only they could hear. Two young college students came walking down the neighborhood sidewalk, talking loudly and lugging skateboards. They were covered in tattoos and body piercings, wearing grunge-style clothing, and carrying a general "who cares?" attitude on their faces.

As they began to walk by a patio that was lined with a dozen rose bushes, the most unlikely of things happened: one of the rough-exterior guys stopped dead in his tracks and began to stare at a stunningly beautiful red rose in full bloom. Mesmerized by this single flower that was reaching up with all its might toward the sunshine, the tough guy took a moment to stop, bend down, and breathe in the sweet, delicate fragrance of that gentle bloom. Why was a little flower able to totally grab his attention and redirect his actions? Because the rose declared the glory of God.

The glory of God is on display everywhere. All we have to do is stop, look, listen, and even occasionally breathe His glory in. You may see His glory in a beautiful flower blossom or in a bee hovering nearby, about to retrieve the flower's nectar. You may see God's glory in the arrangement of the stars in the sky or feel it in the rays of the sun as they warm your body. You may hear His glory in the morning serenade of the birds singing or may observe it in the power of crashing waves on the seashore.

King David was deeply moved by the immensity of God found in nature and by how all creation speaks, and often shouts of, the greatness of God. David realized that God uses His creation as a means of general revelation to all mankind. The beauty, complexity, and creativity found in the heavens above and the world below declare the majesty and glory of God.

God, like a great conductor, has orchestrated His creation to ceaselessly sing His praises and definitively declare His supremacy. All of nature relentlessly reveals His knowledge and unmistakably shines forth His wisdom. The heavens and the earth impressively prove His power for all to see.

One gaze on all that God has created should arrest our attention and force us to stop and take notice of God. Nature can draw us deeper into His presence, lead us into poignant praise, and drive us to our knees in thankfulness, causing us to glorify God with our lives. So the next time you come face-to-face with some aspect of God's majestic creation, take time to stop and smell the roses. Allow yourself to not only be filled with the sweet fragrance of His creation, but to be filled with the even sweeter fragrance of worshiping the God of creation.

June

Then and Now

N O AMOUNT OF HUMAN EFFORT can save you from your sin. No amount of religious activity will bring about your redemption. No humanitarian efforts ever will gain you one ounce of favor with God. No matter how hard you work, you cannot earn God's forgiveness. Church attendance does not give you a "get out of judgment free" card, and no sum of money will grant you an opportunity to buy a house made in Heaven. Faith in Jesus Christ is the only way to be saved from the penalty of sin and to inherit eternal life. Since faith is the only way to salvation, then why was the Law of God given to man? The Law does not repair the broken relationship caused by sin. Only faith can do this. And while we are considering the Law, let us ask the question, does God's law still have any relevance today, or is His Law an old-fashioned, outdated, and obsolete set of rules and regulations?

Paul tackles the issue of justification with the Galatians, making it abundantly clear that justification is by grace alone, through faith alone, in Christ alone. At the same time, he sought to preserve the importance and integrity of the Law, declaring that justification does not come by way of observing the Law, or through works of the flesh, nor by participation in any ceremonies, sacraments, or traditions. Having openly stated his objection to legalism, Paul anticipated the above question would arise in everyone's minds. As if walking a spiritual tightrope between the vast ravine of justification by faith alone and the importance of observing the Law, Paul explained why the Law of God was given.

The Law was given first and foremost to expose man's sinfulness and to reveal God's holiness. The Law uncovers the imperfection of mankind, and shines light on God's faultless character, demonstrating that no one is totally able to live up to God's holy standard. Man cannot follow The Law perfectly, thereby earning salvation. Rather, the intent of The Law was to reveal that humanity is totally incapable of keeping it and therefore, totally unable to save themselves. The Law, therefore, prepares mankind to receive God's gift of grace through Jesus Christ.

We are utterly helpless and hopeless apart from the grace of God given to us through Jesus Christ, and no amount of human effort can ever change our position with God. *Nothing* we can do will ever make us more accepted or more forgiven. The Law, Paul asserted, was never intended to bring about man's justification, but was instead established to reveal mankind's sinful condition and to reveal to humanity their desperately depraved position before God. The Law of God is good, but the grace of God is far better. Where the Law condemns, grace forgives. Where the Law judges, grace justifies. Where the Law dooms, grace delivers.

The Law never will be old-fashioned, outdated, or obsolete because

165

through the Law, we begin to realize our sinfulness and understand that we have violated God's standard for living a holy life. After we realize that we have broken God's Law, we can turn from our sin, surrender to God, and trust in Jesus Christ as our Lord and Savior.

Decide not to live under the guilt and condemnation that comes from trying to live according to the Law; lay hold of the grace and freedom that comes by receiving the grace of God through faith in Jesus Christ.

The Lord is my shepherd. (Psalm 23:1)

A True Masterpiece

JUNE 2

LEONARDO DA VINCI'S *The Last Supper*, Michelangelo's *David*, Van Gogh's *Starry Night*, Beethoven's Symphony no. 5, and Shakespeare's *Hamlet* are just a few of the world's greatest masterpieces. But what makes something a masterpiece? Certainly, a masterpiece must stand the test of time. Also, the work must be able to communicate a message or leave a lasting impression on the audience. Finally, a masterpiece should draw the observer's attention away from the artist and toward the subject, totally captivating his or her attention, causing him or her to temporarily tune out the surrounding world and wholly tune in to the immediate work.

Psalm 23 is a true masterpiece. This verse is one of the most widely known, most beloved, and most commonly read psalms in the Bible. Psalm 23 has been memorized by many, and been a source of comfort to millions. Perhaps most importantly, as with any great masterpiece, we are completely captivated by the subject, the Great Shepherd.

As we gaze at this masterpiece, our attention is unquestionably drawn to the Shepherd, who stands spotlighted among his sheep. His sheep demonstrate a calm and confident demeanor due to the strong presence and tender love of the One who stands watching over them. The presence of the sheep in this masterpiece only serves to enhance the glory and greatness of the Shepherd, as he stands centered among his flock, providing their necessary provisions and ensuring their much-needed protection. He is a Shepherd who diligently makes certain that His sheep want not, worry not, and wander not, as he tirelessly works to steer them, secure them, save them, and sacrifice for them. His calling and His burden is to give all of Himself to the care of those entrusted to him.

As Christians, we are part of Christ's flock, we are the sheep of His pasture, and He is dedicated to providing provision and protection to us, His tender flock. Although physical needs are one aspect of God's provision for and protection of His people, His prevailing preoccupation is with our spiritual welfare. Some say, "the average person is being crucified between two thieves: the regrets of yesterday and the worries of tomorrow." As God's sheep, we can start each day with confidence and assurance that God not only knows our every need, but He is more than able to meet our every need as well (Psalm 23:1).

As a Good Shepherd, He goes before the sheep, leading them from the front and not driving them from behind (verses 2–3). Having gone in front of

His sheep, He knows the way because He has first traveled the path himself, He has surveyed the land, He has seen the dangers, and He knows where the green pastures of safety and rest are found. Then, and only then, does He call out to His sheep, who await the sound of their Master's voice for direction (see John 10:27). Day by day, we walk in the shadow of His goodness and mercy as we travel through the hills and valleys of life, while He protects us with His rod and corrects us with the crook of His staff.

Psalm 23 is a true masterpiece not only because it is timeless and captivating, but the also because it helps us to see the Master more clearly.

Walk in the Spirit, and you shall not fulfill the lust of the flesh. (Galatians 5:16)

The Spirit-Filled Life

JUNE 3

DO YOU FIND that you are constantly struggling with sin? You go to church, you read your Bible, and you pray, but temptation still gets the better of you. Anger boils over, covetousness clouds your vision, jealousy smolders like a hot ember, lust lingers in your mind, bitterness sours the heart, and you are left wondering, *Will I ever have victory over this in my life?* Every Christian is constantly confronted with temptation throughout their lifetime, and one source of that temptation comes from the enemy that lives within us: our very own *flesh.* The *flesh* (as used above in Galatians 5:16) is that place within our hearts that seeks to find fulfillment in anything or anyone other than God. The *Spirit*, on the other hand, is that ever-present part of God's Holy Spirit that dwells within every believer, constantly pushing him or her to seek fulfillment only in God. These two forces push and pull against each other, causing a constant conflict. Although many people find themselves caught in the middle of this conflict, feeling like helpless victims of their own desires, we can break free and experience consistent victory over the flesh.

Paul had firsthand experience with the struggle between the flesh and the Spirit, and he knew this was a very real and regularly reoccurring conflict for believers (see Romans 7). But he also knew a very real and reoccurring way to live above that struggle. A right way and a wrong way exist to approach this battle within us.

Unfortunately, we often go the wrong way first. The wrong way is to try and fight against the flesh, to approach this struggle with an attitude of, *If I just dig in, try harder, or work at it a little more, eventually I will be able to overpower my flesh.* The simple truth is that this technique never will result in any lasting success. What, then, is Paul's solution for this struggle against the flesh? He said, "Walk in the Spirit, and you shall not fulfill the lust of the flesh" (Galatians 5:16).

Walking in the Spirit is not a matter of *fighting* the flesh; rather, walking in the spirit is a matter of *submitting* to the Spirit. This does not mean you are standing up against the flesh; you are simply bowing to the Spirit. The difference is subtle, but significant. When we focus on the flesh, we are more likely to lose to the flesh. When we focus on the things of the Spirit, we enable ourselves to walk in the Spirit. This is a one-step-at-a-time process. That is why *walking* serves as the best illustration of the progression. In walking, you do not receive an instant victory over sin. This is no quick solution. Long-term commitment is necessary to move in a godly direction. The walk requires more than reading your Bible, praying, and going to church, though those are non-negotiable for sure. But walking in the spirit also means to daily focus on the attributes of a living a Spirit-filled life, which includes showing love, joy, peace, longsuffering, kindness, goodness, faithfulness, gentleness, and self-control (see Galatians 5:22–23). As we submit ourselves to the Spirit, yielding our wills to the Spirit, pursuing the attributes of the Spirit and making Spirit-led decisions, we will find that we are walking in the Spirit and will have no time or desire for the things of the flesh.

The degree to which we walk in the Spirit will determine the degree to which we rise above the flesh. No one can live the Christian life the way God wants us to, apart from the help of the Holy Spirit. Allow the fruit of the Spirit to fill your life, and you will not only walk in the Spirit, but you will have victory through the Spirit.

"Delight yourself also in the Lord, and He shall give you the desires of your heart." (Psalm 37:4)

JUNE 4

Our Deepest Desires

DOES GOD PROMISE to give us everything we wish for? Is the Bible saying we should delight in God so we will get what we want in life? Inevitably, someone will look at the above verse and say, "If God gives us the desires of our hearts, then why am I still single?" or "Why am I unemployed?" or "Why haven't I . . . ?" (fill in the blank with any number of unmet wants). Sadly, this verse has been so mistreated and misapplied that many view the verse with a wish-list mentality, mistakenly thinking that as long as they love and look to God, they will eventually get all their hearts desire from God.

But we must be aware that this verse is not some spiritual catchall that can be randomly attached to all our wants and desires, with the expectation that God must give them to us as long as we follow Him. The good news, however, is that when we have the right view of what God *is* promising us here regarding our hearts' desires, God will gladly give them to us; and He will give lavishly!

First of all, we must recognize that some of the desires of our hearts are not good, and therefore, we should never expect God to supply us with those things that are contrary to His Word. The Bible makes clear that our hearts are deceitful (see Jeremiah 17:9) and we must therefore be careful and recognize that we already have a heart problem that can negatively impact our desires. Often our desires are selfish and self-serving, and that means our desires can lead us into temptation (see James 4:1). We must be careful and take time to examine our desires, ensuring they are not spoiled by sin.

As troublesome as some of our desires can be, not all of our wants and wishes are bad. As a matter of fact, some may be decent and upright, but God may still choose not to give us those desires. The question then becomes, "If what I want isn't bad, then why doesn't God give me what I want? Isn't that what

He is promising here?" Regarding this verse, the following is very important to know: this verse is not promising that even if what we desire is good, God must automatically give us those desires. Only when our desires match God's desires will we begin seeing God deliver on this promise and give us the desires of our hearts.

To make sure that we want the right things, God gives us the parameters for His promise by declaring that we must first *delight ourselves in the Lord.* This part of the verse is the necessary piece in properly understanding what God is and is not promising to us. God wants us to find joy and take pleasure in having a relationship with Him. Put another way, God wants us to want more of Him. He wants our desires to be His desires, He wants our thoughts to be His thoughts, and He wants our lives to be a reflection of His nature and character.

Psalm 37 gives us the "how to" for bringing our hearts into alignment with God's heart: through trusting in God, patiently waiting on Him, and committing all your ways to Him. The more we yield to the authority of God's Word, the more our desires will become His desires.

The great challenge is not in God's ability to meet our deepest desires but in our ability to transform our deepest desires into His desires. As we delight ourselves in God and surrender our wills to His will, we will have godly desires that God will enjoy giving us.

Brethren, if a man is overtaken in any trespass, you who are spiritual restore such a one in a spirit of gentleness, considering yourself lest you also be tempted.
(Galatians 6:1)

**JUNE
5**

No Man Left Behind

AS THE ARMY OF MEN slowly advanced in the heavily wooded battlefield, random shots from the enemy riddled the air, sporadically hitting the surrounding trees and causing wood shrapnel to rain down on the troops. As the men used the trees for cover, one soldier, leaning against a thick oak tree, looked back in search of his friend and comrade in arms, only to discover that his friend had fallen by the wayside. Despite the distance, he could still see the agony on the face of his injured friend who was unable to get himself to safety. After pausing for a brief moment, perhaps to pray for protection, the soldier took a deep breath and began running back, zigzagging to avoid enemy fire and risking his life in an attempt to save his fallen friend.

Stories that sound like this one come from every war, stories of great heroism in which men and women risk life and limb to rescue someone in need of help. As Christians, we are also in a war, where many will fall by the spiritual wayside and will need brave men and women to rush to their side. Are you willing to help a fallen Christian get back up?

When we see that a fellow Christian has been overtaken or tripped up by sin, the Bible directs us to go to our fallen comrade and make every effort to rescue him or her from that sinful condition. Jesus gave us the command in John 13 to love one another as He has loved us, both sacrificially and focused on others. But before we run hastily over to our fallen comrades, we should listen to the advice Paul gives in Galatians 6: "Brethren, if a man is overtaken in any trespass, you who are spiritual restore such a one in a spirit of gentleness, considering yourself lest you also be tempted" (verse 1).

First, the directive to go is given to "you who are spiritual." God is not calling super saints, but is calling those filled with the Holy Spirit. Whose lives are governed by God, and produce the fruit of the Spirit. In other words, any Christian living the way God calls us to live is *good to go*.

Second, the purpose of going is restoration. Our job is not to criticize, judge, or condemn, which would be equivalent to kicking a person while they are already down. The goal is to seek to bring healing and hope in lives of the fallen, help them up and set them back on the right path, and encourage them to return to pursuing God wholeheartedly.

Confrontation is sometimes necessary, which leads to the third important guideline. Restoration must be done with gentleness. This means restoring someone quickly, quietly, and caringly. Gentleness is grace in action, and approaches the situation carefully, and carefully always means prayerfully. We need to surround ourselves and the process of restoration with purposeful and persistent prayer so we avoid the, sinful condition we are trying to rescue someone else from. All are susceptible to sin, which means we all must be careful, even approaching the sin of another person, lest that scheming serpent called Satan should turn his head and bite us also.

We are all soldiers in God's army, and as such, we all have a responsibility to help a brother or sister in Christ get back up when sin has tripped them up. Keep Paul's advice in the forefront of your mind, and you will be on your way to ensuring that no man is left behind.

The meek shall inherit the earth.(Psalm 37:11)
Meekness, Not Weakness

JUNE
6

IN A WORLD that believes only the strong survive, where the mindset is success at any cost, meekness has never really been in vogue. In our society, we see the assertive get ahead, the clever capitalize on opportunity, and the rich just get richer. But the meek? Well, they seem to go unnoticed and often get overlooked. This is why some equate meekness with weakness. But the Bible has something quite different to say about meekness. In fact, the Bible declares that meekness is one of the secrets to happiness and usefulness.

The Bible makes clear that meekness is not weakness, based on the fact that the only two people that the Bible described as meek are Moses and Jesus (see Numbers 12:3; Matthew 11:29). When you picture Moses, *weak* would be the last word that comes to mind for the man who stood against an Egyptian pharaoh and led a nation out of bondage, and who wandered in the harsh dessert for forty years and spoke with God on a mountaintop. Moses was a man of prayer who trusted God and was willing to do whatever God asked him to do, no matter the cost.

Then there was Jesus, who rebuked Pharisees, chased out moneychangers, resisted Satan, and endured the cross. That does not sound like someone who is weak.

So, if meekness is not weakness, then what is it? Meekness is power under control and strength under submission. It is authority under authority. Meekness is often used synonymously with gentleness. Meekness is not the result of human wherewithal but is a product of godliness.

The person characterized by meekness is a person who is relying on the strength of the Holy Spirit to guide them into gentleness. The person allowing the fruit of meekness to be displayed in his or her life is a person who is self-controlled, temperate, and not given to excess, but is instead someone who lives in submission to the will of God. Meekness relies on the power of God, recognizes the authority of God, and reflects the nature of God. Meekness receives the blessings of God, refuses the praises of men, and rightfully gives glory to God. As Henry Morris has said, "A meek spirit enables a Christian to maintain composure in the face of opposition, to accept adversity without complaint; promotion without arrogance; demotion without resentment. It produces a peace which no trouble can disturb and which no prosperity can puff up."[28]

As a person walks in meekness, that person walks a path that leads to happiness and spiritual blessing. In God's economy, the meek prevail, not the strongest. God is not looking for weak Christians, but meek Christians. And to those who pursue the fruit of meekness, God promises happiness and blessing.

"Do not be deceived, God is not mocked; for whatever a man sows, that he will also reap. (Galatians 6:7)

JUNE
7

Apples to Apples

WHERE YOU ARE TODAY is a direct result of the decisions that you made in the past, and where you will be in the future is determined by the choices that you will make today. In other words, actions have consequences, and sometimes those actions produce positive results, while at other times they may produce negative results. This is all part of God's universal law known as the law of sowing and reaping. We are all sowing today what we will reap tomorrow. The question then becomes, are we sowing seeds that will yield good spiritual fruit? Every day we are sowing thoughts that will produce intentions, intentions that will produce decisions, decisions that will produce actions, actions that will produce character, and character that will produce a lifestyle. And as we sow a lifestyle, we will reap an eternal harvest.

God's law of sowing and reaping applies equally to every individual, whether he or she is a Christian or not, and has both physical and spiritual implications. A careless and unthinking person never takes into consideration how his or her actions of today will impact life tomorrow. As Tony Evans has said:

It's amazing how many people want to plant unrighteousness, but expect God's blessing. They want to plant bad, but they want to harvest good. They want to sow seeds of wrong, but gather a harvest of right.

But that's not how God's system works. There's something you need to know about sowing. Once you sow whatever you sow, it will grow naturally. The consequences of your sowing are set. You don't have to do anything extraordinary for growth to occur. What you have sown will push up through the ground someday. It's built into the process.

I hope you see the seriousness of this in relation to something as vital as our love for Christ.[29]

With sowing and reaping, we must keep in mind a few other relationships. First, we reap the same type of item that we sow, meaning that if we plant apple seeds, we eventually will harvest apples. To think that if you plant apple seeds, you will harvest oranges is both unrealistic and crazy. In the same way, you cannot sow disobedience and reap blessing. Secondly, we often harvest much more than we plant. For example, one apple seed planted in the ground may yield a tree that produces bushels of apples year after year. Thirdly, reaping occurs after the seeds have been sown, which means our reaping has no timetable. The results may follow soon after the sowing is complete, or the results may be delayed for years.

God will not be mocked. His laws always will yield as He has promised, both in the natural world as well as the spiritual. You cannot plant apple seeds and expect to harvest oranges: apples to apples and oranges to oranges. We cannot sow to sin and hope to harvest righteousness, but if we purpose today to plant seeds of faithfulness and obedience, then we will one day reap the blessings of such productive planting.

Cast your burden on the Lord, and He shall sustain you; He shall never permit the righteous to be moved. (Psalm 55:22)

JUNE

8

What's Weighing You Down?

EVERYONE KNOWS life has ups and downs, highs and lows. But sometimes, life's lows can be so devastating, you feel as though you are emotionally bound in a straitjacket with a cinder block tied around your neck, while you are being pulled deeper and deeper into the depths of despair and hopelessness. Overwhelmed, you become distraught, disillusioned, and discouraged. But as dark as the deepest ocean of despair may be, or as hopeless as the outcome may appear, God can carry the weight of your affliction and keep you from drowning in depression.

King David went through an extremely low point in his life. David's son, Absalom, was rebelling against him and trying to steal the kingdom out from under him. David's friends were walking out on him. And one of his closest friends and confidants, Ahithophel, betrayed their friendship. All this left David feeling disheartened and depressed as he considered just running away and leaving everything behind. Who could blame David for wanting to get away from it all? Many of us have had similar thoughts of escaping from our troubles, but running away from a problem does not make it go away. David knew that the only way to free himself from the crushing weight of despair was to cast the weight of his cares upon the Lord.

David began by turning to God in prayer. Whether your problems are as big as betrayal or as small as suffering from a minor setback, going to God in prayer must be first. As we cast our burdens upon the Lord's shoulders, commit our cares to His watchful eye, and hand over our enemies to the Lord for Him to deal with, God gives us a few promises to reassure us.

God promises that when we surrender our burdens, He will shoulder them and support us. When laden with despair, our tendency is to assume no way out of the pit, no light at the end of the tunnel, and no recovering from the damage. This is not the case. By giving our cares and concerns to God, we place our trust in God's ability to handle them. Our faith becomes a channel through which God transfers His power into our lives, sustaining us through difficulty.

Consider the apostle Peter as he stood on the water with Jesus. As long as his faith was working, and he was trusting and believing in God, he was being upheld. But the minute his faith faltered, he sank. God promises to uphold us, but we must trust in God's ability to do so, or we may feel ourselves sinking deeper into the waters of despair. God also promises that the righteous will not be moved. He is our rock; by anchoring ourselves to Him when troubling waves come crashing against us, we remain secure and immovable because of His power. We may get wet, or even battered, but God will not allow us to be conquered or crushed.

Finally, the Lord promises that as we commit to Him those who have hurt us, betrayed our trust, or turned against us, He will judge them (see Psalm 55:23). We must always let God be the judge, jury, and the implementer of justice, knowing that nothing escapes His sight and His judgment.

If you are carrying a burden today, God can handle it. Nothing is too hard for God, so give it to Him in prayer, trusting in His ability to sustain and support you, no matter what is weighing you down.

Having predestined us to adoption as sons by Jesus Christ to Himself, according to the good pleasure of His will. (Ephesians 1:5)

JUNE 9

Making Sense of Predestination

IS GOD A CONTROL FREAK? Is salvation nothing more than God playing a divine game of eeny, meeny, miny, moe? As individuals, we want to be the masters of our own fate, so the idea of someone deciding for us whether we will go to heaven or hell does not sit well with us. But is this really how the doctrine of predestination works? Few doctrines have caused more division and confusion than the doctrine of predestination. Some people have taken their stance to dogmatic extremes, showing no tolerance for anyone with a differing viewpoint, while others have chosen the path of least resistance and have decided to simply ignore difficult theological issues like predestination. What should we know about predestination? And is there a way for free will and predestination to peacefully coexist?

Let's start with the fact that the Bible does teach predestination. No one can deny or get around this fact. As a biblical concept, then, we need to know what God means when the Scriptures include a word like *predestined*. Predestination, streamlined, means that God has made some choices or decisions in advance. In particular, God has chosen in advance those who will be saved. But wait! Before that ruffles your self-determining feathers, the Bible also teaches that we have the responsibility to believe in Jesus. The Bible teaches that God chooses us, and we also choose Him. God's choice intersects with our choice, and this is why we find difficulty in understanding how both are true. But the Bible teaches that both are true. God predestines us, and we must choose to follow Him. Believe and you will be saved (see Romans 10:9). God has chosen you before the foundation of the world (see Ephesians 1:4). Both are true.

Still struggling with this? Perhaps an example will help. Consider the nation of Israel. They were God's chosen people, but the responsibility to follow God was theirs. They were chosen, but given a choice. The free will of man is never hindered because of predestination. Both are true. One truth does not cancel out the other truth. They are friends, not enemies. We can ever fully understand or settle how and where the election of God and the free will of man meet. God does not tell us *how* both are true, just that both *are* true! Some say, "Try to explain election and you may lose your mind. But try to explain it away and you may lose your soul!"

Where does this leave us? First, we must realize that predestination does not mean that God has charted out every detail of our lives beforehand. We are not preprogrammed robots, forced to obey. If this were the case, then no sin would be in the world and we would have no need for a Savior. Next, in Ephesians the doctrine of predestination is supposed to lead us to a place of praising God for the grace He shows us (see Ephesians 1:6).

However you make sense of predestination and free will does not change the fact that God wants to have a relationship with us, and He is not willing that any should perish. So, choose to accept the choice that God has already made for your life and live for Him today.

"O God, You are my God; early will I seek You; my soul thirsts for You; my flesh longs for You. (Psalm 63:1)

JUNE
10

Waking Up with God

THE SOFT HUES of orange and yellow begin to warn the horizon as the king of the sky prepares to make his morning arrival. A few early birds begin to practice their scales before the choir gathers in the trees. A timer clicks, water begins to drip, and the stout, smoky aroma of fresh-brewed coffee begins to fill the house. Morning has arrived. A new day has begun, filled with brand-new possibilities, unique challenges, and a distinctive twenty-four-hour beauty all its own. How do you start your day? What are your priorities for what lies ahead?

For King David, nothing was more important to him than his relationships with God. David wanted God more than He wanted anything else in his life because he knew that God alone could satisfy the deepest longings of his soul.

The above verse is a reflection of David's daily, passionate pursuit of God. David began his day by seeking God early in the morning. He awoke with a fresh craving for His Creator and would spend the early morning hours pursuing the presence of God. He would pray and wait upon God: "In the morning, LORD, you hear my voice; in the morning I lay my requests before you and wait expectantly" (Psalm 5:3 NIV), he would praise and give thanks to God (see Psalm 63:3-4), and when night came, he was still thinking about His heavenly Father as he lay in bed (Psalm 63:6). How wonderful to have a day filled with such a joy and gratitude for God.

Are your days filled with joy and gratitude for God? Each of us *can* have this type of joy, regardless of our circumstances, when we set aside the beginning of our day to spend with God. This should be a regular time in which we purpose to fill ourselves with the Word of God, willingly fall to our knees and pray to God, and submissively wait upon God.

Now, you may be thinking, *I just don't have that kind of time.* Honestly, yes you do! You may need to make a little sacrifice, and you may have to rearrange your schedule or change your priorities. Something may need to be taken off your plate, or you may have to scratch something off your morning to-do list. If you feel that your days are just too full and finding time is totally impossible, then you may need to take a little extra effort, a little more creativity, or simply a little more diligence to fit time with God into your already full schedule. But one thing is certain: if your schedule is too full for God, then something needs to go.

We should never be content to follow God at a distance. Rather, we should be waking up every day with a hunger and a thirst for God, a craving that can only be met in His presence. If you are struggling to make this happen, then just do it for a few days and see for yourself how the Lord begins to satisfy your soul and grow your hunger for Him.

For by grace you have been saved through faith, and that not of yourselves; it is the gift of God, not of works, lest anyone should boast. (Ephesians 2:8–9)

JUNE 11

Just Add Water

WHEN INSTANT CAKE was developed, the product was a dud at first. The instructions told consumers that all they had to do was to just add water and bake. Cake was now that simple! Yet, the company could not understand why the mix still did not sell well. Then their research revealed at least one of the reasons the buying public felt uneasy about using a mix that required just water to be added: it was simply *too easy.* So, the company changed the formula and called for adding an egg to the mix in addition to the water. This resulted in a dramatic increase in sales.

Does God's plan of salvation seem too easy to you? Is God's grace too good to be true? Grace is Gods "recipe," or way of salvation. No secret ingredient exists that we can add to make God's grace more complete. We cannot do anything to gain God's grace. We cannot buy grace, nor can we work to earn it, and no amount of good deeds will ever nullify our sinful nature. Therefore, to think that man can, by his own efforts, reach the highest standard of holiness set forth by God if he just works hard enough is completely absurd. *For by grace you have been saved* has always been, and forever will be, a work of God completely separate from man's effort. Add even one-tenth of one percent of human energy and grace ceases to be grace.

Faith is the means by which God's gift of grace is received, but we must be careful not to think of our faith as contributing to our salvation in any way. We can add nothing to, nor can we take away anything from, God's grace. If faith were something we added to God's grace, then our faith would become a missing ingredient necessary to make God's grace complete. This would be making faith a work. Faith is not a work that we accomplish for salvation; faith is the acceptance of the work Jesus accomplished for our salvation. Faith does not work for salvation; faith receives salvation.

George Müller said, "Faith does not operate in the realm of the possible. There is no glory for God in that which is humanly possible. Faith begins where man's power ends."[30]

If faith were something we did, a work we completed, then we would have reason to boast, brag, and claim entitlement for our participation in salvation. Faith recognizes the divine nature of Christ, receives the divine work of Christ on the cross, and relinquishes the individual's will to Christ. Faith in no way adds to the grace that God offers. Faith is not the missing ingredient necessary in the recipe of grace; faith only receives the grace that God alone has made.

Grace may sound too good to be true. You may feel like you must *do* something or *add* something to grace, but your salvation does not depend on you. Your salvation depends on God.

As Dwight L. Moody said, "The thief had nails through both hands, so that he could not work; and a nail through each foot, so that he could not run errands for the Lord; he could not lift a hand or a foot towards his salvation; and yet Christ offered him the gift of God, and he took it. He threw him a passport, and took him with Him into Paradise."[31]

Grace can only be received, never earned.

How can a young person live a clean life? By carefully reading the map of your Word. (Psalm 119:9 MSG)

JUNE 12

Mister Clean and Miss Spotless

THE PRESSURE FROM PEERS is powerful! The images from advertisers are explicit! The casual approach to sex is commonplace! Entertainment bombards the mind and assaults the senses with sensuality. Today's youth are maxed out with seductive enticements and are careening headlong on a collision course with temptation. So how can a young person (and every adult, for that matter) stay pure in a sex-crazed culture? How can today's youth avoid trading in the blessings of God for passing pleasures?

As the longest chapter in the Bible, Psalm 119 is an encyclopedia of wisdom that pours forth insight, emphasizing the diverse functions that the Word of God offers. One such function is the cleansing power of God's Word. Crucial to living a clean life and essential for remaining set apart from the worldly influences that are attacking every young person's moral foundation is a persistent dedication to *learn* from God's Word and *live* by God's Word.

The world makes promises it cannot keep and writes checks it cannot cash. Unfortunately for some, these hard truths are discovered only after those promises bounce like a bad check, leaving them empty-handed and unfilled inside. Today's sex-crazed culture proclaims that purity is peculiar, ethical standards are subjective, and moral absolutes are arrogant and arbitrary. God wants to spare every young person from selling his or her self short of God's best and from buying into the dirty deceptions delivered day and night. The solution that will keep us all spot-free is by living according to the Word of God.

Living a clean life begins by taking time to *read* the Word of God. Daily devotion to the Word of God is the best way of remaining spotless against the sinful influences that have saturated the world in which we live. Remaining consistent and persistent with a daily reading of God's Word takes time, effort, and discipline, but the benefits far outweigh any sacrifice in order to make God's Word a priority. Countless forces vie for your time that will inevitably entice you to skimp, slack, and even skip the precious reading of God's Word, but this is where perseverance pays great dividends.

Next, make sure to *heed* the Word of God. Purpose to put into practice what you read from God's Word. Godly obedience shows that you understand what the Word of God says and are committed to following as the Word of God commands. Heeding the Word of God is also a test of whether your love for Him is genuine. Jesus said, "If you love Me, keep My commandments" (John 14:15). In other words, obedience to the Word shows that you love God.

Following these steps naturally will result in a desire to *spread* the Word of God, for out of the abundance of the heart, the mouth speaks (see Matthew 12:34). If you have the Word of God in your heart, then you will be unable to contain it. The Word of God will pour forth effortlessly, cleansing your every conversation and making your words shine even brighter in a dark and dirty world that desperately needs to hear and heed the Word of God.

Take the time to get into God's Word and make this a regular part of your life. Nothing is more important, and nothing else has the power to keep you spotless in this sin-stained, sex-crazed world.

"And He Himself gave some to be apostles, some prophets, some evangelists, and some pastors and teachers, for the equipping of the saints for the work of ministry.
(Ephesians 4:11–12)

JUNE
13

Serving in Your Church

PERHAPS YOU HAVE HEARD the troubling statistic regarding church, which states that only 20 percent of the people do 80 percent of the work. Although that percentage may vary somewhat from church to church, this stat definitely addresses the reality that the majority of churchgoers are not in the habit of serving in their local churches.

Now, let us just get this disclaimer out of the way. You may be taking a break from serving in church at legitimate times. For example, you may be taking off for a short season of rest from your normal ministry load, you may be in a time of transition, or health problems or a tragedy may have temporarily suspended your ministering in church. Any number of legitimate reasons could be found for why you may be taking a break from your regular service in the church. However, with any break should be the understanding that this is only a temporary condition, and you must have intent and desire to return as soon as you are able.

Since we have that out of the way, let us continue. Where do you fall in the previous statistic? Are you committed to serving, or are you sitting on the sidelines?

Misconception has done a great disservice to the work of ministry in the local church. The prevailing misconception that has pervaded the church for centuries is that the work of ministry is for the "professionals," or the clergy. Perhaps you have thought to yourself, *Well, isn't that what we pay them for?* In Ephesians 4, the apostle Paul helped shatter this mistaken belief when he essentially said that the pastoral staff, or the clergy, is there to educate and equip the congregation so the congregation can do the work of ministry in the church. The role of leadership is not to do all the work for the church, but to equip the church to do the work. God has not only given spiritual gifts to every believer in the church (see 1 Peter 4:10), but He has also prepared work for each believer to do in the church (see Ephesians 2:10), and every member should share in the workload (see Ephesians 4:16). Serving in the church is the privilege and responsibility of every church member and was never designed to be the option of every member. Some go so far as to say that when a believer is baptized, they are immediately ordained into the ministry. You might say that upon baptism, you have received your B.S. degree (Baptized to Serve).

A final note about serving: a serving church is a growing church, not necessarily numerically, but definitely spiritually (see Ephesians 4:16). Part of our personal and corporate growth into mature believers is intertwined with our commitment to serve in the church. We desperately need each other if we are going to move forward, make a difference, and grow in Christ. The responsibility is all of ours to share equally but distinctly. By being committed to serving in your local church, you are not only contributing to your own personal growth as a believer, but you are also contributing to the growth of your church corporately. Your service is a God given gift for your church.

Your word I have hidden in my heart. (Psalm 119:11)

Total Recall

JUNE 14

ODDS ARE that most Christians can easily complete this verse from the gospel of John: "For God so loved the world that He gave . . ." And, millions around the world can effortlessly recite the entire Lord's Prayer: "Our Father in heaven, hallowed be Your name . . . (Luke 11:2). But is Scripture memory a thing of the past? After all, why spend the time to commit Scripture verses to memory when you can just open up your Bible and find the passage, or better yet, open a Bible app on a mobile device and have what you are looking for delivered instantly to your screen?

The psalmist declared that by internalizing the Scriptures, we are promoting the work of purification in our lives, we are increasing our ability to live righteously, we are enabling the Holy Spirit to empower us, we are allowing the light of God to illuminate our steps, and we are providing God the opportunity to deposit His wisdom into our lives. A correlation is also made by the psalmist that the more we have processed and personalized the Scriptures, the more likely we will be to live the way God wants us to live. And no small portion of that is the ability to persevere against temptation and stand against sin. No app exists that can do that.

Practicing Scripture memorization is not a thing of the past because memorizing scripture stimulates the work of God in your life today. Committing the Scriptures to memory helps to conform us into the image of Christ, equips us to better share Christ with those who do not know God, adds to our ability to comfort and counsel those who are hurting, and helps us to recognize and defend against deceitful doctrines. Memorizing scripture also moves us forward into maturity in our faith, and will even assist us in our prayer time.

Now, maybe you have tried Scripture memorization in the past and found the practice tedious, tiresome, and time-consuming. Therefore, you decided to postpone or put aside the idea altogether. We have all been there, but this practice does not have to be dreaded, and can actually be exciting, energizing, and encouraging. As you prepare yourself to memorize the Scriptures, know that first, it takes time. But here is the guarantee: if you invest the time, you will eventually succeed at internalizing the truth. Second, it takes repetition. For some, that means rereading a verse repeatedly. For others, it means saying the verse aloud multiple times. You cannot shortcut repetition; the more you practice, the more scripture will stick.

You can use a variety of methods to commit a Scripture verse to memory. Here are just a few. First, begin by choosing a verse that interests you or means something to you. That will help keep you motivated. Second, begin by repeating the location, such as Psalm 119:11. Third, break the verse down into segments. Fourth, reassemble the verse in sections, with the location, and repeat. For example, Psalm 119:11: "Your word I have hidden in my heart." Don't add the subsequent sections until you have that portion down perfectly. Fifth, review and repeat. These are the basics. Apply them, get creative, and make the process personal by adding association or visualization, or by using a chalkboard or notecards. Think outside the box.

If you are not in the habit of memorizing the Scriptures, then why not start right now? I cannot think of a more appropriate verse to start with than Psalm 119:11: "Your word I have hidden in my heart, that I might not sin against You."

Wait...don't go yet. Review and repeat before moving on!

"Wives, submit to your own husbands, as to the Lord."
(Ephesians 5:22)

The S-Word

SSSS . . . sssuuuu . . . ssuubbbbb . . . *submission*. For some women, this is a difficult word to say. For others, the word has been blotted out of their vocabularies altogether. The word *submission* often conjures up images of the Dark Ages, where women were treated as second-class citizens and had minimal rights. Today the idea of a wife submitting to her husband carries negative cultural connotations of inequality and inferiority. But biblical submission is not a bad word; biblical submission does not promote inequality or inferiority, and should not be avoided or ignored. In fact, biblical submission brings freedom and blessing in the marriage relationship.

Alone, this command for submission may seem unfair, confusing, and one-sided. But that is always the danger when we isolate a verse from the Bible and try to make it stand alone, apart from the support of the surrounding setting. Divorcing a verse from its context can lead to misunderstanding and misapplication. The apostle Paul is not promoting unfairness, male chauvinism, or the servitude of women in a relationship. Instead, he is explaining what the dynamics of the marriage relationship should involve and what the order within a marriage should look like, both of which are patterned after the relationship and order found in the Godhead.

Submission has nothing to do with *superiority* and everything to do with *authority*. Take the Godhead, for example. Paul wrote, "But I want you to know that the head of every man is Christ, the head of woman is man, and the head of Christ is God" (1 Corinthians 11:3). Complete equality is found in the Godhead; we see that Jesus Christ places Himself under the authority of the Father (see Philippians 2:6–8). In the same way, wives are equal to their husbands, but are to willingly place themselves under the authority of their husbands. The husband is not superior to the wife, just as the Father is not superior to Christ. But within the Godhead (Father, Son, and Holy Spirit), is a divine order of authority, as well as the unique function and responsibility for each member.

God has established the same kind of authority and responsibility within the family and the church. We understand in the church that God has appointed pastors and elders to oversee the church. They are not superior to other members within the church body, but they have been given authority over the church to perform certain responsibilities within the church. But even they themselves are to be in total submission to Christ, who is the head of the church.

Submission begins when we trust in Jesus Christ as our Lord and Savior. When we acknowledge Jesus Christ as Lord, we agree to give Him full authority over our lives. If a person is unwilling to surrender his or her will to God's will, yield his or her ways to God's ways, and give up self-control for God-control, properly understanding and applying submission will be impossible in any other context.

Submission is a reflection of a person's trust in God. The Christian wife submits to her husband out of her love for the Lord, trust in the Lord, and obedience to the Lord. She is no more inferior to her husband than Christ is inferior to the Father. A wife's submission to her husband is not her cross to bear, but is her joy to reflect Christ in her marriage.

> "Teach me to do Your will, for You are my God.
> (Psalm 143:10)

Knowing and Doing Are Two Different Things

JUNE 16

HAVE YOU EVER asked a question like, "God, what do you want me to do in this situation?" or "God, show me the way You want me to go"? I suspect that after you asked God your question(s) about His will for your life, the stars did not realign to reveal the answer in the sky. You probably did not hear a booming voice echoing out of heaven with instructions on what to do or where to go. And you probably were not visited by one of God's faithful angels with a divine proclamation of God's plan for your life. Do not be discouraged, though. God is not trying to hide His will from you, nor is He trying to keep you from accomplishing His will. Actually, just the opposite is true; God has gone out of His way to help us to both know and do His will.

In Psalm 143, King David had turned to God for guidance. David was in a tough situation as he was feeling the pressure building while his enemies were closing in all around him. David was anxious and worried about what to do next. He did not want to make a mistake, and he did not want to act impulsively or make a rash decision, because his life hung in the balance. Have you ever felt the pressure of a decision weighing on you so heavily that you felt as though your entire future depended on what happened next? Have you ever been so worried or anxious about a decision that you felt overwhelmed? That is exactly how David felt, so David asked God for help. It almost goes without saying, but let's say it anyway. When you do not, know which way to go, the first place to go is always to God.

In David's prayer for help, he asked God for two things: revelation of God's will (verse 8) and a determination to do God's will (verse 11). Certainly, the first step before making any decision is to seek out what God has to say about the subject matter. We diligently seek out God's will from God's revelation. If we want to discover what God's will is, we must look to God's Word. God has graciously given us the Bible. In the Bible, we have His revelation to man, which contains all the information we need to live godly lives. The Bible teaches us, encourages us, and corrects us so that everyone can be prepared to live a life that please God and fulfills His purposes.

The second step is just as important, if not more so, than *knowing* the will of God: we should also be *doing* the will of God. Through doing, we express our faith in God and trust in His Word. Most of us already know enough of what God's will is for our lives, we just need to get busy doing it. For example, we all know that God wants us to love Him with all our heart, mind, soul, and spirit, and we are to love others as ourselves. What would happen if we simply purposed to do what we already know God has told us to do in the Bible? How much would our lives improve, and how much more would we look like Christ? While knowing what God's will is essential, the knowledge amounts to nothing if we do not actually purpose to do His will.

David does not want to simply know God's will; he wants the strength to actually do God's will. "Teach me to *do* Your will," he asks (verse 10, emphasis added). We should pray in similar fashion: "Lord, teach me to *do* Your will!" The best way to learn is by doing. So, the best way for God to teach us to do His will is by giving us opportunities to put into practice what we know from His Word. And the best place to start is by asking, "Lord, teach me to do Your will."

"Husbands, love your wives, just as Christ also loved the church and gave Himself for her. (Ephesians 5:25)

JUNE
17

To Love and to Cherish

ALL THAT IS NEEDED for good marriages to fail is for Christian husbands to do nothing. Husbands, take a minute and remember back to that very special wedding moment when your beautiful bride first made her appearance. As the music began to declare, "Here Comes the Bride," every head turned to catch a glimpse of the woman in the white dress. Time seemed to stand still, and if not for the fact that you could feel your heart pounding inside your chest, you might wonder if this was all just a dream. Mesmerized by her beauty, you did not dare look away, not even for an instant, as you did not want to miss a single second of this moment. As your wife-to-be made her way down the aisle, all you could think was, *I am the luckiest man in the world!* Standing face-to-face and hand-in-hand, you needed all your energy and mental wherewithal to declare, without getting choked up the vows, "To have and to hold, from this day forward, for better, for worse, for richer, for poorer, in sickness and in health, to love and to cherish, 'til death do us part." No other words could summarize so neatly your love and affection for the woman you were marrying.

Now after the "I dos" have been said and the honeymoon is over, husbands, how are you doing with those vows? In particular, how are you doing when it comes to loving your wife? Wait! Before you answer that, in order to accurately consider how you are doing, you need to understand the standard by which you are to evaluate yourself: "Husbands, love your wives, just as Christ also loved the church and gave Himself for her" (Ephesians 5:25). As Christ died for His bride, the church, a husband must be willing to die for his bride, to die to self for the sake of his spouse, to put her health, wealth, and well-being before his own. This includes dying to his dreams and desires so that he might fulfill her dreams and desires. This is love at its highest level; this love is both sacrificial and unconditional, and is a sanctifying and a satisfying love. As Pastor Walter Trobisch once wrote:

> Let me try to tell you what it really should mean if a fellow says to a girl, "I love you." It means: You, you, you. You alone. You shall reign in my heart. You are the one whom I have longed for, without you I am incomplete. I will give everything for you and I will give up everything

for you, myself as well as all that I possess. I will live for you alone, and I will work for you alone. And I will wait for you. . . . I will never force you, not even by words. I want to guard you, protect you, and keep you from all evil. I want to share with you all my thoughts, my heart, and my body—all that I possess. I want to listen to what you have to say. There is nothing I want to undertake without your blessing. I want to remain always at your side.[32]

Men are goal-driven, task-oriented, problem-solving, bottom-liners, so God keeps things simple for husbands by giving us one thing to remember here: husbands, *love* your wives. And if you want to know how to do that, then just look at Jesus and consider all that Christ is to the church, all that He has done for the church, all that He continues to do in the church today, and all that He has promised yet to do for her. This is the standard for a husband's love for his wife. Until you can say you love your wife the way Christ loved the church, there is still more work to be done and more love to be expressed.

Let everything that has breath praise the Lord. (Psalm 150:6)

The Theology of Praise

JUNE 18

A S AN OLD SAYING GOES, "when the praises go up, the blessings come down." I believe that is because something profoundly powerful and remarkably transforming takes place when we praise. When we fully appreciate the place that praise is to have in the lives of God's people, our daily lives will radically and forever change. Praise is not simply something we do when we feel like praising; praise is something we were created for. How is your praise life? Are you praiseful or praiseless?

What is praise? Praise is an act of our wills and an expression of our worship. Praise recognizes God for who He is (adoration) and what He has done (thanksgiving). Praise flows out of awe and reverence for our Maker. Praise gives glory to God and opens us up to a deeper communion with Him. Praise takes our attention off ourselves and our problems and focuses instead on the nature and character of God. Praise recognizes God's authority and remembers God's wonders. Praise prepares us for the power of God to be displayed in our lives and helps us to expand our picture of God. Praise increases and matures our faith in God. Praise fills our minds with who God is—His nature, His character, and His attributes—and praise fills our hearts with the joy of that knowledge.

Why should we praise God? We praise God because God is worthy to be praised. We praise God because praise brings glory to God and because we were created to glorify God (see Isaiah 43:7; 1 Corinthians 10:31). Praise is important in the Bible because nothing is more important than God in the Bible. All nature praises God (see Psalm 148:7–10), the sun, moon, and stars praise Him (see Psalm 19:1; 148:3), the angels praise Him (see Psalm 148:2), and we should praise Him. God delights in the praises of His people because God delights in His people.

So how should we praise? Praise can take on many different expressions. What is most important is that praise should be a genuine expression of your love for God, comes from a pure heart, and does not draw attention to you, but points toward God. Praise should not be distracting, nor be made-up or whipped up. Praise can be public and private, silent or sung, can involve clapping hands or clasping hands, and can be done in the morning or at midnight.

Praise honors God, and we are to live God-honoring lives. We are to praise God when we feel like doing so and even when we do not; we are to praise God in good times and in bad times. If you are having trouble praising God and do not know where to begin, then why not start here? Praise God for His holiness, mercy, and justice (see 2 Chronicles 20:21, Psalm 99:3–4). Praise God for His grace (see Ephesians 1:6). Praise Him for His goodness (see Psalm 135:3). Praise God for His kindness (see Psalm 117). Praise God for His salvation (see Ephesians 2:8–9). Praise God in the morning and in the evening and every minute in between. Praise inside and outside and everywhere along the way. Praise God alone and together and with everyone you meet.

Praise God, because the best theology of praise is one that is reflected every day in a life well-lived.

For we do not wrestle against flesh and blood, but against principalities, against powers, against the rulers of the darkness of this age, against spiritual hosts of wickedness in the heavenly places. (Ephesians 6:12)

JUNE
19

Saints and Soldiers

PART OF LIVING A VICTORIOUS LIFE in Jesus Christ is realizing that you are in an all-out war. The day you become a Christian is also the day that you were enlisted into God's army, instantly becoming both a saint and a soldier. In order to safeguard against becoming a casualty of this war, you must arise to the angelic trumpet call of reveille and prepare for the battle at hand. This war is unlike any other. This war is not of this world. This war is fought on an invisible battlefield where machine guns and missiles are of no use, where helmets and flak jackets provide no protection, and where night-vision goggles and sonar systems give you absolutely no ability to locate the enemy. How, then, do you fight a war where the enemy cannot be seen, where modern weapons do not work, and conventional tactics are insufficient?

First, we must be able to identify our enemy. Paul tells us in Ephesians 6 that our enemy is none other than the Devil. He is also known as "the dragon, that serpent of old, who is the Devil and Satan" (Revelation 20:2). Satan was created with incredible beauty and power, and although he held a high position in the heavenly ranks, he was not satisfied with what God had given him. Because of his pride, he rebelled against God (see Isaiah 14:12). Arrogant and overconfident, Satan led other fallen angels, also known as demons, in an uprising that caused a war to break out in heaven (see Revelation 12:7). Unable to win over God's angelic army, Satan and his rebels were cast out of heaven and now reside among mankind, where they have become rulers of the darkness and a spiritual force of wickedness. The objective of the Enemy is to stop the work of God, the plans of God, and the people of God. He deceives and destroys, he accuses and attacks, he confuses and clouds minds, and he distracts and disorients attention. He is crafty and cunning; he knows he is defeated yet refuses to surrender, and worst of all, he can masquerade as an angel of light. This is the Enemy we face!

Although the war may be invisible, the enemy is very real. And although we may be attacked from those who reside in the unseen realm, that is the dominion where they have already been defeated by Jesus Christ on the cross. Therefore, even though we walk in the realm of this world, we do not fight this war according to worldly tactics because the weapons of our warfare are not found in any tangible arsenal (see 2 Corinthians 10:3). This enemy and his forces cannot defeat the One who has already gained the victory over them; they fight in vain. Therefore, "none of this fazes us because Jesus loves us. I'm absolutely convinced that nothing—nothing living or dead, angelic or demonic, today or tomorrow, high or low, thinkable or unthinkable—absolutely nothing can get between us and God's love because of the way that Jesus our Master has embraced us" (Romans 8:37 MSG).

Even though we are in this war and must be prepared to fight against these evil forces when they come against us, we can still live victoriously in this life. Even though we are behind enemy lines, we are filled with the Spirit of God, giving us the power of God, and enabling us to stand against the enemies of God, confident that "no weapon formed against [us] shall prosper" (Isaiah 54:17).

"The fear of the Lord is the beginning of knowledge."
(Proverbs 1:7)

JUNE
20

The Fear Factor

COUNTLESS FEARS plague the minds of many people today. Some of these fears are common, like arachnophobia, which is the fear of spiders, or acrophobia, which is the fear of heights, and claustrophobia, which is the fear of confined spaces. A few fears are less common, like arachibutyrophobia, which is the fear of peanut butter sticking to the roof of your mouth, or phronemophobia, which is the fear of thinking, or even ablutophobia, which is the fear of bathing. But one fear, exists that, on the surface, seems the most illogical and unreasonable: fearing God. Should people really be afraid of God? If God is caring and compassionate, then why is fear the gateway to a right relationship with Him?

Proverbs is a book of the Bible that is filled with common-sense wisdom. This book contains a series of short and simple life lessons that, when applied, personally lead to godly living. Where the Psalms focus on our worship of God, the Proverbs focus on our walk with God. Each proverb found in this power-packed book shows us what life looks like when we have a healthy fear of God, and what life looks like when we do not. The secret to cultivating the wisdom we need for living a God-honoring life starts by understanding what makes up this fear of God.

The reason that many people struggle with the idea of fearing God is because, all too often, we associate fear with words like horror, terror, and fright. Fearing God is not being frightened of God. Fear of God does not mean that you are trying to run and hide from God like terrified people in a horror movie. God does not want to destroy us, hurt us, or scare us away. Rather, fearing God involves being overwhelmed with a sense of awe for God as we recognize His power, respect His capabilities, and have a humbling regard for His holiness. A. W. Tozer wrote, "I believe that the reverential fear of God mixed with love and fascination and astonishment and admiration and devotion is the most enjoyable state and the most satisfying emotion the human soul can know."[33] The fear of God consists of having a reverence, awe, and adoration for God. The fear of God motivates us to hate evil, provokes us to reject sin, and encourages us to put an end to immoral behavior. To fear God involves seeking God, serving God, and submitting to God. The fear of God dreads to displease God, but does not dread to be near to God, it pursues the purity of God, and it strives to personalize the Word of God.

To fear God is to worship God. To fear God is to live for Him. To fear God is to hate what He hates and love what He loves. To fear God is to begin to recognize His ways, identify His wisdom, and be aware of His Spirit's leading. Fearing the Lord adds life to your years and years to your life (see Proverbs 3:7–8; 10:27). Fearing the Lord is not only the place where true relationship with God begins, but is also the place where we receive wisdom for the walk that follows.

If you feel like you lack wisdom, start afresh with a reverent, awe-inspired, humble fear of the Lord God, because fear is a factor that affects your faith. As Oswald Chambers said, "The remarkable thing about fearing God is that when you fear God, you fear nothing else, whereas if you do not fear God, you fear everything else."[34]

Therefore take up the whole armor of God, that you may be able to withstand in the evil day, and having done all, to stand. (Ephesians 6:13)

**JUNE
21**

Saints in Shining Armor

NO ONE WANTS to be unprepared, ill-equipped, caught off guard, or blindsided, especially when concerning spiritual warfare. As Christians, we face an Enemy that will attack us whether we are ready or not. And considering the fact that we cannot see our Enemy coming, always being ready is vital to our spiritual well-being! The good news is that God provides us every spiritual resource we need in order to stand against the Devil and his army of malevolent misfits.

Every day we dress for what lies ahead. If you are going to the gym, then you wear sneakers and workout clothes. If today's event is a wedding, then we break out the formal wear. Just working around the house? You are likely to toss on some old jeans and a T-shirt. In the same way, we know that every day, a spiritual battle lies ahead, and wearing the right attire is essential. The Bible emphasizes six necessary articles of spiritual clothing: a belt, a breastplate, sandals, a shield, a helmet, and a sword, making us completely prepared for spiritual battle.

First, the belt is the item that holds everything together. And spiritually, our belt of truth, or the Bible, holds all things in place. When we are intimately acquainted with the Bible, Satan's lies cannot deceive us, and false teachers cannot lead us astray. By filtering everything through the Scriptures, we are protected from deception and kept from becoming undone.

The breastplate protects the vital organs, especially the heart, a common attack point of the enemy. The heart is where our emotions reside, and we cannot allow the enemy to attack or manipulate us into feeling afraid or anxious, or feeling unworthy or hopeless. Christ has given us His righteousness, which frees us from trusting in faulty feelings and allows us to stand before God, established and empowered to live a blameless life.

Sandals provide traction and sure footing. Spiritually, the gospel of Jesus Christ provides every believer with the security to stand on the solid rock of Christ, who has provided us peace with God. Nothing and no one can take away the foundation we have in Christ.

The shield provides soldiers with a wall of protection against the arrows of the enemy. Our faith is our shield, providing us with a towering wall of protection. The emphasis here is the trusting faith that results in action. This faith moves mountains. This is the same faith by which Noah built the ark. By faith, Abraham left his home, Moses stood before Pharaoh, the Israelites marched around Jericho, and Peter said to the lame man, "Rise up and walk." By faith, we must trust in and live by the promises of God, where the arrows of the enemy cannot harm us.

The helmet protects our minds, which is where the battle is often won or lost. Whatever we say and do first starts in the mind as a thought. Therefore, our thought lives must be protected and defended at all times.

The final piece in our spiritual arsenal is the *sword*, which is both an offensive and defensive weapon. To become proficient with this weapon takes time and commitment to both study and practice. With this weapon, we are equipped to reprove and rebuke, correct and convince, instruct and exhort.

Today you are heading into battle. Are you properly dressed?

"Dear friend, if bad companions tempt you, don't go along with them. (Proverbs 1:10)

JUNE
22

The Company You Keep

WHAT DO YOU GET when you combine the old adage "birds of a feather flock together" with "monkey see, monkey do"? And no, the answer is not flying monkeys! You actually end up with a biblical principle: we become like those with whom we spend time. No matter the label on this truth—pack mentality, herd instinct, or groupthink—the result is the same: the more time we spend with a particular group of people, the more we will think as they think and do as they do.

Most of us can remember hearing our parents say something like, "Be

careful who your friends are" or "Do not go hanging around with those kids."
Advice like this actually goes all the way back to King Solomon, who was the first
parent in the Bible to give out this kind of advice to his son. The Bible warns us
not to fool ourselves into thinking that hanging out with the wrong crowd will
not negatively affect us, because it will (see 1 Corinthians 15:33). But this type of
peer pressure is not limited to teens in junior high and high school; peer pressure
affects us all. We all want people to like us, which means that sometimes we
can make bad decisions and even worse compromises because we are too
concerned with what others may think about us.

Are you hanging out with friends who are dragging you down? Are you in
a relationship that is causing you to sin? Do you find that the people you know
are causing you to compromise your principles? No one is immune from the
questionable invitations from some friends or coworkers, but do not go along
with them, thinking that your good behavior will rub off on them. It will not. In
fact, the likely effect will be the opposite: their bad behavior will begin to rub off
on you. Their way of rationalizing sin will become your way of rationalizing sin.
Sin that starts out small will grow into a giant of a problem if you do not stop
going in the wrong direction.

What does this mean for you today? Perhaps the time has come to
reconsider who your friends are. Doing this evaluation may even require that
you make some changes, effective immediately. God may be leading you to end
a relationship or make a clean break from some of those non-Christian friends
who have been keeping you from totally following God.

The company you keep is more than just a reflection of who you are; the
company you keep is a powerful force that will shape what you believe and what
you do. This is why you should spend most of your time with people who are
building you up and not bringing you down, friends who are challenging you to
be a better Christian and not enticing you to be a worse sinner. Of course, the
best company to keep is with Jesus. Spending time with Him every day will help
you to think as He thinks and do as He does.

For to me, to live is Christ, and to die is gain.
(Philippians 1:21)

**JUNE
23**

A Win-Win Situation

FILL IN THE BLANK: for me, *to live is* _____? How you answer this
question will determine more than your outlook on life; your answer will
determine how you live out your life. With such an important question that
carries such significant implications, can anyone afford to gloss over , ignore, or
brush the answer aside? People answer this question many different ways. A few
popular responses are: to live is money, or to live is sports. And for some, to live
is happiness, family, or love. Now, nothing is wrong with any of the above, but
none of those "lives" are the ultimate purpose for which we were created. If you
want to live a fulfilling and fruitful life, a life that has meaning in the here and
now but also extends into eternity, then you must live for something higher,
something holier, and something heavenly.

The apostle Paul was writing to the church in Philippi while sitting in a Roman jail cell, and, although you might expect him to need a little encouragement in such a situation, actually, Paul would turn out to be delivering all the encouragement rather than receiving. The Philippians were naturally concerned about Paul's imprisonment and the possibility that he might be executed for his faith in Jesus Christ. But Paul was happy to report that although his freedom would be welcomed, his imprisonment had, in fact, proven to be a very fruitful time of ministry. How was Paul able to be so productive in prison? How could he remain full of joy in such depressing circumstances?

Paul believed that to live is Christ! Charles Spurgeon said of Paul that, "he did eat, and drink, and sleep eternal life. Jesus was his very breath, the soul of his soul, the heart of his heart, the life of his life."[35] For Paul, to live is Christ meant that he had faith in Christ for his salvation, he had fellowship with Christ intimately, he followed Christ practically, he forsook all for Christ personally, and he was filled with the joy of Christ daily. All of this enabled Paul to rise above his circumstances and continue to serve the Lord faithfully and fruitfully. Because Paul believed that to live is Christ, he also believed that to die is gain. Paul understood that the death of a Christian carried certain advantages, as life ends here on earth and eternal life in heaven begins. Life in heaven means freedom from sin, Satan, and suffering. Life in heaven means freedom to worship God perfectly and exclusively. Life in heaven means reunions with loved ones in Christ who have gone before us. But above all the advantages that eternity in heaven provides a believer, the highest and finest reason that death is gain for the Christian is because through death comes immediate conformity into Christ's image and eternal communion with Christ.

No matter how you look at what living means to you, life is what you make it, and for every Christian, we are to make it all about Christ. The Christian life means we are living for Christ, not living for money, love, power, or any other lesser substitute. Christ, and Christ alone, must be the focus of our every thought and the expression of our every action. When you live for Christ today and trust Christ for tomorrow, you always will be able to say, as Paul did, for me, to live is Christ and to die is gain. Now, that is the ultimate win-win!

"Trust in the Lord with all your heart; do not depend on your own understanding. Seek his will in all you do, and he will show you which path to take." (Proverbs 3:5–6 NLT)

JUNE 24

Roadside Assistance

HAVE YOU EVER made a wrong turn, missed an exit, or went in the wrong direction for a while before realizing your mistake? Have you ever come to an intersection and had absolutely no idea which way to go? Or perhaps you have been driving with a GPS and heard the bad news: "Recalculating route!" Knowing which way to go in life is never easy, and neither are knowing what choices to make, or what God's will is in a specific situation, but God has placed a promise in the Bible to point us in the right direction, guide us in the way to go, and, when necessary, help us "recalculate" our route.

You must first trust God completely if you want to know what God's will is for your life, if you are looking to make the godliest decisions possible in the various situations you will be faced with, or if you want to be walking the path that God has chosen for you. The road to righteousness begins with complete commitment, total trust, absolute surrender, and an undivided heart toward God. Trusting God means being able to look past what is visible to the human eye and known to the human mind and seeking to apprehend what is visible to God and known to the mind of God. Trusting God means relying on His Word that has been given to us, the Bible, and seeking to obey what He has commanded us from in His Word.

One aspect by which we demonstrate our trust in God is by depending entirely on Him and not on ourselves, trusting in God's understanding and not our own. Trusting in the Lord with all our hearts means that we place no trust in our own hearts. Unfortunately, we live in a world that says and believes the adage, "Listen to your heart," when God says, "Listen to Me." To be a Christian and to follow your heart means that you are leaning on your own understanding. You immediately demonstrate a lack of trust in God and His Word, which inevitably causes you to go the wrong way. Proverbs 28:26 warns, "He who trusts in his own heart is a fool." We are not to trust in our hearts or in our understanding, because our minds can change, our hearts can waver, and our understanding is limited. God, on the other hand, is immovable, unshakable, unchangeable, all-knowing, all-powerful, and ever present. He knows the beginning and the end. Therefore, He is the only one who can be trusted absolutely and indisputably.

The result of such trust is divine direction, godly guidance, and heavenly roadside assistance. This means placing ourselves in absolute surrender to the Lord's will and His Word, totally abandoning our own natural decision-making process, and fully letting go of our own personal predispositions and individual biases. Then, as we replace them with a complete and total reliance on and recognition of God's sovereignty, totally trusting the all-knowing, all-powerful, ever-present, and eternal God, such trust will result in the revelation of His righteous and His reliable path for our lives.

God has given His people a promise that never fails: if we are careful to follow His directions and take the road less traveled.

Have the same mindset as Christ Jesus. (Philippians 2:5 NIV)

The Right Mindset

JUNE
25

SOME MORNINGS, you just seem to wake up on the wrong side of the bed, which quickly leads to starting out on the wrong foot, and before you realize, your day is going in the wrong direction. What's the culprit? The wrong mindset! But you have the power to choose your thoughts, to choose your attitude, and to decide the direction your day will go, because the outcome of your day (and your life, for that matter) is determined by your approach. All too often we can be guilty of allowing the day to determine our attitudes and actions, when we should determine to make the choice ahead of time, choosing to start our day on the right foot with the right mindset. That way, no matter what happens during the day, we will be heading in the right direction, a direction that honors God in every situation.

Jesus made the choice before He left heaven that He would have the right mindset for His mission here on earth. He made an agreement with the Father to lay down his heavenly glory and come to earth as a man. He purposed in His mind to do the will of the Father and to serve rather than be to be served. He decided that He would live a life of sacrifice, that He would give His life for others, and that He would value humility over haughtiness and selflessness over selfishness. Jesus set His mind on things greater than the physical world (see Philippians 4:8), which led Him to live a life that highly magnified God (see John 17:4). Were some days "easier" than others for Jesus? One would think that days spent with his family working as a carpenter must have been easier than the day He woke up and was tempted by Satan. But the difficulty of a day is not determined by what happens on any given day. Rather, the attitude you possess during that day determines the level of difficulty. Where does this attitude all begin? With the right mindset! Jesus started every day with the right mindset, a mindset that understood the best for every day was found in accomplishing whatever God's will was for that day.

The Bible tells us that we, too, should have the right mindset, and the right mindset is always a mind that is *set* on living for Christ. The right mindset is deciding at the start of every day to do the will of God, to serve rather than to be served, to live a life of sacrifice, to give of yourself for the benefit of others, to value humility over haughtiness and selflessness over selfishness. Will some days be easier than others? Of course, but you can decide whether your day will go in the wrong direction or not.

Compare your thoughts, attitudes, and beliefs with those of Jesus. Do they match? God has given us the ability to think like Christ, which in turn means we can live like Christ. You have the power to choose your thoughts, to choose your attitude, and to decide the direction your day will go. So, take the time right now to cultivate the mind of Christ so that Christ can work through you today.

"The Lord detests lying lips, but he delights in those who tell the truth. (Proverbs 12:22 NLT)

To Tell the Truth

JUNE
26

HERE ARE A FEW famous fibs we hear all the time: "Your luggage isn't lost; it's only misplaced." "The check is in the mail." "I'll start my diet tomorrow." "Money cheerfully refunded." "One size fits all." "Leave your résumé, and we'll keep it on file." "I just need five minutes of your time." "This won't hurt a bit." "Let's do lunch." "It's not the money; it's the principle." Even though we chuckle at these statements because we have all heard them before, lying is a serious offense to God. Try as we might to justify our lies by calling them half-truths or little white lies, a lie is a lie.

The Bible says that we have all lied (see Psalm 119:29), and whether our intentions were good, like not wanting to hurt someone's feelings, or whether our intentions were less than honorable, God hates lying (see Proverbs 6:16–17). Why does God hate lying so much? God hates lying because He is truth. Remember what Jesus said: "I am the way, the truth, and the life" (John 14:6). And since God is truth, lying is impossible for Him (see Hebrews 6:18). Lying, therefore, goes against everything God represents. The truth about lying is that when we choose to lie, we are choosing to behave more like Satan than Christ, because the Bible tells us that Satan is the father of lies (see John 8:44).

Now to some, the conclusion that all lying is sin will sound unreasonable or extreme, too black-and-white, too narrow-minded, and an overly simplistic dismissal of the reality of the difficulty of such an inflexible statement. But as soon as we start to rationalize lying, as soon as we seek to justify an untruth or make excuses for lying, we are in danger of accepting lying as no big deal, when lying is a big deal to God.

The good news about lying is that God is able and willing to forgive us, even when we are guilty of telling a doozy of a lie. If we are guilty of lying, then we should be quick to confess the lie to God and repent immediately. But the best way to handle lying is to simply tell the truth. Honesty is always the best policy, but not necessarily the easiest to practice. Being truthful can be painful, but being untruthful is always worse.

Living a life of honesty is hard work and takes discipline, but honoring God with honesty is worth the effort. Watch your words, think before you speak, and be committed to telling the truth, even when doing so is difficult. If our goal is to become more Christlike, then avoiding lying must be a part of our everyday lives.

Do everything without complaining and arguing.
(Philippians 2:14 NLT)

The Cure for Complaining

JUNE 27

COMPLAINING SEEMS TO BE one of the most commonly accepted sins among Christians. What makes matters worse is that some people see nothing wrong with complaining. We can complain about almost anything: the weather ("It's too hot!"), our food ("It's too cold!"), our taxes being too high, and our bonuses being too low. Then, of course, we complain about traffic, as well as long lines, politics, gas prices, and dropped cell phone calls. We even bring our complaints into church: the sermon was too long, the sermon was too short, the music was too loud, no donuts were served after the service, and the list goes on.

Just so that everyone is clear on the subject of complaining, and to ensure there is absolutely no confusion, complaining is a sin. God clearly and conclusively condemns *all* complaining and commands us to stay away from complaining altogether (see 1 Corinthians 10:10; James 5:9). Complaining is totally off-limits in the life of a Christian, and to make sure we do not try to find a spiritual loophole, we are told in today's verse to do *everything* without complaining. And yes, everything means *everything*!

Paul is encouraging the Philippians to move onward and upward in their relationship with God. He wants them to rise above their circumstances and take charge of their attitudes and actions. Not everything is going to go your way in this life. Not everyone is going to like you or agree with your decisions, and not everyone is going to treat you fairly. Paul knew this all too well, as he was writing this letter from prison, even though he had committed no crime. If anyone had reason to complain, Paul had plenty. But he knew that complaining was not God's way. You may not be able to control what happens to you, but you can control how you respond. And complaining should never be the response.

Does this mean no situation exists in which we can express a complaint? Simply put, no. But when we recognize a problem, we can take steps to fix that problem, and this can and must be done without complaining. For example, if a problem develops in your church, you prayerfully take that problem to the leadership and discuss the problem with them, and do not complain in the congregation. At the core of complaining is discontentedness with God. Complaining says that you dislike what God has allowed in your life. Complaining says, "If I were God, I would do things differently." Complaining tears down instead of building up.

So, what is the cure for complaining? First, we must recognize we are a reflection of Christ to the world, and as such, we are to shine as godly examples. Complaining only serves to dim your light. Next, show some restraint. Keep quiet, or, as Proverbs 30:32 says, "Put your hand on your mouth." Then, find a way to redirect your words: "Let no corrupt word proceed out of your mouth, but what is good for necessary edification, that it may impart grace to the hearers" (Ephesians 4:29). In other words, be encouraging, not discouraging. Finally, find reason to rejoice: "Rejoice in the Lord always" (Philippians 4:4). Complain never; rejoice always!

As much as we might wish that Paul had said, "Do *most* things without complaining," he did not. The command is to do *everything* without complaining. Do not grumble; be grateful. Do not be argumentative; seek to be appreciative. As someone once said, "Instead of complaining that the rosebush is full of thorns, be happy that the thorn bush has roses."

A soft answer turns away wrath, but a harsh word stirs up anger. (Proverbs 15:1)

A Word to the Wise

JUNE 28

WE ALL HAVE TIMES where we can send our words into the air like little hand grenades, carelessly and indiscriminately lobbing them at anyone and everyone who attacks, aggravates, or annoys us, leaving nothing but injured feelings and emotional devastation behind. We are all guilty of having said things we regret. We have all spoken thoughtless words in the heat of the moment that we wished we could take back. What we say and how we say it makes a big difference in the way our words are received and the reactions they will produce in others. Our words can either make a situation worse or go a long way in helping to make a situation better.

The book of Proverbs speaks often of the tongue's power to hurt or heal, to build up or tear down, to comfort or criticize. For example, we read, "A wholesome tongue is a tree of life, but perverseness in it breaks the spirit. . . . A man has joy by the answer of his mouth, and a word spoken in due season, how good it is!" (Proverbs 15:4, 23). Sticks and stones may break a person's bones, but words are far more damaging. Harsh words have started fights, ended friendships, and divided families, while soft words can promote peace, facilitate forgiveness, and diffuse difficulty. How are you doing with your words? Do you find that your words do more harm than good, or the other way around?

The opportunities to respond with a soft answer usually come upon us suddenly, leaving us little to no time to prepare the perfect response. Only the one who possesses a soft heart, a heart that has been made tender toward the things of God, can give a soft answer. A soft heart is one that willingly turns the other cheek when struck. A soft heart chooses to love and not hate, blesses and does not curse, prays when persecuted, and speaks calming words when confronted with someone who is hurling harshness. Soft words come from a soft heart, because our words are a reflection of what is contained within our hearts (see Luke 6:45).

If soft words can only come from soft hearts, then the only way to start speaking softly in sticky situations is by tenderizing our hearts. A tender heart is formed through a faithful persistence to pursue God in His Word. We must allow the Word of God to teach us, correct us, and conform us into the image of Christ that has been revealed to us through the pages of the Bible. A tender heart is also formed in us as we allow the Word of God to create the fruit of the Spirit in us. Gentleness, kindness, goodness, and self-control are all essential if we are going to speak softly. Finally, a tender heart is formed as our minds are transformed. As we think, so we speak. Our hearts are further softened as our minds are steadfastly fixed upon heavenly things.

You can never go wrong with a soft word. Choosing to speak a calm word in a heated discussion is often like water on fire.

Power of Words

A careless word may kindle strife,
A cruel word may wreck a life,
A bitter word may hate instill,
A brutal word may smite and kill;
A gracious word may smooth the way,
A joyous word may light the day,
A timely word may lessen stress,
A loving word may heal and bless.
—Anonymous

> *Yes, everything else is worthless when compared with the infinite value of knowing Christ Jesus my Lord. For his sake I have discarded everything else, counting it all as garbage, so that I could gain Christ.* (Philippians 3:8 NLT)

JUNE
29

From Garbage to Glory

YOU CAN GO TO CHURCH AND MISS CHRIST! You can sing hymns and miss Him. You can listen to a message and miss the Messiah. You can read the Scriptures and miss the Savior. And you can serve in ministry and miss the One you are serving. Essentially, you can be very religious but have no relationship with God. The apostle Paul had an impressive pedigree and was a cut above the rest. He was a talented, well-educated, self-starter who had an impressive résumé of righteous works. He was a who's who among the up and coming rabbis of the day, and he undoubtedly would have been voted most likely to become high priest if God had not literally knocked him off his high horse and changed his life and perspective forever.

After Paul's personal encounter with Jesus Christ on the road to Damascus, he became acutely aware of the fact that what mattered most was not more religious activity. What mattered most was knowing Christ more. Personal righteousness gave way to a personal relationship. Paul considered all his achievements, his family heritage, his education, his success, and his service in the name of religion all garbage compared to the glorious gain of knowing Christ personally and powerfully. Paul realized that the joy of godly living was found in knowing and growing in Christ and not in what he was doing for God. Paul looked upon all his works prior to knowing Christ as rotten and decaying compost. All of his prior work amounted to nothing more than mounds of manure. Sounds disgusting, right? That was Paul's point. He finally saw clearly something that still blinds many today, and that is that religious works do nothing to improve your standing with God. Traditions bring no pardon for sin, and our service to God is not the way to gain salvation from God. Our service to God is only the result of receiving salvation from God. Service is an expression of gratitude, not a means of earning approval. We serve God because God has already saved us; we do not get saved because we serve God. Paul finally understood that good standing with God was not because of tradition, position, or even religion. It was about knowing Christ personally.

All of our good works, when we add them all up, are nothing in comparison to what God has done for us through Jesus Christ. All our good is garbage in comparison to the grace of God. Our treasures are nothing more than trash when compared to the treasures of heaven, and our riches are rubbish when compared to a right relationship with Christ. This does not mean that what we do for Christ is of no value to God and no benefit to others. Paul was one of the greatest missionaries who ever lived, and he did more in his service to God than most of us ever could hope to do, even if we had two lives to live. Is serving God important? Yes. We should all seek ways to serve God with the gifts He has given us. But, our highest priority should not be in spending more time doing things for Christ but in spending more time getting to know Christ better.

Outward religion means nothing apart from an inward relationship with Christ. We are prone to think that the more good we do, the more God will accept us. But what we must all come to see, like Paul, is that when we trust in Jesus Christ, we exchange our righteousness for the righteousness of Christ. We exchange our garbage for His glory.

You can make many plans, but the Lord's purpose will prevail. (Proverbs 19:21 NLT)

Planning for the Future

JUNE

30

SHOULD A CHRISTIAN make plans for the future? Some people believe that planning for the future shows a lack of trust in God today. Maybe you have heard the saying, "By failing to prepare, you are preparing to fail" or "Plan ahead. It wasn't raining when Noah built the ark!" Most people believe that it pays to plan in life, and that if you want to succeed at something, then planning plays an important part of getting you there. But for a Christian, planning is a paradox. We try and plan for the future, yet we know that the future is in God's hands. We are called to wait upon God (see Psalm 27:14) while being urged to take action (see James 1:22). Does planning for the future, then, contradict living by faith?

Planning and faith are not either/or approaches to living the Christian life. For example, Joseph told the people of Egypt to prepare for a coming famine that God revealed was coming (see Genesis 41). David planned for the building of the temple and provided everything Solomon needed to do the job after his death (see 1 Chronicles 22:5). Nehemiah made careful plans and preparations for the rebuilding of the walls of Jerusalem while also waiting on God for the right time to do the job (Nehemiah 1–2). The apostle Paul frequently made plans to visit new cities where he could share the gospel while also making plans to return to old cities where he had planted churches (see 1 Corinthians 16:5). Even Jesus taught on the importance of making plans, as in the story of the wise and foolish builders in Matthew 7:24–27, or when He taught about counting the cost in Luke 14:28–30, and in His teaching concerning the king planning for battle in Luke 14:31–32.

So how can we make sure that we are planning God's way? First, we rest in the fact that God is in control. True, God wants to use you and that He has a plan for your life (see Ephesians 2:10), but do not start making any plans without first seeking His will. Planning and prayer go hand in hand, so do not leave God out of the planning process. Planning ahead is good; just remember that God is the One in control of your future.

Next, when planning, stay flexible! Give God the freedom to adjust your plans so they can better fit His purposes. Also while planning, be committed to honoring God in your life today. Make sure you are living each and every day in a way that honors God and is obedient to His Word. Only then can you be sure that God will remain involved in your plans for the future. As you trust God today, He will guide you into the future (see Proverb 3:5–6).

Lastly, always make plans that keep heaven in mind. As you live for heaven and not this world, the way you plan should be reflected in the fact that you know your future and hope are not found in the things of this world. Keeping that in mind will radically affect the way you plan for tomorrow.

Although we do not know what tomorrow holds because tomorrow is promised to no one, planning ahead still has value. Planning for the future, with prayerful consideration, is good for you and your family. Planning is biblical, shows faith and trust, and establishes your commitment to do what God has directed you to do.

July

I can do all things through Christ who strengthens me.
(Philippians 4:13)

I Think I Can, I Think I Can!

CAN YOU REALLY DO *all* things through Christ? Is this verse some sort of *The Little Engine That Could* optimism, encouraging us to think we can do anything we set our minds to if we simply believe? Well, the tell-it-like-it-is answer is actually no, you cannot do *all* things through Christ. Now, wait. Before you close this book and burn it as heresy, let's keep things in context shall we? Upon further examination, this verse is more about Christ and less about us.

The context of this verse focuses on the God-given power to endure any circumstance, not the power to accomplish any achievement. The apostle Paul had suffered extraordinary hardships in his service to God. He experienced numerous imprisonments, beatings, stonings, and shipwrecks. He encountered weariness, sleeplessness, and hunger. And these hardships do not even begin to cover the emotional and spiritual frustrations and setbacks he faced. But, rather than looking at his circumstances, whether good or bad, Paul looked to Christ to satisfy his every need. The result? Paul was able to say that when he reached the end of his strength, when he was at the limit of his own resources, he knew he could always rely on God's strength and resources. He also knew he had the power to overcome whatever difficulty he faced because of all God had given him through Jesus Christ. In other words, as J. B. Phillips puts it, "I am ready for anything through the strength of the One who lives within me" (Philippians 4:13 PH).

God is not promising to make us supersaints with superpowers, but He is promising us that we will be given the strength and the power to accomplish all that He calls us to accomplish. God is also not promising us that we never will suffer or experience difficulty, but that we will be given all the power that we need to handle the difficulties and demands of this life. Also, God is not promising us financial prosperity, but He *is* promising us that whether we have poverty or prosperity, we are rich in Christ and can be completely content in Him.

God's strength and power that is made available to every believer is sufficient to strengthen us and sustain us in any trial. What we must learn to do is to draw on the deep resources of God, made available to us by faith in Jesus Christ. Our strength for every circumstance comes from Christ, and as we trust in Him, as we turn to Him, and as we allow Him to empower us, we can endure whatever He allows in our lives. As one writer said, "There is strength in Christ not only to sanctify and save us, but strength to support us under all our burdens and afflictions."[36]

Wine is a mocker, strong drink is a brawler, and whoever is led astray by it is not wise. (Proverbs 20:1)

A Sober Look at Drinking

IS ANYTHING WRONG with having an occasional glass of wine with dinner, a cold beer on a hot day, or a toast of champagne during that special celebration? Whether a Christian is ever allowed to drink alcohol has been the source of many personal discussions, and even church divisions, over the years. One side says the occasional drink is okay, because the Bible never comes out and condemns drinking as a sin. The other side says you should stay away from all alcohol all the time because alcohol can lead to drunkenness.

Is one side right and the other side wrong? Or, is this simply a matter of personal preference or an issue of Christian liberty (see Romans 14)? No matter the issue, we must be willing to put aside our own personal preferences concerning a subject and allow the Bible to shape our attitudes and actions.

The best place to begin is with the obvious. The Bible continually and clearly condemns drunkenness (see Ephesians 5:18). From the first example of drunkenness in the Bible with Noah (see Genesis 9:21), all the way to the last mention of drunkenness in the New Testament (see 1 Peter 4), drunkenness is condemned. No wiggle room around or way to justify the issue. Like it or not, drunkenness is sin: end of conversation. What about drinking that does not lead to drunkenness? Is that sin? Nothing in the Bible definitively condemns drinking in moderation as sin, but before you crack open a beer or pop that cork and pour a glass of wine, you must consider something else before taking that next sip.

Although not condemned as sin, drinking *is* considered unwise (take verse above from Proverbs as evidence of that). Famed preacher Martyn Lloyd-Jones once said:

> "Drink is not a stimulus, it is a depressant. It depresses first and foremost the highest centers of all in the brain. They are the very first to be influenced and affected by drink. They control everything that gives a man self-control, wisdom, understanding, discrimination, judgment, balance, the power to assess everything; in other words everything that makes a man behave at his very best and highest. The better a man's control, the better man he is. . . . But drink is something which immediately gets rid of control; that indeed is the first thing it does."[37]

One of the best summations of this perspective came from the apostle Paul when he said, "All things are lawful for me, but all things are not helpful. All things are lawful for me, but I will not be brought under the power of any" (1 Corinthians 6:12).

Although drinking may not be a sin, your drinking could be a stumbling block for someone else. In Romans 14, we are cautioned that although some Christian liberties, or freedoms, are not defined as sin in the Bible, if what we enjoy as a choice may cause someone else to stumble or sin, then that choice is no longer a freedom. For the sake of the other person's well-being, we should avoid the choice. Since love is to be our supreme motivation, the loving thing to do if your drinking may cause another to stumble is to abstain completely.

If you are thinking of doing something that will numb the senses, compromise the conscience, reduce reason, hide the holy, and shroud the spiritual, then seek to take the wisest path for both you and those around you, and simply refrain.

Be anxious for nothing, but in everything by prayer and supplication, with thanksgiving, let your requests be made known to God; and the peace of God, which surpasses all understanding, will guard your hearts and minds through Christ Jesus. (Philippians 4:6-7)

JULY 3

Stressed Out!

EVERY SO OFTEN, life can leave you feeling overworked and overloaded, weary and worn out, exhausted and emotionally on edge. Given the complexities of today's demanding world, you will inevitably experience times when you are feeling stressed-out. But stress, left untreated, can severely impact your everyday life. Physically, stress can cause fatigue, headaches, upset stomach, and sleeplessness. Mentally, stress can lead to forgetfulness and trouble concentrating. Emotionally, stress can leave you depressed, worried, and filled with anxiety. But before stress wreaks havoc on your body and in your life, remember that the Bible tells us we can exchange our problems for peace, we can trade in our anxiety for assurance, and we can live permanently released from the weight of worry.

God wants us to avoid anxiety at all costs, so much so that we are commanded to be anxious for nothing. *Hold on. Wait a minute. What about my finances? Surely, I am allowed a little anxiety here and there over paying my bills, taxes, or credit cards? What about my health? I mean, if I am told that I have an incurable disease, I must have some leeway on the old anxiety meter, right?*

If you think you are entitled to stress out about life's difficulties, think again. "Be anxious for nothing" means we are to be anxious for absolutely *nothing!* No exceptions, no exemptions, no excuses. We cannot avoid all of life's difficulties, but we are never to become a victim of anxiety. Anxiety agitates our attention and stabs at the sensibilities; it beats on the body and causes restlessness in our souls. Anxiety is a sign of distrust in God, and disrupts our communion with Him, leading us to settle when we should be submitting to God. And, for the sake of keeping things simple, anxiety is sin.

Stress can cause us to overreact and jump to conclusions instead of waiting for direction. Stress makes us focus on details and fail to see the big picture. And, stress can cause us to be self-reliant when we need to be God-reliant.

What, then, do we need to do to stop a little stress from turning into sin? We pray. Prayer is the path to the peace that God promises. We must remember that prayer is not designed for us to get what we want out of God; prayer is a way for God to get the selfishness out of us.

Paul is not reducing all of life's problems to a pocket-sized solution. He is not saying that a prayer a day keeps the problems away. What he is saying is that if stress is building, prayer must be lacking. Prayerlessness is a sign of faithlessness. Anxiety enters our heart when our trust in God leaves our minds. Anxiety grows when we allow our problems to become bigger in our eyes than God is in our lives. Prayer helps us to refocus and refuel our faith, which results in a divine transfer of the peace of God into our lives. If you do not know how to start praying in stressful times, begin by thanking God. Even in difficult times, we have much to be thankful for. If you need help, open up the book of Psalms to help you get started.

The next time you feel the pressures of life mounting and stress building, remember: be anxious for nothing and pray about everything.

If your enemy is hungry, give him bread to eat; and if he is thirsty, give him water to drink. For so you will heap coals of fire on his head, and the Lord will reward you.
(Proverbs 25:21-22)

JULY 4

Getting Even with Evil

ENEMIES ARE LIKE SPLINTERS. They always find a way to get under your skin. Enemies in life are inevitable. No matter what you do or do not do, some people will simply not like you, refuse to get along with you, and some people may even cause you some sort of physical, emotional, or spiritual injustice.

How should you treat the person who dislikes you, the one who has slandered your character, mistreated you, and misrepresented you to others? Our natural inclination is to respond with, "Don't get mad; get even!" But God calls us to a higher standard: we are not to lower ourselves by returning evil for evil, but raise ourselves to return good for evil. Some say returning evil for good is Devil-like, returning evil for evil is beastlike, returning good for good is manlike, and returning good for evil is Godlike.

Revenge is never the right response, and payback cannot satisfy a person scorned any more than saltwater can satisfy the thirsty. Although you may never actually respond with vengeful actions toward an enemy, do not be fooled into thinking that inaction is the same as forgiveness. Holding on to hostility and allowing resentment to smolder preserves that person as an enemy in your heart and feeds bitterness.

Instead of seeking retribution whenever you are confronted with an enemy, conquer them with love. God has redeemed people with love, and we are called to redeem relationships with love. God has conquered us, His enemies, with His love. While we were sinners and enemies of righteousness, He loved us and was not willing to repay our evil with evil. Instead, He repaid us with the ultimate good by sacrificing His Son so that we could now become His friends.

Donald Barnhouse has said the way God proved this was:

> When the nations were raging and the peoples imagining a vain thing, He did not move to destroy them. He did not destroy Adam when he sinned, but promised a Savior and began the long course of history so that man could have opportunity upon opportunity to repent

and return to God. . . . He did not destroy us when we were ungodly sinners. He came from heaven to save us. He came into the camp of his enemies and allowed them to do their will against him in order to establish the foundation for our redemption. When we were without strength, when we were enemies, Christ died for us. Note that he did not save us by demonstrating his mighty power in some miracle. He saved us—He saved us by letting us kill him. How astonishing this is! And when he rose from the dead he did not judge those who behaved so wickedly against him. The Jerusalem to which he held out his arms before he died was still the center of his loving thought. He commanded his disciples to go into all the world and preach the gospel to every creature, but he commanded them to begin at Jerusalem. Was this not heaping coals of fire upon the heads of his enemies? And did it not melt the hearts of many?[38]

The coals of God's kindness were not given so that they would burn your enemy to the ground; rather, they should be used to build a bridge through blessing. The coals of kindness replace a cold shoulder with a warm heart, seek to fix rather than fight, and pardon rather than punish.

He is the image of the invisible God. (Colossians 1:15)

Picture Perfect

JULY 5

A PICTURE has an extraordinarily unique ability to capture our attention and captivate our thoughts. A picture is a powerful medium that can communicate more in a single snapshot than often can be expressed through a multitude of words. Pictures seize a split second and memorialize memories. They preserve history and provoke emotion. Pictures of nature can take can our breath away and fill us with awe and wonder. Pictures of people can melt our hearts, make us smile, and cause us to shed tears. Pictures of localities can even motivate us to travel to new destinations. What if we had a picture of God, a snapshot of the Divine, an Instagram of the I am, or a JPEG of Jehovah? Just imagine what that might do.

The Bible is God's personal photo album of Himself. Throughout the pages of the Bible, we see portraits of God, Polaroids of His personality, pictures of His character, and representations of His nature. But one picture stands out as the most comprehensive image of God: Jesus Christ. In Jesus, we see what no man has seen. In Jesus, the invisible God became visible. In Jesus, the mystery of God was revealed.

Jesus is the visual representation of the Everlasting God, the accurate image of the Almighty. He exactly exemplifies El Shaddai. He completely characterizes the Creator. He is fully fashioned after Abba Father. And He lacks nothing as Lord of lords. Like a picture, Jesus helps to give us perspective, brings texture and focus to God, and adjusts our point of view. As one theologian wrote:

If you want to know what God's like, look at Christ. He'll tell you what God is like. If God were man, we would expect Him to be sinless; Jesus was. If God were a man, we would expect Him to speak the greatest words ever spoken; He did. If God were a man, we would expect Him to exert a profound influence on human personality like no other being that ever lived, and He did. If God were a man, we would expect that He would do miracles with ease, and He did. If God were a man, we would expect Him to love, and He did, because He was God, and God cannot be known other than through Jesus Christ.[39]

This is the picture of God, the immaculate image, the sinless snapshot found in Jesus Christ. In the most astounding picture possible, Jesus, as the incarnate God, is able to take our breath away and leave us filled with awe and wonder. He melts our hearts and makes us smile, He causes us to shed tears, and He motivates us to travel to new destinations.

As Jesus is a picture-perfect representation of God, we must not forget that we are to be a picture of Jesus in the world today. For some, we may be the only snapshots of the Savior they ever will see. We must continue to keep our eyes focused on the image of the invisible God so that we may be the best representation of Jesus we can be to those who need to see Jesus.

Veiled in flesh the Godhead see,
Hail the incarnate Deity![40]

As iron sharpens iron, so a friend sharpens a friend.
(Proverbs 27:17 NLT)

True Friendship

JULY
6

A GOOD FRIEND is a gift from God. A good friend is not someone who necessarily agrees with everything you say and do, but is someone who lovingly inspires you to be a better Christian. God is interested in relationships, and after a personal relationship with Him, you have been created to have relationships with others. The book of Proverbs is filled with warnings about the dangers that can come when a person chooses to hang out with the wrong crowd. Poor choices in friendships can lead a person into ruin and away from God. On the other hand, good choices regarding friendships can be both emotionally uplifting and spiritually beneficial.

Take a moment and consider who your close friends are. Do they go to church? Are they living their lives for God? God wants you to have friendships that help you to become a better Christian. But are non-Christian friends still okay to have? Of course! We are called to be salt and light in the world (see Matthew 5:13-15), and so we should do our best to positively influence others as we seek to lead them into a relationship with Christ. Jesus was not afraid to spend time with some pretty irreligious individuals, but He always made a point to share the truth and love of God with them. Jesus never allowed those friendships to negatively impact His most important relationship, which was His relationship with God the Father.

As Christians, our closest friendships should be with other Christians, because godly relationships make us sharp, and ungodly relationships dull our edges. As iron sharpens iron, our friendships should challenge us to make godly choices and decisions. Merely spending time together as Christians will not necessarily sharpen our Christian character. We need fellowship with friends that will include discussions about our spiritual journey and give us opportunities to share with them how we should seek to follow Christ, what He is doing in our lives, and what struggles we may be facing. We should look for ways to "sharpen" one another through the bond of friendship. We can do this by praying together, by encouraging one another through our conversations, confronting a friend in love when he or she may be about to make a bad decision or is struggling with sin, and by sharing what God is teaching us.

Being a good friend is just as important as having a good friend, and true friendship, the way God intended, will bring us joy and help us to grow spiritually.

"For in Him dwells all the fullness of the Godhead bodily; and you are complete in Him" (Colossians 2:9-10)

JULY 7

Cheated or Completed

H.A. IRONSIDE said, "Christ is a substitute for everything, but nothing is a substitute for Christ."[41] Ever since the first time Satan misrepresented God to Eve in the Garden of Eden, the enemy of God has used lies, faulty logic, and unfounded truth in an attempt to misrepresent God. Satan has caused countless multitudes to veer off course, leaving them stranded and broken down on the side of eternity's highway. Satan uses philosophies, false religions, and empty traditions to minimize God, and even remove God completely, as man seeks to understand the purpose and meaning of life. Humanism, legalism, mysticism, pantheism, gnosticism, Mormonism, Hinduism, Buddhism, and most of the *-isms* in the world are nothing more than cheap counterfeits for explaining our existence. Christ is the center of everything, materially and spiritually, and is, therefore, the only complete source of all things pertaining to life and godliness. The centrality of Christ has made Him the center of attack for all things spiritual. We must understand the fullness of Christ's deity, because we stand complete in our faith.

Philosophies professing to explain the meaning of life are nothing new and have not changed much over the years; the only thing new about them is their packaging. The apostle Paul was battling philosophical opinions of his day that are still with us today, beliefs that overemphasize the traditions of men, accentuate an experiential morality, and look toward the physical world in a vain attempt to explain the spiritual realm. Inevitably, any philosophy that diminishes the deity of Christ, minimizes the magnitude of Messiah, or curtails the centrality of Christ as the author, finisher, and sole source of salvation is cheating you out of a genuine faith. In the fullness of Christ, we find the fullness of faith, the totality of truth, the image of the invisible God, and the apex of authority. In the fullness of Christ, we find the completeness of the church, the sufficiency of salvation, the perfection of purity, and the inexhaustible supply of sanctification. In Him is the wholeness of wisdom, the immeasurability of intelligence, the immutability of integrity, the height of holiness, and the one true God. Christ is not merely Godlike; He is completely God, He always has been God, He always will be God, and He never will cease from being God.

Any teaching, tradition, religion, philosophy, value system, moral code, ethical standard, or -ism that in any way diminishes Jesus Christ's absolute authority, complete deity, and exclusive, redemptive power is cheating you out of your future and hope in heaven. But, if in Christ you find the fullness of God, you stand at this moment forever more complete in Him, never needing more, and never receiving less than His fullness.

To be complete in Christ means that I will never lack peace because Christ is perfect peace. Therefore, He is my peace. I will never lack for wisdom because Christ is wisdom. Therefore, He is my wisdom. I will never lack for hope because Christ is the hope of glory. Therefore, He is my hope. I will never lack for anything because He is everything. Therefore, He is my everything, and I stand complete in Him.

"Charm is deceitful and beauty is passing, but a woman who fears the Lord, she shall be praised. (Proverbs 31:30)

JULY
8

Beauty Mark

IF YOU ARE A WOMAN, have you ever looked at the woman described in Proverbs 31 and thought, *No way can I live up to that! I mean, really!*

Just look at her: She is a busy woman who runs a household (verse 27), works hard (verses 13, 25), makes significant business decisions (verse 16), gardens (verses 16), and makes her own clothes (verse 22). She juggles fixing meals (verse 15), keeping the cupboards stocked (verse 14), and volunteering her time to help support worthy causes (verses 19-20), all the while projecting cheerfulness to her children (verse 28) and giving honor to her husband (verses 11, 31). This is all admirable, but seems completely unattainable, because she is no mere mortal woman; she is a superwoman! She is able to leap towering laundry piles in a single bound, is faster than an SUV on its way to soccer practice, and more powerful than a Diaper Genie. But as noble as all these qualities are, the one quality that makes this woman truly beautiful, completely commendable, and absolutely attainable for every woman is her fear of the Lord.

Becoming this kind of woman is not about being amazingly energetic, doggedly determined, and remarkably charitable. Becoming a Proverbs 31 woman is about having a fixed faith in God. This does not mean making sure that every *i* is doted and every *t* is crossed or making sure the to-do list is completed by the end of the day (if you are not careful, you will multitask yourself into the hospital). Instead, becoming this kind of woman is about being unwavering in your love of God. Becoming the Proverbs 31 kind of woman is not about *doing*, but about *being*, and not as much about action as the position of the heart behind every action.

Becoming this kind of woman, a woman of excellence, means that worshiping God is where life begins and ends. This worship loves God with a whole heart, mind, soul, and strength. This worship fears God and seeks to please God through obedience to His Word. This worship consistently meditates on those things that are true, noble, just, pure, lovely, of good report, and virtuous. A Proverbs 31 woman's worship continually prays for her family's physical and spiritual welfare and the welfare of others. Her worship is seen in her faithfulness to use her time and talents all for God's glory. This woman's worship seeks to make the most out of every opportunity that God provides her every day. The worship of the Proverbs 31 woman comes from an inner beauty that does not fade with the passage of time, but only grows lovelier day after day.

Becoming this kind of woman is not out of reach, and is not reserved for only a select few. A Proverbs 31 woman is absolutely attainable, irresistibly beautiful, and worthy to be praised. This woman is marked by true beauty, and she should be admired and cherished because she strikingly symbolizes the message of Proverbs: by fearing God, you can live a life full of wisdom and righteousness.

Work willingly at whatever you do, as though you were working for the Lord rather than for people.
(Colossians 3:23 NLT)

JULY
9

Who's the Boss?

THE CHRISTIAN LIFE should be one that strikingly stands out and is noticeably different in the world. Christians should exemplify enthusiasm, demonstrate diligence, and personify perseverance in all they endeavor to do. There are plenty of tiresome tasks, dreary duties, and cumbersome chores that we all have to do at times, and if we were honest, none of us would say that we necessarily like doing them. No one really wakes up in the morning and thinks to himself or herself, *I can't wait to take out the trash today!* And no one honestly walks over to their neighbor's house, knocks on the door for no reason, and says, "Do you have any laundry that I can fold today?" No one goes into work asking, "Do you have something for me to do that no one else wants to do?" Yet, as Christians, the way we go about completing our responsibilities and working on those chores says a lot about our understanding of who we are working for.

Paul was writing during a time when slavery was widespread, with an estimated sixty million slaves. Work for most was unpleasant, tasks were tedious, and errands were unexciting. Paul wanted to bring hope to those Christian slaves who felt that their situation was hopeless, their work did not matter, and they were insignificant. Paul supplied the slaves with a glimmer of hope as He gave them a glimpse of glory by awakening their awareness to the fact that no matter who their boss was on earth, and no matter what their work situation was, ultimately they worked for God.

Chores and responsibilities take on a whole new meaning when we realize that no matter what we are doing, we are working for God. Whether you have a dream job or a dead-end job, whether you are washing dishes, changing diapers, or running a Fortune 500 company, God sees your labor. He will reward you, not based on the position you hold but on the position of your heart toward the work God has set before you to do. Dr. Martin Luther King, Jr. captured the heart of this truth best when he observed, "If a man is called to be a street sweeper, he should sweep streets even as Michelangelo painted, or Beethoven composed music, or Shakespeare wrote poetry. He should sweep streets so well that all the hosts of heaven and earth will pause to say, here lived a great street sweeper that did his job well."[42]

God sees all, knows all, and is over all, which means that whether we are doing odd jobs, everyday jobs, or household jobs, no matter the job, the chore, or the task, we should seek to honor God in all our efforts as we do our work willingly, eagerly, gratefully, and wholeheartedly for the glory of God. Turn your work into worship as you do all things willingly as unto the Lord.

He has put eternity in their hearts. (Ecclesiastes 3:11)

From Here to Eternity

JULY
10

YOU AND I were made for eternity. We were created with an instinct of the infinite, a realization of the everlasting, and a predisposition for the perpetual. Created by God and in the image of God, we long to find our everlasting purpose, but we are often blinded by temporal trivialities. Turning to the world around us, we seek to find satisfaction, self-importance, and significance, but as we look to the world, we are left feeling disappointed, insignificant, and wanting more. Power does not placate, sex does not satisfy, and gold does not gratify. We have been created in such a way where only one thing can fill the void in the human heart.

The book of Ecclesiastes, written by King Solomon, chronicles his conclusions about life. In the beginning of Ecclesiastes, Solomon expresses the fact that generation follows generation, the earth turns (see 1:4), the sun rises and sets, the wind blows this way and that (see 1:5–6), the rivers empty into the sea but never fill it (see 1:7), and nothing ultimately satisfies (see 1:8). There is nothing new. No one learns from history, so all are condemned to repeat it (see 1:9–11).

Living in the lap of luxury, Solomon sampled everything that life had to offer. If he were here to give us some advice today, that advice might sound a little like this: "I had everything, I tried everything, I was the richest man alive, and money did not satisfy. I had one thousand women, and sex did not satisfy. As king, I had all the power a man could want, and yet I still longed something more. I had luxury homes, the choicest foods, the finest clothes, and the best of everything. I tried the whole enchilada, and at the end of the rainbow, no container of contentment was to be found, no happiness, and no sense of fulfillment. All of that was a complete waste of time." Solomon's dark and dismal outlook on life stemmed from his realization that life lived apart from God is both superficial and senseless. Solomon realized what so many people fail to recognize, which is that fulfillment can only be found in a right relationship with God. French physicist Blaise Pascal said, "This [emptiness] he [man] tries in vain to fill with everything around him, seeking in things that are not there the help he cannot find . . . , since this infinite abyss can be filled only with an infinite and immutable object, in other words, with God himself."[43]

We have been created *by* God to have a relationship *with* God, and when we substitute any person, purpose, or pursuit in the place of God, we never will be truly satisfied in this life. Our relationship with God has been designed to be an unending and everlasting relationship. Consequently, when we fail to put God in the proper place in our lives today, we will be eternally dissatisfied and distressed because we will be left eternally disconnected from God. The only way you will find fulfillment in this life is by living for God every single day. The reward for a life lived pursuing the things of God will take you from here into eternity, complete and full of joy.

"Let your speech always be with grace, seasoned with salt, that you may know how you ought to answer each one."
(Colossians 4:6)

JULY
11

The Spice of Life

NO ONE LIKES TO EAT BLAND FOOD. A pinch of salt, a dash of pepper, or a smidgen of sugar can make all the difference when preparing food. The foods that are most memorable to the palate are the ones that are full of flavor, robust in richness, and have splashes of sweet and subtle swirls of spice. Think of your favorite food for a minute. Chances are, you are not envisioning boiled chicken or plain rice cakes. I suspect your favorite food is something deliciously sweet or sumptuously savory.

No one really wants to eat bland food, and no one really says, "Hey, I want to be a bland Christian!" (Well, at least I hope no one says that.) So, how can we add a little spice to our lives in Christ?

Paul says that the way to enrich our Christian walk is by seasoning our Christian talk. Our words can be sweet or sour, they can be tasteful or tart, and, according to Paul, our conversations should be lightly salted with grace. Salt is most often used to enhance flavor and to preserve food. In our Christian conversations, grace should be the seasoning that is used to enhance and preserve our walk. If we say we have been converted to Christianity, then our conversations must be a reflection of that conversion also. The grace of God that we have received into our hearts must be reflected in our speech, because out of the heart, the mouth speaks. Therefore, grace in our hearts equals grace on our lips.

When our words are seasoned with grace, they enhance conversations as we speak words that are appropriate, kind, sensitive, purposeful, gentle, truthful, loving, and thoughtful. When our words are seasoned with grace, they enhance conversations as we compliment Christ, as we speak the Scriptures, and as we focus on the issues of faith. When our words are seasoned with grace, they act to preserve conversations and keep them from decaying, always seeking to go higher and holier rather than declining into the displeasing. When our words are seasoned with grace, they demonstrate grace and dispense grace to those who are listening.

Salt has another important aspect: salt intake increases a person's thirst. As Christians, we speak a spiritual language in a physical world, and we must be careful to speak in a manner that glorifies God and causes others to be thirsty for the things of God. When our words are seasoned with grace, we will seek to not only edify believers but also to engage nonbelievers with the gospel. When our words are seasoned with grace, they will exalt, elevate, promote, and praise God in whatever company we find ourselves.

Let us seek to make the most of every opportunity when we speak, aiming to be more than bland, rice-cake Christians. When the character, conduct, and conversation of a Christian is seasoned with grace, the recipe makes for a well-seasoned life that brings enrichment wherever it is sprinkled.

A triple-braided cord is not easily broken.
(Ecclesiastes 4:12 NLT)

JULY

Strengthening Your Marriage

12

WHAT MOVIE TITLE best describes your marriage? *One Flew over the Cuckoo's Nest, Cliffhanger*, or possibly *Misery*? On the other hand, maybe you would choose *Life Is Beautiful, Made for Each Other*, or *Love Story*. Every marriage has ups and downs, demanding difficulties, and beautiful blessings. Miscommunication mishaps may occur, and unexpected moments of unspeakable joy will happen as well. Yet, no matter where you would currently rank yourself on the marriage meter, you always have room for improvement, and for making your marriage more like *It's a Wonderful Life* and less like *The Towering Inferno.*

In Ecclesiastes, Solomon tackled the hard issues of life, work, and marriage. He considered the emptiness of so many things in this life, yet, in a moment of relational reflection, he spoke of the value of close relationships. Using the image of threads in a rope, Solomon spoke of the strength that is found when we knit our lives together with others. And although the cord of three strands can pertain to any relationship, this visual is particularly powerful for marriage. At this point you might be thinking, *Okay. That makes two strands, but who is the third strand in the cord?*

Although Solomon has much to say about the advantages of how two people are better than one, the real strength in a relationship, and especially in a marriage, comes from the third cord, which is God. When we invite God to be more than a spectator in our lives, in our relationships, and specifically, in our marriage, we absolutely add strength to that marriage. But keeping God at the center of a marriage takes energy and effort, so here are a few reminders for keeping your marriage God-centered and God-strong.

Begin with *time with God.* Above all, husbands and wives must make their first priority to personally spend time alone with God, reading the Bible and praying. Spouses need to be mutually encouraging one another and assisting one another in setting aside the daily devotional time that is necessary. This might mean that you take turns watching the kids so the other person can get some alone time with God. Or perhaps you may need to get up a little earlier each morning before the day begins to get busy. This aspect of maintaining and further strengthening your marriage is such a nonnegotiable that if your marriage is weak, the start of the weakness likely can be traced back to deficiencies here.

Continue with *time with God together.* The next big strength-builder for your marriage, after God is the center of your lives individually, is to make sure that He is the center of your lives jointly. Read the Bible together and pray together. For some, this may be an everyday occurrence. Other may choose to do so weekly. No magic number is given. Just make sure that whatever the quantity, the time is quality time as well. Also, go to church together. When possible, serve in ministry together. This does not necessarily mean doing the same thing. Use your spiritual gifts accordingly, but when possible, use them together. For example, say that a husband has the gift of teaching and his wife has the gift of hospitality. Maybe you can bring the two together by hosting a small group gathering in your home.

Marriage is a blessing that began in the Garden of Eden and was established by God. When we work to keep God at the center of our marriages, they will be stronger, and we will be on our way to living happily ever after.

For this is the will of God, your sanctification. (1 Thessalonians 4:3)

JULY

13

Slow Down for Sanctification

WE HAVE ALL ASKED THE QUESTION at one time or another: "How can I know the will of God for my life?" At times in life, the will of God may be hard to determine, seem a bit ambiguous, or in general, may leave you somewhat puzzled. However, times also come when God's will is so simply stated in the Scriptures that we can easily read right over and miss the significance of what God is saying. Sanctification is one such aspect of the will of God that can be easily passed over and left virtually untouched, if we are not careful to slow down and think. Let us make sure we are not guilty of sidestepping the significant role that sanctification plays in knowing God's will for our lives.

Sanctification is simply Christ in you. Sanctification is the process by which we become conformed more and more into the image of Christ. When Christ becomes Lord of our lives, we are rescued and redeemed, but we remain imperfect. As we allow Christ to reign in our lives, changing us from the inside out, chiseling away at our imperfections, we become shaped into a more complete resemblance of Christ. The work of sanctification is not instantaneous; this is a process that lasts a lifetime and often can leave a person thinking, *I am not what I want to be, I desire to be more than I am currently, but thank God, I am not what I used to be!*

Sanctification is mostly an issue of submission. This means allowing the nature of Christ to replace the nature of self, yielding decisions and desires to the dominion of Christ, and exchanging our thoughts for His thoughts. Sanctification is part of God's will for our lives daily, completely, and constantly. By our submission to the Word of God, we participate in the work of sanctification in our lives. As we submit, God sanctifies us. As we surrender, God shapes us. Jesus prayed, "Sanctify them by Your truth. Your Word is truth" (John 17:17).

Sanctification is God's will for our lives. Among the many aspects of God's will for our lives, sanctification is God's greatest desire for us, and therefore, should be our most obvious and outstanding pursuit. Becoming more like Jesus is the peak of perfection and the satisfaction of sanctification. To reflect and radiate Christ is to walk in the will of God and is the fulfillment of Gods' highest appeal for our lives. God is constantly working to conform us, and He is relentlessly reshaping us. Because of this, we should have no confusion, apprehension, or hesitation in our minds. Since God has clearly stated that our sanctification is His will for our lives, then do not rush past, gloss over, minimize, or disregard this significant reality. Instead, slow down for sanctification and allow God to use His Word and His Spirit to make you more like His Son.

Better not to vow than to vow and not pay.
(Ecclesiastes 5:5)

Being a Promise Keeper

JULY
14

WHAT WOULD OTHERS SAY about your word? Are you a person of your word? Is your word "as good as gold?" If you say that you will do something, do you follow through? Do you arrive when you say you will arrive, or pay back what you said you were just borrowing? Do you say what you mean and mean what you say? We all have known a person who is always quick to commit but slow to follow through, one who rarely does what they say they will do, or one who hardly ever delivers when promised. If you have ever dealt with someone like this, then you probably have said, "I would rather they just not say they were going to do something instead of committing to do something and not doing it!" Well, that is exactly how God feels when we make promises to Him and fail to follow through with them.

In the Old Testament, God did not require His people to make vows in order to be accepted by Him. But if a person felt led to express their devotion to God through the making of a vow or promise, the provision was there for them to do so (see Deuteronomy 23:21). Even in the New Testament, we see that the expression of devotion through the making of a vow was acceptable. The apostle Paul did so on at least one occasion (see Acts 18:18). The problems come when we make a promise we have no intention of keeping or when we make a promise but delay in keeping it. Both are an offense to God.

Now you may be thinking that you do not make vows or promises that you do not intend to keep, whether to God or to others. But how many times have you promised God at the beginning of a new year that, *this year* was going to be different? This year you were going to (fill in the blank). Maybe you said that this year, you were going to read your Bible and pray every morning, no matter what. Or perhaps this was the year you were going to make serving in church a priority, or any of the other countless "resolutions" that are promised. Also remember those times when vows may have been made because you or someone you loved was sick, and you prayed that if God would just bring healing that you would (again, fill in the blank). Maybe you said you would give a donation, go to church more, or pray more. The simple truth is that we have all made promises to God, such as, "I will do whatever you want me to do or go wherever you want me to go." Or, "I promise I will never do that again." And, if we were honest with ourselves, we would admit that we have all broken a promise or two with God.

How should we approach making promises to God? A vow or promise is completely voluntary. God is gracious and giving, and we do not need to promise anything to Him in order to get something from Him. Our promises are not bargaining chips used to negotiate with God. So, ponder before you promise, and consider before you commit. With every commitment, make certain to follow through to completion. God hears our promises. And once we have made them, God expects us to honor our word. A promise *made* should be a promise *kept.*

Honor those who are your leaders in the Lord's work.
They work hard among you and give you spiritual
guidance. Show them great respect and wholehearted love
because of their work.
(1 Thessalonians 5:12-13 NLT)

JULY
15

R-E-S-P-E-C-T

MANY PASTORS ARE overworked, underappreciated, and often misunderstood. Living in a fishbowl, pastors are coping with criticism, battling burnout, and dealing with disappointment. A pastor provides spiritual guidance, confidential counseling, and hospital visitations. A pastor performs weddings and funerals, spends hours praying and studying the Scriptures, and is expected to lead the church, manage the staff, care for the congregation, preach with passion, and live an exemplary life. A pastor's life is dedicated to serving others, and how you treat the pastor and leaders of your church can go a long way in making their work a delight or drudgery.

God has ordained leadership in the church, and although we are all equal in the body of Christ, and no one person should be exalted above measure, God has called some men to lead the church. With this responsibility comes a certain amount of respect and honor that is due the position. Pastors and elders look after the spiritual welfare of their congregations and therefore deserve our submission and admiration.

Placing the right men in leadership in the early church was essential for ensuring stability, protecting from heresy, defending against the abuse of power, and promoting proper spiritual growth and care. With all the responsibilities pastors face in leading, directing, and caring for the congregation today, the congregation also has a responsibility toward their pastors and leaders, which can be summed up in one word: R-E-S-P-E-C-T.

Respecting your pastors and church leaders begins with obedience (see Hebrews 13:17). When believers do not obey the commands in the Bible or submit to the God-given leadership of the church, they can make life in the local church challenging and counterproductive. God's leaders are led by God's Spirit, and they call God's people to obey God's Word. As such, the response of the people should be one of obedience. Now, no leader is always right, but despite man's limitations, God's appointed leaders should be obeyed, unless they are clearly operating outside of the boundaries of God's will and Word.

Respecting your pastor and church leaders also means accepting them for who they are, appreciating them while giving God the ultimate glory for who they are and what they do, and allowing love to define your relationship. Love is the great Christian catchall because by love, we give grace, practice patience, show sacrifice, manifest mercy, and obey overseers. Other ways to express your respect are praying regularly for your pastors, sharing when you have been impacted by their service, being careful not to criticize, and by rolling up your sleeves and volunteering. Oh, and every now and then, a simple thank you is always appreciated!

Do not take your spiritual leaders for granted. Giving them a good dose of godly respect can go a long way in conveying your gratitude for all they do in their spiritual service for you and unto God.

Remember now your Creator in the days of your youth.
(Ecclesiastes 12:1)

JULY
16

Before It's Too Late

NO DOUBT ABOUT IT: time flies! Well, that is unless you are waiting for water to boil or paint to dry. Those always seem to take forever. Nevertheless, as time goes by, we are often left remarking, "it seems like just yesterday that . . ." or "Where did the time go?" However, when you are young, you feel as though you have all the time in the world, and the temptation is to approach life with a why-do-today-what-I-can-put-off-until-tomorrow attitude. But the one decision where procrastination has eternal consequences, and therefore the one thing we should not put off until tomorrow, is choosing to follow God.

In the final chapter of Ecclesiastes, Solomon is reflecting on his life and has a word of advice for the next generation. Solomon, being the wisest king who ever lived, realized that everything in this life was pointless. He had everything a person could want, and had tried everything this world had to offer. His advice to the next generation was to forget everything else and follow God. Every day that passes brings you one day closer to the end of your life. You have no time to waste in choosing to live for God. Every day that goes by without making a decision to follow God makes a decision to follow God that much harder to make tomorrow.

Do not make excuses like, "My family will not understand" or "My friends will just make fun of me" or "Following God will be easier when I am older." The fact is, making a decision to follow God will never be easier to make than it is today. Sure, peer pressure is always there, and yes, people who try to influence the way you live your life will always be around. But you cannot please all the people all the time. So, why not stop trying to please other people and live to please God?

Making a decision to follow God now not only ensures your eternal destiny in heaven, but also gives your life a present peace, a genuine joy, and a purpose to fulfill. Making a decision to follow God today does not mean that life will be free from future heartache and pain, but does mean that God will use every heartache and painful experience for a good purpose in your life (see Romans 8:28).

If you are putting off your decision to follow God until later, what are you waiting for? Why risk your eternity future, even for a single second? If you have accepted Jesus but have not been putting God first, then do not waste any more time living for yourself. Start today by being honest with God, ask Him to forgive you, ask for the strength you need to make the necessary changes, and then start living for God today. Do not let another minute go by without living for God.

Life is fragile, and time is short. Do not delay your decision to follow God. Do not put off until tomorrow what you can decide today. Trust in Jesus Christ as your Lord and Savior today, take the time to learn what following God means, and begin to make the most of the time that God gives you, before it is too late to decide.

Rejoice always. (1 Thessalonians 5:16)
Mission Impossible?

JULY
17

WE MUST BEGIN AND END this discussion by understanding that *God does not ask us to do anything in the Bible that He will not enable us to accomplish in life.* This is important to start out with because when reading a phrase like *rejoice always,* our first reaction might be to think, *That is impossible! I know I can rejoice sometimes, but I don't think I can rejoice all the time!* But the truth is, as God helps us, what could be seen as an impossible command can become a permanent part of our personality, expressed in and through our lives all day, every day, regardless of our circumstances. Does this sound too good to be true? It is not. Rejoicing is always possible.

The apostle Paul was well-acquainted with hardships, difficult situations, sorrows, and pain. Yet, his ability to rejoice always was never diminished. Paul's emphasis on rejoicing does not mean that Christians are never sad, that we are to trivialize tragedy, or that we should dismiss difficulty. Paul was not promoting the power of positive thinking, nor was he supplying us with a powerless proverb or an appealing adage. What he was doing was giving us the command to live a life that is not defined by our circumstances, a life that responds rightly to our circumstances by rising above them.

At the heart of this command is the word *rejoice,* which simply means to be filled with joy or to reflect joy. Happiness and joy are vastly different. Where happiness depends on circumstances, joy is immune to circumstance. Anyone can experience happiness; but only the person who has a right relationship with God can experience joy. Joy is produced as a person grows in the knowledge and understanding of God and experiences the presence of God personally. Therefore, rejoicing or being joyful is when a Christian reflects the presence of God in his or her life. Rejoicing means responding rightly to all of life's circumstances, whether in crisis or in peace, whether in poverty or in prosperity, responding with a joy that comes from knowing, trusting, and loving God.

Still wondering how to do that, especially during those times when, put plainly, life stinks? Rejoicing, or reflecting the positive presence of God in your life, is usually easier when things are going your way. But, to be joyful when nothing seems to be going your way and life is hard takes perseverance and discipline. Rejoicing always means making the choice to see that God is bigger than all my problems. Rejoicing means holding on to the promises of God. Finally, rejoicing means focusing on who God is, on what God has done, and on what God has yet to do in the world and in your life.

Our circumstances do not define us; we are defined by our position in Christ. Our position is that we have been delivered from death and given eternal life. We are saved and are going to heaven, no matter what happens to us today. Our position means that we have nothing and no one to fear because we belong to God, and He is greater than any problem found here on earth. We are called not to rejoice more, but to rejoice always.

So remember, rejoicing always is possible because *God does not ask us to do anything in the Bible that He will not enable us to accomplish in life.*

"For your love is better than wine." (Song of Solomon 1:2)

Keeping the Love Alive

JULY 18

NO EASY WAY to say this exists: loving another person is hard work. Love involves blood, sweat, and tears, and often means choosing to love even the feelings of love ebb and flow. Sometimes the passion blazes like a flame burning bright, and other times the passion fizzles the fire like a wet blanket. Most married couples remember the giddy, dizzy days of the honeymoon phase of their marriage, when everything was cute, every day involved cuddling, their stomachs were virtual butterfly pavilions, life was fresh, and the relationship was exhilarating. But that period eventually gives way to a deeper, developmental phase. This does not mean that the flame has to fade.

The Song of Solomon takes us back to the ideal of love as God intended, celebrating the romantic love of Solomon and his bride, identified as the Shulamite. As one commentator wrote, "The poem is candid about physical love, singular in regard to commitment and devotion, exalted in its regard for the integrity of both persons, and beautiful in its expression of the care and gentleness shown by both members of the union."[44] This wonderful poem depicts the pure and powerful affection this married couple has for each other while also describing simple expressions of affection that can help every married couple keep the love alive.

While every marriage relationship is different, some similarities can be found regarding cultivating love and affection. Words of affirmation help to cultivate affection. Solomon is not bashful in complementing the beauty of his bride (see 1:8), and men and women both enjoy hearing the occasional flattering compliment on their appearance. Sometimes the subtle and sublime "You look beautiful" will suffice, and other times the comparative compliment is more far more fitting (see 1:9-10). A comment concerning the sparkle in the eye (see 1:15), or the sweetness of a delicate perfume (see 1:12), or the beautiful sheen of her hair (see 4:1) can go a long way toward fanning the flame of love. And you must not overlook the power of simplicity found in repeatedly proclaiming, "I love you" to your spouse.

Along with words of affirmation go acts of affection. Saying "I love you" must be backed up with actions demonstrating your feelings. The place to start is with time together (see 1:4; 2:4). No relationship can stay healthy or burn bright if time is not set aside for each other. Whether this is as simple as date nights or something that takes more purposed planning, spending time together is necessary. Also, do not underestimate the potency of a tender kiss (see 1:2), as a kiss can communicate in the simplest of ways the words "I love you." Finally, a little PDA (public display of affection) can be an acceptable expression of love, whether holding hands, a kiss on the cheek, or a hug (see 2:4). No need to go overboard and become a spectacle like the average teenagers "in love," but a few modest expressions can be heartwarming and endearing.

Maybe a spark is truly what ignites a relationship, but a fan keeps the flame burning bright. So, fan the flame of love and affection in your marriage, and keep the love alive.

Do not quench the Spirit. (1 Thessalonians 5:19)
Life in the Spirit

JULY
19

HAVE YOU EVER SENSED the Holy Spirit leading you to do something? How did you respond? Were you quick to do something? Maybe you were slow to obey. Or, perhaps you even went so far as to ignore the Spirit's prompting altogether. What you do on those occasions when the Holy Spirit of God is tapping you on the shoulder, or maybe even shouting in your ear, will determine whether you are decreasing the Holy Spirit's work in your life or whether you are increasing what the Spirit desires to accomplish in and through your life.

When a person becomes a Christian by believing in and committing his or her life to the lordship of Jesus Christ, God gives that new Christian a gift: the Holy Spirit. This gift is deposited into Christians, sealing them as children of God (see Ephesians 4:30), securing their place in heaven (see 1 Peter 1:4), and sanctifying them for the work God that wants to do in and through their lives (see 1 Corinthians 6:11; 2 Timothy 2:21). But all Christians have a choice: either listen and obey the leading of God's Spirit that now resides within them or choose to ignore and disobey the Spirit, thereby quenching or reducing the Spirit's influence in their lives.

God's Holy Spirit is called the Helper (see John 16:7), and that is because God has given us His Spirit to help us live a God-centered and God-honoring life. The Spirit leads us toward those things that are of God, that honor God, that glorify God, that are true to the nature and character of God, and that help produce those characteristics or the fruit of the Spirit (see Galatians 5:22) in a believer's life. The Spirit teaches us and reminds us of the Word of God so that we can put into practice the truth of God (see 1 Corinthians 2). The Spirit also leads us away from those things that dishonor God, that are contrary to His nature and character, and that will lead to sinful actions.

The Spirit of God wants to work in and through the people of God, to help them reflect the character of God, so that we can accomplish the purposes of God. As John Stott has said, today "there is no need for us to wait, as the one hundred and twenty had to wait [in Acts 1] for the Spirit to come. For the Holy Spirit did come on the day of Pentecost, and has never left his church. Our responsibility is to humble ourselves before his sovereign authority, to determine not to quench him, but to allow him his freedom."[45] Then we will be living unquenched lives, personally and practically, and we will be attending unquenched churches where God is heard, worshiped, and obeyed.

So, the next time the Spirit reminds you of what you have learned (see John 14:26), convicts you of sin (see John 16:8–13), guides you into all truth (John 16:13), leads you in His will for your life (Romans 8:14), or speaks to you (Acts 13:2), be quick to listen and do as you are told by the Spirit. To respond any other way is to diminish His power and work in your life.

Promise me, . . . not to awaken love until the time is right.
(Song of Solomon 2:7 NLT)

JULY
20

The Sex Talk

LET'S TALK ABOUT SEX. I know what some may be thinking: *We can't talk about sex. That's, well, that's taboo for Christians to talk about. It's indecent and improper!* If that describes you, then you might be surprised to know that the Bible actually has much to say about sex, and even considers sex good. After all, God created sex (see Genesis 1:27–28). Sex in the Scriptures is not meant to be shocking, but is instead designed to communicate God's attitude and advice concerning the subject. God created sex not only for procreation, but also as a beautiful expression of intimacy, an expression to be enjoyed within the boundaries of a committed marriage, but not before marriage. Simply put, *love waits*! Unfortunately, few people are hearing that message today and even fewer are practicing it.

Many think that God's commands about sex are just a bunch of rules that take all the fun out of life. They mistakenly believe that having sex before marriage is all part of some relationship compatibility test, subscribing to the idea that that you do not buy a car without taking a test drive, and you do not get married to someone until you know whether you are sexually compatible. But the truth is that God has given us commands about sex not to be a cosmic killjoy, but to preserve pleasure, ensure genuine intimacy, and take away the pain that can come through disobedience. God's command to wait until marriage to have sex is a gracious one, not a heartless one. God wants to protect us from the emotional and physical devastation that inevitably follows sexual disobedience.

Waiting is not only important because God commands us to wait for our benefit, but waiting is also important because marriages cannot survive on sex alone. A healthy marriage will include a healthy sex life, but marriage is so much more than that. Healthy marriages must be built on Christ, not sex. Healthy marriages must practice open and honest communication, must demonstrate mutual respect and trust, and include a mutual love for one another. When these elements are in place before marriage, sex will enhance intimacy. But sex that is practiced before marriage will erode intimacy.

In the Song of Solomon, we see the appeal of the Shulamite woman to refrain from awakening love, to wait until marriage before having sex. And she mentions a key to succeeding is abstaining. Until the wedding in chapter 3, the two people in this poem discuss their attraction for one another in honest but guarded ways. They display restraint and warn of the power and intensity of love. Restraint is essential, and restraint is a discipline that begins by avoiding steamy situations as well as situations that give others the appearance that you might be having sex. The key to restraint in a relationship is not by seeing how far you can go without actually having sex; restraint is seeing how far away from the line you can actually stay.

Do not pressure or be pressured into having sex before marriage. True love will wait. Parents, do not be afraid to have "the sex talk" with your children so they understand God's plan and purpose for sex, and the importance of waiting. Dating couples, you also should have a talk about sex to make sure both people are committed to honoring and adhering to God's commands about waiting for sex before your relationship goes any further. God will bless a love that waits.

That the name of our Lord Jesus Christ may be glorified in you. (2 Thessalonians 1:12)

JULY
21

Glory to God

YOU AND I EXIST to bring glory to God. The question is, how do we do that in the daily routine of life? How do I glorify God at home, when the kids are screaming, the dog is barking, the phone is ringing, and I am running on four hours of sleep? How do I glorify God when I am at work, sitting in front of a computer most of the day? How do I glorify God when the workday is done, and time has come to unwind? How do I glorify God when I finally get to take that long overdue vacation and enjoy some rest and relaxation? How do I glorify God when I get a raise, buy a new car, or make a down payment on a home? What about in more challenging circumstances? How do I glorify God when I am being mocked for what I believe or when I am being persecuted for my faith? Since we exist to glorify God all day, every day (see 1 Corinthians 10:31), for as long as we live and into eternity, in good times and in bad times (see 1 Peter 4:16), being actively committed to glorifying God in the daily routines of life is important.

Glorifying God begins by understanding exactly what bringing glory really means. We glorify God when we seek to make much of God by praising Him and honoring Him through daily obedience to His Word. We glorify God by pointing people to Jesus Christ through our actions and attitudes. This is exactly what the Thessalonians were doing in the midst of some very difficult times. Paul acknowledged that this church was faithful to glorify God even while enduring harsh persecution for their faith. They patiently endured hardship while growing and maturing in their faith and still exhibiting an abundant and steadfast love for others (2 Thessalonians 1:3–4). Now, that is glorifying to God. This church was still growing in God and showing the love of God despite their circumstances! What about us? How can we practically glorify God, no matter our circumstances?

We can practically glorify God in three areas of our everyday lives: *thoughts*, *words*, and *actions*.

First, right thoughts lead to right actions. Godly thoughts will lead to godly actions. If we want to glorify God in the daily routines of our lives, then we must begin by taking control of our thoughts (see 2 Corinthians 10:5), not being held hostage by them. We must resist the worldly way of thinking and approach life and decisions from a biblical worldview (see Romans 12:2). We must learn to say no to our own selfish thoughts and say yes to Christ-honoring thoughts (see Luke 9:23).

Next, the words that come out of our mouths must be seen as a reflection of God in us. Therefore, we must be committed to speaking words that bless others and do not bring harm to others. We must choose words of truth and not deceit, words that encourage faith and not diminish faith. Words are powerful, and we must learn to watch what we say or risk making our faith empty and useless (see James 1:26).

Finally, our actions: simply applying the love standard (see 1 Corinthians 13) to what we are doing or not doing, will go a long way in determining whether our actions are glorifying God or not.

Filter your *thoughts*, *words*, and *actions* through the Bible, and you will find that you are glorifying God in and through the daily routines of your life.

"Behold, the virgin shall conceive and bear a Son, and shall call His name Immanuel." (Isaiah 7:14)

JULY
22

The Immanuel Prophecy

YOU CANNOT SAY you believe in the Bible if you do not believe in the Virgin Birth. Without the Virgin Birth, Christianity cannot exist because no divine birth has occurred. There is no picking and choosing from the Bible; you cannot decide to accept certain portions and throw away others. The Bible is all or nothing. In-between belief or halfway faith to the absolute authority and total trustworthiness of the Bible are not possible. The Bible is entirely accurate, completely reliable, and stake-your-life-on-it factual, and this includes the Virgin Birth. But why a Virgin Birth?

For one, our salvation depends on this event. The Virgin Birth was needed because humankind could not fix the problem of sin. Every person born into this world has a sinful nature, inherited from Adam because he crossed the sin boundary by disobeying God. Now, sin has been passed down to all humankind through the spiritual gene pool (see Romans 5:12). God, in His grace, offers to provide forgiveness of sins and bring healing to the broken relationship between man and God, but that forgiveness and restoration can only come through a perfectly sinless sacrifice. Now, where do we go to get one of those? Nowhere, because none has been available since sin has entered the human race. So, God had to work outside the realm of the natural to produce the perfectly sinless sacrifice He needed. Enter the Virgin Birth.

Through the Virgin Birth, God was able to accomplish that which is obviously supernatural and deliberately divine, that which defies explanation and cannot be explained away. God created the perfect sacrifice in the person of Jesus Christ. Through the Virgin Birth, God was able to preserve the deity of Jesus and His humanity. Through this miraculous birth designed by God, His eternal Son could take on flesh without inheriting the tainted human nature, without receiving that inward inclination to sin that the rest of us were born with. Oswald Chambers wrote,

> Jesus Christ was born into this world; not from it. He did not emerge out of history; He came into history from the outside. Jesus Christ is not the best human being the human race can boast of; He is a Being for whom the human race can take no credit at all. He is not man becoming God, but God Incarnate God coming into human flesh from outside it. His life is the highest and the holiest entering through the most humble of doors.[46]

If not for the Virgin Birth, this miraculous combination of humanity and divinity never would have materialized, and no sacrifice would meet with God's holy standard. The only way God could meet His standard was by giving Himself—Immanuel, God with us—so that God could die for us, so that God could now dwell in us. The Bible is entirely accurate, completely reliable, and stake-your-life-on-it factual. And this Immanuel prophecy is one proof of this.

Let no one deceive you by any means; for that Day will not come unless the falling away comes first, and the man of sin is revealed. (2 Thessalonians 2:3)

JULY
23

The End is Near!

AS BAD AS THE WORLD MAY SEEM TODAY, with many nations experiencing economic collapse, heinous acts of terrorism, the threat of nuclear and chemical warfare, the political hornets' nest in the Middle East, and the escalation of natural disasters, the fact that people are wondering if the end of the world is approaching comes as no surprise.

Many have tried to predict when the end of the world would occur, and some have even claimed to know when Jesus is going to return again to this earth and establish His kingdom. But the Bible is clear that no man knows the day or the hour of these events. Not even the angels in heaven are in the know concerning this information (see Matthew 24:36). And although we do not know exact dates concerning these events, we are encouraged to know some important facts surrounding what is leading up to the end of the world as we know it.

The church in Thessalonica wrestled with the sequence of events related to the end times, and even though Paul covered these issues in 1 Thessalonians, they were still confused. They thought that because they were experiencing life-threatening persecution and perilous trials, they somehow had missed the rapture of the church (see 1 Thessalonians 4:13–18) and were now in the period known as the Day of the Lord. The Day of the Lord, which is covered in the first half of 1 Thessalonians 5, includes events leading up to the return of the Lord Jesus and the establishment of His glorious kingdom. In this period, the catastrophic judgment of God is poured out upon the wicked who inhabit the earth (see Revelation 6:17). In Thessalonica, false teachers were running around and declaring in Chicken Little fashion that the sky had fallen, the sky had fallen, and the end of the world had arrived!

Paul set out to restore hope and eliminate the misconceptions surrounding the Day of the Lord. He reassured the church they were not living in the Day of the Lord because that day could not come until other major events had taken place.

What are those events? First, the rapture of the church must take place, the event where Christ returns (not physically to the earth, which is His second coming). The Rapture is when Christ comes to remove those who are alive on the earth and believe in Him, at which time He will take them up to heaven to spare them the wrath to come. Next, a falling away, or apostasy must occur (2 Thessalonians 2:3), which is the great rebellion and turning away from God that leads to the establishment of a worldwide false religion. Also, the Day of the Lord cannot come until the Man of Sin (verse 3), or the Antichrist, is revealed. The Antichrist will declare himself to be God (verse 4), display false signs (verse 9), and demand to be worshiped by everyone.

As believers, we should be comforted by the reality that God will take His people out of this world before the Day of the Lord and before all the devastation begins. Additionally, we should also be motivated to reach out to the lost and share the hope and salvation found in Christ, so that as many as possible would be saved from hell and from that period of hell on earth. We must avoid far-fetched guesswork about events related to the Lord's return and instead be busy about our present responsibilities to be worshipers of God, waiting patiently for His return, working on what He has called us to do, and witnessing to the world we live in.

And His name will be called Wonderful. (Isaiah 9:6)

Some Kind of Wonderful

JULY 24

IF ANYONE OR ANYTHING has ever deserved to be called *wonderful,* Jesus Christ certainly has. Of the roughly 250 names given to Jesus, wonderful is absolutely appropriate and totally tailor-made for the One whose birth was foretold by the prophet Isaiah nearly 750 years before His birth. Using *wonderful* to describe Jesus automatically raises the splendor of this word above the average, and catapults Him into the realm of the extraordinary because Jesus is anything but ordinary and far from average. Why should Jesus be called wonderful?

His name is called wonderful because His *birth* was wonderful. His birth was predicted in advance and predetermined before time began. His was a birth designed to fulfill the purposes and the promises of God. The birth was unlike any other because in Jesus, the divinity of God joined with the humanity of man in purity and perfection. His was a birth where the stars in the sky were divinely arranged to light the way for wise men to find the newborn King and where the angels were employed to announce the arrival of God's Son.

His name is called wonderful because His *life* was wonderful. His was a life completely sinless and totally selfless, marked by miraculous power and controlled by astounding humility. His life was committed to speaking the word of God and calling people to believe in God. His was a life full of light and devoid of darkness, and he chose to forgive people of evil but refused to rejoice in evil. His life was one that chose to die so that others might live.

His name is called wonderful because His *resurrection* was wonderful. His resurrection continues to bring hope and help. His resurrection promises an eternal inheritance and saving deliverance from eternal punishment. His resurrection dispels doubt and welcomes trust. His resurrection defeats evil, breaks the power of sin and death, and gives life. His resurrection exchanges bondage for freedom and love for hate.

His name is called wonderful because He is unparalleled and unprecedented, preeminent and preexistent. He is supreme and sovereign, all-powerful and all-knowing. His name is called wonderful because He is from everlasting to everlasting, and He is the great emancipator of mankind. His name is called wonderful because He is benevolent and boundless, merciful and mighty, immutable and impartial. He is self-sufficient and self-existent, He is provider and protector, and He is faithful and full of grace. His name is wonderful because He is great and the great I AM.

Someone once said that "in Christ we have a love that can never be fathomed, a life that can never die, a peace that can never be understood, a rest that can never be disturbed, a joy that can never be diminished, a hope that can never be disappointed, a glory that can never be clouded, a light that can never be darkened, and a spiritual resource that can never be exhausted."

Now, that is some kind of wonderful!

Do not grow weary in doing good. (2 Thessalonians 3:13)

Keep up the good work

**JULY
25**

HAVE YOU EVER WANTED to throw in the towel, call it quits, and just move on to something else? Starting something with enthusiasm is easy, but seeing things through until the end is not always easy. For example, how many musical instruments are gathering dust from frustrated musicians? Or how many people have tried to become fluent in a foreign language, only to stop, left with complete discouragement and the limited ability to say, "Good morning," "Good evening," and "Where is the bathroom?" When enthusiasm meets the reality of hard work, weariness can set in, and the temptation to quit is usually not far behind.

This can also happen to us spiritually. After we begin following and serving God, our enthusiasm can be challenged when we are met with the harsh reality that living the life that God has called us to live is hard work. The result is that weariness in doing good can set in.

If Paul warns that we should not become weary in doing good, the implication is clear: becoming weary in our efforts to do good is a real possibility. Why? What would cause us to become weary? Weariness in doing good often comes about when we fail to see the positive results of our labor, and therefore, we can be left wondering, *What difference does any of this make?* Also, if our work goes unnoticed, we can be left feeling unappreciated and that the job is unnecessary. And, of course, we all experience those times when everything becomes a battle, and we are constantly met with opposition. This is a breeding ground for weariness.

Practically speaking, perhaps our weariness is the result of prayers that have not been answered. Or possibly, someone is taking advantage of our generosity. Maybe we are showing love to someone but that love is left unreturned. Sometimes, we may be repeatedly showing forgiveness to someone who only manipulates that forgiveness. Or maybe we are serving faithfully in a ministry that God has called us to, but we are not seeing any fruit and have not received any support from others. Whatever the specific *good* you are doing, whether a work of ministry or a work of obedience to the Word of God, we must not give up or give in to the pressure to quit or stop doing what is right.

How can we keep weariness away? Remember God. First of all, God sees our work, our faithfulness to serve, and our willingness to obey. Even the good works that no one else sees, God sees and God cares. Not only does God see our work, but God will one day reward openly all that was done for Him, even those unnoticed works (see Matthew 6:4). Lastly, God is glorified by our good works (see Matthew 5:16), and bringing glory to God is to be one of the most important things we are to do while here on earth.

Growing weary *in* the work of the Lord is one thing, but to grow weary *of* the work of the Lord is quite another. Never grow tired of giving to God, trusting God, praying to God, obeying God, and sharing God with others. God sees our good, God will reward our good, God is glorified by our good, and God calls us to remain faithful in doing good. So, keep up the good work!

"For you have said in your heart: . . . 'I will be like the Most High.'" (Isaiah 14:13–14)

Me, Myself, and I

JULY
26

IT'S ALL ABOUT ME! That is apparently what Satan thought, and that belief cost him everything. And I do mean *everything*. For humanity, the idea that you could be surrounded by the radiant glory of God, possess immeasurable beauty and power, hold the highest angelic ranking in the universe, enjoy the prized position of leading the heavenly hosts in the praise and worship of Almighty God forever and ever, only to throw it all away because you thought, *It's all about me!* seems unimaginable. Satan gave up heaven and all the blessings of being in the presence of God in exchange for eternal torment because he wanted things his way and not God's way. What a warning this should be for us! If such a favored angel can believe *It's all about me!* then we can, too.

Sin began with Satan, but unfortunately, did not end with Satan. Satan was the first created being to rebel against God because he wanted God's position, God's power, God's preeminence, and God's privileges all for himself. Satan wanted *his* will to be done and not *God's* will. The desire of his heart was "*I will* ascend," "*I will* exalt," "*I will* sit," and "*I will* be" (Isaiah 14:13–14, emphasis added). In other words, Satan made the mistake of believing that what *he* wanted was more important than what *God* wanted.

Satan's mistake also became mankind's mistake when, in the Garden of Eden, Satan convinced Eve that what she wanted was more important than what God wanted, and *her* will came before God's will. Eve believed the lie and ate the fruit, and in that moment, she became the apple of her own eye as she allowed herself to become the focus instead of God.

Satan's problem was that his every want and desire began with *I*, a simple and subtle trap that can catch all of us if we are not careful. Most of us suffer from some degree of spiritual shortsightedness, whereby we allow ourselves to spend too much time focusing and pursuing what we want and do not spend enough time focusing on what God wants. Contrary to what the popular culture says, we are not the center of the universe; God is. Therefore, our every desire should be to fulfill God's desires for our lives. The problem is that just as Satan *said in his heart,* we can be tempted to say in our hearts that everything is about what *I will.* Sin, in the simplest form, is an expression of *it's all about me* instead of *it's all about God.* Sin is what *we* want and not what *God* wants for us, and all about *our* will and not *His* will. We must follow the example of Jesus Christ, who said to God the Father, "Not My will, but Yours, be done" (Luke 22:42).

The once-beautiful angel who wanted to exalt himself above God will be forever separated from the presence of God because he thought, *It's all about me!* Until we truly get to the place in our own hearts where we can say, "It's all about God!" and not "It's all about me!" some degree of separation in our relationship with God is inevitable, because sin separates, but surrendering brings closeness.

Life is not about me, myself, and I; Life is about the Father, Son, and Holy Spirit.

I urge you, first of all, to pray for all people. Ask God to help them; intercede on their behalf, and give thanks for them. (1 Timothy 2:1 NLT)

Conversations with God

MARTYN LLOYD-JONES said, "our ultimate position as Christians is tested by the character of our prayer life."[47] And the famed evangelist D. L Moody, when he was asked at the end of his life if there was anything he would have done differently, responded, "I would have prayed more!"

Have you ever said to yourself, "I wish I had a better prayer life," "I don't pray often enough," "I don't pray long enough," or "I can't seem to keep my mind focused when I pray"? Oswald Chambers said, "The battle of prayer is against two things: . . . wandering thoughts and lack of intimacy with God's character as revealed in His word. Neither can be cured at once, but they can be cured by discipline."[48]

Prayer is a discipline that must be practiced in order to grow deeper in our relationship with God. While prayer is simply having a conversation with God, one thing is certain: everyone can pray more, pray more specifically, and pray more for others.

One very effective way to become more consistent, disciplined, purposed, and precise when you pray is to use the acronym, ACTS, which can help give specificity to your prayers. Simply start your prayer time with the letter *a*, which stands for *adoration*. Adoration is where you express your praise, exaltation, and worship of God. Adoration is expressing your affection for who God is and what He does, and is often made easier by focusing on the attributes of God. Adoration is not the time to start asking God for stuff. Just allow yourself time to express your love and respect toward God.

Next comes the letter *c* for *confession*. Confession is asking God for forgiveness of sins that you have committed and seeking the strength to turn from and resist those sins in the future. Sin hinders our relationship with God, and confession helps bring healing and restoration.

Next, there is *t* for *thanksgiving*. Express gratitude for the many blessings God has given.

Finally, the letter *s* stands for *supplication*. This is where you ask God to supply your needs and the needs of others.

ACTS is not the only way to bring focus and purpose to your prayers, but may help.

One thing that we must guard against is spending the majority of our time always praying for our needs while neglecting the needs of others. How many times have you said to someone, "I will pray for you," only to forget? We must be disciplined to pray for others, because one of the greatest things we can do for another person is to pray for them.

Paul knew the power of prayer and knew that prayer really had an impact and could change lives, so he purposed to pray for others. This is why Paul reminds us in today's verse that a healthy prayer life must include praying for others. Since we are called to "love [our] neighbor as [ourselves]" (Mark 12:31), then we should at least pray for others as much as we pray for ourselves. Just imagine what we might see in the world today if we spent as much time praying for the needs of others as we did praying for our own needs.

Remember, prayer is an act of communing with God. It is about communication, and developing intimacy with God by engaging in conversations with God. Be specific. Be consistent. Be committed. Be purposeful. Be blessed. And be a blessing to others with your prayer life.

> *But those who wait on the Lord shall renew their strength.*
> (Isaiah 40:31)

Hurry Up and Wait

GOOD THINGS COME to those who wait, right? But who really likes waiting? First, the toe tapping begins, then comes the eye rolling, followed by the audible sighing. These are telltale signs that someone is growing impatient. We have all been there, whether because we were standing in line at the DMV, holding number ninety-nine while they were calling for number four, or whether we were sitting in a traffic jam and were already late. Odds are, we have all grown impatient while waiting.

What about with God? Have you ever grown impatient waiting on Him? One reason that waiting is so hard for most of us is because we equate waiting with inactivity. But biblical waiting is not twiddling your thumbs, and definitely not wasting time. In fact, quite the opposite is true. God uses waiting to accomplish some significant work in our lives.

Isaiah was writing to a future generation of Jews who would be taken captive to Babylon, Jews who would have doubts about whether God ever would get them out of this time of captivity. Seventy years is a long time to wait, so Isaiah had to remind the captives that God still cared for them and was still in control, despite the fact they would have to wait for their situation to change.

Waiting is not easy, especially when we are eager for something to happen and expectant for our situation to change. Even the most spiritual person can lose heart, even the strongest believer can become despondent, and even a faithful follower can falter during extended times of waiting. That is, unless we remember that God is still in control and working while we are waiting. The work that God often seeks to accomplish in our lives during times of waiting is the renewing of our strength and the refining of our character.

The renewing of our strength comes as we daily wait upon God and seek His presence. Every believer should stop and make time to be in the presence of God, sitting quietly and listening to God through His Word and by His Spirit, allowing Him to speak to us words of encouragement and even words of correction. By waiting on God daily, our spiritual strength is renewed day to day.

One way God refines our character is by allowing us to go through a season of waiting. A season of waiting often means that God changes or stops some or all of our normal activities so that a more profound work of refining our character can be accomplished. We are a work in progress and in constant need of God's purifying work. Refining is never a comfortable process, but we must wait patiently on God as He works to make us more like Christ.

Biblically, waiting on God is never passive, but is always a process. God may make us wait before we step out in ministry so that He can better prepare us for the future. God may make us wait before moving us on to something else in life so that He can use certain people or circumstances to shape our character.

The next time God has you waiting on Him, don't roll your eyes, don't let out a loud sigh, and don't grow impatient. Instead, keep trusting in God, expecting Him to work, and continue pursuing the presence of God daily while you allow God to renew your strength, refine your character, and prepare you for what He has next.

And I do not permit a woman to teach or to have authority over a man. (1 Timothy 2:12)

JULY

29

Gender Wars

THE DISPUTE concerning the role of women in ministry is not an issue of gender, but an issue of authority. If we are willing to compromise the truth of God at any particular point and for any particular reason, then what we are doing is changing the authority of God's Word to fit our own personal preferences and predispositions, making ourselves the authority and not God. By choosing what we will accept from the Bible and what we will throw away, we have said to ourselves that we know better than God does and refuse to do what God tells us to do. This signals the beginning of spiritual erosion for any individual, church, or organization, and that erosion will continue as long as God's truth is compromised or rejected.

The role of women in ministry has never been free from controversy and likely never will be. But our responsibility as Christians is not to put an end to the gender war controversy concerning the role of women in ministry. Rather, we strive to make sure that we are clear on exactly what God has said concerning the role of women in the church and to make sure that we submit to His authority.

What does God say concerning the role of women in the church? "I do not permit a woman to teach or to have authority over a man" (1 Timothy 2:12). In other words, women are not allowed to be teachers, pastors, or elders in the church. First, Paul's instructions have nothing to do with the equality of men and women in Jesus Christ. Galatians 3:28 makes clear that we are all equal in Christ, end of discussion. But this instruction in 1 Timothy 2 does have everything to do with the way men and women exercise authority in Christ's church.

What the Bible is saying is that women are not to be responsible for the primary equipping of the church through teaching, and they are not called to be leading the church as pastors or elders. What the Bible is not saying is that women never can teach anywhere or in any situation within the church. God has given some women gifts in teaching and leadership, and they should use them to teach and lead or disciple other women (see Titus 2:3–4) or to give spiritual instruction in private as Pricilla did for Apollos (see Acts 18:26).

The New Testament abounds with examples of godly women who, consistent with their assigned roles, served with dignity and led with honor, women whose names will be forever mentioned and remembered with admiration. Most of us have been blessed by the influence of godly women in our lives, and that should cause us to be thankful to God for the many wonderful things women do in ministering in the body of Christ. We must never underestimate the important role that godly women play in the ministry of the church, and churches will have their greatest impact on the world as men and women operate within their God-given gifts, roles, and responsibilities.

"Fear not, for I am with you." (Isaiah 41:10)

Fear Not

*F*EAR NOT! Really, God? That is easy for *You*, to say. After all, You are God! But,for the rest of us here on Planet Earth, this seems a little unrealistic. Quite a few things seem natural to be afraid of, like failure, pain, suffering, loss, embarrassment, punishment, and rejection, just to name a few, not to mention all the daily cares and concerns that can leave a person a bit fearful about the future. What are we to do? How do people like us really *fear not*?

Isaiah had much to say to the future group of Jews who would be held captive in Babylon, and he knew that, as they neared the end of their time in captivity, they would be feeling a bit fearful concerning their future. Although the people had failed God miserably, and their sin caused their captivity, Isaiah wanted to remind them that they were still God's chosen people. He had not rejected them, and they had no reason to fear.

God did not create us to live in fear. Fear came into the world as a result of sin (see Genesis 3:10), and ever since that moment, fear has been a favorite weapon of Satan's. The enemy of God wants us to feel afraid, alone, and helpless, but God wants us to be confident, hopeful, and to remember that we are never alone. As powerful as fear can be, God is greater than *any* and *all* our fears.

Fear is a choice we make that is the result of choosing to focus on our situation more than focusing on God. If "faith is the substance of things hoped for"(Hebrews 11:1), then fear is the substance of things worried about. Fear and faith do not mix. Fear believes the negative; faith believes the positive. Fear can be driven out of your heart if replaced with faith. Faith in the promises of God will kick fear to the curb. You cannot simultaneously be focusing on your fear while trusting God.

When fear invites you to turn away from God, in that moment, you must turn to God's promises. And God gives us a specific promise for facing fear head-on. He promises His presence:"Fear not, for I am with you." You are not alone. God is with you, in all places, at all the times. He is there! His presence is powerful, personal, and permanent. But God does not stop there. He continues to add to the promise of His presence by fundamentally saying, *"Fear not,* for I am your God. *Fear not,* for I will strengthen you. *Fear not,* for I will sustain you. *Fear not,* for I will support you."

Fear not is a promise to be trusted, and a command to be obeyed. As God commanded His people in the Old Testament to trust His promise and to obey His command to fear not, Jesus echoed the same promise and command to His disciples who were in the midst of being fearful (see Mark 6:50).

God is stronger than any struggle; He is all-sufficient, all-powerful, and ever-present. He has all authority and is all-knowing. What have we to fear? When you are alone, feeling abandoned, or being tempted to fear, remember that God's promise to *fear not* comes with the power needed to not fear.

If anyone wants to provide leadership in the church, good!
But there are preconditions. (1 Timothy 3:1 MSG)

Church Leadership

THE EFFECTIVENESS OF ANY CHURCH is largely a reflection of its leadership. If leadership is defined as influence, then godly leadership is godly influence. Godly leaders are to reflect God and point others toward God. They should seek to influence others to imitate and follow Jesus Christ as they exemplify the character and nature of Jesus Christ to others. Godly leaders must lead in a manner that honors the Lord and accomplishes His purposes. What, then, makes someone a godly leader?

Paul wrote to a young pastor named Timothy, who was in Ephesus trying to straighten out some leadership issues in the local church. Paul knew that if the church was going to accomplish the plans and purposes of God, the right leaders must be in place. The desire to be a leader in the church is a noble one, Paul declared, but leadership is not for everyone. As Paul went through a list of requirements that all church leaders are to possess, one thing was crystal clear: leadership is all about *character.* Whether you lead as an elder, pastor, or deacon, you must be a man who maintains good relationships with others and has a good reputation both in and out of the church. Also, you should exhibit good behavior and be spiritually mature.

The suitability for church leadership is not about education, but about integrity. Finding leaders is not about looking for men who have business acumen, but is about seeking men with spiritual wisdom. Leadership is not about having the qualifications, but having the qualities. The men called to lead the church are to live honest, honorable, self-controlled, and model lives. Simply put, the character of Christ must be plainly evident in the life of every Christian leader.

All of the qualities Paul listed are spiritual virtues and character traits that are to mark all leadership. Paul did not outline the duties of the leaders. Rather, he was more concerned with the spirituality, morality, and virtues necessary for a person to be considered for church leadership. As one commentator observed:

> Without question, the standards are high, but that doesn't mean a higher standard for church leaders than "ordinary" Christians. All believers are called to these same high standards of Christlikeness. Paul is not creating a class of the spiritually elite here. He is simply indicating that the church should select its leadership from among people who are generally living up to the ideals of the gospel.[49]

Every Christian, whether in leadership or not, should be striving for spiritual maturity, and these qualities are great goals to keep in mind as you grow and go all out for Christ.

The church cannot progress past the level of its leadership, so having the right leaders in place is essential. This may mean removing leaders or appointing new people to positions of leadership or rewriting bylaws or church constitutions so that only the biblical requirements are used when choosing church leaders.

But the bottom line is clear: godly leadership in the church begins by having godly leaders in place.

August

AUGUST

1

The Purpose-Driven Word

GOD'S WORD always will accomplish God's purposes. God's Word is dependable. His promises are true. What God says, He will do, He will do! Where the Word of God is spoken does not matter, who speaks the Word of God does not matter, nor does when the Word of God is heard matter. God will always see that His Word does exactly what He intends His Word to do. God's Word is greater than the instrument used to proclaim it, God's Word is timeless in its ability to touch a person's heart, and God's Word is unstoppable in its power to transform lives.

This is why we read the Bible. This is why we spend time going to church and listening to sermons centered on the exposition of the Bible. This is why we spend time memorizing Bible verses. We do all of this because within the Word of God is the power to accomplish the purposes of God in and through the people of God.

What are some of the purposes God will accomplish through His Word? The Word of God is the foundation for faith in God (see Romans 10:17), and the basis for spiritual growth (see 1 Peter 2:2). The Word cleanses the life of every believer (see John 17:17), revives the soul of mankind (see Psalm 19:7), and has the power to bring new life (see 1 Peter 1:23). The Word guides the godly (see Psalm 119:105), convicts a person of sin (Titus 1:9), provides encouragement to the faithful (see Romans 15:4),gives wisdom to the worshiper (see Psalm 119:130), and prepares the people of God to do the work of God (see 2 Timothy 3:16-17).

By the word of God, the universe came into existence. By the word of God, humanity was created. By the word of God, the dead have been raised. God's Word is sovereign and supreme, alive and at work, and empowered by God. Therefore, the Word will always accomplish the purposes of God. Because of the power in the Word of God and the promise that it will not return void, we read it, recite it, teach it, preach it, declare it, contemplate it, share it, study it, learn it, remember it, and live it. We should never manipulate it, distort it, isolate it, misrepresent it, change it, add on to it, lessen it, neglect it, or ignore it. And although a time will come when heaven and earth pass away, the Word of God never will (see Luke 21:33).

God's Word may not do what we have planned, but this is not what God promises. The promise is that *God* will accomplish what *He* has planned for His Word. Unleash the power of God's Word by being committed to studying it personally and sharing it openly, because any and all time given to the Word of God is never a waste of time.

Let no one despise your youth, but be an example to the believers. (1 Timothy 4:12)

Youth Ministry

AGE DOES NOT EQUAL WISDOM. The older a person is, the more experience they may have acquired in life, but experience does not translate into spiritual wisdom. A person may be young in years, yet have more wisdom and spiritual maturity than someone twice his or her age. All too often, the attitude toward young people can be summed up in statements like, "Kids today—with their loud music, crazy hairstyles, and disrespect for authority!" or "What do they know? They are only teenagers!" But the truth is that youth is not a waiting room for adulthood. We can encourage and be encouraged, and challenge and be challenged by, younger generations.

Timothy was a young man who loved Jesus. He grew up in a godly home and had a good reputation in the community. When the apostle Paul came to Timothy's hometown of Lystra (which is in modern-day Turkey), Paul saw such a passion and maturity for the Lord in this teenager that he was inspired to bring Timothy along as an "intern" on his missionary journeys (see Acts 16). After fifteen years of traveling and serving alongside the apostle Paul, Timothy was sent to pastor the church in Ephesus and bring some structure and stability to this faltering fellowship. Now in his early thirties, Timothy still was considered very young to be in such a position of leadership, and therefore, he was suffering from a lack of confidence. So, Paul decided to encourage his young protégé to not be bothered by what others may think of his youthfulness, but to instead rise above the opinions of others by choosing to be a good and godly example.

Paul urged Timothy to live a life that was so faultless in word, conduct, love, spirit, faith, and purity that his life would be an example for others in the church to follow. Timothy was to choose his words carefully, realizing that his words would go a long way in helping or hurting his credibility. He was to pay attention to his conduct. He was to make certain to display no difference between what he said and how he lived. He was to exhibit the love of Jesus at all times and in all situations. He was to follow the Spirit's leading, be full of faith, not fear, and remain committed to purity, not perversity.

Timothy may have had a lot to learn in ministry, but he also had a lot to offer the church. If you are an older person, make a commitment to come alongside the young people in your church by supporting them and encouraging them as they follow Jesus. We need to foster an atmosphere in our churches where young people can be mentored and also be allowed to minister. If you are a young person, make a commitment to be a good and godly example to those around you. Seek to represent Jesus in every aspect of your life, and you just might be surprised at how others will admire your maturity despite your youth. As you model godliness to others, you will honor God and will be a real inspiration to others as your example encourages others to honor God.

Behold, the Lord's hand is not shortened, that it cannot save; nor His ear heavy, that it cannot hear. But your iniquities have separated you from your God; and your sins have hidden His face from you, so that He will not hear.
(Isaiah 59:1–2)

AUGUST
3

When God Is Silent

HAVE YOU EVER FELT as though your prayers were going no further than the ceiling? Maybe you have wondered whether God was even listening to you. Well, the truth is, God may not be listening to you. This is not to say God is unable to hear you, but He may be choosing not to respond to your prayers. Now, you may be thinking, *What? Why would God turn His back on me? Doesn't that go against everything God is all about, like forgiveness, love, mercy, grace, and so on? That seems pretty rude of God to ignore me if I am talking to Him.* Sometimes, the reason for the silence is not because of a problem with God, or He is being rude, or that He is unable to respond. Rather, God is choosing not to respond because the problem is with us, and the problem is sin.

The problem of sin comes with bad news and good news. The bad news is that sin separates. The reason sin causes separation between mankind and God is because God is holy, and God's holiness does not allow Him to come near sin. In fact, He must turn away from sin altogether. When Jesus was hanging on the cross as the sacrifice for the sins of all mankind, Jesus, who was perfect, became sin. The point is that even God's own Son experienced separation from God because sin separates. During that brief separation, Jesus cried out in prayer, "My God, My God, why have You forsaken Me?" (Matthew 27:46). But God was silent. Jesus must have wondered, *What happened? What changed? Why won't He answer?* But at that moment, when Jesus took our sins upon Himself, God had no choice but to turn His back on His Son, because sin causes separation from God.

People will experience the separation caused by sin and the subsequent silence of God if they choose to live a life of sin caused by rejecting Jesus Christ as their Lord and Savior. This rejection not only will cause separation while they are alive, but will also lead to eternal separation from God. We have been created as eternal beings, and we will spend eternity either in the presence of God or separated from the presence of God. The good news is if a person believes in Jesus and makes Jesus Lord of his or her life, then God will remove the separation that was caused by sin.

People can also experience a temporary separation after becoming followers of Jesus if they refuse to deal with specific sins in their lives. Perhaps they have allowed pride, anger, lust, greed, or some other sin to dominate their lives. This will bring separation and silence from God. But the good news is that through confession and the turning away from sin, God can bring restoration and remove the separation caused by sinfulness.

Certainly, God will respond with a *no* to our prayers sometimes, and that *no* comes not because of sin but because He has something better for us. So, the next time you feel that God is not listening or appears to be giving you the silent treatment, take the time to examine your life and make sure you have dealt with any and all sin. God is able to hear our prayers, and God wants to hear from us in prayer. Do not let sin get in the way of your prayers.

Now godliness with contentment is great gain.
(1 Timothy 6:6)

AUGUST
4

Greener Grass

IS THE GRASS really greener on the other side? Contentment is a highly prized but hard-to-produce Christian virtue. God wants us to cultivate contentment while the world promotes dissatisfaction. Commercials encourage us to buy newer, go bigger, and want more, causing discontentment to spill over into every area of life. We are growing more and more discontent in our jobs, our marriages, our churches, and our homes. But, even though contentment does not come naturally, the Bible does teach us that we *must* be content (see Hebrews 13:5) and that we *can* be content.

The apostle Paul encouraged his young apprentice Timothy that great value is found when godliness and contentment go hand in hand. While many may look to money or possessions to bring them contentment, they will find that those pursuits will only leave a person unsatisfied and unfulfilled. The problem is that once you finally reach the top rung of the success ladder, something is still missing: contentment.

Contentment does not come easily, and is not a gift given by the Holy Spirit. Contentment must be learned. Even Paul had to learn this quality as he declared, "For I have learned in whatever state I am, to be content" (Philippians 4:11). Paul knew what success was, and he knew suffering well. But he also learned to be content no matter the circumstance. Contentment can be described as an inward satisfaction that is not dependent on outward circumstances, while godliness can be described as simply living a life that pleases God. Godliness is not a haughty holiness or a mystical transcendence, but a life lived purely for the glory of God.

Contentment begins by being rightly related to God and trusting in His sovereign, loving, and purposeful providence. Contentment is knowing that whatever happens in life, God has allowed it, God intends it for good, and God has His glory in mind. In other words, contentment means that you are confident in God's sovereignty and His sufficiency in every situation, whether good or bad. God often uses the bad situations, the problems, frustrations, and concerns we experience in life to teach us how to be content and to bring us to the place where He not only provides for our every need, but He becomes our every need.

Contentment is not complacency, or a defeated resignation that this is your life and you must learn to accept things the way they are. Contentment involves a relentless pursuit of a deeper, more intimate relationship with God while trusting God for everything else. This does not mean settling for second best; rather, contentment means trusting that God knows best. Contentment does not mean that you forfeit ambition, but does mean that you have faith in God's direction. To know God and want nothing but more of God is the secret to contentment. For the Christian, the grass is always greenest wherever God has placed you.

"Before I formed you in the womb I knew you; before you were born I sanctified you; I ordained you a prophet to the nations." (Jeremiah 1:5)

God Is Calling You!

GOD HAS A PLAN for your life. Before you ever breathed your first breath in this world, God already had a specific mission He wanted you to accomplish. Whether you are young, old, or somewhere in between, God has something He wants you to do. He has prepared a work for you, and He has given you the spiritual means to accomplish that work. There is no time like the present to discover your God-given purpose. There is no time like today to get busy with the work God has for you. However, there is one giant hurdle to overcome before you get started, and that obstacle is yourself.

Some times in our lives, when we may come face to face with the plans, purposes, and call of God upon our lives, and almost immediately, we are hit with second thoughts and doubts that can slow us down and even keep us from stepping out. We begin to think, *Is this really what God wants me to do? Isn't there someone more qualified for this work? What if I fail? What if people reject me?* As dangerous as doubts can be, you should know they are common, and you would not be the first person to ask questions like these. Many people in the Bible started out questioning God when they discovered what God wanted them to do with their lives. But you can move past the questions and get busy serving God.

The prophet Jeremiah had doubts and was fearful when He received the call of God upon his life. Jeremiah was a very young man when God called him to be a prophet, or spokesman, for Him. His tenderhearted and compassionate nature earned him the nickname, "the weeping prophet." But this same trait also made him God's perfect candidate for the difficult work of delivering a hard message of coming judgment. We can easily see why Jeremiah was a little hesitant to jump into the ministry. The road would be a long, hard one, full of telling people things they did not want to hear. But this was God's message, and Jeremiah was God's chosen messenger. God reassured Jeremiah by reminding him that his call and commissioning came from God, and therefore, he should not worry, because God would be with him the whole way.

When serving the Lord, we will always have the understanding that we are not able, and we are not adequate. But we must accept the call to serve because God is able, and God is adequate. All service for God begins by recognizing our own insufficiency, but we must quickly move away from the anxiety of our insufficiency and instead trust in the sufficiency of God. When God calls us, we must respond with obedience. Anything less than total obedience is disobedience. Understanding our weaknesses is one thing, but using our weaknesses as an excuse not to participate in the plan God has for our lives is quite another.

Ephesians 2:10 tells us, "For we are His workmanship, created in Christ Jesus for good works, which God prepared beforehand that we should walk in them." Just as Jeremiah had a God-given job to do, so do all of God's people. If you are not sure what God's "job" is for you, then start by doing what you already know the Bible tells you to do (pray, fellowship, worship, obey, and so forth), and pray for God to show you the specific work He wants you to do.

For the love of money is a root of all kinds of evil. (1 Timothy 6:10)

In Greed We Trust

AUGUST

6

MONEY IS NOT THE ENEMY. Money is neither good nor bad, and is both neutral and necessary. Nowhere in the Bible does God call money evil. The Bible also does not condemn those who have money. But the Bible does have much to say about the way we handle our money, as nearly one in seven verses in the New Testament deal with issues concerning money. The reason money is such a talked-about subject in the Bible is because a person's attitude about money and the condition of his or her spiritual life are directly connected.

Having money is not a sin; loving money is. Loving money means that money becomes the driving force and the motivating factor in your life. Money is your security and your sanctuary. Paul warns us that the love of money can open the door for a person to become involved in a variety of other sins that can even, in a worst-case scenario, cause a person to walk away from the faith. The problem is that the pursuit of money is a trap, leading a person deeper into bondage. Many people believe that if they just had a little more money, then they would have the freedom they want and the fulfillment they desire. But the truth is that more money is never enough and only leaves you wanting more.

Paul also added a warning for those in ministry, saying that a pastor should not be in ministry to make a buck. Although a pastor is entitled to earn a living from serving professionally (see 1 Corinthians 9:14), ministry should not be seen as the place to make some easy money or be used to get rich quick.

People are seduced by all that promises that money makes but cannot deliver. The more a person wants money, the less they are inclined to want more of God. Love for stuff outweighs love for the Savior. The things of this world overshadow the Creator of all things. This does not mean that a person must take a vow of poverty to be closer to God. But a person should purpose to pursue God above anything else and find fulfillment in his or her love for God and not love for money. Jesus taught, "No one can serve two masters. For you will hate one and love the other; you will be devoted to one and despise the other. You cannot serve both God and money" (Matthew 6:24 NLT).

Believers need to avoid the love of money at all cost. True freedom and fulfillment can only come from a life devoted to the pursuit of God, not the pursuit of money. We must be more concerned about our character and not our cash. Our greatest treasure needs to be found in the abundant wealth we have in a relationship with God and not the true emptiness that is found in the hearts of those who make money their greatest treasure.

W. Graham Scroggie said, "There are two ways in which a Christian may view his money—'How much of my money shall I use for God?' or 'How much of God's money shall I use for myself?'"

> *"If you will return, O Israel," says the Lord, "Return to Me; and if you will put away your abominations out of My sight, then you shall not be moved."* (Jeremiah 4:1)

Return to Me

AT TIMES IN OUR SPIRITUAL JOURNEY, we can become a bit disconnected from God. This may be the result of focusing too much on our own personal circumstances, making bad choices that can lead us astray, or allowing "stuff" to consume our time and attention. The good news is that even if we have been focusing on the wrong things, or making unwise decisions that have taken us in the opposite direction from God's will, God still stands with open arms, ready to welcome back anyone who is willing to return to Him.

God loves to bless His people. The Israelites, of all people, should have been the first to say amen to that truth because God chose them as His special people. He protected them while they were in Egypt, He delivered them from bondage, He provided for them in the wilderness, and He gave them their own land. But they still found themselves feeling disconnected from God. The problem was that God's people were focusing on the wrong things while failing to remember the right things: the many blessings of God. This resulted in unwise decisions that took them in the opposite direction from God's will. Instead of trusting God, they were turning away from God. Instead of remaining faithful to God, they were committing spiritual adultery. They had abandoned God, and decided they could do just fine on their own. But all they succeeded in doing was making a mess of their lives and driving a wedge between themselves and God.

But God stepped in. Through the prophet Jeremiah, God called the people to return to Him. Instead of rejecting the people for their rebellion, God graciously invited them to return to intimacy with Him. Instead of God saying, "You have gone too far this time," He covered a multitude of sins with His love.

God offers forgiveness and restoration to anyone who is willing to receive them from him. If a disconnect has compromised your relationship with God, of if you feel detached from God, the simple truth is that you have moved away from God. God has not walked away from you, He has not forsaken you, and He has not moved or changed His heavenly address. He stands anxiously awaiting your return to Him.

If you want to return to God, then you need to do a few things to make this desire official. First, respond immediately. The longer you put God off, the more likely you are to never take that final step in the right direction. Next, you must return to God completely. Turning halfhearted to God is not sufficient; you must turn to God with your whole heart. Anything less than complete devotion is not devotion at all. Lastly, you must acknowledge your disobedience, ask God for forgiveness, and then turn from your sin and do not look back.

Whether you have taken just one step in the wrong direction or have been walking in the wrong direction for years, God would say to you today, "Return to Me!"

So never be ashamed to tell others about our Lord. (2 Timothy 1:8 NLT)

Courageous Faith

AUGUST

8

WHEN WE HAVE AN OCCASION to speak for Jesus Christ, the sad reality is we often do not. We know that the gospel can be intimidating to the world, as the gospel exposes man's dark side, man's sinful nature, and declares that a person must turn from his or her sin and receive Jesus Christ as Lord. Others do not always see this as good news, and some react with anger toward the person who proclaims a Jesus-only message. Many have become fearful of sharing the gospel, and that fear has done much to slow the progress of the gospel.

Paul wrote the words of today's verse to his young friend and pastor, Timothy, who was a little discouraged by what was happening in the world around him. Even though Paul knew there was a very real temptation to give in to fear and not share Jesus with others, Paul never gave in to that fear, even when his boldness for Jesus repeatedly landed him in prison. Timothy was experiencing pressure to keep the good news of Jesus Christ to himself. He was tempted to keep quiet because of his shy nature and because of the affliction, persecution, and trials that often came with sharing the truth in a truth-rejecting world. Paul reassured Timothy that we must never be ashamed of some things in life, and, most importantly, we should never be ashamed of Jesus, no matter what.

As a believer in Jesus, you may have some actual apprehensions, just as Timothy did, when sharing your faith in Jesus. You may work in an environment that supports non-Christian values, or you may work with people who question your beliefs on a regular basis. You may have neighbors who are unfriendly toward you because they know you are a Christian, and they go out of their way to avoid you, making everyday life uncomfortable. You may have family members who are antagonistic toward your Christian beliefs and take every opportunity to grill you and put you on the defensive about what you believe. This, of course, does not even begin to take into consideration the millions of people who live under the threat of physical persecution if they open their mouths and proclaim Jesus. All of this can make a person feel a little reluctant to share their faith in Jesus.

Everyone gets a little fearful at times when they are sharing their faith. This is common. We fear others will reject us. We fear people will mock us. We fear that we will not know what to say. We fear the conversation will be way too awkward. The fact of the matter is that some people are going to be offended if you share the gospel. Some people will get angry if Jesus' name is brought into a conversation. Others will want nothing to do with you if you even mention that Jesus is the only way. Talking about sports or the weather is definitely much more comfortable than Jesus, but we have a responsibility to care more about what God thinks about us than to worry about what others might think of us just because we talked about Jesus.

Here is a final encouragement to have a courageous faith and to not hold back in sharing your faith with others because of embarrassment or other reservations. Just remember that God has not given us a spirit of fear, but He has given us the Spirit of power (see 2 Timothy 1:7). This power can conquer all fear because this is the same power that conquered death (see Romans 8:11). *So, never be ashamed to tell others about our Lord.*

"The heart is deceitful above all things, and desperately wicked; who can know it?" (Jeremiah 17:9)

Heart of Darkness

AUGUST

9

HOW KIND IT IS OF OUR GRACIOUS GOD, to conceal from others—what He Himself sees within us; and which if known by others—would alienate them from us, and fill them with disgust! What contemptible creatures we would appear to our friends—if they knew all about us! We may study our own hearts, and if we study them under the cross, it will not injure us—but benefit us. But no man may study his brother's heart—he is not to be admitted into the chambers of idols within. We may form some idea of the hearts of others—by our own.
—James Smith, 1862

At the center of every person beats a depraved and deceitful heart. This is not the most uplifting news in the world, but is both true and important for all of us to recognize. If we do not come to an awareness of our own sinful nature, we never can truly understand or fully experience God's grace.

The heart represents the center of man's will. The heart embodies our inner being, which means that at the very core of every individual is a corrupt will, opposed to God. Any heart that is left unchanged will inevitably lead a person in the wrong direction, away from God. Although no one else can see the darkness found in our hearts, God can. He knows every hidden secret and every evil feeling concealed in the heart (see Psalm 44:21). But this does not stop God from loving us and providing a way for us to change our awful condition.

Since the heart is so important to what we think, say, and do, the necessary change begins as we ask the Lord, like Jeremiah did, "Heal me, O LORD, and I shall be healed; save me, and I shall be saved" (Jeremiah 17:14). We must turn from living lives that seek to follow our hearts and live lives that seek to follow God. We must turn from sin and self and turn our lives over to the Savior. Then, and only then, can the righteousness of God be amazingly transplanted in us through the conduit of our faith in Jesus Christ. Then, beating deep within us will be new hearts (see Ezekiel 36:26) and pure hearts, making us new creations in Christ (see 2 Corinthians 5:17).

With this new heart comes the responsibility to guard it (see Proverbs 4:23) and keep it clean (see Psalm 51:10). The heart needs guarding because even though the Spirit of God through faith in Jesus Christ has renewed it, believers still possess the capacity for sin and selfish pursuits. We are still prone to wander. So, we guard our hearts by remaining alert and attentive, watching and praying, so we can resist the temptation to give in to sin and selfishness (see Mark 14:38). Also, we guard our hearts by trusting God from the bottom of our hearts and no longer trying to figure out everything on our own (see Proverbs 3:5-6). Lastly, the heart needs continual cleansing because we are walking around in an unclean world. Thankfully, every word of God is pure (see Proverbs 30:5), and as we spend time every day in the Word of God, we are washed, cleansed, and sanctified by it (see Ephesians 5:26).

Ask God to search your heart today and reveal to you if anything dishonoring or displeasing can be found, so that God may lead you in the way of everlasting life (see Psalm 139:23–24).

The Lord grant mercy to the household of Onesiphorus, for he often refreshed me. (2 Timothy 1:16)

AUGUST

10

Refreshing Kindness

FROM TIME TO TIME, we all need a little encouragement. Whether we are disheartened by failure, discouraged by circumstances, disappointed by outcomes, or drained from overload, a little encouragement can go a long way in reviving the soul and refreshing the Spirit.

Encouragement is nothing to be trivialized or devalued. Even Jesus knew the importance of encouragement and took steps to receive its benefit. He took His three closest disciples with Him and asked them to watch and pray with Him in His hour of agony in Gethsemane. Also, the fearless and faithful apostle Paul needed the refreshing love and uplifting support of other believers.

One of those very special individuals who refreshed and revived Paul was named Onesiphorus. Some of the lesser-known people in the Bible, like Onesiphorus, were some of the finest of God's servants. Their importance was revealed not in eloquent preaching, but in fearless devotion to Christ and selfless service to the saints in some of the most dangerous conditions. Being a faithful and fruitful Christian is easier when you have the love and support of Christian friends encouraging you along the way.

Onesiphorus was such an encourager. He traveled from Ephesus to Rome to refresh Paul while he was chained in prison. Upon arriving in Rome, finding where Paul was being held prisoner was no easy task, but Onesiphorus was persistent and even risked his own life to come to the aid of his friend and brother in Christ. Onesiphorus could have sent word to Paul from Ephesus to let him know that he was praying for him, but Onesiphorus went the extra mile. In fact, he went the extra five thousand miles so that he might personally refresh one man. Now, that is the heart of an encourager. How uplifting for Paul! Just imagine that first face-to-face reunion, with Paul exclaiming something like, "Onesiphorus! Is that you, my good friend?" as the two men hugged, shed tears of joy, and shared warm smiles in a cold and damp prison cell. Then Onesiphorus might have opened a bag, giving Paul some fresh bread and cheese as they shared some sweet fellowship together.

We should be looking for ways to encourage and refresh others, and although we may have to take some extra effort at times, this effort will be well worth your time. Here are a few practical things you can do to be an encourager like Onesiphorus. First, keep in mind how much encouragement means to you, as this will help you stay motivated to be an encourager. Next, go the extra mile and physically go visit the person in need of refreshing. Power exists in your presence, and just being there is always encouraging. This often goes much further than anything you can say or do for them. Another way to be an encourager is to share the Word of God by reading a promise of God or a blessing found in His Word. So often, a simple reminder from God's Word is as refreshing as a cold drink of water on a hot summer day. Lastly, look for a practical way you can serve that person, perhaps by cooking a meal and bringing that meal to their house as a blessing. Or, you could do something as simple as taking them out for coffee to pray with them.

Onesiphorus serves as a good reminder of the value of Christian encouragement. Take the time today to find someone you can encourage.

For I know the thoughts that I think toward you, says the Lord, thoughts of peace and not of evil, to give you a future and a hope. (Jeremiah 29:11)

AUGUST
11

Back to the Future

HAVE YOU EVER WONDERED, *Does God care about my situation? Is He interested in the day-to-day happenings of my life?* Perhaps you are feeling alone and overlooked by God. Maybe you are a little confused as you try to determine what God is doing in your current set of circumstances, or you may even be unclear about God's future plans for you. One thing is for certain: we all will face difficult and trying circumstances in life, and many times in our spiritual walk with God we will be left confused as to what God is trying to teach us and what He is working to accomplish. But, the answers to these types of questions can only be found by first realizing that God not only cares about you, but He also thinks about you constantly, He is interested in your life today, and He has a plan for your future.

Jeremiah had been telling the children of Israel for years, "The Babylonians are coming! The Babylonians are coming!" but most people paid no attention to his warnings and continued living in disobedience to God. Eventually the Babylonians did invade Israel, and they took many of Israel's best and brightest captive. While the children of Israel were being held as captives in Babylon, the people began to wonder, *Has God forgotten about us? Does God care about our situation?* So, God sent a message of hope to the people through the prophet Jeremiah. Jeremiah wrote to inform the captives that although God would allow them to remain in captivity for seventy years because of their disobedience, He would eventually bring back a remnant of people to their homeland after the captivity was over. God wanted to keep hope alive in the people by reassuring them that even though the captivity was necessary, He still had a good plan for them, and His thoughts toward His people were good, even though times were tough.

If you are feeling forgotten by God or worried that He is not concerned about you or your situation, then you need to know that God's words of encouragement to the Israelites also apply to His people today. Your circumstances in life do matter. God is not detached or disinterested in the happenings of your life; you are treasured in His sight. The psalmist David wrote, "How precious also are Your thoughts to me, O God! How great is the sum of them! If I should count them, they would be more in number than the sand" (Psalm 139:17–18). God is so in love with us that we are constantly on His mind. His thoughts toward us are countless, precious, beautiful, and good. God not only thinks good thoughts toward us, but He also has good plans for our future. That means what God allows in our lives works toward accomplishing those good plans.

Some times in life, we may be left wondering what God is doing, but rest assured, He is bringing us to an expected end. Even though we might not see how, His thoughts toward us are of peace, His plans are to prosper us and not to harm us, and He wants to give us a hope and a future as we trust and turn everything over to Him.

Be diligent to present yourself approved to God, a worker who does not need to be ashamed, rightly dividing the word of truth. (2 Timothy 2:15)

AUGUST
12

Study Guide

HOW WELL DO YOU KNOW THE BIBLE? This is not a question to see if you are good at Bible trivia, nor is this a challenge to see if you can name the books of the Minor Prophets, in order, in less than thirty seconds. This is, however, a deliberate question designed to cause some serious self-examination of the manner, method, energy, and effort used in your personal study of the Bible. The Bible is not your average book, and therefore, should not be approached like all other books. The Bible is a guidebook for living a godly life, and essential for building a God-centered worldview. The Bible is the only source of spiritual truth, and knowing its contents is crucial for forming right theology, which leads to right living. Given the significance of all that the Bible accomplishes, knowing how to study the Bible is very important.

In today's verse, Timothy was being encouraged as a pastor and teacher to give an all-out effort to communicate God's truth as completely and clearly as possible. He was to be fully committed to the accurate examining, interpreting, explaining, and applying of God's Word. His motivation for such diligence was the glory of God and the approval of his work by God. Paul warned every pastor and teacher that the pulpit is not the place to dispense personal opinions, to promote one's own agenda, or even to sponsor worthy social programs. The teacher's chief responsibility is to rightly divide the truth so that he may rightly declare the truth to those who need the truth.

The responsibility to be a dedicated and devoted student of the Bible is not the limited obligation of pastors and teachers like Timothy; this is the responsibility of every Christian to diligently study the Bible and rightly divide the truth. Every Christian is to be fully committed to the accurate examining, interpreting, explaining, and applying of the Bible. So, here are a few suggestions that will help you not only get the most out of your personal Bible study, but also will help you guard against *wrongly* dividing the word of truth.

Start by recognizing the fact that we all come to the Bible with our own set of biases and beliefs, and we all bring those opinions, ideas, and expectations about God, religion, and church with us as well. This is why we must be willing to set aside our biases and beliefs and allow the Bible to be the sole shaper (or even better, the *soul* shaper) of our doctrine and our lives. We cannot manipulate the Bible to fit our beliefs and lifestyle. Rather, we must allow the Bible to form our values, beliefs, opinions, and lifestyles.

Next, always let the Bible speak for itself. Do not believe what others say about the Bible; check it out for yourself and make sure that what you hear or read is in fact what the Bible is saying (see Acts 17:11). As you read, study, and search the Bible, keep all Scripture in the proper context. Use the Scriptures to interpret other Scripture. Don't build a belief around a single verse. And always rely on the Holy Spirit because He is our teacher (see 1 Corinthians 2:13).

Correctly handling the Bible takes diligence, so take the time to study your Bible prayerfully, read it carefully, and obey it joyfully.

"Behold, I am the Lord, the God of all flesh. Is there anything too hard for Me?" (Jeremiah 32:27)

The God of Possibilities

AUGUST 13

DO YOU BELIEVE GOD can do anything? To intellectually comprehend that God can do anything is one thing; to practically and personally believe that God can in fact do anything is quite another. You see, we are all bound to experience things in life that are out of our control, and in those moments when we are caught in the middle of life's uncertainties, we will see if intellectual comprehension gives way to the practical and personal belief that God really can do anything.

Jeremiah found himself in prison for prophesying about the impending destruction of Jerusalem. And, during this tumultuous time in Jewish history, God told Jeremiah to buy some real estate. Now, most of us might have a reaction similar to, "Seriously God? This doesn't look like it's a buyers' market. After all, the Babylonians are conquering the people and seizing their land. I'm not sure that buying property is a wise investment right now."

Since the property was already in the hands of the enemy, this was definitely a bad time to buy, but Jeremiah was obedient nonetheless. He made the necessary arrangements to buy the land and secure the deed of ownership as God commanded. But Jeremiah wondered how God could make good on His promises concerning the land he was buying (see Jeremiah 32:25). In essence, Jeremiah knew intellectually that God could do anything, but he was allowing a mustard seed of doubt to creep in and cause him to question practically how this could be done. God's response to Jeremiah was short and to the point: "Is there anything too hard for Me?"

Does the power of God have a limit? The answer is a resounding *no!* God has infinite and unlimited power. God is able to do anything that He wills to do. Consider this. Which is easier for God to do: heal a person of a deadly disease, or heal a person of a headache? Both are equally possible for God to accomplish;

the when, is simply a matter of if He wills to do it or not. Remember, Jesus said something along the same lines when he declared, "With God all things are possible" (Matthew 19:26). As Max Lucado said, "We forget that *impossible* is one of God's favorite words."[50]

As Christians, we would all agree that God can do all things. We believe in the absolute power of God, but concerning God working things out in our own situations, we can be prone to doubt the reality of God's all-powerfulness. God is able to do so much more than we can conceive and comprehend (see Ephesians 3:20), He is able to save the worst sinner (see Hebrews 7:25), He is able to help those who are being tempted (see Hebrews 2:18), He is able to raise the dead (John 12:1), He is able to heal the sick (Matthew 12:15), He is able to keep us from falling (Jude 1:24), He is able to deliver us (Daniel 3:17), He is able to establish us (Romans 16:25), and He is able to make all things new (Revelation 21:5). Is there really anything too hard for God?

At the end of the day, our hope and trust must rest in the fact that God can do anything, even though some things appear impossible to us. Our God is able because our God is all-powerful. All things are possible because He is the God of possibilities.

All Scripture is given by inspiration of God. (2 Timothy 3:16)

AUGUST

God Has Spoken!

14

CAN THE BIBLE REALLY BE TRUSTED? After all, the Bible is just a random collection of interesting stories? Certainly, the Bible is filled with fascinating people and exciting events, but is far from fanciful folklore. The Bible is unique and unlike any other book. The Bible is not only the best-selling book of all time, the most-translated book of all time, and the most-read book of all time, but the Bible is also the only God-inspired book of all time.

The doctrine of divine inspiration is indispensable to the validity and the authority of the Bible. To degrade, discredit, or discard the Bible is to degrade, discredit, or discard Christianity. Christianity is fundamentally and foundationally built upon the Bible because the Bible is the Word of God, conveyed through man and intended for man: "For prophecy never came by the will of man, but holy men of God spoke as they were moved by the Holy Spirit" (2 Peter 1:21). The Bible comes from God and is therefore entirely error-free. The Bible is divinely authoritative, completely infallible, and eternally indestructible (Matthew 24:35).

God is the author. Therefore, the Bible is totally trustworthy and undeniably dependable, and proof to back that claim up does exist.

The Bible has been proven historically correct. No historical evidence ever discovered has been able to disprove the Bible's account of human history. Historical discoveries only continue to confirm the correctness of the Bible's record of history.

The Bible has been proven archaeologically accurate. No archaeological evidence has ever been uncovered that disproves the Bible's account of civilizations and cultures, going all the way back to man's beginning on earth.

The Bible also has been proven prophetically precise. Hundreds of prophecies recorded in the Bible already have been fulfilled, word for word, with some fulfillments coming centuries after they were written. Many more prophesies yet to be fulfilled that pertain to the second coming of Jesus Christ and the end times are also foretold in the Bible, and they will continue to verify and validate the divine authorship of the Bible.

Jesus also trusted in and relied on the authority of God's Word. He frequently quoted it (see John 4), He repeatedly taught it (see Matthew 5), and He boldly declared its divine origin, saying, "Your [God's] word is truth" (John 17:17).

The more you examine the evidence, the more you become convinced that the Bible is more than a random collection of interesting stories. The Bible is authoritative, authentic, and accurate. We can have confidence in the Bible because the source is credible and has been confirmed both internally and externally. And the Bible must be received, believed, and obeyed as the final authority on all things pertaining to life and godliness.

The Bible is God's inspired Word, and is, therefore, trustworthy. We should read it and apply it to our lives. The Bible is our standard for testing everything else that claims to be true. The Bible is our safeguard against false teaching and our source of guidance for how we should live.

The Lord has spurned His altar, He has abandoned His sanctuary; He has given up the walls of her palaces into the hand of the enemy. (Lamentations 2:7)

AUGUST
15

Wake-Up Call

IF YOU EVER HAVE BEEN GIVEN a speeding ticket, received a less-than-stellar report from a physical exam, or maybe earned a minor reprimand on the job, events like these can serve as a wake-up call, a warning that encourages you to make some changes in your life so that you can stay on the straight and narrow.

God also gives His people wake-up calls to encourage change and to keep His people on the spiritual straight and narrow. Sometimes we ignore the wake-up calls that God sends our way by pulling the covers over our heads and saying, "Not now, Lord. Go away. I don't want to hear this right now!" But, God will continue to use people, events, and circumstances to get our attention and bring us back into a right relationship with Him.

As one commentator has said, "The destruction of Jerusalem revealed an astonishing fact about God: He will go to great lengths to draw His people back to Himself."[51] The people of Judah had wandered away from God. Sure, they were still going through the religious motions, but they were devoid of sincerity and lacked a genuine commitment to God. So, after years of repeated warnings from prophets like Isaiah and Jeremiah, God sent a devastating wake-up call to His people: He allowed Jerusalem to be destroyed. The temple and all its furnishings were pulled down, religious rituals were done away with, and the king and the high priest were removed. God allowed the written Law itself to be destroyed, and He stopped giving visions to the prophets. Now, that is a wake-up call! The removal of these things must have been devastating to the Israelites, but God took these things away to recapture His people's attention and affection.

How many times must God speak to you to get your attention? God does not want you to simply go through the religious motions while lacking the right motivation. He is not looking for more servants; He is looking for genuine worshipers. God wants all of our hearts, minds, and souls, and when we are giving Him anything less than 100 percent of our adoration, affection, and attention, God will discipline those whom He loves (see Hebrews 12:6) to wake us up and snap us out of our waywardness.

Sometimes, God will use extraordinary measures to get our attention. He may use a burning bush, give you a ride in a giant fish, speak to you through a donkey, or, as He did with the Israelites, allow some devastation into your life in the hope of waking you up. But before God goes to extremes, you should know that He would much rather speak to you through the still, small voice of His Holy Spirit and the Word of God.

God can and will use difficult situations to direct us, to correct us, to teach us, and to protect us. He loves us and always has our good and His glory in mind. God will use trials and circumstances to wake us up, turn us away from unholy practices, and teach us the way of godliness. So, the next time God uses something as a wake-up call in your life, resist the urge to hit the spiritual snooze button.

All Scripture is given by inspiration of God, and is profitable for doctrine, for reproof, for correction, for instruction in righteousness. (2 Timothy 3:16)

AUGUST

16

Getting the Most Out of Your Bible

LIVING A GODLY LIFE can only come by spending time in God's Word. If spiritual growth is what you are looking for in your life, then you must rely on the only source of spiritual truth to lead the way. If you want to serve God more effectively, then the Bible is what will equip you to do so (see 2 Timothy 3:17). Knowing God and growing in your relationship with Him means knowing and growing in God's Word. God has given us His Word, the Bible, to empower us to grow spiritually, to enable us to serve Him faithfully, and to glorify Him daily.

Getting the most out of your Bible doesn't require a seminary degree, nor does it involve knowing Greek and Hebrew. But getting the most out of your Bible does require a commitment to read and study the Bible with a willingness to apply the instruction found within. God did not go through the sacrifice of saving our souls only to say, "Okay, I did my part. Now you figure out the rest." Quite the contrary: God continues to guide us and direct us toward godly living as He speaks to us through the Bible. God works through the Bible to produce godliness in us by using doctrine, reproof, correction, and instruction from His Word to produce spiritual growth in our lives.

The entire Bible, from Genesis to Revelation, teaches us God's ways, which is *doctrine*. Doctrine spells out exactly what being a Christian means, communicating what God expects from us, and protecting us from believing in false teachings. The Bible also *reproves* us, which is a nice way of saying that God uses the Bible to show us what we are doing wrong by shining a light on our ungodly conduct. The Bible helps us to see ourselves as we really are, our imperfections and all. This way we can identify accurately the sin in our lives and take the necessary steps toward godly living, which includes *correction*. To simply see our sin or be made aware of our wrong behavior is not enough. We must take action and make corrections, and here, again, the Bible shows us the way to do that. Pleasing God involves changing out our wrong thoughts and actions with right thoughts and actions. Pleasing God means putting off immorality and carnality and putting on righteousness and godliness (see Ephesians 4:22–32). As we continue to follow God, the Bible also *instructs* us, or keeps us going in the right direction.

God has purposed for His Word to accomplish great things in our lives as He uses the Bible to show us truth, expose our rebellion, correct our mistakes, and train us in how to live God's way. The Bible is our guide (see Psalm 119:133), it is our light (see Psalm 119:105), it helps us resist sin (see Psalm 119:11), it revives us (see Psalm 119:25), it strengthens us (see Psalm 119:28), it is the source of faith (see Romans 10:17), it sanctifies us (see John 17:17), it helps us grow strong (see 1 Peter 2:2), and it is our defense against evil (see Ephesians 6:17).

Simply stated, the Bible helps us to know what is right and what is not right, and helps us to know how to get things right and how to stay right. When we allow the Bible to accomplish all this in our lives, then we are truly getting the most out of our Bible.

Through the Lord's mercies we are not consumed, because His compassions fail not. They are new every morning.
(Lamentations 3:22–23)

AUGUST
17

Mercy for the Moment

WE HAVE ALL HAD DAYS where we have wondered, *Can this day get any worse?* You know those days. They chew you up, spit you out, and leave you feeling weak and weary, disappointed and discouraged, and maybe even a little depressed. You can hardly wait for days like these to be over so you can crawl into bed and start fresh in the morning.

What if I told you that God has something that will help you to get through the toughest of days with joy, allowing you to glorify Him in the process? The mercies of God are what make all the difference!

Jeremiah right after the fall of Jerusalem composed five songs of sorrow, or laments, found in the book of Lamentations. The prophecies that God gave Jeremiah had come to pass. God's great city lay in smoldering ruins. The people of God were scattered far and wide, and the outlook was one of despair and desolation. The prophet was consumed with sorrow over the condition of the city and the capturing of the people. Feeling as though things could not get any worse, Jeremiah wrote five songs, which were an outpouring of his soul. But as Jeremiah remembered the mercies of God, things began to change, and the dark clouds of despair started to dissolve. Jeremiah was able to see this was because of the mercy of God that the people were not completely destroyed by the Babylonians. And, because of the mercy of God, the covenant relationship between God and His chosen people was upheld in spite of their unworthiness and unfaithfulness. His mercies made the difference!

The mercy of God implies not only forgiveness for the guilty, but also a tenderhearted compassion for the destitute. God's mercy is more than punishment withheld, but is compassion in action. The mercy of God motivates us and empowers us to live lives that are pleasing to God (see Romans 12:1), and His mercy is an example for us to follow (see Luke 6:36). By God's mercy, we are alive, by God's mercy, we do not stand condemned, and by God's mercy, Jesus took our punishment on the cross. His mercy makes all the difference!

Even though every day is filled with uncertainties, one thing is certain: whatever the day may bring, God will be there to help us because His mercies never fail. His mercies arrive new every morning. They are like His manna in the wilderness: you cannot use yesterday's mercies today, and you cannot store up mercies for tomorrow. Today's mercies are good only for today, and tomorrow's mercies will be good only for tomorrow. God gives us just enough mercy for each day. His mercy makes all the difference!

A new morning truly brings a new start, but the reason mornings are packed with possibilities is not because of a good night's sleep. Rather, the new mercies of God that await us. God's mercy is fresh, current, and relevant for today.

Do not be anxious about the mercy you need from God for tomorrow. Just look to Him today for the mercy you need in this moment, and trust Him for the mercy He promises to deliver to you tomorrow. And remember, His mercy makes all the difference!

"Preach the word!" (2 Timothy 4:2)

The Priority of Preaching

AUGUST
18

SOME PEOPLE BELIEVE that preaching is dead. They say that preaching is an outdated and ineffective way to communicate in our technology-crazed, multimedia, and postmodern world. Critics today are eager to point out that sermons must become events or experiences that engage all of the senses and mix videos, music, drama, audience participation, and visual aids in order get and maintain the attention of the listeners. Today, some believe that a church service must become a Hollywood production in order to be interesting and inspiring.

However, preaching, done as God intended, is not only captivating, thought-provoking, and engaging, but also transforming. Therefore, a priority for every church and the priority of every pastor should be to preach the Word of God.

Preaching is so important to the stability and spiritual growth of the church that Paul commanded Timothy to "Preach the word!" For Timothy and the modern preacher, this command that requires the steadfast commitment to preach the word day in and day out, in good times and bad times, when they feel like it and when they don't feel like it, when people are interested and when they are uninterested. No matter what, pastors are to preach the Word!

Why the emphasis on the Word of God? The Word of God must be preached from the pulpits because the people need to hear from God. The Word of God must be preached because only the Word of God can change a person from the inside out. The Word of God must be preached because the Bible is the only authority and source of absolute truth. The Word of God must be preached because faith only comes by hearing the Word of God (see Romans 10:17). This does not mean that the preacher or the preaching is to be boring. Martyn Lloyd-Jones said, "I would say that a 'dull preacher' is a contradiction in terms; if he is dull, he is not a preacher. He may stand in a pulpit and talk, but he is certainly not a preacher."[52] True, preachers are not there to entertain or put on a show, but their preaching should capture attention, captivate minds, and communicate truth. This certainly should include creativity and imagination and can incorporate videos, music, drama, audience participation, visual aids, and the use of stories and humor as long as these elements never replace or reduce the priority of God's Word in the church service.

Every pastor has the responsibility to preach the Word, to interpret it, to apply it accurately, and to do so with passion and enthusiasm. Every Christian has the responsibility to worship at a church where the Word of God is faithfully and fully preached. Ask yourself, "Was I taught God's Word last Sunday?" You may have been entertained, your funny bone may have been tickled, and you may have even been encouraged, but was the Word of God preached?

John Stott said, "When a man of God stands before the people of God with the Word of God in his hand and the Spirit of God in his heart, you have a unique opportunity for communication."

Preaching is not dead. Preaching is very much alive because the Word of God is alive and active (see Hebrews 4:12).

Let us search out and examine our ways, and turn back to the Lord. (Lamentations 3:40)

AUGUST 19

Soul Searching

SEEING FAULTS IN OTHER PEOPLE is easy, but we may fail to notice them in ourselves, which is why taking the time to do a little self-examination is important so that we can be at our spiritual best. The Bible does not tell us to examine others, but does say repeatedly that we should examine ourselves (see 2 Corinthians 13:5; 1 Corinthians 11:28). Christians who live unexamined lives are not living up to their fullest potential and are, in fact, hindering God's work in their lives.

God's people were in a spiritual time out because of their flagrant disregard for applying the Word of God to their lives. Jeremiah repeatedly spoke in Lamentations 3 of the attitude that God's people should have toward their affliction during their captivity and how their perspective should work to change their outlook toward God, which in turn would change their relationship with

God for the better. Jeremiah told them that their affliction should be endured with hope in God's ultimate plan of restoration (see verse 26), that their affliction was only temporary because of God's compassion and love for them (see verse 31), that God did not delight in their affliction (see verse 33), and lastly, that their affliction was designed to accomplish the greater good of turning their hearts back to God (see verse 40). They were God's people, but they certainly had not been acting as such, which meant a good time was upon them for a little self-examination in order to restore a right relationship with God.

We do not naturally move in the direction of godliness. In fact, if we do not keep a close eye on our lives, we can begin to drift slowly away from faithfulness and nearer to disobedience. No one sets out to disappoint God, and no one strategizes on how to become a wishy-washy believer. But if we avoid regular self-examination of our lives, then wishy-washy is exactly what we will become. This is where the process of self-examination comes into play, because with persistent and purposeful reflection of our spiritual condition, we allow God to move us in the direction of spiritual growth and maturity.

Examining our lives is not subjective self-analysis; rather, this is a spirit-filled analysis of our lives, centered on the Word of God. We should begin by asking God to search our hearts and reveal any sinfulness in our lives so we can see it, confess it, and turn from it. In addition to looking at our sinfulness, we also want to look at our spiritual stability. Here are some starter questions that may prove helpful as you do a little soul searching: Am I living in obedience to the Bible? Am I submitting to the leading of the Holy Spirit? Am I spending time with God daily? Is my life a good reflection of my faith? Can I see positive spiritual changes in my life from year to year? Is my thought life wholesome? Are my words uplifting? Do my actions glorify God?

As Christians, we must regularly take time to do some soul searching and self-examination so that we can better live a life that is both pleasing to God and productive for the kingdom of God.

Slaves must always obey their masters and do their best to please them. They must not talk back or steal, but must show themselves to be entirely trustworthy and good. Then they will make the teaching about God our Savior attractive in every way. (Titus 2:9–10 NLT)

AUGUST
20

Jesus on the Job

BEING A CHRISTIAN is not easy in the workplace. Irreligious ideology is so inescapable in the majority of professional work environments that we often have a difficult time fitting in at the office. Many Christians try not to rock the boat in the workplace so as not to risk being disliked, made fun of, or even fired for choosing to speak up about Jesus. But as Christians in the workplace, we are called to represent Jesus on the job. This is such a blessed and unique opportunity that we have as Christians because for many coworkers, we are the only example and expression of Jesus they may ever experience. With such an amazing and privileged opportunity, how well are you reflecting Jesus on the job?

Slaves in Paul's day had a rotten set of circumstances to deal with in most cases. They would get the dirty jobs, the dangerous jobs, and be forced to do the jobs that no one else wanted to do. Yet, despite the hard and demanding work that was forced upon a slave, Paul called Christian slaves to rise above the drudgery of their work and the hostility of their environment and recognize that no matter what their situation, they still were representatives of Jesus Christ, called to glorify God in the way they did their work. Paul gave the Christian slave, as well as the modern-day Christian employee, several ways to better represent Jesus on the job.

First, show respect for authority by your obedience. Do what you are asked to do, and do it willingly, as your obedience is a reflection of your reverence for God. You might not like the task you are given, and you might think what you are given is unfair or even unreasonable. But as long as you work in that job, you have a responsibility to do what you are asked to do (as long as what you are asked to do is not a sin).

Second, represent Jesus on the job by being well-pleasing in all things. In other words, strive for excellence in all that you do. Work hard and be diligent when the boss is watching or when no one is watching, even seeking to go the extra mile.

Third, represent Jesus on the job by being respectful. Do not talk back or talk behind someone else's back. Do not complain or be argumentative. Show some respect for others, and watch what you say and how you say it.

Finally, be honest. Stealing on the job can take many different forms, from submitting an exaggerated time sheet or padding an expense report to taking office supplies or conducting personal business on company time. Quite simply, whether time or resources, do not take what does not belong to you.

Work weeks seem to be getting longer while weekends seem to be getting shorter, as eight-hour workdays turn into ten- and twelve-hour days. With technology, we are constantly connected, always online, and reachable anytime. Do you know what Paul would say about our work schedules today? "What an opportunity!" What an opportunity to represent God, day in and day out, to many who do not know God personally. What an opportunity to be an example of Jesus on the job and to work in such a way that through your Christian work ethic, others would be attracted to God and want to know more about Him.

"I shall be a little sanctuary for them in the countries where they have gone." (Ezekiel 11:16)

AUGUST
21
My Sanctuary

W E LIVE IN TROUBLED TIMES. The fact that the longer we live, the more troubles we are likely to experience comes as no surprise. Crisis, disaster, and tragedy are no respecters of persons. Whether you are young or old, male or female, rich or poor, difficulty does not discriminate. When trouble comes our way, we can be tempted to think that God is off in the distance, disinterested in our situation, and that He is leaving us to fend for ourselves. Do you believe that?

One of the most difficult aspects of the Babylonian captivity for God's people was not only the strangeness of new surroundings, but also the sadness that came from being separated from their land and from their sanctuary. God's people were feeling alone, isolated, and without hope. They had experienced the crisis of foreign invasion, they saw the disaster of their holy temple being destroyed, and they were living through the tragedy of captivity. We hear their sadness in Psalm 137, where the psalmist said, "How can we sing the songs of the LORD while in a pagan land?" (Psalm 137:4 NLT). Also, even though they had repeatedly turned their backs on God, He still reached out to them in their time of trouble and showed them help and hope.

God promised to be their sanctuary, even though the physical sanctuary where they worshiped was gone. God was providing them the opportunity to worship Him, regardless of their whereabouts, because God would be to them a permanent sanctuary and a place of refuge. God was promising to be everything to His people that they refused to let Him be when they had a physical sanctuary made of stone. God was promising to be a sanctuary that was never to be dependent on a location or tied to a physical building, but a sanctuary, constructed out of the inexhaustible Spirit of God, that would abide with His people wherever they went, God was promising to be a refuge to His people, their strength in every weakness, their help in every trouble, and their peace in every storm. No matter when they needed Him and no matter where they were located, He would be there for them. Having God as their refuge did not mean that God would come in and save the day or that He would fix everything. Rather, having God as a refuge meant that He would work everything for a greater good.

God, through the Holy Spirit, is a sanctuary to His people today. As 1 Corinthians 3:16 reminds us, "Do you not know that you are the temple of God and that the Spirit of God dwells in you?" For every crisis, disaster, or tragedy, for every person who feels alone, isolated, and without hope, God says, "I will be your sanctuary and your place of refuge, no matter where you are and no matter what you are facing." God has made His dwelling place in your heart, and you can take refuge in Him by the Holy Spirit and through His Word because He is a sanctuary to His people.

God longs to be your refuge and strength today. Adversity is inevitable. Crisis is certain. But for those who make God their sanctuary, He is their help and their hope.

We should live soberly, righteously, and godly in the present age, looking for the blessed hope and glorious appearing of our great God and Savior Jesus Christ.
(Titus 2:12–13)

AUGUST
22

Awaiting His Appearing

JESUS is coming back! How does that make you feel? Does the thought of Jesus coming back bring joy to your heart, or cause you to break out into a cold sweat? Or maybe you are completely indifferent to the reality of His return. Your response to the fact that Jesus *will* come again is a real barometer of your current spirituality. Understanding that Jesus will not only come back, but that He could come back at any moment, should radically impact your commitment to live for Him today.

Paul spoke to Titus about the grace of our salvation and how, because of God's past grace that brings salvation, we now live in present grace that brings sanctification as we await a future grace that brings glorification. In other words, grace offers salvation, which leads to godliness, which prepares us for glory. The grace of God is to be a powerful force in our lives, and as Paul puts it in the first part of Titus 2:12, His grace teaches us to say no to ungodliness and worldly passions and to live self-controlled, upright, and godly lives today. One of the marvelous truths implied in this promise is that one day, when our salvation is perfected, we will be glorified, or made fully like our Lord in purity and righteousness. That future encounter, which is to be our happy hope, will bring total and permanent removal of sin from our lives. But until that day, we should be looking forward with anticipation and expectancy as we live rightly and wait patiently for His return.

The heartbeat of Paul's message is that we are to be living in light of His glorious return, living *soberly* or self-controlled today. This means we are to live carefully and responsibly, choosing not to become involved in those things that are harmful and unproductive in our spiritual walks. The idea here is that all things may be permissible for us to do, but not all things are productive for us to do (see 1 Corinthians 6:12). Living in light of His return means allowing the Spirit of God to keep our desires in check because true self-control is allowing the Spirit of God to control self.

Living in light of His glorious return also means that we should live *righteously,* or that we should do the right thing. The perfect standard for what is right is the Bible. Therefore, we should be completely faithful and fully submitted to biblical instruction, which will lead us in righteous living.

Living in light of His glorious return means that we should live *godly* lives, or maintain a right relationship with God. Staying in close fellowship with God means talking to God daily in prayer and listening to God daily by reading the Bible. These two are essential for maintaining a healthy relationship with God.

The great culmination of our salvation is the glorious appearing of Jesus Christ. Jesus is coming back, so we must "live soberly, righteously, and godly," as each of these three characteristics focuses on a different relationship. *Soberly* speaks of our relationship with ourselves, *righteously* speaks of our relationship with others, and *godly* speaks of our relationship with God. These three godly characteristics help us to live spiritually balanced lives while we await His appearing.

"Son of man, these men have set up their idols in their hearts, and put before them that which causes them to stumble into iniquity." (Ezekiel 14:3)

AUGUST
23

Understanding Idolatry

WHEN you think of idolatry, what comes to mind? Perhaps the scene from the movie *The Ten Commandments* immediately pops into your thoughts, where Moses, played by Charlton Heston, comes down from Mount Sinai only to find the Israelites worshiping a golden calf. In his righteous anger, Moses destroys the golden calf. Or perhaps you envision temples in remote lands, filled with carved images where people come and bow down before these statues in empty worship. Both are examples of idolatry. But idolatry goes much deeper than bowing down before statues and worshiping images. Idolatry also includes anyone or anything that has taken the place of God in a person's heart.

God defined what he meant by idol when He told Ezekiel that an idol was anything that a person places before Him, anything that separates a person from God and causes him or her to stumble into iniquity (see Ezekiel 14:7). Idols are not just the carved objects that sit in pagan shrines; they are the cravings, longings, and loyalties that rule over our hearts. The people of Ezekiel's day were guilty of setting up shrines to idols in their hearts, even as they continued to practice their religious rituals. Steeped in idolatry and ungodly worship, the people came to the prophet Ezekiel expecting to inquire of God and hear what God had to say to them. God definitely spoke, but he did not say what they were expecting to hear. God condemned the people for their idolatrous hypocrisies and told the people that their empty idols would fail and judgment was coming their way.

Although we might not be bowing down before carved images, and therefore, think we are free from idolatrous worship in our lives, the truth is that we may still be building shrines in our hearts to something other than God. Perhaps a few questions might help to reveal if any objects of your affection are in danger of replacing the priority and preeminence of God in your life. What do you get excited about? What are you most passionate about? If you had one wish, what would you want most? The greatest affection of a person's heart has become their god. Whatever a person is most loyal to—whether another person, a possession, or a pursuit—has become a god to him or her. Anything that we love more than God Himself should be considered an idol in our lives. God demands absolute loyalty. He must be our primary pursuit, our most prized possession, our master passion, and our utmost interest. We are created to worship God, so if we take God out of our lives, we will replace Him and worship something else.

The Bible warns us about replacing God for something else: "Dear children, keep away from anything that might take God's place in your hearts" (1 John 5:21 NLT). Do not let any person, pursuit, possession, or passion become the primary focus of your attention. Do not let your heart become more interested in something or someone other than God. Keep God as your number one priority.

Speak evil of no one. (Titus 3:2)

Think Before You Speak

AUGUST 24

*P*SSST! Come here for a second! You will never believe what I just heard about . . . ! Our conversations can either be full of grace or overly judgmental. They can be a source of encouragement to someone, or they can be terribly discouraging. They can either be uplifting to the heart or tremendously upsetting to the soul. From the time we were children, we have been taught, "If you can't say something nice about someone, don't say anything at all." Yet despite all the childhood coaching, harmful words are still whispered, gossip still goes out, and slander is still spoken. How can we get past the gossip? How can we leave the slander behind so that we speak evil of no one?

The apostle Paul knew that people often make judgments about God based on what they notice Christians saying and doing. Changed lives are one of the most persuasive proofs of the power of God at work today, but a Christian bad-mouthing someone is a poor reflection on our great God. We are to conduct ourselves in a manner worthy of God, and that includes watching what we say about others. Christians have no business engaging in the destructive habit of speaking evil of others; this behavior simply does not fit who we are meant to be in Christ. Note that Paul is not saying that we are never to talk of or expose the evils of another person. However, we are not to do so with a malicious intent or in a public setting.

What does speaking evil of someone mean? The most common expressions of this destructive speech are gossip and slander. Slander simply means to speak untrue words that intend to do harm to another person's reputation, and gossip is to share unfavorable information about another person. Both types of speech make public what ought to remain private. People often will try to disguise gossip and slander for genuine concern, using phrases like, "I don't mean to be critical. However, . . ." or, "Perhaps I shouldn't say anything, but . . ." And the ever-popular prayer meeting gossip: "We need to pray for . . . because I heard that . . ." If we actively search out and carelessly pass on "the latest news" about someone, then we are guilty of speaking evil.

Jerry Bridges has said,

> We slander when we ascribe wrong motives to people, even though we can't see their hearts or know their particular circumstances. We slander when we say another believer is "not committed" when he or she does not practice the same spiritual disciplines we do or engage in the same Christian activities we engage in. We slander when we misrepresent another person's position on a subject without first determining what that person's position is. We slander when we blow out of proportion another person's sin and make that person appear to be more sinful than he or she really is.[53]

If we are going to refuse to give in to gossip and purpose to stay away from slander, then we must be aware of how hurtful and harmful these kinds of talk are to others, how sinful they are in the eyes of God, and how distressing they are to the Holy Spirit (see Ephesians 4:30–31). One way to stop speaking evil of others is to THINK before you speak, asking yourself questions: Is what I am about to say *true*? Is it *helpful*? Is it *inspiring*? Is it *necessary*? Is it *kind*?

"So I sought for a man among them who would make a wall, and stand in the gap before Me on behalf of the land, that I should not destroy it; but I found no one."
(Ezekiel 22:30)

AUGUST
25

What Can I Do?

EDMUND BURKE said, "All that is necessary for the triumph of evil is that good men do nothing." God is always in search of men and women He can use for His service, but sometimes we are hit with a sense of insignificance, thinking, *I am just one person. What can I do?* We may easily underestimate what one person can accomplish, but God never does. One godly man or woman, boy or girl, can make a dramatic difference in the world, if that person is willing to step out in faith and humility, allowing God to use them.

Ezekiel was a prophet to those who were taken captive during the Babylonian invasion. Through Ezekiel, God explained why He was allowing Jerusalem to be destroyed. He said the people had rebelled, the leaders were abusing their power (see Ezekiel 22:27), the priests failed to point the way (see verse 26), and—the icing on the cake—the prophets were covering up the sins of the priests (see verse 28). God searched but found no one who was willing to stand up for what was right and lead the people into a life of pure and holy worship of Him. Ezekiel pointed out the tragedy of a society in which no one can be found to stand up and be counted for God (see verse 30).

We may feel that if we stand for God, we are just one in a sea of people going the other direction. We can be left asking, "What is the point of standing up against such an overwhelming tide?" But with God, even one individual can make a difference. When all else fails and everyone else is going his or her own way, God is still looking for that one lone person who will stand for Him.

If God were to search around the globe today, would He find anyone willing to stand in the gap? Willing to stand and intercede for people in need? Willing to stand for righteousness? You might be the only Christian in your family, the only Christian in your workplace, the only Christian in your classroom, or the only Christian in your neighborhood. But God may have you there for a reason, and He may be asking, "Will you take a stand for Me where I have you?" God may have placed you exactly where you are so that you can be a godly encouragement in the lives of the people in your world of influence and help lead others into a life of pure and holy worship of Him.

Standing alone is never easy, and being the first one to stand up can be intimidating. But your stance may be what others need in order to see their need to turn to God. And who knows? As you stand up, others may be inspired to stand with you. No one can predict the impact that one person can have when they decide to stand for God. But never underestimate what God may want to do through your life if you simply stand in the gap. Edward Everett Hale put it well: "I am only one; but still I am one. I cannot do everything; but still I can do something; and because I cannot do everything, I will not refuse to do the something that I can do."[54]

I appeal to you for my son Onesimus. (Philemon 1:10)

The Need to Forgive

EVERYONE HAS BEEN HURT by someone. Toes get stepped on, feelings get hurt, and relationships suffer injury. Whether the damage was caused by words or actions, hurtfulness happens. Emotional injuries take time to heal, but they never will completely heal without forgiveness. C. S. Lewis said, "Everyone says forgiveness is a lovely idea, until they have something to forgive."[55] True, forgiveness is never easy, but is necessary. Paul's short letter to Philemon reminds us of our need to forgive.

Onesimus was a slave, and Philemon was his master. Onesimus had wronged Philemon not only by running away, but also by apparently stealing from Philemon. And while Onesimus was on the lamb and hiding out in Rome, he crossed paths with the apostle Paul. As a result of their time together, Onesimus became a follower of Jesus Christ. Now a Christian, Paul encouraged Onesimus to return to Philemon and ask for his forgiveness. But just in case Philemon was hesitant to let bygones be bygones, Paul sent Onesimus back to Philemon with a personal letter and a personal friend named Tychicus (see Colossians 4:7–9) to help smooth things over. Paul did everything he could to encourage Philemon to forgive Onesimus and receive him back, not as just a runaway slave but as a new brother in Christ. And what should motivate Philemon to forgive? He should forgive for love's sake (see Philemon 1:9).

Maybe someone has wronged you, and you find that you are having a hard time letting bygones be bygones. Remember, forgiveness is never easy, but is always necessary. Our God is a God of forgiveness (see Daniel 9:9), and He expects His people to be forgivers too (see Matthew 6:14–15). Forgiveness does not mean we are denying that we were wronged, or that we are excusing the wrong that was committed. But forgiveness is the way God wants us to deal with being wronged. Forgiveness does not mean that all the consequences go away from the wrong that was committed, either. In Onesimus's case, he still would have to make restitution for what was stolen. But forgiveness does not seek to exact punishment on top of repayment. To forgive basically means that a person is pardoned with no strings attached.

What is our motivation to forgive others? We forgive for love's sake. Love demands that we forgive others as "[love] keeps no record of being wronged" (1 Corinthians 13:5 NLT). The love of God toward us is a demonstration of forgiveness and serves as a model of forgiveness for us to follow, "forgiving one another, even as God in Christ forgave you" (Ephesians 4:32). Love also continues to forgive, which means there is no limit to the number of times we are to forgive someone (see Matthew 18:21–22).

Forgiveness is a choice that we make to love someone as God has loved us. Forgiveness believes, "I am forgiven, so I should be forgiving." When we have been wronged, being unforgiving is easy. But for love's sake, we must let go of that wrong and choose to embrace forgiveness. To forgive someone is never easy, but is necessary (see Mark 11:26).

But Daniel purposed in his heart that he would not defile himself with the portion of the king's delicacies.
(Daniel 1:8)

AUGUST
27

Going against the Grain

LIFE IS FULL OF CHOICES, and being a Christian sometimes means choosing to go against the grain. While you cannot control everything that happens to you, you can choose how you are going to respond to what happens to you. Doing what is right in the eyes of the Lord is not always the easiest choice to make, but is always the right choice to make.

Daniel was a godly man who was sent to live in ungodly Babylon. He was one of the young men who was taken captive from Jerusalem and selected to serve in King Nebuchadnezzar's high court. Once in Babylon, Daniel and three of his friends, Hananiah, Mishael, and Azariah, were enrolled in a three-year training program where they were being pressured to conform to the Babylonian lifestyle. They were supposed to eat like Babylonians, dress like Babylonians, and think like Babylonians. Even their names were changed in an attempt to strip them of their identity. But nothing could strip them of their commitment to God.

Daniel and his three friends drew a line in the sand and made the decision that they were going to take a stand for God. They purposed in their hearts not to eat the food that was being provided to them by the king's administration. Daniel and these young men refused to eat food that was sure to be ritually unclean (not prepared according to Jewish Law) as well as morally unclean (offered to pagan idols). This was a courageous choice that could have had devastating consequences, but God chose to honor them because they honored Him.

Daniel and these young men refused to go with the flow. They refused to do something just because everyone else was doing it. The world never will stop trying to make us conform to its way of thinking and living. Therefore, we must have faith and obedience to overcome the temptations and pressures of the world. To take a stand for God tomorrow, we must be committed to Him today. We must be standing *with* God in order to take a stand *for* God.

Our lives are the sum of all our choices, and sometimes making the choice to go against the grain means that we will get a few splinters along the way. But choosing to remain faithful to God is the only way to go. Daniel was a man who had the courage of his convictions. He lived in one the most godless cultures of the ancient world, yet he remained faithful to God. God is looking for people like Daniel and his friends, followers of Christ who will stand by their godly convictions and who will make godly choices that glorify God, even in the face of danger. Therefore, "watch, stand fast in the faith, be brave, be strong" (1 Corinthians 16:13).

Are they not all ministering spirits sent forth to minister for those who will inherit salvation? (Hebrews 1:14)

Angels Among Us

W E ARE NOT ALONE in the universe. I am not talking about strange alien life-forms on a distant planet; I am talking about the fact that angels are among us. From Genesis to Revelation, the Bible makes more than 250 references to the existence of angels and their relationship to God and mankind. Angels reside in an invisible, supernatural realm. Seeing or interacting with them is beyond our natural ability, but God sometimes pulls back the curtain and gives us a glimpse into the invisible comings and goings of these secret agents of God. This may raise the question in your mind about what exactly these angels do.

Despite all the artistic portrayals, angels do not spend their days floating on clouds playing harps. Rather, they are actively involved in the worship and work of God. They are servants of God, sent out by God to do the work of God. And one of the special jobs that angels have is being sent out to minister and care for God's people.

One way angels minister is they *protect* God's people. Perhaps no aspect of the ministry of angels to man is more talked about than the idea of having a guardian angel. While no Bible verse specifically states that a person has a guardian angel, the Bible does teach that angels do guard and protect us (see Psalm 91:11). Angels also *provide for* God's people. God has used angels to provide for the physical needs of others such as delivering food to Hagar (see Genesis 21:17–20), Elijah (see 1 Kings 19:6), and Christ after His temptation (see Matthew 4:11). Angels have been used by God to *guide* God's people into God's will. Angels helped to reveal the law to Moses (see Acts 7:52–53) and spoke to John about the future events found in the book of Revelation. Angels gave instructions to Joseph about the birth of Jesus (Matthew 1–2), the women at the tomb, Philip (see Acts 8:26), and Cornelius (see Acts 10:1–8).

From time to time, we hear extraordinary stories about angelic deliverances of those who found themselves in impossible situations. And, as true as some of these stories may be, they serve to highlight the fact that angelic assistance is not part of the normal, everyday Christian experience. As interesting as angels are to consider, we must remember that Jesus is greater than the angels in every way. He is God's communication to us, He is the Creator and sustainer of all things, He is the reflection of God's glory, He is the One who paid the penalty for our sins, and He is our representative with God (see Hebrews 1:3–4).

Angels have one foot in heaven and another foot in this world. Although we are not usually made aware of their presence, nor are we able to predict if and when they will appear, angels are among us, and God's good and perfect will is to use these powerful creatures to protect, provide, guide, and help God's heirs of salvation. You may have never seen or heard an angel, but one day you will, as we worship and praise the Savior together singing, "Worthy is the Lamb who was slain to receive power and riches and wisdom, and strength and honor and glory and blessing!" (Revelation 5:11–12).

"Our God whom we serve is able to deliver us from the burning fiery furnace. . . . But if not, let it be known to you, O king, that we do not serve your gods, nor will we worship the gold image which you have set up."
(Daniel 3:17–18)

AUGUST
29

Our God Is Able

GOD IS SOVEREIGN. This basically means that God can do whatever He wants, whenever He wants, and however He wants. God is in complete control, and He reigns over everything and everyone. He is all-powerful, He is all-knowing, and He exists everywhere. Nothing is beyond His knowledge and nothing is outside of His ability to control. Knowing this, we must also keep in mind that God only and always exercises His power and authority according to His holy character. God does what He does because He wills to do everything according to His *good* pleasure. God is never pleased to will or to do anything that is evil or contrary to His goodness. Now, the real test of our understanding of God's sovereignty lies in our willingness to trust in God, no matter the outcome.

Shadrach, Meshach, and Abed-Nego (formerly named Hananiah, Mishael, and Azariah) were about to have their understanding of God's sovereignty put to the ultimate test. One day, King Nebuchadnezzar of Babylon set up a golden statue of himself and commanded everyone in his kingdom to bow down before the statue in worship. The punishment for disobeying the king's order was death. Needless to say, everyone in the land fell down before the image in worship. Everyone, that is, except for Shadrach, Meshach, and Abed-Nego. Nebuchadnezzar had them immediately brought into his presence and gave them one last chance to bow down or die. They still refused to bow to his image, and told the king that their God was able to deliver them from death. But even if God chose not to spare them, they still would never give their worship to anyone other than God.

These three young men understood that God was in complete control over their lives. God was sovereign over their situation. They knew that just because God was able to save them did not mean that God would save them. They knew that God might say no to their request for deliverance, but that would not change or negatively affect their willingness to stand for God and even die if necessary. They understood that some prayers are answered with a yes, and others are answered with a no. They knew that some people die young, and others live long lives, that some people are delivered from suffering, and others are not. They also knew that no matter what, God was in control. They truly understood the sovereignty of God, which allowed them to leave the outcome in His hands.

Every day, we are faced with the test of whether we are going to trust God or not. Granted, the test is not a matter of life and death every day, but God wants us to trust Him, no matter the outcome. Are we willing to serve God, even if we are not delivered? Will we continue to trust Him, even if we are not healed? Is God sovereign? Yes. He always has been and always will be. Does God always deliver us from our difficulties? No. But God is always able.

> *Exhort one another daily, while it is called "Today," lest any of you be hardened through the deceitfulness of sin.*
> (Hebrews 3:13)

The Art of Exhorting

WE ALL NEED EACH OTHER. No Christian is an island unto himself or herself. Going to church, blending in, and leaving virtually unnoticed is easy. You can plan to arrive at church right as the worship music begins to play and leave as soon as the final amen is spoken, all the while never involving yourself in any meaningful relationships with other Christians.

Now, what I am talking about is more than just staying after the church service to socialize. This is more than grabbing a doughnut and coffee and sharing pleasantries while the kids run around as though this is the first time they have been allowed to play with other children in weeks. As fine and enjoyable as all this may be, God actually wants us to invest in the lives of those whom we go to church with.

The writer of Hebrews (authorship unknown) has been warning about the dangers of turning away from God. This chapter reminds us of how God delivered the Israelites from the bondage of Egypt and brought them to the edge of the Promised Land. But because the people went backward in unbelief instead of moving forward by faith, they missed out on the blessing of experiencing God's rest. Therefore, they died in the wilderness. After warning the readers that they were in danger of abandoning their faith like the first-generation Israelites who were delivered from Egypt, the author of Hebrews began to explain how to avoid making a similar mistake.

One way to protect against turning away from God or hardening your heart toward the things of God is to work together as a real community of believers and regularly invest in one another's lives. Think of how different the experience of the Israelites might have been if, instead of grumbling and complaining in the wilderness, they encouraged one another and cheered one another on toward the finish line of faith. Never underestimate the importance and influence that exhortation or encouragement can have on a person's faith.

Part of the responsibility we have as a community of faith is to *exhort one another daily*, having a daily, dogged determination to encourage other believers in their faith, as well as a willingness to allow other believers to encourage us in our faith. We must exhort and cheer each other on as we move toward the finish line. When we do this, we help each other to resist sin, to persevere in times of trouble, to continue in good works, and to remain hopeful, faithful, and joyful in all things as we keep our eyes on Jesus. Constant encouragement is necessary because our faith is always under attack.

We need each other like Moses needed Aaron and Hur to help hold up his arms, we need each other like David needed Nathan to rebuke him, and we need each other like the paralytic needed his friends to carry him to Jesus to be healed. If we are going to be all that God wants us to be, then we will need each other's help to get where we are going. True exhorting is nothing more than the art of coming alongside someone and helping him or her along the way.

"I see four men loose, walking in the midst of the fire; and they are not hurt, and the form of the fourth is like the Son of God." (Daniel 3:25)

AUGUST

31

Fireproofing Your Faith

ONE MINUTE everything can be going just fine, and the next minute your life is in turmoil. Trials come in all shapes and sizes and with varying degrees of intensity. Whether the trials are physical, emotional, or relational, no one is immune. With testing comes the question, *What does God want to show me in this situation?*

The trumpet sounded, and the music began to play. The appointed time had arrived. The royal decree ordered everyone in the land to fall down and worship the ninety-foot golden statue of King Nebuchadnezzar, and whoever refused would be thrown into a flaming furnace. Shadrach, Meshach, and Abed-Nego were young Jewish men who served the king faithfully but worshiped God exclusively. They refused to bow down and worship any idol and courageously were willing to die for their faith. Outraged at their defiance, the king ordered that the furnace be heated seven times hotter than normal. The furnace was so hot that the raging fire consumed the men who threw Shadrach, Meshach, and Abed-Nego into the furnace. One minute, these young men were blessed to have the king's favor, and the next they were on the receiving end of his wrath as they were tossed into the fire. But as the king watched, he saw not three, but four, men in the furnace, and they were all unbound and walking around.

Sometimes God chooses to intervene and spare people from going through a trial, and at other times, God allows the trial. But even if God does not deliver you from the heat of a trial, He always will be with you through that trial. God is there to provide a personal and intimate fellowship that often can be experienced only in the fiery trials of life. God told Joshua, "Be strong and of good courage; do not be afraid, nor be dismayed, for the LORD your God is with you wherever you go" (Joshua 1:9).

A point to keep in mind is the fact that Shadrach, Meshach, and Abed-Nego were bound when they were thrown into the fire, but the only things that burned were their constraints. Nothing else was consumed. They not only experienced intimate fellowship with God in the fire, but also found freedom from bondage in the fire. When you go through a trial, do not be surprised if God uses the heat of your trial to burn away anything that might be keeping you in bondage or holding you back from a more intimate relationship with God. The enemy wants to bind us in sin, but God wants to set us free from sin. Jesus said, "Therefore, if the Son makes you free, you shall be free indeed" (John 8:36).

When we consider the trials that God allows us to go through, we must remember a few things, according to Andrew Murray:

First, He brought me here, it is by His will I am in this strait place: in that fact I will rest. Next, He will keep me here in His love, and give me grace to behave as His child. Then, He will make the trial a blessing, teaching me the lessons He intends me to learn, and working in me the grace He means to bestow. Last, In His good time He can bring me out again—how and when [only] He knows.[56]

Every trial is by God's choice, under His charge, part of His preparation, and for His appointed period of time. Remember these truths, and you will help to fireproof your faith.

September

Entering God's Rest

SAINT AUGUSTINE prayed, "Lord, . . . Thou hast made us for Thyself, and our hearts are restless till they rest in Thee."[57] Set aside for the Jewish people was the Sabbath day, a day in which they were to worship the Lord and rest from their work. But the Sabbath day was more than the blessing of a day off; this day was also pointing to something even greater still to come. The "rest" the Sabbath pointed to was a rest found in a relationship with God, in which His people realize they must not work to earn God's approval, but instead find rest in Christ.

In Hebrews, we are reminded of how the Israelites who died in the wilderness did not enter the rest God had provided for them in the Promised Land. They did not enter that rest because they did not believe the promise of God, and their unbelief kept them from enjoying God's rest (see Hebrews 3:19). They did not believe that God would do what He promised He would do for them, and you cannot enter God's rest if you do not believe God or trust in the promise and provision He has made for that rest.

When God completed His work of creation, He rested. God rested not because He was tired or needed a break; He rested because His work was finished. In the same way, people do not need to work for salvation because the work of salvation is finished in Christ. To enter God's rest means to be at peace with God. Entrance into God's rest means to be free from sin because sin has been forgiven. God's rest is perfect, peaceful, sweet, and satisfying, and God offers this rest to every person through a relationship with Christ.

Now, the whole point of God's rest is so that we hold firmly with security to our faith in Christ. Hebrews 4:14 tells us, "So then, since we have a great High Priest who has entered heaven, Jesus the Son of God, let us hold firmly to what we believe" (NLT). This is the entire point of the book of Hebrews. In Christ, God has made a new covenant with man, a greater covenant, which proclaims the superiority of Jesus Christ to everything that has come before. Once we enter the rest of a relationship with Christ, one more rest that God promised awaits us.

Being at peace with God through a relationship with Jesus Christ, we now look forward to our future and final rest that God offers, which is our heavenly rest. This rest that awaits us is even greater than the rest that we now possess in Christ because that rest will provide us with a freedom from all suffering and sorrow, from all sin and Satan. Temptation will be vanquished and nothing will be able to defile us. We will dwell in the immediate presence of God, where we will no longer see in part, but we will behold fully as we see God face-to-face. The glory of God will be our delight, and in Him, we will experience eternal and immeasurable joy. Our worship and rest today is only a foretaste of the rest and worship yet to come. Do not let unbelief keep you from entering God's promised rest; just believe, and you will receive.

Then this Daniel distinguished himself above the governors and satraps, because an excellent spirit was in him.
(Daniel 6:3)

SEPTEMBER

2

A Devoted Life

OUR DEVOTION TO GOD is an expression of our love for God. The more you love something, the more devoted you will become to that which you love. But devotion does not come easy. Devotion takes courage and commitment, patience and perseverance. Devotion also means choosing to do what is right, even when what is right is inconvenient. No one knew this better than Daniel, and from Daniel, we get a glimpse into what a devoted life looks like, and thereby and learn how we, too, can live a devoted life for God.

Daniel had a proven history of commitment and consecration to God that began in his teenage years, when he was first taken captive to Babylon. Now, over seventy years later, there is a new sheriff in town, well, actually a new king on the throne, and Daniel would demonstrate that his devotion to God had not weakened over time. If anything, Daniel was more devoted to God then, in his nineties, than he had been in his teenage years. When Darius took over as king after Belshazzar died (see Daniel 5:30–31), he appointed Daniel to his cabinet and relied on his wise and discerning counsel. Daniel was a man of integrity, and with no spot on his record, no skeleton in his closet, and no secret sins that his enemies could accuse him of. In fact, the only "fault" Daniel's enemies could find with him was that he was *too* devoted to God (see Daniel 6:5). How amazing is that? When others look at our lives, they should find no fault, no spot, and no secret sin. Imagine how great we would feel if the only indictment someone could make against us is that we are *too* devoted to God!

How was Daniel able to live such a devoted life? Two characteristics stand out about Daniel that best highlight his devotion. First, he was faithful in his actions (see Daniel 6:4), and second, he was fervent in his prayers (see verse 10). Faithfulness is simply doing whatever God puts before you to do. Faithfulness is hanging in there until the work is done, consistently allowing God to work in your life and through your life. Faithfulness is doing what is right, not just once, but time and time again, year after year, all for the glory of God.

The fuel for a person's faithfulness is fervency in prayer. Fervency speaks to our level of intensity, passion, and dedication to persistently bring everything to God. Nothing is too big for God to handle, and nothing is too small for Him to take interest in. Times may come when we are tempted to let our passion in prayer fade, or we may be tempted to give up and throw in the prayer towel, but fervent prayer requires an intense commitment to put in the time on our knees before God. Halfhearted prayer has no room in fervent prayer, and you will find no spiritual shortcuts. If you want to live a life that is devoted to God, the place to start is to be faithful in your actions and fervent in your prayer life.

Can your coworkers, friends, family, and even your enemies, charge you with being *too* devoted to God? Is your character above accusation? Remember, your devotion to God is a reflection of your love for Him. So, just how devoted are you?

You have been believers so long now that you ought to be teaching others. Instead, you need someone to teach you again the basic things about God's word.
(Hebrews 5:12 NLT)

SEPTEMBER

3

Growing Pains

HAVE YOU EVER TASTED baby food as an adult? You know, the crushed carrots, smashed sweet potatoes, and pureed peas? To an adult, baby food is not very appetizing, but for a baby with no teeth, this food is not only delicious, but also necessary nourishment. The time will come, however, when every baby moves on from a soft-food diet to one that includes solid foods. What would you think if you saw a teenager in the school cafeteria still drinking formula from a bottle, or a construction worker pulling some Gerber's baby food out of his lunch bag?

In the same way, the time will come when every believer needs to move past spiritual baby food and start taking in solid spiritual food. Otherwise, you are in danger of remaining a spiritual toddler.

By the time the author of Hebrews wrote this letter, his audience was in bad shape. They were having a hard time understanding some spiritual teachings they should have learned long ago. They were becoming spiritually lazy and undisciplined, and therefore, they struggled with some of the elementary principles of the Christian faith. Many of the believers should have grown enough to be teaching others, but instead they needed to be taught the basics of the faith all over again. In essence, they returned to baby food when they should have been eating solid food. Time had come for them to grow up and start acting their spiritual age.

In the same way, how can we make sure that we are not going back to spiritual preschool when we should be moving forward in the school of life? The answer is simple: we must remain disciplined and not become lazy when spending time with God in the Bible and in prayer. The fatal flaw for the recipients of this letter was their lackluster enthusiasm for spiritual truth. The Bible says they were "dull of hearing" (Hebrews 5:11), which means they allowed disinterest to creep into their spiritual life, the result of which was backsliding. Instead of making excuses, we must open our Bibles, and instead of choosing to stay home, we must make an effort to connect with the church, whether by going to a Bible study, a prayer meeting, or a small group gathering. Make steps that help your faith, not hinder it.

Next, share with others (see verse 12). Not everyone is called to be a Bible teacher, but we are all called to be sharers of what God is teaching us. Helping others to grow in their faith is a sign that we are growing in ours. Also important is making sure that you are eating a well-balanced spiritual diet (see verses 13–14). If you are a new believer, then spiritual milk is good. Learning the fundamentals of what Jesus *has done* is important. But if you have already learned those truths, then maybe time has come for you to seek out some spiritual meat to chew on and to begin learning what Jesus *is doing* today.

Lastly, we must be applying the truths we are learning by putting the truth we learn into action daily. We will then not only grow spiritually, but also gain spiritual discernment. Spiritual discernment is the ability to distinguish what is good and evil (see verse 14).

The author of Hebrews begs us to press on to maturity (Hebrews 6:1). Pressing on to maturity is God's answer for the problem of remaining a spiritual toddler. May God help us to grow up in Christ.

> *"Know therefore and understand, that from the going forth of the command to restore and build Jerusalem until Messiah the Prince, there shall be seven weeks and sixty-two weeks."* (Daniel 9:25)

SEPTEMBER
4

Prophecy and God's People

WHY IS PROPHECY SO IMPORTANT? Christians are frequently called upon to explain and even defend why they believe the Bible is true, and prophecy is one of the strongest evidences that the Bible is the divinely inspired Word of God. One of the most powerful prophecies in all of Scripture is found in the book of Daniel. Some have called this prophecy the "backbone of prophecy." Others have gone so far as to say that the key to understanding all prophetic interpretation lies within this prophecy. Regardless, one thing is certain: this prophecy is important! This prophecy pinpoints the exact day in history when the Messiah would present Himself to the world, and does so hundreds of years ahead of time.

Daniel was reading the prophet Jeremiah when he was moved to pray for his people. Daniel asked God to forgive them of their sins, to cleanse them of their unrighteousness, and to bring restoration to Jerusalem. As Daniel was praying, the angel Gabriel appeared and told him about God's future plans for the Jews. Gabriel told Daniel that God's plan would be carried out within a seventy-week period of time (see Daniel 9:24), which meant there would be seventy, seven-year periods of time, or 490 years. After the 490 years, God's purposes for Israel would be complete. At the end of sixty-nine weeks, or 483 years (see verse 25), Israel's sin would be paid for because Jesus Christ would pay the penalty for sin.

This prophecy is so amazing because the details reveal the exact day in which Jesus would enter Jerusalem, declaring Himself to be the Messiah. The prophecy says that the Messiah would come sixty-nine weeks, or 173,880 days (based on the Jewish calendar), after the command was given to restore and rebuild Jerusalem. That command went out when Artaxerxes told Nehemiah to go and rebuild Jerusalem in 445 BC (see Nehemiah 2; Ezra 7:12–13). This began the clock on the 69 weeks. Exactly 173,880 days after that decree, on Palm Sunday, Jesus entered the city of Jerusalem on a donkey, declaring to the world that He was the Messiah (see Matthew 21:4–9). *Amazing!* God's timing is perfect. He is never late but always exactly on time. And just in case you are counting and wondering what happens with the last week in Daniel's prophecy, that is reserved for the book of Revelation and the end times.

These prophecies (and the many others found in the Bible) should convince us of the reliability and authority of the Bible. The Bible is always accurate and entirely reliable. Knowing the Bible can be trusted should strengthen your faith, and should help lead others to faith. Knowing that the Bible can be trusted should give us boldness to declare the truth about God and the truth about mankind's need to have a personal relationship with God through Jesus Christ. Prophecy is not only amazingly fascinating, but impactful to a life-changing degree. Prophecy helps us to view the present in light of God's past faithfulness to His Word, and gives us hope in the future; knowing that what God has said about what is yet to come will surely come to pass.

Abraham gave a tenth part of all. (Hebrews 7:2)

The Ten Percent Plan

SEPTEMBER

5

JOHN PIPER has said "every spending decision is a spiritual decision." Financially, times may be tight for you. You may be feeling fiscally strapped and left scraping the bottom of the money barrel in order to get by. And, as you look at your bank account, writing a check to your church may be the last "expense" you want to meet or that you feel you are able to afford right now. So, you go to church empty handed. Before the pastor steps up to deliver the sermon, you hear the announcement, "And now we will receive this morning's tithes and offerings," and as the collection plate passes you by, you are left wondering what the right thing is to do concerning tithing. You may even be left wondering what a tithe is and whether tithing is something you are really required to do.

We have all heard the word *tithe*, but what does tithing mean? A tithe is a tenth, and tithing means giving one-tenth of what we earn to God. The first time we see someone giving a tithe, or a tenth, is in Genesis 14:20 when Abraham gives a tithe to Melchizedek. Hebrews 7 gives us a brief description of the priesthood of Melchizedek; we see that Melchizedek resembles Jesus Christ because he is a king of righteousness and a king who has neither beginning nor end (see verses 1–3). Abraham recognized Melchizedek as a deserving and faithful priest of God and, therefore, gave him a tithe from the best of the spoils he gained from a recent military victory. He gave freely, and he gave generously. He did not give God his leftovers, but he gave God the best of what he had, and he gave to God first.

God has given us directions for how we should give back to Him (see Leviticus 27:30; Deuteronomy 14:22–23). And the Bible clearly teaches that we should give God a tithe, or ten percent, of what we earn (see Malachi 3:8–12). This is not because God needs our money. Tithing was not created for God's benefit, but was created for our benefit. Tithing was created to teach us how to keep God first in our lives. Tithing shows that we are grateful to God for all He has done and all the ways He has provided for us up to this point in our lives.

Tithing shows that we trust in God to provide for our future as we give to Him in the present. And tithing shows we are committed to join in the work that God is doing in the world today.

Keep a few other things in mind when approaching tithing. First, do not wait until you have paid all your bills before tithing. God's people are called to give the first and best of what they have (see Proverbs 3:9–10), so write your check to God first before using your income for anything else. Do not worry; God will take care of you. He promises (see Malachi 3:10).

Next, give to your local church before you give to any other organization or ministry. The local church is God's primary means of accomplishing His work in the world today, and this is the place where you are fed spiritually. Therefore, give there first.

Lastly, give willingly, and give generously. If you cannot give with the right attitude, keep praying and wait until you can give joyfully (see 2 Corinthians 9:6–7). Remember, God is more concerned about the attitude of your heart in giving than about the amount you are giving. But the best place to start is with a ten percent plan.

Those who lead many to righteousness will shine like the stars forever. (Daniel 12:3 NLT)

Shining Stars

SEPTEMBER

6

THE APOSTLE PAUL was certainly one of the greatest evangelists in the Bible. And while not everyone has the gift of evangelism like he had, we are all expected to participate in evangelism. The hardest part of personal evangelism for most people is simply getting started. The moment comes upon you when you decide to engage a person in a conversation about Jesus, and you begin to notice that your heart is beating a little faster, your palms are getting a little sweaty, and you feel as though you just stepped onto a ledge without a safety harness. But sharing your faith with others, however intimidating, is an act of obedience and a spiritual discipline we must practice. While certainly easier for some people and harder for others, we are all called to build relationships and share Jesus with others whenever possible.

Evangelism is never easy, but will be especially difficult in the period of time known as the Tribulation, that seven-year period preceding the return of Christ to the earth when the Antichrist will become the world leader and literally, all hell will break loose on earth. Daniel is looking into the future and writing about events that will take place during this time, which is certain to be the darkest and most difficult period in all of human history. However, during that time God will have people who, through their wise actions, will shine bright like the stars in heaven as they point others to God and encourage them to walk in the way of righteousness that leads to everlasting life. Daniel reminds us of the importance of evangelism in a world that rejects God. No matter how dark the days are or will be, we should remember that often, when things are the darkest, the light of God shines the brightest.

Now, evangelism is not carrying a sign that says, "Repent or Die!" or "Turn or

Burn!" Evangelism is also not passing out fake $100 bills with the gospel printed on the back, or standing on a street corner, shouting through a megaphone at people. First, evangelism is a way of life. Second, it is a decision to share Christ with others. Can you use tracts, hand out flyers, carry a sign, or stand on the street corner, sharing the gospel with passersby? Yes, of course you can. You may even have some success with this approach. But as we look to the Bible, we see that the greatest evangelists are those who lived a *life* of evangelism, those individuals who pointed others to God by their words and also by their actions.

Getting into arguments, using gimmicks, or oversimplifying the gospel only frustrates people who are in desperate need of the truth. If some tract or tactic helps you break the ice in a conversation, then by all means, use that. But be flexible and allow the Holy Spirit to lead you from there. Seek to build a bridge, not burn one, with the people you talk to. The best way to do that is to ask them some questions about themselves and what they believe.

To be part of the work God is doing in someone's heart is a privilege. And, as we share Christ with others, we, too, are like shining stars to God.

It is appointed for men to die once, but after this the judgment. (Hebrews 9:27)

SEPTEMBER 7

Countdown to Judgment Day

PLEASE DO NOT let the next sentence burst your bubble or ruin your day. We all have an appointment with death. Every day that goes by brings us one step closer to that inevitable appointment, written in God's divine date book. But what happens after that? What happens after we breathe our last breath, after our hearts pump their last measure of blood, and after our spirits leave our bodies like a vapor? After leaving this physical world, we will enter into a new spiritual world where there is a second, unavoidable appointment written down in God's date book. Each person is scheduled to stand before the judgment seat of God. Now, that may sound ominous and intimidating, but you should know a few things before your judgment day appointment.

Our God is a God of mercy and grace, but He is also a God of judgment. After we die, no second chances will be given. No one gets a do-over in life. The decisions we make on this side of eternity will determine the judgment God makes about our eternal destiny. You see, God has established a holy law, or a standard of perfection. To break God's law is to sin against God, and to sin against God means that you must face judgment. The problem is that we have all broken God's law. Therefore, we all must stand before God to be judged (see Romans 14:10).

Not surprisingly, we all have broken God's law. A simple look at the world today provides enough evidence that mankind has some major problems. This problem of sin is a worldwide, past, present, and future epidemic that includes every person who has ever lived and will ever live (see Romans 3:23). The only way to escape the judgment of God is to trust in the provision that He has made, a provision found in Jesus. As John Piper wrote,

Faith in Christ as our righteousness will be our only hope for acceptance with God (Romans 1:16–17; 3:20–26). This is the essence and heart of the gospel. Christ lived for us, Christ died for us, Christ rose for us, Christ reigns for us, Christ intercedes for us, Christ will come for us, and Christ our advocate will be our final judge. Faith in him is key to assurance and life.[58]

If you want to escape the judgment of God, then you must put your trust in Jesus, because without Jesus, we would have no hope on that day of judgment. As one commentator wrote, "To refuse the cross as the instrument of salvation is to choose it as the instrument of judgment."[59]

God's Word clearly teaches that all people—whether saved or not—will stand before God one day to be judged. Since no one is guaranteed tomorrow, the best way to be prepared for the judgment is to live for God today. For some, that means receiving Jesus today, asking Him to forgive them of their sins, and giving Him control of their lives. For others, preparing for judgment means reprioritizing. If you have let other things take precedence in your life, then today is the day to make Jesus your number one priority. Finally, for others, preparing for judgment means renewing their commitment to live a godly life and to serve God faithfully with the time they have left.

Time waits for no one. The clock is ticking, and we are all drawing nearer to that unavoidable appointment with God. The question is, are you ready?

The Lord said to Hosea: "Go, take yourself a wife of harlotry and children of harlotry, for the land has committed great harlotry by departing from the Lord." (Hosea 1:2)

SEPTEMBER

8

The Prodigal Wife

TRADITIONAL LOVE STORIES often sound like this: boy meets girl, boy falls in love with girl, boy and girl get married, boy and girl live happily ever after. That sounds like a beautiful story, right? Unfortunately, this is not the story of Hosea and his wife Gomer (and yes, Gomer was a female). Their story went something like this: boy meets girl, boy falls in love with girl, girl turns out to be a prostitute, boy still marries girl, girl leaves boy for other boys, boy still loves girl, boy buys girl back from a slave market, boy and girl, a little worse for wear, now live happily ever after. But wait, that is not all. This story is more than just a plot for an after-school TV special. An important message from God is just beneath the surface.

Hosea was a prophet during the divided kingdom years of Israel's history. He was the last prophet before the northern kingdom was conquered by Assyria, around 722 BC, and God had a distinct and demanding mission for this prophet. Hosea's mission from God, should he choose to accept it, went like this: "Hosea, I want you to marry a woman who is going to be unfaithful to you, but you are to remain faithful to her. You will love her, but she will be an embarrassment to you. Your marriage, however, is symbolic, and I am going to use your story to teach my people a lesson. In this marriage you will represent

Me, God, and Gomer is going to represent My people, Israel. She will run away and be unfaithful, just as My people have run from me and have been unfaithful to Me. But you are to remain faithful to her because I remain faithful to Israel."

You can almost hear Hosea's response. *Really? That's one monster request, God!*

But Hosea obeyed God, even though doing so was difficult.

The lesson for us is when we as Christians turn away from God and pursue principles and practices that are unworthy and unbecoming of God, we commit the same sort of "harlotries" that Israel committed against the Lord. When we sin and we turn our backs on God, we are being unfaithful to God, and God has the right to let us go our own way. But He does not let us go. He pursues us. And He is faithful, even when we are not.

You may have closed the door on God, but He still stands at the door and knocks. You may have run from God, but no mountain will keep him from climbing to rescue a lost and wayward sheep. No place you can go is too far for God to reach you. No sin is too severe that God cannot forgive you. God wants to not only show you the depths of His love, but He wants to demonstrate the type of love we are to show others.

The story of Hosea and Gomer is definitely not your average love story, but what an amazing, true story and living illustration of God's love toward His people. He has loved us not because we were pure and holy. Rather, He loved us fully knowing that we were the very opposite and took us into a covenant relationship with Himself nonetheless. He did so not because we were good, but to make us good. He also did so not because we were faithful, but to teach us how to be faithful.

By faith we understand that the worlds were framed by the word of God, so that the things which are seen were not made of things which are visible. (Hebrews 11:3)

SEPTEMBER 9

The Creation Concept

IMAGINE A BEAUTIFUL SUMMER DAY. The sun is brightly and gently warming the earth. A light breeze brings a freshness and coolness to the air. The blue sky reveals the great expanse of space by day, and twinkling stars point to distant galaxies by night. Gravity keeps you standing on the green grass, with feet firmly planted, in spite of the amazing speed at which we are both turning and traveling through space. A delicate balance of environmental cycles work together to ensure that life operates continuously, harmoniously, and efficiently.

You are one person, on one planet, in one solar system, out of one galaxy, from one universe. All of these combined make up an entire cosmos, all formed, fashioned, and perfectly framed from the spoken word of God. Out of nothing came everything, from the immaterial came the material, and emptiness yielded fullness as God, in His diversity, creativity, and authority, brought forth creation. By faith, we understand this to be true!

Science and philosophy only offer theories devoid of substantiation for their account of cosmological origins; therefore, man's speculation must succumb to divine revelation. Facts must be accepted by faith, only because no one was present to witness the creation event, with the exception of God Himself. So, we rely on the divine revelation of God's Holy Word, His Word that has been found tried and true and therefore allows us to have faith in the creation account. No sum of scientific investigation and no amount of philosophical pontification ever will be able to arrive at a confirmed cause of creation other than the fact that God created the heavens and the earth. As John MacArthur has said,

> The Christian insists that all truth is God's truth. Some of it—the natural world—is discoverable with our eyes, ears, touch, and intellect. A great deal more of it, however, is not. It is apprehended only by faith, for which the Christian should make no apology. The very attempt to explain the universe, or our own being and nature, apart from God is a fool's effort. These things we understand only by faith in the revealed Word of Scripture.[60]

From start to finish, faith is the foundation of the Bible, because without *faith* it is impossible to please God (see Hebrews 11:6), by grace we are saved through *faith* (see Ephesians 2:8), we live by *faith* (see Galatians 2:20), we stand by *faith* (see 2 Corinthians 1:24), and we walk by *faith* (see 2 Corinthians 5:7).

Understanding that God is the Creator of all things is fundamental to knowing God, knowing yourself, and knowing our relationship to one another. Creation shouts Creator, and design demands Designer. Order does not come from chaos, and faith understands that behind everything visible is the invisible God.

Then the Lord said to me, "Go and love your wife again, even though she commits adultery with another lover. This will illustrate that the Lord still loves Israel, even though the people have turned to other gods and love to worship them. (Hosea 3:1 NLT)

SEPTEMBER 10

Marriage Advice

A STRONG MARRIAGE is the result of investing, and a weak marriage is the result of neglecting. Marriage is a wonderful blessing, but every marriage will go through some hard times. Difficulties, disputes, disappointments, bitterness, frustrations, financial stress, lack of intimacy, and resentment all can send any marriage into a relational tailspin. If you are not careful and prayerful, your marriage will deteriorate, because relationships are either gaining strength or losing speed. If your marriage has fallen on hard times, there is hope. If your spouse seems distant and disinterested, you can regain intimacy. If you are one step away from separation, you can reconcile. Or if things just seem a little out of balance, you can regain stability.

Not only does Hosea provide us with an example of God's love to a people who have rebelled against that love, he shows us what forgiveness and unconditional love look like in a close relationship like marriage. Hosea married an adulterous wife named Gomer who practiced unfaithfulness as a lifestyle.

Eventually she left the prophet and their three children to live with other men. Hosea could have divorced his wife, but despite his pain and personal heartache, he continued to love her.

In the same way, God has called His people to a lifelong commitment and relationship with Him, a marriage of sorts. As believers, we are to be totally faithful to God and not waver in our allegiance to Him. And although God used Hosea's marriage as a representation of His love for His people, some positive and practical marital help is found in the way Hosea loved his wife.

Doing what is easy in the moment may not always be the best thing for your marriage in the long run. Hosea could have chosen the easy way out and called it quits when his wife left him, but he did not. He chose to keep on loving her, even when she was unloving in return. The kind of love displayed by Hosea toward his wife is the same sort of love God displays toward His people. His is a forgiving love, a selfless love, and a steadfast love. It is a love that is unconditional and unwavering. "For better or worse" are not just words we say to describe romantic sentimentality; they are to be a defining characteristic found at the core of biblical and marital love.

Quite simply, you are to love your spouse the way God has loved you. That means when you sin, God shows you forgiveness, so you must extend forgiveness to your spouse. When you are unfaithful, God in His love remains ever faithful toward you, so you must display a love that is faithful, even when your spouse may be unfaithful to you in promise, word, or deed. You must have a love that chooses to go to your spouse and not wait for your spouse to come to you. Your love must seek reconciliation, even when you are not at fault, just as God in His love for you sent reconciliation by sending His Son.

The unconditional love you are to demonstrate to your spouse does not keep you free from hurts or hardships, and loving actions are distinct from loving feelings. But choosing to love always will strengthen a marriage.

Let us lay aside every weight, and the sin which so easily ensnares us, and let us run with endurance the race that is set before us. (Hebrews 12:1)

SEPTEMBER 11

The Amazing Race

NO ONE RUNS IN A MARATHON wearing heavy clothing or added weights, and no Christian can run the race of faith successfully if he or she allows spiritual weights to slow them down. Just picture how strange would it be if, at the starting line of a marathon dressed in nylon shorts, a tank top, and running shoes, you saw standing next to you someone wearing jeans, a winter coat, and work boots! How strange we must look to God when He sees us trying to run the race of faith weighed down with hindrances and slowed by sin. Take a moment to consider if anything is hindering your faith. Is any sin slowing you down as you attempt to run the race that God has set before you?

The Bible uses many different metaphors to describe our life in Christ. The apostle Paul says we are slaves (see Romans 6:22), soldiers (see 2 Timothy 2:3), and farmers (see 2 Timothy 2:6), and here in today's verse, the author of Hebrews says we are runners in a long-distance race. In other words, the life of faith is a marathon, and every marathon requires that we run with discipline and diligence if we want to cross the finish line. Since God saves us, God also starts us in this race, and God sets our course. We are all here for a reason: to live a life that both glorifies God and accomplishes His will. This requires not only faith in God but also perseverance and endurance.

In order to run our race well, we should follow some practical advice to ensure that we finish strong.

First, running the race of faith requires that we run free of any extra weight. Now, a weight is not necessarily sin. More specifically, a weight is anything that does not help you move forward. For the Christian, a weight may be an attitude or an action, materialism or ambition, or may be a hobby or even certain friendships. Your weight might be watching too much television or spending all your free time enjoying a recreational activity. Anything that does not help you move forward in your faith has the potential to weigh you down.

In addition to the hindrances that weigh you down, sin has the potential to slow you down and even disqualify you from the race (see 1 Corinthians 9:27). Certainly, all sin will slow you down, but in today's verse is an indication of a sin that easily ensnares us. Based on the previous chapter in Hebrews, if one sin is above all others that hinders us in our faith, that sin would be unbelief. Unbelief is where you doubt God, distrust God, or deviate from His path, plan, and purpose for your life. All disobedience stems from unbelief.

If you have grown weary running the race of faith, then maybe you are trying to run with added weight that slows you down. If so, then cast off some of those hindrances that weigh you down and drain all your spiritual energy. Maybe sin has caused you to stumble, and other runners are passing you by. Rejoin the race by casting off the sin that has ensnared you, and get back in this amazing race of faith.

"For I desire mercy and not sacrifice, and the knowledge of God more than burnt offerings." (Hosea 6:6)

SEPTEMBER

12

How Well Do You Know God?

WE LIVE IN AN ERA that has been labeled "the information age" where, within minutes—and often even seconds—you can have information delivered to your fingertips. Yet, despite the rapid speed and wide-ranging variety of information that is readily available, many people are still uninformed about God. They do not know who He is, what He is like, why they were created, or what He expects from them. This problem is not new. The apostle Paul spoke of people who were "always learning and never able to come to the knowledge of the truth" (2 Timothy 3:7). Also, in the book of Hosea, we see the children of Israel struggling with knowing how to truly know God. As Christians, we can go through life believing that we know God. After all, we go to church, we read Christian books, we listen to Christian music, and we have emotional experiences with God. But do we really know God?

The children of Israel thought they knew God, but they allowed rote ritual to take the place of a real relationship with God. The significance of today's verse in Hosea, a verse that Jesus Himself quoted (see Matthew 9:13), is not that God was refusing the sacrificial system or burnt offerings that had been an integral part of their religion. God wanted more from His people than merely formal observances or lifeless religious activity; He wanted their worship and their service to come out of a genuine love for Him, and a sincere love for others. The people focused on ceremony, when God was looking for communion, they focused on tradition, when God wanted inward transformation, and they focused on an institutionalized religiosity, when God wanted intimate relationship.

Because sacrifice was an important and essential part of Old Testament worship, this instruction from God must have sounded outlandish to the people. This is the equivalent of God telling Christians today, "I desire mercy, not going to church, and the knowledge of God more than serving in ministry." Now that sounds drastic! This statement sounds so radical to us because going to church and serving God are important and essential parts of our worship. But the emphasis for the children of Israel and for Christians today is the same. Going to church and serving God are important, *but* if we are simply going through the religious motions, while lacking real love, devotion, or knowledge of who God is, then our religious activity is meaningless, and we do not really *know* God. Outward appearance does not necessarily indicate an inward commitment to God.

Does God want our service and sacrifice? Yes! But He also requires that these cannot be done out of some legalistic sense of duty. Our service needs to stem from compassion, kindness, and a consideration for others, and our sacrifice must come from a personal, intimate, and internalized relationship with God that comes from a devotion to His Word.

God said, "For the LORD does not see as man sees; for man looks at the outward appearance, but the LORD looks at the heart" (1 Samuel 16:7). God must have our hearts if our service is to count for anything. Religious activity apart from a personal relationship with God is worthless. If you want to offer the sacrifice of service to God, you must begin with knowing Him personally.

"For whom the Lord loves He chastens." (Hebrews 12:6)

Loving Correction

GOD LOVES US even during times when we may feel like He doesn't. One instance when we are tempted to think that God does not love us is during the difficulty associated with His loving correction. Godly discipline never feels very loving while we are experiencing it, but because God does in fact loves us, sometimes the best way to bring about the needed change in our lives is through discipline. Even though God's motive for His correction is love, and His desire is to bring about sanctification in our lives through discipline, we do not always receive discipline with that in mind. Most of us would be quick to admit that we want God to bless our lives and to work in us and through us. However, when that process involves correction and discipline, our enthusiasm begins to diminish.

Correction is evidence that God considers us part of His family and is a sign of His love for us. Satan, on the other hand, wants us to believe that correction, discipline, or chastening is a sign that God does not love us. This is nothing more than a lie and an attempt by the enemy to turn our hearts away from God. Satan wants us to believe that God is punishing us, but God does not punish His children, He disciplines them. Punishment is associated with penalty, and Jesus paid our penalty for sin on the cross. When we stray, God uses correction to get us back on track. When we sin, God uses discipline to bring us to repentance and to restore fellowship. God uses discipline to mature us. God's discipline and correction are often experienced through difficulties and trying circumstances as He uses them to develop our faith, deepen our devotion, and cultivate our character. Discipline "yields the peaceable fruit of righteousness to those who have been trained by it" (Hebrews 12:11).

Does this mean that all hardships, difficulties, and trials are God's chastening in our lives? Certainly not! All difficulty is not discipline. All catastrophes are not God's correction. Not every hardship or trial we face is the result of sin or waywardness in our lives. We must avoid the categorical condemnation that someone experiencing hardship in his or her life must be doing so because of sin. Sin and difficulty do go hand in hand sometimes, but difficulty also comes about at times because of righteousness in our lives. We can be sure that, no matter what we are experiencing, God intends to use that experience to teach us, conform us, and mature us in our faith.

We do not like to endure hardship, even though we know God has a good reason for allowing hardship in our lives. But instead of losing heart, recognize that our God is a loving God, and He is looking out for our best interests. Instead of fighting the process or correction, cooperate with God and allow Him to work in and through your circumstances to accomplish His will. Instead of asking God to remove the difficulty, remember that the good result that comes from discipline far outweighs the difficulty we must experience along the way.

"For Israel has forgotten his Maker." (Hosea 8:14)

SEPTEMBER

14

Forgetting God

HAVE YOU EVER HAD TROUBLE remembering where you left something? Or, have you ever seen a familiar face approaching, only to be completely unable to recall a name or place or how you know that person? Having those occasional moments in life when your memory goes completely blank is only natural.

But how about things concerning God? Have you ever had trouble remembering the blessings of God in your life? As much as we might not like to admit, the fact remains: we all have a tendency to forget the goodness of God in our lives. Often, the pressures or challenges we face can cause us to forget how God has provided for us in the past, how He has brought us to where we are today, and how He has promised to always be there for us in the future. Taking the goodness of God for granted can be harmful to our faith, but we can take steps to prevent that from happening.

Israel had forgotten God. They did not forget that God existed, but they had forgotten to keep God in the center of their lives. This led them to worship God on their own terms rather than on God's terms, which is not worship at all. Israel had chosen to forget God by no longer trusting in His ways, and instead they began trusting in their own abilities. They gradually neglected their relationship with God by failing to recall the reality of God's goodness and grace in their lives. They were unable to remember God's abundant protection and ample provision in times *past*, which made serving Him faithfully in the *present* nearly impossible. By relying on their own strength and having faith in their own sufficiency, they forgot that all the blessings they had ever experienced came as a result of God's goodness and grace. In sum, their forgetfulness weakened their faith.

By forgetting God and taking His goodness for granted, we can begin to sow seeds of unbelief in our own hearts, which can lead us to disobedience in our lives. Take, for example, when the children of Israel were delivered out of Egypt. As soon as God miraculously brought them through the Red Sea, they instantly forgot, as though their memories went completely blank. They could not seem to remember all the miracles God had just done for them, so they began grumbling, which led to doubting, which led to disobedience. Forgetfulness weakened their faith.

We can do the same today. When the Lord works in obvious ways, trusting Him in that moment is easy. But, as time goes by, we drift toward self-reliance and away from God-reliance. If we want to make sure that we do not take God for granted and begin forgetting the goodness of God, we must exercise our memories.

One of the easiest ways to keep your memory sharp concerning the goodness of God is to *record* and *review* what God has done in your life. Journaling is the easiest way to do this, and is as simple as writing down how God has answered prayers, how He has led you through difficulty, the lessons that He has taught you, how He has provided, what He has delivered you from, and so on. Then, from time to time, review what you have recorded. That way, when your next trial comes, you will be able to say, "God has brought me through before. He will bring me through again." This will help you keep from forgetting God.

Watch out that no poisonous root of bitterness grows up to trouble you. (Hebrews 12:15 NLT)

SEPTEMBER 15

Uprooting Bitterness

INTO EVERY LIFE a little rain must fall. But whether you will let a little rain ruin your day, or not, is up to you. Into every life a little hurt will come. And whether you will let that hurt turn into bitterness and ruin your peace with others or not, is up to you. If you have ever been wounded or offended by someone, then you have been tempted to cultivate bitterness in the soil of your heart. Bitterness always starts out small, like a seed, but can quickly become a troublesome problem that disrupts relationships and diminishes joyfulness as it takes root and grows like a weed.

The author of Hebrews reminds us that although we may have peace with God, we may not always be at peace with those around us. We must make every effort to pursue peace with all people (see Hebrews 12:14). Unresolved anger and unforgiveness eventually will turn into bitterness and can lead to spiritual bondage. Therefore, we must pull up bitterness from the roots before it begins to grow. The author of Hebrews used this picture from the world of agriculture and compared a person who has abused the grace of God to a bitter root. Such a person causes trouble among God's people by disturbing the peace and poisoning relationships. They are like a weed that, when left unattended, slowly chokes out all surrounding life.

Bitterness can affect you and those around you physically, mentally, spiritually, and emotionally. Bitterness grows just beneath the surface and often begins with thoughts like, *I'll never forget what they did* and *they don't deserve another chance.* As Warren Wiersbe has pointed out,

> If somebody hurts us, either deliberately or unintentionally, and we do not forgive him, then we begin to develop bitterness within, which hardens the heart. We should be tenderhearted and kind, but instead we are hardhearted and bitter. Actually, we are not hurting the person who hurt us; we are only hurting ourselves. Bitterness in the heart makes us treat others the way Satan treats them, when we should treat others the way God has treated us. In His gracious kindness, God has forgiven us, and we should forgive others. We do not forgive for *our* sake . . . or even for *their* sake, but for *Jesus'* sake. Learning how to forgive and forget is one of the secrets of a happy Christian life.[61]

Learning to forgive and forget is also necessary for overcoming bitterness. When we are willing to love, we will be willing to forgive.

If you are struggling with bitterness, pray daily for God to forgive you of harboring feelings of bitterness toward another person and ask God to take away those feelings and replace them with compassion. Forgive the other person of the wrong or hurt they caused you, even if they never come and ask you for forgiveness. If you have truly let go of bitterness, you will begin to see that the harsh emotions you have had toward someone will be replaced by compassion, and you will be able to accept that person, even if he or she never changes. Do not let bitterness grow in the soil of your heart. As soon as you see bitterness sprouting, respond by uprooting bitterness and by extending forgiveness and grace.

Break up your fallow ground, for it is time to seek the Lord.
(Hosea 10:12)

SEPTEMBER

16

Field of Weeds

DO YOU FEEL A LITTLE STAGNANT and in need of some spiritual revitalization? Are you ready for God to do a fresh work in your life? Then maybe time has come to break up the fallow ground in your life. Now, perhaps all that does is lead you to ask the question, "What in the world is fallow ground, and why am I breaking it?" Traditionally, farmland was allowed to lie fallow or uncultivated for a period of time to allow the soil to replenish important nutrients so that the soil might become more fruitful for future crops. But during this period of rest, the land would soon become overgrown with thorns and weeds. The farmer then needed to carefully break up the fallow ground in order to clear the field of weeds and prepare to plant for a new harvest. The expression *break up your fallow ground* then means to break away from bad habits, clear your heart of destructive weeds, and prepare for a new harvest in your life.

God's prophet Hosea preached this principle to the people of Israel. They had sown seeds of wickedness and had trusted in their own strength instead of God's strength. They had decided to do things their way and not God's way. They had been planting seeds of wickedness, and they were now reaping a rotten harvest and eating the nauseating "fruit of lies" (Hosea 10:13). Hosea now pleaded with Israel to do things God's way and to start by breaking up the sin-hardened soil of their hearts and to seek the Lord afresh (see verse 12). God promised that if the people would sow seeds of righteousness, they would reap mercy, and God would shower them with blessings.

God is saying to us what He said to His people a few thousand years ago: now is the time to seek the Lord, and today is the day to break up the fallow ground in your life. The process begins by taking the time to pull up the weeds of sinfulness that are in your heart and mind and to plant righteousness in order to reap a harvest of forgiveness and blessing. But to reap the blessings of God, we must be willing to work the plow. If we want to have a bountiful harvest, then we must do the work of cultivating the soil. Tilling and breaking up the ground is always hard work. Pulling up weeds is never easy, but is always necessary if we want to have a harvest with maximum fruitfulness.

Perhaps there are weeds of selfishness that are choking out a harvest of kindness, or the wild plant of fear is hindering the fruit of faithfulness in your life. Unbelief may be growing, neglect for the Bible may be spreading, and a lack of love may be sprouting up. If so, break up the fallow ground and begin to prepare to plant a new harvest. Do not allow yourself to be a fallow Christian who is content to be complacent, more concerned with comfort than conformity, or more focused on self-centeredness than on self-examination.

If you want God to do a new work in your life, then do the hard work of plowing and preparing the soil of your heart and mind. Then get ready to reap the blessing of righteousness in your life.

Remember the prisoners as if chained with them—those who are mistreated—since you yourselves are in the body also. (Hebrews 13:3)

SEPTEMBER
17

The Persecuted Church

IN MANY COUNTRIES IN THE WORLD TODAY, Christians are facing death threats, violence, imprisonment, and even torture because of their faith. Most of us probably will never know what it is like to be beaten for our faith, to suffer imprisonment for believing in Jesus, or to be forced to endure torture for speaking the name of Jesus. Even though we may not personally experience this type of mistreatment, we are all called to share in the sufferings of other Christians around the world who are being persecuted for their faith in Jesus Christ.

It is so easy to forget about what other people might be going through, the hardships they may be facing, the hurt they may be feeling, or the oppression they may be experiencing, if you enjoy the blessings of religious freedom. It is so easy to become preoccupied with our own set of circumstances that we fail to take the time to consider the circumstances of others and how we can support Christians who are enduring horrific situations. We are told in Hebrews that we are to *remember* those who are persecuted and imprisoned for their faith in Jesus because they are part of our family of faith. But what can we *really* do? How can we *practically* help someone who is suffering for Jesus? Here is a simple way to *remember* and help those who are being persecuted: *learn, pray, give, and go.*

First, we need to take the time to *learn* a little bit about what others Christians are experiencing around the world. Online resources are available, books that we can read are aplenty, and we can talk to Christian missionaries so that we can become better informed, and therefore better equipped, to help.

Next, *pray!* Pray globally, pray biblically, and pray practically! Pray globally by lifting up all those who are being persecuted. Pray biblically by praying the Scriptures. For example, pray from Ephesians that persecuted and imprisoned believers would be filled with the wisdom that only God gives (see Ephesians 1:8), that the Holy Spirit would strengthen them in whatever situation they find themselves (see Ephesians 3:16), that they would know the depth of God's love for them (see Ephesians 3:19), that they would know how to share the good news of the gospel of Jesus Christ (see Ephesians 6:19), and that they would have the boldness they need to stand, speak, and live for Jesus (see Ephesians 6:20). From Philippians, pray that their imprisonment would result in the advancement of God's kingdom (see Philippians 1:12) and that the Lord would be exalted, whether in their lives or in the event of their deaths (see Philippians 1:20). Just think how much you would want prayer if you were being persecuted.

Next, *give.* Another way to show support is by giving financial help. Paul thanked the Philippians for sharing with him in his affliction by giving money for his ministry to continue (see Philippians 4:14–16). By supporting him financially, they also encouraged Paul spiritually.

Lastly, *go.* God may open a door for you to go and visit someone who is in trouble. Tremendous encouragement can be found in the physical presence of another believer. Paul wrote about Onesiphorus, who refreshed him by spending time with him while he was chained for Christ in a Roman prison (see 2 Timothy 1:16).

As today's verse reminds us, "Regard prisoners as if you were in prison with them. Look on victims of abuse as if what happened to them had happened to you" (Hebrews 13:3 MSG).

"I will love them freely."(Hosea 14:4)
The Nature of God's Love

GOD'S love is unconditionally, unquestionably, unmitigatedly, and unreservedly free. Money can't buy you God's love, hard work can't earn you God's love, and ability can't win you God's love. There is no substitute for God's love, there is no losing God's love, and there is no limit to God's love. Sometimes we find difficulty in easily receiving the totally undeserved and completely unrestricted love of God, so we try to earn it.

God reminded His people in the book of Hosea that He loved them freely. He was willing to lavish His love upon His people with no need of recompense. God said, "I will love them freely" not because something in them was lovable. Quite the opposite was true. God loved them in spite of the fact that they had acted unlovingly toward God. God said, "I will love them freely" not because they had demonstrated faithfulness. Quite the opposite was true. God loved them in spite of the fact that they had been repeatedly unfaithful and unloving toward God. God said, "I will love them freely" not because His people were demonstrating steadfast obedience. Quite the opposite was true. God loved them in spite of the fact that they had been living backslidden lives. God said, "I will love them freely" not because they had repented. Quite the opposite was true. God loved them long before they ever made a choice to repent and turn to God.

Because of God's love, He offered forgiveness and restoration to His people, and because of His love, He chose to offer graciousness instead of deserved judgment.

The greatest truth in all of Scripture is that God is love. Love is the supreme expression of God's nature and character and is the highest expression of His goodness. All of God's other attributes flow out of His love. God's love is the reason we exist and draw breath, and God's love is the reason He gave His only Son to save us. God's love for us is undeserved. He loves us in spite of our disobedience, our sin, and our selfishness. God does not love us for who we are, but because of who He is. God loves because He is love and has shown us through Jesus Christ that "I will love them freely."

What should be our response to the free love that God extends to us?

Receive it! God freely gives His love to us, so we ought to freely and joyfully receive it.

Share it! Share the love of God with others by inviting them to personally know and experience God's love for themselves.

Show it! Show God's love by loving others the way God has loved you (see John 13:34).

Live it! God tells us that the best way we live out our love for Him is by obeying His Word (see John 14:23).

The more we receive, share, show, and live God's love, the more we reflect the nature of God's love.

Jesus Christ is the same yesterday, today, and forever.
(Hebrews 13:8)

SEPTEMBER
19

Unchanging God

I N AN UNCERTAIN WORLD, we can be certain of one thing: things change. Even the most superficial studies of world history reveal the diversity of change that has covered centuries and impacted cultures. Even in recent years, we have seen changes in technology, culture, philosophy, politics, morals, and more. Change seems to happen so fast that keeping up with all that change can be difficult at times. What about in your own life? How has your life changed in the past year or two, or even five? More than likely, you have experienced many changes in your life over the last decade, whether in the areas of work, family, church, or your own personal or spiritual growth. And while some of those changes may have been good, others may not have been so good. Nonetheless, change is a part of life. As much as people change, and as much as circumstances change, one thing is certain: God *never* changes.

God is undeniably unchallengeable; He is entirely immutable. For His character, nature, or being to undergo any alteration or adaptation is impossible. His power cannot increase, nor can His power ever decrease. He never grows in knowledge, nor does He ever experience a decrease in understanding. He is limitless, timeless, and boundless. He is unfailing, unshakable, and unwavering. He is, has been, and always will be completely perfect and perfectly complete.

The God of the Old Testament is the same God of the New Testament. He is the God found in the Garden of Eden (see Genesis 3), in the Garden of Gethsemane (see Matthew 26:36), and in the garden of glory (see Revelation 22).

He has existed fully and flawlessly from eternity past and will continue into eternity future. He is both the beginning and the end of all things (see Revelation 1:11). He created all things formerly (see Colossians 1:16), He is upholding all things currently (see Hebrews 1:3), and He will make all things new imminently (see Revelation 21:5).

By faith in Jesus Christ, we can have a relationship with the one and only unchanging thing in the universe: God. He is the unchanging God who never will go back on His promises, who always will honor His Word, who never will adjust or amend His plan of salvation, and who always will be gracious, merciful, holy, and loving. He always will do what is right, good, pure, and true to His Word. God's nature does not change. Therefore, His plans are perfect, His promises are permanent, and His commandments are constant.

A. W. Tozer said, "In God no change is possible; in men change is impossible to escape."[62] Knowing that God never will change means knowing that no matter the difficulty, God is dependable. It means that no matter the trial, God is trustworthy. It means that no matter the instability, God remains steadfast. It means a "new" religion will never exist to replace God's plan of salvation for all mankind throughout all generations.

What an abundant source of comfort and an endless fountain of joy that is found in the immovable and immutable nature and character of God! And although God may change our circumstances, our circumstances never will change our God.

Tell your children. (Joel 1:3)

Passing Your Faith on to Your Kids

FAITH IS ALWAYS one generation away from extinction. No matter how much someone may love and serve God, they cannot believe for someone else. No matter how much you love your kids, they must develop their own faith and their own personal relationship with God. With all of the great children's ministries and youth programs in churches today, parents may be tempted to simply leave their children's spiritual development to the church. But God wants parents to take the lead, nurturing their children spiritually, and parents can help instill in their children the importance of personalizing their faith in God in some practical ways.

God spoke to parents and grandparents through the prophet Joel, as the elders and leaders of Judah were urged to tell their children about all that God had done among them. In particular, they were to share presently and perpetually about the recent locust plague that swept across the land, causing widespread destruction. This plague of locusts was important to memorialize not only as a reminder of God's discipline for disobedience (see Deuteronomy 28:38, 42), but also because as a foreshadowing of a future devastation that would be far greater than the plague of locusts: a reference here to the coming Day of the Lord. Joel's challenge to keep this story alive by repetition throughout the generations reveals the importance of the event, as well as the importance of communicating the works of God to our children, our children's children, and so on down the family tree, so that they, too, might know God personally, worship Him devotedly, and serve Him faithfully.

Sharing the works, wonders, and ways of God with the next generation begins in the home. Parents must take charge of telling their children about the wondrous works of almighty God. Children also must not only hear about God from their parents, but also see a personal relationship with God in their parents' own lives. Nothing will help your children processes and personalize the issues of the faith you are trying to teach them more than if they can observe you living out your faith before their very eyes.

If you find difficulty in talking to your kids about God and spiritual issues, then maybe some practical advice will help you get started.

First, make a regular time for family devotions, whether this is a weekly time or something you do daily. Consistently reading the Bible and praying together as a family is imperative. Also, take advantage of dinner time to reinforce what you are teaching them. Use meal time as a natural time to talk about "God stuff." Keep things simple, and look for natural ways to guide the conversation toward spiritual subjects.

Next, look for ways to talk about God in the normal routine of your children's everyday lives. As they deal with peer pressure and friends, as they face athletic or academic competition, as they wrestle with homework and sibling rivalries, your children will readily present you with opportunities to teach them about God.

Parents, take the time to tell your children about God and encourage them to spend planned and purposeful time with God, and they will be well on their way to having a personal faith in God.

Let us continually offer the sacrifice of praise to God.
(Hebrews 13:15)

SEPTEMBER

The Sacrifice of Praise

21

PRAISING GOD is easy when the sun is shining, the bills are paid, your job is secure, and your health is good. When rain is pouring down, money is tight, you are unemployed, or the doctor gives you bad news, praising God is a little more difficult. In other words, times in your life may come when you just do not feel like praising God because of your circumstances. However, if praising God were always easy, then it would not be called a sacrifice of praise. If you are currently having trouble praising God, then perhaps a fresh look at how to offer the sacrifice of praise will help.

Praise plays an important role in our walk with God. The Bible tells us that we were created to praise God (see Isaiah 43:21). Therefore, praise and worship need to be top priorities in the life of every believer. If we are honest with ourselves, we would admit we have times when we feel like praising God, and other times when we do not. Job must not have felt like praising God when he lost his family and his possessions in what seemed to him like the blink of an eye, but the fact remains that he was still able to offer praise to God in the middle of his grief (see Job 1:21). Paul and Silas certainly did not like being beaten and sent to prison for serving God, but they were still able to praise God at midnight while they were chained in prison (see Acts 16:25). How were they and others in the Bible able to offer praise and worship to God while experiencing painful circumstances?

We must not confuse our ability to praise God *in* painful or difficult circumstances with praising God *for* painful or difficult circumstances. In life, we all will experience pain, sorrow, disappointment, discouragement, and many other difficulties. God does not expect us to pay Him phony platitudes when we are suffering. Bad things are bad things, and bad things happen to good people. But we can still offer God honest and genuine praise.

How does this happen? When we focus on the fact that God is always good, we can praise Him even when life is not so good. Psalm 106 calls us to "praise the LORD! Give thanks to the Lord, for he is good!" (Psalm 106:1). Our praise can only be unchanging and unhindered in a life that is ever changing and frequently hindered if we keep our praise always and forever focused on the goodness of God himself and not on the constantly changing circumstances of life. Our praise is not to be situational, but sacrificial. Part of offering a sacrifice of praise means that we are able to praise God even when we feel hurt, helpless, and unhappy. This demonstrates that we are able to see that God is greater than our circumstances and that He can still work bad circumstances for good.

Our praise never will be inhibited if we keep God at the center of our praises, not looking for what God can do *for* us, but praising who God is *to* us. Our praise is an expression of our faith and trust in God, and no matter how difficult the circumstances, those who know and trust God always have much to praise Him for. So let us offer the sacrifice of praise continually and thankfully.

Declare a holy fast, call a special meeting, get the leaders together, round up everyone in the country. Get them into God's Sanctuary for serious prayer to God. (Joel 1:14 MSG)

SEPTEMBER

22

Hungry for Change

FASTING AND PRAYER are important and powerful spiritual disciplines. Through fasting and prayer, the Holy Spirit can transform our lives, our churches, our communities, our nation, and our world. When God's people fast and pray with the proper biblical motivation, God will hear them, heal them, and help them (2 Chronicles 7:14). The road to personal and communal revival is paved through fasting and prayer.

The nation of Israel had suffered a terrible invasion, one that left everything utterly destroyed. Crops were devastated, homes were torn apart, the land lay in waste, and the army that leveled such a cold-blooded attack was none other than an army of locusts. That's right. Grasshoppers! In the wake of such an overwhelming attack, the prophet Joel encouraged the people to gather everyone together in the sanctuary and seek God through fasting and prayer. Times of great trouble and trial often prompt people to seek God, and Joel knew that the people, as well as the nation, needed a spiritual breakthrough, and the only way for the process of restoration and revival to spread throughout the nation was if God's people humbled themselves by seeking Him through fasting and prayer.

Are you hungry for change in your own life? Are you looking for a spiritual breakthrough? The place to begin is with fasting and prayer. Fasting and prayer is the way to a transformed life. Fasting and prayer are not manipulative tools used to change God's mind, speed up His answer, or influence His will. Instead, fasting and prayer prepare us individually to hear from God as we eliminate distractions and concentrate our attention on Him. We all have areas in our lives in which we could use a spiritual breakthrough. Perhaps you have a habit that needs to be broken or a habit that needs to be started. Perhaps you have an attitude that needs to change or a sin that has become a hindrance. Whatever and wherever the spiritual breakthrough is needed, do not be surprised if change is found through fasting and prayer.

Perhaps you remember the story in Mark 9 where the disciples tried and failed to cast out a demon. Casting out demons was something that Jesus had previously given them the power to do (see Mark 3:14–15), but here they completely lacked the ability to do so. When they asked Jesus why they were incapable and ineffective, Jesus responded by saying, "This kind can come out by nothing but prayer and fasting" (Mark 9:29). The disciples needed a breakthrough. Where they previously had seen God do amazing things in and through them, now they were feeling powerless. Jesus said to them that the way to see a spiritual breakthrough was through fasting and prayer.

When you fast and pray, keep in mind that although some people say they are going to fast from chocolate or TV, the nature of a biblical fast is to go without sustenance and nourishment for a period of time while you seek the Lord and rely on Him for your strength. Also, biblical fasting always includes serious prayer. If you have a real hunger for change, if you are ready for a spiritual breakthrough, if you want to see God do some amazing things in and through your life, then begin to practice the spiritual discipline of fasting and prayer.

My brethren, count it all joy when you fall into various trials, knowing that the testing of your faith produces patience. (James 1:2–3)

SEPTEMBER
23

The How-Tos of Trials

SOMEONE ONCE NOTED that the Christian life is lived either coming out of one trial or going into another one. Why is that? Simply put, God is in the refining business.

The book of James reads like a how-to manual for your faith. Fundamentally, the Bible can be divided into two categories. The first category deals with how to *know* God, which is the theological aspect, and the second category deals with how to *follow* God, which is the practical aspect. The book of James largely deals with the how-tos regarding *following* God, as James challenges believers to live out their faith every day. Although James does not say so outright, he is a strong supporter of the idea that actions speak louder than words. Therefore, Christians should be loudly proclaiming their faith in God by the way they live their lives.

For the Christian, life in the real world means that trials are inevitable, and James points out two important and practical things to remember when we go through trials. The first is *perspective*, and the second is *purpose*. Outlook determines outcome, and attitude determines action. If trials are going to produce the proper outcome in our lives, then we must look at trials with the proper perspective, which means that we are to have an attitude of joy. James is not saying that trials are joyful experiences, or even that we should enjoy going through trials. Rather, we must make the decision to *find* the joy in every trial. James says we should "count it all joy." In other words, we are to make a careful and deliberate decision to evaluate our trials in light of what God is doing in and through them. This, in turn, produces a joy within us. The joy is not found in the trial itself; the joy is found in God, who is working through the trial.

Our joy is first found in God, whom we know is working in the trial.

Second, our joy is strengthened as we understand God's purpose for the trial. And yes, trials have a purpose; they are not random, and they are not coincidental. God is not trying to sabotage or destroy our faith; He is working to strengthen our faith. Trials are designed to test our faith. The word *testing* here carries the idea of confirming our faith or attesting to our faith. Temptation is different from testing. God always tests us to bring out the best; Satan tempts us to bring out our worst. Trials are designed to bring out the best in our faith. Trials make us more valuable, but they do not make us more precious in God's sight. He loves us the same. His love does not increase or decrease; His is always a supreme, all-out love. The value is found in our usefulness in serving God. You see, we become more valuable in our service to God as we patiently endure trials. As we endure trials, God shapes us and prepares us to be used even more by Him.

How long must we endure, and how long will God keep us in the trial? Let us take a lesson from a silversmith who holds the silver in the hottest part of the flame. He never lets it go and never takes his eyes off what he is working on, because if the costly metal is left in the fire a moment too long, it becomes worthless. How does a silversmith know when the silver is refined and when he should remove it from the heat? He knows the silver is refined when he can see his reflection in the silver. God wants to see His reflection in us, and He will leave us in the heat of a trial for as long as it takes for us to reflect His image more clearly.

Will you be a reflection of Him today?

"I will restore to you the years that the swarming locust has eaten." (Joel 2:25)

SEPTEMBER

24

God Restores

WHEN WE IGNORE GOD, life has a way of unraveling. When we fail spiritually, we have a tendency to want to avoid God. When we fall into sin, our hearts gradually become hardened to the things of God. But no matter how your life may have unraveled, how many times you may have failed, or how far away from God's will you may have wandered, God can still bring restoration to your life. Though the consequences of sin may continue, and though the effects of disobedience may linger, God still restores.

God's people had been ignoring God and avoiding His warnings. They had gradually allowed sin to take over as they routinely practiced idolatry. Their hearts were becoming hardened from repeated disobedience, and now they were entrenched in waywardness and life was unraveling. In light of God's recent judgment against the Israelites, the prophet Joel urged the people to wake up, repent, and turn back to God. Joel, reminded them of the graciousness of God and His promised blessings if they turned from their sin and returned to Him:

> Then the Lord *will* be zealous for His land, and pity His people. The Lord *will* answer, . . . "I *will* send you grain and new wine and oil. . . . But I *will* remove far from you the northern army, and *will* drive him away into a barren and desolate land. . . ." He *will* cause the rain to come down for you. . . . "So I *will* restore to you the years that the swarming locust has eaten. . . ." "I *will* pour out My Spirit. . . . I *will* show wonders in the heavens and in the earth." (Joel 2:18–20, 23, 25, 28–30, emphasis added).

But God's restoration can only come after personal repentance.

Perhaps you are feeling as though sin has been eating away at your life. Like the swarming locusts, you may feel as if all the good in your life has been stripped away, and you are standing in a barren wasteland, wondering how you got there and whether you will ever see fruitfulness in your life again. You know that time has been wasted and mistakes have been made. But God can forgive you, and, even better, God wants to forgive you. As James Montgomery Boice wrote,

> Opportunities may have been lost, but God can give new and even better opportunities. Friends may have been alienated and driven away, but God can give new friends and even restore many of the former ones. God can break the power of sin and restore a personal holiness and joy that would not have been dreamed possible.[63]

God is looking to bring restoration to your soul, and God wants to heal the brokenness in your life. But God's restoration can only come after personal repentance. When we confess our sin to the Lord, He is quick to forgive our past and to fill our future with hope. When we turn from our sin and disobedience, God is ready to bring good out of wasted years. God is more than able to restore our souls and lead us into the land of blessing, but we must pay attention to God's wake-up calls and be quick to respond. It is never too late for God to bring restoration to your life, but we must first understand that true restoration begins with personal repentance.

Each one is tempted when he is drawn away by his own desires and enticed. (James 1:14)

Making Sense of Temptation

SEPTEMBER 25

LIFE IS FULL OF TEMPTATION, and the pressure to sin is both powerful and persistent. Temptation has existed from the beginning of mankind and will continue to mislead as long as people are born into this world. Yet, as common as temptation is, and for as long as it has been around, very few people have learned how to deal with it successfully and sufficiently. To deal with temptation successfully, we must understand it accurately.

James began his epistle by discussing trials, and in his characteristically rapid-fire approach, he quickly moves to the subject of temptation. Separating the two is important, because trials and temptation are distinctly different. Where trials are designed to bring about growth and blessing, temptation, if not dealt with properly, brings about sin. Where trials work from the outside in, temptation works from the inside out. Where trials come from God, temptation never comes from God: "Let no one say when he is tempted, 'I am tempted by God'; for God cannot be tempted by evil, nor does He Himself tempt anyone" (James 1:13).

Where does temptation come from, then? James could not be clearer on the subject: the source of temptation is not God, or even the Devil, but man's own sinful heart. If not for our own desires, temptation from the Devil or the world would never even be a possibility. Temptation takes place when we are lured toward something that appeals to a desire, want, or craving, and in our excitement we fail to notice the danger of the cleverly camouflaged hook that is ready to ensnare us.

Temptation is a given. No one is exempt; everyone must face temptation.

The question is, are we prepared for when temptation tempts? When preparing ourselves to resist the lure of temptation, we need to know that temptation is most powerful when our personal time with God is neglected. When we are at our weakest, temptation is felt the strongest. Conversely, temptation is at its weakest when we are spiritually strong.

If you want to stay strong spiritually and avoid temptation, then start by spending more time in prayer. Consistent and persistent time with God goes a long way in strengthening you to stand against temptation. Do your best to avoid compromising situations altogether, but if you find yourself in a place or with some people where you are being tempted to do something you know you should stay away from, then simply leave. Just walk away. Leaving, knowing you avoided giving in to temptation, is better than staying, and hoping you can avoid giving in.

Most importantly, be in the Bible. Time studying, memorizing, reflecting on, and reading the Bible is the single most important way to be prepared for when temptation entices. The word of God will guard your heart, protect your mind, and help safeguard your thoughts. If all temptation starts with a thought, then the more you think about God and His Word, the more you will be able to resist temptation.

"And it shall come to pass that whoever calls on the name of the Lord shall be saved." (Joel 2:32)

How Great a Salvation!

SEPTEMBER 26

SALVATION IS GREAT because God is great. Salvation is a picture of the majesty of God's mercy. Salvation portrays the grandeur of God's graciousness, contains the boundless blessings of God, is overwhelming in opulence, and unparalleled in power. Salvation is complete in its capability to save, eternal in its extent to save, and absolute in its assurance to save. Salvation's comprehensiveness cannot be contained, its cost cannot be calculated, and its availability cannot be restricted.

The apostle Peter preached from Joel 2 at Pentecost, just after the Spirit of God was poured out on the early church disciples. And at the end of his sermon, salvation came to three thousand new believers that day. How great a salvation! Peter and everyone there that day in Jerusalem were witnesses to God's predictive power and accomplishing authority as Peter declared, "This is what was spoken by the prophet Joel" (Acts 2:16). Here, God began to fulfill this prophecy by pouring out His Holy Spirit in a new way, making His Spirit available to all who believe. How great a salvation! This boundless outpouring of the Spirit of God continues today and will continue until the second coming of Christ, as all who receive salvation also receive the gift of God's Holy Spirit and are empowered by God's Spirit to live, serve, and worship God according to His Word.

How great a salvation that God makes available to all, available to anyone and everyone who wants to receive the grace of His salvation. No one is too rich, too poor, too smart, or too uneducated to receive this grace. All are invited to receive this salvation.

The time is not too late to accept what God has offered, for *whoever* calls on the name of the Lord shall be saved from death. *Whoever* calls on the name of the Lord shall be spared from the penalty of sin. *Whoever* calls on the name of the Lord shall be delivered from the wrath of God. Salvation is available for everyone, and the simple requirement is that you *call* on the name of the Lord. Believe and receive, trust and pray, confess that Jesus *is* Lord, and receive Him *as* Lord over your life. How great a salvation!

Salvation is one of the greatest words ever conceived, and we could expound its splendors forever. But to truly understand the greatness, we must first experience salvation for ourselves. The threefold experience of salvation is made up of justification, sanctification, and glorification. Through salvation, we are at peace with God, as He has declared us righteous, forgiven of sin, and freed from sin's penalty. Through salvation, we are being made to reflect the image of God. He is sanctifying us, changing us, and making us a new creation in Christ. And through salvation, we will one day be glorified, forever freed from the influence of sin, and forever and finally changed into His image. How great a salvation!

Be doers of the word, and not hearers only, deceiving yourselves. (James 1:22)

SEPTEMBER 27

Just Do It

WE ALL KNOW that eating healthy is good for us. If you eat healthy foods, they can help prevent disease, boost your immune system, and increase your energy and stamina. But even though everyone knows the benefits, not everyone eats healthy.

We all know that regular exercise is good for us. Exercise can help you manage your weight, help you sleep better, lower your cholesterol, increase muscle strength, and lead to good mental health. But even though everyone knows this, not everyone exercises.

We all know that obeying God's Word is good for us: "All Scripture is given by inspiration of God, and is profitable for doctrine, for reproof, for correction, for instruction in righteousness" (2 Timothy 3:16). The Word makes us "wise for salvation" (2 Timothy 3:15), is a sword for defense (see Ephesians 6:17), and "blessed are those who hear the word of God and keep it!" (Luke 11:28). But even though everyone knows this, not everyone obeys God's Word.

James is not seeking to *beat up* the body of believers, but he is trying to *build up* the body and encourage believers to get up and get busy obeying God's Word. Application is always where the rubber meets the road in the Christian faith. As Jesus said, the true test of our love for God is in our willingness to *do* what God tells us to do: "If you love Me, keep My commandments"(John 14:15). Obedience is accomplished one step at a time, and as Oswald Chambers said, "One step forward in obedience is worth years of study about it."

James knew the importance of studying the Bible and growing in our knowledge and understanding of the truth, but also equally important, to *living* the Bible. After revelation comes responsibility, after principles comes practice, after belief comes behavior, and after creed comes conduct. Right thinking leads to right living. If good theology is the foundation of the Christian life, then godly living rises naturally from that solid foundation. To simply know the truth is never enough; at some point, we must begin to live the truth. Likewise, we must not simply embrace the truth; the truth we believe must, at some point, embrace us. Simply knowing what to do is not the same thing as doing it.

Warren Wiersbe said, "Many people have the mistaken idea that hearing a good sermon or Bible study is what makes them grow and get God's blessing. It is not the hearing but the doing that brings the blessing. Too many Christians mark their Bibles, but their Bibles never mark them! If you think you are spiritual because you hear the Word, then you are only kidding yourself."[64]

Martin Luther, the father of the Protestant Reformation, said, "The world does not need a definition of religion as much as it needs a demonstration."

The next time you have the opportunity to put into practice what you have read and learned from the Bible, do not waste any time; just do it!

This message was given to Amos, a shepherd from the town of Tekoa in Judah. (Amos 1:1 NLT)

SEPTEMBER
28

Not-So-Famous Amos

HAVE YOU EVER FELT like a small fish in a big pond? Feeling small and insignificant in such a big world is easy. Add to that the humdrum of life's repetitive routine, which can occasionally leave a person wondering if what he or she is doing really makes a difference in the grand scheme of things, and the feeling increases. If you are currently feeling this way or know someone who is, then take heed and take heart, my friend, because God likes to take ordinary people and use them for extraordinary purposes.

Amos was a nobody from nowhere, yet God saw in him a somebody whom He could do something with. Amos was not a religious leader, he did not have a formal education, and he was not well-to-do. He lived in the boondocks of Tekoa, five mile southeast of Bethlehem, where, according to his own account he said, "I'm not a professional prophet, and I was never trained to be one. I'm just a shepherd, and I take care of sycamore-fig trees. But the LORD called me away from my flock and told me, 'Go and prophesy to my people in Israel'" (Amos 7:14–15 NLT). God saw in this little fish some big potential, and He decided to do the unexpected with an unlikely person. God turned this simple sheepherder into His sanctified spokesman.

What kind of qualities is God looking for in the man or woman whom He uses? Is He looking for the person with the longest list of credentials after his or her name? Is He looking for the natural born leaders? Is He seeking a superstar? Not usually. True, sometimes God will use a big name to get the job done, the well-educated to communicate His message, or the well to do to accomplish His plans, but more often, God chooses to use the ordinary. In fact, this happens with such regularity that you could say that using the ordinary is God's method of choice. The Bible even goes so far as to say, "Remember, dear brothers and sisters, that few of you were wise in the world's eyes or powerful or wealthy when God called you" (1 Corinthians 1:26 NLT).

Why does God regularly select the insignificant in the world's eyes to do something significant? The reason is so that "no one can ever boast in the presence of God" (1 Corinthians 1:29 NLT).

God will confound the wise by anointing the foolish. God will shame the strong as He empowers the weak. God will skip over those who lean on their own understanding, trust in their talents, depend on their own knowledge, or rely on their family name. Instead, He will raise up the weak and the weary, the little and the lonely. He will show them His greatness, and they will become strong in the Lord and in the power of His might.

Willingness is more important to God than influence, and weakness goes much further than strength in God's economy. Often, the faithfulness to do that which appears insignificant displays immeasurable significance in the eyes of God. The gateway to usefulness is not whether you are able, but whether you are available. Your usefulness is not determined by whether you are talented, but whether you are teachable. It is not whether you are "with it," but whether you are willing. That is how a not-so-famous Amos became the first of the prophets to write down the messages he received from God.

But if you favor some people over others, you are committing a sin. (James 2:9 NLT)

SEPTEMBER
29
Don't Judge a Book by Its Cover

WE ALL HAVE A FEW FAVORITE FRIENDS we enjoy spending time with, friends that we are drawn to, friends that we can kick off our shoes and let down our hair with, friends with whom we just share a certain chemistry. But is having a few favorite friends the same as showing favoritism?

James cautions Christians not to show favoritism or partiality, going so far as to declare that partiality is a sin. Is this a condemnation against having favorite friends and choosing to spend more time with them? Not at all. James is talking about when we allow what we see on the outside of a person to affect how we treat that person. This is the essence of the principle of partiality that James is spelling out, and is very similar to what God told Samuel in 1 Samuel 16 when He said, "Do not consider his appearance or his height. . . . People look at the outward appearance, but the LORD looks at the heart" (verse 7 NIV). Favoritism is when we let the outward appearance of a person affect our actions toward that person. A person might be a different skin color, have body piercings or tattoos, or wear what we consider to be odd hairstyles. We may first see someone's age, clothing, or nationality and develop an instant dislike for him or her. Bottom line, anytime we let something we see on the outside keep us from loving someone, we are showing favoritism.

Here is a modern take on James' illustration of favoritism: Sunday morning service is about to start, the grounds are clean, the stage is set up, the bulletins are printed, and the ushers are in place and ready to welcome people as they arrive. Today, you are an usher, and you notice two new visitors. The first visitor pulls up in a new Mercedes and is wearing a nice silk Tommy Bahama shirt (this is California, after all) and expensive gold-trim Ray Ban sunglasses. You (as the usher) think, *Great!* You are quick to welcome him: "Good morning! Welcome to (insert your church's name here)! So very glad you could visit today. Allow me to show you to a seat. Would you like to sit up front today? Here you go. Enjoy the service! If I can help in any way, let me know, and don't forget to stop by our visitors table for a free gift on your way out!"

As you get back to the door, visitor number two makes his way up. He is riding an old bicycle, his jeans are a little dirty, he has sun-beaten skin, and, well, he does not smell like roses. You think sarcastically, *This is great, just great.* You begin to talk to him. "Hello. Are you here for the service today? Would you like to sit in our fellowship hall or outside on our patio this morning?" After you show him to a seat, you decide that someone should keep an eye on him.

Anytime we make a judgment based on outward appearances, we have broken God's royal law, which says, "Love your neighbor as yourself" (James 2:8).

When we look at the life of Jesus, whether you were rich or poor or whether you were a teacher or a tax collector, those things did not matter to Him. He would talk with you if you were a politician or a prostitute. He would eat with you if were a leader or had leprosy. He would not look up to you if you were the high priest, and He would not look down on you if you were a harlot. He always exhibited love toward everyone.

So, the next time you are tempted to treat someone a little differently, based on what you see on the outside, remember that if you judge a book by its cover, you are showing partiality.

Hear this word, you cows of Bashan, who are on the mountain of Samaria, who oppress the poor, who crush the needy, who say to your husbands, "Bring wine, let us drink!" (Amos 4:1)

SEPTEMBER
30

The Real Housewives of Samaria

IN THIS VERY SARCASTIC RANT against the wealthy women of his day, Amos, made clear that oppressing the poor in order to get what you want was a disgrace. Amos called the women of high society "the cows of Bashan." Not a very flattering image, but would be similar to calling someone who was wealthy and powerful today a "fat cat." Bashan was in the area now called the Golan Heights, a region located northeast of the Sea of Galilee and well known for good grassland that produced expensive livestock. The poor people in Amos' day often were overlooked and shamelessly oppressed by the rich, as many of the wealthy women pushed their husbands to support their expensive lifestyles. Their only concern was chewing the cud of their own wealth. The mistreatment of the poor was a widespread problem, not only limited to the housewives of Samaria.

God has much to say in the book of Amos about caring for the poor, and when God revealed to Amos that He was about to bring judgment upon His people, He cited Israel's treatment of the poor as a reason. In Amos 8:4, God said that Israel had "trampled" the needy and robbed the poor during their time of prosperity. The poor were the victims of greed and mistreatment, and because no one else was looking out for them, God would make sure they were not overlooked.

In the New Testament, God continued to show His care and concern over the treatment of the poor by stating in James 5:4–5, "Indeed the wages of the laborers who mowed your fields, which you kept back by fraud, cry out; and the cries of the reapers have reached the ears of the Lord. . . . You have lived on the earth in pleasure and luxury; you have fattened your hearts." Look, making money is not wrong, and being rich is not a sin. But God *is* concerned with how we earn money and how we use money. God never endorses materialism, and God pays attention to the way we treat others, especially the poor (see James 5:1–6). To live in unrestrained luxury is dangerous, especially when we do so at the expense of others.

You may not be able to keep up with the Joneses down the street with their huge home, new cars, and expensive clothes, but playing the game of "the person with the most toys wins" is not a biblical approach to handling your wealth. And just as you can always find someone who has more than you, finding people who have less than you is even easier. What you should be asking yourself is not how much more can you get, but how much more generous can you be? Are you looking for ways that you can be a blessing to others?

Throughout the Bible, God calls His people to have a loving concern for those in need. After all, life is not about you. Life is about loving God and loving others. How well do you love others with what God has given you? What is your love level today?

October

A Faith That Works

IN EVERY CHURCH, some will say they believe in Jesus, but they do not live for Jesus. James would say if that describes you, you need to wake up and smell the coffee, because you are not really a Christian. If your life is not a testament to biblical truth, if you do not have works that support your worship, then your faith is meaningless. *Wow. Really, James? Aren't you getting a little carried away?*

Well, consider the fact that even Jesus warned us, "Not everyone who says to Me, 'Lord, Lord,' shall enter the kingdom of heaven, but he who does the will of My Father in heaven" (Matthew 7:21) will enter. James is challenging individuals to think through what real faith looks like by insisting that faith is only genuine when evidence supports that faith.

James does not contradict the truth found elsewhere in the Bible, truth largely coming from the apostle Paul, that says we are saved by grace alone, through faith alone, in Christ alone. James knew a person could do nothing to add to what Jesus Christ finished on the cross; he was simply choosing to emphasize a different aspect of faith. Where Paul focused on the *root* of salvation, which is faith in Christ, James focused on the *fruit* of salvation, which is faith in action. Where Paul focused on what *precedes* salvation, James focused on what *follows* salvation. The two are not mutually exclusive; they are correspondingly complete. Both Paul and James would agree with the statement, "Though we are justified by faith alone, the faith that justifies is never alone."[65] True, we are saved by grace and not by works (see Ephesians 2:8). However, we must remember that to simply say, "I believe" is not enough if we then turn around and do nothing else to support that belief.

James added a little emphasis to the issue by saying, "You believe that there is one God. You do well. Even the demons believe—and tremble!" (James 2:19). No doubt, James was hoping for a little shock value with this statement, as he referenced a dead, demonic faith. You see, it is possible to know all the facts about God but still not have a true faith in God. Demons actually know their facts quite well. They know there is one God. After all, they once lived in Heaven (see Revelation 12:9). They believe in the deity of Jesus (see Matthew 8:29). And they know that hell is a real place (see Luke 8:31). Yet, despite what they *know* to be true, they do not *live* like it is true. Therefore, they have a dead, defective faith.

Our works *prove* our salvation; they are not the *process* of our salvation. By our actions, we declare what we believe. Salvation is not found in our works, but our salvation is what causes our works. Faith produces works. Works reveal faith. A saving faith is always an active faith. It is not faith *and* works that save a person. It is not faith *or* works that saves a person. But a faith *that* works truly reflects genuine salvation.

"Prepare to meet your God." (Amos 4:12)

Proper Preparation

MEETING WITH GOD takes purpose and preparation. Without a doubt, every person needs to be prepared for the day when he or she will stand in the presence of God, and only those who have placed their faith in Jesus Christ truly will be prepared to meet their Maker on that day. But how well do you prepare to meet with God in your personal times of worship? Do you take time to prepare your heart and mind before your devotional time? Do you prepare to meet God before you worship at church?

The prophet Amos saw that the people had drifted away from God. They had become selfish, corrupt, and idolatrous. Their lives were tainted with outward forms of religion, which lacked a foundation in the truth, so Amos challenged the people to stop wasting time in vain worship and pointless pursuits and to prepare to meet God. They needed to prepare themselves by forsaking their love for wealth and their lack of love for the poor. They needed to prepare themselves by setting their hearts and minds on God and not on false religion. And they needed to prepare themselves by confessing and repenting of sin.

Every day, we are exposed to ideas, images, and ideologies that can corrupt our spiritual sensibilities. Therefore, we should take time to prepare ourselves before we meet with God. Here are a few suggestions that may prove helpful as you prepare to meet God in your times of worship. Much like the children of Israel, we may need to forsake a pursuit or passion that is leading us away from God or clouding our spiritual vision in order to prepare ourselves to meet with God. We may need to be more focused and purposeful in setting our hearts and minds on God and obeying His Word rather than being self-focused. Lastly, we may need to confess and repent of sin that has been hindering our walk with God.

You can also do a few things physically when preparing to spend time with God.

First, *be rested.* You will not be ready to hear from God if you cannot stay awake, so as a practice, get the needed rest before your devotions, before church, before Bible studies, before prayer meetings, and so on.

Next, *be relaxed.* Psalm 46:10 reminds us to "be still, and know that [He is] God." Take a few deep breaths, calm your heart, and focus your mind on God before you plan to spend time with Him.

Also, *be ready.* Expect to hear from God. The psalmist prayed, "Open my eyes that I may see wonderful things in your law" (Psalm 119:18). Being ready means expecting that God will speak. Being ready means being early to church or Bible study. Rushing into God's presence never will properly prepare you to meet with God. Make sure you give yourself enough time to prepare.

Be reverent. After all, this is the God of the universe whom you are preparing to meet with, so do not enter His presence flippantly or halfheartedly.

Finally, before every act of worship, *be prayerful.* Pray something as simple as, "Lord, I come to worship you in spirit and in truth. Speak to me and help me submit and surrender to Your will."

Taking the time to prepare before rushing into the presence of God is both reverential and beneficial.

But no man can tame the tongue. It is an unruly evil, full of deadly poison. (James 3:8)

Taming the Tongue

DO YOU LIKE RIDDLES? See how well you do with a couple of brainteasers. What lives in a cage, is surrounded by a jagged fence, and is walled in on all sides? Or, how about this one? What is often held but never touched, always wet but never rusts, often bites but is seldom bit, and to use it well, you must have wit? For the answer to each of these riddles, just open your mouth and stick out the answer. That's right: the tongue!

God, in His creative diversity, has fashioned many different kinds of tongues in his living creatures. Take, for instance, the anteater's tongue, which is a two-foot long tongue which can extend and retract up to one hundred fifty times per minute and can catch up to thirty thousand ants in a single day. Also, consider the tongue of the archerfish, which uses its tongue much like a squirt gun to shoot its prey.

The Bible also mentions the different kinds of tongues that are found in us: the flattering tongue (see Psalm 5:9); the proud tongue (see Psalm 12:3; 73:9); the lying tongue (see Psalm 109:2; Proverbs 6:17); the deceitful tongue (see Psalm 120:2); the perverted tongue (see Proverbs 10:31; 17:20); the soothing tongue (see Proverbs 15:4); the healing tongue (see Proverbs 12:18); the destructive tongue (see Proverbs 17:4); the wicked tongue (see Psalm 10:7); the soft tongue (see Proverbs 25:15); and the backbiting tongue (see Proverbs 25:23). Which tongue best describes the way you speak?

James emphasized the importance of not only watching what we do as Christians, but also watching what we say as Christians. James believed that if Jesus is Lord of our lives, then naturally, Jesus also should be Lord over our language. How many times have you said something you wish you could take back? You may have said an unkind or unloving word or told a joke that was unbecoming of a Christian. The simple truth is, we are all guilty of saying things that we should not have said. We have all seen where a careless word caused conflict, a hurtful word caused heartache, or complaining words caused discontent. All of these are examples of people using their tongues to shoot down, like the archerfish, rather than to build up, like a Christian should.

So how can a person tame the tongue or control his or her conversation? According to James, this control is impossible to exercise on our own. But do not worry; this is not another riddle. The answer is found in God's Word. First of all, no *man* can tame the tongue (see James 3:8), but *God* can (see Mark 10:27). Second, the real problem with the tongue starts in the heart: "For out of the abundance of the heart the mouth speaks" (Matthew 12:34). We speak words that come from our hearts. Therefore, taming the tongue begins by taming our hearts and filling them with God's Word. If our hearts are abundantly filled with God's Word, then our mouths will speak from the overflow, and our words will be words of edification, exhortation, and encouragement. We will speak kind words, gentle words, loving words, and words of blessing. Therefore, taming the tongue begins by taming our hearts.

The next time you feel the desire to use words that are more hurtful than helpful, words that shoot down rather than support others, take a moment and ask the Holy Spirit to help tame your tongue.

"Behold, I am setting a plumb line in the midst of My people Israel." (Amos 7:8)

Setting Things Straight

OCTOBER 4

THE MEANS BY WHICH WE MEASURE our lives will go a long way in determining the outcome of our lives.

When constructing a building, an important skill to have is knowing how to measure straightness. Without a straight line, a true standard to guide the building process, and without knowing what level is, a building is in danger of crumbling. This is why builders throughout the centuries have used plumb lines as a measuring standard. A plumb line is nothing more than a piece of string with a weight attached to one end. The string hangs down vertically so that gravity can pull the weight toward the ground, producing a straight line. This simple—yet clever—device reveals that which is straight and that which is crooked.

How can we determine what is straight and what is crooked in our spiritual lives? In a vision from God, the prophet Amos saw God standing by a wall with a plumb line in His hand, revealing that the wall was built true to the plumb line, ensuring that the wall was straight. This was God's way of saying to Amos that He was about to check Israel to see if the nation was plumb or upright before God. The sad reality was that God's people had become crooked because of corruption. Sin had bent them out of shape, and they were in danger of crumbling.

Allowing the many pressures and priorities of life to bend us out of shape is easy. If we abandon godliness as our primary pursuit, we can easily become a little warped by worldliness. Fortunately, God has given us a standard by which we can measure spiritual straightness, where we can live plumb, straight, and upright in the sight of God.

What is God's plumb line for His people? Well, certainly, He does not want us to compare ourselves to others in order to determine whether we are doing things right. Nor are we to look at the world we live in to measure how well we are living. Only one true standard, only one accurate plumb line exists: the Bible. The Bible is the standard by which we are to measure our lives and determine whether we have become bent out of spiritual shape. When God lowers His plumb line into our lives, and reminds us of what His Word says, He reveals when our lives are out of alignment with His will, and we should be glad that God has taken the time to correct us. God does not use His plumb line to destroy us but to build us up.

A wall out of plumb requires physical correction, and a life out of plumb requires spiritual correction; otherwise, ruin is sure to follow. How do we measure up to the plumb line of the Bible in our relationships with others, those in our family, our workplace, and our community, especially in our churches? By focusing on God's plumb line, we can see where we are out of alignment with God's will and can work to set things straight.

Therefore, be patient, brethren, until the coming of the Lord. (James 5:7)

OCTOBER 5

The Virtue of Patience

*B*E PATIENT! How can such a simple command be so difficult to put into practice? After all, life is full of frustrating situations and exhausting events that drain our energy and try our patience. Take a moment and test yourself to see how well you do on the patience scale. For example, how long do you wait before you honk your horn when the person in front of you fails to notice that the traffic light has turned green? Or, how long before you roll your eyes and let out a sigh when the checkout line you have chosen is not moving? How long until you tell your kids to "take it outside" when they are running around in the house in hyper play mode? What about with God? Have you ever asked God to hurry up? The simple truth is that we all can be impatient at times. But part of spiritual maturity is growing in our ability to put patience into practice.

James knew people struggled to be patient in the face of life's many difficulties, but he also knew that Christians have the added stresses and strains of suffering persecution as the result of their faith in Christ, all of which only makes practicing patience that much harder.

But James is not without encouragement. He gives three illustrations of how we can grow in our ability to put patience into practice, even in difficult times. First, like a farmer, we are called to be patiently waiting for the spiritual harvest that God is preparing. Of course, we must work the field by tilling the soil, planting the seeds, and tending to the crops, but God is the one who brings the harvest. So, we must wait on God to produce the produce in due season. Like the prophets of old, we are called to remain faithful to represent God and proclaim His message, even if that means enduring hardships because of our faith. And, like Job, we are called to wait for God to accomplish His plans and purposes in and through our lives, even when that includes suffering, knowing that our suffering is never meaningless.

We all need more patience with each other, more patience with our families, more patience with our friends, and more patience at work. Patience means being able to accept whatever God gives us, or whatever God chooses not to give us, patiently accepting either outcome without complaining. And yes, the command *be patient* is easier said than done. But as we practice patience, we also grow our ability to be patient. Patience is an attribute that develops like a muscle: the more we exercise it, the more it grows. In other words, in developing more patience, no gain comes without some pain.

Patience is a virtue we are called to have, regardless of the afflictions or aggravations we face. We are, therefore, to remain patient, no matter the difficulty or the suffering. As believers, we are called to face trials patiently until

Christ returns, remembering that God is always in control, and He never wastes our suffering.

> *"I will send a famine on the land, not a famine of bread, nor a thirst for water, but of hearing the words of the Lord."*
> (Amos 8:11)

OCTOBER

6

Hunger Games

RUMBLE . . . GRUMBLE . . . GROWL! What is that noise? If you have ever missed a meal, then you are familiar with the sounds of a hungry stomach. Not long after hunger sets in, you begin to become completely preoccupied with thoughts of satisfying your growing appetite. Every living creature needs some type of nourishment to survive, but man is the only creature that has a *higher* appetite that also must be fed. Man has a spiritual hunger that is only nourished by feeding on the Word of God.

When you miss a spiritual meal, you should begin to feel the rumbling, grumbling, and growling of your Spirit, and your thoughts should begin to be completely preoccupied with how you can satisfy those spiritual hunger pains.

The nation of Israel was experiencing a time of great prosperity. The economy was strong and unemployment was low. Physically, they were satisfied, but spiritually, they were starving. God's people had allowed their pride, their preoccupation with possessions, and their interest in idolatry to become more important to them than worshiping and serving God. And when the prophet Amos warned them of their need to repent and return to God, they would not listen. So, because God's people would not listen to the warnings of Amos and other prophets, God promised to send a famine "of hearing the words of the LORD" (Amos 8:11). God's people had not wanted to listen to the message of God, so God decided that He would silence His messengers. Only then would God's people develop a hunger for His Word.

Although many people claim to be Christians today, a definite turning away from biblical truth is occurring. Many people are not letting the Word of God guide their lives. They are becoming spiritually malnourished by allowing psychology, popular culture, and philosophy to influence their decisions instead of God. People are seeking to accumulate "stuff" rather than accumulate riches in heaven. Even people who profess to be born-again Christians are simply not spending enough time reading God's Word and applying His Word to their everyday lives. And if you do not study the Word, you certainly cannot live according to the Word. The only hope is to develop a genuine hunger for the things of God.

We must ask ourselves whether or not we are fully feeding on God's Word. If we want to grow spiritually strong, we must feed on the only source of spiritual nourishment that God has provided, which is His Word. We will never find our spiritual sustenance in the confections of carnality or in the junk food of false spirituality. Nothing can be substituted for the meat of the Word.

Do not skip a meal, do not starve your spirit, and do not play games with your spiritual hunger. Take the time to daily feed on the Word of God.

Is anyone among you sick? Let him call for the elders of the church, and let them pray over him, anointing him with oil in the name of the Lord. And the prayer of faith will save the sick. (James 5:14–15)

**OCTOBER
7**

The Prescription for Healing

NO ONE LIKES BEING SICK. From seasonal sicknesses to serious illness, from starving a cold to feeding a fever, being sick is no fun. Whether you take an over-the-counter medicine in an attempt to manage your symptoms, sip a cup of chicken noodle soup to fend off the chills, or undergo chemotherapy for cancer, the truth is that sickness is everywhere and affects everyone. As you look at the ministry of Jesus, you cannot miss the fact that Jesus healed many different people who suffered from many different sicknesses. But what about today? Does God still heal people?

As James begins to wrap up his power-packed letter, he sets his sights on suffering and sickness. James boldly declares that healing can be found through the prescription of prayer. But is James giving us a universal formula for healing? Is healing as simple as anointing someone with oil, praying for them, and then by faith they receive healing? If that is true, then what about all the people who *have* prayed for healing yet have never received this healing in this life? Did they tamper with the "James formula"? Did they lack the faith to be healed? Or, did they have some secret sins in their lives that prevented the healing process? How do we explain that good, godly people sometimes pray for healing and are not healed?

Take, for example, Joni Erikson Tada. As a young girl, she became a quadriplegic after diving into shallow water. When medicine failed, she became convinced that God would heal her. So, "she brought together a group of friends and church leaders and set up a private healing service. The week before the service she publicly confessed her faith by telling people, 'Watch for me standing on your doorstep soon; I'm going to be healed.' On the scheduled day, the group read Scriptures, anointed her with oil and prayed in fervent faith. . . . [She] did everything right and seemed to have met all the conditions, yet she was not healed."[66] She followed the "formula," so why was she not healed? In the Bible, many faith-filled saints have prayed for and never received healing. Even the apostle Paul, Timothy, and Trophimus struggled with sickness.

How do we reconcile the fact that God heals some people and not others? First, we must understand that the choice of whether to heal or not resides in the sovereignty of God and not in the desires of man. Is God able to heal? Yes! Does God heal people today? Yes! Does God heal everyone? No! Why not? Put simply, if God's will is for a person to be healed, and the healing will glorify God, then God will heal that person. Now, if you are asking yourself, *Well, God says that we are healed by His stripes, right?* (See Isaiah 53:5.) The answer is yes. *But . . .* this healing is related to our spiritual health and the forgiveness of sin and not our physical health.

So, what is God's prescription for healing? Even though healing resides in the sovereignty of God, we are still instructed to come to Him with our requests.

We may miss out on His healing touch in our lives if we fail to ask in faith. But no matter God's answer to our request for healing, we must always remember that the answer is up to God. Maybe that healing will happen now, or maybe we will have to wait until heaven for full healing. But in the meantime, remember that God's grace is sufficient for any sickness, and His strength is made perfect in any weakness (see 2 Corinthians 12:9).

"Though you ascend as high as the eagle, and though you set your nest among the stars, from there I will bring you down," says the Lord." (Obadiah 1:4)

OCTOBER
8

Falling for Pride

ALTHOUGH OBADIAH is the shortest book in the Old Testament, the book addresses one of the biggest problems that people deal with: the issue of pride. Pride was the very first sin, and will likely be the very last sin as well. Unfortunately, the sin of pride is often trivialized and dismissed as "no big deal," which only serves to make pride an even bigger deal. The full extent of the destructive nature of pride is evidenced by the fact that this was the sin of Satan, the father of all sin. His pride caused him to say, "I will ascend above the tops of the clouds; I will make myself like the Most High" (Isaiah 14:14 NIV). And, pride tempts a person to take the first bite of the cleverly disguised bait that lures him or her into believing that he or she is the most important person in the world.

Obadiah was writing to warn of the fall of Edom that was coming because of their pride. The Edomites were the descendants of Esau, the brother of Jacob. An intense sibling rivalry between these two brothers continued with their descendants. Edom was a great kingdom where the people carved great cities out of rock. The city of Petra is one of the great cities of the Edomites, and because of the impenetrable nature of a city such as Petra, the Edomites felt safe and secure. They felt strong and shrewd. The result was that they trusted in their resources, their reason, their riches, and their relationships instead of trusting in their relationship with God. They thought they were untouchable and indestructible, but they were very wrong. Little did they know, they were about to fall from greatness at the hand of God because of their prideful practices.

How about you? Are you trying to run your life without God? Do you trust in your wealth, wisdom, and wherewithal to get by instead of trusting in God to direct your life? If you said yes or even maybe to any of these, you are in danger of falling for pride, just like the Edomites did, and the result will be a spiritual nosedive. The essence of pride is living without God by dismissing your need for God, taking the position of authority in your life that is reserved for God and God alone. Pride deceives people into thinking they are something different than they really are, and blinds them from seeing the reality of pride's depravity.

How can we avoid falling for pride's invitation to be puffed up with self-importance?

The only countermeasure to pride is that of humility. Humility begins by confessing that we do not have adequate resources, reason, riches, or relationships outside of God to live a God-honoring life. Humility also means that we must submit to God and refuse to make decisions or take action before first seeking counsel from God's Word. Next, humility seeks to serve others even before serving self.

Pride is a tool that a person uses in order to exalt himself or herself, but ironically, that same tool that will cause a person to be brought low. The Bible tells us, "Humble yourselves in the sight of the Lord, and He will lift you up" (James 4:10).

In his great mercy he has given us new birth into a living hope through the resurrection of Jesus Christ from the dead, and into an inheritance that can never perish, spoil or fade. This inheritance is kept in heaven for you. (1 Peter 1:3–4 NIV)

OCTOBER
9

Hope for Today

CAN A PERSON SURVIVE in this world without hope? The significance of hope is never fully appreciated until all hope is gone. Have you ever lost hope? Perhaps a bad situation you expected to get better only got worse, or the good news you were waiting for never came, or the situation you thought would change simply stayed the same. When circumstances are such that seemingly no chance, no cure, no change, no cheer, no confidence, and no consolation can be found, you can be left feeling like life is hopeless. Opportunities to lose hope abound, but you can receive an infinite supply of heavenly hope that will keep you going, even when you experience the worst that life has to offer.

Being a Christian in the early years following Jesus' earthly ministry was tumultuous to say the least. Persecution was on the rise while Christian freedoms were on the decline. The apostle Peter recognized that Christians were being distressed by various trials (see 1 Peter 1:6), and were in danger of losing all hope. Peter knew that hope dramatically affects a person's behavior, and when a person has hope in Christ, everything changes. For example, holding on to a heavenly hope that promises eternal life and a heavenly inheritance gives a person the ability to see past current stresses and pressures and enables him or her to respond with a Christlike attitude and faithful conduct.

If you want to take hold of the living hope that God makes available so that no matter the stress or pressure, you will have enough hope for the day, then pay close attention. Hope for today begins with the realization that biblical truth is absolute truth. Biblical hope is not finger crossing, wishful thinking, or pie-in-the-sky dreaming. Nor is biblical hope "I hope so" believism. Rather, biblical hope is a confident conviction in God. Our hope for today is reliable because the Bible is reliable. Our hope for today is a living hope because the Bible is alive and active. Our hope for today is an unconditional certainty because the resurrection of Jesus Christ is an unconditional certainty. Jesus is alive, and therefore our hope is alive. Life without Christ is hopeless, whereas life in Christ provides endless hope.

This life never will be free from pressure and persecution or from suffering and sorrow, but when a Christian is filled with hope, he or she never will be overcome by life's difficulties. Hope for today means that we are willing to endure hardship today for the promised peace of tomorrow, and we are willing to live sacrificially today for the blessed inheritance of tomorrow. Hope for today means that "for to me, to live is Christ, and to die is gain" (Philippians 1:21).

Hope lights the way. Hope looks ahead. Hope lifts our spirits. Hope provides strength. Hope produces patience. Hope moves us forward. Hope abides with us. When all else fails, hope never does because Christ never fails. Set your hope completely on God, and He always will give you enough hope for today.

"But Jonah got up and went the other direction to Tarshish, running away from God. He went down to the port of Joppa and found a ship headed for Tarshish. He paid the fare and went on board, joining those going to Tarshish—as far away from God as he could get." (Jonah 1:3 MSG)

OCTOBER
10

You Can Run, but You Can't Hide

HOW FAST do you think you need to run in order to outrun God? How far is far enough to travel so that God cannot find you? Do these questions sound ridiculous? That's because they are. You can choose to run from God, but you most certainly cannot hide from God. You cannot go anywhere to escape God's presence, and you cannot keep any thought secret from God, because God is both ever-present and all-knowing. But do you think this stops people from trying to run from God? Not at all.

As ridiculous as this may sound, one of God's prophets thought he could outrun Him. He thought he could travel far enough away from God that God either would not be able to find him or would not care enough to go after him. That prophet's name was Jonah. One day, God spoke to Jonah and called him to go and preach to the people living in the city of Nineveh, the capital of the brutal Assyrian empire, and the largest city in the world at that time. But, when God told Jonah to get up and go on this mission of mercy to Nineveh, Jonah got up and went in the other direction. Nineveh was east of Israel, and Jonah decided to go west toward Spain. That does not seem very prophet-like, now does it? What would cause a servant of God to go against God? Jonah's reluctance was the result of fear, national pride, and simple disobedience.

Running from God is never a good idea, and will likely lead a person to make a series of other bad decisions, just as Jonah did. The first of Jonah's bad decisions was to go *down* to Joppa, a step that led him away from God and would lead to more downward decisions. This is the nature of sin; sin always takes a person further and further down, further and further away from fellowship with God. Next, Jonah found a boat that was going in the opposite direction of where God had told him to go. Whenever you are heading in the opposite direction from the will of God, you can be sure that the enemy will have a ship ready and waiting to lead you away from God. As F. B. Meyer pointed out, "Because the ship happened at that moment to be weighing anchor and the sails [were] filled with a favoring breeze, Jonah might have argued that his resolution was a right one. Whether he did or not, there are many times in our lives when we are disposed to argue that favoring circumstances indicate the right course."[67] We must not let the opportunity of circumstances outweigh the specific call of God on our lives.

Finally, Jonah paid the fare to get aboard the ship and sail away from God's will. Sin always comes at a high price, and we will inevitably pay the fare for sin as long as we choose to sail away from God's will.

This portion of Jonah's life illustrates the foolishness of disobeying God, regardless of the reason. God's command does not change just because we run from God. Our running is just going to cost us extra until we obey. Whether we feel like running away from God and His will, as Jonah did, or put our own wants before God's will, this is still disobedience, and we are still running away from God.

If you believe that God is calling you to a specific task, then get up and go in the direction He is calling you to go. Do not run from God, because no matter where you go, you cannot hide from Him.

But you are a chosen people, a royal priesthood, a holy nation, God's special possession, that you may declare the praises of him who called you out of darkness into his wonderful light. (1 Peter 2:9 NIV)

OCTOBER
11

Called to Be a Minister

IF YOU WERE A PRIEST OR PASTOR, would you live your life any differently than you are today? Would you get rid of anything in your home that may not seem appropriate for priestly living? Would you purposely *stop* doing something because the activity would not be fitting for a pastor to be caught doing? Perhaps your favorite TV show is a little too risqué, or having a couple of drinks out with friends is not the best example. Would you *start* doing something because the activity just seems right to do as a minister, like helping the poor or visiting the sick? Odds are, if you were part of the priesthood, you would begin looking at your life a little differently because, after all, ministers are required to live a more pure and holy life than the average believer, right?

Well, not to burst your religious bubble or anything, but if you are a Christian, then *you are* a priest. At this point, you might be thinking, *Me, a priest? You have got to be joking! I never attended seminary. I have not been ordained, and I do not get paid to work in a church.* That all may be true, but the fact remains that every Christian *is* part of a holy priesthood, chosen by God, belonging to God, set apart by God, and called to serve God as a consecrated minister to proclaim the love of God to those around us. Like it or not, ordained or not, you are in the ministry. You might not be part of the more public aspects of ministry that involve preaching from a pulpit or corporately carrying out the sacred sacraments, but you are still called to be part of the priesthood of Jesus Christ.

Throughout the Old Testament, priests were considered a separate spiritual group. Seemingly a cut above the rest, they were charged with doing the daily spiritual work of ministry as they offered sacrifices to God and served as mediators between God and man. But the New Testament position of every believer is one of a royal priest. All God's people have access to God. All God's people can enter His presence and be heard by God personally. We have this wonderful privilege not because we have been to seminary, not because we are superspiritual, but because we belong to Christ, our Great High Priest.

Ministry is not the sole responsibility of church "professionals"; ministry is the calling and responsibility of every believer. See yourself as God sees you: part of the priesthood of believers. This means that we are all equal before God, we all have equal access to God, we all are equally called to live a life worthy of the priesthood of believers, and we all are equally called to serve God completely. Ministry may not be your vocation, but God has appointed every believer to the priesthood, thereby making ministry your obligation.

Welcome to the ministry! Now that you are a part of the priesthood, should you be living your life any differently today?

From inside the fish Jonah prayed to the Lord his God.
(Jonah 2:1 NIV)

OCTOBER

12

Not Your Average Fish Story

THE STORY OF JONAH AND THE WHALE is a very fascinating one and causes some people to ask, "Do you really believe in the story of Jonah? I mean, really, a man swallowed by a giant whale? Something smells a little fishy to me!" If you are a Christian, you have probably come face-to-face with the doubtful and undecided person who has questioned the truth of stories like these. Skeptics love to attack the miracle of Jonah and the whale (or big fish, as you may know the story). But if a person is unwilling to accept this miracle, then odds are that they are unwilling to accept any miracle in the Bible.

The issue with the story of Jonah is not really the miracle of a man being swallowed by a whale and living to tell the greatest fish story ever. No, the issue is with God. The bottom line for the skeptic is, either God is able to perform miracles, or He is not. The issue is an issue of faith. The only point we will make about God's ability to perform this miracle, or any other miracle for that matter, is this: if God can create the universe, then certainly God can control everything within the universe, including a whale. But as amazing as miracles are, and as amazing as the miracle is of Jonah surviving after being swallowed by a whale, miracles are only tools used by God to accomplish His purposes. So then, what is the purpose behind this fish story?

God had a plan to reach the people of Nineveh with a message of mercy, and Jonah was to be a part of that plan. But Jonah refused and tried to run from God (bad idea, by the way). As Jonah tried to run away from God, his plans for escaping went terribly wrong. While attempting to sail away from the will of God, Jonah was thrown overboard. God, in His power and providence, unforgettably got Jonah's attention while Jonah was floating in a sea of disobedience. God brought a giant fish to swallow Jonah and changed Jonah's method of transportation from that of a ship to a fish. One led him away from God, and the other brought him back to God.

The belly of a whale certainly is not a great place to spend a three-day weekend, but the time does provide a person with a great opportunity for some alone time to reflect on decisions and choices that have been made. During Jonah's stay in the sauna of the fish's stomach, he had a change of heart and finally turned to God in prayer. Jonah could have prayed on the dock, on the shore, or even on the ship, but this experience was needed to bring Jonah to a place of total surrender. God could have justly let Jonah die and then chose someone else to do the job, but in His merciful sovereignty, He chose to spare Jonah's life and grant him a second chance.

At times in life, we may go astray, we may move off the path that God has set for us, and God may bring us to the place where we feel like we are in the belly of a great problem. What should we do? Turn to God.

Jonah was wrong, so God isolated Jonah inside the stomach of a smelly fish and did not end his "vacation" until the prophet was willing to return to obedience. While God often will be merciful to His people, we can never use this as an excuse to remain in the place of disobedience. Do not wait to be in the belly of a problem to choose obedience. Choose to follow God's will today, and spare yourself your very own fish story.

For to this you were called, because Christ also suffered for us, leaving us an example, that you should follow His steps. (1 Peter 2:21)

OCTOBER
13

Follow the Leader

THE STORY IS TOLD that during the American Revolution, a man in civilian clothes rode past a group of soldiers repairing a small defensive barrier. Their commander was shouting instructions but making no attempt to help. When the rider asked why he was not helping the men, he responded with great self-worth, "Sir, I am a corporal!"

So, the stranger apologized, dismounted, and proceeded to help the exhausted soldiers. When the job was done, he turned to the corporal and said, "Mr. Corporal, next time you have a job like this and not enough men to do it, just go to your commander-in-chief, and I will come and help you again."

The man was none other than President George Washington.

The world has always been in need of positive role models, people with integrity, and leaders who lead by example. Everything that Jesus did on earth is a perfect example for us to follow. The way in which Jesus trained His disciples was not purely academic; he did not require reading books and writing papers. Rather, his teaching involved following Him around and seeing how He ministered to people and how He responded to different life situations. When Jesus first called the disciples, the message was simple: "Follow Me!" Peter reminds us now, years after Jesus' death and resurrection, that the message has not changed, and the best way to live a godly life is by following in the footsteps of Jesus.

Jesus left us an example to follow, but if we are honest, we would admit that walking in the footsteps of Jesus is not easy and would be downright impossible if not for the help of the Holy Spirit. Many people say they want to follow Jesus, and that is great! But what does following in the footsteps of Jesus really mean? Following Jesus is more than accepting a religious belief system; this is a way of life. Following in the footsteps of Jesus means that we are putting feet to our faith. Following Him implies that we are moving forward, that we are taking action, and that what was important to Jesus is also important to us.

What would happen if believers who were genuinely interested in following in the footsteps of Jesus looked for ways to exemplify Jesus in the everyday routines of their lives? How would Jesus want me to walk through suffering? How would Jesus want me to show submission? How would Jesus want me to demonstrate patience? How would Jesus want me to live out mercy? How would Jesus want me to exhibit meekness? How would Jesus want me to reveal grace? How would Jesus want me to embody godliness? How would Jesus want me to endure hardship? How would Jesus want me to demonstrate compassion (and so on)?

If we are going to follow in the footsteps of our Lord and Savior, then we must be dedicated to glorifying God in all that we do, because Jesus was dedicated to glorifying God in everything He did. If we are going to follow in the footsteps of Jesus, we must be determined to spend quality and quantity time in prayer with God because that is what Jesus did. If we are going to follow in the footsteps of Jesus, we must be committed to the Word of God because Jesus was the Word made flesh.

If you are ever in doubt as to what you should do, then look to Jesus and follow His lead.

The people of Nineveh believed God's message, and from the greatest to the least, they declared a fast and put on burlap to show their sorrow. (Jonah 3:5 NLT)

OCTOBER
14

Desperate for Forgiveness

THIS IS ONE of the most incredible chapters in the Bible, and the book says much about the power of repentance and the nature of God. This is a case in which God was about to destroy an evil nation that was an enemy of the Israelites, but God changed His mind when He saw the repentant hearts of its people. When you sin and fall short of God's standard, are you desperate to regain intimacy with God through prayer and repentance? The Ninevites were so convicted of their sin that not only did they fast, but they also made their animals fast. And not only did they put on sackcloth, but they made their animals wear sackcloth. They were desperate for God's forgiveness. How desperate are you for God's forgiveness?

When Jonah went to Nineveh, he delivered a message of judgment, a message of doom and gloom in which he declared, "Forty days from now Nineveh will be destroyed!" (Jonah 3:4 NLT). No promise was given of forgiveness, no reference to God's love, and no mention of mercy. Jonah basically was saying, "You are all going to die!" But the people listened nonetheless. They were cut to the heart, and they repented. And "when God saw what they had done, and how they had put a stop to their evil ways, he changed his mind and did not carry out the destruction he had threatened" (verse 10 NLT).

Widespread revival broke out in one of the most evil cities of the ancient world because the people of that city were overwhelmed by their sin. They saw their need for God, they desperately sought God's forgiveness, and were committed to changing their behavior. Are you that desperate for God's forgiveness? Or, have you grown calloused toward your sin? Are you taking the grace of God for granted? Or, are you urgently pursuing the forgiveness of God?

Feeling bad about sin and confessing your sins to God but still choosing to change nothing is possible. Repentance means that you must take responsibility for your sin and make a commitment to change your sinful action or attitude. Repentance is not feeling sorry about your actions; repentance means that you understand that your sin grieves God, and you commit to change your behavior in order to please God. This is what the Ninevites did (see verse 8), and is also what we must do if we are desperate for the forgiveness of God.

Real repentance can only be found in a close, personal relationship with God, and being real with God by confessing our sins and changing our behavior is crucial. No sin is so great as to be beyond the reach of God's grace. The question is, have you come to the place where you are desperate for God's forgiveness? Are you desperate enough that God is more important to you than your sin? Are you desperate enough that you are willing to turn everything over to God and walk away from that sin once and for all?

Forgiveness is a miracle of grace, and God is eagerly waiting for all who are desperate for His forgiveness. As the psalmist David declared, "Oh, what joy for those whose disobedience is forgiven, whose sin is put out of sight!" (Psalm 32:1 NLT).

Always be prepared to give an answer to everyone who asks you to give the reason for the hope that you have. But do this with gentleness and respect. (1 Peter 3:15 NIV)

OCTOBER
15

To Everyone an Answer

HAVE YOU EVER FELT overwhelmed and underprepared when defending your faith in Jesus Christ? After all, you must contend with countless philosophies, numerous religious systems, and various viewpoints, and trying to keep track of all the different information out there can be challenging and confusing for most Christians. Inevitably, all Christians will find themselves in a situation where they are forced to defend their faith, and the apostle Peter challenges us to always be prepared to share with anyone and everyone who may ask us why we believe what we believe.

Christians need to be ready to give an answer to others as to why they have hope in Christ. But, with busy lifestyles and endless demands on their time, many Christians never have taken the time to really think through their beliefs, and therefore, feel uncomfortable and unprepared when called on to defend their faith. But you do not have to have a doctorate in theology or have studied apologetics to be properly prepared to give an answer to those who ask.

To properly communicate your faith in God to others, you must first have personal communion with God. The first step in being prepared to share your faith is having a solid foundation. Your personal relationship with Jesus must be a priority, which means that you need to be dedicated to spending time in prayer, time reading and studying your Bible, and time in fellowship with other believers.

Second, know the basics. This does not mean that you have to be an expert, but every Christian should be acquainted with a few basics like these: Jesus Christ is the only way to salvation (see John 14:6), we are saved by grace and not by works (see Ephesians 2:8–9), Jesus Christ is the Son of God (see John 11:25), Jesus Christ came in the flesh (see Matthew 1:23), Jesus rose from the grave (see Matthew 28:6), the doctrine of the Trinity (see 1 John 5:7), the Bible is the inspired and inerrant Word of God (see 2 Timothy 3:16), and we are given the Holy Spirit at the moment of salvation (see Ephesians 1:13).

Third, make sure that you spend more time studying your Bible than you do studying false philosophies. The best defense of your faith is to know your faith inside and out, which means knowing your Bible.

Fourth, pray for wisdom and ask the Spirit of God to give you the right words (see James 1:5).

Lastly, be able to explain the gospel message clearly. The point of defending the faith is so that you might have an opportunity to lead someone to Christ. So, be ready to seal the deal with the salvation message.

Defending your faith is not always easy, and usually means you will be mocked, ridiculed, and labeled as narrow-minded or dogmatic at times (or much worse). But none of this should discourage you from responding in love. Some say that people do not care how much you know until they know how much you care. So, be ready to give everyone an answer for what you believe, but above all, be ready to give that answer with gentleness and respect, even if you do not receive the same treatment.

Then the Lord said, "Is it right for you to be angry?"
(Jonah 4:4)

Anger Management

OCTOBER
16

SOMETIMES, THE SLIGHTEST THING can send a person into a fit of anger. Do you have a short fuse? Do you find difficulty in keeping angry feelings from erupting like the Yellowstone geyser Old Faithful? Anger is a common emotion that can have serious consequences. We all handle anger differently, but no matter how we express our anger outwardly, anger is sure to take its toll inwardly. Anger gnaws at our souls and sabotages our health. Anger strains our relationships, especially our relationship with God. And although everyone must deal with anger, not everyone deals with anger correctly.

Jonah was a prophet who had a battle of wills with God. He repeatedly wanted to do things his own way, while God wanted him to do things *His* way. When Jonah resisted and ran from God, God made Jonah fish bait and had him swallowed by a great fish. This gave Jonah a few days to reconsider and repent of his stubborn willfulness. Once Jonah agreed to do things God's way, he was redirected and recommissioned by God. Yet, despite the detour, God's plan remained the same, which was to use Jonah as His spokesman to offer mercy to the Ninevites. Jonah obeyed but would become angry with God for showing mercy to the enemies of the Jews. When the people of Nineveh repented and God relented from destroying them, Jonah got mad at God for being gracious and compassionate, which is ironic, since Jonah recently enjoyed the benefits of God's grace and mercy himself. Why was Jonah so angry? Very simply, Jonah did not get what *he* wanted, so he got mad.

If we were honest with ourselves, we would see that our own anger often can be traced back to the same reason. We get mad when we do not get our own way. Other variations of the same idea are, we get mad when we are not treated the way we want, when we do not get what we want when we want it, when things basically go in a way we do not prefer, or when we do not receive what we think we deserve. Our pride gets hurt, and we get angry. What happens next is a very predictable pattern for anger to follow.

Jonah's anger caused him to lose perspective (see Jonah 4:3), become irrational (see verse 3), make accusations, even against God (see verse 2), try to justify his own actions (see verse 2), and even isolate himself (see verse 5). These are all warning signs that we or someone we love are being led astray by anger. Anger begins to cloud our judgment and negatively influences our thinking, and we need to watch for the warning signs.

So how can we handle anger in a way that is healthy and not harmful to others or ourselves?

First, be aware that not all anger is a sin, and when we are justified in having a righteous anger, we still must be careful not to allow that anger to lead us into sinful actions.

Next, be aware of what makes you angry, and be watchful for those anger signs. When frustrations mount and anger begins to bubble up, *confess it* to God (see 1 John 1:9), *change it* into godly alternatives (see Ephesians 4:32; Colossians 3:12), and *commit it* to God and allow Him to work things for your greater good. Then, *continue it* as often as you need until you begin to properly manage your anger.

And that water is a picture of baptism, which now saves you, not by removing dirt from your body, |but as a response to God from a clean conscience. It is effective because of the resurrection of Jesus Christ. (1 Peter 3:21 NLT)

OCTOBER
17

Why Baptize?

HOW CAN WE UNDERSTAND AND EXPLAIN this mysterious ordinance of baptism and the role the act plays in the life a believer today? As Max Lucado has said,

> The human mind explaining baptism is like a harmonica interpreting Beethoven: the music is too majestic for the instrument. No scholar or saint can fully appreciate what this moment means in heaven. Any words on baptism, including these, must be seen as human efforts to understand a holy event. Our danger is to swing to one of two extremes: we make baptism either too important or too unimportant. . . . One can see baptism as the essence of the gospel or as irrelevant to the gospel. Both sides are equally perilous.[68]

Baptism in the early church was often the very first act of obedience for a new believer in Christ. New believers felt an urgency to fulfill this ordinance with haste. Baptism was more than just going through the spiritual motions, and more than empty tradition. Baptism was an important first step that signified a believer's new life in Christ.

The purpose behind baptism is threefold.

First, baptism is a public, outward *expression* that reveals a personal, inward commitment to Christ. The expression is to be the evidence of an inner change that has occurred in the person's life when, through faith, he or she trusts in Jesus Christ for salvation.

Second, baptism is a believer's *identification* with the Father, Son, and Holy Spirit (see Matthew 28:19). Baptism also identifies a believer with the message of the gospel, with other believers, and with the death, burial, and resurrection of Christ (see Colossians 2:11–12; Romans 6:4).

Third, baptism is an *illustration* representing a profound spiritual truth, signifying a believer's death to his or her old life and his or her resurrection as a new creation in Christ (see Romans 6:1–8; Colossians 2:12). In other words, baptism is an *expression* of our faith, an *identification* of our faith, and an *illustration* of our faith.

We are to be baptized because Jesus commanded us to do so (see Matthew 28:19), and Jesus demonstrated how to do so (see Matthew 3:13). Water baptism is *not* an act of salvation, but is a byproduct of our salvation. Baptism is a sign of our sanctification, a clue of our cleansing from sin, and a symbol of our commitment to the great commission of Christ to the church. Baptism is an act of obedience, and as an act of obedience, the act should be preceded by our repentance and followed by our submission to God.

Baptism is much like a marriage ceremony; both are public declarations of love. In a baptism, we are publicly declaring our love and commitment to Jesus, and in a marriage ceremony, we are declaring our love and commitment to another person. So, why baptize? Baptism is the way in which we show that we have died to our old way of life through the death of Jesus and live a new life through the resurrection of Jesus. We come up from the waters of baptism cleansed from our sin in the same way that water cleanses us from dirt.

Listen to what the Lord is saying. (Micah 6:1 NLT)

Are You Listening to God?

OCTOBER
18

SOME PEOPLE HAVE SAID that God has given us two ears and one mouth so that we can listen twice as much as we speak. God has given us the privilege of prayer, where we can speak to Him and pour out our hearts to Him. But, we can be so eager in our desire to talk to God that we do not take the necessary time to stop and listen to Him. And the reality is, we cannot listen to God if we are always talking. Learning to listen to God is an exciting aspect of our journeys with God that can lead down a path of great joy and fulfillment in our walks with God. God has much to say to each one of us about life and godliness, but are we listening?

God definitely wants us to listen to Him, but like the nation of Israel, we can ignore His voice and veer off course, if we are not ready and willing to pay attention to what He has to say. Micah called the people to listen to the Lord. God had a case to bring against His people because they had failed to listen and respond to God's Word. God's dispute with Israel took the form of a legal proceeding, as though God had taken Israel to court. If God's people had only listened to Him in the first place, they would not be suffering this scolding by God. But God's mercy is great, and although the people had not done a great job of listening to God in the past, they still had hope, if they were willing to listen to Him now.

A person can easily doubt whether they are hearing from God. Who would not love hearing from God as easily as getting a personal e-mail from heaven every time God had something to say to us? Or, perhaps we could have a special ringtone that went off every time God wanted to speak to us directly. Listening to God is not quite that easy, but we can learn to listen to Him.

The best way to start learning to listen to God is by spending time in the Bible. This is the primary way God communicates to His people today. So, if you want to listen to God, then take the time to hear what He is saying in His Word.

Next, listening to God involves examining your circumstances. Often, God will lead you through certain circumstances to speak directly into your life. Also, sometimes, God will use other people to speak into your life. Perhaps a word of encouragement will be spoken to you, a word of exhortation, or even a word of rebuke. Do not dismiss the godly counsel of those whom you know and trust in the faith. Take a moment and listen to others as they speak into your life. God also may speak to you through the still, small voice of His Holy Spirit. Here, God may give you peace about a decision, or make you uneasy about a direction you are planning to go.

God speaks in different ways at different times for different reasons. So be attentive, be thoughtful, be prayerful, be expectant, and be patient. Hearing from God is not so much a matter of whether He is speaking; hearing from God is more a matter of whether you are listening.

Give all your worries and cares to God, for he cares about you. (1 Peter 5:7 NLT)

Because He Cares

OCTOBER 19

LIFE ON THE THIRD ROCK from the sun has its share of cares and concerns. With each passing trip we take around the luminary giant, more and more reasons seem to arise for us to become apprehensive, anxious, fearful, uneasy, and concerned. From our finances to our fitness, from our personal appearances to our personal relationships, from our work to our well-being, we are at risk of being needlessly overloaded with an abundance of anxieties. The question is no longer, "What am I worried about?" Rather, the question has become, "What do I do when worry begins to flare up?"

Peter tells us that if we want to live carefree Christian lives (not careless, mind you), then we must give all of our cares to God; and yes, all means *all*!

Every past, present, and future care, every "big" care, and every "small" care must be turned over to God. We cannot hold on to a little care here, or hide a little worry there. God is interested in *all* our cares, no matter the size and no matter the shape. God is asking us to turn them all over, totally and completely, into His capable hands. The reason God wants to relieve us of our burdens is because *He cares for us*. Peter knows that we desperately need to remember this truth, because when we fail to remember that God cares for us, then our cares can begin to overwhelm us.

Worry focuses on the short-term, leading us to forget that our problems will not last forever. When we worry, we often make our problems last longer than necessary. By worrying, we are choosing to hold on to our concerns, rather than turning them over to God. Our worry often blinds us to the fact that God cares for us! The temptation when we worry is to think that God does not care about us and does not care about our situations. But nothing could be further from the truth. The truth is that God cares for us more than we know.

If you are in need of a little reminder today of some of the ways God has demonstrated His deep care for you, then just remember this: He created you (see Psalm 139:13), He died for you (see Romans 5:8), and He has forgiven you (see Ephesians 4:32). He has given you His Spirit (see 2 Corinthians 5:5), His Word (see 2 Timothy 3:16), and His righteousness (see Philippians 3:9). He knows you by name (see John 10:3), and He even knows the number of hairs on your head (see Matthew 10:30). If God cares for the smallest sparrow, then you can be certain that He cares more for us, whom He has created in His very image (see Matthew 6:26; Genesis 1:27).

You matter to God! He is interested in every aspect of your life, whether something seems extraordinarily small or universally gigantic. Remember, God cares, and He wants to help. Remember that casting your cares upon God does not mean that you can be irresponsible. Do what you can, and trust God to take care of the rest.

He has shown you, O man, what is good; And what does the LORD require of you but to do justly, to love mercy, and to walk humbly with your God? (Micah 6:8)

OCTOBER
20

Bumper Sticker Theology

IF YOU DO ENOUGH DRIVING, you eventually will become familiar with bumper sticker theology. This is where people use bumper stickers to broadcast their religious beliefs and opinions. With quick quips and short one-liners, people make statements like, "My Karma ran over your Dogma" or "Stop Global Whining." Christians are no exception. They, too, have taken their faith on the open road with bumper sticker theology, boldly proclaiming, "Honk if you love Jesus!"; "God is my copilot!"; "God allows U-turns"; or "Do you follow Jesus this close?" If you are a Christian that likes short phrases that capture spiritual truths, then Micah has the verse for you, delivering a one-verse summary of what God wants from our lives.

The people of Israel came to the prophet Micah and asked him, "What does

God want from us?" In other words, they were asking God, as most of us have asked, "Show us what you want us to do!" or "Just give us a sign!" They were seeking God's direction and His requirements for godly living. The prophet's response was a simplified summation of the law of God, a little Old Testament bumper sticker theology if you will, by delivering three short spiritual truths for everyone to live by. Micah told the people that what God wanted from them was to *do justly, to love mercy, and to walk humbly with God.* And although bumper sticker theology is often a little superficial, Micah's advice is far from shallow spiritualism.

These three truths are not designed to be applied like a bumper sticker, where you stick it and forget it. These truths are to be essentials for living in harmony with God.

To *do justly* simply means to do what is right. Often, doing what is right means that we must be willing to do what is right according to the Bible, regardless of the consequences. We are to live responsibly and act rightly in all our relationships, and we are to treat others how we want to be treated.

To *love mercy* means to show kindness, even when unearned and unreciprocated. We love many things in the world, such as being right, having power, and being successful, but do we love being merciful? Do we love being kind when someone is unkind to us?

To *walk humbly with your God* means to daily live dependent upon God, to rely on God's resources and not man's resources, and to submit to God's will over self-will.

These three truths represent more than mere bumper sticker theology. They represent qualities that every believer needs to understand and practice. Therefore, the next time you are wondering what God wants you to do, just remember that He has shown you what is good and what He wants from you. So, start here.

I will always remind you about these things. (2 Peter 1:12 NLT)

Spiritual Sticky Notes

PARENTS HAVE A FULL-TIME JOB reminding their kids to do things they already have been taught to do, like, "Wash your hands before you eat," "Pick up your clothes off the floor," and "Brush your teeth before you go to bed." Some say that because our minds have been affected by sin, we forget the things we should remember and remember the things we should forget. Therefore, we use shopping lists to remind ourselves of things we need to buy, we use calendars to remind ourselves of appointments we need to keep, and we even go so far as to place sticky notes on everything to remind ourselves of things we are likely to forget. What about our spiritual lives? Do we need regular reminders of the issues of our faith?

C. S. Lewis said, "We have to be continually reminded of what we believe."[69] The apostle Peter would completely agree. Repetition is the key to learning, and Peter was committed to constantly reminding believers of what was important.

Peter wrote this epistle to as an eternal reminder of important spiritual truths. And even though his audience knew and was grounded in many of the truths he was writing about, he knew that hearing them again was important for them to stay grounded in their faith, and this is just as true for us today.

Why do we need to be constantly reminded of what we believe? Well, being reminded of spiritual truth gives us hope, protects us from error, keeps us going in the right direction, and helps us resist sin. And we must not ignore the fact that we are all prone to forget. One of the great enemies of the Christian mind is forgetting spiritual truth. So, we must work to counter our forgetfulness by weekly listening to the preaching of God's Word, by reading and rereading through the entire Bible, by meditating on what we read and hear from the Bible, and by committing verses of the Bible to memory through repetition. Part of learning is applying what we learn, and although we may have heard something a hundred times, until we apply that truth to our personal lives, we may need to hear the same truth a hundred more times. How much you know is not what is important; more important is whether you are you using what you know.

Reminding is the nature of ministry, and is also one the jobs of the Holy Spirit (see John 14:26). The closer the Word of God is to our lips, the deeper the Word is rooted in our hearts. As we live out our days, no greater work is to be done than to remind one another of spiritual truth. People do not need our counsel as much as they need to hear the counsel of God. Take the time to leave yourself, or someone you know, a spiritual sticky note as a reminder of things we are prone to forget about God.

The Lord will be a light to me. (Micah 7:8)

Let There Be Light

OCTOBER
22

MOST WOMEN LOVE CANDLES and use them for decoration, aromatherapy, and relaxation, while most men see candles exclusively as a light source, reserved for power outages and other emergencies. In fact, the entire candle business is oriented toward women, with candle scents like Lilac Blossom and Juniper Breeze. If candle makers want to get men to buy candles for their own relaxation and aromatherapy, they need to create scents like Grilled Rib Eye and Fresh-Baked Bread! While candles are often used as amenities, light is more than just a convenience; light is a necessity.

The Bible often uses the image of light when speaking of God: "God is light and in Him there is no darkness at all" (1 John 1:5). Jesus, speaking of His identity and relationship to God the Father, said that He was the light of the world (see John 8:12). Additionally, John explains how Jesus is a light that shines in the darkness (John 1:1–5). When used to describe the Creator, light is often a reference to His glory, His goodness, and His righteousness. The Scriptures describe the experience of God's light as the greatest blessing any human being can enjoy. Micah knew that the greatest blessing in his life was the fact God was his light, a light that brought warmth and comfort, a light that promoted growth and fruitfulness, a light that illuminated his path and gave him direction, and a light that dispelled darkness and brought protection.

Have you experienced the blessing of having God as your light? We live in a spiritually dark world, and God is the sole light source,. By virtue of our fallen condition, we are in a constant state of darkness and are thereby separated from the light of God. But, in Christ, we are reconciled to God and now can experience fellowship with the light. The Bible is clear that those who experience God's light are to walk in the light as God is in the light (see 1 John 1:7), walking in the light of God's will and Word.

Because God is light, when He gets involved in our lives, He begins to illuminate those things in our hearts that we may have kept in hidden in the dark shadows. The best and most freeing thing we can do is to allow God to shine the light of His Word into the recesses of our hearts so that He can purge and purify them. And as we enjoy the light of God's goodness and grace in our own lives, we must not keep that light to ourselves. Instead, we have a responsibility to share the light of God with a world that is trapped in darkness (see Matthew 5:14–16).

Let God be the light of your life. Recognize that He is a necessity and not an amenity. God is not a mystical accessory in our lives. He is not there for ornamental enrichment. Rather, He is as indispensable, just as light is to life.

There will be false teachers among you. They will cleverly teach destructive heresies.
(2 Peter 2:1 NLT)

OCTOBER
23

Don't Drink the Kool-Aid

NO ONE EVER EXPECTED that it would happen, especially with this model congregation. They provided a heated swimming pool for underprivileged kids, horses for inner-city children to ride; they gave scholarships for deserving students and provided housing for senior citizens. They even had an animal shelter, medical facility, an outpatient care facility, and a drug rehabilitation program. Walter Mondale wrote that the pastor was "an inspiration to us all." The Secretary of Health, Education, and Welfare cited the pastor's outstanding contributions: "He knew how to inspire hope." Where are they now? Where is this model congregation—dead! One day their pastor called everyone together—spoke to them about the beauty and certainty of death—then proceeded to give everyone cyanide laced Kool-Aid—when it was all over 918 people were dead—including the pastor, Jim Jones.[70]

False teachers have always been trying to get people to drink their lies and swallow their poison. They have laced the truth of God with cyanide adulterations, hiding behind pseudo religiosity instead of inspiring real change. They have been dividing and weakening the church of Christ since its inception by manipulating and misapplying the truth for their own advantages. False teachers know the truth, but deliberately distort the truth in order to deceive others, often for personal gain, selfish ambition, or even to satisfy others.

Whatever their motivations are, false teachers are nothing more than hell's bartenders, serving up deadly cocktails of half-truths mixed with deceit and deception, leading to spiritual intoxication. Christians must be cautious and watchful so they do not drink the strange brew that false teachers are serving up.

How can you detect the deceptiveness of false teachers? False teachers emphasize experience over truth, they depend on charisma over correctness, and they bring confusion and not clarity. They promote division rather unity, elevate personal desires over moral absolutes, deny the deity of Jesus, use eloquence to sidestep error, exploit their followers, and are more concerned with convincing others of their opinions rather than searching for the truth.

To help you determine whether someone is teaching truth or promoting a twisted reality, consider a few questions: Where does their message come from? What is at the center of their message? What does their message promise?

The source of the Christian message is the Bible, and nothing else! The center of the Christian message is salvation through faith in Jesus Christ, and the promise is a new life in Christ now, and an eternal life in heaven later.

The church always will be subject to the heresy of smooth-talking false teachers. Christians must understand how they operate and be alert for their presence within the body of Christ. While we must not be quarrelsome over nonessential matters, we should never be afraid to stand against those who might pervert or subvert the fundamentals of the Christian faith.

Let us, in love, help those who are in bondage to false doctrines and keep ourselves firmly grounded in the essentials of the Christian faith.

Where is the god who can compare with you?
(Micah 7:18 MSG)

OCTOBER
24

Nothing Compares to God

WHO IS LIKE GOD? We cannot fully comprehend an incomprehensible God. Grasping that which is invisible, immaterial, and immeasurable is impossible. As the magnificent Designer of an amazing universe, He is unconstrained by physical parameters. Nowhere exists where He has not been and nowhere exists where He cannot go. He is both outside of our time and space continuum, yet able to enter at any given moment. He is infinite yet intimate, abstract yet authentic. He is self-sufficient, self-sustaining, and self-perpetuating.

"Where is the god who can compare with you?"

The prophet Micah knew that God is unique and unlike anyone or anything else in all of existence. And although his question is a rhetorical one, Micah nevertheless attempts to explain why our great God is like no other. Micah mentions that God is unsurpassed in His judgment and in His deliverance, unparalleled in His guidance and in His forgiveness, unmatched in His faithfulness and in His compassion, and unrivaled in His mercy. What Micah understood about God gave him a greater confidence in God and elevated his worship of God.

"Where is the god who can compare with you?"

Our God is all this and so much more, and we must work to expand our view of God so that we can go deeper in our worship of Him. Consider that God has always existed and always will. Keep in mind that God is all-knowing and all-powerful. He is unchanging, unending, and unequaled. There is none like God in power, in knowledge, or in wisdom. God has authority over death, and by His word things come into existence. Nothing is impossible for God, and nothing can stop His plans and purposes from being carried out. He holds the universe together, He is the source of all truth, and His truth is eternal.

"Where is the god who can compare with you?"

As outstanding as God is, He is also personal. He miraculously became personal to humanity by becoming man in the person of Jesus Christ. He inexplicably becomes personal by depositing His Spirit inside all who trust in Him for salvation. He repeatedly becomes personal as He continually transforms His people into His image. He practically becomes personal as He speaks to His people through the Bible and His Holy Spirit. He generously becomes personal as He allows His people to become partners with Him in accomplishing His perfect plans.

"Where is the god who can compare with you?"

The answer is simple: *There is none*! Nothing compares to our great God, and nothing ever will.

May the reality of His majesty move you to go deeper in your worship of the One who has no equal.

The Lord is not slow in keeping his promise, as some understand slowness. Instead he is patient with you, not wanting anyone to perish, but everyone to come to repentance. (2 Peter 3:9 NIV)

OCTOBER
25

The Patience of God

GOD IS PATIENT. We are not. We want what we want, right when we want it. God, on the other hand, is able to remain calm and not become irritated while He is waiting. We often reveal our impatience when we ask questions like, "How much longer is this going to take?" God is not in a hurry, because God is on a totally different timetable than we are. God's schedule is so much different than ours because according to God's clock, one day is like a thousand years and a thousand years are like one day (see 2 Peter 3:8). God has existed from eternity past and will continue for eternity future, which explains why His view of time is a little different than ours. The problem arises when people mistake God's patience for His approval.

In Peter's second epistle, he refers to doubters who were questioning the promises of God. In particular, these skeptics were saying that since Jesus had not yet returned, the promise of His return must be a lie. Peter was quick to stress that the reason Jesus had not returned was because God is longsuffering with sinners. Longsuffering is God's ability not only to delay the execution of His wrath for a period of time, but also to delay that wrath to show grace toward sinners.

God is not blind, unable to see the evil that men do; *God is not* deaf, unable to hear the cries against such evil; and *God is not* weak, unable to stop evil. What is happening is that *God is not* willing that any should perish, so He patiently holds off His return so that many might be saved.

God is patient because He does not want people be to be lost for all of eternity. By His patience, He is giving people time to turn from sin and trust in Jesus. God's patience toward us is incredible, and because God *is* patient, countless numbers of people have trusted in Jesus for their salvation while we wait for the return of Christ.

The patience of God extends beyond salvation and continues to benefit people on a daily basis. How often have you enjoyed the patience of God? Can you count how many times God could have dealt harshly with you because of your sin, but He did not? God waits patiently for us to repent when we are being stubborn and disobedient, something for which we should be continually thankful.

We are all going to stand before God to give an account one day, and we must not abuse the patience of God by waiting to repent. Whether our repentance is leading to salvation or repentance leading to obedience, do not mistake God's patience for His approval. Is there something in your life that you have not repented of? Be thankful that God, in His patience, is willing to wait for you to ask forgiveness and to turn from your sin.

Be wise. Do not test the limits of God's patience. Do not wait for His discipline. Instead, do what is right and turn your heart toward God today.

You will cast all our sins into the depths of the sea.
(Micah 7:19)

The Sea of Forgetfulness

OCTOBER
26

WE ALL MAKE MISTAKES! We all slip up! We all sin! This should come as no surprise to you, but what may surprise you is that once God has forgiven you, He never will bring up your sins again. He will not throw them back in your face, He will not hold them over your head, and He will not use them against you. God does not want you to live under the constant condemnation of your recent faults and past failures. Dwelling on past mistakes and wallowing in self-pity is so easy when you have failed others and God, but your sins do not have to haunt you because God has permanently forgiven and completely forsaken your sins (see Ephesians 1:7; Psalm 103:12).

To think that a holy and righteous God would willingly forgive and remove all record of our transgressions is amazing. But no matter how difficult you may find this to believe, it is still true. If you have confessed your sins and turned your back on them, the Bible clearly teaches that you are forgiven (see 1 John 1:9). But something in us wants to keep dredging up our sins. If God chooses not to remember our sins anymore (see Isaiah 43:25), then why do we? Why do we always allow the Devil to dig up some spots or blemishes from the past and wave them in our faces, when all our sin has been completely covered by the blood of Christ? Do not try to dig up what God has buried. Do not relive what God has chosen not to remember.

Many people struggle with letting go of their past mistakes and moving forward in the freedom of forgiveness. Although some of our sins may have a few lingering consequences, we do not have to keep punishing ourselves as part of the atoning process.

God not only forgives us of our all our sins, but He also sends them into the deepest part of the ocean. God has tied a millstone around each sin, sinking it to the darkest depths of the ocean floor, never to see the light of day again. God will not dredge forgiven sins up again. He will not seek to use them as leverage against us. They will remain forever submerged in God's sea of forgetfulness. We just need to remember not to try and raise them up from the depths of the sea floor.

As a Christian, whether or not you feel forgiven, you are! Leave your faults and failures where God has sent them and where they belong: in the sea of forgetfulness.

Grow in the grace and knowledge of our Lord and Savior Jesus Christ. (2 Peter 3:18 NIV)

OCTOBER
27

Growing in Grace

LITTLE CHILDREN LOVE TO MEASURE THEIR GROWTH. Houses the world over have the incremental pencil marks on walls and doorposts, marking the growth spurts of their kids. However, growth is gradual and is something that is noticed over time, not spontaneous or instant. No one wakes up five inches taller than they were when they went to sleep.

Spiritual growth is much the same. Spiritual growth is not spontaneous or instant, and happens gradually, and no one goes to sleep one night and wakes up the next morning as a spiritual giant. But measurable growth, and visible changes should become evident over time , which mark our growth in Christ. As believers, Peter's final challenge to us is to make sure that we are growing in grace.

Grace is unmerited favor, undeserved kindness, and unearned blessing. Grace is God giving to us, not on the basis of what we have done, but in spite of what we have done: "For by grace you have been saved through faith, and that not of yourselves; it is the gift of God" (Ephesians 2:8). Peters impulsive, go-get-'em attitude provided him with plenty of opportunities to receive grace from the hand of Jesus, and is undoubtedly the reason that his final words encourage us to grow in grace.

Growing in grace starts when we receive the grace of salvation, given to us by God through Jesus Christ. That moment plays out as though God plants a seed of grace within us, a seed that must be nurtured if it is going to grow. The nourishment for such a seed is tied directly to the Word of God and the knowledge of God. Peter reminds us back in 1 Peter 2:2 that if we want to grow, then we must have a desire to feed on the Word of God.

Growing in grace often means that the lessons of grace taught in the Word of God are learned through our life experiences. Most of what Peter learned about grace came from his mistakes. After he denied the Lord three times, Jesus came to Him and extended grace to him, restoring him to ministry. The apostle Paul experienced grace through difficulty that he endured. Paul had a thorn in the flesh, some sort of anguish or trial, yet despite his repeated prayers and petitions for God to remove that thorn, God saw it as an opportunity for Paul to grow in grace (see 2 Corinthians 12:9).

Growing in grace is tied to our growing in the knowledge of Jesus Christ from His Word and from our personal experiences with God's Word in our lives. From our first experience with grace to our last, the more we grow in our knowledge of Jesus, the more we will understand about grace. And the more we grow in our knowledge of grace, the more we will understand about Jesus.

God is good. (Nahum 1:7 MSG)

The Goodness of God

OCTOBER
28

GOD NOT ONLY *DOES* GOOD, God *is* good. Odds are, we have all said , this and meant it. But do we really know what the *good* in "God is good!" really means? Are we speaking of the same *good* as when we say, "It's all good," "Good job," or even "Good dog!" In general, when we use the word *good* to describe people, places, or things, we are using good to show some measure of approval or appreciation. But when we say that *God is good*, so much more than just appreciation and approval is expressed. How are we to comprehend God's goodness, and what should our response be to His goodness?

God not only causes all things to work together for good as Romans 8:28 says, but He is also the standard for goodness. In fact, Jesus said, "No one is good—except God alone" (Luke 18:19 NIV). The goodness of God is related to the perfection of His being and the kindness of His actions. The goodness of God is connected to His moral uprightness and His loving compassion. God is always and absolutely good, He is independently and fundamentally good, and He is good in nature and good in character. Every good gift comes from God (see James 1:17), which means that all goodness in the world has its origin in the goodness of God.

Everything God does is good. His works, His plans, and His purposes are all good. He is good in His benevolence, and He is good in His chastisement. He is good in His judgment, and He is good in His forgiveness. He is good when He spares us from suffering, and He is good when He allows us to go through suffering. He has never been able to do anything but good and never will cease to be able to do good.

How does the goodness of God impact your daily life? How does His goodness help you live the Christian life? If we are to "be" good and "do" good, these can only be accomplished with God's help. The Bible is clear that no one is good, and no one can do good apart from God (see Romans 3:10–12). But the more we allow God to have His way in our lives, the more of His goodness we will experience and the more we can reflect His goodness to others. Only as we experience God and His goodness can we ever hope to be good or do good.

God is good, all the time, even when our circumstances may not feel good or even be good. God is still good. Everything God does is good, and everything God is working to accomplish is good. God even will take the bad stuff that happens to us and still use it for His good.

Take time throughout your day today to consider some of the ways that God has been good to you, and thank Him for the fact that He not only does good but also is good. God is good!

If we confess our sins to him, he is faithful and just to forgive us our sins and to cleanse us from all wickedness.
(1 John 1:9 NLT)

What to Do When You Have Blown It

SOMETIMES LIFE is going along just fine when, all of a sudden, we say something stupid or do something foolish. Regardless of what we might have said, or how we may have messed up, one thing is certain: we have all blown it at one time or another. As much as no one likes to admit when they have blown it, to admit, "I have sinned" is even harder. But, if we want to get right with God, and if we want to clear away any spiritual barriers that may have developed, the first thing we ought to do after we have blown it is to confess our sins to God.

The apostle John recognized that, as much as every Christian wished that he or she no longer sinned after trusting in Jesus for salvation, the fact remains: we all still sin. And instead of denying our sins or pretending they do not exist, we should be quick to confess our sins to God, knowing that He is ready and willing to forgive us and cleanse us from all unrighteousness.

Confession is more than a healthy practice; confession is the responsibility of every Christian. The more time we spend with God, the more aware we become of our faults and failures and the more we comprehend the depth of our own sinfulness. But God never convicts us of our sin to drive us away from His presence. Rather, His conviction, which comes by the Holy Spirit, is intended to draw us closer to Him and make us more like Him.

When we confess our sins to God, we are saying, "God, I agree with You. I have sinned." Confession is not informing God of something He did not see in us or know about us; confessing is agreeing with what God already sees in us and knows about us. Confession means that we come clean with God: no more secrets and no more attempting to deny or cover up our sins.

How can we make sure that we confess our sins correctly and completely?

First, confession should involve examination. Examine what God calls sin while also examining your own heart for sin.

Next, do not procrastinate regarding your confession. Do not put off until tomorrow what you know needs to be confessed today.

Also, be specific. Call your sin what God calls your sin. If the sin is lust, call it lust. If the sin is bitterness, call it bitterness.

Next, ask God for forgiveness. And once you have asked Him for forgiveness, accept His forgiveness. Move forward knowing that you are forgiven and cleansed, and do not hold on to your sins. Leave them with God, and walk in the freedom of His forgiveness.

When we sin, the best thing we can do is to confess the sin to God immediately so that we can experience His forgiveness and cleansing in our lives. As difficult as admitting, "I have sinned" may be, confession is the fastest way to reestablish a right relationship and intimate fellowship with God. Do not put off until tomorrow what needs to be confessed to God today.

The just shall live by his faith" (Habakkuk 2:4)

Living by Faith

OCTOBER 30

THE CHRISTIAN LIFE is the most wonderful and the most challenging experience anyone could ever hope to live. At the core of Christianity stands one word: faith. No other single word could so wholly encapsulate the message of the Bible and the purpose of the Christian life. In the happy times and the hard times, God's challenge to His people remains constant: live by faith.

The book of Habakkuk records a conversation between God and the prophet Habakkuk concerning a situation that troubled the prophet. Habakkuk was upset by the ungodliness and immorality that was spreading throughout the land of Israel. When Habakkuk asked God how long all this corruption would last, he got an answer that he did not like. God replied that He was not ignoring the wickedness of His people; in fact, He intended to raise up the Babylonians to discipline the pigheadedness of His people. This made Habakkuk even more confused and prompted him to ask God why He would use an infamously evil nation to discipline His chosen people. God's response to Habakkuk's concern was essentially, "Even though you don't understand all my ways and reasons, Habakkuk, what I want you to remember is this: *the just shall live by his faith."*

This verse is so important to the Christian life that it is repeated three times in the New Testament, once in Romans (1:17), once in Galatians (3:11), and once again in Hebrews (10:38), each time emphasizing a different aspect of this great truth.

Living by faith means that we live day to day, trusting God because His character never changes and His Word never fails. Living by faith means resting in the promises of God. Living by faith, as one writer put it,

> means trust, dependence, clinging to God; it means living and moving and having one's being in him alone; it means relying on him for the breath one draws, for the direction one takes, for the decisions one makes, for the goals one sets, and for the outcome of one's living. . . . Faithfulness means placing one's whole life in God's hands and trusting him to fulfill it, despite all outward and inward circumstances; despite all personal sin and guilt. Faithfulness is life by God's power rather than by one's own . . . ; and therefore it is truly life, because it draws its vitality from the living God who is the source of life.[71]

Living by faith does not mean that we live by serving or by sacrificing or by trying to be "spiritual." Living by faith does not mean living by our emotions, nor does it mean living by our IQ. No, living by faith means that we will not always know what God is doing and will not always understand how God is working, or even why God is doing what He is doing. What we do know is that God is in control, and we are to have faith in Him and His ways. We come to God by faith, we are justified by faith, and we are to live our lives by faith.

We will experience times in life when we, like Habakkuk, do not understand all that God is doing. But God has not changed, and His Word for us today is still the same: the just shall live by faith.

> "Do not defile yourselves by turning to mediums or to those who consult the spirits of the dead. I am the Lord your God." (Leviticus 19:31 NLT)

OCTOBER
31

Trick or Treat

HALLOWEEN. The holiday conjures up images of black cats, jack-o'-lanterns, witches, ghosts, and of course, candy. We cannot forget all the snack-sized candy! Halloween has become big business, second in sales only to Christmas. But is Halloween a harmless holiday or a day filled with evil and darkness? Are Christians overreacting about Halloween? And are Halloween alternatives like Harvest Festivals really any different?

For many, Halloween means little more than putting on a costume once a year and going around asking for free candy. For others, Halloween is an excuse to dress up and go to a costume party. Still others see the holiday as an opportunity to get scared out of their wits by visiting a haunted house. However you approach this spooky holiday, Halloween's origins can be undeniably traced back to pagan beliefs and rituals. Some of those beliefs and rituals centered on seasonal harvest preparations, while other beliefs and rituals embraced occult practices involving spiritism, divination, and superstition.

Halloween is not mentioned in the Bible, but some of the practices associated with this mysterious day are, like fortune telling, witchcraft, and séances. Whatever uncertainties Christians might have about the current position this holiday should have in their lives, one thing is clear: Christians are not to engage in any of the dark practices often tied to this day. As the Bible says, "For once you were full of darkness, but now you have light from the Lord. So live as people of light!" (Ephesians 5:8 NLT), and "don't become partners with those who reject God" (2 Corinthians 6:14 MSG).

What else should Christians consider as they approach Halloween?

First, Christians should not respond to Halloween superstitiously. We have the truth of God's Word on our side. Evil spirits are no more lively and menacing on Halloween than they are on any other day of the year. In fact, Satan prowls around every day, seeking whom he may devour (see 1 Peter 5:8). But God has triumphed over Satan and all evil through Jesus Christ (see 1 John 3:8).

Next, Christians should respond to Halloween with wisdom. The biggest trick on Halloween is most likely going to come from the social situations that promote sinful behavior like drunkenness, promiscuity, and other wrong behavior. Use wisdom by simply avoiding those tricky or tempting situations.

Lastly, Christians should see the unique opportunity that Halloween provides for sharing the gospel, whether in conversations with those who celebrate Halloween or those who come to your door trick or treating, or by participating in a Christ-centered alternative.

God never said that trick-or-treating is an abomination, or that all who ask for free candy are defiling themselves. But completely dismissing this day as innocent and innocuous is naïve. Whatever your personal view of Halloween is, celebration of the holiday is a matter of conscience before God. While definitely a unique holiday, just like any other day, what you make of it is what is important. So you can either seek to glorify God, or you can put God aside.

But whether you go asking for treats on this day or not, do not be tricked into thinking a dark side to this day does not exist. Christians are to be separate from the world and should use wisdom when approaching any day that has an associated dark side.

November

"Praisefulness"

"PRAISE THE LORD AND PASS THE SALT!" Some days, that is the sum total of our praise to God. While this may be sad, the truth is that we simply do not spend enough time praising God. Some may be feeling as though life is not giving them much to praise God about at the moment. For others, life may seem full of go, go, go, or work, work, work, which has left them feeling hurried and harried most of the time. Any of these conditions can leave us with a lackluster praise life.

Sure, when some "big" blessing comes along in our lives, we are quick to give God the proverbial pat on the back. And, before we dig into the food on our plates, we feel compelled to stop and pay God some polite praise for His provision. But does God not deserve more praise than that? No matter what your life condition, the problem of "praiselessness" (we will just make that our word for today, okay?) is a problem of priorities and a problem of perspective.

Habakkuk had been troubled by God's plans for Israel, which is understandable. Few men could remain unaffected by news of a coming invasion by a scary enemy. This impending invasion meant that Habakkuk had a choice to make: either he could let fear and frustration lead him to complain about God's plans and purposes, or he could trust God's plans and purposes and begin praising God. Two things in particular helped Habakkuk choose the right path of praisefulness over praiselessness: prayer and reflection on the past.

First, Habakkuk prayed (see Habakkuk 3:1). Prayer is often the best place to start when we need an attitude adjustment. God wants us to seek His face, to hear His voice, and to catch His vision, and prayer helps us to check our perspectives and get our wills in alignment with His will.

Next, Habakkuk considered the past (see verses 3–16). Habakkuk poetically reflected on some of the ways that God had worked in Israel's past to accomplish His plans and purposes, which boosted Habakkuk's confidence in God for his current circumstances. Reflecting not only on God's past faithfulness in the Bible, but also on His past faithfulness in our own lives, should give us attitudes of praisefulness. Because Habakkuk was able to keep the right perspective, he was able to praise God. Habakkuk knew that, even if everything around him fell apart, he would still be able to sing joyful praises to God because God was His strength (see verses 17–19).

Praise teaches us to be joyful and thankful regardless of our circumstances. Praise prepares us for God's service and helps us to see beyond our present circumstances to the possibilities that lie ahead because of our faith. Praise teaches us to turn our eyes away from circumstances and focus on God, whose plans are always good for His people, even if His will allows us to go through hard times. By focusing on our problems instead of praising God, we become self-centered and self-absorbed. Praise refocuses us and gets our attention off our problems and back on God, where our praise and focus belongs.

God gives us more than enough reasons every day to praise Him. Although we may not always be able to choose what happens to us, we can choose how we are going to respond to what happens to us. No matter how busy you are today, no matter how tough your situation is, choose praisefulness over praiselessness. You never will regret your choice.

Do not love the world or the things in the world. (1 John 2:15)

NOVEMBER

2

Living in a Material World

W E LIVE IN A MATERIAL WORLD, and if we are not careful, we can become material people. We dress to impress, we drive in style, we enjoy good food, and we appreciate the finer things in life, but these tastes can come at a high price. Let's face it. Things cost money, and nicer things cost even more money. And that usually means that we need to spend a lot more time working to make the money we need so we can buy the things we want. While chasing after the finer things in life is not all bad, we often get so preoccupied with the pursuit that we can miss the finest thing in life: God.

A tension exists for every Christian to live *in* the world but not to love the world. John cautions Christians not to take their salvation for granted by loving the world or the things of the world, because love for the world means the love of God is not in us. Now, we must understand here, that the *world* here is not referring to nature. Of course, Christians should appreciate God's creation the most because we know the Creator, and God considers His creation "good" (see Genesis 1:10). Also, the *world* is not referring to human beings, because people are created in the image of God (see Genesis 1:26) and are loved by Him (see John 3:16). Instead, what John is referring to when he says that we are not to love the *world* or the things of the world is the world system. The world system is a way of thinking and living that embraces the attitudes and beliefs of the world over the standards of God. This attitude causes some to want what they do not have and to trust in what they do have.

Are you wondering whether worldliness has become a distraction in your life? Are you unsure whether the pursuit of finer things has become a preoccupation? If so, consider the following: Are you satisfied with what you have? Or, are you always looking for the next, the newest, and the latest thing? Do you own anything that you would have a difficult time letting go of? What brings you more joy: your stuff or God? Be aware that John is not saying that everything material is evil, and he is not saying that we never can enjoy the things of this world. That is not the point. But if anything in a Christian's life diminishes his or her delight in God or the desire to do God's will, then he or she is in danger of loving the world more than God.

Loving God and living for the world are mutually exclusive. We cannot do both. Either we love God and live for God, or we love the world and live for the world. Just because we live in this world does not mean that we have to live for this world.

Keep yourself from becoming a material person by loving what God loves and pursuing the finest thing: God.

He will take delight in you with gladness. With his love, he will calm all your fears. He will rejoice over you with joyful songs." (Zephaniah 3:17 NLT)

Our God Sings

JOSIAH WAS KING IN JUDAH after Assyrian invaders had carried the northern kingdom of Israel away. During the early part of his reign in the kingdom of Judah, not learning from Israel's mistakes, the people descended deeper into sin and rebellion against God. In the eighteenth year of Josiah's reign, the Book of the Law was found and read to the people. This caused Josiah to humble himself before God (see 2 Kings 22:19), and he began an amazing reformation in Judah that he started by renewing the covenant between God and His people (see 2 Kings 23:3). These were the days of Zephaniah the prophet (see Zephaniah 1:1).

However, despite all that King Josiah did, his efforts were too little, too late. The reforms were good, but they did not last long. The result was the kingdom of Judah fell into the hands of the Babylonians. But, in the midst of Judah's defeat, the prophet Zephaniah spoke up and offered a word of hope to bless the people during those dark days, a word of hope that continues to bless God's people today.

What could be so deeply encouraging to God's people that no matter the circumstances, one can rejoice? The word to God's people, past, present and future, is this: God delights in you, God loves you, and God rejoices over you in song! What a thought: God rejoices over every person who finds his or her salvation in Him. God joyfully sings songs over His people. More longed-for are the songs of God for His people than the sweetest song of any nightingale. More marvelous are His songs to hear than the most angelic of voices. How blessed is the child of God to hear that our great God sings over His people. What a word of encouragement!

When God made creation, He did not sing, but merely saw that it was good. But for the redeemed of God, He feels such joy that He chooses to express Himself in a love song, a song He sings for His own. Except for the time when Jesus sang a hymn with His disciples at the Last Supper (see Matthew 26:30), this is the only place in the Bible where we read of God actually singing. God rejoices over you and me with singing. How amazing!

What should be the effect of such an astonishing truth be? With His love, He will calm all your fears. We may be worried about the future, we may be fearful about our circumstances, and we may be saddened by our sinfulness, but God's love is greater than any fear. And because we are now and forever clothed in the righteousness of Christ, He delights in us, He loves us, and He sings over us.

Knowing that our God sings over us should dispel the deepest fear, drive out the darkest doubt, and dismiss the innermost disquiet of your soul.

But whoever has this world's goods, and sees his brother in need, and shuts up his heart from him, how does the love of God abide in him? (1 John 3:17)

NOVEMBER

4

Helping Hands

AS YOU EXIT THE FREEWAY and approach the stoplight, you see the weather-beaten face and begin to read the cardboard sign: "Will work for food" or "Homeless, please help!" While walking on the streets of a big city, you cross paths with someone holding out a paper cup, asking for spare change. Ordinarily in these situations, thoughts run through your mind like, *Should I stop and help?* Or *how do I know they won't spend this money on drugs or alcohol?* What is a Christian to do? Are we expected to help everyone who is in need?

The apostle John had much to say on the subject of love, and one thing he strongly emphasized was that love in action was evidence of genuine faith. John presented love as the proof that we have passed from death to life (see 1 John 3:14). Our love is not measured only by the supreme sacrifice of laying down our lives for others (verse 16) but also by our willingness to lay down our material stuff for others. John said that one practical way that a Christian can and should demonstrate his or her love in action is by kindness and a willingness to lend a helping hand to a fellow Christian in need (see verses 17–18). If God expects us to give our lives for one another, then surely He expects us to give our stuff for one another.

John's emphasis here is undeniable. Love shows itself through action, and one action we are to be practicing is lending a helping hand to our fellow Christians in need. This does not mean that we ignore the stranger on the street corner. Love and compassion always should be on our minds when helping those outside the church.

But, we should also be discerning when helping someone who we know nothing about. Perhaps the best way to help people you pass on the street who ask for change, work, or help is to offer to buy them food. If they are truly in need, they will accept your offer and be grateful for the assistance. This may give you an opportunity to share with them what they need most, and that is a relationship with Jesus. John knows that we cannot help everyone in need. That is unrealistic. However, when we discover that a fellow believer is in need, and we have the ability to help them, love demands that we help. In other words, love for Christ demands that we help those in Christ who are in need.

Now, if we are going to help our brother or sister in need, then we must first have the resources necessary to meet his or her need. These may be financial resources, material resources and possessions, or the giving of our time and talents. Warren Wiersbe tells the story of a young mother who "admitted . . . that she never seemed to find time for her own personal devotions. She had several little children to care for, and the hours melted away." He writes, "Imagine her surprise when two of the ladies from the church appeared at her front door." The women came to her house every day so that she could have a quiet time in her room, which helped the busy young mother develop her devotional life.[72]

John says that if we have the resources, we must be willing to take action and help.

Do not harden your heart to the needs of others. Be willing to give generously of your resources. Do you know someone in your church who needs help? Go and see if you can lend them a helping hand today.

This is what the Lord Almighty says: "Give careful thought to your ways." (Haggai 1:7 NIV)

NOVEMBER

5

Think about It

HOLINESS IS HARD WORK. Charles Spurgeon wrote,

There are times when solitude is better than society, and silence is wiser than speech. We should be better Christians if we were more alone, waiting upon God, and gathering through meditation on His Word spiritual strength for labour in his service. We ought to muse *upon the things of God, because we thus get the real nutriment out of them.* . . .Why is it that some Christians, although they hear many sermons, make but slow advances in the divine life? Because they neglect their closets, and do not thoughtfully meditate on God's Word.[73]

The people of Jerusalem in Haggai's day had some unfinished business with God. After returning from Babylonian captivity, they had enthusiastically finished a foundation for the new temple. But after a couple of years, the rest of the building project came to a standstill, and for the next sixteen years nothing more was done. You would think the people would not have been so selfish and thoughtless. After all, they had just come from living in exile because they were selfish and disobedient. Now they were back in the land and back to their old tricks. They were living as though the whole Babylonian experience never happened. So, the Lord sent the prophet Haggai to tell the people to consider their ways and get back to work.

Failure to consider our ways as we walk with God eventually will mean that we either do something we should not do, or will fail to do something we know we should do. Holiness only comes as we give ourselves to God and walk in His ways. Do you have unfinished spiritual business with God? Perhaps you have regressed in your walk with God. Perhaps you need to renew some of your spiritual practices, like going to church and having a quiet time with God every day that includes reading your Bible and praying. Or perhaps you need to take some time to fast. Perhaps you need to stop and "consider your ways" (Haggai 1:7 NKJV).

Your spiritual growth will not just happen by itself. Take some time to consider your priorities. In light of God's priorities for His people, think about the direction your life is currently going. Have you been growing closer to God lately, or have you been putting God off? If you discover that you are putting Him off, you need to reprioritize: no more procrastinating, no more making excuses, no more putting off the unfinished things that God is trying to accomplish in and through your life.

Holiness is hard work. Are you willing to put in the time and effort by giving careful thought to the direction you are going, to the way you are growing, and to the time you are spending with God?

The proof that we love God comes when we keep his commandments. (1 John 5:3 MSG)

Proof of Life

IN THE CHRISTIAN LIFE, obedience is the proof of spiritual life. Unfortunately, obedience has received a bad rap in the world today. When a word like *obedience* is mentioned, it immediately evokes the negative image of doing something that you do not want to do. But for the Christian, obedience should not be seen as a chore but as a reflection of one's love and devotion for God.

There are three reasons we obey, according to Warren Wiersbe:

> We can obey because we *have to*, because we *need to*, or because we *want to*.
>
> A slave obeys because he *has* to. If he doesn't obey he will be punished. An employee obeys because he *needs* to. He may not enjoy his work, but he *does* enjoy getting his paycheck! He needs to obey because he has a family to feed and clothe. But a Christian is to obey his Heavenly Father because he *wants* to—for the relationship between him and God is one of love.[74]

Why do you obey God?

John tells us that love for God is more than a feeling. Love for God includes obedience to God. Without obedience, saying that you love God is nothing more than phony flattery. John insists that for the child of God, the commands of God are not burdensome. In fact, the child of God not only *wants* to keep the commands of God but *enjoys* keeping the commands of God. Love for God will result in love for God's commands. God does not say, "Keep my commands, and you will love me." No, what He says is, "If you love Me, keep My commandments" (John 14:15). Obedience is not the requirement for salvation; we are saved by grace. But obedience is definitely a sign of our salvation.

No one can keep all the commands of God perfectly, but it should be our aim to keep Gods commands as perfectly as possible with the help of the Holy Spirit. The guaranteed way to know you are in the center of God's will is considering whether you are obeying His commands. And the only way to experience all that God has for you is to walk in complete and continued obedience to God.

Do you find the commandments of God to be nothing more than harsh rules and tiresome regulations? Or, do you enjoy doing what God tells you to do? If you say you love God, then you must not run from God's commands but run toward them. Our love for God is expressed through our obedience.

Love delights to do God's will because it understands the cost and sacrifice of God's love for us. Jesus loved to do God the Father's will and daily lived to do His will—and so should every Christian. Obedience is the proof of our spiritual lives.

"I am with you says the Lord." (Haggai 1:13)
Enjoying God's Presence

THE COMPANY OF A CLOSE FRIEND often can be extremely encouraging. His or her mere presence can be enough to lift your spirits, bring some much-needed reassurance, and make you feel loved and appreciated.

As you comprehend the reality of God's presence in your life, you will experience even more encouragement and comfort as the presence of God provides you with everything you need. Are you enjoying God's presence in your life? If not, you can start today.

The message to Haggai was brief but extremely powerful: "I am with you." What more did God need to say? What more could God offer? Is anything more precious or more powerful than the presence of God? The declaration "I am with you" is more than the reality that God is everywhere; this is a personal promise of His presence to His people.

"I am with *you*" (emphasis added). God makes His power available to His people through the closeness of His company. When God's people come to the realization that the all-powerful God makes His particular presence available to His people personally, these words should produce deep joy within the heart of every believer. What confidence, and what contentment!

Oswald Chambers said, "Having the reality of God's presence is not dependent on our being in a particular circumstance or place, but is only dependent on our determination to keep the Lord before us continually. Our problems arise when we refuse to place our trust in the reality of His presence."[75]

Forgetting that God is with us can be easy simply because we cannot see God. So, how can we take experiencing the presence of God in our lives from theory to reality?

First, our faith is the assurance that God's presence is with us. Believers are given God's presence as soon as they place their faith in Jesus as their Lord and Savior (see Ephesians 1:13). His presence is a certainty, but experiencing and enjoying God's presence takes cultivation that only happens as fellowship with God is practiced. Fellowship with God is accomplished by spending time, listening to what God has to say, through the reading of His Word and by communicating with God through prayer.

Further fellowship with God is developed by spending time with God's people. And, as our fellowship with God increases, we enjoy and experience the reality of His presence in our daily lives.

No shortcuts exist to experiencing the intimate fellowship of God's presence in your life. But walking in the reality and power of God's presence brings enjoyment beyond any other.

God is with you! He goes before you, He walks behind you, He stands with you, He never will leave you alone, and He never will take His presence from you. What an encouragement we have in knowing that God has promised to be with us. Take time today to nurture and enjoy the promise of His presence in your life.

For everyone born of God overcomes the world.
This is the victory that has overcome the world,
even our faith. (1 John 5:4 NIV)

Victorious Faith

A S CHRISTIANS, even though we are on our way to heaven, we still live in a real world that is full of real conflict, chaos, and challenges. Our world has its fair share of trials, temptations, and traumas, all of which point to the fact that living the Christian life is not easy. And although this life can be thought of as a struggle, a battle, and even a war, we must remember the victory is ours in Jesus. We have overcome the world, because Jesus Christ has overcome the world.

The apostle John was writing to first-century Christians who were well-acquainted with the cruelties of this world. Many Christian communities experienced severe persecution by refusing to worship the Roman emperor. They were therefore considered disloyal subjects and radical dissenters. They were living in a culture that embraced evil and rejected good. The Christian life was not easy then, and still is not easy today. Sometimes the pressures of life are intense and the outlook appears bleak. But John confidently declared, "For everyone born of God overcomes the world. This is the victory that has overcome the world, even our faith."

Being an overcomer of this world is not dependent on what we do; our victory is solely based on what God has already done. The battle has been won. The war is over. Jesus has done what we could not. He defeated sin, death, and the devil. We must remember that evil never will overwhelm the Christian because by faith, we have overcome the evil of this world. The enemy of God wants us to think that we can be overcome and defeated, when in fact, our faith in God makes that impossible. Faith saves us, and faith keeps us. By faith we walk, and by faith, we are able to overcome this world.

Our faith overcomes the world, as God gives us the power to break free from the enslaving power of sin. Our faith breaks the enticing spell of the world's charm, as we are now able to see the truth that this world has nothing of eternal value to offer us. Our faith helps us to overcome "all that is in the world—the lust of the flesh, the lust of the eyes, and the pride of life" (1 John 2:16), as our faith leads us into obedience, freedom, and joy.

As overcomers, we should live with the hope of knowing our future is secure, no matter how hard this present life may be. As overcomers, though our circumstances may change, our future is secure. As overcomers, we should live knowing that we have all the necessary help we need to live victoriously over all that is in the world. As overcomers, we should live *from* victory, not *for* victory, because the victory is already ours by faith in Jesus.

I have removed your iniquity from you, and I will clothe you with rich robes." (Zechariah 3:4)

The Ultimate Stain Lifter

AFTER SPENDING A FEW HOURS working around your house, planting flowers, pulling weeds, raking leaves, cutting grass, or doing some other equally dirty household chore, nothing feels quite as good as a warm shower. With a little soap, shampoo, and some elbow grease (or a loofah sponge if you prefer), the dirt is washed away in a matter of minutes, and presto, chango! You feel squeaky clean again. Now, that's refreshing! Salvation, on the other hand, is not a matter of cleaning yourself up. Washing your sins away is not as easy as taking a warm shower and scrubbing your guilt away. In fact, nothing you can do will wash away the grime of sin.

The Bible records a vision that Zechariah saw in which Satan accused Joshua, a high priest, as he stands before God. As Joshua was likely performing his priestly responsibility of representing the people before God, Satan was right there to accuse him. Joshua was seen in filthy clothes, signifying his and the people's sin, and, as Satan was pointing out how unfit Joshua was to stand before God, the Angel of the LORD rebuked Satan and said to Joshua, "See, I have removed your iniquity from you, and I will clothe you with rich robes." This is such a beautiful picture of salvation, as God is the one to take away Joshua's filthy clothes and replace them with clean garments. This vision is an illustration of how God cleanses us of our sin through Jesus Christ.

We must realize one important fact about this story. God does not tell Joshua to go clean himself up, and God does not ask us to go clean ourselves up before we come to Him. Salvation is not a matter of getting right, or cleaning yourself up, before you come to God. If that were the case, none of us would ever be able to come to God. We come to God as we are, filthy, dirty, and grimy because of our sinfulness, and God cleanses us. Only God can make a sinner acceptable. Only God can wash the stain of sin away!

We must recognize that we are sinners, unclean and undone before God. But, by faith, we accept and allow Jesus to clothe us in new, spotless garments. No amount of good works can ever undo our uncleanness because "all of us have become like one who is unclean, and all our righteous acts are like filthy rags" (Isaiah 64:6 NIV). We must know and never forget that we are made righteous, clean, and upright in the sight of God, not because of anything we have done, are doing, or ever will do. Our cleanliness is utterly and completely based on what God has done through Jesus, and only through Him, we will be able to stand in the presence of God, cleansed.

Satan will try and convince you that you are worthless and that because of your sinfulness, you never will be good enough to stand before God. With every accusation, we must remember, "we have an advocate who pleads our case before the Father. He is Jesus Christ, the one who is truly righteous. He himself is the sacrifice that atones for our sins" (1 John 2:1–2 NLT). Jesus is the ultimate stain lifter. He removes the stain of our sin, and presto, chango! We are clothed in the robe of His spotless perfection. We are squeaky clean before God because of Jesus Christ.

Now this is the confidence that we have in Him,
that if we ask anything according to His will,
He hears us. (1 John 5:14)

Pray by the Rules

THERE IS POWER IN PRAYER. Moses interceded and turned God's wrath away from the people (see Exodus 32:7–14). Hezekiah prayed, and God extended his life by fifteen years (see Isaiah 38:1–5). And Peter was freed from prison because of a prayer meeting (see Acts 12:1–16). When a person is praying according to God's will, their prayers are unstoppable. But how should we pray? What should we pray for? Can we be sure that God always hears our prayers? And can we be confident that He will answer when we pray?

This promise from 1 John is all-inclusive and all-encompassing. The promise is remarkably reassuring and profoundly powerful, but carries one condition: our prayers must be according to God's will. Some believe that to add, "if the Lord wills" to the end of your prayers shows a lack of faith, but nothing could be further from the truth. Jesus Himself prayed, "Father, if it is possible, let this cup pass from Me; nevertheless, not as I will, but as You will" (Matthew 26:39). So, how can we be sure that we are praying according to God's will?

First, we must pray according to what the Bible teaches. God never will go against His Word, so to pray for anything that contradicts what He has already revealed to us in the Bible is foolish. James 4:3 tells us, "You ask and do not receive, because you ask amiss." Also, praying according to God's will means that we must ask, believing: "And whatever things you ask in prayer, believing, you will receive" (Matthew 21:22). Jerry Bridges has said,

> When I do not have faith, I'm saying one of two things: either God cannot answer this prayer or God will not answer this prayer. If I say He cannot, I'm questioning His sovereignty and His power. If I say He will not, I'm questioning His goodness. To pray in faith means that I believe God can and I believe God will insofar as it's consistent with His glory, because God is good.[76]

Next, praying according to God's will means we are praying from a place of purity in our personal lives. If we are praying to God from a place of sinfulness, meaning that we are living in state of habitual sin, then God will not hear or answer our prayers until we deal with our sin. The only prayer God will hear or answer when we are in sin is a prayer of confession, repentance, and forgiveness. Once our sins have been properly dealt with, we can resume our regular prayer lives once again.

Finally, praying according to God's will means that we are praying from a place of close proximity to Jesus. Jesus made this promise: "If you abide in Me, and My words abide in you, you will ask what you desire, and it shall be done for you" (John 15:7). We must be spending time with Jesus and living in obedience if we want to see fruitfulness from our prayerfulness.

If you want to experience the power of prayer, then you must pray by the rules. When we hunger for God's will to be done and pray accordingly, we can pray with confidence that God hears our prayers and will answer them for our good and His glory.

"Not by might nor by power, but by My Spirit,' says the Lord of hosts." (Zechariah 4:6)

Might Does Not Make Right

NOVEMBER
11

ETTING GOD'S WORK DONE is not a matter of big biceps or big brains. You do not have to be one of those huge, no-neck Nordic weight lifters named Argon or Eggart to move mountains for God, and you do not need to have a PhD to share the gospel. But times will come when you are following God that you will find yourself in difficult or even impossible situations, and no amount of skill, strength, or smarts will enable you to accomplish the work of God before you. However, when you become a Christian, God gives you one resource that can enable you to get His work done His way: by His Holy Spirit. Your successfulness in serving God is largely dependent on your yieldedness to the Spirit of God.

Zerubbabel, the governor of Jerusalem, was faced with what seemed like an impossible task. After leading the first group of God's people back to Jerusalem from captivity, his mission was to rebuild the temple of God, which at that time was nothing more than a pile of rubble. As the work began, the people were met with persistent opposition from the outside and increasing discouragement from the inside, all of which left Zerubbabel frustrated and facing failure.

God decided to send the prophet Zechariah to strengthen the faith of Zerubbabel and to encourage the Jews who were working on the rebuilding project. The message of encouragement to Zerubbabel and the temple construction crew was that success would come not as a result of their own dogged determination or because of their own skill, strength, or smarts, but " 'by [His] Spirit,' [said] the Lord" (Zechariah 4:6).

God's work must be done God's way. Are you facing difficulty while trying to accomplish God's work? Have you reached what seems like an impossible situation while serving God? Has discouragement hit you like a ton of bricks? Know this: the solution to your difficult situation is not found by rolling up your sleeves and trying to just get the work done. The solution is not found by assembling the most skilled team or throwing money at the project. The solution is found by trusting in and turning to the Spirit of God.

God's work is a spiritual work; therefore, only spiritual resources will ever get God's work done the right way. God's work cannot be accomplished by the strength or skill of man. His work must be done spiritually, which means by the leading and empowering of God's Holy Spirit. What may seem impossible with man is not only possible with God, but also easy for God.

The Spirit of God is able to accomplish what man cannot. Where man is unable, God is fully able. God intends for us to accomplish great things for Him today, but we must be fully yielded, filled with, and anointed by His Holy Spirit for those things to become realities. Do not look to man's strength to accomplish God's work, because God reminds us that, 'not by might . . . but by [His] Spirit,' He will accomplish His work.

It has given me great joy to find some of your children
walking in the truth. (2 John 1:4 NIV)

NOVEMBER
12

Walk in the Truth

THE BEST EVIDENCE that a person knows the truth is whether they also walk in the truth. The truth is not only to be something intellectually understood; truth is something to be lived out in everyday life. Just as Jesus was the personification of truth, His children are to be a living representation of truth. To know the truth is good, but to walk in the truth is even better. Nothing glorifies God more than when His children walk according to the truth.

The apostle John was overjoyed at the fact that the children of this "elect lady" (2 John 1:2) were walking in the truth. Nothing brings greater joy to the heart of a parent than knowing that his or her children are walking in the truth, and nothing brings greater joy to our Heavenly Father than when He sees that His children are walking according to the truth.

How can we make sure we are "walking in the truth?"

Walking in the truth begins by knowing, believing, and accepting the truth, accepting that Jesus Himself is "the truth" (see John 14:6), that the Word of God is "truth" (see John 17:17), and that the Holy Spirit, given to every believer, is the "Spirit of truth" (see John 15:26). Walking in the truth means making the deliberate and disciplined choice to have the pursuit of God become the habit of one's life. Walking in the truth means having our thoughts, words, and actions governed by the truth of God's Word. To walk in the truth means to know the truth, believe the truth, and obey the truth.

Living the truth never has been popular. The path of Truth always has been and always will be the more difficult road to walk, because those who do not live according to the truth are always "surprised when you no longer plunge into the flood of wild and destructive things they do" (1 Peter 4:4 NLT). There is a lot of pressure to live as the world lives. Christian students face the pressure at school to compromise the truth and go with the crowd, and Christians in the workplace feel the pressure to compromise their convictions about the truth in order to keep their jobs secure. But no matter the pressures we face, we must walk in the truth. We are not to just fill our heads with theological truths; we are to live out biblical theology in school, at work, in our families, with our friends, and in our neighborhoods. We must determine to walk in the truth of God's Word, because the way we live either points people toward Jesus Christ or away from Him.

Our understanding of the truth is demonstrated by our walking in truth. As we apply the truth of God's Word to our everyday life experiences and allow that truth of God's Word to shape our attitudes and actions, we will bring joy to our heavenly Father as He see His children walking in the truth.

"Do not despise these small beginnings, for the Lord rejoices to see the work begin." (Zechariah 4:10 NLT)

Starting Out Small

IN ORDER TO REACH THE TOP, we must be willing to start at the bottom. We must prove ourselves, pay our dues, and show we are reliable. And that means we have to be willing to start out small if we want to be used by God in a big way. That is why, when serving God, we are not to despise the days of small beginnings. The only problem is, the days of small beginnings are easy for us to dislike. After all, small beginnings come with lots of hard work, little encouragement, and plenty of obstacles. You may be looking at your life today and wondering why nothing is happening. You are anxious to be used by God and have big plans regarding all that you want to do to impact the world for Christ. But God may be saying, "You are not ready yet. I need to prepare you first." So, what should you do next?

As Zerubbabel began working on the temple, he was met with difficulties and disappointments that caused the building project to come a grinding halt. So, God decided to send Zerubbabel some encouragement, by way of the prophet Zechariah, to remind him that the work must go on and that he was not to give up, even though the work was hard and may have been moving along at a snail's pace. And because Jerusalem was not as the city used to be, some of the Jews were thinking, *Why bother? What's the point?* But God still had a great and glorious plan, and the way to get there meant starting out small.

You may be destined to do great things for God, but along the way, you are sure to face lots of hard work, little encouragement, and plenty of obstacles. But, do not despise the early days of a new work, because every big work started out as a small work. When God leads us to start out small in our service for Him, we must not look down on humble beginnings. What may look like a small thing to you may only appear that way because you cannot see God's big picture. Every journey begins with a first step, and we are never to take those first small steps for granted, no matter how small they appear to be.

Everything you are learning today is preparation for something you will do tomorrow. Do not let small beginnings stop you from thinking big, but remember that moving forward is a one-step-at-a-time process. You may have to watch others lead before God calls you to lead others, you may have to spend years studying before God allows you to teach, you may be required to sweep floors before God gives you a stage, and you may have to learn a new language before God sends you to the mission field.

What has God called you to do? Are you in the day of small beginnings even now? Do not be in such a hurry to be used in a big way that you miss the small lessons that God is trying to teach you now. Faithfully do the small things that God has placed before you to do, and leave it to God to bring the big things your way.

Diotrephes, who loves being in charge . . . (3 John 1:9 MSG)

NOVEMBER
14

"What's in It for Me?"

THE CHURCH is not exempt from the go-getter mentality, with people who are driven to succeed, who want to get ahead, who are looking to be recognized, and who like to call the shots. Now, ambition can be a good quality in a person, but left unrestrained, can be very dangerous. The paradox of ambition is that too little ambition can produce laziness, and too much ambition can produce pridefulness. Should Christians, therefore, renounce the get-up-and-go attitude? Not at all! We just need to be clear about whose glory we are seeking.

The apostle John wrote a letter (well, more like a postcard) to one of his close friends named Gaius. Gaius was a good man with a good reputation. He loved God's Word, and he loved God's people. But Gaius had a problem, and that problem went by the name of Diotrephes. Diotrephes was an ambitious, power-hungry member of the church who did not just want to serve in the church, he wanted to run the church. People who love to be in charge, who are proud and self-centered, and who seek places of power and positions of prestige have always been in the church. Unfortunately, pride is completely incompatible with living a godly life. Pride, by nature, drives a person to seek his or her own glory and not God's. When our desire is for our own advancement, we cannot also be seeking God's glory. We cannot serve two masters. Either we are seeking to glorify God, or we are seeking to gratify ourselves.

The spirit of a Diotrephes can show itself in the church in many different ways. There may be a person who always wants to dominate discussions, a person who always feels the need to offer his or her opinion all the time about everything, or a person may try to usurp someone's authority. Or the person may be a board member, a pastor, a teacher, a musician, or a small group leader in the church. Whoever is acting like Diotrephes would be wise to remember this warning from the Old Testament: "Are you seeking great things for yourself? Don't do it!" (Jeremiah 45:5 NLT).

If your approach to ministry is, "What's in it for me?" and if you want to be famous instead of making Jesus famous, then you are not yet ready to serve in the church. Take a moment to make sure your motivations are right before God.

Leadership is not only important in the church, but also necessary. But the type of leaders whom God wants ministering in the church is a servant leader, not selfish leaders. How much would Diotrephes have preferred to be remembered this way: "Diotrephes, who loves glorifying God . . ."!

"Behold, your King is coming to you; He is just and having salvation, lowly and riding on a donkey." (Zechariah 9:9)

NOVEMBER
15

A Day Unlike Any Other

THE DAY STARTED OUT like any other day for this ancient city. As the sun began to rise over the Eastern Gate, people slowly made their way onto the cobbled roads. Vendors started setting up their booths and unloading their carts of merchandise, as the streets were being lined with bushels of dried figs and dates, crates of olives, sacks of lentils, and colorful handwoven tapestries. By midmorning, the hustle and bustle of life in Jerusalem was in full swing, and the pungent smell of fish coming from the Fish Gate mixed with the sweet aroma of fresh-baked flatbread, as merchants and consumers began bartering for goods. Yet, despite all the outward appearances, this was no ordinary day. In fact, the day would become a day unlike any other.

One of the extraordinary aspects of this particular day was this day had been spoken of several hundred years earlier by the prophet Zechariah. This ancient prophet of God spoke of a great and glorious day when Jerusalem's Messiah and King would arrive. Zechariah declared that when God's great King came to His people, the people should welcome Him and rejoice because this King was coming not to conquer the people, but to show compassion to the people. One way this unique King would demonstrate His mission of mercy was to come riding on a donkey.

Kings rode on horses when they wanted war, and they rode on donkeys when they wanted peace. Nearly five hundred years after Zechariah's prophecy, Jesus rode into Jerusalem on a donkey. Some welcomed Him by shouting, "Blessed is He who comes in the name of the Lord!" and others rejoiced by shouting "Hosanna in the highest!" (Matthew 21:9). Some of the people took their tunics and laid them down on the road, while others cut branches from palm trees and placed them before Jesus as He rode into the city.

An old saying goes that the two most important days of your life are the day you were born and the day you figure out why you were born. For Jesus, this day was His public proclamation of why He was born. He came to this world to die so that others may live. He came to bring peace between God and man. And He entered the ancient city of Jerusalem on this anything but ordinary prophetic day so He could accomplish that mission.

Unfortunately, many people misunderstood Jesus' arrival that day, thinking that He came for earthly reasons, causing them to entirely miss the true purpose of His mission. Many people today still misunderstand Jesus' arrival and welcome Him and rejoice with wrong expectations. They want a king who will solve all their earthly problems, when Jesus came as the only King who could solve all our spiritual problems.

Zechariah's prophecy was intended to help people of every generation recognize and rejoice in who their great King is and why He came. Have you welcomed Jesus as King of your life? Do not let today be a day just like any other day. Do not let the sun rise and set while failing to stop and rejoice in the knowledge that Jesus came to be the spiritual King of your life.

And if He is not currently ruling and reigning as King over your life, then start now by accepting Him as your King, making today a day unlike any other.

But you, dear friends, . . . [build] yourselves up in your most holy faith. (Jude 1:20 NIV)

Faith Builders

FAITH IS THE FOUNDATION upon which our spiritual lives are built. The stronger our faith, the stronger our spiritual lives will turn out to be. But building a strong faith does not happen by accident, and does not happen without using a little spiritual elbow grease. You must be proactive if you want to see consistent spiritual growth in your life. There is no such thing as a passive approach to building up your faith. No matter how long a person has been a Christian, the work of building oneself up is never finished. And, if we were completely honest with ourselves, we would acknowledge we could use a little help in the area of strengthening our faith, more times than we would like to admit.

Jude, the half-brother of Jesus, was a defender of the faith, and as such, he encouraged all Christians that the best way to contend for, or defend, the faith (see Jude 1:3) is to be strong in one's own personal faith. Practically speaking, Jude was dealing with some ungodly people who had wormed their way into the church and were spreading some damaging doctrines in an attempt to undermine the faith of as many Christians as possible. So, Jude called on Christians to contend for the faith by carefully building themselves up in their precious faith. Basically, sometimes the best offense is a good defense.

The building up of a person's faith is the direct result of time spent in God's Word. Building up of one's faith cannot happen apart from the source of one's faith, because "faith comes by hearing, and hearing by the word of God" (Romans 10:17). Being a student of the Word is the best way to strengthen your faith.

Also, according to Jude, praying in the spirit (see the second half of verse 20) is another important aspect of strengthening ourselves in the faith. Praying in the Spirit may sound strange at first, but since the Spirit seeks to point people to Jesus, praying in the Spirit simply means being guided by the Spirit to pray for those things that are consistent with the life, ministry, and teachings of Jesus. And since Jesus and the Word are one (see John 1:1), the best way to pray in the Spirit is to pray according to the Word of God.

Finally, being built up involves remaining in the love of God (see verse 21). The words of Jesus should come to mind here: "If you love Me, keep My commandments" (John 14:15). Keeping ourselves in the love of God means that we are purposefully practicing biblical obedience as we wait patiently and expectantly for the return of Jesus.

The responsibility of building up our faith falls upon your own shoulders. Whether you will put in the elbow grease needed to become strong in the faith is up to you. Take the time to study the Bible with purpose and passion, pray, being led by God's Spirit and not your own desires, and make practicing obedience part of your daily to-do list. Then you will see your faith grow stronger day by day.

"Woe to the worthless shepherd, who leaves the flock!"
(Zechariah 11:17)

Step Up or Step Down

SHEEP NEED A SHEPHERD. Although sheep are cute and cuddly, sheep are also far from being the smartest creatures in the animal kingdom. To give you an idea of their intellectual inadequacies, sheep can wander in circles for days looking for food, all while edible grass is within sight. Add to that the fact that sheep are easily frightened, prone to wander, and totally defenseless, and you have an animal in need of some serious help.

God calls His people sheep. While not the most pleasing of portrayals, this comparison is true all the same. Like sheep, we easily worry, we are prone to wander, and we are vulnerable to attack. Therefore, we need some serious help. God has appointed shepherds to help His sheep, shepherds who will love and care for God's people, and who, if need be, will lay down their lives to protect the sheep (see John 10:11).

But Israel had a problem. They were plagued with worthless shepherds who were not looking out for the best interests of the sheep. Rather, they were more concerned with themselves and what they could get from their position. The religious leaders who were entrusted by God with the welfare of the people were to care for the people and lead them into fields of faithfulness and obedience. But they had grown lazy and greedy, caring more for their own glory and gain than for the spiritual health and wealth of their flock. They had become worthless shepherds who did more harm than good. Zechariah envisioned the day when a Good Shepherd would replace the bad ones that plagued Israel. However, this Good Shepherd initially would be rejected, and His sheep would be scattered (see Zechariah 13:7), all of which eventually would be fulfilled by Jesus, the Good Shepherd (see John 10).

Just like Israel, the church also has had problems with worthless shepherds, "shepherds" who are more concerned with themselves than with the sheep, "shepherds" who are nothing more than hirelings. Jesus said, "But a hireling, he who is not the shepherd, . . . sees the wolf coming and leaves the sheep and flees. . . . The hireling flees because he is a hireling and does not care about the sheep" (John 10:12–13). Hirelings are more interested in what the sheep can do for them than what they can do for the sheep. They are in the business for the money, the power, the prestige, and the perks, but not for the sheep. They like to be in charge, but do not want the spiritual responsibility that comes with being in charge.

All of us, not just leaders and shepherds, need to watch our lives and our motivations for why we do what we do. We need to practice what we preach, and we need to be more concerned with others than ourselves. We need to be committed to sacrificially caring for those entrusted to our oversight, whether in the home or in the church, a commitment that goes as far as willingly laying down our lives for someone else.

If this has not been your approach, if you have not been lovingly leading, then you have two choices: step up or step down. Either step up to the standard that Jesus set as the Good Shepherd, or step down and let someone else lead.

The Revelation of Jesus Christ, which God gave Him to show His servants—things which must shortly take place.
(Revelation 1:1)

The Jesus Exposé

TO MANY, the last book of the Bible reads like a strange mystery novel, full of shadowy figures, catastrophic events, and eerie symbolism. Add to that the glorious snapshots of heaven and horrifying images of a hell on earth, and you have a book that scares some, confuses others, and leaves many scratching their heads, wondering what to do with all they read. But this book of the apocalypse, or the unveiling, is a magnificent exposé of Jesus Christ and the events leading up to and including His glorious appearing at the Second Coming. This book is not intended to baffle believers but to bring blessing to all believers who read and heed its contents (see Revelation 1:3).

The book of Revelation is an open book that reveals God's plans and purposes for His people. Written by the apostle John while he was imprisoned on an island called Patmos, the Alcatraz of his day, John tells of the "things which must shortly take place," events that explain the future of the world, the victory of the church, the glory and majesty of God, the political, social, and religious battles against the Antichrist, the judgment of sin, and the fulfillment of promises and prophecies given as far back as the Old Testament, all culminating with the creation of a new heaven and a new earth. What else can you say but wow? Yet, John did not write this book to "wow" us or entertain us; he wrote this book to encourage us.

So, what *do* you do with a book like this? Before you look at the book of Revelation and think it has no bearing on your life today because it is all about future events—events that mostly take place after the church is removed from this earth—think again. Nothing could be further from the truth. This book is bursting with blessing and packed with pertinent truth for your life today. One of the main reasons John was given this message to share with the churches of his day was to bring comfort and encouragement to the Christians who were experiencing ruthless and unrelenting persecution. And that comfort and encouragement continues bless God's people today.

Also, as you read and study this amazing book, you will notice that the prevailing theme is the final victory of Jesus and the subsequent victory of His people. There is no missing the book's central figure, Jesus Christ. And, this book will teach us to adore Him even more as we witness the unfolding of His wonderful plans and purposes.

Biblical revelation always brings blessing. Wherever you are reading in the Bible, you always will be blessed as God gives us revelation into His heart. And, the promise of Jesus Christ's coming should be to all Christians at all times a motivation for obedience and consecration. As mysterious as the book of Revelation may appear at times, just remember the book is simply an exposé of our great Lord and Savior, Jesus Christ.

God will be king over all the earth, one God and only one.
What a Day that will be! (Zechariah 14:9 MSG)

What a Day!

THE DAY IS COMING when Jesus will rule and reign on this earth as King. On this day, all the wrongs will be made right and good finally will triumph over evil. All creation has been eagerly longing for this day since its impressive inception. On this day, God will assert His supreme right to govern this earth. Yet, as that day draws near, the Antichrist and his army of underworld mercenaries will approach Jerusalem, poised and ready to attack, prepared to tear down and destroy God's holy city. Jerusalem will appear to be doomed, all hope will seem to be lost, and Satan will be on the verge of fulfilling his grand plan of annihilating the remnant of God's chosen people, once and for all. But, in that moment, help will come from the sky as the King of kings descends from heaven, leading an army of saints and angels. Jesus' feet will touch down on the earth at the very same place they left on the day that He ascended. As He sets foot on the Mount of Olives, immediately the mountain will split in two. This will set in motion a series of cataclysmic occurrences that include changes in the geography and topography as the earth receives its long-awaited King. *What a day that will be!*

As God's holy city is secured, His enemies smashed, and His people safeguarded, the Lord will begin to rule with a rod of iron from Jerusalem for a thousand years. Zechariah describes this glorious period of time when Jesus returns to the earth and reigns on the throne in Israel. In that day, Jesus will establish His kingdom on earth and will reinstate the Feast of Tabernacles as all the people who survive the Tribulation will be ordered to come to Jerusalem yearly to celebrate this feast. Any nation that refuses to come and worship will experience drought and plague.

Prophetically, Zechariah described what will happen in that day when Jesus comes back, but consider something else that relates to you practically. God, the Creator and King, has a plan and purpose for your life that can only be discovered as you submit and surrender your life to His authority and as you worship Him completely. To refuse to submit to Him, and worship Him as Lord of lords and King of kings, will only lead to a spiritual drought in your life.

We must live in expectation of His kingdom come, and we must live for His will to be done on earth. But that begins by submitting and surrendering our hearts to Him today—not tomorrow or the next day—today! Allow God to rule and reign over every aspect of your life. Allow God's plans to become your plans. Many people call themselves Christians, but they are not willing to submit *all* to Jesus. Before Jesus comes to rule the earth, He wants to rule in hearts.

Are you looking for His kingdom to come? Are you waiting eagerly for His will to be done on earth? Then allow Him to take His rightful place on the throne of your heart today. Allow God to rule and reign in your life completely so you can look ahead and say, "What a day that will be!"

> *"I have this against you, that you have left your first love."*
> (Revelation 2:4)

Rekindling the Romance

FALLING IN LOVE is a wonderful feeling! Colors seem a little brighter, the sky looks a little bluer, and flowers smell a little sweeter. Even food tastes a little better. Your days are spent looking for ways to express your feelings: a small gift here, a heartfelt note there. Your love is not containable. An energy and excitement fills the air, as your thoughts constantly drift to your newfound love.

Do you remember how you felt when you first fell in love with Jesus? Remember the energy and excitement that you felt as your thoughts constantly drifted to your newfound love? Everything seemed brighter, bluer, and better. But sometimes, that love fades as bills pile up, illness hits, and the business of life is allowed to creep in, causing your thoughts to begin to drift away. And, before you know it, you are taking God for granted.

On the surface, everything seemed to be going just fine for the Ephesian church. They were busy serving God, brilliantly standing against godless heresies, and boldly enduring persecution for their belief in Jesus. But they had one problem, a big one. Although they were busy laboring for Jesus, they were no longer loving Jesus as they once had. They were taking God for granted.

This romance that we have with God is more than emotion; this romance involves continually doing those things that will keep our love alive. Become so busy serving God that we actually forget to spend time cultivating our love relationship with God is possible, and before we realize it, we are in danger of losing our love for God. We must guard against letting our relationship with God become merely routine.

The good news is God has some advice that will help us rekindle the romance with Him (see Revelation 1:5).

First, *remember.* Remember back to that time when things were fresh and filled with the desire to be in God's presence. Remember that time when your love for God was all you could think about, and you were overwhelmed by His love for you. Remember when you were willing to go anywhere and do anything because of your love.

Next, *repent.* Stop going in the wrong direction right now, turn around, and start going in the right direction. Stop allowing things to interfere with your love for God by turning away from a lackluster love for Him.

Lastly, *return.* Go back to doing those things that you did in the beginning of your relationship with God, when your love was alive and active.

If your love for God is not stronger today than your love for Him once was, in the beginning of your relationship, then start today to take the necessary steps to return to Him. The time is never too late to return to your first love and rekindle the romance.

Give thanks to the Lord, for he is good; his love endures forever. (Psalm 107:1 NIV)

Cultivating Thankfulness

GIVING THANKS should not be a once-a-year tradition. Giving thanks should be more than something we do just before stuffing our faces with turkey and trimmings. Why, then, are we not more thankful? The truth is that we simply do not take the time to stop and think. The cares, concerns, and choices of this life choke the tree of gratitude, causing the fruit of thankfulness to never flourish. Thanksgiving is really the product of careful cultivation. The fruit of thankfulness is born out of a deliberate determination to think about God, to consider all that we possess in Him, and to do so continually, not sporadically. By giving thanks, we are declaring that circumstances do not affect our thankfulness. Rather, thanksgiving ripens as a result of a healthy relationship with God.

As Warren Wiersbe points out,

> Some people are appreciative by nature, but some are not, and it is these latter people who especially need God's power to express thanksgiving. We should remember that every good gift comes from God (James 1:17) and that He is (as the theologians put it) "the Source, Support, and End of all things." The very breath in our mouths is the free gift of God. . . .
>
> Thankfulness is the opposite of selfishness. The selfish person says, "I *deserve* what comes to me! Other people *ought* to make me happy." But the mature Christian realizes that life is a gift from God, and that the blessings of life come only from His bountiful hand.[77]

No matter where we look, we can see that God is good, and that thanksgiving should be the recognition of His goodness. If you are having trouble today finding something to be thankful for, then consider thanking God for the following: God has triumphed over sin and death through his Son, Jesus Christ; God causes all things to work together for good for those that are His; God uses trials to make us more like Him; God is faithful, even when we are faithless; God's Word is true; we can trust God's promises; evil will not last forever; Heaven is real; when we are weak, God is strong; God's grace is sufficient; nothing can separate us from the love of God in Christ Jesus; our salvation rests on God and not on us; with God all things are possible; God never will leave us or forsake us; God has given us His Spirit to help us; and God will finish the work He started in us. God can do more than we can imagine.

If thanksgiving has become a day you celebrate rather than an attitude you are cultivating, then consider this: thanksgiving helps us overcome evil (see Ephesians 5:3), is an act of obedience (see Psalm 50:14), is an expression of worship (see Hebrews 13:15), is an aspect of the will of God for your life (see 1 Thessalonians 5:18), and cultivating an attitude of thanksgiving is an example to other people (see 1 Chronicles 16:8).

The more time you spend thinking about God and His goodness, the more you will be cultivating thankfulness in your life.

"I have placed before you an open door that no one can shut." (Revelation 3:8 NIV)

Understanding God's Open Doors

CHRISTIANS SOMETIMES SPEAK in a strange language called "Christianese," using phrases like "Washed in the blood," "It's a God thing!" and "God has opened a door," all of which can cause people to walk away from conversations scratching their heads and feeling a little confused. However, most of these puzzling phrases are nothing more than variations on verses found in the Bible that have been turned into common Christian vocabulary. Take, for example, "an open door," which can be found here in Revelation 3. But what is an open door in the spiritual sense, and how can a person recognize it?

Quite simply, an open door is a God-given opportunity for ministry. The idea of an open door is used a few times in the New Testament. Paul spoke of an open door when he came to the city of Troas to preach the gospel (see 2 Corinthians 2:12), and he also prayed that God would open a door so that he could minister the message of Christ while in chains (see Colossians 4:3). Here in the book of Revelation, God is also opening a door, or an opportunity for the church in Philadelphia to minister for Christ.

God opens the doors of opportunity for His people from time to time, and these opportunities can come in a variety of shapes and sizes. But a few things remain constant, regardless of the shape or size of the open door.

First, open doors of opportunity come from God and are for the glory of God. When God opens a door, no one can shut that door. The only question is whether a person will walk through. God opens doors of opportunity so that we can use our time, treasures, and talents to share the Word of God and to declare the gospel of Jesus Christ. Also, when God opens a door of opportunity, we must make the most of whatever opportunity He gives us.

But sometimes God will close a door because He has something better planned. Paul wanted to go to Asia to preach the gospel, but God closed that door on Paul's plans (see Acts 16:6). Just as important as it is for us to go through the doors that God opens, it is equally important that we do not try and pick the lock on God's closed doors or go searching for an open window. We need to understand that God may be using a closed door to correct us, to redirect us, to prevent us from making mistakes, or to prepare us. The timing may not be right, the place may not be right, or we may not be right for the job, so we need to make sure to let go of our own agenda and trust God when we face a closed door.

The wise Christian will keep watch and wait patiently for God's open doors, and then make the most of whatever opportunity God provides. So, be ready to minister for Him and to speak the life-giving Word of God to those who need to hear when those doors open.

The burden of the word of the Lord. (Malachi 1:1)

A Pastor's Burden

GOD'S CALLING TO PREACH OR TEACH starts with a burden for His Word. Pastors live under a God-given burden for the Word of God. Pastors must be able to communicate God's Word to young and old, to the wise and the unwise, to the avid reader and the comic strip-only reader. He must have a word for the happy and the sad, to the healthy and the sick, for those ready to live for God, and for the ones who do not even know their need for God. He needs to encourage and challenge, he must call for commitment and change, he must instruct and inspire, and he must do all of this in less than forty-five minutes, week after week. Why would someone willingly submit himself to such scrutiny, such pressure, and such responsibility? They do so because part of God's calling them to be a pastor includes giving them "the burden of the word of the LORD."

"Malachi" means messenger, and this messenger was called to give God's message to God's people when they needed it the most. He did so because God gave him a burden for the word. Malachi holds a unique place in the Bible because he is the one who delivered the final message from God to His people until the time of Jesus. Four hundred years of silence followed the message of Malachi until God's next messenger, John the Baptist, arrived on the scene.

Malachi was in Jerusalem during the years between Nehemiah's return to serve King Artaxerxes (see Nehemiah 13:6) and the time when he came back to Jerusalem. Malachi was particularly concerned with the corruption of the priests who were abusing their power and position while serving the Lord during this period of time. He saw that the abuses from the priests had a trickledown effect that caused God's people to be apathetic toward the things of God. So, Malachi spoke as every "messenger" of God should speak, and that was with a God-given burden to declare God's word to God's people so that God could work in their lives.

God still uses messengers to deliver His message to His people, and every person called to deliver that message should first have a burden for the Word of the Lord. As the apostle Paul said, "Woe is me if I do not preach the gospel!" (1 Corinthians 9:16). No one should step into pastoral ministry if they think they can do something else; only those who can do nothing else are the ones with a genuine calling to be God's messenger.

To be responsible to speak God's Word is a heavy burden. To prepare a message is a burden, not only because of the time and energy, but also because of the personal experience that goes into the declaring God's Word. No preacher can truly prepare a message unless he has first experienced that message. Also, a burden is delivering God's message. Standing before God's people declaring that God has given you a message to speak is not easy. But above all, being a minister is a burden because God's messengers must give an account to God for everything they have said. Even though these are burdens in the sense that they are heavy weights to carry, God will help those whom He has called carry the weights with joy.

The desire to enter full-time ministry should be a God-given desire only. Full time ministry should be confirmed by the Word of God and include a burden for God's Word. This burden will motivate you to seek to win the lost, to encourage the saints, and to inspire believers to receive and apply the message God speaks through His appointed messenger.

"Since you are like lukewarm water, neither hot nor cold, I will spit you out of my mouth!" (Revelation 3:16 NLT)

NOVEMBER
24

Do You Make God Sick?

DOES JESUS LOOK AT YOUR LIFE and want to throw up? That may sound a little harsh, but saying that you believe in Jesus and living like you do not need Jesus makes Him want to throw up. That is the background to this strong warning delivered to the church in Laodicea, and it is still a necessary warning for Christians today.

Laodicea was an amazing city with a booming economy. They were famous for their black wool trade and were well-known for their therapeutic eye cream. They were so well-off financially that after an earthquake leveled the city around AD 60, they were able to completely rebuild their own city without any outside assistance. They did not need anyone's help, and they did not need anyone's money. They were totally self-sufficient. Well, they did have one exception to this self-sufficiency: they needed water. Because Laodicea had no water source of its own, inhabitants were forced to build an aqueduct to deliver water to their city, water that arrived lukewarm and was known to cause vomiting because of a high mineral content. Much like the lukewarm nature of their water, the church in Laodicea was becoming lukewarm spiritually, and this was turning Jesus' stomach.

Jesus cannot stomach a lukewarm faith, and unfortunately, many in the church today are in danger of being spit out of the mouth of Jesus for having a halfhearted faith. Having wealth is fine, but trusting in wealth actually will leave you bankrupt spiritually. A lukewarm person is someone who claims to be a Christian but does not live like a Christian ought to live. Oh, many people would probably consider most lukewarm individuals "nice people," but just being a nice person does not please God. A lukewarm person regularly goes to church but does as little as possible when serving, giving, and loving others. A lukewarm person does not want to offend people by speaking about Jesus, so they rarely do because they care more about what others think of them than what Jesus thinks about them. A lukewarm person sees nothing wrong with telling the occasional white lie or going out and drinking a little too much. Lukewarm people say "I love the Lord" but live like they love the world.

Actions always reveal a person's spiritual condition, and when following Jesus, you must leave no room for indifference, or for playing both sides of the moral fence. So, if you are becoming indifferent to the things of God, then listen to the strong warning from Jesus and determine to be useful, to live passionately, to stand out, and to live a life that is blazing hot for God instead of making Him sick with a halfhearted faith.

God said, "I love you."
You replied, "Really? How have you loved us?"
(Malachi 1:2 MSG)

You Are Loved!

YOU PROBABLY HAVE HEARD IT BEFORE. In fact, you probably have heard it a million times before: God loves you! Yet as often as you may have heard it, the question remains: Do you believe that God loves *you* personally? Maybe you need a little help today really believing and receiving the truth that God loves *you*. Would you be surprised to know that you would not be the first person to wonder about this? God's chosen people had their doubts about God's love for them, and when God said to them, "I love you," they responded by saying, "Oh yeah? Well, prove it!"

How could God's people be so blind? Was God's love for them not obvious? All they had to do was look at the past and recall all that God had done for them. But still they doubted, and still they lacked confidence in God's love for them. So, God reminded them of how he chose them to be a holy nation set apart *by* God and set apart *for* God. God's choice was not based on who they were or what they did; God loved them and chose them because of His self-determining choice to do so. Throughout the Old Testament, we see that God repeatedly demonstrates His love for His people countless times and in countless ways, simply because His will was to love them.

Thousands of years have passed since God spoke those words to His people, and still God is saying to His people today, "I love you!" Are you having trouble accepting God's love? Are feelings of unworthiness interfering with the reality of God's love for *you*? Have experiences in your life made enjoying the genuineness of God's love for you difficult? When God says, "I love you," is your response "Prove it"?

How has God proven His love for you? He has proven His love with the searing pain of a shredded back and the sting of exposed nerves; with the distorted vision from eyes that were beaten shut and the inability to move as hands and feet were pinned to splintery wooden beams; with each short, agonizing gasp for air as suffering stole strength and dying drained life. Does God love you? Just look back at all that God has done for you at the cross, and you will see an unconditional love that is obvious and irrefutable. God chose *you*. God cares for *you*. God died for *you*. So yes, God loves *you*! You can do nothing to make God love you more, and you can do nothing to make God love you less.

Sometimes the difficulties of life make us doubt God's love for us. But do not let doubt and unbelief keep you from believing and receiving the fact that God loves *you*! Remember, God proved His love on the cross, and nothing and no one can take away the reality that *you* are loved!

Behold, a throne set in heaven, and One sat on the throne.
(Revelation 4:2)

Heavenly Minded

H OW DOES ONE EVEN BEGIN TO DESCRIBE that which is indescribable? How does one respond to glory inexpressible? And how can a person accurately perceive the imperceptible? Apart from God, these are impossible. No doubt that is why God helps us to understand a little more about what heaven will be like as we are given a divine glimpse into some heavenly happenings. The glimpse is not only so wonderful, astonishing, and more than the mind can process, but is also a glimpse that can help us live for God today.

John was given a backstage pass into the throne room of God, where he was given permission to take a snapshot of what he saw. The snapshot depicted God in radiant splendor, bright and colorful, surrounded by twenty-four elders casting crowns at His feet as the sound of lightning and thunder echoed in heaven, while four living creatures, full of eyes, never ceased from proclaiming, "Holy, holy, holy, Lord God Almighty!" That is quite a snapshot!

David Wilkerson has said, "This throne room is the seat of all power and dominion. It's the place where God rules over all principalities and powers, and reigns over the affairs of men. Here in the throne room, he monitors every move of Satan and examines every thought of man."[78] In the throne room, God accepts the praise, honor, and glory that He deserves as a heavenly worship service unlike any this earth has ever experienced is taking place. In the throne room, God oversees the creation from His heavenly headquarters as He dispatches angels, dispenses blessings, and distributes strength. The throne room is the hub of all heavenly activity and the worship center of the universe.

This snapshot of glory is not given just so we would have a better understanding of the state of worship in heaven; we are given this snapshot of glory so that we would become better worshipers of God today. Simply put, we were created to worship God, and we will spend eternity worshiping God, so work on becoming better worshipers of God every day is important. We will spend eternity praising God in heaven, but today we are exhorted to worship God in everything we do (see 1 Corinthians 10:31), and we should be constantly seeking opportunities to give Him the praise, honor, and glory He is due in the here and now.

Keeping this snapshot of glory permanently in view in our minds will help us to be praiseful people, no matter what this earth gives us to deal with, and will help prepare us for the praise in which we will be participating in eternity. We must never forget that God is on the throne and that nothing happens without His awareness, nothing surprises Him, and nothing is beyond His control: absolutely nothing!

This glimpse of God seated on the throne in heaven should always serve as a reminder of God's sovereignty, His greatness, and His authority. God is in control, and one day we will be in His presence, singing like the angels, "Holy, holy, holy, Lord God Almighty!"

So, stay heavenly minded so that you may accomplish all the earthly good that God has for you.

"For the Lord God of Israel says that He hates divorce."
(Malachi 2:16)

NOVEMBER
27

Unhappily Ever After

DIVORCE HAPPENS. Of course, divorce should not happen, but does anyway. Divorce is never easy, sometimes messy, often complicated, and, every time, divorce is emotional. Living in a society where half of the marriages end in divorce, everyone will be affected by divorce sooner or later. The way we experience divorce may be through a close friend, a family member, a neighbor, or even yourself, who has gone through the heartache of a divorce. With such a far-reaching impact, what God has to say about divorce is important to know.

First and foremost, God says that He hates divorce. Malachi warned the people of his day to "take heed to your spirit" (see Malachi 2:16) and not to have casual attitude toward divorce. He challenged the people's approach to divorce by indicating that if divorce was being considered, that was because of a problem with their hearts. Jesus took this idea a step further when He said, "Moses, because of the hardness of your hearts, permitted you to divorce your wives, but from the beginning it was not so" (Matthew 19:8). God was the one who created marriage, and His plan from the beginning was to bless man with the covenant of companionship. So, by breaking that commitment, we break our covenantal agreement with God and our spouse. Divorce never was in God's blueprint for marriage, and even though God makes a few allowances for divorce, divorce is never God's best. He never commands divorce, and He never wants divorce to be our first choice.

As much as God hates divorce, he still loves the divorced. God does not hate the person who has chosen to divorce, and He does not hate the person who is a casualty of divorce. Remember, Jesus went and offered help to a woman who had been divorced five times. Jesus offered her forgiveness, hope, healing, and a new life (see John 4). And Jesus is there for all who have gone through divorce, offering them forgiveness, hope, healing, and new life.

Where does all this leave a person today? If you're single, recognize that marriage should not be entered into lightly. Do not be in a hurry to marry the first compatible person who is ready and waiting to tie the knot. Go slow, stay pure, and keep God in the middle of your relationship.

If you are married but are having some marital trouble, remember that God wants your marriage to work! He wants you to stay married, so commit to keeping your eyes on God. He can help, hurts can be healed, forgiveness is available, and rebuilding can occur. Give your marriage everything you have, and give God the chance to work.

If you are happily married, then keep it up. Let your marriage be an example to others, do not judge someone who is divorced, and continue to nurture your relationship with your spouse and God.

And finally, if you have been through a divorce, seek an end to hostilities with your ex and be open to the possibility that God may even bring a restoration of your relationship. Either way, remember that God does not love you any less because you have divorced. He has not branded your forehead with the letter *D* for all to see. He wants to bless your life, and He still wants to use you tremendously. Divorce does not mean that you are destined to live unhappily ever after. Recovery may not be an easy road, but healing is possible.

> *It also forced all people . . . to receive a mark on their right hands or on their foreheads, so that they could not buy or sell unless they had the mark.* (Revelation 13:16–17 NIV)

NOVEMBER
28

Life in the End Times

CELL PHONE TRACKING, digital fingerprints, and RFID (Radio Frequency Identification) chips all may sound like the high-tech know-how you see in spy movies. But could all this technology actually be paving the way for a one-world government and something known as the mark of the Beast? Sound a little too conspiracy theory for you? Well, the Bible does speak of a coming time when the world will be in chaos and crisis, and a one-world government, economy, and religion will emerge. Satan will be behind it all, leading many people away from God.

God definitely wants us to have an awareness of future events. The Bible is filled with insight into what lies ahead. One happening which garners much speculation is the mysterious mark of the Beast. This mark will identify the followers of the Antichrist and induct them into a false worship system that will seal their eternal fate. No one will be able to buy or sell without this mark, and those who refuse to take the mark will be executed. John MacArthur says, "The pressure to give in to the worship of Antichrist will be far worse than anything ever experienced in human history. Life will be virtually unlivable, so the people are forced to bow to the demonized king, not prompted merely by religious deception, but also by economic necessity."[79] During this troubled time, Satan will give great power to the Antichrist and False Prophet, convincing the world to worship them instead of God.

No one knows for sure when all this will take place, but when you look at the condition of the world today and examine the "signs of the times," one thing is certain: we are close. Important to keep in mind, as one commentator has said, is that "John was writing to believers to help them maintain a realistic view of good and evil in the midst of intense persecution. Today, as we watch televised reports of death and disaster around the world, and as we experience pain and suffering in our own families, . . . we too need to maintain a godly perspective."[80] God has placed a limit on evil and what Satan can get away with, but we must stay focused on God if we want to live the life that He has called us to in this dark (and getting darker) world.

God tells us of these and other future events not only to remind us that God knows the future and that nothing happens without His permission, but also so that His people would see just how important living for Him today is! Do not be the person who looks back and wishes that he or she had paid better attention in church. Do not be the person who wishes that he or she had worshiped God sooner. Life in the end times can be avoided by living for God today.

"Will a man rob God?" (Malachi 3:8)
Stealing from God

THE BIBLE IS CLEAR that we are all stewards, supervisors if you will, over what God has given to us. When real spiritual change has taken place in a person's life, then a noticeable change in perspectives, priorities, and in the management of possessions will take place. No longer is everything about making money, saving for retirement, and striving to live the good life. Life becomes about how to use what God has given us for His glory, and part of that stewardship involves giving back to God. When we fail to give back to God what He has already given to us, we are actually stealing from God.

In Malachi's day, the people were not giving back to God. In particular, they refused to give God tithes and offerings. By choosing to keep what they had for themselves rather than give back to God, God said they were actually stealing from Him. And not only were they stealing from God, they were also stealing from the priests and the poor. God did not need the people's money, but God did want the people to change their perspectives, priorities, and the way they managed their possessions. By holding on to what God had given them, the people were hindering the work of the ministry and hurting the people who would benefit from their giving. God goes on to declare to His people that there are consequences for disobedience, and there are blessings for obedience (see Malachi 3:10).

As important as consistently and generously giving tithes and offerings is, withholding these are not the only ways we can steal from God. How do you know if you are stealing from God? Are you holding back on God with your time and your spiritual gifts? You see, God has given each of us more than just material possessions to be stewards of and give back to Him. He has also given each of us time and spiritual gifts, which He also expects us to give back to Him consistently and generously.

We steal from God when we try to keep our time all to ourselves, time that should be given to God in prayer, time that should be given to God in personal worship, and time that should be given to God in serving and helping others. God wants our time. Also, we steal from God by not discovering our spiritual gifts, gifts that are intended to bless the body of Christ, gifts that have been specially chosen by God for us to use, gifts that produce spiritual blessings in the lives of others and produce joy in the life of the person using them. By holding on to what God has given to us, we can hinder the work of the ministry and withhold that which would benefit and bless others.

Just as Malachi tried to reawaken the people to their responsibilities in the area of giving, God's Word should reawaken us and stir our hearts to reexamine our lives and see if we are stealing from God when we should be giving to God.

> And then I saw all the dead, great and small, standing
> there—before the Throne! And books were opened.
> Then another book was opened: the Book of Life. The dead
> were judged by what was written in the books, by the way
> they had lived. (Revelation 20:12 MSG)

NOVEMBER
30

Judgment Day

A DAY OF JUDGMENT is coming, and some people believe their good works will act as some sort of get-out-of-hell-free card. One day, every person will stand before God and give an account for the way they have lived their lives. For Christians, judgment day takes place at the judgment seat of Christ (see Romans 14:10), where God will look back over their lives and examine how they have served God with their time and talents. The result will be a heavenly awards ceremony where each believer will receive rewards based on his or her service.

For non-Christians, judgment day will be at the Great White Throne of God (in Revelation 20), where God will examine their lives and reveal why they are not going to heaven.

For our names to be written in the Book of Life, we must throw away the idea that our names are written in God's Book based on whether we were "good enough" or did enough good works to get in. Let us just be clear: no one is good enough, and no one's works ever will get his or her name on the guest list!

The apostle Paul reminds us that we are justified by faith in Christ and not by our works (see Ephesians 2:8–10; Galatians 2:16). Nonbelievers can never *be* "good enough" or *do* enough good to get into heaven. God's standard for admission into heaven is complete perfection, and the only perfect person who has ever lived, and ever will live, is Jesus. That means our works just will not get us into heaven. A believer's name is written in the Book of Life solely on the basis of his or her faith in Jesus Christ and not on his or her works.

John's purpose in describing the Great White Throne judgment is clear. With stark simplicity and straightforward honesty, he exposes the eternal consequences of rejecting God's saving grace found in Jesus. Those who reject God's grace and mercy in this life will inevitably face God's judgment in the life to come. That means there is no time to waste because no one knows how much time they have left on this earth. Tomorrow is promised to no one, so get rid of the incorrect idea that if you are just "good enough," then God will let you into heaven. That is not how heaven works. Faith, and faith alone, is your ticket into heaven.

Are you ready to meet God? If you are a believer, then you need to ask yourself this: am I living the kind of life that is making the most of every opportunity to serve God, knowing that I must give an account of my life? And if you are a nonbeliever, ask yourself this: am I prepared to stand before God on my own merits?

Why stand before God then and make Him your judge when you can stand before God now, making Him your Savior? The only get-out-of-hell-free card is the one given by the grace of God to those who place their faith in Jesus.

December

CHRISTMAS is certainly a wonderful time of year, filled with sights, sounds, and smells that flood our senses, captivate our minds, and trigger cherished memories. Now that Thanksgiving, Black Friday, and Cyber Monday have passed, 'tis the season for baking cookies, pulling out those beloved holiday decorations, wearing that obnoxious reindeer sweater, drinking a year's worth of eggnog in only a few days, going to Christmas parties, and—we can't forget—untangling hundreds of feet of twisted Christmas lights. 'Tis the season when the fragrances of seasonal coffees dance through the air like sugar plum fairies, when the twinkling of colorful lights illuminate neighborhoods like runways at an airport, when cheerful songs of white Christmases and winter wonderlands can be heard playing in the background everywhere you go, and when people happily replace the traditional "good-bye" with a seasonal "Merry Christmas!"

The Christmas season is definitely the most wonderful time of the year, but not for any of the above reasons, even though all those particulars add nostalgia to seasonal experience. The real reason this time of year is so special is because the world celebrates the birth of its Savior. This time of year, we celebrate the reality of the redemptive plan of God, in which God's long-awaited Messiah entered into the world, in matchless splendor and remarkable humility. This time of year, the goodness of God's great love for mankind has been so clearly revealed.

Christmas is the season when families come together and the name of Christ echoes in the air. 'Tis the season when everyone seems a little nicer, a little more giving, and even a little more forgiving. 'Tis the season when those who do not worship Jesus at any other time of the year find themselves compelled to worship Him. 'Tis the season when we should certainly celebrate, with great joy and excitement, the real reason for the season. Although we may need to put forth a little extra work, 'tis the season to keep Christ in all our celebrating, bargain hunting, and family gatherings. The reality is that, with the endless distractions that only increase during this time of year, we need to remember, in everything we do for the season, why we are celebrating in the first place.

As the Christmas season gets underway and you are knee-deep in frosting and cookie dough, as you get ready to talk with that weird relative you only see once a year, and as you wait in lines that never seem to end, remember, 'tis the season to celebrate Jesus' birth. Then, and only then, will this truly be the most wonderful time of the year for you and your family.

Why am I discouraged? Why is my heart so sad? I will put my hope in God! (Psalm 42:5 NLT)

Hope for the Holidays

AS WE CELEBRATE THE UPCOMING HOLIDAY SEASON, we must remember that not everyone looks forward to the holidays. For some, Christmas reminds them of things that ought to be, but are not. While Christmas is a time of love, some people feel very unloved. Many people spend the holidays surrounded by large, wonderful families, but some experience hostility when family gets together, while others have no family to spend the holidays with at all. Whether someone is feeling troubled by painful memories or remembering loved ones who have passed, the hurt of loneliness hits especially hard during the holidays.

The Bible talks of how King David was feeling depressed and how he refused to let those feelings get the better of him. He would not allow himself to sink into the deep pit of despair. Rather, as he vividly described his feelings, he also described his decision not to be ruled by his emotions. David chose to remember God and to consider His grace, and He began to praise God for His goodness.

If the sentimentality that surrounds the holidays is intensifying your hurt, then know this: Christmas is all about delivering hope to those who are hurting. If you feel the tinge of loneliness coming on, know that God cares for you, and remember that He knows about loneliness firsthand. Jesus experienced the greatest loneliness imaginable when He was forsaken by God the Father on the cross (see Matthew 27:46). But Jesus was forsaken so that we can be forgiven. He was willing to be separated from God temporarily, so that we never would have to live one second without God, because God has promised, "I will never leave you nor forsake you" (Hebrews 13:5). For the person out of work, for the struggling single mother, for the sick, sad, and disheartened, you can have hope.. The birth of Christ is God's highest expression of hope!

But, how can you take delivery of this hope practically this season? By doing just as King David did: decide not to let your emotions get the better of you. Holiday hurt and loneliness are opportunities to draw closer to God. At the heart of hurt and loneliness is a lack of dependence on the sufficiency of God to meet every need. Therefore, God often will use times of deep hurt and loneliness to teach people that God is all we really need. We must learn to lean on Him more and let go of those crippling emotions, stop looking to others to fill the void, and focus on the peace and happiness that only God can provide. This is the message of Christmas: God has come near. And as a result, we never have to walk alone.

If you are feeling lonely this holiday season, then take the time to "draw near to God and He will draw near to you" (James 4:8). Allow His goodness and grace to give you hope for the holidays.

"Behold, the virgin shall be with child, and bear a Son, and they shall call His name Immanuel," which is translated, "God with us." (Matthew 1:23)

Unwrapping His Presence

W HAT DO YOU WANT MOST THIS CHRISTMAS? I would venture to guess that your response would not be another fruitcake, a gift card for Weight Watchers, or a Chia Pet. After all, what do you say when you get one of those "special" gifts at Christmas? "Hey! Now, there's a gift!" or, "You shouldn't have! No, really! You shouldn't have!" or "Yeah, I really don't deserve this!"

However you respond to the unusual and unwanted gifts you may receive this Christmas, God has given all of us a gift that was specifically designed to bring us comfort and joy not only this Christmas, but 365 days of each and every year.

No matter what presents you get this Christmas, the newness eventually wears off, gifts get broken, and before you know, the gifts are collecting dust in a closet. The gift of God's presence is the only gift that continues to bring joy to the hearts of all who have received Jesus. Jesus has many names in the Bible: the Alpha and the Omega (Revelation 1:8), King of kings and Lord of lords (Revelation 19:16), and Messiah (John 1:41). One of the most precious names of all for Jesus is Immanuel, God with us. At the center of the Christmas message is a God of love who desires to be with us. And on that very first Christmas, God gave mankind the gift of His presence in the person of Jesus Christ.

God with us is an amazing thought that stands at the center of Christmas and the Christian faith. Because God is with us as Christians, God has given us the ability to live as He has called us to live. Since God is with us, we will never walk alone, no matter how alone we may feel. *God with us* means that God has given us the ability to accomplish great things for His glory because all things are possible with God (see Luke 1:37). *God with us* reminds us that, in the midst of a fallen world that is filled with broken relationships and broken lives, God remains near.

Experiencing the reality of God's presence in our lives is not a matter of receiving the perfect gift, nor is receiving His presence a matter of being in the right place at the right time. Rather, experiencing His presence is a matter living in the awareness of His continual presence among us..

So, when the time comes this Christmas morning to unwrap your presents, keep in mind that the greatest gift came wrapped in swaddling clothes, and the gift of God's presence is a gift that can be enjoyed all year long.

"Herod will seek the young Child to destroy Him." (Matthew 2:13)

Dealing with a Grinch

W HETHER THEY ARE FAMILY, friends, coworkers, or acquaintances, we all must deal with difficult people, and the holidays are no exception. Those grouchy Grinches, selfish Scrooges, cold Jack Frosts, and angry

Burgermeisters can all put a damper on the Christmas spirit and make the holiday season a chore rather than a joy.

One of the worst killjoys in all of Christmas history had to be King Herod the Great. Prideful and addicted to power, this "king of the Jews," as he was known, hated anything that threatened his authority. His paranoia led him to kill anyone he suspected of opposing him, which included in-laws, sons, and even his wife. So, when wise men from the East came to Jerusalem, reporting the birth of a newborn King of the Jews, and that they had traveled a long way to worship Him, you can imagine the fear and fury this provoked in this psychotic king's mind. When the wise men left for Bethlehem, they had reached an agreement with King Herod that they would return to Jerusalem and tell the king where he could find Jesus. But, having been warned by God in a dream that Herod intended to kill Jesus instead of worshiping Him, the wise men went home a different way. After word reached Herod of the wise men's secret escape, the king chose to respond in a violent and vengeful rage, killing all the babies in Bethlehem under the age of two.

Like Herod, many people remain unaffected and unchanged by Christmas. Instead of worshiping God because salvation has come through the birth of Jesus, some respond with hostility toward God and unfriendliness toward anyone who shows even the slightest hint of Christmas spirit. How can we keep ourselves from becoming Grinch-like, and how should we respond to those whose good nature is lacking this season?

First, do not let someone's lack of joy rob you of your joyfulness. Keeping a proper perspective will help in maintaining your joyfulness. So, when difficult people threaten to steal your joy, remember the wonder that is the Christmas story, and keep in mind the pronouncement of the angel: "I bring you good tidings of great joy which will be to all people" (Luke 2:10).

Next, have some compassion. You never know what difficulties, hurts, and hardships others are facing, and perhaps God has placed you in their lives to help them know God personally and help them heal. Be willing to show them some loving-kindness; your acts of kindness can often be a better witness than your words.

Finally, be committed to praying for these people regularly, and when God gives you an opportunity to speak to them, pray that God would give you wisdom in choosing the right words.

We cannot control difficult people, and we cannot change them. But with God's help, we can love them better, understand them more, and find a positive way to deal with them, especially during the Christmas season.

What can I offer the Lord for all he has done for me?
(Psalm 116:12 NLT)

What Do You Give to God, Who Has Everything?

DECEMBER 5

NVARIABLY, ONE PERSON ON YOUR CHRISTMAS LIST each year is impossible to shop for. You hope this person will drop hints, letting you know what he or she would like this year, but this seldom happens. You walk the malls endlessly in hopes of stumbling upon that perfect gift, but you cannot find anything that he or she does not have already.

In the same way, what can a person give to God, who has created everything, who has given us all things that pertain to life and godliness in Christ (see 2 Peter 1:3), and who continues to do exceedingly abundantly above all that we could ask or think (see Ephesians 3:20)?

Well, of course, you can buy nothing for God, because He needs nothing, which certainly makes finding that perfect gift to give Him a little harder. But we can give precious and personal gifts to God, gifts that He desires, gifts that matter to Him, and gifts that honor Him for all that He has done and continues to do for us.

One of the many precious gifts we can give to God is our obedience (see John 14:15). By giving God our obedience, we are demonstrating our submission to His sovereignty. We can give God our love (see Matthew 22:37), which reveals the priority of His position in our lives. We can give God the gift of our praise (see Psalm 108:1), which is an expression of our appreciation for God. We can give glory to God (see Psalm 29:2), which is our way of showing recognition to the fact that God is the source of everything good. We can give God our service (see Hebrews 12:28), which is an acceptance and acknowledgment of our purpose in the body of Christ. We can give God our thanks (see 1 Thessalonians 5:18), which is evidence of our gratitude to God for who He is and what He has done for us. We can give God our best (Colossians 3:23), which honors God because we are a reflection of Jesus to the world around us. We can give God our bodies (Romans 12:1–2), which means we are to be living sacrifices, freely giving ourselves to the One who freely gave Himself for us.

Even though God needs nothing from us, we have plenty of gifts we can give him that He would like to receive from us, gifts that reflect our gratefulness and honor His graciousness.

So, if you are wondering what to give God this year, start by giving yourself totally and completely to Him. That is the best gift that you can give to God, who has everything.

There was in the days of Herod, the king of Judea, a certain priest named Zacharias, of the division of Abijah. His wife was of the daughters of Aaron, and her name was Elizabeth. (Luke 1:5)

DECEMBER 6

Breaking the Silence

HAS IT BEEN AWHILE SINCE YOU HEARD FROM GOD? Do you feel like you have been faithful to follow God day in and day out this year, but if the truth were told, you have recently felt as though God were distant? As Christmas approaches, and another year begins to wind down, and many people tend to be a bit more reflective about their lives and their relationships with God. Perhaps, as you look back over the past year, you are saying to yourself, "I am not perfect, and I have made my fair share of mistakes, but I have been living rightly before God and serving Him faithfully. But even so, God still seems silent."

God's people had not heard from Him in four hundred years. Can you imagine, after a history of God's leading and speaking to His people, that generation after generation heard nothing from Him? No prophets were speaking, no angels had been visiting, and no Mount Sinai moments from God had happened, that is, until God broke those years of silence with an angelic visit to Zacharias the priest.

Zacharias and his wife Elizabeth were righteous, obedient, and blameless before God (see verse 6), but they lacked the one thing they wanted most: a child. For years, they had been praying that God would give them that precious addition to their family, but year after year, God was silent. And now they felt as though their prayer would forever remain unanswered, as they were past the age of having children. Little did they know that God was working behind the scenes and was about to break His silence with a miraculous blessing.

Zacharias means "God remembers," and his wife Elizabeth's name means "His oath." Together they mean "God remembers His oath." You see, God made a promise back in Psalm 89: "No, I will not break my covenant; I will not take back a single word I said. I have sworn an oath to David, and in my holiness I cannot lie: His dynasty will go on forever; his kingdom will endure as the sun" (verses 34–36 NLT). God made an oath to David that one of his descendants would have an eternal reign, and Jesus is that descendant. Zacharias's son, John the Baptist, would be the forerunner for Jesus and would break God's silence to the people of Israel by preparing the way *for* and pointing people *to* Jesus.

Zacharias chose to remain faithful to God in his service as a priest, and he was faithful in his prayers for a child, even when God was silent. Zacharias could have easily stopped praying, became bitter, and stopped serving the God who was not providing the child that he and his wife so desperately wanted.

As Christmas is rapidly approaching, do not give up on God just because you may be going through a season of silence. Rather, remain a faithful, obedient, and blameless servant, because God often breaks the silence with His people while they are busy, about His business.

Set your minds on things above, not on earthly things.
(Colossians 3:2 NIV)

DECEMBER 7

The Dangers of Christmas

CHRISTMAS CAN BE DANGEROUS! *Wait . . . Christmas? Dangerous?* Exactly. If we are not careful, Christmas can be just that: dangerous. One of the most troubling aspects of the Christmas season is the persistent commercialization and widespread materialism that have become a "normal" part of this holy holiday. You experience pressure to have your house looking magazine perfect, finely decorated on the inside and brightly lit on the outside. You feel pressure to buy your kids the latest and greatest gifts that the season has to offer, and as the pressures build, the bank account dwindles, which all add up to danger. While absolutely nothing is wrong with gift giving and receiving or decorating and celebrating, we need to be careful to avoid some of the dangers that can come with Christmas.

First, keep your mind set on eternal things! If you want to navigate through the holidays with your heart right, then you must start by keeping your head straight. The whole reason we give gifts is because God gave us the gift of His Son. We may need to make a little extra effort to stay focused on the eternal meaning of Christmas while in the middle of all the earthly madness, but, and this is very important, we must not allow anything to hinder a heavenly mindset this holiday season.

Next, as you participate in the annual exchanging of gifts, keep it simple! The temptation here is to spend more money than you have. But really, if you don't have the cash, then don't buy the gift. Be creative. You can always save some money by making or baking some of your gifts. Most people appreciate the thought, time, and effort that go into a gift more than the cost of the gift, not to mention that some of those baked gifts taste delicious.

Also, practice gratefulness. You may not have everything you want in life, but odds are that you have more than you need, so be grateful for what God has given you. That, of course, means reaching beyond the physical blessing of cozy comforts and personal possessions and extend into the spiritual riches that every single believer enjoys in Jesus Christ. Practicing gratefulness is simply a great way to keep the proper perspective.

Finally, because Christmas is about Jesus, find ways to bring Jesus into more of your everyday holiday celebrations. Perhaps this means giving cards or gifts that promote or praise Jesus instead of the innocuous greeting cards or gifts that have nothing to do with the real meaning of Christmas. Perhaps you can read different parts of the Christmas story throughout the holidays, or maybe you can give out a gospel tract when buying or giving your gifts. The fact of the matter is, the more ways you seek to bring Jesus into your everyday holiday routine, the more heavenly minded you will be.

If you want to avoid the dangers of Christmas, then keep the right mindset by setting your mind on things above and avoiding preoccupation with the worldly side of Christmas.

"I am the light of the world. He who follows Me shall not walk in darkness, but have the light of life." (John 8:12)

DECEMBER

8

Christmas Lights

CHRISTMAS LIGHTS are a big part of the holiday season. As December rolls around, you are sure to see strands of glowing lights all over the place. They cover Christmas trees and hang from houses, they are situated on shrubs, and, if you look closely, you can even find them covering the occasional car! From tree trunks to rooftops, Christmas lights do more than fill the night sky with twinkling brightness; they also go a long way in preparing our hearts for Christmas day, as they remind us that the light of the world has come so that we never have to walk in darkness.

Israel had been living in a perpetual state of darkness for many centuries. They had been rebellious against God and refused to walk according to His Word. Then, in the fullness of time, Jesus was born as a light sent to illuminate this dark world. Jesus' birth fulfilled what the prophet Isaiah spoke when he said, "The people who walked in darkness have seen a great light" (Isaiah 9:2). Then one day, centuries later, while in the city of Jerusalem, Jesus declared to the people of Israel that He was the light of the world. He promised that if anyone was willing to follow Him, they would have the light of life and would never walk in darkness again.

December is the darkest month of the year. You get up in the dark, you have breakfast in the dark, and then, by the time you get home from work or school, the sky is dark again. The simplest way to drive out darkness is to turn on the light. Light and darkness cannot occupy the same space at the same time, and light always overpowers darkness (see 1 John 1:5). When we trust in Jesus as our Savior and purpose to follow Him, the darkness in our lives disappears. God forgives our sins and lights the way for us to walk in holiness. Jesus came as the light. He came to dispel the darkness. And without Jesus, a person walks in darkness. Unfortunately, not everyone wants to walk in the light. Some prefer to stay in darkness because they love sin more than they love the Savior (see John 3:19–21).

If you are struggling with sin, if you are stumbling along in the darkness, or if you are wandering away from Jesus Christ, then turn on the light and come back to Jesus today. Jesus is always the answer. He came to light the way so that no one needs to stumble around in the darkness.

Living in this dark world, we must continue to walk close to Jesus, who is the Light of Life. The closer we walk with Him, the brighter His light shines in and through our lives.

So, the next time you see some Christmas lights wrapped around a tree or decorating a neighborhood house, allow those lights to serve as a reminder that Jesus is the Light of the World, and He came so that we might never walk in darkness.

But Christ has rescued us from the curse pronounced by the law. When he was hung on the cross. . . . For it is written in the Scriptures, "Cursed is everyone who is hung on a tree." (Galatians 3:13 NLT)

DECEMBER

9

The Real Christmas Tree

FOR MANY, Christmas does not officially begin until a Christmas tree is chosen. The yearly tradition of trudging off, bundled with hats and gloves, to pick out the perfect Christmas tree is often a favorite family activity that creates many special memories. And when selecting a Christmas tree, everyone has his or her personal preferences. The perfect tree must have the right look, feel, and smell, must be perfectly shaped, and must be the most beautiful tree around. Once home, the Christmas tree takes center stage and is decorated with lights and ornaments as part of the holiday celebration.

But another tree, a tree that we do not often associate with Christmas, a tree that is more than merely a customary centerpiece to our celebration. Yet, this tree is central to the Christmas story.

For God, Christmas could not begin until He first chose a tree. This tree had to be perfect and perfectly shaped, not because the branches would be decorated with ornaments or wrapped in lights, but because upon this tree, the Light of the World would hang. Unlike the Christmas trees that garnish our homes, this tree would not be beautiful to look at, even though its significance is beautiful to all who ponder its purpose. This tree would not have presents neatly positioned underneath. Instead, underneath this tree, crooked men would cast lots for the Savior's clothes. Underneath this tree, religious leaders would mock and ridicule the God they claimed to know. Underneath this tree, the Savior's mother would watch and weep as her Son suffered. And underneath this tree, the blood of Jesus would form a puddle. Jesus could have come down from the tree where He hung, but if He did, man would have been lost for eternity.

When we think of Christmas, we usually think of birth, not death. But Jesus was born to die. We cannot escape the reality that the Savior born in a manger would grow to be the Messiah who would die on the cross. Christmas is all about God coming into this world to save humanity from sin and death, so logically, Christmas should also acknowledge the sacrifice of Jesus' death. Most people like the idea of a baby coming into the world, because something is cute, innocent, and pure about a newborn. But the world was not in need of a child; the world was in need of Christ.

Christmas is truly a joyful time in which we should celebrate and rejoice that God was willing to come and save us from our sins. As you prepare to bring a Christmas tree into your home, keep in mind the real Christmas tree that eventually became the cross of Christ.

Mary responded, "Oh, how my soul praises the Lord. How my spirit rejoices in God my Savior! For he took notice of his lowly servant." (Luke 1:46–48 NLT)

DECEMBER
10

Mary's Song

DURING THE HOLIDAYS, Christmas music fills the air with songs like "O Come, All Ye Faithful," "What Child Is This?" and "Silent Night." Christmas would not be the same without our favorite songs. But Christmas music is more than seasonal schmaltziness. As we listen to Christmas carols and holiday choruses, our minds can begin to become set on things above and help us to position our hearts in alignment with the true spirit of the season.

After Mary received word that she would be God's chosen vessel to carry and nurture God's only Son, she went to visit her relative Elizabeth. No doubt still recovering from seeing an angel—and processing the astounding news that she would give birth to God's Son—Mary was able to spend some time talking with her family and contemplating all that was told to her by the angel of the Lord. A little while after arriving at Elizabeth's house, Mary sang her own Christmas song of praise to God, a song so magnificent that the lyrics are forever preserved in the pages of the Scriptures and they serve as a wonderful encouragement to our faith.

With poetic prose, Mary's song not only revealed her understanding of God's plan for her life, but also expresses her humility over being chosen by God. She expresses her realization of the presence of God in her life and discloses that Mary was no stranger to the Scriptures. Mary's song is packed with Old Testament references, carefully structured and beautifully poetic. In her song, Mary rejoices even though she sees herself as a simple servant. Imagine being selected for this tremendous job and how undeserving and unfit Mary must have felt! She must have felt blessed to be chosen, but this would also be a challenging blessing as well.

Sometimes, a song is the fastest way into God's presence, and living with a sense of the reality of God's presence in our lives is often simply achieved by worshiping Him through song. The Christmas season gives a unique opportunity to bask in God's presence as Christmas songs flood the airwaves. Enjoy this opportunity to reflect on the many gifts that God has graciously blessed you with, and worship Him through the songs you hear and sing.

Read Mary's song of praise for yourself in Luke 1 and reflect and rejoice over the blessing of God's kindness. Sing songs of praise, and worship the King. And with every Christmas chorus you sing, be reminded of the goodness that God has shown to you.

"As You sent Me into the world, I also have sent them into the world." (John 17:18)

DECEMBER

11

Your Christmas Mission

C HRISTMAS SHOULD REMIND YOU that you are on a mission. For Jesus, Christmas is the beginning of the story of His earthly mission. Jesus came into the world to seek and save the lost, and His entire life was clearly lived out in fulfillment of that mission. When Jesus came to earth, He came to offer mankind a new relationship with God, a personal relationship with God, which meant that Jesus always was on the lookout, on the go, and on the job when fulfilling His God-given mission. And just like Jesus, we have been given a similar mission from God.

God wants you to be on the lookout, on the go, and on the job, reaching out to the people He has placed around you with the truth about Jesus. And because Christmas is part of God's story, this is an especially good time to be on the lookout for opportunities to live out your mission. God has called you to live and work side by side with people who need to know Jesus. The problem is, we can come up with all sorts of excuses as to why we should not follow through with the mission God has given us. We say to ourselves, "I don't know enough about the Bible" or "What will they think of me?" or "I might lose my job!" We can explain away the mission, believing that someone else will reach those people, when, in fact, God has strategically placed you in your family, in your neighborhood, and in your job so that *you* can be the one to reach them.

If you need a little help getting started, here are a few suggestions to get you moving in the right direction. Pray by name for those around you who need to know Jesus. Prayer is always the best place to start. Consider giving the occasional Christ-centered gift to your unsaved friends or family members. This is an easy way to get the message out there, and those gifts open the door for follow-up conversations. Invite someone to go to one of your church's Christmas services or events, and then take him or her out to dinner afterward and casually talk about the experience. Finally, you can always do a random act of kindness: shovel a driveway, deliver a meal, help a family in need in your neighborhood, or even coordinate a family or neighborhood service project for a worthy cause.

None of this is meant to be a Christmas guilt trip, but to serve as a reminder that as believers, we are all on a mission, and there is no better time than Christmas to talk about Christ. Doors are opened and hearts are more receptive to the message. So, step up, because God has sent *you* out!

The generous will prosper; those who refresh others will themselves be refreshed. (Proverbs 11:25 NLT)

DECEMBER
12

An Example of Generosity

WHATEVER YOUR PERSONAL CONVICTIONS are about Santa Claus, an example of generosity is found at the heart of the real Saint Nick. Nicholas was a Christian living in the fourth century, born in what is now Turkey (not the North Pole). Even though he had a difficult life, which included being orphaned at a young age, he would grow up to become a strong defender of the Christian faith and was considered an outspoken troublemaker by the Roman Emperor Diocletian, who wanted him to stop preaching Christianity. As a result of his evangelism, he spent many years in prison and was eventually released when Constantine took over as the Roman Emperor. (Yes, that is right: Kris Kringle had a criminal record.)

Although Nicholas was believed to have performed several miracles in his lifetime (none of which included making reindeer fly), he was best known for his generosity. As traditions indicate, he was so selfless that he helped a poor neighbor pay for his three daughters' weddings. In an attempt to remain anonymous and mindful of Jesus' words, "But when you do a charitable deed, do not let your left hand know what your right hand is doing, that your charitable deed may be in secret; and your Father who sees in secret will Himself reward you openly" (Matthew 6:3–4), Nicholas snuck up to his neighbor's house at night and dropped a bag of gold coins through an open window when each of the neighbor's daughters came of age. Eventually, the father discovered that the gifts came from Nicholas and shared his story.

Do what you want with Santa Claus, but the real Saint Nick was a believer who dedicated his life to serving God, and he stands as an example of generosity for all of us to follow.

Nothing and no one should ever take the place of Jesus, especially at Christmas time, but we can certainly learn valuable lessons from Christians like Nicholas. The Bible is clear that God loves when a person gives generously and cheerfully (see 2 Corinthians 9:7), especially when every effort is made to give without drawing attention to his or her self.

The secret to success is not found in gathering more, but in giving more. Christmas is a time when we are reminded of just how much God has given to us, and should motivate and move us to be hilariously generous givers. Take some time this season and consider how you might show a little extra generosity to someone.

> *And behold, there was a man in Jerusalem whose name was Simeon, and this man was just and devout, waiting for the Consolation of Israel.* (Luke 2:25)

DECEMBER
13

Simeon

WAITING IS A PART OF LIFE, and during the holidays when lines are longer and traffic is heavier, you cannot go anywhere or do anything without waiting. Waiting is also a part of your Christian life. You cannot go anywhere or do anything for God without first waiting on God for answers and direction. Tucked away in a corner of the Christmas story is an example of a man who patiently and joyfully waited on God.

Simeon was an elderly man who had been promised by the Holy Spirit that he would not die until he had seen the promised Messiah, referred to in today's verse as "the Consolation of Israel." But with that promise came a long period of waiting. We do not know exactly how or when the Holy Spirit revealed this to Simeon, but what we do know is that he believed this promise, and believing all the while, he waited with great anticipation for that day. Something is heartwarming about picturing a white-haired and weathered Jewish man, faithfully waiting on God with a glimmer in his eye and a spring in his step, because he knew that before he died, he would see the fulfillment of God's great promise.

Simeon's incredible moment finally came eight days after the birth of Jesus when Joseph and Mary brought Jesus to the temple. This day was one of dedication for the family, and for Simeon, a day for celebration. Nothing special about Simeon qualified him to take up Jesus in his arms and bless Him (see Luke 2:28). He had no special priestly credentials and no special authority. He simply was a "just and devout" man who walked with God (see verse 25).

Simeon was a man who knew how to wait on God. He waited expectantly, he watched with anticipation, and he lived joyfully. How are you waiting on God? Whether you are waiting on God to answer your prayers or to direct your steps, or whether you are waiting for the second coming of Christ, you should be waiting expectantly, watching with anticipation, and living joyfully. To wait expectantly means that you believe the answer is just around the corner, due to arrive at any moment. Your heart is full of hope, and you live each day eagerly waiting for God's answer. You are looking forward and moving forward. Do not give up! Do not stop believing! Stay focused on what God has for you, remembering that God's power is limitless. Simeon lived for one thing, he waited for one thing, he prayed for one thing, and he cared for one thing. And when he eventually saw God, he essentially said, "Now I can die" (see verse 29).

If you are waiting on God for an answer to a prayer, for direction on which way to go, then remember Simeon, whose name means "God hears." He is an example of how God honors those who watch and wait patiently on Him.

For prophecy never had its origin in the human will, but prophets, though human, spoke from God as they were carried along by the Holy Spirit. (2 Peter 1:21 NIV)

The Twelve Prophecies of Christmas

T HE CHRISTMAS STORY is the greatest story ever told, and, even better, is the fact that the story is jam-packed with fulfilled prophecy. Most people who want to read about the birth of Jesus turn to the New Testament for the most detailed look at the Christmas story, but we must not overlook the fact that much in the New Testament is fulfillment of Old Testament prophecies, which were written hundreds of years before.

God had been planning this event for a long time. He gave us signs, or prophecies, to look for along the way so that we might know that He is God. Prophecies like the twelve listed below give us our earliest preview into God's blueprint for Christmas.

1. Jesus would come from the line of Abraham. This prophecy is found in Genesis 12:3 and was fulfilled in Matthew 1:1.
2. Jesus the Messiah would be born of the seed of woman. This prophecy is found in Genesis 3:14–15 and was fulfilled in Matthew 1:18.
3. Jesus would be a descendant of Isaac and Jacob. This prophecy is found in Genesis 17:19 and Numbers 24:17 and was fulfilled in Matthew 1:2.
4. Jesus' mother would be a virgin. This prophecy is found in Isaiah 7:14 and was fulfilled in Matthew 1:18–23.
5. Jesus would be born in the town Bethlehem. This prophecy is found in Micah 5:2 and was fulfilled in Luke 2:1–7.
6. Jesus would be called out of Egypt as a child. This prophecy is found in Hosea 11:1 and was fulfilled in Matthew 2:13–15.
7. Jesus would be a member of the tribe of Judah. This prophecy is found in Genesis 49:10 and was fulfilled in Luke 3:33.
8. Jesus would be the Son of God. This prophecy is found in Psalm 2:7 and was fulfilled in Matthew 1:20.
9. Jesus would be from the House of David. This prophecy is found in Jeremiah 23:1–5 and was fulfilled in Luke 3:23, 31.
10. Jesus would be presented with gifts at His birth. This prophecy is found in Psalm 72:10 and was fulfilled in Matthew 2:11.
11. Jesus would be God with us. This prophecy is found in Isaiah 7:14 and was fulfilled in Matthew 1:23.
12. As a result of Jesus' birth, children would be killed. This prophecy is found in Jeremiah 31:15 and was fulfilled by Herod in Matthew 2:16.

The temptation with a list like this one is to skim over or even skip the list altogether. Please do not skim or skip this list, however, because to shrug off prophecy, especially prophecy about Jesus, is to miss an opportunity to see God's love, mercy, and faithfulness in action. God has given us prophecies like these so that we might see His plans and purposes come to fruition, so that we might know His Word is reliable, and so that we would know He is in complete control. God uses biblical prophecy to prove His credibility and to convince us of His authority in the universe. Biblical prophecy provides irrefutable evidence for God's existence, proves that God has a purpose for mankind, and more specifically, proves He has a purpose for your life.

God's use of prophecy in the Christmas story should, therefore, motivate us to know Him more personally, trust Him more completely, and follow Him more fully.

After the celebration was over, they started home to Nazareth, but Jesus stayed behind in Jerusalem. His parents didn't miss him at first. (Luke 2:43 NLT)

DECEMBER 15

Keeping Christ in Your Christmas

WITH ONLY TEN DAYS LEFT until Christmas Day, most of us are feeling the pressure of the holiday hustle and bustle. A few last-minute gifts are still left to buy, and those little "thinking of you" presents you baked or bought for your friends and neighbors are packaged and ready to be dropped off. The turkey or ham has yet to be ordered, and a handful of Christmas cards are sitting on the kitchen counter, waiting to be addressed and mailed to have any hope of arriving before Christmas Day. Whatever remains on your get-it-done-before-Christmas list, make sure that you do not let the Christmas commotion keep you from fixing your eyes on Jesus.

Once, when Jesus was twelve years old, He wandered off from His parents. Mary and Joseph had journeyed from Nazareth to Jerusalem to celebrate the Passover as a family, but when the feast was over and the family was making their way home, they realized that Jesus was nowhere to be found. A whole day passed before they realized Jesus was gone. This was not because Jesus' parents did not care about Him; the fact of the matter was they simply lost sight of Him.

Before you are quick to condemn Jesus' parents, have you lost sight of Jesus this Christmas season? Oh, you still love Jesus and your faith is not faltering (or anything drastic like that), but with the busyness of Christmas, have you actually allowed yourself to simply lose sight of Jesus? This can happen ever so slowly and slightly as the little things begin to take over, and with time being in short supply, the first thing to suffer is your spiritual walk. Time in God's Word takes a backseat in your overloaded and overbooked life, prayer becomes a luxury you cannot afford, and before you know, you have lost Jesus in the crowd.

If you need a little help keeping Christ in your Christmas schedule, then perhaps a few seasonal suggestions will help.

First and foremost, do not skimp on your quiet time with God. If you need to get up a little earlier or stay up a little later, then just do so, because so much of your ability to survive the season is found in consistent time with God.

Also, keep worship a part of your Christmas celebration. Go to that extra holiday concert at church or the additional candlelight service and be refreshed through the expression of your worship. In your home, you can set up a nativity scene so you can have a visual reminder of the reason you are running around like crazy. You may want to plan a family service project for the month of December, maybe serving at a food bank, visiting a local nursing home, or sending a special gift to a missionary. And try taking the time to read the Christmas story in Luke 1–2, before the unwrapping storm begins on Christmas morning.

However you choose to celebrate, and whatever your Christmas traditions are, the important thing is that you do not lose sight of the fact that Christmas would not exist without Christ!

"Glory to God in the highest, and on earth peace . . . !"
(Luke 2:14)

DECEMBER

16

Peace on Earth

WHEN THE ANGELS DECLARED on Christmas day, "Glory to God in the highest, and on earth peace . . . !" Were they joking? Really, can there be peace on an earth that is filled with fighting? Add to that the fact that Jesus made clear that He did not come to bring peace on earth. He said, "Do you suppose that I came to give peace on earth? I tell you, not at all, but rather division" (Luke 12:51). So, did the angel get the message wrong? Did he make a mistake in his Christmas declaration? Not at all. The answer lies in the type of peace that was being promised.

As Rick Warren pointed out,

> There will never be peace in the world until there is peace in nations. There will never be peace in nations until there is peace in communities. There will never be peace in communities until there is peace in families. There will never be peace in families until there is peace in individuals. There will never be peace in individuals until we invite the Prince of Peace to reign in our hearts. Jesus is the Prince of Peace. [81]

Jesus did not come to *bring* peace; He came to *be* our peace! We read in Colossians 1:19–20, "For it pleased the Father that in Him all the fullness should dwell, and by Him to reconcile all things to Himself, by Him, whether things on earth or things in heaven, having made peace through the blood of His cross." And again, in Ephesians we read, "For He Himself is our peace" (2:14).

Although peace among men is a good and godly ambition, peace will never happen unless man first experiences personal peace with God, the peace that the angel promised on that first Christmas day. This promised peace comes only when a person accepts that Jesus Christ is the only way to peace with God. This promised peace was delivered that Christmas night and is available for all men to receive when they take delivery of the salvation offered through Jesus Christ.

But another aspect to the promised peace offered to mankind on that first

Christmas cannot be overlooked. In addition to peace with God, when a person believes in Jesus, he or she also can have a peace that surpasses circumstances. Regardless of what is happening in the world around you, you can experience the personal and practical peace of God in your heart because of the Holy Spirit. Jesus said, "Peace I leave with you, My peace I give to you; not as the world gives do I give to you. Let not your heart be troubled, neither let it be afraid" (John 14:27). Jesus provides an inner rest for the soul of man through the Holy Spirit.

Remember the words of the heavenly host at the birth of Jesus this Christmas, reflect on how God has made peace with Him possible for you to have, and enjoy the peace that He freely gives to His own.

When Joseph woke up, he did what the angel of the Lord had commanded him and took Mary home as his wife.
(Matthew 1:24 NIV)

DECEMBER

17

Christmas's Unsung Hero

SOMETIMES, THE BIBLE can leave us with more questions than answers. In the Christmas story, we are introduced to an important person who is both intriguing and a bit inconspicuous. Joseph, the earthly father of Jesus, was given the unique privilege of raising the young Messiah as his own son. But for a person with such a significant role in Jesus' life, significantly little is said about him, leaving us with more questions than answers. After all, what was raising God like? What can you teach the One who knows everything? Did he ever mistakenly punish Jesus for something his brothers did? And did Joseph ever give Jesus a piggyback ride? Inquiring minds want to know! We do not know much about Joseph, so much is left to speculation and imagination, but what we do know about Joseph serves to be both an inspiration and an example to us all.

Joseph was a man of integrity who was entrusted with a great responsibility. Try to imagine for a moment God deciding whom He would choose to raise His Son. God chose Joseph to be the earthly father of Jesus just as much as He chose Mary to be the mother of Jesus. The Bible tells us that Joseph was a righteous man (see Matthew 1:19), and we can see an illustration of this when Mary told Joseph that she was pregnant. Joseph had every right to be angry because he knew that this child was not his. And with Mary's apparent unfaithfulness, Joseph not only had the right to divorce Mary, but under Jewish law, he could have demanded that she be put to death by stoning. Instead, he chose to show her kindness, love, and mercy. Joseph could have walked away if he wanted to, but he stood by Mary, even though doing so meant going through life being thought of as a man married to an immoral woman.

Joseph was also a faithful man who lived out his beliefs. On more than one occasion, when the angel came to Joseph with God's will for him and his family, Joseph responded in obedience. He was obedient to take Mary as his wife (see Matthew 1:20, 24), he was obedient to flee to Egypt when warned of Herod's coming wrath (Matthew 2:13–14), and he was obedient to return to Israel when the coast was clear (Matthew 2:20–21). He did not let life's uncertainties and unknowns keep him from living in a present obedience to God. He did not have all of life's answers, even though he was raising the One who did, but he did know that if God said do it, he was going to do it.

What about us? Our lives are also filled with unknowns and uncertainties just like Joseph's life was, and we have the same choices to make: Will we obey or disobey? Will we be faithful or unfaithful? Will we be loving or unloving? Although we do not know much about this man, we do know he is a wonderful, biblical example of integrity, faithfulness, and obedience.

The next time you consider the Christmas story, do not overlook this godly man. Be reminded of the fact that God is still looking for people who will respond when God calls, just as Joseph did.

"Behold the maidservant of the Lord! Let it be to me according to your word."(Luke 1:38)

DECEMBER
18

What about Mary?

ALL HOPE OF LIVING A NORMAL LIFE would soon be over for Mary, as this young teenage girl was about to receive a visit from the angel Gabriel with a life-changing message from God. After recovering from the shock of an angelic visitor, Mary heard the news that she had both found favor with God and was being chosen to bring forth the Son of God! *What?* Mary must have thought to herself something like this: *Surely there had to be a queen somewhere better suited to give birth to the King of the universe? Wasn't there a woman of better pedigree or higher social standing that could be chosen for this assignment?* As normal as these skeptical thoughts might have been, we do not see any hint of wavering in Mary. She indicates no trying to refuse this awesome responsibility, and she offered up no excuses as to why she was not the best choice. No, Mary bravely and modestly responded, "Let it be to me according to your word."

The news of her pregnancy would shock and embarrass her family, especially her husband-to-be, who would have had every right to call off the wedding due to unfaithfulness. After all, who was going to believe a virgin was pregnant by God's Holy Spirit and that the baby was the Son of God (see Luke 1:35)? Mary was facing a life filled with hurtful heckling (see John 8:41), frequent dirty looks, and constant cold-shouldering. But Mary would not be swayed from her devotion to God, and even though she naturally would have been flooded with waves of fear and faith, this was the burden she bravely agreed to bear.

When considering Mary, many people take one of two extremes: either they ignore Mary and the important role she played in bringing forth the Messiah, or they make too much of Mary, exalting her above measure. How should we treat Mary? Mary is worthy of respect and adoration, not just because of the role she played in the Christmas story, but also because of the example she is for every Christian. Mary readily surrendered her will to the will of God. She considered herself a servant of God, and as a servant, she lived in submission to God. We can see no wonder that God chose her. What an example for us to follow!

Is your life submitted to God like Mary's was? Do you consider yourself a servant of God, willing to do whatever God's Word says to do? If you want to experience the blessing of God's ongoing power in your life, then you must be willing to live surrendered and submitted to His will. Mary was not perfect or sinless, but she was faithful to follow God, regardless of the shame and suffering she would face, and she is a great example to us all this Christmas.

The angel Gabriel was sent by God to a city of Galilee named Nazareth. (Luke 1:26)

Gabriel, God's Messenger

DECEMBER

19

THE ANGEL GABRIEL dwells in the presence of God (see Luke 1:19) and always stands ready to do God's will at a moment's notice. When the fullness of time had arrived, God called him forward and gave him the most important mission of his existence. As Gabriel likely knelt before the throne of God, he received the details of this sensitive and splendid mission. Surely, Gabriel did not fully comprehend the totality of what his message would mean to the universe. How could he? How could any angel fully grasp the scope of what God was planning (see 1 Peter 1:12)? Regardless of Gabriel's limited understanding, the one thing he did know—to borrow the words of Tennyson—was that his was "not to reason why, [his] but to do [or] die." Gabriel had been given a message, and nothing was going to stop him from delivering that message.

The Christmas message delivered by Gabriel was so important because contained within this message is the reality that nothing is impossible for God (see Luke 1:37). As Mary received the message from Gabriel, she needed to be reassured that God was able to do more than she thought possible. Most of us certainly can relate to the need for an occasional reminder that nothing is impossible with God when we are facing "impossible" situations.

This Christmas message was so important because the reality that man could be saved from sin and reconciled to God is revealed in the message. Supernatural God was going to break into the natural world and do the unthinkable: become man so that He could save mankind.

This Christmas message importantly contained the reality of God's love, for no other representation could so completely demonstrate the love of God.

This Christmas message is because shown in this story is the reality that God lives up to His Word, and He will satisfy every promise yet to be fulfilled.

The angel Gabriel was faithful to do deliver God's glorious message to an unsuspecting world, a message that is full of joy and hope, love and redemption, a message that today's unsuspecting world still needs to hear. As Romans 10:14 reminds us, "How, then, can they call on the one they have not believed in? And how can they believe in the one of whom they have not heard? And how can they hear without someone preaching to them?" (NIV).

God has given all of us the responsibility of delivering His Christmas message to the world. Are you willing to be God's messenger to those around you? Why not start today?

December 20

Now there were in the same country shepherds living out in the fields, keeping watch over their flock by night. (Luke 2:8)

The Shepherds' Joy

GOD DEFINITELY made some unusual choices surrounding the birth of Jesus. One such choice was inviting shepherds to be the first to worship the newborn King. Shepherds were social outcasts and religious outsiders. They were underprivileged, uneducated, and unsophisticated. They were rough and tough characters who lived on the outer edge of society, and because of the work of caring for sheep, they were ceremonially unclean, which meant they were not allowed to be an active part of worship. As a result, most people avoided them at all costs. So, for the average shepherd, life was lived on the outside looking in.

As irregular as the choice may seem for God to choose to invite shepherds to be a part of this great and glorious day, this was the type of choice that would mark the life and ministry of Jesus. Jesus would live a life that invited the outcasts in. He touched the untouchables. He ate with the unclean. He spent time with the unwanted. God chose shepherds to be a part of this glorious day because to Jesus, we are the sheep of His pasture, and He came to be our Good Shepherd (see John 10).

As our Shepherd, He knows us, and we know Him. As our Shepherd, He defends us with His staff and corrects us with the crook. As our Shepherd, He is willing to leave the other sheep when we wander off. And as our Shepherd, He freely laid down His life for us. God's choice to include the shepherds on that special day was representative of Jesus' identification with them.

The shepherds had nothing to offer Jesus. They were not theologians who could understand the implications of fulfilled prophecy. They were not like the Magi who would arrive later, bringing expensive gifts for the infant King. They were simple people who lived simple lives, and all they had to offer were themselves. After all, is that not the point of the gospel? All are invited to come to Jesus, and in God's new social order, the last shall be first, the poor shall be rich, the least shall be the greatest, and the humble shall be exalted.

Let us be like the shepherds, who responded immediately to the invitation to come and worship God. Let us be like the shepherds, who left the presence of God forever changed and full of joy. Let us be like the shepherds, who went away praising God and proclaiming all that they had seen and heard. Let us be like the shepherds, who were filled with immense joy as they worshiped at the birth of their Savior that Christmas night.

December 21

"Where is He who has been born King of the Jews? For we have seen His star in the East and have come to worship Him." (Matthew 2:2)

Wise Guys

FOR THE WISE MEN, the journey to see the newly born King of the Jews was going to be a long and difficult road. They would devote countless hot and dusty days riding on the backs of camels, hard days that would give way to harsh nights spent trying to sleep on the cold desert floors of rough-and-ready campsites. Day after day, night after night, week after week, their path was plotted and their course was charted, not by map and compass, but by a divinely placed star (see Matthew 2:9) that would light and lead the way to the very baby who one day would call himself the Light of the World (see John 8:12).

But before ever leaving their likely home of Babylon, these wise men from the East had a decision to make. What gifts would they bring for an infant king? Expensive clothes? Fine linen blankets? What about a hand-carved baby's rattle? Not exactly. These wise men decided that the best gifts to bring would be gold, frankincense, and myrrh.

If you are thinking those gifts do not exactly sound like they are child safe, you are right. However, they are very proper and prophetic. First, gold is the metal of kings, and when gold was presented to Jesus by the wise men, this was a confession of his kingship. Then, their gift of incense was also significant and symbolic because incense was commonly used in temple worship., so this gift would point to the fact that Jesus Christ is the great High Priest. Lastly, their gift of myrrh would represent the death of Jesus, as myrrh was most commonly used as part of the burial process. When Jesus was being wrapped for burial, a large mixture of spices and myrrh was used to prepare His body for entombment (see John 19:39).

These men truly were wise guys, because when seeking Jesus, they did whatever it took. They traveled as far as they needed to travel, did their research, and looked into the Scriptures. They were willing to follow God's leading and go wherever He led them. And, at the core of their wisdom, was their desire to worship. Their quest was serious and their search was careful, but above all, their worship was genuine.

The wise men are not just supplemental additions to manger scenes (even though they technically did not arrive until one or two years later); they are reminders to us that if we have not found Jesus, we should be willing to do whatever we must to find Him. If you are serious about your search for Jesus, God will light and lead the way through the pages of the Scriptures until you find Him.

If you have already found Christ, then offer Him your gold by letting Him rule as King over every aspect of your life. Offer Him the incense of your worship, for He is our High Priest, the One who sacrificed Himself on God's altar so that we might be forgiven. And finally, offer Jesus your myrrh and willingly die to your sins, for Christ willingly died to pay for them.

"And she will bring forth a Son, and you shall call His name Jesus, for He will save His people from their sins."
(Matthew 1:21)

DECEMBER
22

What's in a Name?

IN THE BIBLE, we often see great value placed on a person's name. Names were often prophetic and occasionally descriptive of the character and nature of the person holding that name. On several occasions, God assigned a new name to one of His chosen people, and by renaming them, God was essentially giving them a new life or a new mission. Sarai became Sarah, Abram became Abraham, Jacob became Israel, Simon became Peter, and Saul became Paul. And ever since the angel of the Lord declared to Mary that her Son would be named Jesus, His life and mission was being declared to the world.

There is just something about the name of Jesus. His name is sweet to the saved and antagonistic to the unsaved. The name Jesus is both unifying and divisive. For some, His name is a beautiful word of praise, and for others, nothing more than a harsh expletive. You can talk about God and religion with many for hours, but mention the name of Jesus, and conversations have a tendency to get ugly or to abruptly come to an end. Why is one name so polarizing among people?

The divisiveness exists because the name of Jesus means "Savior," and was given to Him because "He [would] save His people from their sins." The reason the name of Jesus is the cause of so much division and controversy is because "there is no other name under heaven given among men by which we must be saved" (Acts 4:12). And the sad truth is that people do not want to admit they are sinners. They do not want to admit they need a Savior, and they do not want to admit that Jesus is the only way to heaven. Because Jesus was sent to be our Savior, we are in need of saving. Jesus saves us from the guilt of sin by forgiving us and washing away our sin by His atoning blood. He saves us from the power of sin by sanctifying us through His Holy Spirit. He saved us from the penalty of sin when He took our chastisement upon Himself on the cross. And He will save us from the presence of sin when He comes to take us from this world to dwell with Him in heaven.

This is the message of His name, and the message of Christmas, that Jesus came to save us from our sins, and one day every knee will bow and every tongue will confess that Jesus Christ is Lord (see Philippians 2:10–11). One day, Jesus will bring a final end to all sin and usher in a new heaven and a new earth forever.

This Christmas, remember that the name of Jesus is the most beautiful of all names, and His name will forever stand as reminder of His life and His mission. What's in a name? In the case of Jesus, His name is salvation.

There was no room for them in the inn. (Luke 2:7)

Have You Made Room for God?

DECEMBER
23

THE CHRISTMAS SEASON is a busy season. Everyone knows that during this special time of year, a frenzied factor is added to life. All the normal stresses and strains of the everyday routine remain during the holiday season, only now errands and responsibilities that come with the season's festivities are added. Yet, most of us find a way to make room for it all. We make room for family and friends to come and visit, we make room for lights and decorations to adorn our houses, we make room for the parties and the presents, and we even make room by rearranging furniture so we have space in our homes for a pine tree to live. But with all the ways that you make room for the seasonal merriment, have you actually made room for Jesus?

The first Christmas was also a busy one. Orders came from Rome that Caesar Augustus wanted everyone in the entire Roman world to be counted. This meant that everyone was compelled to stop what they were doing and return to their hometowns to be registered. A census like this was important to governments because the numbers helped them plan taxation, prepare for military campaigns, draft labor projects, and much more. God used this census to move Mary and Joseph to Bethlehem so that His plans and purposes could be fulfilled surrounding the birth of His Son.

After the lengthy journey from Nazareth to Bethlehem, Mary and Joseph, pregnant and expecting, finally arrived in Bethlehem. They approached a local innkeeper for a room, but his inn was bursting at the seams due to the influx of people traveling for the census. Preoccupied, he turned them away and indifferently pointed them to a nearby cold, dark, smelly stable, where they could stay the night. The innkeeper was too busy and had no desire to make room for Jesus.

Too many people today are acting like the innkeeper concerning Jesus. They are too busy to stop and see what is right in front of them. They are simply unwilling to make any effort or accommodation for Jesus in their lives. Oh, Jesus may decorate a mantle, He may fill a manger, or His name may drape over a railing in your home, but no room has been made in your heart for a relationship with Him.

If Jesus is nothing more than an ornament that only comes out once a year and then is packed up and put away until next year, then take the time today to get to know Him. And if you have simply allowed things in your life to get too filled with "stuff," then stop, refocus, and make room for Jesus.

While they were there, the time came for the baby to be born. (Luke 2:6 NIV)

DECEMBER
24

Not-So-Silent Night

IT WAS THE NIGHT BEFORE CHRISTMAS and all of heaven was bustling, for the King of glory would soon be descending. All the angels were gathered around Heaven's throne to see what would soon become the world's greatest mystery. As the night was fast approaching, the earth was unaware that Creator God soon would be there. Weary and worn from their long journey's plight, Mary and Joseph found shelter and prepared for a not-so-silent night.

With shouts of pain and tears of joy, the night would be long for the mother of this boy. Animals were all around and a chill was in the air as the Son of God would soon enter the world with no fanfare. Mother and father would wrap him in ragged cloth and place him in, of all things, a trough. While the shepherds made their way there, you can only imagine that Jesus' parents prayed a thanksgiving prayer. As the shepherds shouted their praise and the angels sang with all their might, God's glory shone clear on this not so silent night.

What do you have planned for the night before Christmas? For some, this day means braving the shopping madness to get those last-minute presents, batteries, and forgotten ingredients for Christmas Day. For many parents, tonight will be a long night filled with hours of frustration caused by the simple phrase "some assembly required." This is a night of wrapping presents, eating cookies left for Santa, and childlike excitement as the morning glory approaches. But whatever your plans may be for your night before Christmas, you must not lose sight of the message of this not-so-silent night in Bethlehem.

Even though the event seemed like nothing flashy, His birth was much to celebrate, for this event that would change the course of human history. What God did on that not-so-silent night is beyond comprehension and can only be understood and experienced in the heart of man by the power of God's Spirit and because of the gift of His grace. Despite the dark and dismal surroundings, that night in a cold, damp manger, the glory of God shone all around, lit up the darkness, and revealed the glory of the good news that born today in the city of David was the Savior who is Christ the Lord.

Make a point in the midst of your not-so-silent Christmas Eve to take the time and consider God's condescension, meditate on this magnificent manger scene, reflect on the meaning of the angels rejoicing, and stop to remember the Savior who was willingly wrapped in swaddling clothes. Ponder His mission of peace, and go to sleep glorifying God for what He was willing to do for mankind . . . all of which started on this not-so-silent of nights.

Every good gift and every perfect gift is from above, and comes down from the Father of lights. (James 1:17)

DECEMBER
25

Christmas Gift

CHRISTMAS DAY HAS FINALLY ARRIVED. Kids are waking up before dawn, full of excitement, as parents, still half asleep, are filling themselves with coffee. The peaceful scene of presents perfectly placed under a charmingly decorated Christmas tree is about to give way to a tornado of eagerness that will tear through living rooms, leaving nothing but wrapping paper wreckage and ribbon remains thrown about. If you were to interview parents about what they saw on Christmas morning, the story might sound something like this: "One minute everything was fine, then all of a sudden, the house began to shake as shiny paper, red stockings, and cardboard boxes began to form a funnel cloud of glimmering gifts. The whole thing was over as suddenly as it began; we never knew what hit us!"

Do not let Christmas come and go in a whirlwind without taking time to consider the awe-inspiring gift that God has given to each of us.

The greatest of gifts ever given has come in the person of Jesus Christ. Jesus is God's gift to this world, and wrapped up in this single gift from God are countless other gifts. On Christmas day, of all days, we should take the time to at least reflect on a few of these wonderful blessings that come wrapped up in the world's greatest Christmas gift.

Consider that in Jesus, we have been given the gift of salvation (see Matthew 1:21). Christmas, after all, is God's redemptive plan come to life. In Jesus, we have been given the gift of God's Word (see John 1:1, 14). Jesus is

God's Word come to life and an example of what life looks like when a person lives in perfect harmony with God's Word. In Jesus is the gift of hope (see 1 Peter 1:3). Because of Jesus' life, death, and resurrection, we have a living hope that offers security to our souls and sets our focus on eternity. In Jesus, we have the gift of peace (see John 14:27), peace that steadies our emotions and calms our anxieties (see Philippians 4:7). In Jesus, we have the gift of eternal life (1 John 5:11), never-ending, glorious life in the presence of God. In Jesus, we have the gift of access (Hebrews 4:14–16). Because of Jesus, we now can come directly to God personally in prayer, as Jesus is our High Priest.

Christmas is here because Christ came, and we give gifts because God gave us the gift of His Son. So, as you enjoy all the gifts you have been given by family and friends, why not take the time to enjoy all the gifts we have received in Jesus?

Be very careful, then, how you live—not as unwise but as wise. (Ephesians 5:15 NIV)

Now What?

DECEMBER 26

THE PARTY IS OVER, and soon the cleanup will begin. The lights will come down, the tree will be taken to the curb, and stores will discount holiday leftovers. Parents will look for receipts to give their children, who are eager to take off to the mall and exchange all the clothes that were thoughtfully picked out for them. Then, of course, is the odd feeling you get when you wrap up baby Jesus and place Him in a box, not to be opened again until next year. Something just feels wrong about putting God in a box. December's gifts will turn into January's bills, and before you know it, life will be back to normal. In the wake of Christmas and with a new year approaching, you might be asking yourself, *Now what?*

As believers, we are to live wisely. Our lives are to be lived in the will of God and are to demonstrate that we belong to God. Therefore, since we belong to God, we need to make sure that our decisions glorify Him daily. Are there any ways to make sure that we are going in the right direction? One of the ways we can ensure that we stay on track with God is by taking a simple test. Oh, no, this is not one of those old Scantron forms that require a number two pencil to fill in the multiple-choice bubbles. No, this is more like a true or false test, and will help define the dos and don'ts of living out your faith:

1. *The world test.* Is it worldly? Will it make me worldly to do it? (John 15:19, 1 John 2:15–17)
2. *The quality test.* Is it good for me physically, emotionally, and spiritually? (Romans 12:9b)
3. *The temple test.* Can I do it when I remember my body is God's temple and must not be marred or misused? (1 Corinthians 6:19)
4. *The glory test.* Will it glorify my Lord, or will it on the other hand possibly bring shame to His name? (1 Corinthians 6:20, 10:32)

5. *The blessing test.* Can I honestly ask God's blessing on it and be sure I will not regret doing it? (Proverbs 10:22, Romans 15:29)
6. *The reputation test.* Is it apt to damage my testimony for the Lord? (Philippians 2:15)
7. *The consideration test.* Am I being considerate of others and the effect this might have on them? (Romans 14:7, 21)
8. *The appearance test.* Will it look bad? Does it have the appearance of what is wrong or suspicious? (1 Thessalonians 5:22)
9. *The weight test.* Could this slacken or sidetrack me in running the Christian race? (Hebrews 12:1, 1 Corinthians 9:24)
10. *The coming of Christ test.* Would I be ashamed to be found doing this when He comes again? (1 John 2:28)
11. *The companion test.* Can I invite Christ to go with me and participate with me in this? (Matthew 28:20b, Colossians 3:17)
12. *The peace test.* After having prayed about it, do I have perfect peace about doing it? (Colossians 3:15a, Philippians 4:6–7)[82]

Once the last holiday party is over, all the decorations are finally put away, and you are left wondering what is next in your life, then keep this test handy as you examine your life choices and inspect your decisions, and keep you headed in the right direction. The test is great to revisit whenever you are wondering, *What's next?*

Then Jesus said to them, "Follow Me." (Mark 1:17)

Following Jesus

DECEMBER 27

JESUS WANTS US TO FOLLOW HIM wherever He leads. Following Jesus is not always easy, and truth be told, we may not always want to go where He leads. But a true follower will go, nonetheless. Following Jesus means that a person is willing to surrender everything in his or her life to Jesus. Jesus must be first in his or her life, not second, not third, and not a slice in life's pie chart. He is the whole pie. Is anything holding you back from following Jesus 100 percent?

As Jesus was walking along the Sea of Galilee, He called out, "Follow me" to a few disciples. Who could have ever anticipated that those two simple words would forever change the course of their lives? Notice that not one of these men hesitated to drop what they were doing to follow Jesus. Not only did they drop what they were doing, but they completely gave up everything familiar to follow Jesus into the unfamiliar. As R. Kent Hughes said, "By and large they knew little more than the deck of their boat, the currents of the lake, and the handful of people in the marketplace. Their conversation consisted of trade talk, local gossip, family affairs, and Galilean politics."[83] Now they would talk of spiritual matters, heavenly kingdoms, and religious standards. They would give up their comfortable routine of life to spend every day with Jesus, always would be on the move, living hand to mouth, with no place to lay their heads.

But they also would see great things as they watched Jesus perform miracles, heal multitudes, and preach to thousands. They would watch as Jesus bucked the religious system, fought the traditions of men, and silenced every argument. They would witness the worst sinners being saved and the holiest of religious leaders rejecting God. They would learn from His teaching, be blessed by His praying, and be given His power. They would laugh together, cry together, and face life together, all because they were willing to leave their nets and follow Jesus.

Is following Jesus any different for us today? Jesus still invites us to follow Him. Forever changing our conversations from the ordinary to the extraordinary, no longer do we simply talk of worldly matters, but we talk of spiritual matters. We still see Jesus perform miracles, heal individuals, and speak to thousands. Jesus still challenges the religious systems, fights the traditions of men, and can silence every argument. Sinners are still being saved, and holy religious leaders are still rejecting God. We are still learning from His teaching, being blessed by His prayers, and given His power. We laugh together, cry together, and face life together.

Following Jesus still requires faith, obedience, submission, surrender, sacrifice, trust, and perseverance, but if you are willing to leave your "nets" behind and follow Jesus wherever He leads, you never will regret your decision.

"In the same way I loved you, you love one another."
(John 13:34 MSG)
Love Is a Verb

DECEMBER
28

WHAT IS THE SINGLE GREATEST ATTRIBUTE IN THE BIBLE? Love! Love is greater than all the spiritual gifts, and love is so significant that Paul says we are nothing and our works amount to nothing without love (see 1 Corinthians 13:1–2). Of the three greatest virtues, faith, hope, and love, love ranks number one on the list (see 1 Corinthians 13:13). Keep in mind that to talk about love is easy, but the tough work of living love is much harder. Love, as God intended, is more than a feeling. Love involves commitment, sacrifice, and service. In other words, love is a verb.

The Christian life is all about love: how God loves us and how we are to love others. Love starts by accepting Christ's love for us and continues as we commit ourselves to expressing that kind of love in our lives and in our relationships. Love demands that we slow down, stop, and make time for others. Love requires us to look at people as God looks at them. Love starts with our attitudes and is realized through our actions. Love seeks to understand people and respond to them in kind. Love endures provocation without indignation. Love is not theoretical; love is to be tangible. Love wears no masks; love is totally transparent. Love has no ulterior motives; love's one desire is to glorify God. When presented with an opportunity to do evil, love chooses what is good. Love sees what needs to be done and does it. Love listens to people and finds ways to help. Love is what is needed most in the world, in the church, and in the home. Love is choice; love is an act of our wills. And love is a verb.

Our ability to love like Jesus is tied to our ability to abide in Jesus. Feeding on the Word of God fuels love. Love is nurtured in fellowship with other believers. Love keeps our ears tuned in to the voice of the One who is love (see 1 John 4:8). Trying harder to love does not produce love; love is the natural outcome of a life that is submitted to the Holy Spirit. Since apart from God we cannot love the way that He intends us to love, we must grant God the freedom to express His love through us. With God as the supplier of our ability to love, we can never say we have loved enough, that we have exhausted the supply of love, or that we have paid off our debt to love others.

The greatest picture of love is Jesus. His nature, His character, and His life were examples of love in action. If we seek to love as Jesus loved, then love always will be a verb.

Fully carry out the ministry God has given you. (2 Timothy 4:5 NLT)

Fulfill Your Purpose

DECEMBER
29

MINISTRY IS NOT JUST FOR PASTORS; ministry is for everyone. God has a plan for your life, a job for you to do, and a unique position that only you can accomplish in the body of Christ. Some ministry we are all called to carry out, regardless of our gifts. For example, we are all called to share the gospel, to make disciples, to love and serve others, and so on. But also, God has chosen specific gifts, ministries, and activities for you in particular to carry out. If you have been saved, then you need to know that you have been called to serve in ministry. Now, before you begin to make plans to quit your job, you should know that ministry is simply serving God. Although the word ministry can refer to a full-time, professional career choice, generally, ministry means serving as God has called and gifted a person to serve. What God has called *you* to do is going to be unique and different from what He has called someone else to do. But we are all called to serve, and God wants each one of us to be faithful to complete the ministry that He has given us.

As the apostle Paul was nearing the end of his ministry, he took a moment to remind his young protégé Timothy that faithfulness was the key to fulfilling his God-given ministry. Paul told Timothy that yes, there would be opposition, yes, there would be suffering, and yes, there would be trials and temptations, but he must endure these things in order to fulfill his ministry. God never said that ministry would be easy, but He did say it was essential that we serve (see 1 Peter 4:10).

Fulfilling your ministry begins by discovering your gift. God has given each one of us a spiritual gift that we are to use as we serve Him. Your gift will help you determine the *what* and the *where* of serving God. Once you figure out the *what* and the *where*, get busy! Start serving in your local fellowship as soon as possible, and remember that we are not serving so that we have something to boast about or as way of earning favor with God. We serve for the glory of God.

How wonderful that God has a specific ministry for each of us, a special job for us to do (see Ephesians 2:10). Work to fulfill your ministry with integrity, diligence, excellence, and perseverance.

So, discover what your role in ministry is and then be faithful to that ministry for as long as you live.

For God knew his people in advance, and he chose them to become like his Son. (Romans 8:29 NLT)

DECEMBER

30

Becoming Like Jesus

GOD WANTS YOU TO BE LIKE JESUS. True, God loves you just the way you are, and nothing you can do can make God love you any more or any less than He already does, but because of God's love for you, He wants *you* to become *less* and *Jesus* to become *more* in your life. A day will come when we will be made like Jesus perfectly and completely (see 1 John 3:2). But until that day, we are to be living and growing more and more like Jesus here and now, which means that we are to reflect His character and exemplify His conduct in all that we say and do, in every situation and in every setting. Sound difficult? Well, difficult, yes, but not impossible, because God is not only on our side, He is inside of us.

For us to talk about Jesus is not enough, to praise Jesus is not enough, and for us even to say that we love Jesus is not enough. We need to be living like Jesus. Too many Christians say the right things, but live the wrong way. Too many Christians lift up the name of Jesus with their voices, but drag His name through the mud with their lives. Too many Christians sing halleluiah choruses, but live with things hidden in their closets.

What does to become more like Jesus even mean? For starters, God wants you to get rid of your bad habits (see Colossians 3:5–7). God wants you to put off your old way of thinking and acting and to begin thinking and acting as you were created to think and act (see Colossians 3:10). Living like Jesus means that you will be able to look back over weeks, months, and years and see that you are not the same person that you once were. Living like Jesus is being able to say that Christlikeness is increasing in your life.

Becoming more like Jesus is the goal of our spiritual growth, and is accomplished by living each and every day with that goal in mind. Practically, some of the ways you can keep that goal in mind is by making sure that you read your Bible, do what God says, die to self, put others first, walk in love, show kindness, be thankful, stay committed, use wisdom, and pray without ceasing. Certainly, Christlikeness involves more than these ten practices, but this is certainly a good place start as we seek to become like Jesus.

If we should all want one thing as we say good-bye to this year and hello to the next, that one thing is how we can be more like Jesus. Maybe this past year was not so good for you in regard to growing in Christlikeness. As unfortunate as that is, the good news is that the past is the past, and today you can say good-bye to that past and hello to a new year. Finish out this year by committing to become more like Jesus in the year to come.

"Yes, I am coming soon." (Revelation 22:20 NIV)
Famous Last Words

A PERSON'S FINAL WORDS can say a lot about what is important to him or her. For example, Napoleon cried out, "Josephine!" before he breathed his last breath. P. T. Barnum's final words were, "How were the receipts today at Madison Square Garden?" And former President Grover Cleveland's last words were, "I have tried so hard to do right." Few words ever spoken have had a more far-reaching impact on the world than those of Jesus, and as the Bible comes to a close in the book of Revelation, we have the final words of Jesus in the New Testament: "Yes, I am coming soon."

The return of Jesus Christ is an important part of God's redemptive plan, which was foretold by prophets, affirmed by angels, and taught by Jesus. In fact, the Old Testament speaks more about Christ's second coming than His first, and in the New Testament, Jesus mentions His return more than His death. One out of every thirty verses in the Bible makes reference to the time of Christ's return. What are some things we should know about Christ's return?

His return will be literal (see Acts 1:10–11), His return will be dramatic (see Matthew 24:27), His return will be unexpected (see Matthew 24:36), His return will be seen by all (see Revelation 1:7), and His return will seal Satan's fate (see Revelation 20:2, 10). Why is Christ's return such a big deal? Because His return is the culmination of God's plan for humanity. Order will be restored, all things will be made new, and God will reign supreme.

Although we do not know the day or hour of His coming, we are to live in light of His return. What if you knew that Jesus was coming back a week from today? Would you live any differently? Would your priorities change in any way? Why not take some time today to consider how you might start off the new year living in light of His soon return? The Bible encourages us that the best way to live waiting for Christ's return is to be watchful (see Matthew 24:42), to be expectant (2 Peter 3:13), to be ready (Matthew 24:44), and to live rightly (2 Peter 3:14). In other words, looking forward to the day that Jesus will return is intended to encourage us to live godly lives now.

The return of Jesus is to be a constant reminder that feeds our faith, keeps our hope alive, and encourages us to do His will. The Bible teaches His return, Jesus declared His return, and we are to live in light of these final words of Jesus. He is coming soon! If the reality of Christ's soon return has not radically impacted the way you live your daily life, then perhaps you have become more concerned with *what* is yet to come rather than *who* is yet to come. Because Jesus can come any day, let us live for God every day.

Leap Year

Now I saw a new heaven and a new earth, for the first heaven and the first earth had passed away. (Revelation 21:1)

All Things New!

LEAP YEAR

A DAY IS COMING when hurts will be history, when sorrows will subside forever, when death will disappear into obscurity, when tears no longer will trickle down a troubled face, and when mortality will give way to immortality. A day is coming when there will be no more physical or emotional pain and no more brokenness in the world, there will be no more broken bodies, broken hearts, broken relationships, and broken lives. A day is coming when God will make all things new.

In the first two chapters of the Bible, we see how God created the first heaven and the first earth, prepared for the first man and the first woman. God prepared a perfect and beautiful place for them to live called the Garden of Eden, where even God could be found walking in the cool of the day. Unfortunately, the first sin was committed in this same place, bringing death into the world and thereby vandalizing God's creation. What followed this fall of man were the preparation, reception, and continued proclamation of the redemptive work of God through Jesus Christ. All of this leads us to the final two chapters of the Bible, where God's original intentions for the creation are fully and finally realized.

In order to properly understand the Bible and live lives that glorify God, we must never lose sight of God's big picture. "In the beginning" (Genesis 1:1) gives us the context for creation. "For God so loved the world" (John 3:16) gives us the redemptive plan for God's creation, and "Behold I make all things new" (Revelation 21:5) provides the culmination of creation.

One of the best ways to live a life that honors God and works toward accomplishing all that He has planned for your life is by living in light of heaven. If you are not looking forward to life in eternity, then you are reducing your ability to be effective for God today. The Bible tells us that we are to be looking ahead and living for heaven because "there's far more to life for us. We're citizens of high heaven! We're waiting the arrival of the Savior, the Master, Jesus Christ" (Philippians 3:20 MSG). This heavenly reminder keeps us motivated to share the hope of heaven with others and keeps our eyes off the hardships found here on earth, as we wait patiently for the new heaven and new earth.

A day is coming when body and soul will be as God had always intended. A day is coming when sin will no longer bind. A day is coming when creation will be as the Creator intended, and we will dwell in the brightest light imaginable as we live in the light of God's glory, as we rejoice in His holiness forever, and as we see Him face to face. A day is coming when God will make all things new!

Appendix
Spiritual Gifts

Romans 12
- *Prophecy:* speaking for God and giving His message
- *Ministry/serving:* seeing tasks that need to be done and using the needed resources to accomplish them
- *Teaching:* the ability to take the Word of God and convey it to God's people in such a way that it can be clearly understood and applied
- *Exhorting/encouraging:* to come alongside to comfort and challenge someone to live the life God has called him or her to live
- *Giving:* the ability to give financially to the work of the ministry with an attitude of cheerfulness and generosity
- *Leadership:* the ability to motivate and work through others to accomplish God-given goals
- *Mercy:* compassion for those who are in need or suffering, and the ability to help bring them comfort

Ephesians 4
- *Evangelism:* the ability and desire to communicate the Gospel message
- *Shepherd/pastor:* the ability to care for the spiritual needs of God's people

1 Corinthians 12
- *Word of wisdom:* the ability to apply biblical truth, often in a specific situation
- *Word of knowledge:* the ability to receive God-given facts (insight) about a situation
- *Faith:* exceptional ability to believe and trust in God's ability to work
- *Healing:* the gift in which God is able to heal the sick (mentally, physically, and emotionally) through you
- *Miracles:* God's working through you to accomplish something supernatural
- *Discernment:* the ability to make a distinction as to whether someone or something is speaking truth or error and whether it is of God
- *Tongues:* the ability to speak in a previously unknown language for the purpose of edification
- *Interpretation:* the ability to interpret tongues
- *Apostle:* a person who is sent out as messenger of the Gospel to new areas
- *Helps:* supporting others and freeing them up for other ministry
- *Administration:* the ability to plan, guide, and organize in order to accomplish tasks

Endnotes

1. Alan Richardson, *Genesis 1–11* (London: SCM Press, 1979), 128.

2. Charles R. Swindoll, *The Grace Awakening* (Nashville: Thomas Nelson), 152–153.

3. John Foxe, *Foxe's Book of Martyrs* (Lawrence, KS: Digireads.com Publishing, 2011), Google e-book, 119.

4. Philip Graham Ryken and R. Kent Hughes, *Exodus: Saved for God's Glory* (Wheaton: Crossway Books, 2005), 666.

5. C. S. Lewis, *The Complete C. S. Lewis Signature Classics* (New York: HarperCollins, 2002), 220.

6. Arthur W. Pink, *Exposition of the Gospel of John* (Grand Rapids, MI: Zondervan, 1968), 78.

7. See Revelation 19:1–9.

8. Karl Barth, quoted in Alfred P. Gibbs, *Worship: The Christian's Highest Occupation* (Kansas City, KS: Walterick Publishers, 1950), 63–64.

9. Robert Murray M'Cheyne, *The Works of Rev. Robert Murray M'Cheyne: Complete in One Volume* (New York: Robert Carter & Brothers, 1874), 138.

10. Norman Geisler and Ron Brooks, *When Skeptics Ask* (Grand Rapids, MI: Baker Books, 1990), 23.

11. Geisler and Brooks, 23.

12. H. A. Ironside, *John: An Ironside Expository Commentary* (Grand Rapids, MI: Kregel, 2006), 498.

13. Keith Krell, "A Saved Soul, A Wasted Life (Judges 13:1–16:31)," *Bible.org*, last modified June 15, 2010, https://bible.org/seriespage/saved-soul-wasted-life-judges-131-1631.

14. Dr. Frank Minirth, *What They Didn't Teach You in Seminary* (Nashville, TN: Thomas Nelson, 1993), 165.

15. See Soren Kierkegaard, *Concluding Unscientific Postscript*, trans. and ed. Alastair Hannay (New York: Cambridge University Press, 2009).

16. J. I. Packer, *Knowing God* (Downers Grove, IL: InterVarsity, 1973), 80.

17. Charles Spurgeon, *Faith's Checkbook* (MobileReference, 2010), "June " http://books.google.com/books?id=8T6AdZaOENIC&printsec=frontcover&source= gbs_ge_summary_r&cad=0#v=onepage&q&f=false.

18. Charles G. Trumbull, as quoted by Donald Grey Barnhouse, *Epistle to the Romans*, part 1 of the printed radio messages (Philadelphia, PA: The Bible Study Hour, 1953), 1982.

19. Note on Romans 10:1, *The Word in Life Study Bible*, New King James Version (Nashville, TN: 1996), CD-ROM.

20. R. H. Mounce, *Romans: An Exegetical and Theological Exposition of Holy Scripture*, The New American Commentary, vol. 27 (Nashville, TN: Broadman & Holman, 1995), 266.

21. Oswald Chambers, *The Oswald Chambers Devotional Reader: 52 Weekly Themes*, ed. Harry Verploegh (Nashville, TN: Thomas Nelson, 1990), 65.

22. Quoted in Roy B. Zuck, *The Speaker's Quote Book: Over 5,000 Quotations and Illustrations for All Occasions, Revised and Expanded* (Grand Rapids, MI: 2009), 268.

23. G. Campbell Morgan, quoted in James Stuart Bell, *The One Year Men of the Bible: 365 Meditations on Men of Character* (Carol Stream, IL: Tyndale House Publishers), 16.

24. Charles Haddon Spurgeon, *Sermons Preached and Revised by the Rev. C. H. Spurgeon*, sixth series (New York: Sheldon and Company, 1860), 25.

25. Henry M. Morris, "The Resurrection of Christ—The Best-Proved Fact in History," Institute for Creation Research, accessed January 23, 2014, http://www.icr.org/ChristResurrection/.

26. *Bits & Pieces,* May 28, 1992, 15.

27. Charles R. Swindoll, *Job: A Man of Heroic Endurance* (Nashville, TN: Thomas Nelson, 2004), 24.

28. Henry Morris, "The Meek of the Earth," Institute for Creation Research, accessed February 26, 2014, http://www.icr.org/article/2586/.

29. Tony Evans, *Returning to Your First Love: Putting God Back in First Place* (Chicago: Moody, 1995), 167.

30. George Müller, quoted in Ron Rhodes, *1001 Unforgettable Quotes About God, Faith, and the Bible* (Eugene, OR: Harvest House Publishers, 2011), 83.

31. D. L. Moody, *Twelve Penny Addresses* (London: Morgan and Scott, 1884), 12.

32. Walter Trobish, *I Loved a Girl* (New York: HarperCollins, 1989), 4.

33. A. W. Tozer, *Whatever Happened to Worship?* (Camp Hill, PA: Christian Publications, 1985), 36.

34. Oswald Chambers, quoted in *The Westminster Collection of Christian Quotations,* Martin H. Manser, ed. (Louisville, KY: Westminster John Knox Press, 2001), 322.

35. C. H. Spurgeon, *Morning by Morning: Daily Readings for the Family or the Closet,* s. v. "Jan. 7" (New York: Sheldon and Company, 1866), 7.

36. Jeremiah Burroughs, *Rare Jewel of Christian Contentment* (Mulberry, IN: Sovereign Grace Publishers, 2001), 23.

37. Martyn Lloyd-Jones, quoted in R. Kent Hughes, *Ephesians: The Mystery of the Body of Christ,* ESV ed. (Wheaton, IL: Crossway, 1990), 171.

38. Donald Barnhouse, quoted in Sermon Central sermon by Zak Saenz, Digital Edition.

39. Bernard Ramm, quoted in John MacArthur, *Jesus Silences His Critics* (Chicago: Moody, 1987), 94.

40. Charles Wesley, "Hark! the Herald Angels Sing".

41. H. A. Ironside, *Luke* (Grand Rapids, MI: Kregel, 2007), 89.

42. Dr. Martin Luther King, Jr., quoted in Kevin J. Navarro, *The Complete Worship Service: Creating a Taste of Heaven on Earth* (Grand Rapids, MI: Baker, 2005), 60.

43. Blaise Pascal, *Pensées,* trans. A. J. Krailsheimer (London: Penguin, 1995).

44. *The Word in Life Study Bible* (Nashville: Thomas Nelson, 1996), digital edition.

45. John Stott, *A walking embodiment of the simple beauty of Jesus,* digital edition.

46. Oswald Chambers, *My Utmost for His Highest for the Graduate,* James Reimann, ed. (Uhrichsville, OH: Barbour, 2006), 126.

47. D. Martyn Lloyd-Jones, *The Christian Soldier: An Exposition of Ephesians 6:10–20* (Grand Rapids, MI: Baker, 1998), 342.

48. Oswald Chambers, quoted in Mary Ann Bridgwater, *Prayers for the Faithful: Fervent Daily Prayer and Meditations for Christians Serving Around the World* (Nashville: B&H Publishing Group, 2008), 178.

49. *The Word in Life Study Bible,* digital edition.

50. Max Lucado, *Max on Life: Answers and Insights to Your Most Important Questions* (Nashville: Thomas Nelson 2011), 31.

51. *The Word in Life Study Bible,* digital edition.

52. D. Martyn Lloyd-Jones, *Preaching and Preachers* (Grand Rapids, MI: Zondervan, 2012), 100–101.

53. Jerry Bridges, *Respectable Sins: Confronting the Sins We Tolerate* (Colorado Springs, CO: NavPress, 2001), 161.

54. Edward Everett Hale, quoted in Jeanie A. B. Greenough, *A Year of Beautiful Thoughts* (Philadelphia: George W. Jacobs & Co., 1902), 172.

55. C. S. Lewis, *The Complete C. S. Lewis Signature Classics* (San Francisco: HarperCollins, 2002), 66.

56. Andrew Murray, quoted in V. Raymond Edman, *They Found the Secret: Twenty Lives That Reveal a Touch of Eternity* (Grand Rapids, MI: Zondervan, 1984), 117–118.

57. Saint Augustine, *Confessions,* 2nd ed., F. J. Shreed, trans. (Indianapolis, IN: Hackett Publishing, 2007), 3.

58. John Piper, "There Is No Partiality With God, Part 2," *DesiringGod.org,* January 31, 1999, http://www.desiringgod.org/sermons/there-is-no-partiality-with-god-part-2.

59. Philip Hughes, *A Commentary on the Epistle to the Hebrews* (Grand Rapids, MI: Eerdmans, 1977) 388.

60. John MacArthur, *The MacArthur New Testament Commentary: Hebrews* (Chicago: Moody Press, 1983), 294.

61. Warren W. Wiersbe, *Be Rich (Ephesians): Gaining the Things That Money Can't Buy* (Colorado Springs, CO: David C. Cook, 2010), 129.

62. A. W. Tozer, *The Knowledge of the Holy* (New York: HarperCollins, 1961), 50.

63. James Montgomery Boice, *The Minor Prophets: An Expositional Commentary* (Grand Rapids, MI: Baker Books, 2002), 142.

64. Warren W. Wiersbe, *The Bible Exposition Commentary,* vol. 2 (Wheaton, IL: Victor Books, 1989), 347.

65. J. I. Packer, *Concise Theology: A Guide to Historic Christian Beliefs* (Wheaton, IL: Tyndale, 1993), 160.

66. Bruce Barron, *The Health and Wealth Gospel* (Downers Grove, IL: InterVarsity, 1987), 176.

67. F. B. Meyer, *Our Daily Homily,* s. v. "Jonah 1:3," *PreceptAustin.org,* accessed April 1, 2014, http://preceptaustin.org/jonah_commentaries.htm#1:3.

68. Max Lucado, "Baptism: The Demonstration of Devotion," *Max Lucado.com,* accessed April 1, 2014. http://maxlucado.com/read/topical/baptism-the-demonstration-of-devotion/.

69. C. S. Lewis, *The Business of Heaven: Daily Readings from C. S. Lewis* (Boston: Houghton Mifflin Harcourt, 1984), 77.

70. David Walls, Max E. Anders, *Holman New Testament Commentary 1&2 Peter, 1,2,&3 John, Jude,* (Nashville: B&H Publishing, 1999), 123.

71. Elizabeth Rice Achtemeier, *Nahum–Malachi* (Atlanta: John Knox Press, 1986), 46.

72. Warren W. Wiersbe, *The Bible Exposition Commentary,* vol. 2, 512.

73. Charles H. Spurgeon, *Morning and Evening,* s. v. "Morning, October 12" (Peabody, MA: 2010).

74. Warren W. Wiersbe, *The Bible Exposition Commentary,* vol. 2, 483.

75. Oswald Chambers, "Dependent on God's Presence" in *My Utmost for His Highest,* ed. James Reimann (Grand Rapids, MI: Discovery House, 2006), 20.

76. Jerry Bridges, "Praying in Faith" *Decision* magazine, March 28, 2013, http://billygraham.org/decision-magazine/march-2013/praying-in-faith/.

77. Warren W. Wiersbe, *Be Complete: Become the Whole Person God Intends You to Be* (Colorado Springs, CO: David C. Cook, 2008), 52–53.

78. David Wilkerson, "The Path to the Throne," *WorldChallenge.com,* August 2, 2004, http://sermons.worldchallenge.org/en/node/1112.

79. John MacArthur, *The MacArthur New Testament Commentary: Revelation 12–22*, (Nashville: Thomas Nelson, 2000), 63.

80. *The Word in Life Study Bible*, digital edition.

81. Rick Warren, *The Purpose of Christmas* DVD Study Guide (Grand Rapids, MI: Zondervan, 2008), 37.

82. Eugene A. Wood, "Training Manual for Local Church Visitation" (master's thesis, Dallas Theological Seminary, 1980), *Bible.org*, https://bible.org/illustration/romans-14.

83. R. Kent Hughes, *Mark: Jesus, Servant and Savior*, vol. 1 (Wheaton, IL: Crossway, 1989), 37.

Scripture Index
OLD TESTAMENT

GOD EVERY DAY / 365 LIFE APPLICATION DEVOTIONS

NEW TESTAMENT

CHRISTMAS DEVOTIONS

Discovering God's Will for Your Life:
Your Journey with God
by Michael Lutz

Your Journey with God possesses something that other books of this kind do not have: a fresh approach!

A few of the chapter titles are as follows:

- "You Talkin' to Me?
- "I Object!"
- "Watch the Road!"
- "Follow Your Dreams"
- "Detours, Obstacles, and Rough Roads"
- "Are We There Yet?"

Readers will truly be inspired and truly enjoy their journey as they find out how to listen to God's voice, remain in His will, and progress in HIS plans for their lives.

ISBN: 978-0-88270-831-7
TPB / 192 pages

Prayers That Change Things

by Lloyd Hildebrand

More than 160,000 copies have been sold. These mass-market paperbacks contain prayers that are built from the promises of God and teaching that is thoroughly scriptural.

978-1-61036-105-7
MMP / 192 pages

978-0-88270-012-0
MMP / 232 pages

978-0-88270-743-3
MMP / 232 pages

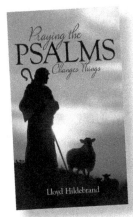

978-1-61036-126-2
MMP / 216 pages

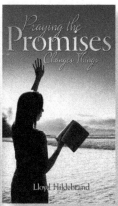

978-1-61036-132-3
MMP / 248 pages

978-1-61036-141-5
MMP / 256 pages